The Lettered Indian

BROOKE LARSON

The Lettered Indian

*Race, Nation, and Indigenous Education
in Twentieth-Century Bolivia*

DUKE UNIVERSITY PRESS
Durham and London
2024

© 2024 DUKE UNIVERSITY PRESS
All rights reserved
Project Editor: Liz Smith
Designed by A. Mattson Gallagher
Typeset in Minion Pro by Westchester Publishing Services

Library of Congress Cataloging-in-Publication Data
Names: Larson, Brooke, author.
Title: The lettered Indian : race, nation, and indigenous education in twentieth-century Bolivia / Brooke Larson.
Other titles: Race, nation, and indigenous education in twentieth-centuryBolivia
Description: Durham : Duke University Press, 2024. |
Includes bibliographical references and index.
Identifiers: LCCN 2023005380 (print)
LCCN 2023005381 (ebook)
ISBN 9781478025467 (paperback)
ISBN 9781478020653 (hardcover)
ISBN 9781478027560 (ebook)
Subjects: LCSH: Escuela Profesional de Indígenas de Huarizata (Bolivia)|IndiansofSouthAmer ica—Education—Bolivia—History—20th century. | Education—Aims and objectives—Bolivia. | BISAC: HISTORY / Latin America / South America | SOCIAL SCIENCE / Ethnic Studies / American / Native American Studies
Classification: LCC F3320.1.E4 L377 2024 (print) | LCC F3320.1.E4 (ebook) | DDC 371.829/98084—dc23/eng/20230607
LC recordavailableathttps:// lccn.loc.gov/2023005380
LC ebookrec ordavailableathttps:// lccn.loc.gov/2023005381

Frontispiece: Peasants vote to organize a local school, 1934. Courtesy of Carlos Salazar Mostajo, *Gesta y fotografía: Historia de Warisata en imágenes*, photo no. 96.

Cover art: Miguel Alandia Pantoja, *Lucha del Pueblo por su Liberación, Reforma Educativa y Voto Universal*, 1964. Mural (detail), Museo de la Revolución Nacional, La Paz, Bolivia. Courtesy of Gobierno Autónomo Municipal de La Paz, Oficialía Mayor de Culturas, Dirección de Espacios Culturales, Unidad de Museos Municipales. Photograph by the author.

For Carter

Decolonization, which sets out to change the order of the world[,] ... cannot be accomplished by the wave of a magic wand, a natural cataclysm, or a gentleman's agreement. Decolonization is a historical process: In other words, it can only be understood, it can only find its significance and become self-coherent, insofar as we can discern the history-making movement which gives it form and substance.

—FRANTZ FANON,
The Wretched of the Earth

CONTENTS

xi	Preface	229	6. Enclaves of Acculturation *The North American School Crusade*
1	Introduction		
23	1. To Civilize the Indian *Contested Pedagogies of Race and Nation*	269	7. The Hour of Vindication *Rural Literacy and Schooling in the Age of Revolution*
70	2. Lettered Aymara *The Insurgent Politics of Literacy and Schooling*	315	Epilogue *Silences, Remembrances, and Reckonings*
110	3. Warisata *Forging an Intercultural School Experiment*	339	Acknowledgments
160	4. Whose Indian School? *Revenge of the Oligarchy*	345	Notes
		423	Bibliography
		465	Index
192	5. Instigators of New Ideas *Peasant Pedagogies of Praxis*		

PREFACE

Book ideas often have a way of germinating for long periods of time, quite unbeknownst to the future author. I first stumbled on the theme of this book, quite unknowingly, in the summer of 1966, when I participated in an NGO (nongovernmental organization) program in rural education on the outskirts of Pátzcuaro, in Mexico. Like some well-intentioned projects transporting the beneficence of First World technologies, aid, and expertise to parts of the "Third World," this one backfired. But on a personal level, it taught me something about the ethical ambiguities that rural development projects can engender. Those unintended lessons resurfaced many decades later as I set out to study the history of rural schools in the Bolivian highlands.

But first things first. My initial encounter with the subject of Indian schooling began happily enough. Our work crew's task was to help lay the stone foundation of a future educational and conference center. In sight of the glistening waters of Lake Janitzio, we chipped away at rocks, filled wheelbarrows, and pushed our loads downhill to the construction site, a short distance from the lakeshore. There, we were told, a local Mexican work crew (working under the direction of a Mexico City architect, who never actually showed up that summer) would begin building an international conference center. Once finished, the gleaming center would become the destination of NGO development officers, agronomists, rural sociologists, development economists, and various educators—all of them eager to advance the Green

Revolution by exchanging ideas and designing policies to raise living standards, improve the rural workforce, and modernize the countryside in Mexico and other parts of Latin America.

Ineffectual as we were, our tiny do-gooding group seemed to be doing no harm. One day, however, we traveled to the far side of the lake to pay a visit to George M. Foster, the Berkeley anthropologist. This encounter was a disaster. Instead of endorsing our collective work project, Foster delivered a stern lecture about the potential environmental and cultural damage that the Green Revolution, writ large, could unleash on the region's fragile lacustrine ecology.[1] Did we not realize that capitalist farming would eventually erode the topsoil? That modern irrigation works would drain the lake, turning its waters brackish from pesticide runoff? And what would happen to Janitzio's local fishing industry, the traditional livelihood of local villages? How, then, would local communities stem the migratory tide of Tarascan youth, abandoning their parched lands and dry lake beds for the throbbing metropolis of Mexico City or en route to the northern border?

Presented with this dystopian picture, our group faced a moral dilemma, and our work ethic quickly disintegrated. We split into warring factions: the true believers in our project continued hauling rocks; the moral skeptics went on strike. At night, we debated the issues Professor Foster had raised and voted whether to work or strike. As for me, I left the rock pile and spent the remainder of the summer involved in a local literacy project, teaching a small group of Tarascan young women how to read and write in Spanish. It was a wonderful experience, but I soon discovered that even in that nightly literacy class, I had not yet extracted myself from the local NGO project, preaching the gospel of Western progress to local campesinos. Indeed, the textbooks I used in the classroom were actually agro-modernization primers for peasants! Several years ago I came across those illustrated readers. Published in 1958 by the Centro Regional de Educación Fundamental para América Latina, a transnational NGO based in Pátzcuaro, one of the textbooks was aimed at male campesinos in the region. It told the story of a traditional Tarascan fisherman being urged by a visiting white engineer to "give up the old ways" and switch to modern chicken-raising, with the promise of credit and loans from the Credit Bank. Another textbook promoted the benefits of literacy among the illiterate men of the peasant community, so they could overcome their "shame" by learning their letters, recover their sense of honor, and join the modernizing national community. Peasant women were ciphers in those stories, except as apron-wearing wives and helpmates in the chicken-raising industry.[2] In the time-honored tradition of Mexican adult literacy training, I was helping to socialize my young students in accordance with the patriarchal values of agrarian modernity and national integration.

As I thought about this experience, though, I realized that my complicity was only half the story; and in this case, the textual *medium* (the peasant alphabet reader) was probably far more significant than the intended moral *message*. My students giggled at the textbook's illustrations of the ideal hen farmer and his happy housewife, but they were deadly serious about mastering the rudiments of Spanish literacy. However ideologically freighted their textbook, those young Tarascan women pursued the mastery of alphabetic literacy for their own purposes and at great personal sacrifice. They had dropped their daily work, walked the long road to school each night, and willed themselves to learn spoken and written Spanish so that they might widen their horizons, empower themselves, and improve their life chances. That much was clear from our informal classroom conversations. Looking back from the distance of now, I can appreciate how the very act of mastering their letters represented a courageous act of cultural self-empowerment—a way of pushing against the entrenched odds of growing up poor, rural, and female in the mid-twentieth-century Tarascan highlands. There were, as I later came to understand, multiple narrative threads and layered complexities to the history of local literacy and rural school politics in Michoacán's villages and elsewhere in rural Mexico. Since those days, Mexican scholarship on rural education has exploded. Interdisciplinary research has decentered state-centric approaches to reexamine the dynamic interplay among regional and local stakeholders under shifting cultural and political circumstances in postrevolutionary Mexico.[3] In Bolivia, by contrast, it would take another two decades for ethnographic and historical scholarship on the theme of Indigenous and peasant schooling to finally catch fire.

In the meantime, this formative field experience banished any implicit notions I might once have had about the normative neutrality of knowledge, literacy, and learning. It opened my youthful eyes to the underlying politics of knowledge and schooling, culturally situated forms of learning, and the potentially transformative meanings that "popular education," broadly defined, might signify to marginal rural constituencies. Refracted through the decades, my memory of that summer of fieldwork in Michoacán—the rock pile fiasco, the anthropologist's admonishment, the pamphlet's chicken-farmer allegories, and the nightly reading circle—sharpened my intuitive appreciation for the manifold, often contradictory ways that literacy, knowledge, and schooling acquired symbolic and strategic value in traditional rural societies situated on the margins of modernity. I could not have known then that decades (and several books) later, I would be back at the drawing board, thinking critically about the contested histories and politics of rural education—this time, in the context of Bolivia's tumultuous history of neocolonial violence, nation-making schemes, and Indigenous social movements.

Introduction

There are two human inventions which may be considered more difficult than any others, the art of government and the art of education; and people still contend as to their very meaning.
—IMMANUEL KANT, *Thoughts on Education*

When Kant penned his "thoughts on education" in the early nineteenth century, philosophers had long debated the subject. He was influenced by Jean-Jacques Rousseau's 1762 work, *Emile*, the eighteenth century's most popular treatise on education. That essay had conjured a utopia of emancipation, one where the child's spirit and intelligence were elevated not through the deadening routines of formal schooling, but through the airy experiences of life and nature. The "natural child," once liberated, would evolve into a virtuous citizen.[1] To Kant, on the other hand, formal education was the prime instrument of civilization, but also the irrefutable index of superior Western virtues. The unschooled child—and, by extension, the unschooled masses—embodied the innate primitivism of human impulses: an unbridled "lust for freedom," "beastly urges," and "unruly behavior." The savage child, buried within the body and soul of the Everyman, had to be exposed to civilization's disciplinary regimes before he could qualify for entry into the social compact of citizenship.

By implication, Kant's logic adhered to the world's division of advanced and primitive regions as well. The inhabitants of "savage nations," he believed, were condemned by nature to languish forever in "a kind of barbarism."[2] Broadly conceived, his imperial cartography mapped nations and continents along the binary of civilization/savagery—a nineteenth-century literary trope that threw shadows of pessimism and doubt across the utopian schemes of Western state-builders, especially as they fixed their gaze on the colonized regions of the world. Like Kant, post-Enlightenment men of science and letters invoked the authority of "race science" to cast "savage subjects" out of the modern citizen-state on the premise that they were innately uneducable and thus ungovernable by the light of reason. Yet despite his certitude about the twin pillars of civilization, Kant had to concede that "the art of government and the art of education" defied common understanding among enlightened statesmen in his own day. "People still contend as to their very meaning," he noted in 1803, with a hint of exasperation.[3]

If, in Kant's view, European philosophers had difficulty coalescing around ideas of modern statecraft, imagine the epic challenges facing Spanish American elites as they tried to adapt European political ideals and institutions to their own ravaged societies and multiracial populations in the aftermath of the Independence wars! A state administration must fill the power vacuum; generals on horseback had to yield to men of laws and letters, trained in modern educational establishments that did not yet exist. From the onset of republican rule, education reform became an obsessive concern. Angel Rama writes, "The unanimous call for *education* rivaled the clamor for *liberty* during these years . . . because the organization of an educational system was [deemed] indispensable to the [new] political and administrative order."[4] Advocates of secular education faced daunting social challenges (and not only the opposition of the Catholic Church). They had to school a labor force composed of millions of enslaved people, impoverished free people of color, Indigenous peasants inhabiting remote villages and haciendas, and motley plebeian crowds of mixed racial and ethnic heritages—all struggling, in one way or another, to break free of oppression and rise above their humble origins. Outside the urban enclaves of "lettered cities," literacy rates were dismally low: much less than a quarter of the population was considered to be functionally literate (that is, able to decipher the meaning of written Spanish letters and words); and many fewer could both read and write. If, as Eric Hobsbawm argues for nineteenth-century Europe, "the progress of schools and universities measures that of nationalism," Latin America's new republics had enormous work ahead of them if they hoped to foster national consciousness and forge strong, unified nation-states.[5] Conjuring new nations out of the racial fragments of the old empire and instilling a unifying sense of national belonging to peoples living on the margins hinged on modern educational systems capable of socializing an incipient citizenry.

But as the mystique of education inflated nationalist expectations, it also precipitated decades of discord and debate among Latin America's erudite writers, pedagogues, and politicians.[6] For some, the theme of education was a framing device for utopian thinking. Writing in the radical Enlightenment tradition, Simón Rodríguez, Simón Bolívar's famous tutor, argued that the true republic would be forged by public schools and consolidation of a national language—the constitutive elements for instilling a sense of peoplehood in Latin America's fragmented and inchoate societies. Rodríguez's egalitarian values and utopian spirit opened a vein of progressive educational reformism in Latin America that inspired generations of advocates and practitioners of "popular education," down to the present day. If the ideals of republicanism were to flourish, he argued, the public school must cultivate the reasoning ability of its citizenry, and not simply produce legions of elite *letrados* (lawyers, scribes, literary writers, etc.).[7] His Latin American critics, however, called for the application of Europe's latest disciplinary methods: classroom drills, monitorial routines, and other innovations plucked from the harsh Lancaster model of schooling designed for the children of Britain's laboring class. Domingo Faustino Sarmiento, Argentina's preeminent man of letters and educational reformer, was a famous skeptic of democratic schooling (although he was a great admirer of New England's "common school"). He believed deeply in the value of public schooling, not only to open young minds to the light of reason but also to reform unruly behavior and instill in the child an abiding sense of moral and civic duty. Sarmiento's hardline pedagogy was compatible with Kant's strictures calling for "the inculcation of habit in the youngster's preparation that he or she may follow faithfully the rules of conduction imposed from above," notes Mark Szuchman.[8] Beyond this erudite circle of liberal statesmen and pedagogues, Latin America's elites often looked askance at the republican fervor for public school reform. Either they dwelled on the impossible odds and intrinsic limits that blocked modern statecraft and public education reform, or they worried about the potential threat that rural schooling, once implemented, would pose to the prevailing political and social hierarchies.

During the late nineteenth century, the entwined intellectual movements of "positivism" and "race science" only intensified debate over the education problem in Latin America. Latin American modernizers put their faith in the power of positivist thinking—that is, they invested their efforts in higher education reform and technical training institutes. Their purpose was to produce a young technocratic elite to meet the imperatives of Latin America's age of commodity exports and incipient industrialization. Positivist educational reform (spreading through Brazil, Argentina, Chile, and Mexico from the 1870s on, and later in the Andean nations) was seen as an institutional and cognitive arm of scientific state-building, economic progress, social uplift, and racial integration. Yet such modernist aspirations were stymied by the ascendance of "scientific racism," particularly variants of French race theory and social Darwinism. Race-thinking, predicated on the primordial powers of biology, nature, climate, and/or history, shook the modernizers' faith in the power of modern technology, market capitalism, and social reform to call forth the glories of economic prosperity and racial progress. Out of existential interest, many progressive Latin American statesmen eschewed the most doctrinaire theories of genetic determinism, and instead preferred to frame racial difference as a function of geography, climate, social evolution, or culture. Such "soft theories" of racial inequality opened cracks in the body politic for remedial interventions by statesmen, scientists, and pedagogues—all of them wielding the latest disciplinary tools and social policies designed to turn the racial situation around (toward whiteness or *mestizaje*).[9] Meanwhile, European theories of race often projected doleful images of racial hybridity and degeneration, and they nurtured an "aristocratic revulsion for [the idea of] democracy, incipient mass society, and the mixing of peoples."[10] Precepts of scientific racism even threatened to undermine Sarmiento's celebrated faith in the remedial power of public schooling to solve Latin America's racial problems. Although he did not completely abandon his belief in education as the solution to Latin America's racial backwardness, a toxic (particularly anti-Indigenous) racism infected his evolving ideas, policies, and attitudes toward the subject later in his life.[11] By the 1880s, Sarmiento had become a conflicted man of two minds, a split public persona: while he still championed enlightened school reform, he was also the purveyor of racial determinism. And his racial imaginary was the dark filter through which he perceived the need to conquer the Indigenous inhabitants of the pampa. Once he was president, Sarmiento acted on that conviction. In 1879–80, he ordered a new military operation (euphemistically named "Conquest of the Desert") to eradicate the "barbarian hordes" (gauchos, Indians, and caudillos) from the Argentine frontier.[12] In this one tortured soul, we perceive an evolving war of ideas and sentiments that raged between the utopian promise of educational reform and the dystopian threat of racial determinism. That pernicious war of ideas would play out on many platforms in different times and places.

Beyond the southern periphery of Argentina, where the plains rise into the northern hill country and then ascend into the high Andes, the "Indian problem" could not be resolved through military assault, certainly not on the genocidal scale of Argentina's military conquest. The challenges of nation-building were particularly daunting in the fledgling Andean republics. The void of statelessness in the Andean countryside, and the persistence of colonial norms and racial hierarchies (tribute, communal landholding, indirect rule, caste divisions, etc.), threw up structural barriers to projects of integrative nationalism. Dense settlements of Quechua- and Aymara-speaking pastoralists and farmers, laborers and traders, had subsidized the colonial enterprise for three centuries and continued to serve as the semicolonized rural workforce, even as the rural Andes were swept into transatlantic currents of capitalist modernity. Campaigns of ethnic cleansing would not, and could not, be seriously entertained as a conceivable "solution" to the Indian problem under the aegis of the civilizing state.[13] Alternative solutions would have to be engineered by criollo state-builders, eager to pacify the interior frontiers, integrate the Indigenous population, and improve the racial composition of their Andean republics. Under those circumstances, liberal-positivist elites in Bolivia, Peru, and Ecuador were not apt to disavow the potential agency of education and government, even if they had existential doubts about the Indian's ultimate capacity for cultural assimilation. Indeed, many statesmen and intellectuals embraced the mystique of education as the best, and perhaps the only, pathway toward cultural unity, modernity, and nationhood. In their feverish imaginaries, the exalted figure of the public school teacher, trained in the "normal" (teacher-training) institute, would carry the Kantian torch of enlightened governance and education into the rural Andean hinterlands.

The Lettered Indian explores the contested politics of governance and education that unfolded in the Bolivian Andes, roughly between the early

1900s and the 1970s.[14] Through layered narratives, this book explores the rural Indian school as a contested site and symbol of knowledge, power, and identity during the political and cultural formation of neocolonial modernity. The book's geopolitical focus is the politically volatile highlands of La Paz, traversing the ethnic borderland of Aymara rural networks and the white urban metropole in the city of La Paz. A preliminary note: this book does not offer an institutional or policy-oriented history of education of twentieth-century Bolivia. Instead, I have drawn widely from a rich interdisciplinary scholarship to explore rural schooling, both in discourse and practice, as an intercultural battleground over wider social issues of race, nation, and education in the making of postcolonial Bolivia.[15] Thus, the book's seven chapters (each of which is interpretive and synthetic and begs for further inquiry) toggle among four arenas of action: a shifting state-centered analysis of educational policy, debate, and ideology; a regional ethnography of Indigenous repertoires of vernacular literacy and school activism; an interethnic sphere of struggle and mediation among radical middle-class educators, urban intellectuals, and working-class activists; and the transnational domain of pedagogical ideas and informal empire. Using multisited and multifaceted approaches, I hope to shed new light on the disparate social groups involved in the politics of governance and education (broadly defined) in Bolivia's racially fraught political environment. As a whole, this book is grounded in ethnographic and historical detail while also fixing its sights on the distant horizon of national and transnational historical change. As we shall see in due course, rural Indigenous communities were both the object of educational reform policies and the source of active peasant protagonists, who often became the driving force behind the expansion of rural schooling. Through their actions and words, Aymara people (in particular) became the subjects of their own (oral and written) history of struggle for literacy and schooling, and the agents of their own emancipation from the scourge of "slavery and ignorance"—the compounded oppression of body and mind that Indigenous people often used to characterize the essence of their racial subjugation. This, then, is their history, which I have reinterpreted within the wider framework of Bolivia's tumultuous and halting journey toward modern nationhood.

Although anchored primarily in the highland regions of La Paz, this book casts its net widely to include a range of disparate criollo and Indigenous characters from both sides of the internal colonial divide, including those interstitial groups who trespassed on the ethnic borderland, and a few foreign interlopers who ventured into the Bolivian Andes to dabble in rural school reform at particular times and places. While keeping an eye on the wider transregional horizons, I use the lens of ethnographic history to catch sight of some of the local drama unfolding on the ground. There, Indigenous activists actively engaged in fighting for literacy, lands, schools, and the rule of justice as Bolivia transitioned from a dual republic (an institutional hangover from colonial and early republican times) to a centralizing and modernizing state, albeit one cleaved by race and ethnicity, social class, and geography. As political circumstances changed during the 1930s and early 1940s, new educational practices became the seedbed of radical pedagogies, articulated to wider agrarian movements and coalitional class politics. Grassroots peasant movements, and their expanding political repertoires, opened new subaltern spaces for popular education, rural syndicalism, and citizenship practices to flower in the 1940s, helping to catalyze explosive sociopolitical change in the 1950s. By mapping this rough terrain of tutelary peasant politics and insurgent literacy practices over five decades, then, this book unearths some of the constitutive elements of a decolonizing political counterculture that surfaced in the Aymara highlands (and, later, the Quechua valley regions) at key political conjunctures in Bolivian history.

Below, I sketch the book's narrative framework, conceptual orientations, and interwoven themes.

Enlightenment Fictions, Racist Fears

The book begins by mapping the political geography of the northern Altiplano, an unfolding internal frontier defined by ethnic conflict, the dispossession of communal landholdings, the spread of hacienda servitude, and growing state incursions. Around 1900, the new capital of La Paz became a spatial concentrate of political power, oligarchic wealth, and the state's civilizing ambitions. To unshackle the Aymara-speaking Indian child from the Kantian state of barbarity and backwardness was, for Bolivia's liberal-positivist reformers, the state's indisputable civic and moral imperative. But the establishment of rural schools that would teach Indians their letters, and thus prepare them for the rights and privileges of (male) enfranchised citizenship, threatened to remake Bolivia into a multiracial polity—a utopia that was as remote as it was dangerous in the eyes of the ruling oligarchy.

Chapter 1 ("To Civilize the Indian") explores the contradictory impulses that both impelled and subverted Bolivia's first modern efforts at governance and education along the ethnic frontier of La Paz during the early twentieth century. Race and education worked at ideological cross-purposes in the modern psychology of the ruling oligarchy. Prescriptive tutelary schemes were vested in the power of schooling to change the outward behavior and inner character of the Indian subject. But social policy reforms unleashed virulent reactions whenever they threatened the status quo ante. Bolivia's enlightened men of science and letters were often, themselves, the progenitors of anti-Indigenous racism. They indulged in cosmopolitan ideas about racial determinism—ranging from social Darwinian strictures against degenerative race-mixing, to climatic racial determinism (claiming that different racial groups were destined to live in separate climate zones), to Eurocentric notions about Anglo-Saxon racial superiority. Each strain of racial theory carried policy implications for how the problem of Indian schooling should be addressed—but bundled together, kinetic ideas about race and education constituted a special field of knowledge (which I call "tutelary race-thinking"). This protean field focused on the putative benefits or dangers, possibility or impossibility, of educating the rural masses and how educational policy should be crafted to fit the peculiar racial needs of the nation. Even Bolivia's optimistic reformers were pulled apart by contrary racial prescriptions. To educate the rural masses was to assimilate, rehabilitate, preserve, and/or segregate the population, sometimes all at once! On one point, however, there was a sense of certitude: the country's racial future and national viability pivoted on the outcome of this ongoing battle.

With the Indian education problem unresolved, the Liberal state's first federal effort at educational reform was bound to fail. As chapter 1 shows, however, several important precedents were set. The Montes regime (1904–7; 1914–17) created a few elementary schools and dispatched a small band of itinerant teachers into surrounding provinces. Meanwhile, pedagogical thinkers built castles in the air about the power of "national pedagogy," capable of transforming the primitive Aymara Indian into an obedient and efficient farming class. But liberal zealousness was matched by conservative fear, and in the realm of ideas, the agency of enlightened educational reform ran up against determinist theories about race, climate, and culture. On a practical level, the Liberal Party's enemies warned against the danger of lettering Indians, lest they breach the literacy/suffrage divide and clog the political sphere with yet more lawsuits, mass petitions, and vindictive manifestos. Schooling the Indian could be perilous, they warned, if it were to upend the racial caste hierarchy. Thus, if the rural village school was heralded by social reformers as an evolutionary conveyor belt, moving the lowly *indios* upward from savagery toward civilization, its expansion was thwarted by landlords, conservatives, and provincial authorities, vested in the ancien régime and fearful of Aymara sedition.

In the end, Bolivia's ideologues of race and education bowed to the dictates of "scientific pedagogy" that proclaimed the Indian race to be educable. Furthermore, the viability of the Bolivian nation depended on educational reform: without an assimilated Indian mass of Spanish-speaking farmers and laborers (constituting some 80 or 90 percent of the population around 1900, depending on official racial stats and categorizations), Bolivia could not function as, or even claim to be, a cohesive nationality. Only the practical policy question remained to be solved: How should public instruction be tailored for, and delivered to, Bolivia's school-age children of the Indian race?

This chapter follows the twisted logic of educational advocates and skeptics—both the cosmopolitans and their various critics—who agonized over the Indian problem and its putative solution. It argues that after almost two decades, Bolivia created a blueprint of public education reform, especially tailored to its "peculiar" racial environment. The upshot was a policy plan that split public schooling into two segments, urban and rural, both designed to meet the differential educational needs (mental and manual) of mestizo and Indigenous children. Indian children of the countryside would receive a lesser education. They would be exposed to a "minimal" (usually two-year) curricular course, and they would be immersed in the "national" (Spanish) language in the classroom while gaining "practical knowledge" suitable to their rural milieu, cognitive deficits, and basic subsistence needs. More widely, the goal of rural schooling was to enhance the quality and discipline of the rural Indian workforce while introducing the Indian to lessons in cultural hygiene. Regionalism and ethnicity loomed large in early twentieth-century tutelary race-thinking, making the ethnic "Aymara race" the immediate target of Liberal government school reform and turning the provinces surrounding the white metropole of La Paz into ground zero.

As always, the dynamic interplay of racial theories and pedagogical propositions was profoundly shaped by unfolding political circumstances and by tensions on the ground in particular historical moments. Government school policy (albeit still more imagined than real) was driven by contradictory colonialist needs of racial assimilation and class segmentation. Rhetoric aside, Liberal state school policy walked a fine line between its goal of civilizing the Indians (i.e., bringing them into the nation as efficient workers and loyal patriots) and its fear of disrupting the fragile racial order in a region where "race war" and "rebellious Indians" were a chronic source of white fear. Engineering this delicate balance drove Bolivian elites to scour the Western world for pedagogical ideas and aid. Europe brimmed with a variety of educational models, and Belgium sent a young pedagogue who helped Bolivia set up its first modern school system in the early 1900s. Other Bolivian educators drew inspiration from North America's Indian boarding school model of acculturation and from the "Negro industrial institutes," a pillar of the Deep South's system of racial segregation. How those eclectic foreign pedagogies were applied to the scientific diagnosis (and institutional remedy) of Bolivia's "Indian education problem" continued to shape the elites' ongoing arguments about the vagaries of race, nationality, and education reform until well into the twentieth century.

Andean Literacy before Schooling

Indigenous school activism and aspirations taking place in the margins of the Aymara hinterland could scarcely be imagined, much less contained, by the *paceño* oligarchy in the early twentieth century. Chapter 2 ("Lettered Aymara") pivots to resituate the story of school activism that flourished in the outlying provinces of La Paz. It sketches out the wider play of forces that stoked the fires of peasant aspirations for literacy and schooling between 1900 and 1930. As I seek to show, rural school expansion (uneven and tenuous though it was) sprang from the spontaneous actions and organized campaign of Aymara peasant authorities, for whom alphabetic literacy, documentary culture, and judicial politics had become weapons of combat in their legal struggles to defend or reclaim their original title deeds to colonial landholdings. Engaging in subversive appropriation, Aymara political authorities transformed the civilizers' ideal of the "educated Indian" into a lettered warrior, a bilingual and literate interlocutor capable of challenging the Liberal state's ruthless policy of territorial annexation and the oligarchy's racial theories that legitimated it. Resituated in the Aymara hinterland, the prosaic "alphabet" school was transformed into a symbolic site of subversive political activism among a spreading oral/literate network of Aymara and Quechua people.[16]

Although Aymara school-based activism was particularly intense in Bolivia's northern Altiplano in the early 1900s, it ran concurrently through the veins of Andean peasant society in various times and places.[17] Traumatic moments of social threat and violence could suddenly inflate the currency of Indigenous bilingualism and literacy, spurring Andean peasant leaders to hone their Spanish legal skills; hire bilingual scribes, notaries, lawyers, or other representatives; and otherwise go to great lengths to produce the bureaucratic and legal paperwork in their dogged pursuit of justice and collective voice—a deeply ingrained folk-legal tradition of judicial politics and representation that had come down through the centuries of living under Spanish colonial rule. Andean colonial caciques had wielded the legal protocol and technologies of Spain's "empire of letters" to negotiate and contest the colonizers' rules of governance, coercion, and oppression that burdened the colonized peasantry. Judicial politics, resistance, and tactical uses of alphabetic literacy (or, to borrow Rolena Adorno's compound idea, "writing and resistance")[18] were baked into the mud bricks of Spanish colonial hegemony and endured, albeit on a more diffuse and local level, during the postindependence era of Andean nation-building.[19] Although most rural people still inhabited monolingual villages and rarely came into direct contact with the criollo world of alphabetic literacy, vernacular literacy practices flowered in many Andean regions. Agrarian flare-ups, write anthropologists Frank Salomon and Mercedes Niño-Murcia, suddenly inflated the symbolic and tactical value of literacy learning in rural villages, already engaged in the defense of community as a primordial value among their kinsmen.[20] The turn of the twentieth century was such a conjuncture in the southern Peruvian Andes and northern Bolivian Altiplano. There a booming export trade in wool and the spread of the railroad turned the traditional pastures and cropland of the high plains into coveted real estate, newly vulnerable to *latifundismo* and predatory state policies. As Joanne Rappaport shows, parallel developments engulfed the Cauca region of southern highland Colombia. Their old covenants of communal landholding broken, Indigenous communities under siege began trafficking more heavily in legal, notarial, and archival documents. At such times, the roving *indio letrado*—slandered by city elites as a *tinterillo*, or "ink spiller"—became a colloquial Andean stereotype of the racially ambiguous interloper who incited, and represented, litigious Indians in their courtroom and political battles.[21]

This book traces similar insurgent developments on the Bolivian Altiplano, where local land conflicts flared into a regional movement of *caciques-apoderados*, fighting for their rights to lands, schools, and justice under the Liberal rule of law.[22] Linking the politics of literacy and schooling to the wider

Andean struggle for communal land restitution, I trace the "textual imprints" of Aymara peasant authorities who, through their bilingual intermediaries, played a vital role in mobilizing discursive and tangible support for their right to local elementary schools (as promised by Bolivia's 1874 Constitution). Individual protagonists can provide glimpses of the lived experiences of rural activists who took up the cause of Indian schooling. Accordingly, the story is threaded with textual fragments extracted from government records, court cases, newspaper editorials and articles, literary works, and other official or semiofficial documents. These "autoethnographic" sources (to use Mary Louise Pratt's term) were "authentic" lettered artifacts, although mediated by legal protocol, translation, and various tactical considerations, in which "colonized subjects [undertook] to represent themselves in ways that engage[d] with the colonizer's own terms."[23] As Andean ethnohistorians have documented, some Andean peasant leaders mastered the craft of interethnic communication. Deploying the protocol and media of their oppressors, Andean activists dispatched mail and messages; mobilized court and political challenges; published newspaper articles and notices to sway public opinion; and conducted research in the archives to buttress their arguments over disputed land claims. More than simply a medium, literacy came to define an objective of Aymara communal politics. Because Aymara leaders invoked colonial law to secure traditional land rights and liberal law to secure the right to education, their quest for land and schooling became inextricably linked by the 1910s. In tracking several Aymara literacy instructors and activists— from Bolivia's powerful caciques, and their appointed legal advocates, to the anonymous rural teacher—we can partially unearth the half-buried, muffled voices of "rustic illiterates" who founded village schools; demanded the right to education in elaborate petitions and lawsuits; denounced incidents of violence; advocated for the cause of Indian education; or imagined what cultural decolonization might come to mean in a more inclusive, pluralist society. In the course of their activism, some Aymara leaders engaged in adversarial literacy and developed an incipient kind of popular education through their public denunciation of criollo acts of racial persecution, stolen lands, purloined documents, and pillaged schoolhouses. Where texts allow, I open a window into wider political horizons, where identities of indigeneity were articulated within the ideals of communal autonomy and citizenship equality. In several cases, Indigenous petitions from the 1920s and 1930s advanced the causes of Indian territorial repatriation, schooling, and integration into a "renovated" multiracial nation that might yet come to be.

The Rise and Fall of Warisata

A remarkable communitarian school project that flourished on the Altiplano in the 1930s opens another portal into the Aymara world of rural school activism. Chapter 3 ("Warisata") takes a close ethnographic look at the intricate local dynamics of communal school-building in the turbulent political environment of the 1930s. I seek to show that, by most measures, the construction of that "escuela-ayllu" marked a fundamental turning point in Bolivia's tortured history of Indian/state relations. Working amid the threat of violence in the heart of "*gamonal* territory," criollo educators and Aymara peasant leaders collaborated in a unique experiment in communal restitution, self-governance, and community-based schooling.[24] During its formative history, this ayllu-school expanded the existing boundaries of Indian education, invented new pedagogical norms and practices, set up its own governing and judicial structure, and demonstrated to the outside world the oratorical skills and emancipatory aspirations of Aymara authorities. People across the Altiplano were pulled into its magnetic field—precisely the thing that made this fragile school enterprise so "dangerous" in the eyes of conservative elites.

Why and how this Indian school eventually became iconic, a flash point of debate and an object of violence, will emerge in the course of the book's overarching narrative. But my immediate purpose in chapter 3 is to explore the enabling conditions and social tensions that shaped this groundbreaking project of liberatory schooling and the innovative ways that the school complex was used to reconstitute an expansive geo-cultural space of autonomy in the heart of the Omasuyos province. Had the communitarian school remained a strictly local affair, it might never have attracted much attention, either then or now. But by the late 1930s, Warisata's geopolitical reach and symbolic currency had exploded beyond all expectation. As its fame grew, streams of Indigenous visitors converged on the school for civic holidays, such as the "Day of the Indian" (established in 1937); other Indigenous pilgrims came by flatbed truck or muleback simply to see the school with their own eyes. From the city of La Paz came youthful dissidents, artists, craftspeople, and teachers to see and celebrate the school, or to stay and participate in this inspiring and creative endeavor. A group of revolutionary leftists wondered aloud, Might this cultural project of Indian redemption offer an alternative exit from Bolivia's shameful history of violence and internal colonialism? (Many were skeptical.) As Warisata's fame spread overseas, progressive educators made their way to the school from places as far away as Lima, Santiago, Mexico City, and New York.

That it flourished for almost ten years in the heart of Omasuyos' hacienda zone was no small miracle, as I hope to show. Warisata represented a novel experiment in intercultural schooling. Adapting itself to the geography and culture of the region, the *parlamento de amautas* (council [or parliament] of wise elders), in collaboration with the teachers, created the original *núcleo escolar*, designed to pull outlying "orphan" elementary schools (barely subsisting on their own) into its protective orbit. By the mid-1930s, Warisata had evolved a pedagogy of civic democracy, agrarianism, and intellectualism that broke down the racial-neocolonial division of labor and radiated a bold ethos of emancipation into the surrounding area, where many rural people lived on haciendas as *peones* attached to their overlords. Arguably, however, its very success proved its undoing. Warisata's growing fame, as well as Elizardo Pérez's troubled association with the populist regime of Col. Germán Busch (1937–39), brought about its political demise. For nothing threatened Bolivia's neocolonial order more than the promise and possibility of a rising cadre of educated Aymara youth aligned with radical teachers and intellectuals who, in turn, were building networks of solidarity across Latin America.

As chronicled in chapter 4 ("Whose Indian School?"), the oligarchy's looming fear of Indian emancipation (rehearsed as "race war" or "communist sedition") unleashed waves of microaggression that swelled into organized state violence in the early 1940s. In hindsight, it is perhaps easy to understand how the oligarchy's assault on the ayllu-school movement at its height would come to represent a tragic episode, and a squandered opportunity, in the political life of modern Bolivia. Dramatic though it was, the state's preemptive act of violence against this monument to Indian emancipation perpetuated Bolivia's longer, deeper history of anti-Indigenous racism, neocolonial violence, and lost opportunities in the field of Indigenous education. Once again, traumatic events lay bare the underlying cultural violence of internal colonialism, rooted in the oligarchy's denial and fear of the educated Indian. At the same time, though, Bolivia's postwar generation of populists, leftists, and nationalists lobbied desperately for "the incorporation of the Indian" into a unified national culture.[25] While the socialist parties and militant trade unions looked to the vanguard action of the urban proletariat, the conservative elite sought to shore up the old regime by recycling the earlier civilizers' mission, thinly disguised in the anti-Indianist rhetoric of "mestizo" assimilation during the early to mid-1940s. Either way, the left and the right imagined the future of assimilated campesinos in a mestizo nation. The utopian ayllu-school of Warisata apparently had no place in either nationalist scheme.

Of course, there would be no going back to the old reign of oligarchic parties responsible for the disastrous Chaco War and, later, for the state's assault on Warisata. The rise of a powerful spate of leftist parties, followed by the blood-drenched miners' strikes in 1942 and a cycle of peasant strike actions beginning in 1942, marked a political point of no return in the slow decay of the old order—a full decade before the Movimiento Nacional Revolucionario (MNR) seized the reins of power in 1952. The compounded political shocks of violence at the state level—its frontal assault on Warisata and its program of "Indigenal education," followed by the military's massacre of striking tin miners in Catavi—provoked the moral fury of Bolivia's postwar generation of urban dissidents, rural trade unionists, leftist teachers, displaced veterans, and a roving band of peasant organizers (*dirigentes campesinos*).

Peasant Syndicalism and Popular Education

Revisiting this tumultuous decade, chapter 5 ("Instigators of New Ideas") resituates the locus of Indigenous education in the wider, informal terrain of peasant politics and popular education, rooted in the nascent post–Chaco War movement of peasant syndicalism that spread from the Quechua villages of Ucureña, Cliza, and Vacas in the Cochabamba valleys up into the western Aymara highlands of La Paz and Oruro during the early 1940s. By invoking Gramsci's axiom of "politics as [intrinsically] educative,"[26] this chapter throws light on the emergent political repertoire of agrarian/left activists and their infrastructure of rebel communication, transregional associations, and practices of political socialization (later dubbed *concientización*).[27] More than simply an organized movement of rural trade unionists, with strong alliances to leftist and labor groups in the distant cities, the highland peasant movement sprang from the older *comunario* league of interconnected ayllus, still trying to restore their traditional land rights. But the postwar generation of caciques now shared the political stage with a new breed of rural activist, a roving professional organizer who stirred up Indigenous discontent in dispersed pockets of rural Cochabamba, Oruro, and La Paz. Feared and persecuted by the landed oligarchy, the "rural dirigente" (a peasant leader with ties to rural syndicalism) began to rearticulate the defensive struggle of Aymara communities with the radical class politics of hacienda laborers, as two flanks of a militant peasant movement. Chapter 5 focuses on how these activists operated on the ground and the subversive role that popular education played in this emerging peasant movement.

To catch sight of this submerged sphere of educative politics, my discussion traces the work of several rural dirigentes who founded rural schools and peasant unions, organized local assemblies and regional peasant congresses, circulated radical print literature, and apprenticed in participatory citizenship practices—all the time laying the infrastructure of an emerging peasant movement.[28] Building up from the pluralist base over the early 1940s, this insurgent peasant politics of knowledge and learning culminated in the nationwide Indian Congress of May 1945. The gathering represented a watershed political moment: the first nationwide conference, organized by regional peasant committees from around the country, until the whole ordeal was hijacked by the government at the very last minute. But the real story here is the grassroots mobilization of material and intellectual capital that leveraged and sustained this unprecedented Indigenous political project in the face of landlord threat, obstructionism, and persecution. A national Indigenous association, representing hundreds of dispersed peasant assemblies, translated local grievances into a visionary political agenda of justice and reform. As performance, the Indian assembly was a stunning show of force. Like most mass gatherings of marginalized or oppressed people, it represented a display of collective self-empowerment, a monument to the organizing capacity and solidarity work of Indigenous activists and teachers, and an unmistakable sign that Indigenous people were both honing their oratorical and organizing skills and broadening their base of ethnic solidarity and class identity.

In the end, however, the Indian Congress devolved into a colonial hall of mirrors—one that offered its Indigenous constituents a breathtaking glimpse of the horizons of *possibility*, along with a disheartening lesson in the structural *impossibility* of Indigenous self-education and emancipation within Bolivia's rigid neocolonial order. In microcosm, the 1945 congress represented a clash of political agendas, a political contest between the populist state and a militant peasant movement, and the momentary advantage fell to state authorities. Under the populist antics of Col. Gualberto Villarroel (1943–46), the Indian

Congress devolved into a high-stakes drama over the vexed relationship between race, nation, and citizenship that could not possibly be resolved within the prevailing social order, and Villarroel's days were numbered, in any event. By late 1946 and 1947, with Villarroel dead and gone, the Bolivian state resorted to desperate measures, using military technology to crush the rural movement and secure the old oligarchic order. But the unintended lessons of that failed Indian Congress were manifestly expressed in the escalation of peasant strikes and other kinds of rural disturbances (the spread of rural labor unions, leftist revolutionary party operations, and peasant militias). There would be no "negotiated" Indian/state hegemony after all.

Pastoral Indians, Imperial Incursions

During the 1940s, Bolivia's domestic disturbances resonated in the wider hemispheric arena as the country's volatility became a source of growing concern to officials in the US Department of State, its embassy in La Paz, and a small group of international diplomats, aid donors, and social scientists. North American diplomats were already well versed in Bolivia's postwar politics of economic nationalism and anti-imperialism by the late 1930s, when the military regime of Col. David Toro (1936–37) expropriated the Bolivian holdings of Standard Oil. Diplomatic relations were patched up once the conservative oligarchy came back into state power and Bolivian tin became a strategic resource in World War II. From then on, Bolivia's domestic situation became an object of US intelligence and surveillance, as well as a target of economic (and, later, military) aid, institutional modernization, and strong-armed diplomacy. In turn, Bolivia's relationship with the hemisphere's hegemon would become ever more contingent, complex, and clientelist.

While Washington's wartime priorities and Cold War relations with Bolivia have attracted much scholarly attention, chapter 6 ("Enclaves of Acculturation") explores North America's cultural and political strategies of incursion into rural Bolivia as its agrarian crisis deepened. Even before World War II was over, US social scientists and engineers were eager to stabilize Bolivia's laboring and peasant classes and contain the appeal of leftist, nationalist, and communist ideologies. The tin mines were the main focus of concern, for obvious reasons, but eventually Washington's field agents began to understand how labor stability and communist containment would depend on pacifying the Indigenous peasantry, the geo-cultural reservoir of the urban labor force.

Development, stabilization, and democracy were strategic imperial goals that soon brought Bolivia's Indian problem into sharp focus.

Exploring the linked themes of rural development, cultural hygiene, and Indian schooling, this chapter scales up the narrative analysis to examine the imperial geopolitics of knowledge and the attendant rural school reform policies that converged on the Bolivian Andes between 1940 and 1949. It traces how transnational forces of rural development and strategic intelligence catapulted the country's Indian problem onto Washington's wartime agenda, thus bringing the hoary issues of race, labor, and education into the playbook of diplomats, technicians, and teachers. A well-funded American school reform policy (under the Truman-era "cooperative services") became the new site and conduit for US programs of "rural extension education." That gendered model of resocialization introduced a complex of agrarian workforce training, family norms and homemaking, and community-based programs of social hygiene (designed to eradicate the cultural defects and primitive lifeways) of the Indian. Bolivia became a testing ground for US disciplinary programs, designed to habituate Indians into becoming hard-working, modernizing, self-regulated farmers. Armed with new pedagogical guidelines and goals, newly trained rural teachers became the project's foot soldiers, who were sent off to targeted rural communities to solve the Indian problem—one body, household, school, and community at a time.

By the end of the decade, the US-run Servicio Cooperativo Interamericano de Desarrollo Educativo (SCIDE) won a major concession from a reluctant Bolivian government: North American educators were granted permission to take over and rehabilitate the remnants of Warisata. Armed with the latest theories and methods of "functional education," North America technicians were put in charge of Warisata (along with several other *núcleo escolares*), where they instructed Bolivian teachers-in-training how best to educate and acculturate "their Indians." Where once the original ayllu-school of Warisata had drawn a stream of pedagogic pilgrims from across the Americas, it now became a North American showcase of modern agriculture, public hygiene, homemaking, good work habits, and consumerism. With astonishing strategic foresight (or perhaps it was just a twist of fate?), the United States had burrowed into the interior affairs of Indian education politics at a time of escalating agrarian unrest and growing anti-Americanism—almost as if in anticipation of the 1952 revolutionary upheaval—a decisive political moment in the long struggle for Indigenous citizenship and justice.

From the Threshold of the Rural School: Rethinking the Bolivian Revolution

Bolivia's trajectory of popular mobilization and oligarchic reaction reached a cathartic moment of rupture and transformation in the uprising of April 1952. Catapulted into power by an armed coalition of miners, workers, peasants, and radical middle-class dissidents, the MNR had an urgent mandate to dismantle the oligarchic order, open the political system, and redistribute property and power to Bolivia's laboring classes and secure its base of popular support. The MNR's cascade of civic and social reforms, together with its coalitional governing structure with the country's powerful labor confederation, signaled the depth and intensity of political transformation during the early years of MNR political rule (1952–64). This historic episode of political mobilization and change was, by most measures, an integrative revolution that swept away all but the vestiges of the neocolonial order. Or so it seemed at the time.[29]

Chapter 7 ("The Hour of Vindication") locates the struggle over Indigenous education at the axis of Indigenous mobilization and the MNR's historic mandate to shape a modern patriotic citizenry, train an efficient agricultural labor force, and inculcate a spirit of civic loyalty to the popular revolution. Although agrarian reform (1953–54) quickly took political precedence, education reform (1955–56) propelled the revolution's ethos of democracy and integrative politics of cultural nationalism. That populist framework could be read, and reworked, in multiple and contradictory ways. For Aymara activists, the 1952 insurrection invoked a collective sense of "social revindication," to borrow the poetry of one peasant petition. The authors of this visionary proposal approached the overthrow of the old order as a precipice in time, a moment that called for a moral reckoning with the past sins of oligarchic violence, denial, and alienation of communal lands. A profusion of peasant petitioners, long accustomed to lobbying state authorities for schools and other rights, seized the moment to make their voices heard. The swell of rural unrest only amplified their political demands for lands, schools, unions, and justice in the wider public sphere. On the ground, plots of lands were seized; haciendas were invaded and occupied; Indian petitions flooded the office of the new president; and Indigenous leaders mobilized the paperwork to demand plots of ex-hacienda land or the restitution of communal landholdings. The quiet (and largely forgotten) underside of agrarian transformation was the peasant crusade for schooling that resurfaced in the early 1950s. In mobilizing for the right to elementary literacy schools, an onrush of rural petitioners demanded "the alphabetization of the Indian!"

From the margins, we can perhaps take the pulse of Indigenous aspirations: in the communal act of building a local school, without the fear of landlord retribution; in the heightened demand for rural teachers and schools, government aid, and NGO collaboration; in the scramble for popular literacy and schooling; and in the outflow of Indigenous youth to the cities in search of new educational and livelihood opportunities. Amid the political ferment, the prosaic village school became a potent symbol of dignity, autonomy, and inclusion. On the Bolivian Altiplano, where Aymara communities had long struggled for community schools and cultivated a tradition of vernacular writing, the revolutionary promise of redemption was enshrined in the schoolhouse. It represented the aspirational space wherein Indigenous children would be released from racial oppression of "ignorance" and "illiteracy" by learning how to read and write in the dominant language. Historically denied their constitutional right to formal schooling, and punished by local potentates or state violence for having tried to claim it, rural people now had a chance to redeem the sacrifices of their forebears. At the most prosaic level, the pursuit of cultural empowerment and emancipation came in the shape of the alphabet reader.

At the same time, the rural elementary school became an indispensable tool of the new state, and there was no time to waste in the aftermath of insurrection. The overnight explosion of Bolivia's mass electorate (following the promulgation of the universal "vote and voice" in 1952) amplified the party's need to secure the loyalty of the masses and integrate them into a unifying national culture under the hegemonic state.[30] Much as Eric Hobsbawm described for western Europe, Bolivian state officials looked to the rural primary school as "the secular equivalent of the church ... imbued with revolutionary and republican principles and content, and conducted by the secular equivalent of the priesthood, or the friars."[31] To "bolivianize" the Indian majority, to instill in the Indigenous peasantry a strong sense of patriotic loyalty to both nation and party, was the holy grail of the MNR's newly trained rural teachers, the "apostles of Indian education." Resocializing the masses would require a massive state apparatus: rural schools, public hygiene, culture brigades, political propaganda, and mass media campaigns, all filtered through government offices, a network of rural teachers, official peasant militia and agrarian unions, and various US and other foreign aid agencies.

From the outset, Bolivian statesmen, intellectuals, educators, *indigenistas*, and artisans looked to postrevolutionary Mexico for inspiration. In particular, Bolivians admired Mexico's nationalist, aesthetic, and educational campaigns that projected a unifying mestizo identity while also repatriating its authentic Indian heritage through the venues of folklore, mural art, and archaeology.[32] Exalting the Indian heritage, while marginalizing the despised "indio" from the modern polity, would be the road toward unity and modernity that Bolivian cultural nationalists hoped to travel. But if the MNR drew lessons from Mexico's project of national integration, it also depended heavily on US material aid, development programs, and technical expertise. From early on, Bolivia's Commission for Education Reform (CRE) worked assiduously with US and UNESCO teams to build a "functional" (or "fundamental") program of rural education. Its primary purpose was to fashion a new revolutionary ideal—the modern campesino—through the application of programs in rural extension, community development, and Indian acculturation.

Even as MNR officials looked abroad for funding and inspiration, they faced a daunting domestic challenge: fifty years of failed school policy now had to be reckoned with. Emblematic of that failure was the unresolved Indian problem, in the assessment of MNR officials. Standing before dozens of international delegates to the 1954 indigenista congress, held that year in La Paz, Vice President Hernán Siles Suazo confessed to the group that the Indian was still Bolivia's "greatest problem."[33] Although he was clearly angling for international aid and solidarity, this confession was a telling sign that Bolivia's new regime was determined, one way or another, to "solve it." As this chapter will argue, the MNR's conception of rural education recycled a brand of tutelary race-thinking encapsulated by that signal colonial trope. The MNR devised a series of institutional and rhetorical ways to dissolve, disappear, or marginalize the Indian problem in the process of converting the despised indio (symbol of the feudal-colonial past) into a "modern campesino" subject (celebrated as agrarian worker, comrade, and citizen). Embedded racism was buried just below the surface of revolutionary, populist, and class rhetoric. The MNR's rural education policy was indicative, as it was still predicated on the underlying racial-colonial logic of "separate and unequal" schooling that had governed the pedagogy of Bolivia's early civilizing elites. Officially, rural elementary schooling would be "universal, obligatory, and free" under the MNR regime, yet also downscaled to provide a minimum of schooling to the school-age children of the rural masses. Literacy brigades would invade the countryside, but the curriculum would cater to the nation's functional need to anchor the Indian laborer on the land (particularly in the harsh environment of the Altiplano to which the Aymara peasant was uniquely adapted). The MNR's 1955 Education Code also doubled down on the state's larger goal of Indian assimilation into a unifying mestizo nation. Social and civic integration were vigorously promoted, but on the condition that the rural masses shed their native cultural traditions, languages, and identities (a process long dubbed *castellanización*). Indo-Mestizo unity opened civic spaces for the decorative folkloric Indian or the acculturated campesino, but foreclosed the utopian quest for a genuinely postcolonial, multiracial democracy—both democratic and inclusive, but true to its complex cultural heritage of resilient indigeneity, racial mixing, and interethnic mobility. Such were the profound contradictions that delimited the MNR's "negotiated" hegemonic order, as viewed through the optic of educational politics.

Yet, looking across the long arc of social history, it is hard not to perceive in this half-century battle over Indigenous education a high-water mark in Bolivia's cultural politics of revolution. Even before the MNR state could erect an apparatus of popular nationalism and educational reform, the rural school had surfaced, once again, as an impromptu yet potent symbol of Indigenous freedom from slavery and illiteracy (the twin evils of the racist-colonialist order). As the age of agrarian and education reform unfolded in tandem, the village school opened new horizons of possibility for the Aymara "children of '52" (and for other rural people across the highlands and valleys). Andean peasants had established a precedent on which to build their ambitions and demands for "social revindication." For the revolution's children and youth were, in a crucial symbolic way, the cultural heirs of the famous caciques of the 1910s and 1920s; the once-celebrated emancipatory school movement of the 1930s; and the militant peasantry that fought for rural unions, schools, and citizenship through the 1940s. And they too would leave an emancipatory legacy for their heirs.

Eventually, toward the tail end of the twentieth century, the Bolivian state would finally have to accommodate the country's vibrant multiethnic heritage and bank on the possibility that the country's ethnic diversity was not the scourge of the colonial past but, potentially, its greatest cultural asset. This book plots the long, difficult journey toward that belated social revelation.

1

To Civilize the Indian

Contested Pedagogies of Race and Nation

What should we do with the Indian? Will he be susceptible to even the most rudimentary education? ... What future awaits the Indian, the nation?
—ALFREDO GUILLÉN PINTO, *La educación del indio*

From the mid-nineteenth century, the ideal of universal education inspired Latin America's liberal elites, eager to cast the light of reason into their shadowy interior backlands. If Latin America's lettered elites had any hope of extending the apparatus of government into the unruly countryside, they would have to mount civilizing projects under secular agents of the state. A vanguard group of schoolteachers would be dispatched as the foot soldiers wherever statesmen proclaimed *la instrucción pública* (along with European immigration) to be the panacea of poverty, ignorance, political instability, and cultural backwardness in their own interior frontiers. Their positivist faith in the power of education to mold bodies, hearts, and minds would become the driving motif of state hegemony and the nation-building project for much of the twentieth century. Thus was born the sentimental ideal of *pedagogía nacional* in Argentina, Chile, Bolivia, and elsewhere in Latin America during the early 1900s.[1] A unifying nationalist trope, the notion soon devolved into a terrain of conflict in which competing educational proposals were permeated by racial anxieties, civilizing theories, and nationalist utopias in the reimagining of the modern Latin America nation-state for the new century.

The social stakes, and embedded challenges, involved in constructing a unifying national pedagogy were particularly dramatic in the Bolivian Andes, for in many ways, Bolivia in 1900 was not yet a "nation"—if, by that, we mean a cohesive "imagined political community" nestled within an ideological, legal, and institutional apparatus of modern state rule. Quite the contrary: the legacy of colonialism, violence, and indigeneity had produced a quasi-citizenship republic in name only. Alberto Flores Galindo's description of mid-nineteenth-century Peru as a fictitious "republic without citizens" fits the Bolivian case, certainly as late as 1899. But times were changing. Outside the new capital of La Paz, Bolivia's arid highlands provided fertile terrain for the new governing elite to entertain ideas about how to pacify, civilize, and thus redeem the Indians who inhabited the provinces surrounding the city. In 1900, it began devising plans to provide schooling for the children of the popular and peasant classes. By any measure, Bolivia's need for rural public schooling was dire: 73 percent of the country's population (roughly 1.6 million) lived in rural areas, largely beyond the reach of the state; Indians composed well more than 50 percent of Bolivia's racially classified population; and only 16 percent of Bolivian school-age children were registered as having had "some schooling."[2] (And those numbers did not begin to accurately assess the country's woeful lack of a state-run educational infrastructure in the countryside at the turn of the century.) Even more than the glamour of spreading iron rails, the expansion of secular schooling was heralded as the answer to Bolivia's social and racial problems.

The more urgent mandate, however, was to create a network of elementary schools that reached deep into the countryside, where an (allegedly) inert mass of Indians waited to be exposed to the light of reason, instructed in the habits of industry and piety, immersed in the national language, letters, and culture, and schooled in their patriotic duties to the Bolivian nation. A tiny vanguard of progressive educators gave voice to the nationalist idea that Bolivia's material and racial progress—indeed, its very existence as a cohesive nationality—depended on the state's ability to apply the amendment in Bolivia's

1874 Liberal Constitution (art. XIV) that entitled all the nation's school-age children to basic education in schools that were "universal, secular, obligatory, and free." For a quarter of a century, that democratic ideal lay dormant as Bolivia went through cycle after cycle of crisis—the War of the Pacific (1879–83), chronic partisan upheaval, rampant *caudillismo*, a massive Aymara uprising (1899), a simmering border war with Brazil (1900–1903), and successive years of highland drought and crop failure. But by 1900, there were glimmers of hope. Bolivia's modernizing Liberal government, it seemed, was at long last prepared to launch a pedagogical revolution in the rural Aymara heartland of La Paz and beyond.

But official educational reform also raised troubling dilemmas. How might the penurious state build an apparatus of schooling without adequate funding, physical schoolhouses, trained teachers, school supplies, or bureaucratic functionaries? What kind of pedagogy should be designed for the rural schoolchild, barely conversant in Spanish (at best) and usually needed in the fields and pastures of the peasant family farm? How to fulfill Bolivia's liberal constitutional promise of universal schooling without releasing streams of semiliterate voters, litigious Indians, or plebeian cholos into the white metropole? Many conservatives were dead set against the idea of spreading rural literacy and schooling. Even Bolivia's progressive "educationalists" were haunted by doubts about the racial character and future of the nation. Was Bolivia on the road to whitening, or trapped in a spiral of racial degeneration? No wonder the young normal-trained teacher Alfredo Guillén Pinto sounded exasperated when he asked his compatriots, rhetorically, what Bolivia should do about the Indian problem (see the epigraph). In 1919, after two decades of educational debates and reforms aimed at the Andean peasantry, this educator was still plagued by racial doubts about the Indian as a viable tutelary object. He wondered, Would the Indian child be receptive to "even the most rudimentary education?"

This chapter explores how Bolivia's modernizing elites struggled to overcome their internal rivalries and existential doubts as they cobbled together a racialized national pedagogy—one specifically crafted to lift the restive Aymara Indians out of "a state of savagery" without disturbing the neocolonial caste hierarchy or unleashing a new "race war" in the city's outlying rural provinces. We begin by scoping out the geopolitical and regional contexts in which the newly ascendant paceño elite tried to define the state's civilizing/assimilationist mission as it mobilized the instrumental knowledge and institutional reforms needed to carry it out. Elite arguments over Indian education provides a fractured lens through which to view the remaking of urban La Paz into a white metropole as the Liberal oligarchy tried to launch a new public education system in its outlying Aymara provinces—already submerged in territorial conflicts over the state's predatory land reform policies.

The Civilizers' Imperative: Constructing the White Metropole

To urban elites, the indelible sign of progress was the smoke-belching locomotive chugging across the vast horizons of the Altiplano. Bolivia first caught the feverish desire for railroads in the 1870s, when an erstwhile North American investor imagined a rail system that would link Bolivia to Brazil, around the same time steamship service was introduced on Lake Titicaca. Though that initial railroad scheme failed, by 1900 Bolivians began laying an iron skeleton of glistening rails and telegraph lines across the high desert plateau. New rail lines linked Bolivia's interior population centers on the Altiplano to the mining towns, the lake, and Chile's Pacific ports (Guaqui to La Paz, 1905; Oruro to Viacha, 1908; Arica to La Paz, 1913; and Viacha to La Paz, 1917). In Bolivia, as everywhere else in Latin America, modernizers wrote paeans to the miracle of the steam locomotive. Not only would railcars haul manufactured goods from Europe's industrial economies and ship out Bolivia's raw mineral ore; they also promised to shatter the provinciality of the cramped Bolivian worldview. Romancing the railroad became a literary cliché. One Bolivian enthusiast wrote, "More than transporting mere material objects, [the railroads] open new channels to social doctrines and introduce tolerance with [the coming for foreign] immigration. Liberty grows and widens with the variety of opinions and beliefs that comes from contact among diverse nationalities. Its impulse is irresistible."[3] Bustling overseas commerce, European immigrants, and the prospect of prosperity tracking alongside the glistening rails: here was the apparent panacea for Bolivia's doleful state of backwardness. Here, too, was the remedy for the country's "fatal illness" of small minds and petty concerns—the putative pathology of isolation and provincialism. Writing in the early twentieth century, Ignacio Calderón envisioned an expanse of rails that would collapse Bolivia's vast "empty" frontier, by reaching across the tropical expanse of territory lying to the east of Cochabamba and connecting the country's mining and rubber enclaves to the world market.[4]

Paradoxically, shiny railway cars threw into stark relief the region's economic backwardness, encapsulated by ancient Andean traditions of transport and communication. Bolivia's vertiginous geography of mountains, valleys, and ravines had challenged even the most confident European engineers. Tortuous mountain trails, for centuries constructed and maintained by Indigenous labor parties, continued to bear the heavy and constant traffic of pack animals and their drivers, who hauled tropical fruits, coca, cacao, coffee, and other crops up from the Yungas and other warm places on the eastern escarpment of the Andes to the highland peasant markets of La Paz and Oruro. Traditional kinship networks of trade and reciprocity, along with a brisk trade in these crops and manufactured goods, lubricated those ancient arteries of trade. A passage in the National Census of 1900 noted that "the vast interior commerce of Bolivia, carried on in this [ancient] form, is a peculiar surprise for all foreigners who visit the country, because this traffic is entirely in the hands of Indians."[5] The upkeep of those interior mountain paths was the responsibility of municipalities, which in turn was foisted on rural Indigenous communities. A holdover of colonial tribute, obligatory work maintaining those roads, especially after heavy rains, continued to burden rural communities in the early twentieth century. In later years, the federal government tried to regulate the civic obligation on public works projects (building and repairing roads, aqueducts, bridges, etc.) through policies of road work obligations. But in 1900 the country's circulatory system still depended on Andean modes of communication and transport—from the ceaseless traffic in animal caravans, to the network of roadside inns (*tambos*) to aid the long-distance traveler, to the "inexhaustible" mountain guide and mail carrier (*postillón*) still performing the Indian's colonial tributary obligation. The stark contrast between animal and machine was best captured on the page by Alcides Arguedas, who described the ubiquitous Indian *pongo* and his mule train carrying a load of crops, firewood, or other wares to the landlord's urban townhouse.[6] Arguedas understood the Aymaras' aversion to the predatory merchant, but he deplored the race's "refractory" attitude toward the march of progress:

> The conquests of the white neither interest nor impress [the Indian]. Yet there, in their rural villages, lost in the distance, are [signs of progress]: nail-studded posts sunk into the ground every so often; the posts are strung with vibrating threads of iron and copper. Yet [the Aymara] does not know their use, nor does he suspect their usefulness. Trains leave him indifferent. For

twenty years, they have steamed noisily across the Altiplano, but only recently have [the Aymara] realized that they can transport men in short periods of time across long distances. Now he sometimes travels by passenger train, but he never transports his harvested crops, preferring to truck his crops on the backs of his burros or on thick sheepskins on his slow and stoical llamas.[7]

The jarring sight of the camelid lumbering alongside the iron rails, or under the telegraph's vibrating copper threads, evoked this binary landscape of tradition and modernity. But Arguedas's stereotypical Indian was not the only figure stuck in the past. He also criticized the country's provincial landlords and merchants who saved the freight cost of rail transportation by continuing to deploy the labor services of their serf-like *colonos*. Few Liberal statesmen and writers, the same men who extolled the marvels of the railroad, broke with this anachronism of rural life. For the hacendado, the old transport system of "the mule and the Indian"—archaic, dusty, and woefully inefficient—was an entrenched tradition of Bolivia's highland agrarian order.

Would the railroad really usher in a new age of civilization and modernity, sweeping this ancien régime away in its wake, as the positivists envisioned? A few skeptics on both the right and left ends of the ideological spectrum wondered about the inexorability of "universal" progress following rapidly in the tracks of the railroad. Viewed from the white metropole, the Aymara Altiplano seemed to be trapped in a time warp—an immense and desolate plateau, inhabited by primitives stooped in servitude on autarchic estates, and located in a temporal netherworld—hovering somewhere between the mechanical mirage of modernity and the iron grip of the colonial past. Even many sunny positivists wondered about the nation's destiny. In rhapsodizing about the railroad, Calderón provided two indices—*the number of railroads and schools*—by which "the progress and culture of modern peoples are measured. By this criterion," he admitted, "we Bolivians do not have much to be proud of."[8]

Looking out from the arid basin of La Paz toward the glacial peak of Illimani glistening in the luminous thin air and the cordillera framing the northeastern edge of the vast Altiplano, the city's urbane elites must have taken comfort in the fact that, as of late, the city had been undergoing a modern face-lift. The city's dusty carriage road led down from the Altiplano into the cavernous bowl of the city, where a grand boulevard paved the way into the city center. Gas lanterns lit the night sky in central plazas; bustling salons offered imported teas and coffees; noisy streetcars carried ladies and gentlemen to

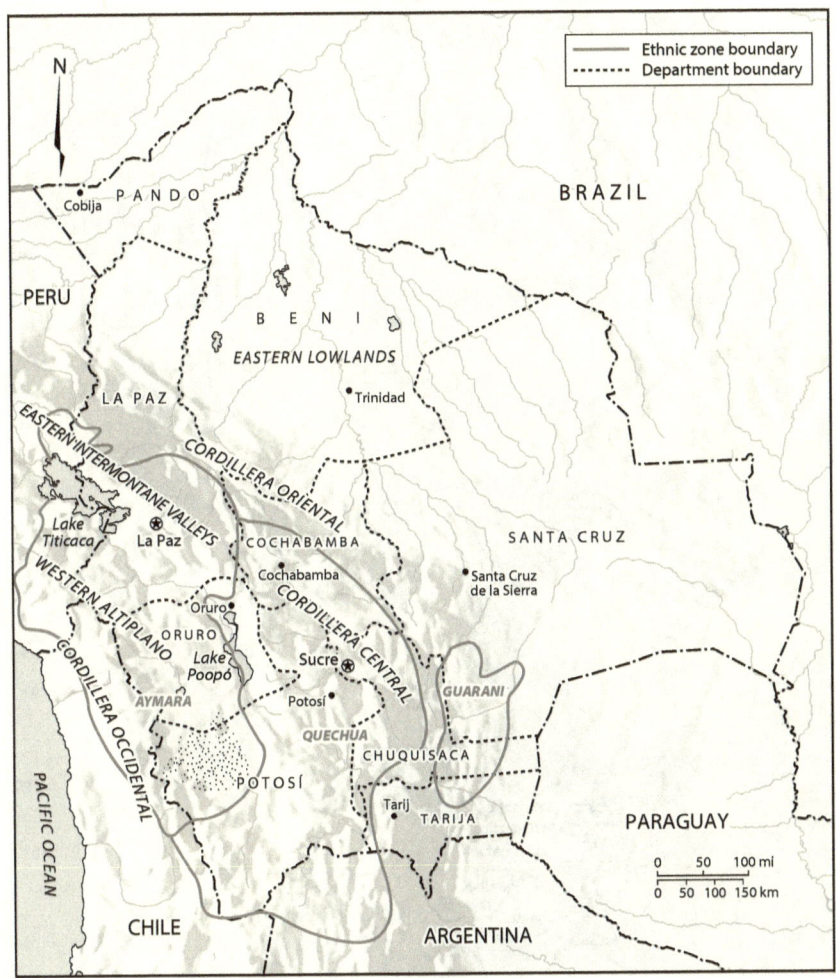

MAP 1.1. Bolivia. Map by Bill Nelson.

shops, salons, and each other's townhouses; and corner newsstands offered the reading public a cornucopia of print matter. The growth and transformation of downtown La Paz, notes Javier Sanjinés, was "the clearest geopolitical expression of the modernizing impulses" of the new ruling elite (see fig. 1.1).[9]

But as any foreign observer could plainly see, the metaphorical lettered city was no oasis of civilized whiteness. The city's vibrant and diverse population was made up of urban artisans and laborers; market women and domestic servants; and the ceaseless traffic of peasants, traders, and transient day

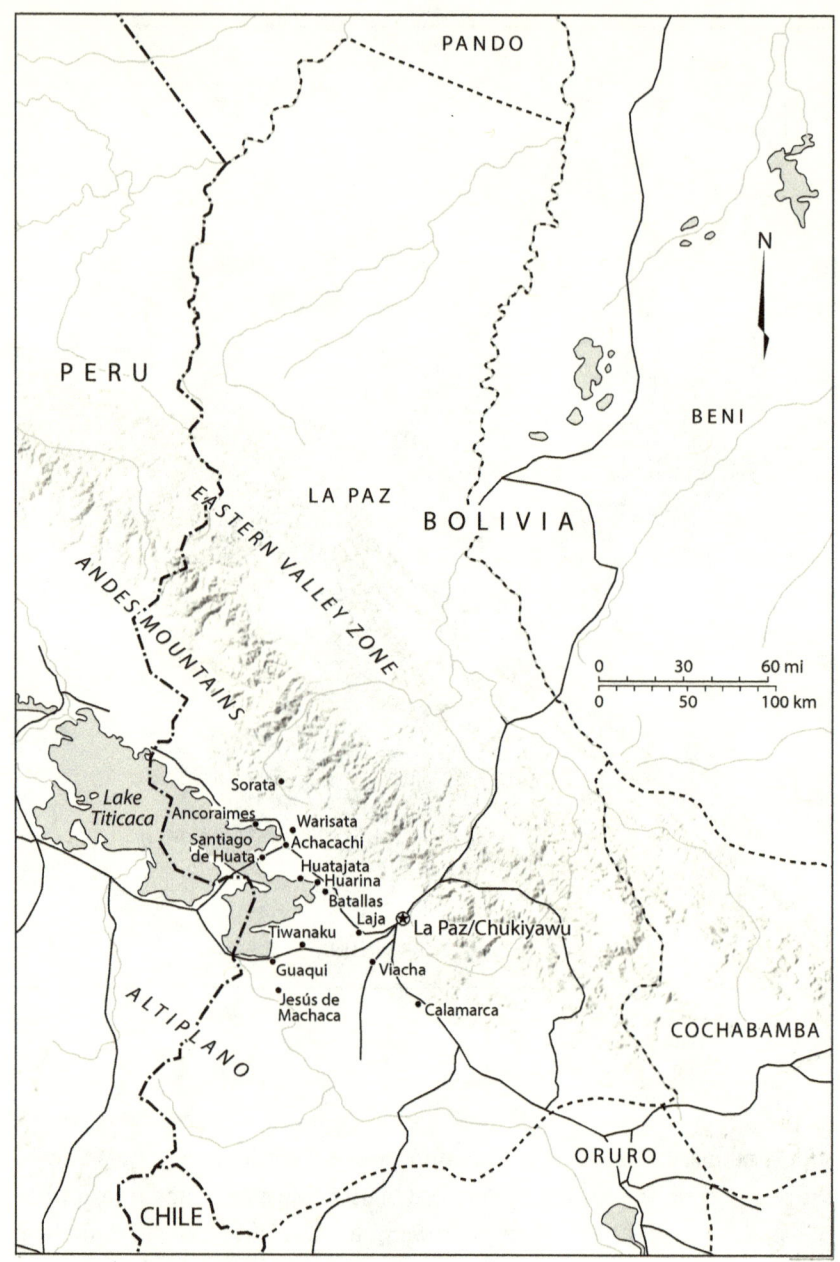

MAP 1.2. The region of La Paz. Map by Bill Nelson.

FIGURE 1.1. Elegant modernity in the capital city of La Paz, ca. 1910. A quintessential sign of urban progress, the cable car was restricted to white passengers. Indigenous people were forbidden to walk, much less congregate, in downtown La Paz. Photo by Julio Cordero, courtesy of the Julio Cordero Family Archive.

laborers. In his early nineteenth-century visit to the city, the French naturalist Alcide D'Orbigny[10] traced the roots of the city's vitality to its strategic location at the colonial crossroads of overland trade routes and its proximity to the densely populated Aymara Altiplano.[11] To the east of La Paz, on the other side of the towering Cordillera Oriental, lay the rich coca fields of the Yungas, a region that massively exported coca to the Potosí silver mines. To the west, across the high desert plateau and down through the western mountains, across the coastal Atacama Desert, lay the vital Pacific port of Arica, a major maritime depot for the southern Andes. Although the city of La Paz lay far from Alto Peru's iconic silver mines of Potosí, it prospered from prospecting in nearby gold mining. Long after the traveling French scientist passed through Bolivia, the region's sputtering gold mines faded from memory before the economic explosion of industrial tin mining in southern Bolivia, Oruro, and the southern border of the Department of La Paz. But for all those economic fortunes, the city's name was a historical misnomer—wishful thinking on the part of Spanish colonists. The geopolitical location of La Paz—and the region's long history of colonial violence, labor extraction, and interethnic trade—constituted powerful countervailing factors that both fueled the city's colonial and mercantile prosperity and periodically shook its very foundation under the threat of Aymara peasant insurrection and siege. More than a century had passed since Túpac Katari and his troops had laid waste to the city in the early 1780s, but that trauma was still deeply embedded in the political culture and collective memory of the city's ruling elite, making a mockery of the city's name.[12]

Set against the "melancholy" landscape of the Altiplano, the motley city of La Paz appeared to be a jumble of adobe huts and stone buildings tucked into deep canyons and clinging to steep mountainsides. Peering over the edge of the great plateau into the crevice of the city, the Frenchman was stunned by the vista: "In [the city of] La Paz," he wrote, "not only is the mass of the population indigenous, and speaks nothing but its primitive language, but [its] national dress also dominates ... [which is,] if not the most picturesque, at least the most original."[13] Dark colors, intricate weavings, and homespun wool textiles clothed the bodies of Andean men and women, marking them as country folk. By contrast, the city's laboring and plebeian communities (the "cholo" inhabitants) displayed a kaleidoscope of colors and textures assembled from both manufactured and handmade pieces of clothing—a sartorial amalgam of Indigenous and mestizo, rural and urban identities. In 1830, the roving French scientist recognized that the city of La Paz was, in reality, two intertwined spatial and racial communities—the Aymara city of Chukiyawu and the criollo (white) city of La Paz—whose distinctive origins and geographies had become inextricably linked under the early republic (see fig. 1.2).[14]

In the early 1900s, the European traveler would not have encountered a fundamentally different cityscape outside the city center of power and commerce. The national census of 1900 confirmed the city's vibrant ethnic amalgam. Indians still greatly outnumbered the urban population of whites and mestizos.[15] But the census commissioners were puzzled by their numerical findings. What was indisputable was the Indian population's surprising long-term demographic resilience and proportional weight: "At the present, the proportion of the indigenous race, including the savages [the civilizers' label for the country's eastern lowland "nomads" and "tribes"], is the same now as it was 54 years ago," the census reported.[16] The census revealed the *persistence* of the Indigenous population over the previous fifty-odd years. Yet

FIGURE 1.2. A sartorial portrait of caste division. A mestiza matriarch stands behind two children: one boy born to the white criollo elite, the other a child of Indigenous parents. Courtesy of the Julio Cordero Family Archive.

that observation of Indian population continuity seemed to contradict the specious social Darwinian doctrine of the "survival of the fittest" (a phrase coined by the positivist philosopher Herbert Spencer) in the context of harsh environmental pressures. How could the Indian population have sustained itself? Drought, famine, and pestilence—the usual triad of death among the impoverished peasantry—had plagued the Bolivian highlands since 1878. And the havoc that nature wreaked was compounded by the scourge of alcoholism, "notably decimating [the Indians'] ranks."[17]

According to Bolivia's official census of 1900, the first of its kind, the obdurate Indian race was doomed to extinction:

> For a long time, a noteworthy process has been unfolding in Bolivia—the slow and gradual disappearance of the indigenous race.... [Thus] after a brief interim, following the progressive laws of statistics, we will have an Indian race which, if not completely obliterated from the everyday scene, will be reduced to its minimum expression. This will be to the good, considering the fact that, if there has been an obstruction to civilization, it has been the Indian race. [It] has been essentially refractory to innovation and progress, and refused tenaciously to accept any customs not transmitted by tradition over the ages from its remote ancestors.[18]

That strikingly social Darwinian conclusion—that the Indian population was in exorable decline due to its innate unfitness, its refusal to adapt, and the deleterious effects of the social and physical environment—was not presented as an unalloyed finding, however, for if carried to its logical conclusion, the inexorable forces of "natural selection" would leave the Bolivian countryside denuded and depopulated. Over the long run, the scourge of racial degeneration and decline would do "grave harm to industry and agriculture."[19]

But even the official census takers could not decide, definitively, which way the evolutionary wind was blowing. Was the Indian population destined to be absorbed into the "superior" racial strata of whites and mestizos within a couple of generations, thus whitening the complexion of the country until it resembled its admired neighbor, Chile? Or did the sheer demographic weight of Bolivia's Indigenous population, and the government's failure to attract European immigrants, cast doubt on the civilizers' hope for evolutionary progress toward whitening? Indeed, the census numbers could be turned around to buttress the arguments of Bolivia's "racial pessimists" who, borrowing from the theories of Gustave Le Bon, worried about the degenerative forces of race mixing. Other race-thinkers fastened on the genealogy of the ancient Aymara race and the country's indelible racial caste divisions.[20] One notable footnote in the 1900 census commented that after three centuries of colonialism, "Bolivia still offers the spectacle to the traveler of being two divided pueblos that [must] encounter each other. The cultured and civilized element [is] reduced to a few cities, which appear to be surrounded by thick Mongoloid walls that are nearly impossible to traverse. Only steps beyond them, [the traveler sees] immense tracts of Indian land, with their *rancherías* as in the time of the Incas."[21]

Borrowed from the impressions of D'Orbigny, the author of these words was very much a man of his time. Manuel Vicente Ballivián was a patrician member of the elite, a distinguished writer, president of La Paz's Geographic Society, and the man in charge of the 1900 census commission. It was Ballivián who presided over the ambiguities and contradictions that marred the census results.[22] What was the country's racial future? Were the Indians poised on the evolutionary brink of extinction, as the white Darwinian "optimists" insisted? Or, having survived three centuries of colonialism, were the highland Aymara and Quechua races a permanent part of Bolivia's somnolent rural landscape? This uncertainty only intensified the racial anxieties and arguments among Bolivia's vanguard civilizers. Perhaps the census's most disheartening diagnosis was the apparent "incapacity of the Indians to civilize themselves, [because they] swim against [the tides of] history and experience."[23]

As we shall see, this clash of racial and evolutionary prognoses would vex the state's leading pedagogues over the first two decades of the twentieth century and beyond. Within the governing elite, disagreement over the racial fate of the nation filtered down into educational policy debate. Should the state design a national pedagogy to assimilate the Indian race? Were they educable? Might they be rendered socially and morally "fit" for inclusion in the modernizing state? Or did *la indiada* represent a pathological and dying race of people, as Bolivia's racial pessimists insisted? On the other hand, a growing chorus of indigenista teachers and writers advocated for the rehabilitation and preservation of Bolivia's Indigenous majority. Who else, they wondered in Brechtian fashion, would grow the food, herd the animals, transport the firewood, dig the aqueducts and roads, fight the border wars, and provide the servile labor to La Paz's upper classes? Should not the rural school incubate the country's essential rural workforce?

Although fraught with twisted logic and contradictory impulses, race-thinking and school policy helped articulate the paceño elite's will to subdue and civilize the Aymara hinterland. This geo-racial project was, above all, a neocolonial endeavor that shared much in common with other such endeavors taking place across the interior of Latin America in the late nineteenth and early twentieth centuries. Racializing the hinterlands, La Paz's white metropole sought to "reinvent [the Indian] as backward and neglected [and] encode its non-capitalist landscapes and societies as manifestly in need of the rationalized exploitation [and cultural improvement] that [the modernizing oligarchy] would bring," in the words of Mary Louise Pratt.[24] Bolivia's prestigious Geographic and Anthropological Societies, the 1900 census, various racial inventories and diagnoses, and other cultural technologies provided the knowledge and devices with which the civilizing state would pacify the native, improve the race, and eventually forge the homogenized nation-state. In the early 1900s, then, a growing circle of civilizers and indigenistas (including statesmen, intellectuals, educators, medical doctors, scientists, etc.) carved out a public space for positing the "irrefutable truths" about Bolivia's race problem and for prescribing the enlightened intervention of science and the state. Focusing their diagnostic gaze on the Indian, these new pedagogic and scientific authorities remained largely impervious to the agency, voice, and aspirations of Indigenous people themselves, the object of this neocolonial knowledge enterprise (see fig. 1.3).[25]

Lurking just beneath the surface calm, the real or perceived threat of Indigenous uprising inevitably recast the Indian question in stark, apocalyptic terms. On a cold night in February 1899, in the town of Mohoza, peasants confronted a squadron of Federalist soldiers, took them hostage, moved them into a parish courtyard, and executed them one by one. Local townsmen also perished at the hands of the rebels before the Federalist army captured, imprisoned, and executed almost three hundred men—not just the presumed culprits but also countless others. The insurrection was quelled, but urban elites felt under constant siege. Just a month earlier, *El Heraldo* had warned of "the war of the races that threatens the nation."[26] White fear was most palpable in the city of La Paz, situated as it was amid the dense concentration of Aymara villages, networks of ayllus, and clusters of servile peones living precariously on haciendas. Hemmed in, the city's jittery urban elites felt vulnerable and "isolated ... from contact with the other civilized towns" in the Republic.[27] The city's air was saturated with allegorical stories of Indian savagism and Aymara depravity.[28] Silvia Rivera notes that in the aftermath of the 1899 rebellion, images of Aymara *barbaridad* were indelibly imprinted "on the collective perception of the criollo society" and would be for decades to come.[29]

Reeling from the aftershocks, the ruling liberal elite of La Paz began to frame its civilizatory agenda in apocalyptic terms. The official solution to the "Indian problem" would supposedly come from the benign workings of social evolution, civilization, and assimilation. Otherwise, it would require a bloody campaign, engineered by the Bolivian state along the lines of North America's genocidal wars against the Native peoples in its own western territories. Mimicking a North American imperial slogan, *El Heraldo*'s 1899 editorial threw down the gauntlet: the Bolivian government must either civilize or exterminate the Indian race if it wanted to secure the social peace:

FIGURE 1.3. Studio portrait of an Aymara man, ca. early 1900s. In traditional dress, this dignified figure poses as the "exotic Indian" for the Western gaze. Courtesy of the Carpenter Collection (LOT 11356-26), Prints and Photographs Division, US Library of Congress.

In Bolivia, there is a numerous population of ferocious, stupid [Indians] who resist progress [and] ... now threaten the collective and individual security of others. [They] need to be educated to change or, at least, modify their savage nature.... The only remedy is to blend our populations, forge the nation, and erase the differences that the Indian race presents. And to do that, there are only two solutions: *to imitate the Yankees in their [military] campaigns against the redskins ... or to try to arrive at the same result under the beneficent and modifying influence of [public] instruction.*[30]

Mere months after the 1899 uprising had subsided, President Pando (whose Federalist army had captured, killed, and imprisoned dozens of Aymara rebels) set his sights on the "beneficent influence" of schooling. It was seen as the Liberal regime's best hope of pacifying the Indian hinterland, uplifting the race, and saving the nation.

The Beneficent Influence of Public Instruction

Following the Liberals' military and political victory, Pando's regime took a hard look at the country's decrepit infrastructure of rural schooling. Census figures in 1900 revealed the shocking scope of Bolivia's challenges: nationwide, 20 percent of the population was literate. In the Department of La Paz, only 12 percent qualified as literate (and many of them could read but not write).[31] Still fewer people had any formal schooling—around 2.3 percent of the population in 1903.[32] The numbers bespoke a radical urban/rural disparity, underscoring "the total void" (Alfredo Guillén Pinto's descriptor) of primary schooling in the countryside: for example, in 1917, out of some 104,000 children (six to ten years old) living in rural areas, only about 3,500 had access to schooling.[33] Almost 90 percent of the nation's population lived in rural areas where, except for the occasional parish, private, missionary, or municipal school, few primary schools could be found. To the extent that primary schooling existed at all, it was largely confined to the cities and provincial towns.

The material poverty and institutional fragility of rural schools was laid bare by the government's first school inspection tours. President Pando dispatched his able minister of education (Samuel Oropeza, a lawyer from Chuquisaca) to report on "the deficiencies in elementary schooling." Oropeza was appalled by what he found. The country lacked physical plants for elementary schools, and the few he visited were dark, dank, filthy, and ill equipped. Furthermore, primary schools were failing to teach children how to read and write in the "national language" of Spanish. To remove this terrible obstacle to modern nationhood, Oropeza wanted to abolish traditions of rote learning, impose curricular reform, and organize remedial programs to compensate for the abysmal condition of primary schools.[34] More shocking was Manuel Paredes's 1906 report on the human toll that the scourge of drought and famine had afflicted on his own province of Inquisivi. "All these schools," he wrote, "are housed in disastrous rooms, true hovels, lacking hygiene and furniture. In most schools, the child must bring a sheepskin to put on top of a bundle of straw or on the ground. He uses adobe bricks or an empty box for a desk." As for the schoolteachers, "All of them are ignorant, reduced to a state of beggary, deprived of respect, held in contempt by the plebe, and abused by cantonal authorities. Under such conditions, they are incapable of introducing signs of vitality to the semi-civilized population, where 80 percent is illiterate."[35]

Most lay schools were municipal establishments, lying outside the jurisdiction of the federal government. In the early 1900s, Bolivia counted some 760 primary schools, but almost all of them (95 percent) fell into the camp of the towns and municipalities, or else they were parish schools under Church or missionary control. The plan to impose federal authority over public schools ran up against the tyranny of the provinces.[36] The Liberal state also wanted to coax the Catholic hierarchy into the modern, secular age. Church-state tensions were never far below the surface of public life during the Liberal era, although Bolivia's Liberal Party was not as stridently anticlerical as liberal elites in either Mexico or Argentina were. Indeed, both the Pando and Montes regimes cultivated a sense of tolerant "agnosticism" toward the Catholic Church, in the words of Françoise Martínez.[37] With woefully inadequate resources, the Bolivian government relied on Catholic missionaries to conduct the civilizing work among "savage" tribes inhabiting the immense eastern lowland territory that lay beyond the reach of the Bolivian state and civil society. Thus, in 1906, Montes modified article II of the 1874 Constitution to permit Catholic missions to operate in the eastern lowland territories (where Franciscan and other missionaries were already ensconced, in many cases).

Compartmentalizing the civilizing/education mission, the scheme delivered the lowland tribes to Catholic and Protestant missionaries while assigning the schooling of highland Aymara- and Quechua-speaking peasantries largely to the secular state and municipal councils.[38] This racial/spatial bifurcation between religious and secular schooling refocused state authority on the densely populated highland zones, but it did not begin to address the underlying obstacles to elementary schooling—the country's staggering rate of illiteracy and absenteeism; the lack of a basic school infrastructure; abject rural poverty; the paucity of trained teachers; and the state's severely limited jurisdiction, budget, and regulatory bureaucracy. Faced with such structural problems, the Liberal regime would try to turn the tide and begin building, brick by brick, a centralized system of public ("fiscal") schooling.

On paper, the Liberals' education reform mission seemed eminently possible. Under the state's rationalizing reforms, the Liberals hoped to make public primary schools "universal, obligatory, secular, and free" (as promised by article XIV in Bolivia's 1874 Liberal Constitution). Without the fiscal means to build an adequate infrastructure, however, the Pando regime concentrated on the intangibles of curricular reform. Pando's 1901 Central Plan called for standardizing school rules and routines and modernizing the national curriculum. Ideally, the standard course of study would include such secular subjects as reading, writing, and grammar; arithmetic; geography; and *urbanidad* (cultural norms and conduct). (Catechism was included as a small concession to the Church.) This academic menu was to be served up in primary schools for students in the towns and cities. A positivist in spirit, Pando also promoted technical institutes for the sons of the elite (he wanted to train more engineers and entrepreneurs and fewer lawyers). But his populist impulses inclined toward "popular instruction" (*instrucción popular*).[39] He hoped that by disseminating "useful knowledge," schools would quicken the march of industrial progress and in turn, following the model of Argentina and Chile, throw open the gates to European immigrants. Practical training in trade schools, Pando believed, would prepare future generations of Bolivian farmers, miners, and workers to be able to compete with the armies of industrious immigrants who in theory would soon be flooding the country.[40]

After the landslide election of Ismael Montes in 1904, the Liberal Party carried forward the mantle of federal school reform. Montes's right-hand man in this endeavor was Juan Misael Saracho.[41] With the political wind at his back, this minister of education was brimming with Spencerian optimism: "Our century is eminently pedagogical, in which all the conquests of progress emanate and flow toward the grand ideal of humanity's incessant improvement through the perfection of educational means, of all kinds," he proclaimed in 1907.[42] A new Central Plan called for a regulatory bureaucracy to enforce a new uniform set of rules on all school establishments, including an obligatory curriculum of moral and academic subjects as well as practical skills (differentiated under the rubrics of *la educación* and *la instrucción*, respectively). Saracho's transformative education plan would prepare "a virtuous and industrious citizenry" to participate in a well-ordered, culturally homogeneous modern polity. Students would be put through a rigorous five-year elementary curriculum encompassing twelve subject matters: "Reading, Language and Spanish Grammar (*gramática castellana*)"; "Arithmetic and Notions of Algebra"; "Lessons on Objects"; "Writing and Linear Drawing"; "General Geography of America and Particular [Geography] of Bolivia, and National Borders, with Notions of Universal Geography"; "Elementary Geometry"; "Notions of Cosmography, Physiology, and Natural History";

"History and Constitution of Bolivia, and Notions of Universal History"; "Notions of Physics, Chemistry, and Hygiene"; "Moral, *Urbanidad*, and Religion"; and "Gymnastics and Music." An additional course, "Domestic Economy and Handicrafts," would be available to girls, while the old-fashioned "scholastic" subjects of religion and Latin would be eliminated.[43]

Rhetoric aside, the Liberal category of "universal" knowledge was an imaginary realm within which operated the strictures of geographic, racial, and gender hierarchy. The national curriculum was framed as an assimilationist device—to lift all children and set them on a path toward Western culture, civility, and progress. Ideally, the state's modern school system would bridge the dreary chasm, forged by centuries of colonial oppression and evolution, separating the mestizo and criollo children of the urban elites from Indian kids of the rural poor. Yet the constitutive principle of the Liberals' education reform was to perform precisely the opposite function—that is, to cater to and reinforce the racialized neocolonial divide between the unacculturated rural Indians and the urban population of semi-assimilated mestizos and privileged ("criollo") whites. In effect, the government's curricular plan subverted its own integrative goals, creating an indelible and unequal urban/rural divide in public schooling. This foundational reform, tentatively worked out in the realms of policy, administration, and the curriculum, would eventually harden into an unshakable doctrine. As this book will show, this official schism in school ideology and policy—although largely symbolic in the early 1900s—would legitimize and reinforce the systemic racism, inequality, and institutional neglect that actively "underdeveloped" public schooling for the rural poor through successive cycles of state crisis and educational reform well into the twentieth century.

From the outset, there were immediate policy ramifications that discriminated against Indigenous children. Supposedly adjusted to their cognitive deficiencies, state-run rural elementary schools would offer their pupils a "minimal" curriculum. The discrepancies surfaced in the differential curriculum for urban and rural schools. While (theoretically) the urban child would study twelve subjects during a five-year cycle of schooling, the peasant child would attend two-year remedial *escuelas populares y Rurales*. Their course of study would consist of four subjects: language and literacy; morality and religion; elementary geography of Bolivia and America (with patriotic lessons about Bolivia's borders, sovereignty, and stolen coastline); and an elementary history of the patria and constitution. Without grade levels, these rustic schools would group children by age or aptitude in the one-room schoolhouse. Most lessons would be delivered orally. Public school teachers were instructed to tell stories using chalk, the blackboard, and laminated pictures, if available. Armed with the latest methods, modern teachers would habituate the children to puzzle out the pronunciation and word meanings on the pages of their reader. Teachers were told to quiz their pupils regularly on the content of the words they had read—even if the Aymara-speaking pupil was barely conversant in Spanish. The Bible's scriptural passages would supply the text for teaching kids their letters while also inculcating piety and morality. Any teacher who lacked the Bible or a modern reader to use in the rustic classroom was advised to hand out fragments of Bolivia's 1874 Constitution as an efficient way to teach reading and civics at the same time.[44]

Thus would the Liberals' secular curriculum perform cultural miracles, by infusing in the Indigenous child a love of patria, a modicum of civic awareness, and a semblance of spoken and written Spanish. Having recently imposed universal military service, the Montes regime also looked on the rural school as a seedbed of disciplined army recruits once schoolboys came of age.[45] Here, then, was the transcendent Liberal plan for civilizing the Indian and consolidating a true sense of national identity. Public instruction offered Bolivia a way "to redeem ourselves and that enormous Indian mass, which could [potentially] form the central nerve of our nationality in the future." Nothing less than *la nacionalidad* was at stake, and "we have not a moment to lose!" Minister Saracho proclaimed in 1904. "We need to forge [*cimentar*] Bolivian nationality, at any sacrifice, with a solid [system] of moral, intellectual, and physical education."[46]

The Congress was not in accord, however. Before the ink had dried, Saracho was denied congressional funding to build a string of permanent rural schoolhouses.[47] Desperate, he did an end run around the obstructionist legislators by organizing a tiny program of roving teachers that he grandly called "ambulatory schools" (*escuelas ambulantes*).[48] As he envisioned the plan, this cadre of itinerant instructors would each be assigned to an Indigenous province or urban parish. There they would teach school for fifteen days before moving to another locale. Walking or riding by horseback, the ambulating teachers would commute between two rural towns or villages, ideally traveling no farther than five or six kilometers. In the Aymara cantons, they would visit all the ayllus and *rancherías* (rural hamlets) to dispense the light of reason and deliver their lessons to the gathered schoolchildren. If teachers received an urban assignment, as some did, they would be expected to visit various Indian parishes and military barracks. The teacher's grand objective,

Saracho explained to the legislators, was "to make accessible even just a minimum and occasional instruction."[49] But even that threadbare proposal did not open the congressional purse strings. In one last appeal, Saracho begged his fellow statesmen not to "abandon the unfortunate Indian race to his traditional ignorance." And he appealed to their pathos and conscience to fund public schooling for "the race that pays tribute and bears the onerous burdens of private and public service."[50]

Here, then, was an ameliorative way for Bolivia to redeem its moral debt to the oppressed Indian race without disturbing the underlying colonial order of caste. Saracho's grand strategy was to convert the raw politics of racial fear in the white city into a modern civilizing campaign, one that was driven by a righteous sense of moral rectitude to bring the light of learning and reason to the Indians. Draw inspiration from the United States!, he urged his skeptical colleagues, for the Americans had proven it was possible to domesticate even their most "bellicose and refractory Indian" tribes. So too could Bolivia. Indeed, the task would be far easier for the Bolivian state, he said, because the Quechua and Aymara Indians were ideal subjects for schooling and civilization. They were more placid, anxious to improve their lives and acquire a modicum of "culture." (He made no allusion to the 1899 incidents of violent unrest, the state's drawn-out punitive trial, or the eruption of rabid racism in the years since.) Armed with chalk and readers, a new generation of teachers would "redeem the Indian from the abject ignorance into which he was born" and incorporate him into the currents of "national progress of the whole order."[51]

The more inflated the rhetoric, however, the more penurious the school program. In the end, Saracho's grand mission boiled down to a group of about twenty roving teachers carrying the torch of civilization into the Aymara hinterland. Scaled back, Saracho's program targeted a small radius of Aymara communities in the provinces of Sicasica and, to a lesser degree, Pacajes and Omasuyos. Those zones lay within easy reach of urban La Paz and its emissaries of itinerant teachers, school inspectors, and visiting political dignitaries—including President Montes himself. Moreover, those outlying provinces were home to intensifying land conflicts and boundary wars, recently inflamed by the Liberal land reforms, a new wave of divestiture, and the resurgence of Indian litigation in defense of their traditional land claims. Sicasica's spectral image, for example, was that of an Aymara breeding ground of savage rebels and dangerous allies. Even before the 1899 rebellion, the Liberal Party had long sought political alliances with some of the ayllus and communities throughout the region, and the Montes regime was eager to move beyond the 1899 crisis and rebuild his patronage network among ayllu authorities in key villages and towns.

The inauguration of Saracho's school plan in the village of Ayoayo provided the perfect opportunity for Montes's entourage to leave the safety of the city, travel to Sicasica, and inaugurate the *escuela ambulante* program in the company of Aymara ayllu authorities from the region. This official *visita* exhibited all the trappings of a formal colonial visitation with Indian caciques, with the exchange of ritual offerings and favors asked. Montes offered a gift of school supplies to the gathered *hilacatas* (Indigenous authorities) while asking in return for their cooperation (allowing the teachers to enter the communities, round up pupils, establish an official school). And looking ahead to the next electoral cycle in 1907, Montes anticipated that, in cementing this intercultural alliance with local hilacatas, he could expect the Liberals to win the vote of semiliterate Indians in the region.[52]

In the meantime, Saracho dispatched his apostles. He had planned to use a grid to assign teachers on the basis of population density and need, but few provincial officials provided the demographic data. Saracho never obtained the funds he needed to purchase enough school supplies, and in any event, the didactic materials he had ordered from the United States were lost in transit. The plan was a disaster. His new national curriculum gathered dust in the minister's offices; most teachers reverted to mind-numbing methods of recitation; and the erstwhile itinerant teachers encountered difficult, if not openly hostile, conditions in the countryside.

Throughout the early 1900s, a dark fog of racial fear still hung over the Aymara Altiplano, where ayllus were engaged in a low-intensity war against encroaching haciendas, or where haciendas had recently assembled fragments of usurped communal landholdings and, in the process, dispossessed or reduced hamlets of "ex-comunarios" to servile colonos. In such a climate, racial fear cut both ways: the arrival of a white teacher could bring down the wrath of local hacendados, their administrators (mayordomos), or provincial authorities. In the paranoid mind of the *latifundista* or *corregidor*, the roving literacy teacher was a natural suspect—an outside agitator, a thinly disguised Indian ringleader, or possibly another sort of disrupter. But the reticence of Indigenous people to engage with the itinerant teacher, at least at first, might also have derived from toxic undercurrents of racial fear and hostility—an embedded feature of neocolonialism. Many rural teachers were stymied by fear and suspicion stirring among the Indigenous people, whose children they hoped to teach.⁵³ Indigenous people, in turn, worried that the newly arrived teacher was acting on behalf of the military, assigned to infiltrate the rural provinces and drag young men into the army.⁵⁴ Or were the teachers really thinly disguised tax collectors, land surveyors, "labor hookers" (*enganchadores*), cattle rustlers, or myriad other parasites who had traditionally fed off Indigenous labor and land? Various motivating pressures were surely at play: the "rational" peasant calculation of risk and reward, or the powerful fear of reprisal, or the reticence of parents to give up the essential daily labor of their own school-age child in their own fields and pastures or on hacienda lands. One itinerant teacher showed up on the edges of a hacienda to begin his reading lessons with the children, only to be met by aggressive Indian authorities. They refused to deliver the village's school-age children or permit the school to function at all—because, as they tersely explained, they were "Indians of the hacienda" (as opposed to Indians of the free "ayllu" community). School apparently had no place on the semifeudal estate, where the landlord had forbidden his colono tenants to learn how to read and write, or where a sadistic mayordomo was used to enforcing the lord's will with impunity. In this case, ironically, the interlocutors were Indians "belonging" to the hacienda owned by none other than the "pedagogic president," President Montes himself!⁵⁵

This odd encounter provides a rare glimpse of the ragged patchwork of ephemeral rural school endeavors. The primary school campaign was, as I have suggested, largely rhetorical. Materially, the federal state's effort to found permanent schools was confined to isolated enclaves, surrounded by an ocean of unschooled Indigenous people and serviced, largely, by a tiny flotilla of federal teachers. The church and municipalities held their own institutional grip on Bolivia's elementary schools, while the vast majority of rural children of the highlands did not attend school at all.

But as we shall see in chapter 2, concurrents of vernacular literacy were beginning to flow through the veins of the Aymara Altiplano—precisely through those ayllus and villages where the occasional itinerant teacher discovered a surprisingly receptive environment. There, Indigenous authorities enjoyed more social space to initiate or negotiate the intercultural arrangements for school provisioning than did semibonded populations of colonos subsisting on estate lands, in the shadow of the landlord and his overseer. But more salient to this comparison is the functional value that literacy skills accrued in many Aymara ayllus and communities during the early 1900s. Mastering literate and litigious practices was becoming a practical imperative of Aymara caciques in their escalating legal battles over Indigenous land claims. Agrarian disputes inevitably inflated the value and aura of Spanish literacy (and, by extension, the cultural currency of the village school) within the confines of local Aymara society. For both structural and conjunctural reasons, then, the itinerant schoolteacher was apt to encounter a more receptive community among the people of the ayllus than among the peones of the hacienda. Nor was that all. The ayllus of Sicasica, Omasuyos, Ingavi, and other nearby provinces had become the provenance of peasant *solicitudes*, documentary requests for state-sponsored teachers or schools. One village even petitioned for a tribunal of examiners (*mesa examinadora*) to make an appearance at their comunario school of Aigache so that their pupils might display their knowledge and earn their certificates of graduation before the white dignitaries.[56]

Saracho's modest program of itinerant teachers did meet with limited success in the working-class barrios and immediate hinterlands of La Paz. The mere presence of the state, and the official promotion of elementary schools, opened a narrow channel of opportunity for rural communities to solicit state support and protection for their fragile school enterprises. Of course, Saracho was eager to claim an exalted legacy, thanks to his novel program of ambulatory schoolteachers.[57] The Indian, he exuded, "unabashedly embraces and collaborates with the [school] proposal, once his natural suspicion is allayed." Indeed, "in many communities, where the maestros ambulantes are working, their enthusiasm is so great that the Indians themselves have offered to construct permanent schoolhouses at their own expense."[58] So heartened was Saracho that he announced the expansion of the ambulatory schools into the provinces of Pacajes, Omasuyos, and possibly even the Department of Potosí.[59] The prospect of forging a true "nationality," through the extension of a federal network of rural elementary schools, seemed almost at hand. "If the government and [provincial] authorities persist in this [noble] labor," Saracho gushed, "the day is not far off... when the Indian will hold in his hand the letter of citizenship."[60]

It was precisely this linked association between Indian literacy, schooling, and citizenship, however, that appalled and terrified the Bolivian oligarchy. Already by 1907 and 1908, a vocal opposition to the Montes regime accused the Liberal Party of mobilizing unruly mobs of "illiterate" Indians and cholos to rally and vote for the party (breaching the legal requirements of enfranchisement). Montes's pursuit of electoral clients among the urban and rural poor was a red flag that stirred up a powerful backlash, even within the

Liberal Party. By the 1910s, men like Bautista Saavedra repudiated the Liberal Party by denouncing the whole premise that literacy should be the basis of rural schooling.⁶¹ Not only did the rural alphabet schools threaten to open the floodgates of electoral democracy to the rabble, but the very prospect of arming Indians with Spanish letters and the legal tools they needed to combat their enemies in the courts, ministries, and public sphere was threatening to upset the delicate balance of racial and class forces in rural La Paz.

But this conservative reaction to Liberal education reform would take time to materialize. In the meantime, prominent Liberal educators of the early 1900s began to scan the wider horizon for European theories of race and education that might help Bolivia advance its own civilizing project in the backlands of La Paz.

Study Abroad: Civilizers in Search of Pedagogical Solutions

Nineteenth-century Europe had long been the province of "the grand tour" among aspiring intellectuals and political leaders from across Latin America. Early Spanish Americans broke free of their imposed provinciality in the early nineteenth century: once the Spanish Crown lost its imperial grip on the colonies, overseas trade channels opened, new ideologies shot across the Atlantic, print capitalism exploded, overseas travel quickened, and Spanish American elites turned (often ambivalently) to Europe and North America for lessons in how to govern their own war-torn republics. Even before European doctrines of liberalism and positivism swept across Latin America, the role of formal education became an obsessive concern among the first generations of statesmen. They looked enviously to Europe's advancements in secular public schooling—its centralized hierarchy of schooling, standardized curricula, pedagogical theories, didactic materials, certified corps of normal-trained teachers, and host of monumental universities, libraries, laboratories, and museums. This apparatus of public and private education held great allure for Latin America's vanguard of liberal-cosmopolitans. A few Spanish American republics sponsored educational and administrative pilgrimages to the Old World, in hopes of schooling its own administrators and educators in the latest pedagogical ideals.⁶² Whether state-sponsored "educational commissions" or studious individuals making the rounds on their own, these traveling pedagogues were on assignment to gather educational ideas and materials needed to set up systems of public instruction in their home countries.

The nineteenth-century Argentine titan of letters Domingo F. Sarmiento became the supreme exemplar of the cosmopolitan pedagogue, trekking through Europe and North America in search of the latest educational ideas and institutions. For two years, Sarmiento made the rounds of cities and towns in Spain, Italy, France, Switzerland, and Germany (as well as the edge of North Africa) in what would become the iconic pilgrimage of Latin American educators and writers. News traveled widely, thanks to the encyclopedic book and articles he wrote about his worldwide journey.[63] Surprisingly, however, it was not the lycée in the glittering European metropolis but the humble primary school in the snowy fields of New England that truly captured Sarmiento's pedagogical imagination, for during his travels, Sarmiento had stumbled on the educational writings of Horace Mann (who had recently returned from his own grand tour of Europe's educational institutions). Toward the end of his years abroad, the Argentine sojourner set off for Massachusetts to meet with the famous Mann.[64] Once there, Sarmiento was astonished to find near-universal literacy among white New England people—everyone, from the local pig farmer to the town councilman, seemed to be reading newspapers, books, and broadsheets.[65] Having studied educational programs in the great capitals of Europe, Sarmiento was most impressed by North America's legally compulsory "common school." It was the ubiquitous elementary school, along with the normal school, that constituted the foundation of North America's electoral democracy and industrial progress, he believed.[66]

In the early 1900s, Bolivian Liberals were swept into these transnational currents of educational reformism. Education Minister Juan Misael Saracho was determined to unlock the Bolivian nation from the prison of its own geographic isolation and cultural provincialism. Chile—the seedbed of Sarmiento's formative educational activism—provided especially fertile ground for Bolivian positivists and educators to widen their horizons by studying and observing the country's advanced institutes of learning. By 1900, Chile boasted six pedagogical institutes, including the prestigious Instituto Pedagógico of the University of Chile. All of them were founts of positivist philosophy and pedagogy.[67] More broadly, Bolivians admired Chile's stable parliamentary government, economic prosperity, and influx of white immigrants. Hoping to capitalize on the recent thaw in Bolivian/Chilean relations, Montes launched a robust program in educational diplomacy. In 1906,

Bolivia sent sixty scholarship students to Chile, where they were assigned apprenticeships in "professional studies" (medicine, engineering, commerce, arts, and teaching) with sixty-eight Chilean professors and twenty-five visiting German educators. (Other students were sent to Argentina, Peru, and a few to Europe and the United States.) Upon returning to Bolivia, the newly trained teachers were expected to disseminate their professional knowledge through public lectures and demonstrations, in professional journals, and by inspecting schools for the government.[68] Meanwhile, Bolivia's Liberal regime organized its own grand tour of foreign educational establishments. A much-heralded "educational commission" was appointed by Saracho in 1905: the positivist professor Daniel Sánchez Bustamante was dispatched to Chile, where he toured its showcase public schools, collected textbooks, and studied the latest curricular reforms (particularly in Chile's institutions of higher education).[69] Unlike Sarmiento's revelation about Anglo-Saxon miracles of universal literacy and public schooling, Sánchez Bustamante was dazzled by Chile's model institutions of higher education in the technical fields of science, engineering, architecture, teacher training, and so on. Bolivia needed poets, philosophers, and lawyers pouring out of its universities far less than it needed trained technicians, pedagogues, and entrepreneurs, he believed.

The Chilean visit turned out to be a dress rehearsal for a grand European tour. Daniel Sánchez Bustamante's Chilean sojourn was so successful that before he had unpacked his trunk, he was appointed by Saracho to lead a grand pedagogical expedition to the capitals of Europe. His main traveling companion, Felipe Segundo Guzmán, was a lawyer and journalist who signed on as the commission's "secretary." Hardly a sidekick, Felipe Guzmán chronicled their European sojourn as they met with distinguished educators; visited schools, museums, libraries, and institutes of higher education; gathered teaching materials; observed classroom techniques; and interviewed the professors of several normal institutes.[70] Upon their return to La Paz in 1910, the secretary's earlier dispatches were published in an essay collection titled *El problema pedagógico en Bolivia*. While his eminent colleague Sánchez Bustamante retreated into the interior bureaucracy of the Liberal government (briefly serving as minister of education), it was Felipe Guzmán who sought ways to disseminate the ideas and inspiration he had acquired during their European pilgrimage.

Guzmán had collected a trunk load of inspirational impressions and ideas. From Berlin, he extolled the German trade schools that were training workers to take their place in the industrializing economy. Knowing Montes's obsession with modernizing the Bolivian military, he wrote admiringly about the military academies they had visited in both Prussia and France, where soldiers were disciplined to defend the national flag in times of strife and advance civic morale in times of peace. In France, Guzmán mused, "military education is, above all, moral education," and it could also be so in Bolivia, he averred. To destroy the vestiges of caudillo politics, the officer class would have to fulfill its sacred duty by educating its own squadron of soldiers in the virtues of patriotism. With mass illiteracy and lack of primary schools, Bolivia's modern army barracks must also serve as incubators of Indian acculturation.[71] But the French educational system (modernized in the 1870s) also offered lessons in civic education and cultural assimilation: along with roads and rails, print and newspapers, the ubiquitous elementary school was transforming "peasants into Frenchman," in the famous phrase of historian Eugen Weber.[72] Here French education was masterful (and ruthless) at enforcing a policy of linguistic assimilation on France's rich oral patchwork of vernacular dialects. A uniform national curriculum took aim at what Eric Hobsbawm calls the "world of words"—where the language of "illiterates" was almost entirely oral, and consequently the official language of the nation "was of no significance except, increasingly, as a reminder of their lack of knowledge and power."[73] Public schools, along with newspapers, novels, military, and bureaucratic centralization, were advancing the battle lines of linguistic nationalism throughout much of western Europe by the late 1800s. No doubt the two Bolivian sojourners, thinking about Bolivia's massive population of monolingual native speakers, were keen to study how public education was advancing the interior frontier of linguistic unity and literacy.[74]

Meanwhile, while they were overseas, the itinerant Bolivian educators became erstwhile students of "racial character," and they devised their own crude racial-national typology to guide their pedagogical aspirations for Bolivia. Accordingly, the German was "vigorous, tall, and erect" in stature, but had a belly and was a little heavy; the Frenchman, of slighter build, was alert, nervous, with shoulders of uneven height, and thrust forward; the Englishman was slim, tall, and similar to the Swede, but a little lazier; and the Swede was almost always taller, straight-backed, muscular without being plump. But the most striking feature of Guzmán's typology was the Swede's superior "disposition": he had an air of repose, a preternatural serenity, and robust health.[75] Why did the Nordic race represent the acme of a civilized people?, he wondered. Was it biology or environment, evolution or culture?

Heredity was at the root, according to these eminences: the blood of "primitive Germans" and "valorous Vikings" ran through the veins of the modern Nordic race, shaping a supposedly superior civilization. But the powers of education apparently played a codeterminant role. Guzmán pointed to Nordic racial and moral "superiority" as scientific proof that the Swedish system of modern schooling—and particularly its curricular emphasis on vigorous exercise—was the secret to its bio-cultural progress. "There are astute educationalists," Guzmán asserted in 1908, "who attribute this [superior] character of the Swede to the practice of physical exercise."[76]

A risible but well-meaning version of educational utopianism, the new pedagogy of sport would build the nation's musculature and instill self-disciplinary vigor in Bolivian youth. In this eugenic brand of tutelary race-thinking, notions of evolution, culture, physiology, and nation were conceptually conflated, presuming that enlightened state policies (social hygiene, physical education, behavioral reform, and other disciplinary programs) could heal the body politic and set Bolivia on course toward a healthy, culturally homogeneous society in the space of a generation or two.[77]

Once back in Bolivia, Felipe Guzmán honed his oratory and journalistic skills. In a series of twenty-five newspaper essays (published as *El problema pedagógico en Bolivia*), he developed his ideas about the laws of human evolution (on a trajectory that would culminate in "Nordic" standards of beauty, physical grace, and intelligence), articulated with his positivist faith in the miraculous (proto-eugenic) powers of modern education and social hygiene to improve the race. Like so many tutelary race-thinkers of his day, Guzmán worked at the dynamic axis of biological and cultural determinisms, trying to harmonize his social Darwinian impulses with his buoyant optimism regarding pedagogy's potential to lift up the Indian race. In just a few more years, the emerging eugenics movement would inject science and policy into the idea of "racial improvement"; but in the meantime, the mystique of scientific pedagogy offered enlightened civilizers the knowledge and tools they believed they needed to accelerate the evolutionary process of whitening in the heart of the Bolivian Andes.

The magical synergy of evolution and education: this was the potent solution that suffused the tutelary race-thinking of Bolivia's civilizers. In his collected essays, Felipe Guzmán mapped his ontological argument about Bolivia's evolutionary racial advancement through "crossbreeding," on the biology side, onto his template of educational reform, on the cultural side:

We postulate that the civilization of the Indian... has to traverse several periods [of time]. The first [evolutionary stage] will result from the crossing [of the Indian] with the white, as well as from its alphabetization. The result of this process will be the hybrid [race], called the cholo. [During this second stage of racial-cultural development], the cholo will display the most antisocial characteristics, from the moral point of view. For he conserves the physical resistance [i.e., strength] of the Indian and [some] of the intellectual qualities of the white race. Yet the cholo is but a transitory race. Civilization will not be detained, once education and race-crossing become the driving forces of this process. Thus, from the cholo is born a more civilized product and, in the third period, by virtue of the [Lamarckian] law of the inheritance of acquired characteristics, the anomalies of the cholo will be erased in part, until this evolution arrives at the [superior] moral, intellectual, and social level of the dolichocephalic white.[78]

In this evolutionary scheme, the white European immigrant makes no appearance in the pedagogue's imagination, probably because Bolivia's European immigration policies had failed thus far. Nor does the figure of the "mestizo" symbolize the stable amalgam of Indian and white in this evolutionary scenario. Rather, it is the "transitory," racially hybrid, plebeian class of urban Aymara people, categorically denigrated as cholo, that was viewed as the vector of gradual miscegenation. Invoking the neo-Lamarckian idea that newly acquired traits could be passed through the blood to the heirs, Guzmán was confident that the cholo race (once "improved") would serve as the hereditarian conduit toward national whitening.[79] What, then, of the country's Indian majority? "We have in Bolivia," he wrote, "the autochthonous element as the great majority. Although useful in the spheres of agriculture and mining, it is *always a negative factor* for the advance of culture."[80] Yet Guzmán was confident that Europe's imperial "impulse of civilization" would eventually penetrate the Bolivian backlands. Before the teleological forces of Western progress and civilization, "sooner or later the civilizing impulse would reach [the Indian] to crush him or lift him up." Either way, he believed, the Bolivian Indian was destined for extinction.[81] Writing against the pessimistic theorists of racial degeneration, Guzmán had faith in the redemptive power of European virtues (morality, science, good habits of industry, physical vigor, and beauty) if they were properly inculcated in the populace.[82] Most of his newspaper columns were recipes for how to pound those European virtues into the hearts and minds of Bolivian youth.

But Guzmán also defended himself against indigenista critics, such as Franz Tamayo, who accused him of slavish Eurocentrism. In his defense, he insisted that European models must be filtered and adapted to the Bolivian racial and environmental milieu. Thus, the psychology and cognitive capacity of the Bolivian child, for example, had to be investigated scientifically. Bolivia's racial makeup had to be properly classified and characterized before educational policies could be effective. In the end, this quintessential civilizer insisted on the possibilities of racial improvement: "The Indian, in possession of modern knowledge, habituated to live conscientiously, and with another set of habits, could become the most powerful factor in the nation's rapid aggrandizement."[83] Here, in distilled form, was the official Liberal doctrine of civilization-as-whitening that was to lead Bolivia into the future of racial harmony and homogenization.

Dissonance and Dissent

Sometimes a random event can shake the convictions of crusading reformers. Another social tremor in the Altiplano, a vociferous group of caciques petitioning for land and justice, an act of gamonal violence against a fledgling rural school project: all such eruptions were bound to shake the civilizers' confidence in their own ability to engineer Indian assimilation and chart the nation's pathway toward whiteness through the application of enlightened reform.

For Felipe Segundo Guzmán, however, it was a small incident that unsettled his own deep-seated convictions. In 1910, he had a unique opportunity to test his grand civilizing agenda as the new director of Bolivia's first boarding school for Indians, established to train Bolivia's first corps of "teachers of Indians." Located in the urban La Paz barrio of Sopocachi, the school drew its first students from "various Indigenous centers." The curriculum was designed to train the next generation of maestros ambulantes in literacy, manual labor skills, and other forms of useful knowledge.[84] But more than instilling didactic skills, the normal school would resocialize the Indian pupil through daily disciplinary and work routines, Spanish-language immersion (*la castellanización*), and their exposure to civilized norms and desires. Encouraged by what he had heard about North America's Indian boarding schools, Guzmán was confident that after a short immersion in boarding school culture, Indian youth would display good manners and clean habits, facility with spoken Spanish, and a moral conscience. To that end, the schoolmaster had fashioned an environment of bourgeois "comforts"—the school's dormitory was outfitted with cots and mattresses; a toilet was located in the school patio; and students dined in a comfortable, well-appointed dining room.

The civilizer's grand delusions! He reported that each night, after the school's curfew, "the *indiecitos* would leave their cots and sneak downstairs to sleep on the bare floor, covering themselves with their ponchos, where they slept better than on the dormitory's straw mattresses. Eating in the dining room disgusted them; they preferred to eat in the kitchen, dispensing with silverware; and the bathroom caused them horror. In my eagerness to try to change their customs, I did nothing but bore the Indigenous children," he confessed to Congress in 1922. Then, one night, the children stole past the sleeping guard, escaped through the school's front door, and took off for their distant villages.[85] Years later, Guzmán could laugh about the incident in public. But at the time, the midnight flight of students cast doubt about the wisdom and viability of the Liberals' tenuous civilizing project.

At its apogee, the Liberals' civilizing mission collided with a vociferous group of conservative churchmen and literary indigenistas. Indeed, the Bolivian elite was torn by the very prospect of formalizing a system of public education for the rural masses. Church authorities and municipal governments resented the state's encroachment on their traditional turf. Provincial authorities and latifundistas denounced the very idea of educating the Indian, while they hounded local teachers or forbade their tenants to found a local school. Liberalism's conservative enemies denounced the party's electoral tactics, including its desire to spread literacy, schooling, and suffrage among its Indian clientele. A kernel of anti-Liberal dissent was also germinating among a small group of conservative intellectuals and writers—cosmopolitan men of education, privilege, and property, but also landowners wedded to feudal forms of labor exploitation and increasingly disenchanted with Liberal political hegemony. Indeed, as Marta Irurozqui has argued, the Indian question was turning into a larger proxy war on Liberal Party legitimacy, a sign of the deepening partisan divide within the oligarchy.[86]

One partisan skirmish broke out over the Indian question (i.e., what to do about the Indian problem), just as the Liberal government was unveiling its civilizing plan. Around 1910, an eclectic group of politicians, writers, and intellectuals assaulted the plans and pretensions of cosmopolitan liberalism. They deplored Liberal Party dominance and its fawning Eurocentrism; warned against "Jacobinist" doctrines of popular citizenship; and debated the place of the Indian in the modernizing Bolivian nation. Civilization's poster boy, Felipe Guzmán, was mocked for trying to "plagiarize" foreign educational programs rather than designing an authentic national pedagogy suitable to a country so radically different, evolutionarily backward, and racially diverse as Bolivia. Out of this debate emerged a conservative strain of Bolivian *indigenismo*, an ambivalent mix of racial, telluric, and Romantic sentiments that venerated the "pure Indian" within an incipient nationalist discourse in the early twentieth century. This strand of race-thinking was infused with a regionalist inflection and indigenista spirit which, together, reified the Colla— the ancient "ethnic race" of the Aymara and Quechua inhabitants of the high plateau. The Aymara emerged as a singular object of paceño literary revisionism. Reconfigured as the ethnic/regional essence of Bolivian Indianness, the Aymara was condemned and feared for its latent savagery, yet bathed in the literary glow of Romantic nostalgia. Infused with the millennial mystique of Time, Nature, and the Land, the redemptive Aymara Indian was admired for his energy, endurance, and stoicism, and for having adapted to the harsh climate of the high plateau. By this Romantic measure, the Aymara were both exalted and scrutinized as a specimen of Bolivia's purest "Indian type," in contrast to the semi-acculturated Quechua race of Indians, who inhabited the eastern belt of intermontane valleys. In the pages of criollo poetry, essays, and sociological treatises, the studied Aymara subject was variously characterized in functional terms (as Bolivia's essential high-altitude farmers), in bio-cultural terms (as the present-day heirs of the ancient Colla), and in spiritual terms (as Bolivia's most pristine, least contaminated Indian race). Sentimental ethnic portraits invoked the shaping forces of race and environment (*raza y medio*) to mystify the telluric power of the Altiplano in the millennial shaping of the Collasuyo region and Colla race. Literary scholar Javier Sanjinés notes how "this discourse on the autochthonous generated ambivalent racial sentiments of pride, nostalgia, and fascination with the Indian, while at the same time [showing] repugnance for any breaking of racial boundaries that could not be rationalized and strictly controlled by mestizo-criollo consciousness."[87]

This literary school, enriched by elements of nationalism, mysticism, and pragmatism, was crystallized in the 1909–10 newspaper essays of Franz Tamayo (1879–1956). At the time, his essays (republished in 1910 in Buenos Aires as *La pedagogía nacional*) resonated with the new literary generation in Latin America, which had grown skeptical of Enlightenment values and the spiritual vacuity of Western materialism. The young poet Tamayo gave voice to this growing disenchantment, turning for inspiration to Germanic Romanticism (where he discovered his own cultural lineage and intellectual roots as a mestizo, the offspring of a German immigrant father and Indigenous mother) as a way to reclaim the nativist and folkloric essence of Bolivian nationality. Drawn to the generic "Indian" (for he rarely distinguished between Indigenous ethnic and linguistic groups), Tamayo paved Bolivia's literary path toward a small measure of racial tolerance, but one strictly limited by the existing caste hierarchy. His frenzied literary production was primarily fueled by his animosity toward the reigning Liberal Party, and his immediate nemesis was Felipe Gúzman, who was barely back from his sojourns in Europe. Excoriating the civilizer's naive and imitative ideals, Tamayo urged his readers to turn their gaze inward to rediscover Bolivia's authentic moral character. Only then, he proclaimed, could Bolivia fashion a unique national pedagogy, especially suited to the Bolivian racial milieu.

Meanwhile, he argued, the Bolivian Indian must become the object of sustained scientific investigation and careful tutelage. From German Romanticism to Western science, Tamayo mixed literary fantasy with scientific authority to craft an antiassimilationist project that would uplift but preserve the essence of indigeneity as he imagined it to be. But he also insisted that official educational reform be guided by Western scientific study. Preserved and then rehabilitated, the Bolivian Indian (Tamayo believed) must first be "studied, disciplined, and exalted under an enlightened, paternalistic, and authoritarian political order," writes Sanjinés.[88] Here, then, was Tamayo's prescription: the pure Indian must become an object of clinical investigation to determine whether the race was educable. Assuming so, the nation needed to design a genuine *pedagogia nacional* that might accommodate Bolivia's autochthonous races, while still bringing the country into the modern age.

In 1910, the Tamayo/Guzmán debate over Indian education defined the incipient schism between Bolivia's rival schools of liberal civilizers and conservative indigenistas. Tamayo's forays into German Romanticism notwithstanding, he later emerged as Bolivia's most prominent cultural nationalist, telluric indigenista, and precocious advocate of cultural mestizaje. At the time, however, Tamayo's eclectic literary musings about race, ethnicity, and national pedagogy were not widely shared, even in conservative circles. Indeed, his passionate call for a national pedagogy was provoked, in large part, by a sudden and unwelcome development in the political sphere. In 1908 and 1909, the Bolivian government decided to invite a European "scientific pedagogue" to help Bolivia reorganize its system of public schooling—starting with the founding of the first normal school. The Liberal oligarchy staked its hope for the country's racial improvement and cultural integration on a modern, European-styled system of public schooling. To accomplish their mission, Bolivian liberal statesmen turned to a brilliant young Belgian educator, a man who had never before stepped foot in the Andes.

The Belgian Mission

Toward the end of their European travels, Daniel Sánchez Bustamante and Felipe Segundo Guzmán had visited Belgium's famous pedagogical institutes. There they met a rising star in Europe's firmament of scientific pedagogy. At the age of twenty-seven, Georges Rouma had already apprenticed with famous teachers of pedagogy and acquired a reputation as an expert in speech pathology. He worked with children with speech defects, but his research interests focused on the influence of the social environment on child development. As an educator, Rouma wanted to understand how the microenvironment of the modern classroom (where an "integral pedagogy" was practiced) might govern the norms of social behavior.[89] By any measure, he was an impressive fellow. Quite taken with this preternaturally mature educator, the Bolivians proffered an intriguing invitation: Rouma was asked to advise the Bolivian government on how to establish a functioning public school system. His initial task would be to design and run the country's first normal school in the city of Sucre.

It was an intriguing invitation he couldn't refuse. Reversing the direction of the Latin American pedagogical pilgrimage, Georges Rouma left his comfortable perch in Belgium and, in 1909, set out for the New World by steamship. Stopping in the port city of Buenos Aires, he dazzled his audience with a lecture series on the sociology of education, complete with charts depicting the biological and environmental factors that shaped the character of the "superior [European] man."[90] From there, Rouma traveled by train across the pampa, northward toward the border between Argentina and Bolivia. He arrived in Sucre in April 1909 to great fanfare (see fig. 1.4). The city was decked out in honor of the country's centenary celebrations of Independence and to welcome President Montes, who had come to welcome the Belgian and to inaugurate the country's first teacher-training school. A monument to Bolivian nationalism on its anniversary, Montes (a great booster of public instruction) invested the normal school with the mystical capacity "to revivify the national soul," "unify our aspirations," and forge the "indissoluble bonds of a loyal and true fraternity."[91]

Once the civic festivities were over and Rouma had a chance to get his bearings in this strange new land, the scales dropped, one by one, from his eyes. He immediately saw that behind the soaring rhetoric, Bolivia's new teacher-training institute was but a tiny pilot program. Its first graduating class in 1911 numbered but six students (rising to only twenty-three in 1915, and thirty-nine in 1920).[92] To compound matters, Rouma's very presence provoked public outcry from the Catholic hierarchy, anti-Liberal conservatives, and cultural nationalists (men like Franz Tamayo), all of whom repudiated his European liberal, scientific, and secular values. He had become a convenient scapegoat of the Liberal Party's critics, defectors, and ideologues. Even more disheartening were the "structural obstacles" that stood in the way of Rouma's bold reform agenda. Public schooling was in shambles: "One cannot even speak of an effective system of [public] instruction," he complained in 1913. The country's primary schools were woefully insufficient, "and those that do exist are [often] installed in houses that do not correspond to schoolhouses; they lack almost all the necessary teaching materials, and the teachers are youths without any special preparation.... [They] take up the profession as a last resort, and leave at the first opportunity," he observed.[93] What Bolivia needed most, he came to realize, was not a fancy normal school for the sons (and a few daughters) of the white criollo elites, but a vast and dispersed network of rural primary schools for the country's Indigenous children.

Yet his mission seemed daunting. Through Rouma's imperial gaze, the Bolivian Indian seemed inscrutable and the country "illegible" (to borrow James Scott's metaphor)—it was a crazy quilt of ecologies, regions, races, and ethnicities. When first contacted in Brussels, Rouma could scarcely locate Bolivia on the world map, much less fathom its complex diversity of Indigenous cultures and languages. But once he fastened on the rural elementary school as a prime goal, the Belgian turned the Bolivian Indian (broadly defined) into an object of intense scientific investigation, delving into the nature of the native's "disposition" (in terms of physique, psychology, personality, and environmental adaptation). The research project was driven by two functional questions (long familiar to local indigenistas): Was the Bolivian Indian really educable? And, if so, how should Rouma's scientific pedagogy be adapted to fit the Bolivian racial and environmental milieu?

Thus, Rouma was one of the first investigators to bring fieldwork, race science, and educational policy into one diagnostic and prescriptive framework.

FIGURE 1.4. Portrait of Georges Rouma, early 1900s. Invited in 1909 to help Bolivia establish a modern school system, the young Belgian advanced the "science of pedagogy," much to the ire of Conservatives and Church authorities. Photographic Collection, ALP, reprinted from *Fuentes* 9, no. 4 (2010).

In 1913 and 1914, he mounted a major ethnological research project to devise a hierarchical "bio-typology" of regions and racial groups. His aim was to measure environmental influences on Bolivia's Quechua and Aymara races. Weighing the differential influences of biology, culture, altitude, climate, and environment on the physiology and psychology of his human subjects, he would use that data to craft an educational reform program uniquely suited to Bolivia's national needs and diverse socio-racial ecologies. The research design targeted three "racial types" to investigate: "pure" Aymara, "pure" Quechua, and "mixed" Quechua and whites. He then situated each sample population within its distinctive environmental setting, so that region, altitude, and climate could be calibrated as variables in measuring and explaining patterns of differentiation. Next he plotted those differentiated biotypes along the incline of social evolution, from the primitive to the more assimilated state of development. Lest they fail to control for variations in ecological and social conditions, Rouma limited his sample to groups of tenant laborers working on haciendas in key regions of the vertical landscape. Safety and convenience also played a role: Rouma pointedly wanted to avoid contacting comunarios living in the ayllus, because of their inherent "volatility." Doing its advance work, his research team extracted permission from large landowners, who gave Rouma permission to choose his specimens and conduct his physical examination (see fig. 1.5). Landlords and their administrators would help facilitate the research by compelling their colonos to cooperate with the visiting scientists.[94]

The operation was almost dragnet-like. By prior arrangement with the landlord, Rouma's roving research team would swoop down on his tenant farmers, ideally catching them unawares. The element of surprise was a useful tactic, he later explained, because "the Indian is very impressionable, vulnerable, and susceptible to 'bad spirits' that can trigger rebellion.... They are always on the edge of rebellion, so we did not want to give them time to rebel."[95] Twenty-five young men (somewhere between the ages of twenty-five and thirty) were rounded up and steered to the makeshift field station, where they were subject to all manner of poking and probing as the scientists measured their weight and height, their chest circumference, the length of their limbs, and the size and shape of their cranium. There would be the usual "scientific" mugshots, frontal and profile, to gather the somatic data for deducing the collective subject's physiognomy (personality type, psychological disposition, and moral character, i.e., their supposed susceptibility to criminality or to efforts of cultural uplift and instruction).

This research methodology was commonplace among European and North American race scientists (particularly in the discipline of anthropology and its sub-branch of study, anthropometry). Rouma had read Arthur Chervin's three-volume 1908 anthropological treatise, *Antropologie bolivienne*—the first "scientific race study" of Bolivia's Indigenous populations of its kind. Chervin, who had never actually stepped foot in Bolivia, used his forensic collection, along with a collection of photographs, to measure, rank, and type the various races in Bolivia. Chervin tracked Bolivia's evolutionary progress through the gradual workings of miscegenation and assimilation (offering implicit confirmation of the Liberals' civilizing mission). Under Rouma, the field researchers were remarkably efficient: they conducted their experiments in one site within the span of a long day, so as not to disrupt the hacienda's work rhythms. A medical doctor examined the subjects' maladies and dispensed

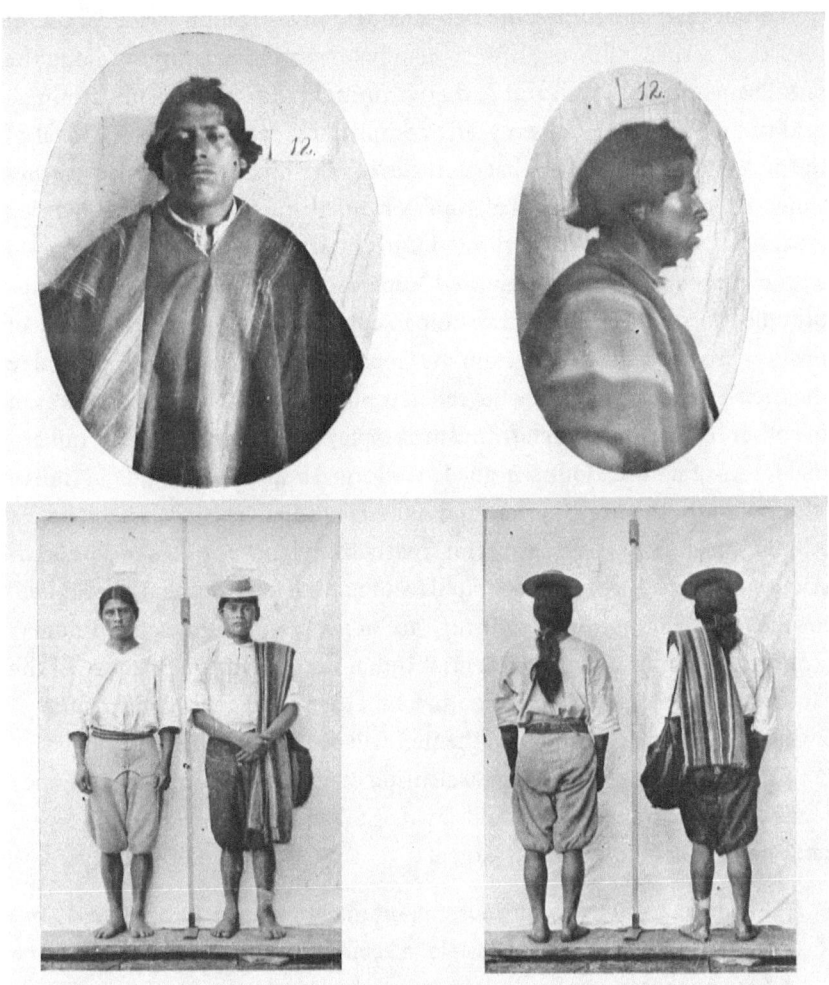

FIGURE 1.5. Samples from Rouma's data bank of "racial" and "regional" types of Bolivian Indians. Rouma's findings were used to "redeem" the unique vigor of the Aymara laborer working on the high plains. Rouma, *Les indiens Quitchouas et Aymaras des Hauts Plateaux de la Bolivie*.

basic medicines, while the scientists coaxed their subjects' cooperation by dispensing bags of coca leaves and cigarettes. Still, they encountered resistance. Everywhere they went, the scientists had to convince their research subjects not to fear them. Rumors raced through the countryside that the white-coated doctors were thinly disguised agents hunting for Indian conscripts under Montes's new law of "universal conscription."

For all their difficulties, the Belgian's field investigation yielded a pile of statistical results, allowing him to map his research conclusions along the familiar axes of bio-cultural and environmental determinisms. Rouma's grid of race and regionalism vastly complicated Tamayo's literary ideal of the pure Indian. He argued that centuries of race-mixing in Bolivia's warmer valley regions had produced a "superior" socio-racial type. Racial hybrids (specifically, the semi-acculturated Quechua Indians who had interbred with mestizos and whites) displayed "superior physiological traits" and thus occupied the highest rung of the human evolutionary ladder. His sample of positive crossbreeding came from the Cochabamba region of Caraza, where the men were classified as being tall, strong, and brimming with life.[96] On the other hand, climatic determinism also played a decisive role. The millennial forces of nature, Rouma argued, had forged a species of highland Indian (the Colla—both pure Quechua and Aymara ethnicities concentrated on the Altiplano) who displayed a superior "masculine vigor." The cold, alpine landscape constituted "a better geographic and natural environment," he argued, for the forging of a strong, enduring race of people.[97] In this sense, Rouma's work helped crystallize the essential Indian as an enduring feature of the landscape, ontologically tied to nature, and therefore logically the country's essential agrarian labor force (a theme I will return to below).

Here, then, was the Belgian's scientific contribution to the swirling polemics that continued to vex and divide La Paz's liberal, conservative, and nationalist ideologues. He explained,

> [The Indian] is not only the most important ethnic element [in Bolivia], but an element that will be impossible to replace. In Argentina and Chile, the autochthonous Indian has, little by little, completely disappeared. The lands he cultivated and pastures where his flocks once grazed were taken by European immigrants, who raised abundant harvests, bringing wealth and prosperity to those nations. In those countries, the expropriation [extinction?] of the Indian was entirely favorable to [the progress of] those nations.
>
> By contrast, if the Indian [race] were to disappear in Bolivia, it would not be replaced [by European immigrants]. In effect, the Indian is admirably adapted to the high-altitude lands of the high plateau. He works hard under the most severe conditions without any discomfort in the thin air. It is not the same for the European. Breathing is slower; fatigue is greater; sleep is longer; energy is sapped by the high altitude.... The rigor of agriculture is almost impossible for Europeans. The obvious result is that the European peasant

will not settle on the high plateau, and will never perform the work of the soil that the Indian does. *The Bolivian Indian, in the end, is indispensable.*[98]

What, then, was to be done? How might the "problem of indigenous education" be resolved, given this implacable truth? Rouma offered one practical answer—"farm-schools" (*les fermes-ecoles*): "I see no other way than the creation of farm-schools, vast establishments that could simultaneously develop the method of industrial exploitation and the systemic education of selected groups of young Indians."[99] Each pupil would acquire the intellectual, physical, and moral aptitudes befitting a universal "general culture" through a diffusion of work skills and habits suitable for growing crops and raising animals in Bolivia's mountainous environments. He envisioned self-sufficient, farm-school complexes mushrooming throughout the provinces, presumably without placing any fiscal burden on the state. The farm-school's most valuable harvest would be the pupils themselves, for they would be the bearers of useful knowledge and good work habits. Their ultimate mission, he said, was to return to their ancestral villages to instruct the rural inhabitants in modern farming under the watchful eye of tutelary authorities.

Rouma's utopian scheme never saw the light of day. Always bereft of public funding, he had to scale back his expectations and instead settle for the establishment of three rural normal schools. They were created as rural, satellite normal schools—pale reflections of the national pedagogic institute in Sucre. Following Rouma's logic of ecological and racial diversity, each normal school was planted in a distinctive environment: Umala, founded in 1915, was planted on the Altiplano; Colomi, established in 1917, was located in the valleys of Cochabamba (and later transferred to Sacaba); and Puna, founded in 1917, was placed in the remote highlands of Potosí. These small boarding schools were designed expressly for the "natural environment" of the Indian (*el propio medio del indio*). There the normal students were trained to teach the arts and crafts of modern farming suitable to the local ecology. Still a novelty and blessed by Rouma's prestige, the rural normal schools attracted "the best graduates of the Sucre normal school," according to Suárez Arnez.[100] Umala's teaching staff, for example, included Vicente Donoso Torres (who would become Bolivia's leading educational administrator in the early 1940s), Luís Crespo, and Juvenal Mariaca. Their charge was to teach "little but well, everything reasoned and practical." Special consideration would be given to Spanish-language immersion as the medium for the rapid incorporation of the masses into the national culture. Native languages were dismissed as being merely oral, and thus deficient and ultimately consigned to extinction.[101]

Although his farm-school utopia did not materialize in those formative years, Rouma had a crucial impact on tutelary race-thinking in Bolivia: he brought the prestige of science to advance a foundational premise—namely, that the prime mission of the rural "farm-school" was to prepare the next generation of Indians (the nation's *uniquely adapted* workforce for Bolivia's mountainous regions) for a lifetime of manual labor in Bolivia's highland crop fields, pastures, and mines. In epistemic and institutional ways, Rouma's scientific pedagogy had inadvertently provided Bolivian educators with the imprimatur for modernizing the neocolonial system of caste. By 1918 and 1919, his thesis was beginning to sway Bolivian public opinion, eclipsing the Liberal cosmopolitans' moral investment in the civilizing mission.[102] Timing and Liberalism's collapsing currency were also crucial. Around then, Manuel Vicente Ballivián (a scientist, writer, and geographer, and the Liberal Party's man in charge of Bolivia's 1900 census) reversed his earlier social Darwinian prognosis about the natural and inevitable disappearance of Bolivia's Indian race. The new doxa was both pragmatic and preservationist—the Indian was a permanent feature of the Bolivian landscape, and state educational policy must reflect that harsh new reality. Ballivián put it well: "If we know [the Indian's] defects, we must also realize that, at present, he is our only agriculturalist, herder of cattle, laborer in the mines. . . . *For such work, the Indian is irreplaceable.*"[103]

The Irreplaceable Aymara: Race into Labor

By the early 1920s, that racial axiom had begun to focus on the unique ethnic metabolism of the Aymara people, which had supposedly allowed them to endure "the privations and painful work with more consistency and resignation than any white man [i.e., the hoped-for European immigrant] could ever sustain."[104] Two years later, Jamie Mendoza applied his prestige as a medical doctor to explain Indians' innate capacity for endurance and praise their ability to survive under oppressive work conditions. Nature and geography, he argued, had endowed the race with a "Cyclopean energy."[105] Ultimately, Mendoza's explanation rested on the telluric mystique of the high plateau and its surrounding snow-capped mountain chain. The *macizo boliviano*, he argued, had shaped the character of the native inhabitants through millennia, and this telluric power of the land held the keys to Bolivia's national destiny. Race science, environmental determinism, and scientific pedagogy converged on the ontological premise that the Aymara ethnic race must be preserved and rehabilitated to perform its millennial function as the nation's "indispensable" high-altitude labor force. Race was becoming naturalized as a rural underclass, anchored by geography, climate, ethnicity, and subsistent necessity in the countryside.[106]

Also, by 1920, Bolivia's first cohort of professional indigenista pedagogues had been hatched from Rouma's normal school movement, and they displayed intense interest in solving the putative Indian problem. But many had become disenchanted with the Liberals' hollow promises of rural school reform. When the young educator Alfredo Guillén Pinto published his 1919 thesis, *La educación del indio*, it gave him a chance to lash out at the Liberal establishment's failure to effect change: "Until when?" he demanded to know. Two decades of Liberal rhetoric, and still the moral question haunted the nation: "What shall we do with the Indian? Will he be susceptible to even the most rudimentary education?"[107] This rhetorical question had long framed variant imperial civilizing projects up and down the Americas—ever since Jacksonian policies of Indian removal spurred passionate debate in the United States, and later in the century when a host of international fair expositions began to propagandize the civilizing progress that North American government agencies had made in regard to their own "savage" Creeks, Choctaws, and Cherokees, not to mention the Apache and other nomadic peoples being felled by disease, guns, or territorial dispossession.[108] In the 1920s this racist trope—what to do about the "Indian problem"—still haunted writers, scientists, and pedagogues in many parts of the Americas.

In search of answers, Bolivia's first generation of professional teachers had turned to the wider world. Some got to study abroad in Chile, Argentina, and other places, just as their own cosmopolitan tutors had trekked across Europe in search of the West's latest pedagogical models. Increasingly, however, it was the allure of North American models of school reform that attracted this new cohort of Bolivian educators. Of late, Bolivian and North American circuits of ideas, men, and capital had become entangled. Bolivia's tin and railroad booms had drawn North American investors, bankers, and diplomats into the country, while Bolivian diplomats eagerly pressed for US aid and investment. Old World ideas and pilgrimages were rapidly being eclipsed by new inter-American circuits of imperial technology, diplomacy, and knowledge. North America's industrial prowess, obsession with material progress, progressive evolution of civilization over savagism, militarist expansion into ancient tribal territories in the West, and aggressive overseas empire in the Caribbean, Central America, and the Philippines, along with the acute problems of racial violence and segregation policies in the Jim Crow South: all these developments in the Colossus of the North drew the keen interest of Bolivian civilizers and social reformers (as well as the repulsion of anti-imperialists). As Roy Harvey Pearce has argued, viewed from afar the history of American civilization would appear to some admirers as a three-dimensional juggernaut—"progressing from past to present, from east to west, from lower to higher."[109] From the Bolivian Andes, the metaphysics of US cultural and material progress must have seemed inexorable and compelling to vanguard nation-builders. But the idea of emulating the expansionist materialism of the Yankee imperium was also repellant to many. Like the force field of a powerful magnet, North America has historically exerted strong counterforces of attraction and repellency among Bolivian social reformers, as we will see in later chapters.

On a practical level, however, Bolivia's tutelary race-thinkers were especially intrigued by North America's Indian education policies. How would the Yankee engineers of Indian schooling close the giant evolutionary gap that separated its Anglo white people from the tribal "savages" who roamed the western plains? As we shall see in chapter 6, Bolivia would learn firsthand about US educational technologies when a small cadre of American educators swept into the country to redesign its rural school system. In the early 1900s, however, North America's influence was still rather opaque. In fact, there appears to have been little real understanding of US Indian policy beyond vague impressions: in 1905 Saracho, for example, had alluded to an illusory Washington program that had sent teachers to domesticate its "most bellicose tribes" in order to promote his own program of ambulatory schools to the Bolivian Congress.[110] But local educators' interest in El Norte grew as Bolivia's educational reforms sputtered. In the 1920s, a few normal teachers evinced keen interest in North America's pedagogical policies and tutelary race-thinking. Its famous boarding schools for Black and Indigenous students—particularly the institutes of Carlisle (in Pennsylvania), Hampton (in Virginia), and Tuskegee (in Alabama)—became objects of intense curiosity. To the Bolivian onlooker, those segregated trade schools for Blacks and Indians appeared to be efficient incubators of racial assimilation, social discipline, and vocational training. The Carlisle Indian Industrial School, for example, proudly displayed the "civilized Indian" in reports penned by religious and government authorities, and in the glossy brochures and propaganda that circulated widely, making that school an icon of a modified, work-oriented assimilationist policy.[111] Their pupils were being schooled to fit into North America's "Jim Crow" racial order while imbibing the Christian and capitalist values of obedience, piety, hard work, cleanliness, and self-reliance.[112] A new cosmopolitanism was emerging in Bolivia, but this time it was oriented toward North America's compounded pedagogic logic of assimilation, segregation, and subordination. The Tuskegee Institute and its famous Black founder, Booker T. Washington, were held in high regard. Alfredo Guillén Pinto, a newly minted *normalista* (i.e., a teacher with formal training) and acolyte of Georges Rouma, penned a paean to "Bvoker Wásington [sic]," the "Black Moses" of North America's industrial school movement, founded for the benefit of the descendants of enslaved people.[113] His colleague, Enrique Finot, adapted Rouma's farm-school idea to argue for special Indian boarding schools modeled after Tuskegee and Hampton.[114] And in 1923, in his *Ensayo de filosofía jurídica*, Ignacio Prudencio Bustillo beseeched his fellow educators to study the North American example of industrial training. Abolish "verbalistic and charlatan education!" he urged them. Replace it with "practical education," taught on "'model farms,' like those set up in the United States by Booker T. Washington for the education of the Negro." In schools like those, he said, the Bolivian Indian could learn how to cultivate the land using modern methods.[115]

Ironically, it was Felipe Segundo Guzmán, once the quintessential cosmopolitan and civilizer, who became the most fervent admirer of North American institutes for black manual labor training. Like the other Liberal educationalists of his day, Guzmán had embraced the oracle of modern education as the state's prime instrument for inducing bio-cultural progress through assimilative pressures. "School the child properly," went the mantra, "and you civilize the race." But that belief was more contingent, more ephemeral, than expected. At least three experiences pried loose Guzmán's youthful conviction: the 1910 boarding school fiasco; the fury he unleashed from powerful indigenista critics like Franz Tamayo; and the pseudoscientific revelation of Georges Rouma, who, upon "discovering" the true nature of Bolivian Indians, decided the country needed to create separate farm-schools to both sustain and upgrade its essential rural Indian workforce.

By the early 1920s, during his own term as Bautista Saavedra's minister of education, Guzmán had done a complete about-face on the issue of Indian schooling: "We all know that the Indian of the Altiplano is irreplaceable in his environment," he told the Congress in 1922. By that logic, the nation should build special, segregated farm-schools to train the Indian in agriculture and the manual arts. The curriculum would include gymnasium, hygiene, and love for and duty to the patria. Above all, the student would be disciplined to control his unruly impulses. Further, Indian children would be taught by teachers of their own kind in schools spatially separated from the city, just as Rouma had advocated. The model for Guzmán's pedagogic plan: North America's special "work-schools" designed for its "retarded ethnic elements." Schooling the Bolivian Indian would be reduced to "a rudimentary form of instruction" in manual labor skills. The boarding school of Hampton (Virginia), "with its retarded negroes and Indians," he explained to the legislators, "is almost identical to the one we are proposing for our Indians of the Altiplano." Its curriculum would be "strictly tailored to the mental capacity of the Indian, to which evolution has brought him." This plan for a segregated system of schooling, then, was set forth as the modern solution to the country's "autochthonous problem."[116] Guzmán's speech apparently did not loosen the congressional purse strings, but it did provide this former civilizer with a political platform for realigning his own ideological position in favor of a neocolonial national pedagogy of racial separatism and class inequality.

This history offers an eerie reminder that Eurocentric civilizing discourses and North American race doctrines were often mutually constitutive elements of modern neocolonialism, and never more so than in the Bolivian Andes. Such admiring allusions to North America's segregated school system inevitably plucked it out of context. Bolivian education reformers rarely alluded to those institutions as products and pillars of systemic racism in the Jim Crow South— the perverse confluence of abjectly racist ideas and attitudes; segregationist laws, policies, and policing; the rollback of Black rights to citizenship; and a southern political culture of domestic terrorism (white vigilantism, serial lynching, Black Codes, a carceral system of forced labor, and punitive laws, etc.).[117] That repulsive underside of American racial separatism was conveniently suppressed in the discourses and policy debates of most Bolivian educators. What Bolivian educators admired was the manifest disciplinarity of American educational policy, which aimed at civilizing and assimilating subaltern laboring classes of Blacks and Natives while, at the same time, rationalizing and reinforcing the country's rigid geo-racial and class hierarchy. Here, then, was Bolivia's whitewashed pedagogy of neocolonial modernity.

Educational utopia lay just beyond the reach of the governing class, however. After twenty years of governance and education reform, the Liberal Party had failed to build a viable apparatus of rural elementary schools. Structural impediments blocked the efforts of even the most vigorous reformers, men like Montes, Saracho, and Rouma. The federal state could not muster the institutional willpower to impose even a modicum of educational reform on the outlying rural provinces. Its half-hearted schemes and feeble efforts ran up against the bulwark of feudal landlords and provincial power holders. Hacendados routinely forbade, or pillaged, local school initiatives on their estates (defying a series of presidential decrees); and rural bosses often ran teachers out of town, lest they stir up trouble. And even Bolivia's progressive educators were stymied by their own racial ambivalence and partisan infighting. Yet if the governing elite failed to provision most Indian children with functioning primary schools, its cabal of tutelary race-thinkers harvested a rich set of ideas, polemics, and policies that converged, around 1920, in a coherent neocolonial pedagogy of race and nation—a framework that legitimated the basis of caste inequality that would endure, more or less intact, for decades to come. Viewed from a distance, and across time, the tarnished legacy of this "golden age of Bolivian education reform" was dismal indeed.

Yet, perhaps not surprisingly, the Liberal oligarchy's educational initiatives (its stream of pronouncements, arguments, actions, decrees, policies, and reversals) raised social expectations, even as it dashed hopes. Indeed, the Liberal era of failed school reform produced one of those ineluctable, unintended social consequences that can shift the ground under the sandal-clad feet of Indigenous peasants. In this case, the Liberal obsession with Indian education as the putative solution to the nation's race problem opened narrow spaces for Aymara school activism to take root and flower in the harsh political climate of the Altiplano.

2

Lettered Aymara

The Insurgent Politics of Literacy and Schooling

Those who attack [our schools] are responsible for the backwardness of Bolivia.... They are the eternal enemies of the Indian race because they want to keep us in [a state of] ignorance.
—"Solicitud de Manuel Choque y otros pidiendo que se cumplan los decretos para la instrucción," March 3, 1928

One bright crisp morning in September 1929, the bustling streets of La Paz were turned into a picturesque theater. About one hundred Aymara people marched in military formation down the city's central boulevard. The patriotic parade, along with the throbbing crowd of plebeian spectators, wended its way through downtown La Paz and spilled into the city's grand civic spaces, where Indians were still forbidden to congregate by municipal law. The spectacle of Indian schoolchildren carrying the Bolivian flag and marching to the drums and trumpets astonished many street-side spectators. The next day, *La Razón* spotlighted the scene: "The famous caciques of our department [of La Paz], having traveled into the city from distant provinces," proudly led several delegations of Indigenous schoolchildren. Lest the reader become alarmed that Indians were flooding into La Paz, the reporter assured him that the Indians' sole purpose for converging on the city was to display their patriotism and to demonstrate that despite their rural isolation from "our civilized cities..., [they] are nonetheless eager to promote their own cultural advancement."[1] What better proof than the sight of schoolchildren from the provincial cantons of Ancoraimes and Achacachi marching through the "civilized city" of La Paz?

Not only that, but the sheer number of Indian schoolchildren astonished the journalist. They seemed to him to have materialized out of nowhere—for, as he noted, very few state-sponsored schools served children in the rural backlands. But here was live evidence that village schools had cropped up across the countryside. Clearly, this reporter had rarely ventured beyond the city limits, or imagined that the Aymara community was anything but a desolate camp of prostate Indians, indifferent to their own "cultural advancement." The parade evidently challenged such assumptions. The reporter commended the Indians for sustaining rural elementary schools without costing the state "even one centavo of the national budget [for education]." Was this procession of caciques and schoolkids, then, not manifest proof that "in spite of the barbarous acts of local *corregidores* and other perverse elements," a hidden cultural revolution was unfolding in the countryside?[2]

In this chapter I shift perspective to ground the narrative in the Aymara rural periphery while also enlarging the spatial and temporal framework to examine the historical provenance of this nascent school movement in La Paz's outlying provinces during the late nineteenth and early twentieth centuries. Building on the foundations of Bolivian scholarship, this chapter situates this reporter's fleeting impressions in nested historical, regional, and ethnographic contexts to draw out the political pressures and cultural motives that drove Indigenous school activism.[3] Although his tone was patronizing and naive, the journalist's impressions were insightful. Something truly significant, yet still almost invisible, was happening in the paceño countryside. As this chapter will show, the Aymara legal campaign in defense of communal land rights powered an autonomous Indigenous school movement. Eventually it took on a dynamic of its own making as literacy became a weapon of combat in an escalating battle over the legality of traditional land claims and ongoing boundary disputes.

Ethnographers have long understood literacy as more than simply technology, appropriated and redeployed by Indigenous peoples involved in mediating and contesting the rules of colonial hegemony. Brian Street warns scholars against "setting up a false polarity between the 'technical' and 'cultural' aspects of literacy" (or, for that matter, between orality and literacy). Rather, he urges us to approach literacy practices "as they are encapsulated within cultural wholes and within structures of power."[4] Writing about the Nasa peoples of southern Colombia, Rappaport and Cummins reinforce Street's conceptual point: "Literacy [is] more than a technology: [it] is better understood as a set of practices deeply embedded within social, political, and economic realities."[5] As practiced by Aymara-speaking authorities and their intermediaries, the production of literate knowledge and their textual artifacts was usually a collaborative intercultural affair—the living legacy of a "distinctly colonial culture of communication."[6]

Precisely because of such innovative techniques and counter-hegemonic purposes, Indigenous practices of reading and writing occupy a critical place in this unfolding story of how the peasant desire for elementary schooling took hold, and what it signified for rural power relations in a pivotal time period, when the traditions of communal landholding were being threatened by liberal divestiture laws and the booming land market. In that crisis, the battle over land rights provided fertile ground for (what I am calling) insurgent literacy practices and community-based alphabet schools to develop, more or less, in tandem. This chapter begins, therefore, by exploring how the politics of literacy and schooling in the rural Andean world became inextricable from the escalating legal warfare over communal land rights. Anchored in the northern Aymara Altiplano, where the post-tributary political crisis was deep, long-running, and relatively transparent, this chapter highlights the emerging ethnic movement of caciques-apoderados, who fought to defend their traditional landholding rights and, in the process, coveted and acquired a host of legal and literacy skills needed to argue their cases in the cultural medium of their oppressors. Thus, precisely at the moment Bolivia's assimilationist state was devising a school system to civilize the Indian (yet also curb the spread of popular literacy), Aymara communities were reinventing their relationship to the white lettered metropole. Rural modes of literacy and schooling acquired enormous cultural currency during the escalation of Aymara battles over their traditional land rights. Eventually, the local alphabet school itself became the object of ayllu and community initiatives, quite apart from the state's grand design to educate and assimilate the Indians. This chapter traces the origins of the Aymara drive to acquire literacy, knowledge, and civil justice—motives that ultimately fired up the ambition to found a local school, even under the threat of violence. Because of the diffuse nature of official sources on the topic, this chapter must rely on fragments of oral testimony captured by Aymara-speaking Bolivian researchers in the 1980s and 1990s. But a remarkable stream of cacique petitions, along with news clippings and several insightful government reports, attends to the subject of Indigenous schooling in surprising ways. Most striking is the emergence of Eduardo Nina Quispe, one of Bolivia's first advocates for a nationwide program linking Indigenous education and territorial restitution. What this Aymara educator was advocating, some seventy years ahead of his time, was the principle of Indigenous citizenship set within the boundaries of a reimagined multiethnic Bolivia.

In broad strokes, then, this restive political landscape—from the late 1800s to the eve of the Chaco War (1932–35)—provides the dynamic context within which the regional Aymara politics of communal land defense, insurgent literacy, and local school initiatives were to play out. Watching the patriotic parade of schoolchildren marching through the streets of La Paz in 1929, neither the newspaper man nor the astonished criollo spectators might have known that Indigenous people had been fighting for the right to land, literacy, and schooling for some thirty years.

Landscapes of Lettered Caciques

Across the Andean highlands, the arrival of rails, markets, and mercantile capitalists began to dramatically alter the ideological and political landscape after 1870. Bolivia's booming export markets in minerals and other extractive goods sent powerful undercurrents into remote regions of the interior Andes, where, until then, Indigenous communities had managed to secure a precarious (if penurious) social peace under the post-Independence republic. Land inflation and the growing urban market for food crops began to attract entrepreneurial attention as investors eyed Indian land and labor as potential commodities in the incipient agricultural market and as a hedge against their speculative activities in mining, banking, or commerce.[7] So it was that market capitalism began to insinuate itself into the "Indian backlands," transforming Aymara and Quechua communal lands into a scarce, valuable, and conflict-ridden commodity. Capitalists began to covet large pockets of fertile fields and pastures along the shores of Lake Titicaca; the rich llama and alpaca herds of the province of Omasuyos beckoned the land speculator; and many an entrepreneur was ready to seize advantage of the region's dense concentration of ayllu lands, potential tenant laborers, and geographic proximity to the booming city of La Paz.

Around the turn of the century, meanwhile, Bolivia's liberal oligarchy was busy designing a grand scheme for Indian pacification and assimilation (see chapter 1). Bolivian modernity demanded that the state set up a bureaucratic apparatus for the privatization of Indian lands by abolishing the communal order, selling off parcels of land, and distributing individual land titles to a new class of petty landowners. The legal and institutional vehicle for this massive enclosure was the 1874 Law of Divestiture (Ley de Ex-vinculación). Beyond the letter of the law, the new agrarian reform represented a fundamental shift in power relations and modes of representation that had governed Indian/ayllu relations since colonial times. By proclamation, the law ruptured what historians have called "the colonial tributary pact"—that folk-legal "contractual" arrangement of colonial domination under which the king of Spain had bestowed his Indigenous subjects with corporate rights to land in exchange for their obedience, labor, and tribute.[8] Colonialism's hegemonic bargain (communal land rights for all manner of tribute and labor) had survived, in modified form, the transition to Republican rule. But by the 1860s and 1870s, the prospect of agrarian capitalism and land speculation (together with the decline of state revenue from Indian tribute) prompted Bolivia's governing elites to dismantle the neocolonial pact, a prospect that threatened to disturb the intricate web of communal landholding and labor relations, as well as ritual and political forms of self-governance.[9] Bolivia, with the highest per capita concentration of tribute-paying comunarios, was the last Andean nation to carry out this modernizing agrarian scheme.

Years later, the Jesuit anthropologist-activist Xavier Albó took note of the bitter historical paradox that burdened the oligarchy's internal colonization of the Altiplano. As the ruling elite heralded the bio-cultural miracles of Western civilization, the nobility of the wage-earning working class, and the promise of market capitalism, Bolivia's political elites unleashed a tidal wave of latifundismo and fortified a rentier class of feudal landholders, which pushed the country back into the dark ages. In the wake of this agrarian retrogression, masses of rural peoples were dispossessed, evicted, or reduced to an abject state of servitude ("slavery") on primitive haciendas. In search of an agrarian utopia of yeoman farmers and modern farming estates, the Liberal state instead became the midwife of a grotesque rebirth of agrarian feudalism, entrenching racial caste and servile relations that would prevail in many highland regions for the next several decades.[10]

This ominous realignment of property and power relations, along with the deepening geo-racial divide between metropole and hinterland, unleashed a wave of Indian petitioning and lawsuits. A new generation of lettered and litigious peasant activists took up the mantle of the apoderado (legal representative, carrying a *poder*, or power of attorney) to mediate conflicts and advocate on behalf of aggrieved Indian communities in the courts and public sphere.[11] They organized an informal guild of Indigenous apoderados (bearing a variety of ranked titles, such as "apoderado general," "cacique-apoderado," or the maximalist title "cacique apoderado general"), which evolved into a sprawling ethnic movement that had few contemporary counterparts in the greater Andean world. Under (mostly) Aymara leadership, this defensive land-based movement spun off from spiraling conflicts over land claims (including inter-ayllu boundary disputes), but by the 1910s the cacique-led movement had coalesced around the growing imperative to defend, protect, and/or restore Indian access to communal landholding rights under (their own interpretive readings of) colonial and republican laws.

Soon enough, Indigenous protestors and petitioners were moving from local disputes and retail lawsuits to wholesale strategies of political contention. Ayllus pooled their resources and entrusted their cases to a small cadre of Indigenous apoderados. Most were comunarios who had come up through the civil-religious channels of rotative community service. They had acquired the essential experience and skills of the *tramitador* (legal/bureaucratic fixer), becoming specialists in navigating Bolivian law, bureaucracy, and the notarial culture. Most apoderados worked closely with a small group of Indigenous scribes and secretaries (*escribanos* or *qilqiris*). Based in the city of La Paz or in surrounding provincial towns, bilingual Aymara escribanos crafted letters, manifestos, and even newspaper notices. Their rich communicative repertoire (mixing oral, written, ritual, and print forms of expression) reflected the fact that Aymara activists began to diversify their strategies, crafting and broadcasting messages in the wider political and public spheres. Like the iconic "indio ladino" of colonial times, but deploying the new technology of their day, these Indigenous intermediaries stepped up to fill the interethnic gap that had separated the lettered Hispanic metropole from the rural mass of monolingual native speakers. Displacing the "mestizo sphere" of petty officialdom and intercultural mediation, Indigenous scribes and notaries worked closely with leading Indigenous political figures—the venerable caciques apoderados generales, such as Santos Marka T'ula and Francisco Tanqara—to prepare legal documents, translate and record the spoken words of Aymara petitioners, decipher archival records, read aloud government edicts, publish newspaper notices, and compose the occasional manifesto.

The scope and intensity of this literate and litigious activity remained somewhat diffuse in the years leading up to the triumph of the Liberal Party in 1900. Yet early flashes of an incipient comunario movement were unmistakable. In 1880, for example, peasant leaders (from the ayllus of Callapata, in Oruro) gave a power of attorney to Juan Mamani, who was charged with the task of carrying ayllu documents (specifically, a 1646 *título de composición*) to present in Congress to the Bolivian senators. The documents would prove, they hoped, that their ancestors had duly purchased "absolute rights" to their communal lands and, on that basis, the litigants had rightful claims to their ancestral lands under the new Liberal laws.[12] By the 1890s, legal resistance had become more collective and ambitious. In 1894, a peasant network from across the whole Department of Oruro put forth a mass petition demanding the restoration of ancient ayllu lands and the definitive end to the unpaid labor obligations and illegal liens that burdened Indigenous communities. The petition reminded the judge that under republican law, the Indian was no longer responsible for paying tribute or serving on corvée labor projects.[13] Here an incipient discourse of Indian rights operated along the seams of inherited colonial/customary law (the basis of Indian communal land claims) and civil/constitutional law that prohibited provincial authorities from conscripting Indian labor.

The very act of mass petitioning compelled far-flung Indigenous communities to bind together, thickening their underground networks of communication and exchange, and transforming local grievances into a broad platform of peasant demands. Historian Carlos Mamani's research uncovered an extensive web of Indigenous leaders and apoderados that stretched across the Bolivian highlands, tying the ayllus of Sakaka (in the Department of Potosí) to the distant Aymara-speaking barrios of San Pedro, located on the outskirts of La Paz. Led by Diego Kharikhari (of Sakaka) and Feliciano Espinoza (of San Pedro), their 1889 petition was signed by some twenty-five men, hailing from Aymara and Quechua communities throughout the Departments of La Paz, Oruro, and Potosí. Their driving concern was to establish their legal authority to defend their *collective* inherited rights and protections to the commune under a mix of colonial and republican decrees. They called on the state to recognize and respect their Indian apoderados and to shield them against provincial predators.[14] A collective voice in the wilderness, they demanded that the state ratify the right of Indigenous people to represent their lawful interests (including their inherited rights to communal land) at the very moment Bolivia's ruling elite was plotting ways to silence and marginalize the Indian race through state-sponsored devices of territorial displacement, local forms of labor subjugation, and racial terror.

In such a climate of racial violence, this represented an astonishing achievement: by 1900, an informal guild of lettered Indians had emerged as a unifying force of voice and mediation. In the process, multiple local lawsuits were conglomerating in broad counteroffensive strategies. A 1904 petition submitted by Patricio Mamani (apoderado general for all the rural communities in the canton of Ayoayo, province of Sicasica) demanded that the government's land commissioners conduct a formal review (*revisita*) of all colonial documents. On the basis of the Indigenous *recopilación* of colonial documents, the petitioners asked the state to conduct an official reinspection of their land claims, based on colonial title deeds and other old documents. Once those documents had been inspected and ratified, the state would be compelled by the 1883 law protecting "pro-indiviso" communities to restore all stolen and usurped lands to their rightful owners—in this case, the ex-comunarios of Ayoayo.[15] Deploying the logic of the rationalizing bureaucratic state for opposite ends, the peasant petitioners insisted that the land commissions use their modern instruments (the land survey, boundary inspection, property register, cadastral map, etc.) to reverse the government's legal divestiture process. Once the collected colonial titles were carefully reviewed, the state would be compelled to create a new cartography of ayllu territories. Property lines and landmarks would be used, they reasoned, to reinstate the true, original owners to their ancestral territories. Utopian in its boldness and scope, the Ayoayo peasant demand drew on a long colonial tradition of legal and institutional resistance through the mechanism of revisita. In seventeenth-century Huamanga, to take but one widely known example, a stream of Indian petitioners pressured the colonial state to organize new inspection tours of their lands and communities. This tactic mushroomed into a wider strategy, transforming the institution of revisita into a battleground as rural communities throughout Peru's central highlands insisted that colonial inspectors take new inventories of their diminished lands, herds, and populations. (There was a good deal of subterfuge involved in this strategy, as rural people plotted ways to shield their resources from the prying eyes of colonial *visitadores*.) But in classic form, Indigenous resistance borrowed, and inverted, the official script (in this case, the colonial revisita) to halt, obstruct, or mitigate the harsh system of tributary extraction.[16]

Times had changed, of course, and many rural communities had come to rely on their so-called tributary pact with the republican state to stave off the incessant encroachments and threats to their communal lands. But the devastating impact of the 1874 land reform law, followed by successive waves of land grabbing, had turned the revisita into a new political battleground. The very purpose of the *mesa revisitadora* (as the official inspection tour was called) became a political contest between opposite logics and unequal social forces. The state's official mission was to dismantle the commune in the name of a modernizing agrarian regime (albeit granting minimal exception to those ayllus that could prevail in the courts). For Indigenous apoderados, an official review promised the opportunity to reconstitute the communal order, piecing together all the legally claimed lands that had passed (illegally) into private hands. As far as Indigenous petitioners were concerned, there was no ambiguity behind their clamor for an official reinspection of their customary tenure rights. Their openly counter-hegemonic strategy called into question the legitimacy of *all* divested, sold, or usurped lands that had been carved out of ancient ayllu jurisdictions since the time of Melgarejo.[17] Pending an official revisita of Indian land titles and other documents, the Aymara legal campaign threw shadows of doubt on the very legality of hacienda ownership in some parts of the Altiplano. Bolivia's rural property regime was turning into a murky state of legal limbo.

After the turn of the century, rural conditions deteriorated further. Land values spiked; the state's divestiture process proceeded apace; and racial tensions deepened in the aftermath of the 1899 uprising. Privatization of ayllu lands—the division of a territory into private lots and sale of title deeds—was met by a new wave of anguished opposition. A new generation of Aymara activists coalesced around a mix of legal strategies, direct actions, and political propaganda campaigns. There were internal leadership adjustments within the sprawling network of Aymara and Quechua authorities and their apoderados. Some caciques fortified their position by tracing their genealogical descent from colonial chieftains. In search of authority and authenticity, Aymara leaders reconstructed a quasi-mythical lineage of the office of hereditary *cacicazgo* by upstreaming to sixteenth-, seventeenth-, and eighteenth-century documentary names and titles of noble caciques (the post was formally

FIGURE 2.1. A group portrait of the cacique-apoderado movement, around 1920. Poised at the center of the first row is their leader, Santos Marka T'ula. Kneeling, he holds his staff of office and wears a silver cross. Photo by Julio Cordero, courtesy of the Julio Cordero Family Archive.

abolished following the great uprisings of the 1780s). *Caciques de sangre*, their title conflated with that of the official legal apoderados, began to appear as the leading signatories at the bottom of peasant petitions. Bearing this "double" mark of hereditary and appointed authority, they began representing broad swaths of the rural population, sometimes even the totality of *la raza indigena* (see fig. 2.1). Mass peasant petitions began carrying the imprimatur of Aymara and Quechua leaders, including the five leading Aymara-speaking apoderados covering the Department of La Paz: Santos Marka T'ula, Francisco Tanqara, Prudencio Callisaya, Faustino Llanqui, and Eduardo Nina Quispe. In one petition, historians Roberto Choque and Cristina Quisbert identified a sprawling web of ninety-six "named" caciques-apoderados from across the departments (forty-six in La Paz, twenty in Oruro, fourteen in Potosí, and sixteen in Cochabamba).[18]

Irradiating from the epicenter of rural La Paz, the cacique-apoderado movement extended its reach into the distant provinces and eventually surfaced in the Departments of Cochabamba and Chuquisaca. In the valleys of Vacas and Tapacarí, for instance, Andean peasant activists crafted petitions demanding their "absolute right" to their original lands; other petitioners, representing colonos, denounced the actions of abusive landlords or provincial officials.[19] In Chuquisaca, Indigenous juridical skills and strategies evolved to fit the region's entrenched seigneurial regime. Where the great estate had early colonial roots, the prospect of litigating colonial title deeds to restore ownership to long-lost communal lands was increasingly seen as a lost cause. Instead, Indigenous activists became adept at mobilizing the mass petition demanding their inviolate right to "protection and guarantees" (*amparo y garantías*) under republican law.[20] The mass petition, shaming the Indians' predatory class of oppressors, became the currency of rural protest, especially after the Chaco War, as agrarian militancy ripped through hacienda zones, peasant unions began cropping up, and socialist and anarchist organizations gained ground in places like Cochabamba and La Paz. But long before the arrival of agrarian activists, the political and legal activism of Aymara and Quechua authorities, combined with the developing literate and legal skills of native petitioners, mobilized in ways that won small but important victories. Although the caciques' legal campaign never managed to roll back, or reverse, the expansion of haciendas across the Altiplano, the outpouring of lawsuits, petitions, and newspaper notices amounted to a deliberate public opinion campaign that sometimes astonished the urban elites. Not only did Andean activists hone the technologies of legalism, literacy, and print culture to spread the word; they also fashioned the elements of a syncretic utopia of communal and civil rights, predicated on the possibility that a form of "indigenous citizenship" might be made to flourish within the legal-institutional framework of the Bolivian nation-state.[21] As we will see later in this chapter, this matrix of indigeneity, territorial justice, and citizenship crystallized in the utopian vision and activism of the Aymara educator Eduardo Nina Quispe.

In the pursuit of communal land and justice, the caciques' expanding repertoire also began to embrace the ideal of "public instruction" in the late 1910s and 1920s. The clamor for alphabet schools grew organically out of this larger Aymara political movement as the power of the written word became inextricably linked to Aymara aspirations for land, justice, and autonomy. Although the newspaper reporter was unaware of it, La Paz's "famous caciques" leading the 1929 parade of schoolchildren carried the battle scars of this long civic struggle for ethnic empowerment and justice. Wielding pen and ink, the caciques had become the primary interlocutors and advocates for Bolivia's "illiterate" masses who clamored for alphabet schools to fill the void left by decades of failed state policies.

The Caciques' Archive

Through skillful petitioning, rural activists crafted petitions that appropriated and transformed the sites and symbols of Western civilization—the pen, the archive, and the school. For if the colonial archive guarded the secrets of the state, as Michel Foucault would say, in the Bolivian Andes it also housed the ancestral documents that were the key to contemporary legal campaigns for the restoration of communal justice in the face of agrarian and state violence. And if legal writing could be deftly deployed as a combat weapon by Indigenous activists in their ongoing battles, it was the lowly primary school that promised to deliver the power of literacy to the unlettered masses and thus might open the sluice gate to a better future, beyond the wall of Bolivia's racial caste system, which kept the deracinated peasant entrapped in a state of "slavery and ignorance."

But it took a jolt of racial violence in 1914 and 1915 to catalyze the transregional league of cacique-apoderado activists, who began to operate within the instrumental and symbolic matrix of literacy, the archive, and the school. We can catch a momentary glimpse of this opaque landscape, if we (narratively) track the comings and goings of several itinerant Aymara activists. The precipitating event began rather uneventfully, in a long, dusty overland trek to Peru's colonial archive. In 1913, two mestizo lawyers and an Aymara apoderado, hailing from the ayllu of Illata in the province of Pacajes, set off across the high plateau and down through the western cordillera to the Chilean coast, en route to the sprawling Peruvian capital of Lima. The national archive, site of the old Audiencia (high court of the Peruvian viceroyalty), was their main destination, though they might also have visited a public notary's office. The old imperial vault housed thousands of colonial documents, including royal land-title deeds of settlement and sale (*títulos de composición y venta*)—the legal currency they needed to prove their claims to their ancestral *tierras de origen*.[22]

When Martín Vázquez (along with several mestizo lawyers) left his village of Illata for the capital of Peru, he was undertaking an ancient tradition, the judicial pilgrimage. Much like the religious pilgrims seeking salvation, these judicial pilgrims were on a redemptive secular mission to renegotiate the terms and traditions of their rights and obligations under colonial law. They followed the caravan trade routes to Lima, Sucre, and Buenos Aires, the seats of Spanish colonial bureaucracy, law, and power. Where corruption was endemic in the provinces, Indigenous petitioners carried their petitions and lawsuits up through the imperial chain to the viceregal capitals, and even beyond to the overseas Council of the Indies.[23] Indeed, Martín Vázquez's 1913 overland journey to Lima (site of the old Audiencia of the Viceroyalty of Peru) brings to mind the 1779 judicial pilgrimage of Tomás Katari, who walked more than a thousand miles, from the highland town of Macha to the port city and viceregal capital of Buenos Aires, to find justice. In that fateful trek, Katari carried petitions denouncing the tyranny of local caciques and the collusion of corregidores and even the ministers of the Audiencia of Charcas (the governing body of Alto Peru, located in the city of Sucre).[24] The circumstances were not so very different in 1913. Like Katari, Vázquez spoke little or no Spanish and did not claim noble cacique heritage. As apoderado, however, he was vested with the authority (and collected funds) to carry out this archival expedition in preparation for the collective lawsuit. At this stage of the judicial process, Vázquez's Peruvian mission was to gather archival documents that could later be used in the defense of Qallapa's ancient land claims in Bolivian courts.

The expedition to Lima yielded fruit, and the group hurried home to Bolivia with their haul of affidavits (*testimonios*) of documents, evidence of "absolute ownership" (since "time immemorial") of their communal lands.[25] Years later, several elders recounted how Vázquez brought back from Peru notarized copies of ancient documents, tangible proof that their ancestors had faithfully served the Crown through their payments of labor "service [as mitayos] in Potosí in 1500, 1600, 1700."[26] Fired up, the group began spreading the word about their cache of land titles (probably facsimiles and affidavits of the original documents). Here we have only hints of what may well have been a far-flung operation dealing in the inflationary paper currency of colonial title deeds (hand copied or printed). On the other hand, the wide diffusion of facsimiles of archive documents made perfect cultural sense, since the apoderados' wholesale strategy was to litigate their documents, while also demanding a revisita of their thick corpus of old papers, being collected from all sorts of repositories, archives, and public notary offices everywhere. But in the jittery racial climate of La Paz, this archive pilgrimage was bound to trigger a harsh reaction on the part of landlords and elites, ever wary of itinerant Indian "troublemakers." In early 1914, Vázquez and other caciques watched with horror as policemen apprehended them and confiscated their "ancient papers." A year later, the documents cropped up again. But this time, they provided the prosecutor's "prime evidence" in the criminal trial of Martín

Vázquez and the Monroy lawyers. They were on trial for their "crimes of subversion, tumult, and others."[27]

It is worth pausing for a moment to focus on the aftermath of Martín Vázquez's archive expedition because it throws light on the Aymaras' flourishing underground scribal economy. What little we can garner from these sources must be filtered, of course, through the layers of racist sentiment and prosecutorial bias in the trial testimonies, organized by La Paz's prefect, subprefect, and lesser officials. But there are a few signposts pointing to semiclandestine activities of lettered caciques, their mestizo "co-conspirators," and the alleged Indian uprising (*sublevación*) that was brewing in early 1914. The trial's formulaic protocol aside, these transcripts open a window into the vernacular literacy practices that provoked the wrath of the oligarchic state.[28]

The prefect's criminal case against Vázquez, the Monroy lawyers, and several other "accomplices" revolved around criminal accusations of fraud and extortion. That is, the Bolivian state sought to wipe out Vázquez's bounty of archival documents by alleging their fraudulent nature. Moreover, the crime was compounded by theft: Vázquez and the lawyers were charged with using the scam to bilk the Indians of hundreds of bolivianos.[29] More worrisome to Bolivian authorities was the Lima expedition's insurrectionary aftereffects. The (allegedly) phony documents, the prosecutor said, had ignited false expectations that the Liberal government would soon ratify the Indians' colonial titles, thus proving beyond a doubt that the comunarios were in legal possession of their ayllu holdings in Qallapa and elsewhere. Exhibit A of this "vast conspiracy" was a 1914 broadsheet (*boletín*). Stamped with a fake official seal, the circular announced the arrival from the archive in Lima of "ancient and authentic titles from the time of the King of Spain." Moreover, the court accused the Indian conspirators of profiting from (what it saw as) counterfeit documents: notarized facsimiles (or duplicates) of the original archival documents that could be ordered "for a small fee with a few days' notice."[30]

We can only surmise that a prodigious underground commodity market in copied land titles was flourishing: the boletín, seized by the police in a raid, offers tangible evidence that Vázquez and his comrades had spread the news that notarized (probably boilerplate) colonial land titles were available for purchase. Printed copies of the announcement circulated briskly through the oral and literate arteries of rural society, carried by itinerant laborers, traders, and *chasquis* (Andean messengers who trotted over mountain passes, from tambo to tambo, village to village, carrying mail, documents, rumors, and news). Another clue to this flourishing underground market was Vázquez's magnetic attraction in the final days of 1913 and early 1914. Aymara authorities streamed into the city of La Paz, drawn by the possibility that they too could use this paperwork to leverage their own legal negotiations with the Bolivian state, or they could sign on to the broader legal challenge being mounted by a web of Indigenous apoderados.

Apparently the seized documents comprised the prime evidence the prosecution needed to make their case against the "conspiratorial machinations" of these lettered Indians. The diffusion of "ancient and authentic [land] titles" was viewed by state authorities as a brazen act of political subversion. More apparent evidence of "Indian rebellion," brewing in the provinces of Pacajes, Sicasica, Loayza, Ingavi, and Los Andes, was forthcoming in late March 1914. According to the subprefect of Pacajes, caciques had streamed into downtown La Paz, clustering in knots of whispering "conspirators" who plotted their nefarious schemes. And those schemes apparently surfaced in a half-finished manifesto, cobbled together by Vázquez and other Indigenous leaders, during a nocturnal meeting convened in a rustic hall near La Paz's municipal cemetery.[31] According to the research of Carlos Mamani, the Indian manifesto demanded that the state end compulsory military service (a crushing burden borne almost exclusively by young Indigenous men); enforce the abolition of colonial tribute (which continued to be levied in many rural places, despite its legal abolition in 1874); and end all forced labor services, including the onerous provincial burden of carrying mail over long distances. Also on the agenda were two crucial civil demands: the right of Indians to enter the market (to sell their crops, enter wage labor relations, move freely, and be released from relations of bondage on the hacienda); and the right to send their children to public elementary schools under the protection of state law. The overarching Indigenous strategy had not changed—the manifesto articulated the mixed logic of colonial heritage and contemporary civil rights as the moral and legal basis for restoring the commune under the modern republic.[32]

This semiclandestine assembly, and the broad postcolonial platform it was beginning to build, would never see the light of day, however. Vázquez and the peasant leaders in attendance were found guilty of "lies and conspiracies" and of "chimerical vindications"—because they had demanded the abolition of the territorial tax and the end to unpaid turns of gang labor. But it was the subversive nature of the paperwork that most troubled authorities: "The Indians spend huge sums of money on writings and useless publications;

[they are] distributed in great profusion among the Indian masses [*la indiada*], who have taken [them] as their patents of exemption from all the taxes and services imposed on them by the Congress and government." This flurry of archive papers, complained the prefect of La Paz, had stirred up agrarian unrest and was causing "total demoralization among the provincial and cantonal authorities."[33] What most alarmed state authorities, however, was the assembly's plan of assault on Bolivia's private property regime and bonded labor: the 1914 assembly was in the process of assembling a massive cacique archive of documents, and it planned to insist on a "general review" of all colonial land titles and boundary lines pertaining to "all the original lands."[34] This nonviolent movement of decolonization, negotiated through the channels of legal and political discourse, posed a mortal threat, both real and imagined, to the status quo ante. The government prosecutor and his witnesses warned that a brewing "Indian uprising... [aimed at] overthrowing the nation's political regime and establishing a strictly Indian government."[35] In a tone dripping with condescension, one newspaper reporter warned that if the Indians were to get their way, they would "soon become property owners of estates, presently owned by various gentlemen [*caballeros*]."[36]

But there was nothing amusing about the government's brutal reaction. With the imprisonment of the Monroy lawyers and Martín Vázquez, the Liberal state and its provincial underlings began to crack down on the cacique movement. As brutal as the physical repression was, it was the state's persistent use of symbolic violence—specifically, the confiscation of the archival documents—that energized the caciques' defensive tactics in the aftermath of the 1914–15 reprisal. Over the next five years, the Bolivian Andes were crisscrossed with archival paper trails as Santos Marka T'ula (who in 1919 was given the title "cacique apoderado general") took up the mantle of collecting and litigating colonial title deeds—not only to replicate what was confiscated but also to gather up, produce, and circulate a variety of documentary materials in the ongoing "search for justice." His obsession was to *create and circulate a subaltern archive*, a tangible and symbolic centerpiece of the Aymara cultural armory. In practical terms, the caciques had learned not to collaborate with predatory mestizo lawyers (Vázquez's hired lawyers, for example, were accused of betrayal and extortion). In the meantime, Marka T'ula secured working relationships with trusted Aymara scribes (men like Rosendo Zalerio in Sucre, and Leandro Condori Chura in La Paz). Although Marka T'ula spoke very little Spanish, he was a principal signatory on copies of official papers, and he would often listen to documents being read aloud

FIGURE 2.2. Delegates, bearing their staffs of office and a bundle of documents. To the left stands Leandro Condori Chura, in Western dress. Next to him is Rufino Willka, a powerful cacique of ayllus and communities in the Omasuyos province. The other two figures are unidentified. Archive of the Alcalde de Potosí, reprinted in Condori Chura and Ticona Alejo, *El escribano de los caciques apoderados*, 100.

by his *qilqiri* (secretary and scribe), Condori Chura (see fig. 2.2). Working with the scribe, he dictated the contents of a political document and often committed to memory the essence of colonial title deeds in his keeping. And he brought deep cultural and contextual knowledge to those reading and writing sessions, making it seem to Condori Chura that they jointly read the Spanish documents, navigating the oral/scribal divide as if they were two individuals folded into one.[37] This, too, was a dangerous business, however. Like Vázquez before him, by 1916 Marka T'ula had become a marked man in La Paz. Closely watched, stalked, and persecuted, the cacique-apoderado (and the men and mules that usually accompanied him) moved stealthily by night, along mountainous paths, smuggling the "contraband" paper bundles between state archive, notary office, and courthouse. Arrested and imprisoned in 1914, 1917, and 1918, Marka T'ula resorted to smuggling messages out to the other caciques. Once released from Bolivia's jungle labor camp in late 1918, this consummate chiefly authority resumed the ceaseless "work of reconstructing his documentary holding," scouring the land for "all the ancient deeds belonging to our community."[38]

The caciques' prodigious search for old papers reminds us that the tangible sediments of the past (particularly copies of composición documents) were embedded in rural village life throughout the Andes.[39] Historian Waskar Ari, working closely with local authorities, unearthed numerous "cacique archives" dispersed in rural villages throughout highland Bolivia.[40] Local village archives might house the debris of past colonial court battles or government business, but those same textual fragments also formed the elements of communal history and moral memory.[41] Indeed, Andean ethnography has shown us how scribal tradition was (and still is) woven into the everyday rituals and governance of communal life in traditional ayllu-communities.[42] Olivia Harris's fieldwork in northern Potosí reveals the persistent ritual value of local documentary collections. Old documents, she writes, "are celebrated with offerings and guarded from the eyes of those outside the immediate group to whom they belong. Thus, paradoxically, documents not only represent the crystallization of knowledge through writing, but also ... a direct communication from the ancestors who first obtained them, and who entrusted them to their descendants."[43] The colonial title deed might also serve as a ritual artifact to mark the community's seasonal and ceremonial calendars. In many rural communities, for example, colonial documents were taken out of strongboxes and unwrapped from protective sheepskin coverings so their contents could be "read" or recited from memory in civil-religious ceremonies. At the beginning of each year the K'ulta authorities of rural Oruro carried their community's portable archive as they retraced the ancient boundaries and marked the sacred landmarks within the vast Asanaqi territory, once the territorial homeland of their ancestors. Through this ritual performance, community authorities established themselves as rotative custodians of the communal patrimony. For a year they would serve as the community's spiritual and political authorities and keepers of the communal archive, entrusted with protecting the ancestral heritage, inscribed in their colonial documents and in the land.[44] The esoteric power of ancient papers was rekindled in those intimate ritual spaces of the Indigenous community. Remembering the times of the caciques, Leandro Condori Chura described how he and his kinsmen routinely blessed and made offerings to their documents (*hay que hacer wilancha*).[45] On the occasion of a legal battle or petition campaign, peasant leaders might pay homage to their ancient titles by sacrificing a sheep or llama, or sprinkling its blood on the site where bundles of documents were to be blessed, opened, and read. Such precautions were to be taken if, as folk wisdom had it, the dangers of collective amnesia, or the "nakedness of ideas," were to be guarded against.[46]

But in the course of the caciques' struggle, Marka T'ula turned not to ritual sacrifice but to Bolivia's national archive to secure the tangible evidence of "our laws," as the caciques might say. This time, however, Marka T'ula was not extracting copied documents from that repository; rather, he was entrusting his sacred paperwork to the Archivo Nacional de Bolivia. In 1921 and again in 1923, Marka T'ula deposited in Sucre's venerable national archive (and later in the Archivo de la Paz and several other archives) several dossiers of Indigenous documents that he had been gathering and assembling over several years. As custodian of this documentary patrimony, Marka T'ula reversed the usual direction of the paper trail—a stream of legal papers now flowed from the rural periphery into the urban center, from the villages and provinces into the state's central vault of documentary holdings. There, in the Bolivian National Archive, the documents would be catalogued and stored, available for reference by Indian pilgrims in search of their own communal patrimonies in later years. It is possible that some of this Indigenous paperwork from the early twentieth century was funneled into the archive's famous documentary collection, "Tierras e Indios, 1549–1824," which many historians, myself included, have examined over the years.[47] Protecting their archival patrimony from the "snatchers" and placing it under lock and key in the state's vault was a strategy devised under duress, but it meant that peasant pilgrimages to the archive would continue as long as rural people continued their search for truth and justice through oral and documentary memory.

The Archivo Nacional de Bolivia—that august repository designed by Spain to guard "the secrets of the state" in Alto Perú—was turned into an unlikely strongbox containing the legal paperwork of Indigenous people trying to reclaim their colonial rights, safeguard their communal heritage, and challenge the state's vicious program of land divestiture.

Contraband Schools and Clandestine Teachers

In the meantime, Santos Marka T'ula and the league of caciques-apoderados began to advocate for rural schools. Apart from some Catholic and Protestant missionary schools, rural La Paz still had almost no state-sponsored school establishments; elementary schools, run by municipalities, mainly served the children of local mestizo and Creole people. In the 1910s, at the height of Georges Rouma's campaign for scientific pedagogy, Bolivia's first experiment in rural Indian normal schools was already in a shambles, and the nation still lacked a pool of teachers trained for, and channeled into, the nascent sector of public instruction. Yet despite those structural limits, there were narrow, often circuitous, pathways to formal schooling—meaning, basic instruction in speaking and reading (and sometimes, even writing) the Spanish language. Their journeys often led to dispersed sites of basic literacy instruction: a municipal primary school located in a provincial mestizo town; a Protestant missionary school; an urban night school run by the meatpacker's guild; and the military barracks.

Leandro Condori Chura's experiences are illustrative. Born in the ayllu of Wanqullu, near the village of Tihuanaku, he spent his early years tending sheep until a local priest, serving as the boy's patron, offered to send him to the local municipal school so he could learn his letters. He lasted a year before escaping from the humiliating taunts and beatings he had to endure at the hands of other schoolchildren. Thereafter, he worked on improving his Spanish-language skills, eventually becoming adept at speaking, reading, and writing a rustic, Aymara-inflected dialect of Castellano. Over time, Condori Chura used his bilingual intercultural skills to mediate the Aymara/Quechua/Spanish language divide, master the basic notarial protocol, and build a clientele among native litigants anxious to defend their lands and to conduct other bureaucratic business in the city of La Paz. He received streams of Indigenous delegates, took their dictation, helped them assemble dossiers of petitions and letters, and composed short telegraphic messages, often printed in leaflet form. When Martín Vázquez returned from Peru with copies of colonial documents, it was Condori Chura who wrote and distributed the notice announcing their arrival. Later he became a close counselor to Marka T'ula and, in the late 1920s, helped promote a major urban Catholic organization sponsoring Indian education. As an indio letrado, Condori Chura built a long and illustrious career, but it was the transformative power of literacy that gave his long life its deepest meaning and inspired profound reverence. Speaking to anthropologist Esteban Ticona, the elderly scribe expressed his belief that literacy and schooling were the keys to an emancipatory future, the vehicles for moving beyond the dark ages of colonialism, feudalism, and illiteracy, "because not knowing how to read was [how it was in] the time of obedience, like that of the old people or the ignorant children [of today]" (see fig. 2.3).[48]

FIGURE 2.3. A rural school in the early 1900s. A rare scene of prosperity: the school has furniture, a globe, and well-appointed pupils—signs of the Liberal government's short-lived effort to provide Indian children with basic education (with the help of US aid). Courtesy of the Carpenter Collection (LOT 11356-26), Prints and Photographs Division, US Library of Congress.

With formal schooling largely out of reach for rural youth, an alternative pathway to rudimentary literacy ran through the military barracks. The Liberal state had introduced the ideal of universal conscription about the same time it touted universal public education. The program was slow to go into effect, but by the late 1920s the military was training and resocializing hundreds of Aymara men each year.[49] Many ex-conscripts headed to the city and the mines, looking for a decent livelihood or to shed their rustic ways and move into the plebeian ranks of the cholo working class. Others, however, took their newly acquired alphabet skills back to their rural communities and put them to use in the cacique-led comunario movement. Peasant communities began to see a few ex-soldiers return home from the battlefront or from prison camps in Paraguay, bringing with them newly acquired literacy skills and a sense of patriotic self-sacrifice and entitlement to basic citizenship rights. Some peasant families looked more favorably on the military as an opportunity to educate their young sons and empower their communities with the next generation of literate apoderados.[50] By the 1920s, many Aymara petitioners felt they had a better chance to get government help setting up a school if they directed their appeal to the Ministry of War or to individual members of the military's high command. Delegations of Aymara petitioners added the Ministry of War to their judicial and archival circuits as they traveled the land in pursuit of communal lands, schools, and justice. Not surprisingly, many educators and statesmen supported Montes's policy of military conscription as a convenient way to enforce the castellanización of the male Indian while subjecting the conscript to a severe disciplinary regime. In 1929, the director of the Colegio Nacional Ayacucho echoed the patriotic sentiment of most military officials: the Aymara children made inherently good soldiers and should be trained accordingly. The institute boasted it would expunge all traits of Indianness from the newly hispanized and disciplined young recruit, now ready and prepared to defend Bolivia's national sovereignty against its aggressive neighbors or to quell social unrest in the provinces.

Or was he? This question became a flash point of debate in the 1920s. Some indigenista educators, like Daniel Sánchez Bustamante and later María Frontaura, feared the barracks were producing a dangerous new breed of Indian, one that was both armed and educated. In 1921 in the aftermath of a massive upheaval in the region of Jesús de Machaca, those warnings had come to seem prophetic. In that jittery racial climate, the Aymara acquisition of military training, along with a rudimentary knowledge of the nation's laws and letters, posed a growing risk to the landed oligarchy. Having traveled beyond the village, acquired military training, and perhaps picked up a modicum of Spanish language and letters, was not the ex-conscript capable of becoming a rebel ringleader?

Such racial anxieties in the white metropole were not totally unfounded. Marcelino Llanqui's traumatic experiences as soldier, teacher, and rebel is a well-known case in point.[51] Born in one of the twelve ayllus surrounding the mestizo town of Jesús de Machaca, he was the son of Faustino Llanqui, a prominent apoderado in the growing Aymara land-claims movement. Armed (metaphorically) with "guns and letters," Marcelino emerged as a catalyst in the grassroots village school movement beginning to spread across the Altiplano. Around 1920, he organized a primary school in the ayllu of Qalla. Like Saracho's "itinerant teachers," Marcelino became an itinerant literacy instructor among the nearby communities of Yawiri and Qhunqhu. There he assisted an older schoolteacher, Pablo Choque, before expanding the radius of his literacy teachings even further. Amid heightened racial tensions, the town vecinos of Jesús de Machaca began to accuse the caciques and teachers of stirring up lies and conspiracies. Their main target was Marcelino—"the hybrid cacique Marcelino Llanqui[, who] has started to incite the Indian population, by posing as ambulatory preceptor, without any title [of apoderado] from the communities. [In alliance with the Republican Party,] . . . he wants to make the Indians adhere to this revolution, meaning the extermination of the white race so that . . . Indians can govern themselves."[52]

From alphabet teacher to rebel leader of an apocalyptic race war! Paranoid provincial elites had turned this literacy teacher into a poster child of the dangerous indio letrado. In fact, Marcelino did put his literacy skills at the service of the caciques' land-recovery project: he composed and signed political petitions and trafficked in other documents. A village elder described Marcelino Llanqui's lettered activism: besides being a cacique, "he was literate, he was a teacher, and well, he was also a professor. That's why he became a leader. . . . He always went about distributing papers to [the ayllus] of Sullkatiti Arriba, Ch'ama, Achuma, and Kuypam Qhunqhu." Here, roaming the rural backlands of the Altiplano, Marcelino quietly engaged in the insurgent politics of literacy—spreading "seditious" ideas and teachings about Indigenous peoples' inherited rights to communal lands and the nature of their colonial oppression. Through that political and didactic activity, Marcelino helped forge the connecting links of Bolivia's sprawling cacique movement during the 1920s. In the eyes of town mestizos, Marcelino embodied "a civilized Indian who knows how to read and write and has served in the military . . . a fact, that without a doubt, [has] equipped him to prepare an *insurgent plan* against [the soldiers stationed at the] Albaroa Regiment."[53] Condemned as a hybrid civilized/savage Indian, Marcelino Llanqui quickly became a target of military firepower unleashed on peasant protests surrounding the town of Jesús de Machaca in mid-1921.[54]

Marcelino Llanqui was not the only clandestine teacher who plied the ayllus of Machaca with incendiary documents. In a remarkable series of interviews between Aymara-speaking elders and Esteban Ticona in 1990, several men and women expanded on each other's recollections to paint a vivid picture of the "first educators" who came into the villages of Qalla and Yawiri to teach the children their first letters. One elder, Primitivo López, recalled what his father had told him: "In contraband we had to educate the children, in hiding, [and] paying money from our pockets, selling many products, that way we made them teach [the children]." He continued: "They say that from that time [under Saavedra's regime], they learned how to read and write. My father told me that 'we learned clandestinely; no one helped us. That's how we learned to read and write, that's how we founded our school.'"⁵⁵ To Ticona's question about the method of instruction, López responded: "They taught us in Aymara and Castellano. Primarily to read in Spanish and then to understand the meaning of the word in Aymara: [the teacher would ask], 'What does this word mean?'" Other elders elaborated on the storied origins of Indigenous schools in their region. Toribio Calle recalled how "many years ago, in the time of the caciques, the vecinos forbade there to be schools.... They did not want us to learn to read... only to serve the patron in the hacienda." His kinsman, Rafael Calle, remembered his father telling him how he had learned to read under the tutelage of two teachers in Qalla, and later in Achirhiri: "'We would learn [our letters] clandestinely, one time a week or maybe once a month; that's the way we learned,' he told me."⁵⁶ In this humble remembrance, we catch a glimpse of how "contraband" schools and "clandestine" literacy teachers underwrote a hidden cultural revolution unfolding in villages across the Altiplano.

The Village School: Communal Site of Hope and Fear

Through the recorded voices of these village historians and the fragmented testimonies that crop up in written petitions, we may catch glimpses of this shadowy world of contraband schools and clandestine teachers. Across the region, the story of the first village school is a tale of local hardship and heroism, fear and courage, achievements and setbacks for many rural communities in "the time of the caciques." Coaxed by their interlocutors, many Aymara men and women focused their remembrances on the material hardships and sacrifices that those *escuelas de pitanza* (schools of pittance) required of local families of a rural community. In 1985, Placido Jacinto, a village elder of Jach'a Junt'u, told a member of the collective THOA (Taller de Historia Oral Andina) how his father once wove woolen cloth (*bayetas*) to pay for the son's classes: "My father wove cloth, so I could study, year after year."⁵⁷ In many cases, the earliest village schools were held in private homes or a local chapel. Juan Yujra remembered how "we learned to read and write in small chapels or we had the teacher go to one or another of our houses... [because] in those days, there were no state schools and we learned with private teachers."[58] State inspectors noted in 1931 that most rural Indian schools had neither shelter nor furniture. They seemed to float among sites and settle in hidden places, wherever the teacher landed and called his students together.[59] Communities sometimes shared a roving preceptor, soliciting coins or crops to pay him or her whenever they could. One woman recalled how, in those times, "you learned how to read and write by paying a teacher monthly, each one paid what he could afford, maybe two or three bills, which was worth a lot in those days. In those days only our own people taught us, the *q'aras* [whites] did not want to teach us."[60] Where outside mestizos or q'aras did serve as local schoolteachers, perhaps in one of the few state-sponsored primary schools in the region, it was not unusual for tensions to erupt and angry petitioners to denounce the teachers' abusive behavior or other vices. Drunkenness, ignorance, idleness, physical abuse, or racial slurs on the part of the teacher was reason enough for peasants to demand that the state eject the instructor from their local community and its fiscal school. In that way, too, local Aymara authorities tried to make the state accountable to the community for the teacher sent to instruct their children.[61]

As the grassroots campaign spread, communities became more vested and involved in the "free functioning" of their local village schools. Converting the tenuous arrangement among villages and itinerant literacy teachers into a permanent network of physical schoolhouses would require support from the whole community. Community lands would be identified and donated; families would organize work parties (*faenas*) to lay the school's stone foundation and put up its adobe walls; all families would contribute their quotas of fees and labor to keep it functioning; local authorities would periodically assemble to deliberate over the rules and rituals that would govern relations between the school and the community. By 1930, a fragile web of village schools had managed to survive a decade of state indifference and landlord hostility. An Indigenous petition printed in *La Rázon* announced that "we have been sustaining our schools at our own cost, so we can educate our children in each one of our ayllus." As we shall see below, this news came as a surprise to many government officials.[62]

Establishing a village school, an enterprise involving risk and sacrifice, played a key role in local statecraft and the ritual life of the rural community. Like the ancient parish church, the school was often a gathering place of worship and governance, where the entire community—the elected cabildo staff-holders (*varayoc*), local teacher, priest, peasant families, and so on—would convene to commemorate its founding or initiate a new school cycle (and, in later years, to perform civic holidays, or *fiestas patrióticas*). An improvised altar (or *mesa*) often would serve as the site of community offerings, libations, recitations, prayers, blood sacrifices, and other ritual expressions of the community's hope that the school (and its embodied subjects) would flourish. Ritual offerings also functioned as a way to shape the school as a syncretic space in which the introduction of school lessons (primarily the ABCs) commingled with local forms of knowing, ideally in a symbiotic relationship.

With the founding of a village school often came the reinvention of local tradition. Contemporary Andean ethnography throws light on the spiritual ways a local community might integrate the village school into the fabric of social life. A litany of prayers and libations might be offered up to regional tutelary deities—to "our *kawiltus, ceros, y montañas*," as in the incantations of the Quechua-speaking people in the southern village of Chari, for example, or through orations to the sacred ancestral powers (*w'akas*), earth mother (*pachamama*), and mountain deities (*achachilas*) in accordance with Aymara ceremonial customs in the northern Altiplano. Those deities were called on to be the spiritual guardians of the schoolchildren, the teacher, and community.[63] In the Aymara village of Qaqachaca, for example, the local school served as both ritual object and sacred site of communal renewal.[64] Through their fieldwork, Denise Arnold and Juan de Diós Yapita have studied the metaphorical ways that rural people made sense of the painful process by which Aymara-speaking children try to master alphabetic literacy. A special prayerful refrain marked the initiation of Qaqachaca's school year. It was a time to gather and bless the schoolchildren. Like the community's sheep being put out to pasture, its children were released from their daily cycle of farm chores (pasturing the animals, for example) so they might "graze on letters." Prayers were said so that "the children [would] read well and also grasp well what they [had] learnt."[65] Other ceremonies involved nocturnal libations in the name of the pupils, along with blood offerings of rams, sheep, or llamas in the name of the school—ritual offerings to safeguard the success and well-being of the pupils and the good work of the schoolteacher. In some rituals, alphabetic letters were inscribed with animate powers, and schoolchildren were willed to conquer or corral the wayward letters—as the shepherd child corrals his flock. According to Arnold and Yapita, the villagers' orations expressed sympathy for the Aymara child struggling to master the alien sounds and script of the foreign (Spanish) tongue. Other local rituals revealed a sense of ambivalence toward the intrusive role of the schoolteacher. Village elders often measured a teacher's competence by how well their pupils could recite the alphabet, or read simple words in Spanish. But communal prayers and libations also beseeched the deities to protect the schoolchildren from danger or misfortune, and to fortify them so they might muster the "physical strength to struggle against the enemy letters" and thus learn to read more quickly.[66] In his oral history work, David Llanos's elder Quechua informants in the community of Chari remembered how they would make offerings of sweets (wrapped in wads of sheep's wool), incense, and chunks of llama fat in exchange for the deities' protection of the ayllu children. Malignant spirits would be warded off and the children protected from the dangers of plague, illness, and persecution during their daily treks to and from school. And elders prayed that children would be steeled for the harsh disciplinary conditions sometimes awaiting them in the classroom.[67]

Courage, terror, hope, and outrage: the oral and written testimony of the early Aymara school movement is suffused with this potent mix of emotions. This profound sense of cultural ambivalence makes it all the more remarkable that many rural communities mounted urgent petition drives for schools. During the 1920s, the lowly school was transformed into a cultural weapon in the armory of activist peasants mobilizing against violence and servitude. In 1924, at the beginning of the scramble for state authorization of rural schools, a group of caciques, *originarios*, and agregados reached an accord "to raise their voices in unison, asking for instruction for our defiled race."[68] They expressed outrage that *los señores de provincia* were using lies and calumny to silence the anguished voices of the Indian and crush their battle for education. Equally insidious were the rumors and threats flying around the countryside: "We have learned that the vecinos work against us, by spreading rumors that those Indians who learn to read and write will be punished, their fingers severed and their eyes plucked out. With these lies . . . they want to spread discord among us, and all so they can exploit Indian labor."[69]

Such practices of gamonal fear-mongering could paralyze whole communities, sow discord, and keep parents from sending their children off to the local school. In 1924, Paulino Quispe and José Sirpa reported that many comunario families were keeping their children home from school, and they asked the prefect to order all his lesser authorities to guarantee the safety of all families "so that without fear of any kind, they will send their children, both boys and girls, to school." In later correspondence, Quispe and Sirpa expressed frustration at the fear and reticence of families to send their children to the village school, "the sacred corner the Supreme Government has granted us to found [schools] in our communities and estancias."⁷⁰

Years later, anthropologists William Carter and Mauricio Mamani collected stories in the village of Irpa Chico about the terror that stalked its rural inhabitants. Rumors warned that the first children in a village to learn to read would have their tongues cut out; children who looked at books would have their eyes plucked from their skulls; and whoever learned to grip a writing utensil would have his fingers severed.⁷¹ When such horrific images were not summoned by the "primitive" peasant imagination, they were most certainly the source of many children's nightmares in darkened huts across the Altiplano, for rural terror was as real and pervasive on the Bolivian Altiplano as it was in the antebellum South, where fear saturated the humid air and a whole legal apparatus reinforced planters' prohibition of slave literacy before the Civil War.⁷² In Bolivia, proscription did not come from formal laws and institutions as in the American slave South; rather, it sprang from within the neocolonial domain of symbolic and physical violence and intimidation that targeted the lettered cacique, the roving literacy instructor, or the schoolhouse itself. In the countryside, where state promises of legal protection had little tangible effect, a host of provincial oligarchs wielded the threat of violence with impunity. And much as Andean peasants strove to bring schooling into their reach, their actions often unleashed a wave of fearful rumors, news, and stories (and flash headlines in newspapers), all of which served as a potent deterrent, as Quispe and Sirpa reported in 1924. Symbolically, the school had come to crystallize the ambivalent feeling of hope in the future and terror in the present, especially in those places where schooling was prohibited by the local landowning class and the threat of punitive violence hung heavy in the thin air.

Hiding in Plain Sight

Endemic violence notwithstanding, by the end of the 1920s both Indigenous and official sources began to register the scope and achievements of the grassroots school crusade. By then, the frenzied production of Aymara pro-school petitions channeled a stream of information to Bolivia's Ministries of Education, War, and Government. Occasionally those petitions advanced claims about the Aymara promotion of rural schools. In a thick docket of legal documents dated 1928, various caciques (including Marka T'ula, Dionico

Paxipati, Feliciano Condori, Rufino Villca, Antonio Quispe, Mateo Alfaro, Santos Cornejo, and others) looked back over the decade and assessed the impact of school-building in rural Indigenous areas. They reported that village Indian schools had spread to communities in Caquiaviri, San Andrés de Machaca, Callapa, and Ulloma (all in the province of Pacajes); in Achacachi, Ancoraimes, Santiago de Huata, Tiquina, Copacabana, Huarina, and Laja (the province of Omasuyos); in Italaque, Ilabaya (province of Larecaja); in Taraco and Tiwanaku (province of Ingavi); and in Chulumani (province of Sud Yungas). Although they provided no precise estimates, they were rightfully proud of the geographic scope of their school movement. Moreover, they demanded that the government step up its civic responsibility to support this independent school movement in moral and material ways.[73]

A year earlier, Bolivia's Ministry of Education had registered a dim awareness of Indigenous school activity. A 1927 ministry report titled *Cuestiones indigenales* issued a surprising summary:

> For some time in these parts, the increase in indigenous schooling has been enormous. In some cases, Aymara military veterans who came out of the barracks with a smattering of Spanish letters returned to their villages to teach and take up the cause of Indian education.... Other times, it was [the communities] themselves that solicited help from the government to install schools in their villages. They request the necessary school materials and offer to subsidize the occasional costs of sustaining the school. In this way, they have *founded hundreds of school establishments* over the past few years.[74]

It was beginning to dawn on a few government authorities that "hundreds of school establishments" had sprung up with the benefit of little or no tangible support from the state. The minister's impression was confirmed in the early 1930s, thanks to a new government initiative to survey and inspect all nonmunicipal schools throughout the provinces of La Paz. In 1929, the newly autonomous Dirección General de Educación Indígena (DGEI) began to plot ways of bringing "wild literacy" and unregulated local schools under its administrative control.[75] But first the bureau needed to know just what was out there. Extending the reach of the state into the most remote corners of the sprawling department was an ambitious project that exceeded the state's bureaucratic capacity. Furthermore, the effort soon ran up against the cataclysmic events of the Chaco War (1932–35) and, like most other social reform projects, immediately succumbed to the urgency of national crisis, the fall of oligarchic rule, and the devastating effects of that war. Yet for two years, in 1931 and 1932, the new DGEI organized inspection tours of La Paz's rural schools. School inspectors were instructed "to direct and organize the private Indian schools of the Department of La Paz."[76]

Their assignment was difficult, since the inspectors had no way of knowing the actual number or location of most rural schools, many deliberately hidden in parishes, huts, or open-air sites, away from the threat of landlord or municipal reprisals. Furthermore, state inspectors were few in number and ill equipped. On the other hand, the ministry continued to be besieged by peasant petitioners requesting state authorization and subsidies for local schools. Many villages were anxious for the inspectors to sanction their existing local schools, so they could get state protection from the tyranny of landlords and a meager portion of the promised school supplies.

In 1931, under the supervision of Erasmo Tarifa Ascarrunz, rural school inspectors fanned out across the Altiplano, visiting some sixteen rural schools in Achocalla, Viacha, Santiago de Huata, Ancoraimes, and Guarina. They also toured ten night schools for trade union workers and migrants in the working-class barrios of La Paz. They were appalled by the dismal conditions of the rural schools. Most lacked even rudimentary furniture and supplies (tables, benches, chalk, etc.), and many classes still met in chapels, huts, or under trees. As monitors of the state, the inspectors also questioned rural teachers who occupied their posts without possessing the mandatory "certificates of competence and morality." For many rural Aymara teachers did lack credentials. They were recruited by local communities to teach reading and writing—rudimentary skills they themselves may have acquired in the course of managing the community's ancient titles in ongoing legal and bureaucratic struggles or else at the knee of a literate parish priest.

Yet it was the sheer scope of this ad hoc rural school movement that most impressed school inspectors. In 1931, they counted some 187 Indigenous schools, with a student matriculation of 8,079 and 155 "certified teachers," located in the province of Omasuyos alone. Extrapolating from their sample, they estimated that *"more than 500"* rural Indigenous schools were scattered across the vast Department of La Paz, a number that appeared to confirm the impression that the spread of literacy and rural schooling had mainly become the province of the rural communities and their peasant authorities.[77] In the 1932 survey, we catch another glimpse of the predominance of community-based schools, thanks to a partial state survey of various categories of rural schools. That year, school inspectors managed to inspect 240 Indian schools throughout La Paz, accounting for almost half the estimated 550+ rural schools that existed in the department. The inspectors grouped the newly matriculated 240 schools into four categories: 170 Indian community schools; 36 hacienda-based schools; 32 Protestant missionary schools; and 2 parochial and convent schools. The initial impression was confirmed by this partial sample: peasant-sponsored schools (*escuelas privadas indígenas*) greatly outnumbered all other categories of rural Indian primary schools. It came as no surprise that the schooling of hacienda peasant children had lagged far behind the flourishing rural school initiatives of comunarios.[78] That skewed ratio only underscored the power of landlords to crush both the desires of their tenants and repeated state mandates to landlords to school the children of their hacienda laborers.

By the early 1930s, there was no escaping the fact that the Aymara movement was the driving force behind rural literacy, education, and communal empowerment. Powerful confirmation came in 1932 in the form of a widely discussed book, *Hacia el futuro indio*. The book was notable for its redemptive evaluation of the Indian, its "declaration of Indian rights," and its advocacy of universal schooling—namely, for the purpose of "instructing, educating, and providing opportunities for [Indian] incorporation into [the nation's] active forces."[79] Its author, María Frontaura Argandoña, the country's most prominent woman teacher and indigenista, called on the state to pass a comprehensive agrarian law to promote rural education and industrialization: "implanting centers of obligatory primary schools for the Indians, establishing agricultural courses in livestock ranches and haciendas; and creating vocational courses." An acolyte of Georges Rouma and his ideal of practical ("farm-school") education, she also realized that it was Bolivia's rural people, not the urban pedagogues of grand designs, who had built a fragile infrastructure of elementary schools. The nation's professional teachers, she argued, should throw their support behind this great public project, tapping the hidden network of rural schoolteachers: "On the high plateau and in the valleys of the cordillera, there are hundreds of humble Indigenous teachers, self-taught, self-sacrificing, and so generous that, even without any material or moral support, they have carried the mantle of educational instruction to their race."[80] Taking a page from Rouma's treatise, she urged the state to fortify its rural normal schools as training centers for Indian teachers so they could staff the hundreds of "humble little schools" that already served Indigenous communities.

In 1931 and 1932, La Paz's state school inspectors confirmed their astonishing first impression: "For a time of approximately ten years in this area, the Indian race has been building an unusual movement in favor of their own education and at the cost of their own efforts."[81] But why did rural teachers insist on making their students memorize the alphabet? What was the value of the written word to the Indian?, they wondered. Reporting what he had heard during his inspection tour, one interlocutor translated the Indian's fervent desire for schooling in stark functional terms: "so that our children will know the laws and thus would not permit any abuse"; "so that our children are not the victims of lies and injustices that we must suffer."[82] Peasant petitioners clamored for alphabet schools, in a word, to empower themselves and their communities in the face of hostile outside forces. That the functional value of Indigenous education could cut both ways—serving as both a technology of racial assimilation and/or a weapon of cultural combat—was a novel insight for criollo administrators blind to the potential of Indigenous agency, desire, and initiative in the field of rural schooling. One inspector tried to explain this discovery: "The Indian does not promote the education and instruction of his race to improve his conditions and natural tendencies, whether through the 'professionalization' of farming or cattle-raising. His concept [of education] is different: he sees in the Indigenous READING MAN [EL HOMBRE LEÍDO] the means to defend his interests, until now unjustly ignored. For the Indians are convinced that they are the main victims of the parochial judges and corregidores and other lettered officials [letrados] in their ordinary life."[83]

As the inspector saw it, "the social character of the Indian school movement, built by the Indian," was driven by the peasant's need to enter the dominant political sphere and do battle against injustice, corruption, and discrimination: "The Indian wants to 'intellectualize himself' so as to take reprisals against the hacendados." Accordingly, the inspector proposed urgent state action, a major overhaul of the nation's rural schools, and new protective laws. Only then, he told the minister of education, could "a rational and [state-]directed education [reform project] correct these concepts among the aboriginals." How to wean the Indian away from his litigious and politicized obsession with mastering literacy? The partial answer, the inspector said, was to restore the state's protectionist policies toward the Indian: the state should "dictate laws that protect [the Indian] and guarantee fair judicial trials." State protection, together with state-run schools, would hasten the day when the Indian would emerge as "a positive factor in the nation's greatness."[84]

Despite its paternalistic tone, the inspector's report was a playback of the vocational prescription of an earlier generation of pedagogic reform. Already, by the 1910s, Bolivian educational strategies for the masses (like those in much of the rest of Latin America, Europe, and the United States) had gravitated toward the model of agro-industrial training to preserve and upgrade the country's indispensable aboriginal workforce. Paternalistic laws and civilizing work-oriented schools provided the formula. Yet over the course of the 1920s, the Bolivian state had virtually abdicated its role in providing primary schools for the children of its rural masses. Instead, feckless politicians (notably Bautista Saavedra) issued a series of unenforceable laws requiring large haciendas and communities to set up their own local schools at their own expense. And that nonsolution was part of the problem, since most landlords ignored the fiat, while many rural communities were already establishing such schools! By 1930, a few troubled education officials began to express alarm at the government's malign neglect of the rural school system, and how it was the peasant community that was sustaining the "wrong kind" of schooling for nefarious purposes in the countryside.

The diffusion of local alphabet schools was taken as a clear warning to conservative statesmen that things had gotten out of hand. The "indio leído" had become a social menace to society and politics at a time when the state had relinquished its control over the proper education of the Indian underclass. Once again, Bolivia's leading educators proposed a special curriculum: the Indians should be instructed in farm skills and good work habits in state-run schools. The minister of education was forewarned: it had become too dangerous to allow Indians to "intellectualize" themselves.

"To Renovate Bolivia": Eduardo Nina Quispe's Bold Proposition

The man who probably best embodied the "self-intellectualizing" indio leído was Eduardo Leandro Nina Quispe, the venerable Aymara activist and teacher. Nina Quispe's journey toward political literacy and activism began when he was marked as a troublemaker and expelled from the hacienda where he had tended the landowner's crops and herds. He embodied the lived trauma of neocolonial violence and dispossession when, in 1905 and 1906, the Montes regime applied the coercive apparatus of state power to usurp communal lands throughout the canton of Taraqu.[85] Reduced from a landholding comunario to the semienslaved colono, and subject to the perverse whims of the landlord, the expelled "ex-comunarios" of the Taraqu region carried much of the burden of legal and social protest against this historic crime of the Liberal oligarchy. As agrarian tensions spread, Nina Quispe had to abandon his community for the relative safety of the city. Many years later, the elder scribe Condori Chura explained to Esteban Ticona the meaning of the term *indio lanzado*. It was a category applied to the generation of Aymara activists caught in the violence of dispossession. As victims of threat and persecution by white landowners and mestizo officials, they were "expelled" from their dispossessed ayllu-communities without ever having abandoned the struggle to reconstitute the stolen communal lands and free their kinsmen (the "ex-comunarios") from the ignominy of dependence and "slavery" on the hacienda.[86] They were loyal to the cause, but victims of the moment. The trauma of continuing persecution, following the shocking murder (in January 1920) of Prudencio Kallisaya (Taraqu's most powerful apoderado-activist), drove Eduardo Nina Quispe to flee Taraqu for the city, where he sought his livelihood amid the bustling working-class and artisan neighborhoods of La Paz. Eventually he found a place of refuge among members of the city's meatpackers' guild. He attended night school, worked in a bakery, and later opened a school in his home for a few elementary school children. By the late 1920s, he had laid a new foundation for carrying forward the fight to restore communal lands to their rightful owners and to spread literacy and schooling throughout the countryside.

Thus began Nina Quispe's career as an Indigenous educator and intellectual. Looking back on his lifework, Nina Quispe described his pedagogical orientation in classic terms—combining the moral education of his pupils with basic instruction in literacy. By moral education (*la educación*), Nina Quispe meant that he taught his pupils "to respect one another and to understand the meaning of justice." He also taught them the consequences of certain vices—namely, alcoholism and thievery. Regarding literacy instruction, Nina Quispe explained that he used "the simple method" of writing letters of the alphabet on the board and then asking the students to pronounce each letter until it was "engraved on their memories." His method of literacy instruction through memorization and repetition was common to most rural and municipal primary schools.[87]

Nina Quispe's humble career might never have come into view had he not been "discovered" by a woman reporter in 1928. The chance meeting took place at an exposition of municipal schools in the city of La Paz. As the journalist Ana Rosa Tornero made her way through the salon, looking at the pedagogical materials and schoolwork on display, she stopped to look at a colorful drawing of a woman dressed in mourning and posing against the backdrop of snow-capped mountains. When she asked about the picture's significance, Ana Tornero was told that the woman represented a bereft Bolivia, still mourning the loss of her seacoast (following Bolivia's military defeat in the War of the Pacific). As she reported this incident later in a news article, it was this momentary exchange with Nina Quispe that had "awakened" Tornero to the realization that "the Indian race," or at least this particular specimen of the race, was not so insular or ignorant as she had always believed. Amazed, the woman gushed that the Indian was actually "versed, in his own way, in History and Geography; he [even] knows about the territories that once belonged to us."[88]

And so began a lively exchange between the educator and reporter on Nina Quispe's lifework as an Aymara teacher in La Paz. When the interviews were transcribed and published in October 1928, the reading public learned that Nina Quispe had established his night school in La Paz with virtually no subsidy from the state. Asked about his views on the Indian question, the reporter was delighted to find Nina Quispe taking a "progressive" position on the Indian question. For example, she wanted to know, What did Nina Quispe think of Indians continuing to wear their traditional homespun clothing? He gave a judicious response: "It would be better that we exile the poncho. Our clothing makes outsiders look at us with suspicion, and they immediately point the photographic machine at us. Besides, the difference in our clothing provides them the chance to categorize us as human beasts."[89] The journalist seemed pleased by this modern sartorial position, though not without asking Nina Quispe to pose in front of her own photographic machine. She concluded her news article with an appeal to the noblesse oblige of her readers, asking them for compassion, not contempt, as they contemplated Bolivia's ethnic landscape: "Has not each one of us felt compassion for those hermetic and errant beings who wander across the Altiplano, staying hidden and masticating [coca] for the pain and misery of their race?"[90]

Ana Tornero's discovery of this enlightened Indian (the exception to the rule of the "hermetic and errant" Aymara Indian) redounded to the benefit of Nina Quispe, at least in the short run. Before long, the educator was appointed by the education ministry to serve as the new "Director of the Night School of Indians." The impressive title came with no salary, though he was promised a few school supplies (fifty notebooks, pencils, and readers, including a textbook called *Progreso* by Pablo Pizno).[91] And for a brief time in 1930, Nina Quispe was appointed to serve as General Director of Indian Education in the newly created (and not yet funded) department under the Ministry of Education. For a moment, in 1929 and 1930, La Paz's progressive educators delighted in this figure of a "modern Indian," and they extolled him as an exemplary gentleman and patriot—living proof (if they still needed convincing) that even the bellicose Aymara race was eminently civilizable and educable. And to some degree, Nina Quispe took pains to cultivate that public image, partly because it served his deeper political interest—"to wipe out illiteracy among our own kind" and redeem the Indian race (see fig. 2.4).[92]

On the surface, Nina Quispe's words and deeds were innocuous enough, and he became the model of the assimilated Indian, a superb exemplar of the beneficent influence of education and civilization. How could there be any doubt? In September 1929, Nina Quispe and several other teachers celebrated the founding of a new mutual aid society, the Sociedad de Educación Indígena Collasuyu (Collasuyu Society for Indian Education). Its mission was to support rural communities (with a modicum of aid and advice), so they could each establish a primary school. The new organization's reference to the "Collasuyu" gave prideful reference to the ancestral Aymara kingdoms that flourished on the high plains under the Inca Empire. But since late colonial times, the name had also come to signify the natural territorial homeland of rebel Aymara ayllus and communities. And in 1929, the term surely served as a sly allusion to—perhaps a code word for—the long-simmering territorial ambitions of the cacique movement, which had long been fighting for the wholesale restitution of communal lands. Meanwhile, the Collasuyu Society tooled up, organizing a "great congress" of Indigenous teachers who were to stream into the capital from all 768 cantons in the nation. Convened in August 1930, the assembly met to elaborate a pedagogical plan for "the future development of the activities within the teaching profession."[93] Sensitive to the possible racial backlash, Nina Quispe was careful to prepare the ground by casting the event as a venue for expressing the Indians' patriotic sentiment.[94]

On the surface, then, the Collasuyu Society looked very much like any other Creole philanthropic organization that promoted Indian education.[95] But Nina Quispe was no Uncle Tom disguised in a poncho, nor was he posing as Bolivia's counterpart of Booker T. Washington—the figure that still inspired so many elite educators who promoted a separate school curriculum in agro-industrial training in farm-schools (see chapter 1). By the early 1930s, Nina

FIGURE 2.4. Eduardo Nina Quispe, about 1932. This photograph appears in Nina Quispe's long petition to the Bolivian president, in which he proposes a bold plan for a pluralist, inclusive "renovation of Bolivia." Nina Quispe, *De los títulos de composición de la Corona de España*.

Quispe was tying his pedagogical ideals to a radical nativist plan for restoring an Aymara-Quechua homeland, created out of an imagined ethnic geography of restituted ayllu lands. The metaphorical Collasuyo in this educator's political imaginary was summoned as a project of Aymara ethnic nationalism, a utopia of Indian liberation and territorial repatriation that would reposition the Aymara and Quechua majority at the geopolitical center of the Bolivian nation.[96] One clue to the radical nature of Nina Quispe's utopian project is buried in his 1932 pamphlet *De los títulos de composición de la Corona de España: [. . .] Títulos de las comunidades de la República. Renovación de Bolivia*. In a fragmented fashion, Nina Quispe created a long string of associations that linked the solution of the so-called Indian problem to the moral renovation of the whole Bolivian nation. By "renovation," Nina Quispe was referring specifically to the repatriation of Indian lands in nine departments, seventy provinces, and 768 cantons.[97] Just as he recognized that Indians made up "virtually the totality of the nation," he reminded the public that Indian lands were dispersed throughout the entirety of the nation and needed to be reallocated, according to the ancient colonial titles of "composición." What is more, the educator called for the reordering of Bolivia's internal administrative boundaries so as to fortify its external borders (*fronteras*) with Brazil, Paraguay, Argentina, Chile, and Peru. His allusion to Bolivia's ongoing crisis of territorial sovereignty, and the country's frequent boundary flare-ups, was a clever rhetorical ploy: here Nina Quispe assumed the role of political diplomat and statesmen, reminding the public that Bolivia's political borders were still vulnerable, even after the republic's wrenching territorial losses to Chile in the War of the Pacific, and to Brazil in the rubber war at the turn of the twentieth century. His words must have struck a sensitive chord among Bolivian statesmen, since by then military conflicts were already intensifying along the Bolivia/Paraguay border in the Chaco zone.

The very audacity of addressing matters of "grave national concern" gave Nina Quispe a platform on which to speak about a variety of civil, agrarian, and racial issues vital to the nation. He also used the text to discard Bolivia's racialized notion of national pedagogy in favor of a reimagined postcolonial order that would restore the territorial sovereignty of Bolivia's Indigenous majority. The proposed "renovation of Bolivia" was predicated on the political will of the Bolivian state to remap and fortify Bolivia's internal administrative and property boundaries as well as its vulnerable political borders.[98] There were wider strategic implications to this argument: in effect, Nina Quispe was warning the Bolivian government that if it were to secure the country's political borders (and, presumably, rally the mass of conscripted Indian soldiers to protect them), it would first have to enfranchise the country's Indigenous majority by restoring their own territorial sovereignty (on the basis of colonial land deeds) and protecting their civil right to schools and legal protection—an ingenious argument. Indeed, Nina Quispe harbored a precocious "pluri-nationalist" vision of Bolivian nationhood, almost a century ahead of its time.

While Nina Quispe cultivated a nonthreatening public persona and navigated the channels of civil society, politics, and government, he never broke rank with the restorative comunario project. In fact, he surfaced in the public eye only in the late 1920s, after years of semiclandestine solidarity work promoting schools and justice in the countryside. Leandro Condori Chura, the scribe, remembered Nina Quispe traveling around the countryside and helping people to formulate their petitions while raising people's expectations. Speaking to Esteban Ticona many years ago, Condori Chura tried to capture the influence that Nina Quispe came to wield over many peasant communities during the 1920s. Foremost was his ability to communicate. Nina Quispe knew how to simplify his message, saying in Aymara: "'The land belonged to us; it is ours and no one else's; it does not belong to the *mistis* [mestizos], nor to anyone else.'" He was a powerful persuader, an optimist, whose mantra was "'We are going to win.'" As his reputation spread throughout Taraqu and Viacha, his political stature rose, and eventually he acquired the title of apoderado general.[99] In that capacity, however, Nina Quispe's relationship to the "blood caciques" may have been an ambivalent one. Marka T'ula's faithful scribe criticized Nina Quispe for always "mixing things up," and becoming "tangled up" in the confusion over his own legal logics and strategies—did the apoderado want Indians to civilize and assimilate themselves through schooling? Or to forge an autonomous Collasuyo, a subaltern state within a state? Over the late 1920s, Nina Quispe's intellectual and educative work seemed to vacillate between those contradictory goals.

Arguably, though, Nina Quispe's strategy of "mixing things up," of negotiating the tensions between Andean-emancipatory and criollo citizenship discourses, may also have been a sly tactical ploy at a time when the comunario movement itself was coming into greater contact with urban laboring and professional groups. The Aymara educator's political quest for Indian emancipation was driven by both nativist and popular impulses, and his strategies pulled him in those two directions—toward the rural Andean world, on one side of the divide, and toward the urban sphere of the lettered elites and working-class communities, on the other. He often made the rounds among haciendas and communities in the countryside, founding branches of the Collasuyu Society and aiding peasant leaders in their school petition campaigns. At the same time, he reached out to politicians and indigenista intellectuals, such as Arturo Posnasky and Jaime Mendoza. He sought out members of the military academy, officials in the newly created DGEI, and its technical inspectors (in charge of surveying Indian rural schools). It seems clear that the more public Nina Quispe made his commitment to the comunario crusade, the more he had to assure the criollo public that he was a safe, civilized Indian—loath to brew conspiracies or stir up rebellion.

And no wonder he took care to cultivate that benign image (*el indio permitido*, in the apt phrase of the scholar-activist Silvia Rivera): in the early 1930s, once again Bolivia's political climate was rapidly deteriorating, thanks to the brewing border war with Paraguay and the uptick of Indigenous unrest in the countryside. The press, too, was turning hostile again. In 1932, the Salamanca regime established the Legión Cívica, charged with advancing an "internal front" against Bolivia's domestic enemies ("communists") who were accused of threatening the public order in this time of war. Nina Quispe's political and educative activism put him at the top of the Legión's blacklist of spies and enemies, the presumed instigator of a brewing Indian-communist conspiracy. In 1933, two ominous articles in *La Razón* accused him of fomenting a "vast subversive conspiracy," plotting to overthrow the government, and working to found a "communist Indian republic" under the name of "Collasuyu."[100] As the storm clouds gathered in the Chaco, the Bolivian state began tracking him as a roving danger to the nation. Nina Quispe was arrested and thrown into prison in December 1933. A political exile in his own land, he languished behind bars for six long years.[101]

Like so many other Indigenous authorities who were rapidly moving onto the national political stage, Eduardo Nina Quispe—the quintessential Aymara educator and visionary—became another casualty in the oligarchy's escalating internal war against the emergence of self-empowered Indigenous people. This time, however, the state's persecution of Aymara "troublemakers" was executed in the name of the "social defense" of the patria, just as the Chaco War was exploding along the southeastern border with Paraguay, and just as Bolivia's Indigenous school movement was breaking new ground.

3

Warisata

Forging an Intercultural School Experiment

The spirit of the Indian has survived; the mission of the Indigenal school is to give to him new vitality; to modernize him without abandoning his traditions; to civilize him without destroying his old culture and institutions.
—ELIZARDO PÉREZ, *Warisata*

We could not simply educate the Indian. We had to attend to ... the imperatives of justice and freedom, and ... the return of agricultural lands to the Indian.
—CARLOS SALAZAR, interview with author, 1990

The innovative communal school of Warisata was located at the confluence of three streams of cultural aspiration and social action. Flowing out of the white metropole, a cadre of young idealists poured their indigenista spirit into the work of building a unique agricultural school, where the Indian might be taught to modernize his way of life without abandoning the land for the city or forfeiting the virtues of his millennial culture. For Elizardo Pérez and his cohort, Warisata provided a social laboratory, the perfect site for testing their novel pedagogical ideals against harsh reality. From the very outset, the indigenistas' well-intentioned imperial endeavor became entangled with an Aymara regional network of peasant community activists involved in legal battles over ayllu land; defining the scope of ethnic and civil rights; and fashioning a moral language of protest and anticolonialism (see chapter 2). Amid this political ferment, a grassroots school movement was spreading—and this development opened the space for a unique community-school experiment in intercultural dialogue and cooperation to flower. Once planted in the arid soil of the Altiplano, the *escuela-ayllu* (as it came to be called) drew on the ideas, anguish, and energy of Bolivia's radical and bohemian youth, in search of answers to the barbarities of the Chaco War and the backwardness of Bolivia's feudal-like regime of estates and servile tenants.[1] Might Warisata provide a beachhead of Indian emancipation? Was it an alternative route by which the nation could travel toward a more just, integrated, and sovereign nation?

This chapter revisits the origins and development of Warisata during the tumultuous 1930s, when these three groups of stakeholders brought starkly different cultural aspirations and political agendas to this educational experiment. As I will show, the school was primarily the creation of Aymara peasant leaders, whose commitment, authority, and cogovernance provided the material and moral pillars of the escuela-ayllu. Governance and education, the peasant school and community, I will show, were mutually constitutive elements in this remarkable collaborative endeavor. It was the ayllu (broadly speaking) that forged the escuela, just as the escuela reconstituted the inter-ayllu lineaments of the ancient *marka* (an extended network of ayllus oriented around a town settlement).

Casting an ethnographic eye on the main protagonists, I probe the interior workings of Warisata—from the first encounters between white schoolteachers and Aymara leaders in 1931–32, through the creative endeavors involved in constructing a self-governing and emancipatory Indian school during the early to mid-1930s, to the arrival of urban dissidents, and finally to Warisata's explosive cultural impact on the surrounding region and nation toward the end of the decade. The school caught the brisk winds of social change: the shocks of the Chaco War (1932–35); the rise of a "military socialist" regime under Presidents David Toro and Germán Busch in the postwar era (1936–39);

and the explosion of mass and leftist politics in the late 1930s and early 1940s. By 1938, Warisata (and the offshoots of communitarian schooling in other regions) had captured the imagination of youthful political dissidents. Radical teachers and artists, delegations of politicians, and a stream of distinguished foreign visitors began making pilgrimages to the Bolivian Altiplano to bear witness to this oasis of progressive Indigenous schooling. Inevitably, the more symbolic capital Warisata accumulated among progressive educators, intellectuals, and leftist activists (both inside Bolivia and overseas), the more it was seen as a threat to the status quo ante. Even at the height of its fame, Warisata's fate seemed to hang in the balance.

Sorting through various memoirs, oral histories, government reports, and newspaper articles, I try to dispel the mystique that has suffused the oft-told history and national narrative of Warisata that hides as much as it reveals. Bathed in nostalgia, the escuela-ayllu has become an iconic symbol of Indian liberation among competing indigenista and nationalist narratives. Likewise, we must avoid the partisan trap of cynicism and critique (from both the left and the right) that misuses hindsight or theory to dismiss Warisata as simply an anachronistic experiment in educational philanthropy, one doomed to fail. Either way, historicizing this intercultural pedagogical experiment cries out for deeper contextualization, enabling us to begin to understand why and how that school came to occupy such a contested place in the history and historiography of Bolivian nation making.[2] Here I focus on Warisata during the 1930s, only briefly mentioning the broader history of Bolivia's "núcleo" peasant schools that cropped up in different regions during that same decade.[3] Borrowing insights and images from Elizardo Pérez's rich memoir, a cache of new documents, several oral accounts, and the abundant historical ethnography, this chapter begins by situating the early school project in its regional, temporal, and Indigenous contexts. It then traces the intricate art and craft of local governance and education which, through the uneven process of negotiation, collaboration, conflict, and compromise, came to define the school's communitarian ideals and pedagogical practices. Underlying this story of intercultural creativity and tension lies a darker question (which we take up later in this chapter and in the next one): How and why could this brilliant star, fixed in the firmament of Indian school experiments across the Americas, have flickered out so soon?

An Indigenista Educator: The Making of Elizardo Pérez

Elizardo Pérez was, like all of us, a product of the contradictory social and ethical impulses of his own time. He grew up in a time of intellectual and political ferment, when the ascendant paceño oligarchy argued over the implications of their diagnostic studies of the nation's primordial "Indian problem." Bautista Saavedra's "defense" of Aymara criminality competed with Alcides Arguedas's diagnosis of racial degeneration, while Franz Tamayo's Romantic redemption of the "pure" Bolivian Indian threw open another channel of social reformism and indigenista critique. In 1910, the problem of Indian education had exploded on the pages of La Paz newspapers, dividing the Liberal civilizing project of Indian assimilation (a project of "cultural genocide," some critics would later say) against an eclectic group of telluric indigenistas, scientific pedagogues, and conservative oligarchs, who loosely coalesced around an incipient rehabilitation plan based on Indian segregation, paternalist protection, and work-oriented schooling (see chapter 1). Pérez came of age in that highly charged atmosphere, when the social and moral stakes of Bolivian nationality seemed to hang in the balance.

Thanks to the 1909 founding of Bolivia's first normal institute, the young Pérez had a chance to translate his nascent ideas about race, nation, and education into a four-year course of pedagogical study. In the pastoral white city of Sucre, the air crackled with the latest educational philosophies. A brainchild of Georges Rouma, Sucre's normal school introduced students to liberal and scientific values: the free exchange of ideas, hands-on ("active") forms of learning, laboratory experimentation, coeducation, the study of child psychology and the cultural and environmental milieu in which schooling would take place.[4]

The first cohort of normal students also bore witness to Rouma's growing awareness that Bolivia's future depended on the introduction of formal schooling to Bolivia's vast majority of illiterate, unschooled children. They learned from Rouma that the art of pedagogy depended on scientific research on the human object of educational reform—namely, the children of Bolivia's Indigenous majority. In short, they witnessed the Belgian's discovery and diagnosis of the Indian problem as he got to know the lay of the land. The results of Rouma's 1913 field research in anthropometry were presented in no uncertain terms: not only did Indians make up the country's numerically dominant majority, he revealed, but the country's "ethnic element" would also "be impossible to replace."[5] The irony was inescapable. A white European, brought over to show Bolivia how to whiten its population through modern school reform, now proclaimed that he had discovered an unavoidable truth—Bolivia could never expunge its Native population from the nation. Nor should it. The Indian, he believed, must be preserved and trained up to fill the national need for hardworking peasant farmers. That called for model "farm-schools," specifically tailored to Bolivia's diverse ethnic and rural environments. Ironically, Rouma's science eventually led him to the same doctrinal conclusion that his greatest detractors and critics had been promoting for several years (ever since Franz Tamayo had proposed, in 1910, that a special national pedagogy be designed for Bolivia's peculiar racial and natural milieu).

Drawing from those two sources of ideas—the scientific pedagogy of Rouma's practical farm-school plan and Tamayo's racial-telluric school of "autochthony"—Pérez developed his own strain of indigenista pedagogy. The mission of the school, he believed, was to preserve the millennial cultures of the Aymara and Quechua peoples. Their strength and vitality rested on the very cultural survival and achievements that had sustained them during four centuries of colonial oppression. Shaped by the forces of nature, culture, and evolution, Bolivia's autochthonous races were molded to fit the country's varied altitudes and climates. Jaél Oropeza de Pérez (Elizardo's widow, a college-educated and trained schoolteacher in her own right) remembered her husband's guiding assumption: "The Indian in his essence is an agriculturalist. He loves the land, the Pachamama. He should not be pulled from the campo, or left desolate and abandoned. And besides, the campo was the future of Bolivia."[6] On that score, the Aymara Indian was the most extraordinary specimen of cultural survival and adaptation before the punishing forces of nature, having evolved a way of life capable of "conquering the hostile environment."[7] Early on in his career, then, Pérez began formulating his basic orientation to Indian education. As with Tamayo and Rouma, Pérez's doctrinal pedagogy was quite simple: the rural school curriculum must be adapted to the peculiar characteristics of the human and natural environment in which it was to function. In abstract terms, he conceived of "*la escuela indigenal* as a [social] organism of integrative functions and aboriginal roots."[8] In blunt material terms, Pérez's indigenista pedagogy rested on two existential pillars, *fuerza y trabajo* (strength and work).[9]

After graduation from Normal, Pérez returned to La Paz (see fig. 3.1). There he secured a government post as a rural and municipal school inspector. By

FIGURE 3.1. Elizardo Pérez, in 1917. As a recent graduate of Bolivia's first normal school, his pedagogical ideas aligned closely with those of his mentor, Georges Rouma. Salazar Mostajo, *Gesta y fotografía*, photo no. 18.

horseback, Pérez traveled through the provinces of Loaiza, Sicasica, Los Andes, Omasuyos, Camacho, Muñecas, Caupolicán, and Inquisivi. What must it have been like to travel over this vast high plateau to towns and villages, in search of village, fiscal, and municipal schools to inspect on behalf of the Ministry of Education? Pérez could see the miserable condition of most schools. He sometimes distributed school supplies from government dispensaries, and he often found himself trying to solve local disputes in the towns and parishes he visited. Meanwhile, it was disheartening to see Indigenous corvée laborers building a school on the outskirts of a town, only to see it fill up with the children of urban mestizo townspeople (*vecinos*). When Pérez was not making inspection tours, he taught the children of servile colonos in a rustic elementary school, established on the grounds of a hacienda.

Pérez's years of rural itinerancy gave him valuable field experience, an ethnographic introduction to the community organizations and cultural norms that governed social life of the ayllu on the Aymara Altiplano. He had shed the Creole's racist blinders enough to appreciate the integrity of communal self-governance, its agrarian cycles, and forms of oral memory and ancestral knowledge. He was impressed by the resilient forms of ayllu organization, even after it had been absorbed by encroaching haciendas in the Omasuyos province. Community traditions and authorities, he noted, still functioned in accordance with ancient agro-ritual traditions of crop rotation, communal labor parties (*faenas*), and spiritual offerings to the deities and ancestors. He watched as farmers and herders "mobilized labor and determined the exact calendar dates to begin planting, fallowing, and harvesting," and he admired how Aymara farmers understood the effects of climate and season on their seedlings. But the rural people he observed were also savvy commercial farmers. The condition of illiteracy, he had come to realize, was not equivalent to isolation or ignorance. Most Indigenous people could not read or write, he noted, but when it came time to commercialize their crops, the Indians were shrewd traders and sharp accountants.[10]

One day in 1917, Pérez's inspection tour took a surprising turn. Leaving the bowl of La Paz, he traveled toward the provincial capital of Achacachi, a town bloated with officials, lawyers, merchants, and partisans of the new Republican Party (including its founder, the prominent politician and landowner Bautista Saavedra). Passing through the dusty town, Pérez traveled eastward toward the cordillera, where he planned to inspect several rural and municipal schools in the region of Warisata. There he stumbled on a private little school (*escuelita particular*) built by the local community and run by an

Indigenous teacher, Avelino Siñani, a man with deep roots and wide connections in the Aymara communities of the province. As Pérez later reflected, this encounter would turn out to be serendipitous—years later, the two men would forge an unshakable bond in their joint endeavor to create a unique community school at the very site of this first meeting.

In the meantime, in that momentary encounter Pérez crossed the racial divide to speak a few words with this erudite Aymara man "in a natural way"—a simple exchange that would change his life. Pérez sensed immediately that he had breached the wall of racial prejudice and white arrogance to discover a man of true character, wisdom, and dedication. Years later, he reflected on the weight of poverty and oppression that burdened this extraordinary man: "In another setting [*medio*], or in another epoch, Avelino Siñani would have been a man esteemed by society; but he was destined to be born and to live in the sordid feudal environment of the Altiplano, a place that was degraded and obscurantist, adverse to [his] kind of spirit." Dressed as an Indian (*kolla*), his face etched by a lifetime of hardship and struggle, Siñani instilled in Pérez a paternalist feeling of reverence and respect. One could sense, he later wrote, that this man had a soul "so pure, like that of a child, and so strong, like that of a giant."[11]

Here Pérez elaborates his first impressions of Siñani, a man who shattered racial stereotypes of the rebellious Aymara, in the noble act of having founded an elementary school for local children. Had this Indigenous man not opened a pathway to Indian redemption and integration, not through senseless acts of insurgent violence but through the promise of education? "Such was the meaning of his school, in whose humility I contemplated in silence, the most radiant auroras for Bolivia."[12] Pérez captured this remembrance in his memoir as a sort of spiritual epiphany: he had discovered an Aymara Indian who shared his ideals; a man of strength and integrity who had invested his hope for Indian redemption in a humble alphabet school. But while Pérez extolled the Indian literacy instructor, he denigrated the "mere alphabet" school, the symbol of Bolivia's antiquated system of public schooling. With the white oligarchy of La Paz and his normal-trained colleagues, Pérez shared a deep distrust of semiliterate cholos and Indians who were "misusing" their rudimentary knowledge of reading and writing to breach the electoral system, flood the courts with their lawsuits, and otherwise make political mischief in the public sphere. Nor is there much evidence that Pérez fully appreciated the use-value of literacy within Aymara rural society, where various ayllus and communities were anxiously litigating and defending their ancestral ayllu lands in this region of rampant latifundismo. Be that as it may, it was this fleeting human encounter between the white teacher/inspector mounted on horseback and the short Aymara literacy teacher on foot that first kindled the flame of mutual trust and reciprocity. Pérez quickly arranged to hire two mules, and off they rode to the town of Copacabana, on the shores of Lake Titicaca. There Pérez requisitioned a few school materials (and even a wall clock) for Siñani's schoolhouse. More than a decade later, Pérez's reencounter with Avelino Siñani would make possible his dream of cofounding and collaborating in the building of a unique Indian community school on the site of their first meeting.

Long before they met up again, however, the young idealist had to reckon with the hypocrisy and failure of government school policy in the rural domain. As Pérez traveled through the Aymara hinterland, he saw signs of trouble everywhere. In 1917, he noted the virtual evaporation of Saracho's famous escuelas ambulantes (only one had been converted into a tangible, permanent schoolhouse); still more alarming was the closure of Bolivia's first three rural normal schools (Umala, Puna, and Sacaba), on the order of Bautista Saavedra (1921–25). Meanwhile, Saavedra had purged Daniel Sánchez Bustamante from the Ministry of Education and consigned his heralded 1919 education reform to the dust heap. In fact, the federal government seemed to be in full retreat from its federal responsibilities of governance and education. Saavedra's supposed solution to the problem of schooling the rural masses was to outsource it to large establishments (haciendas, mines, and ayllus). In 1923, they were ordered to establish private schools for the school-age children in their midst. There would be no guaranteed state subsidy, no federal teachers, no protection, and no enforcement forthcoming. Meanwhile, Saavedra's oligarchic racism and populist bravura were unmasked in the face of Indigenous unrest. While he sometimes courted favor with urban artisans and a few caciques in the province of Omasuyos, and while his regime eased tensions around the communal land issue, Saavedra belonged to the conservative landholding oligarchy and was thus an unmitigated enemy of Liberal reform. He had barely ascended to the presidency in 1921 when the ayllus surrounding Jesús de Machaca exploded in fury against the pressures of new liens and persecution by abusive provincial authorities. Though few vecinos were killed in the local skirmish, this new episode of "Indian rebellion" triggered a scorched-earth military campaign against not just the local Aymara perpetrators but ayllu settlements throughout the whole region. The firepower of a full regimen of soldiers ricocheted through the villages.[13] Pérez didn't know how many people had died or fled, but the violence left an indelible scar on his psyche. Years later, having traveled to Jesús de Machaca to establish a new school, Pérez gathered local testimonies about the "terror and hatred" unleashed by Saavedra in 1921. Pérez asked himself, How could government school officials possibly hope to win the trust of Indigenous people if those people still associated genocide with the governing class? Eventually, with a sense of angst, Pérez would try to reconcile his belief in the transcendent power of Indigenous education with the feudal-bourgeoisie's implacable opposition to educational and agrarian reform.[14]

Not all was so bleak, however. New educational reforms were stirring in the late 1920s, toward the end of President Hernando Siles's term (1926–30). His charismatic minister of education, Bailón Mercado, had initiated important reforms: the granting of university autonomy to Bolivia's public universities; the establishment of an independent body, the Consejo Nacional de Educación (CNE), and a new agency in charge of "Indigenal education," the Direccion General de Educación Indigenal (DGEI). Suddenly it seemed that Bolivia had turned over a new leaf. In the meantime, Pérez was named director of a new residential Indian school in the working-class barrio of Miraflores. Pérez no doubt felt honored, but he soon realized the urban Indian normal school stood for everything he morally repudiated: it was located in a "contaminated" urban setting; was filled with mestizo students; possessed no agricultural lands; offered no active (agrarian) curriculum; and tortured its students with rote exercises and boarding school routines. In short, it was based on the old assimilationist model that Pérez had come to detest. By 1930, the young educator was convinced that the Indian must be taught moral values and technical skills that would prepare him for his "destiny" as Bolivia's indispensable agricultural laborer. In that sense, Pérez was an acolyte of the Belgian educator Georges Rouma and adhered to his farm-school model—but with the proviso that its pedagogy must be adapted to fit (and take advantage of) Andean norms and customs. Specifically, he called for school programs that tapped into Andean practices of labor sharing (*mink'a*) and reciprocity (*ayni*). In effect, those traditional forms of communal labor would effectively subsidize the cost of organizing a community-oriented school while also giving the local ayllu an abiding stake in this public work project (or *obra*).[15]

Unsurprisingly, Pérez quit the boarding school directorship after only fifteen days. The moment of truth had arrived. The minister of education called his bluff, telling him, "Go off into the Aymara outback and test your outlandish ideas!" So, with Bailon Mercado's blessing, but without a government purse,

Pérez set off again across the Altiplano, this time by truck, in search of the ideal ayllu. There, far from the contaminants of urban civilization, he would create the Indian school of his dreams.

In Search of the Primordial Ayllu

In the winter of 1931, the young man set off in search of a pristine Aymara village where he might establish a rural school "in a purely Indian environment."[16] He headed toward Lake Titicaca, where fishing and agricultural settlements, a benign climate, and the stunning lacustrine landscape beckoned. But after a short stay in Santiago de Huata, Pérez felt the area was spoiled by mestizo towns and latifundias. He pushed on:

> I was not looking for an *aldea* [small town], heir of colonial and republican vices, but for an ayllu where the Indian reality would be vital. Besides, I knew that if I established a school in a mestizo town, it would be the Indians who would build it, with the sweat of their own labor, while only the sons of the mestizo town-dwellers would take advantage of the school's urban location. My school would have fallen into the same trap as did [the normal school of] Miraflores, where the students ... were the sons of the provincial gamonales who, once they graduated, turned into the new exploiters of the Indians, attaching themselves to the landlords who lived from pongueaje and servitude. By contrast, my dream was to create a school in an Indian environment, to which the autochthony would bring concord. It would be an "indigenal school" whose mission would benefit directly the Indians and their children.[17]

Turning eastward, Pérez took the road through Achacachi, gradually climbing the plain toward the base of the volcanic snow-capped mountain of Illampu. Stopping briefly in the bustling provincial town, he informed the local authorities of his mission to locate a peaceful rural community, where he might build his school with "the cooperation of the Indian in lands and work."[18] As if by providence, the Achacachi officials directed him eastward, to the region of Warisata, where small clusters of comunarios and smallholders inhabited lands outside the hacienda zone. Almost fifteen years had passed since his encounter with Siñani, but Pérez must have had Siñani in mind as he headed out of Achacachi toward the ayllu region of Warisata.

According to his memoir, Pérez's odyssey was rewarded by a jubilant community welcome, as if the prodigal son had come home. Pérez remembered the speeches, festivities, and—most crucially—the fraternal embrace of Avelino Siñani himself. As he recounted, this euphoric reunion sealed their "common destiny" to build a great rural school center in the heart of ayllu territory. Yet Pérez wasted no time asserting his tutelary authority: soon he was laying out the conditions under which the municipality, landlords, and the surrounding ayllus would donate lands and labor to build the school. A roadside site was marked off, and organizational plans were established. "We were in perfect accord," recalled Pérez.[19] But as he unfolds the story, we begin to perceive how imperfect that "perfect accord" was turning out to be.

In the warmth of the noonday sun, the Altiplano is deceivingly benign. "Geography and nature" served as the stunning backdrop of his chronicle, and also as a metaphor for formidable challenges Pérez was about to face. The physical location turned out to be punishing to this urban transplant. He apparently had forgotten how much harsher the Altiplano becomes as one moves away from the mitigating influences of Lake Titicaca. And, indeed, it is certainly easy to be fooled. By day, Warisata offers a stunning high-altitude landscape of bright sun, brilliant sky, and arid pampa, flanked by Ilampu's soaring majesty. But by night, temperatures routinely plummet to below-freezing levels, creating in effect a unique diurnal contrast which the Incas and earlier Andean civilizations had used to process high-energy, freeze-dried foods (*chuño*, for example). But it was the sheer brutality of the Altiplano's winter winds and cold nights that humbled Pérez: "We are talking about a high plateau, situated between Lake Titicaca and the cordillera, whose frequent winds swirled and scoured the plains. The climate was frigid, the plain inclement. And everything was dominated by the snowy mountain peaks of the Illampu, whose vista reduces man to a religious silence, so awed is he is by its grandeur and snowy splendor." Later, ayllu families would teach Pérez about the region's rich and varied resources that could be tapped for communal-school projects. But initially Pérez had to learn how to adapt and survive in the campo, for he was determined to inhabit the "life of an Indian and with the Indian, while [he] planned out the project and overcame environmental obstacles." Meanwhile, "the plain was hostile!"[20]

But nature was not his worst natural enemy. The region's confusing land tenure patterns threw up another obstacle. Soon enough, the region's complicated and contested history of landholding punctured Pérez's telluric utopia. Disheartened, he came to realize that Warisata was "not exactly an ayllu, but a zone of latifundias, where freeholding Indians belonging to the [ancient] ayllu hardly numbered a dozen." As the scales dropped from his eyes, Pérez saw that "Warisata had been [largely] absorbed by the hacienda; it was functioning as a territory that was subject to the exploitation of the landlords of Achacachi, men who had slowly divested the Indian and converted themselves into the owners of almost all the zone."[21]

So Warisata had not escaped the Liberal oligarchy's enclosure movement after all. Archival land records tell part of the story. By the early 1900s, Warisata, located along the moving edge of the latifundia/ayllu frontier, had become a zone of intense agrarian warfare. The fact that a vestigial network of communities still existed in this area was largely thanks to the counterforce of Aymara tenacity and legal resistance. Using the 1883 "pro-indiviso" clause of the 1874 agrarian reform, a group of local apoderados had managed to protect a portion of the "customary lands of Guarizata [sic]," as registered in the records of the Mesa Revisitadora in the late 1880s. At that time, the community counted some two hundred registered comunarios, who claimed a territorial expanse of some 3,400 hectares, including high-altitude cropland (fields of ocas, bitter and sweet potatoes, quinoa, barley, rich sheep pastures, and an irrigation network). Not only its fertile pastures, glacial waters, and croplands, but also its interecological location made the Warisata area attractive to latifundistas. Since Inca times, the area had been a way station for traders and travelers, and their llama caravans, moving between the dense settlements along Lake Titicaca and the warm maize valleys of Sorata, lying along the eastern slopes of the cordillera. The wonder is that any ayllus had managed to survive at all. By 1930, Warisata's lands and families were living in the shadow of several large haciendas, such as Umapusa and Chijipina on its southern border, and Taypi Pararani on its northern border.[22] Many comunario families still clung to small parcels of land in name only, having mortgaged fragments of their communal and family-held lands (*sayañas* and *tupus*) to a multitude of covetous merchants, bankers, and hacendados, most of them based in the nearby town of Achacachi or in the city of La Paz.[23] A few peasant families (for example, the Siñanis and the Rojas) had managed to stave off despoliation by diversifying their livelihood activities into retail commerce, day labor, and the pack animal industry. But Warisata's patchwork of land tenure and contested boundaries inevitably spelled trouble. From the outset, Pérez realized that the school would be plagued by incessant land conflicts and boundary disputes, as well as the growing hostility of local landlords and provincial authorities who policed the region. The situation carried ominous implications: How could a bold project of Indigenous education flourish in colonized land dominated by hostile vecinos and semifeudal hacendados?

Pérez was not easily deterred, however. He envisioned an expansive enterprise—a school complex to be assembled from donated parcels of cropland and large swaths of pastureland cutting across the contested boundaries of ayllu, hacienda, and smallholding. Most of the original land donations came from prominent Aymara families: Siñani, Quispe, Mamani, Choque, Huallpa, Apaza, and Poma. Several landlords also donated land at first: the Mendoza, Monterrey, and Gutiérrez families.[24] Years later, in 1936, the question of land scarcity induced Pérez to solicit the government to annex more lands for the school. That hope was dashed, however, when President José Luís Tejada Sorzano (1934–36) was swept from power.[25] Just as Pérez had feared, the ayllu-school became mired in land conflicts among comunarios, smallholders, landlords, and the ayllu-school itself (whose influence continued to radiate outward into surrounding areas). This low-intensity war corroded its original land claims, tied up scant resources in court battles, chipped away at communal solidarity, and eventually threatened the very legitimacy of the escuela-ayllu. From its inception, then, Warisata teetered on "the margins of legality," a situation that would haunt the school community over the course of the 1930s.[26]

Another challenge surfaced when it came time to negotiate the school's educational mission and the authority of the schoolmaster. That Pérez and ayllu authorities were not "in perfect accord" became all too clear to him in the days and weeks following Pérez's ceremonial welcome in 1931. At the moment the physical work of construction was to begin, Avelino Siñani and the other community leaders suddenly were nowhere to be seen. They had mysteriously disappeared on the very week that Pérez (accompanied by three newly contracted teachers) had returned to the work site to begin baking adobe bricks for the school's foundation. The white teachers worried they'd been abandoned, like orphans left alone with their utopian dreams. Would the community collaborate, offer its labor and land for this joint endeavor to a city man who had appeared suddenly in their village with a trunk full of ambitious plans and a few delusions? Years later, Pérez explained this tense moment of watchful waiting: "The Indians looked at me with suspicion, thinking perhaps that the new teacher was not much different from the other [q'aras] that they had known."[27] Would he make rural people haul rocks and perform other menial work to build a school, largely for the benefit of Achacachi's mestizo children? Corvée work on public roads, irrigation ditches, mail carriage, and other public works was only too common in the Bolivian Altiplano, and Pérez worried that he was viewed as just one more *enganchador* (labor contractor, or "hooker") in search of unpaid work parties. For days thereafter, life and work became ever more difficult for Pérez and his fellow teachers: "In the solitude of the pampa, we seemed to be the only living beings. The Indians did not come near us. They made us feel our isolation, and life began to become more difficult."[28] To make matters worse, the municipality of Achacachi did not ratify their initial land donations; the Ministry of Education reneged on any commitment of funds for the school (other than the teachers' meager salaries); and, at the first opportunity, the three teachers decided to desert the construction site. They had fled Warisata while their boss was away in La Paz, trying to lobby the education minister for material support.

Then came the crucial breakthrough, as Pérez later chronicled. Early one morning Avelino Siñani showed up at the work site to help lay a cement floor. Siñani and Pérez labored at it, side by side, until nightfall. As dusk approached, that shared experience of hard labor was turning into a daylong performative act that had shattered, in real and symbolic terms, the rigid racial caste divide between the white overseer/administrator and the Indian laborer/*peón*. Perhaps more than any other incident, the visible act of labor sharing established a fragile bond of trust and respect that radiated out into the community as rumors and images circulated. As filtered through the veil of nostalgia, we can infer from Pérez's memoir that Siñani trumpeted a message of moral redemption to the itinerant white educator: "We have not abandoned you to your fate," he assured Pérez. "Although the pampa might seem desolate to you, thousands of us have watched you... making mud adobes with your calloused hands; [we have seen you working] from five in the morning until sundown. All this we know,... nothing you do goes unnoticed. From the folds of the mountains... and from our huts, we are observing you."[29] He continued, "Soon the Indian families of this sacred land will approach you. They will lift up the pampa and the mountains, and as one man, the entire community will fulfill its duty and give of themselves all that they must. And of course, beginning tomorrow, I will come each day with my wife and little daughter, Tomasita."[30]

As recorded years later, Pérez's sentimental prose (speaking, as Pérez always did, as the benign ventriloquist for Siñani) is saturated by paternalism, nostalgia, and self-regard. Yet the vital fact remains: Warisata's families did ultimately decide to show up at the school's construction site and to stake a claim in this school venture. That they did so speaks well of Siñani's stature and sway as an *amauta* (wise elder) of the surrounding ayllus and ex-ayllus (see fig. 3.2). It also

FIGURE 3.2. Avelino Siñani, in 1939. Siñani was a literacy instructor who, years earlier, had mobilized local support for a local school establishment in Warisata. Salazar Mostajo, *Gesta y fotografía*, photo no. 4.

marked the beginning of an extraordinary intercultural educational project, a moment crystallized for posterity in a formal photographic portrait of the three cofounders: Elizardo Pérez, Avelino Siñani, and Mariano Ramos (see fig. 3.3).

True to his word, Avelino Siñani returned the following morning, bringing along other members of his family and two burros, ready to transport wood, stone, sand, and other building materials. Soon thereafter, the Siñani clan was joined by dozens more men and women who organized themselves into work parties doing all sorts of tasks—laboring in the construction of the buildings, laying out gardens, growing crops, fashioning school furniture, digging irrigation ditches, operating the school kitchen, and participating in the school's internal organization and coadministration. Rare photographs, later collected by Carlos Salazar, capture the dynamism of Warisata's communal work enterprise—Indigenous families, with their burros, oxen, tools,

FIGURE 3.3. Iconic image of Warisata's official cofounders, 1932. *Left to right:* Mariano Ramos, a seasoned community elder, holding a whip (a traditional symbol of authority); Elizardo Pérez, holding a tool; and Avelino Siñani, holding an alphabet reader. Salazar Mostajo, *Gesta y fotografía*, photo no. 1.

and labor, participating in all facets of the school's construction and planting; a group of women, in their bulky black shawls, doubled over the soil as they planted seeds; and the students baking bricks in the hot sun for the walls of their school building.[31] Years later, as Warisata's critics attacked the school for its alleged "exploitation" of unpaid Indian labor, Pérez and other champions of the school were forced to defend the use of labor-sharing customs, particularly the practice of ayni.[32] A stream of labor contributions came from five nearby ayllus. As Pérez hoped, it was predominantly Indian labor that ultimately subsidized the construction of Warisata's school buildings and, later, cultivated the school's planting fields.

Called to defend this practice, Pérez took pains to demonstrate how the Indian's "spirit of voluntarism" had resolved the school's initial labor problem. As time went on, Warisata's governing council experimented with a mix of draft and voluntary labor parties, both based on a loosely organized system of rotation. Inevitably, there was internal dissension. School authorities ran into resistance from many colono Indians, who feared the whip of the

FIGURE 3.4. The school was built, brick by adobe brick, by a communal labor force, involving peasant families, students, and teachers. In 1935, they began laying the foundation of the main building, the *pabellón México*, named in honor of Lázaro Cárdenas. For lack of material resources, the project was temporarily abandoned until outside aid could be secured in later years. Salazar Mostajo, *Gesta y fotografía*, photo no. 84.

landlord or expulsion from their leaseholds if they participated in the school project. Once the initial euphoria had worn off, it became more difficult for the school's administration and Indigenous governing body (*el parlamento de amautas*) to mobilize collective labor parties, and some local families opted out of the ayllu-school's labor demands, particularly if they had no children attending it. By the mid- to late 1930s, the school operated largely as a self-sufficient enterprise, building into the curriculum basic manual labor stints in the school's ever-expanding area of orchards, gardens, crop fields, and workshops. The school eventually supplied its own labor needs, drawing on the study body and their families to participate in all facets of the school economy, self-governance, and ritual life. Ingeniously, Pérez's "integral curriculum" included vocational training: What better way to train students in modern construction, maintenance, artisan crafts, and gardening skills than to channel their labor power into the growing, diversifying community school project itself (see fig. 3.4)?[33]

From almost the outset, cooperative labor arrangements, along with hands-on training in the mechanics and discipline of farm labor, were practical subjects folded into Warisata's communal culture and pedagogy. There was no top-down mandate or mita-like impositions. Rather, the mobilization of local labor to build and run the school was the subject of lively communal discussion, debate, consensus, and vote that took place within the school's parliament of amautas, among the school's staff, and in local peasant assemblies. By late 1931, Pérez reported, "hundreds of Indians [were] working happily without salary, united through the *ayni* or *achacalla*, the fraternal institution of Aymara labor." In Brechtian detail, he described an idyllic scene: some Indians making adobes, cutting stone, clearing earth with the power of their oxen; others threshing wheat with their sticks to the rhythm of song. Working together, they raised the adobe walls of school buildings "and the [metaphorical] walls of their own spiritual edifice that they were building, so as to recuperate their faith in their [Indian] destiny."[34] These joyful scenes took place toward the end of September 1931, when some four hundred people regularly joined the work party. It was then, too, that Pérez managed to acquire two trucks from his brother, Raúl, to transport all sorts of building materials to the site. The whole community turned out to witness the delivery of those materials, after weeks of frustration and uncertainty. It seemed to clinch the implicit "pact of reciprocity" that Pérez was hoping to negotiate with communal families.

Finally, after some fifty days of hard work, Pérez felt he had gained the trust of the community.[35] He credited that moral victory to his own willingness to shed the trappings of white privilege, dignify the physical work of the peasant, and live under the Spartan conditions of the rustic campesino: "When they saw that the professor lived with them, ate their food out of a clay plate [*chúa*], slept on a hard bench covered by straw, and that, above all, he was one of them, they felt their caution recede, as their fear of being deceived and exploited also faded away."[36] Certainly, Pérez had passed an implicit ethical test, thanks to his sense of honor, respect, courage, and conduct. He even fancied that he had transgressed—even dissolved—the racial/ethnic divide as he Indianized his own image and became "one of them." But Pérez leaves no doubt in the reader's mind: he could never have achieved what he set out to do without the trust and collaboration of local peasants.

Indeed, the man most responsible for Warisata's origins was Avelino Siñani, whose work in the field of Indigenous education sprang from the furrows of the Aymara literacy movement that had flourished on the Altiplano during the late 1910s and 1920s.

The Making of Aymara Educators: Avelino and Julián Siñani

Avelino Siñani's success in "delivering" Warisata to Pérez's school project was helped considerably by his local status and history of political activities throughout Omasuyos and beyond. The Siñani family's education and relative mobility helped to catapult two brothers, Avelino and Julián, into positions of authority in the emerging Aymara peasant movement during the 1910s and 1920s. Both men, albeit in different ways, acquired the apoderado's skills of intercultural mediation, and they used those skills (literacy, proficiency in the Spanish language, legal writing, bureaucratic experience, and political contacts) to represent local communal or trans-ayllu interests. Although neither Avelino nor Julián carried the title of apoderado, Avelino was known throughout eastern Omasuyos as an itinerant literacy instructor. His older brother, Julián, earned the prestigious title of "cacique principal" of Omasuyos and Larecaja in the mid-1920s. In their distinctive ways, then, these brothers were involved in converting their vernacular literacy skills into weapons of peasant cultural empowerment and identity-making.

Avelino's story is better known because of his later involvement in Warisata and the legacy of testimony left by his own politically active daughter, Tomasa Siñani de Willka. Her testimony throws light on her father's underground literacy and political work in the region.[37] One of twelve children, Avelino was born in Warisata in 1881—ironically, the same year that the state's land commissioners were beginning to survey, partition, and privatize communal lands throughout the Altiplano, beginning in the province of Omasuyos. He was sent to the lakeshore town of Huarina to be educated in a municipal "mestizo" school, where he was exposed to rote memorization, alphabet drills, and rudimentary reading lessons. It was the kind of "alphabetizing school" that indigenista pedagogues like Franz Tamayo and Elizardo Pérez came to deplore. And true to form, he used his newly acquired Spanish language and literacy skills to "meddle" in electoral politics under the dominant Liberal Party machine. President Montes sought him out to drum up Indian partisan support at election time, turning Avelino into the "transgressive cholo" (stuffing the ballot box) in the eyes of La Paz's conservative letrados.[38] His electoral activities also brought offers of money, clothes, and other gifts—all of which he refused, according to his daughter.[39] In any event, Avelino's uneasy alliance with the Liberals turned him into a pariah and object of persecution by provincial authorities and landlords. He eventually fled to the city of Oruro, where he picked up rudiments of the Quechua language, worked for a spell in the tin mines, and plowed his earnings into pack animals, a mule train that would carry his wares to distant towns. Still later, Avelino made another career change: he became a literacy instructor among the children and adults of haciendas and ayllus in Omasuyos—in places like Chikipa, Suñasiwi, Qutapampa, and Umaphusa.[40] As a roving trader and teacher, "alphabetizing" his students, Avelino joined legions of other Aymara literacy instructors who carried on their semiclandestine activities in the shadows of huts and chapels. But not for long: by the 1920s, the work had become more risky and Siñani a marked man, identified by local authorities as a *cacique agitador*. Guilty by denunciation, he was arrested, imprisoned, and whipped in Achacachi's jailhouse. By the time he encountered Pérez again, in 1931, he had become a legendary figure in the underground literacy movement, and authorized to speak on behalf of Warisata's peasant families in his unfolding relationship with the white schoolmaster.

Julián Siñani, Avelino's older brother, was even more deeply enmeshed in the transregional network of Aymara caciques and apoderados, all of them engaged in legal battles over communal land titles. Julián's title and signature were scrawled across numerous legal petitions and other documents in the early 1900s. On some papers, he authorized himself as the "cacique principal" of Omasuyos (and its twelve cantons); on other documents, he signed for the Indians of the Larecaja province (with its twenty-three cantons). Versed in Spanish letters, he helped craft Indigenous denunciations and demands on a whole range of issues: the Indian right to literacy and education; the landlords' "wicked exploitations" of Indian labor and ignorance; the latifundistas as despots and "absolute owners" who ruled with impunity; the government's corrupt hypocrisy and racial discrimination; and the avarice of provincial officials. His target was not just the evil and corrupt behavior of rural elites, but the underlying structures of internal colonialism. The backwardness and ignorance of the Indian race, he implied, was not a question of biology, cultural inferiority, or even material deprivation—it was, rather, a result of the elites actively denying Indians access to schooling. Inverting the civilizers' logic, he argued that the cause of rural backwardness rested squarely with the nation's elites and their provincial agents.[41] Like Avelino, Julián Siñani also expressed the impulses of a social reformer. For example, he wanted federal authorities to circulate handbills to provincial towns and villages so that their bilingual teachers and apoderados could break the barriers of geography, language, and isolation to disseminate important news about government laws and policies.[42] Because of his stature as cacique and unyielding critic of Omasuyo's provincial authorities, Julián suffered a crueler fate than his younger brother did. His niece Tomasa tearfully recalled how Julián Siñani, condemned to a decade of imprisonment and intermittent torture, was treated like an internal prisoner of war or an escaped slave. Chained, he was forced to walk across the high plains and down through the mountains, from Achacachi to the distant valley town of Sorata.[43]

This brief chronicle of the Siñani brothers illustrates the divergent pathways that Aymara activists sometimes took to reach their common goal. Clearly, Julián was the more militant of the two leaders, while Avelino performed the patient spadework of the radical literacy worker, slowly cultivating the political consciousness and cultural power of the community's adults and children, one by one. Whereas Avelino had manipulated Liberal Party politics to advance his project of lettering Aymara men and generally spreading popular literacy and suffrage, Julián incorporated himself into the heart of the cacique movement and directly confronted the legitimacy of the state's divestiture laws and its abusive provincial elites. But both men looked on the rural school as a critical instrument in the armory of the Aymara-led Indigenous movement. And both had suffered the brunt of the oligarchy's racial fear and endemic violence, which routinely shadowed Aymara teachers, activists, and other authorities in the course of their everyday activities.[44] Without fully realizing it, Elizardo Pérez had stumbled onto this network of Aymara political activists that had flourished for more than two decades.

The Parliament of Amautas

From the outset, the social construction of Warisata was the product of intense intercultural conflict and compromise. But at its core, Warisata rested on the pillars of communal self-governance and comanagement (*co-gestión*) of the ayllu-school. Both functions converged on Warisata's parlamento de amautas, an ad hoc decision-making body composed of Aymara elders (see fig. 3.5).[45] The amautas, the esteemed and wise elders of the community, mediated relations among the director, schoolteachers, community authorities, and the local *padres de familia*, the parents of school-age children who were becoming ever more involved in school activities and policy-making. Avelino Siñani (amauta), Pedro Rojas, and Mariano Ramos (both mallkus) stepped forward to serve as Elizardo Pérez's initial interlocutors, but they needed to widen the pathways toward self-governance through the means of direct peasant participation and representation in an overarching assembly (or parliament). As Pérez quickly appreciated, the entire community became stakeholders in the school project.[46] Local institutions of communal self-rule (for example, a deliberative council [*ulaka*]; rotative turns of service, moving up through the civil-religious hierarchy; and communal forms of social discipline) set the cultural earthworks on which the school organized its governing process. But the art of everyday statecraft was situated mainly in the council of amautas. Pérez described their ad hoc afternoon meetings in the early days:

> After work, we sat in a circle on the rocks and ground so we could talk about the day's work or make new plans. What marvelous days! ... Hundreds of Indians [were] working without salary, happily, united through the ayni or achocalla, the fraternal work institution of Aymara labor.... In those twilight meetings I realized the value and persistence of ancient indigenous institutions. [One of them was] the Consejo de Amautas, which began to germinate spontaneously and flower into a central organism of the school, the motor that provided the force and oriented its activities. It began to meet more regularly over issues raised by Indians themselves. In those meetings, they planned work, named commissions, began to take attendance, regulate work turns making the adobes or other jobs, and in sum, organized the machinery of production that produced and maintained the school.... [And] all that effort represented a process of self-determination![47]

Such improvisations rapidly evolved into institutionalized patterns of school governance and regulation. Pérez himself had a strong hand in shaping the council: he helped to structure its internal composition around ayllu authorities (the amautas, *mallkus*, and hilacatas) and also to organize "commissaries" in charge of regulating specific aspects of school life, including the regulation of communal labor, physical construction of the school, agriculture and public works, day-to-day operations, and administration of justice and discipline within the school and in the larger community. The parliament had no official president or board of directors (*mesa directiva*). Pérez and the other teachers would attend the meetings and sometimes speak, but it was the amautas and hilacatas who set the meeting agenda, discussed the issues, and gathered consensus to make decisions. Warisata's teacher-activist, Carlos Salazar, later recalled that the school's director was often present but did not control the discussion. It was a genuinely communal assembly: peasant representatives from various ayllus would gather on Sunday evenings in the school's dining room, because it was not so cold there, and would raise issues from the floor. "The parliament was an elastic body, where the Indian (as padre de familia of a school child) spoke without any pressure or fear; and that was a magnificent thing."[48] Peasant women were always present in the meetings, though they rarely spoke up; to speak in a public forum was to violate the community's gender norms. But as time went on, some of the *madres de familia* did speak up—sometimes in outbursts of recrimination against their own husbands. Reluctant to release their daughters from their daily domestic tasks, some fathers resisted the parliament, saying that girls had little need to master their letters, because it was the male prerogative to acquire literacy and conduct bureaucratic business in the public domain. Still, the principled issue of coeducation dogged them, and Warisata's primary and secondary schools eventually began to matriculate girls.[49]

As often happens with civic organizations, the governing council became more bureaucratic and layered during the mid- to late 1930s.[50] The parliament was reorganized into three major divisions: communal governance continued to reside with the council of amautas; pedagogical rules and methods were in the hands of Warisata's teachers; and students from the secondary work-school and the normal school (established only at the end of the 1930s) elected their own spokesmen.[51] Most disciplinary power resided in the commissions charged with mobilizing communal work parties and coordinating various economic activities.[52] Warisata's hilacatas went around the villages, tapping peasant families for donations of land and labor, not to mention the pressure they exerted on families to enroll their school-age children at the start of each school year. The massive physical effort to build a boarding school (with its component of elementary day-students) often placed enormous pressure on the local population. On one occasion, the parliament of amautas sent news that it would need one hundred people, along with their pack animals, to cut and carry limestone from a quarry some twenty kilometers away. One frigid night, caravans of llamas and mules converged on the quarry, where people cut the stone, loaded the pack animals, and hauled it back up over the mountains until noon of the following day.[53] Meanwhile, the ayllu-school's agricultural commission regulated the rotation of seed and fallow in the school's "experimental" planting fields, in accord with the traditional agro-ritual calendar and labor turns. Other commissions mobilized workforces for road and irrigation works. One of the community's greatest feats was the channeling of volcanic lake water from Illampu to reservoirs near the school.[54]

Such heroic feats of Indian cooperation and self-sacrifice were part of the lore of Warisata, brought vividly to life in Pérez's chronicle. But times were changing, and as Warisata established itself and grew its student body, its work-oriented curriculum began channeling primary and secondary students into all facets of construction, farming, artisan production, and school maintenance. By the late 1930s, Warisata's student body had ballooned into some five hundred students of various ages.[55] The combined labor force of community and school eventually built an enormous physical complex: a two-story school pavilion (*pabellón*), surrounded by croplands, pastures, gardens, and artisan workshops. By 1937, the school had become economically self-sufficient, thanks to its abundant crop yields and bustling craft industries.[56]

Warisata's parliament also assumed a crucial judiciary role, meting out punishment and adjudicating local disputes. As it expanded its jurisdiction, it briefly eclipsed the authority of Achacachi's provincial bureaucracy as the source of local adjudication. Peasants usually accepted the Justice Commission's judgment without much dispute. The commission rarely charged fines but did not hesitate to punish local transgressors through banishment or even corporal punishment.[57] And, indeed, the council's disciplinary controls sometimes led to internal debates. Warisata's school authorities, with the consensus of the parliament, eventually prohibited all forms of corporal punishment in the school environment, although the occasional flogging was not unknown.[58]

Locally, the parliament of amautas became an axial point of negotiation between teachers and elders, the school and the community, as it emerged as an alternative tribunal of justice throughout the wider region. Rather than take their land disputes to the corrupt court of Achacachi, Aymara people often registered their grievances with the ad hoc "peasant court" at Warisata. Sometimes the council would dispatch the "commissioner of justice" to investigate peasant complaints about an incident of violence or abuse, by interviewing the hacendado or mayordomo accused of wrongdoing. By the mid-1930s, it was not unusual for roving peasant investigators to travel among the largest haciendas of the region looking into cases of possible landlord abuse. Although Warisata's tribunal of justice had no means of enforcing its will, and there was no jail on the premises, it deployed print media to name and shame local culprits and denounce injustices.[59] Instead of succumbing to Achacachi's corrupt provincial court, Aymara people sought retribution in Warisata's makeshift court, broaching everything from boundary transgressions to acts of personal violence.

FIGURE 3.5. Warisata's Indigenous governing body, the parlamento de amautas, in 1931. Those members posing here included (*from left to right*) the maximal leaders (*mallkus*), Pedro Rojas and Mariano Ramos (seated). The others present were identified as hilacatas, or communal authorities from the area. Salazar Mostajo, *Gesta y fotografía*, photo no. 2.

The school's expanding ad hoc jurisdiction of justice and self-governance had obvious ramifications for the school's staff. To be a teacher in this school system was to serve as advocate, counselor, and adjudicator among Indigenous families and, more broadly, to engage in the low-intensity warfare between Indians and their immediate oppressors. "All the teachers, especially elementary school teachers, extended the arm of this alternative system of justice . . . at great risk," remembered Carlos Salazar many years later. So wherever a local school was founded (within the Warisata network), it was viewed by political authorities as a potential site of subversive activities.[60] A new wave of retaliation made it ever more dangerous for Warisata's legal adjudicators to venture out into the surrounding area or investigate incidents of racial violence.[61] As local landlords cracked down on their colonos in the late 1930s, forbidding them to work in or send their children to Warisata, the parliament dispatched its own authorities to intervene in landlord/peón conflicts. Newspaper notices were weaponized to censure or shame local potentates.[62] It cut the other way as well: Pérez was targeted in dozens of lawsuits and newspaper denunciations, condemning his putative crimes, insults, and transgressions, and the sin of betraying his own social class. Danger stalked him everywhere. It was so risky for Pérez to drive the school truck along the road through Achacachi that the parliament decided to post sentinels on the perimeter of the school area and assign bodyguards to accompany him on his motor trips across the Altiplano.

Aymara Voices of *Revindicación*

Meanwhile, the vibrant cultural practices of everyday life in the greater Warisata area continued unabated. Autonomous modes of judicial politics, ongoing dialogues and exchange, fiery oratory, and other forms of communication—all these cultural developments were transforming the ayllu-school into a zone of free expression, in which larger pedagogical, social, and moral issues were debated in the Aymara language, without fear of censorship.[63] Once Warisata's parliament arrogated to itself the right to arbitrate and administer justice, it became a site of Indigenous political discourse that reverberated across the Altiplano. Salazar, the young teacher who arrived in Warisata in 1936, bore witness to this assembly of political debate: "I did not speak Aymara very well, but I stayed the length of those long sessions that began at six o'clock on Saturday evenings and usually lasted until midnight during those frigid Altiplano nights. I stayed because I wanted to listen to how the Indian spoke, finally exercising his right to speak, to voice an opinion."[64] Recalling those late-night sessions, and hearing about the great debates that had gone on in the parliament during the formative years of Warisata, Salazar paused to reflect on his experience:

> In those assemblies, the Indians did not collapse the compass of their debate to the problems involved in running the school, but they realized that Bolivia was filled with Indian comrades with problems similar to their own. They discussed things that widened horizons and opened up the world—for example, the grave issue of the Chaco War that unfolded in 1932, barely a year after the school's foundation. Warisateños heard about the coercive mobilization of Indian troops in the South, and they began to talk about Bolivia as an Indian nation, and about other Indian nationalities, such as in Peru, Ecuador, or Mexico.[65]

The nation's crisis of the early 1930s arrived at the threshold of the new Warisata school, and the community and teachers had to decide how to respond to the state's aggressive drive for military conscripts. As the Chaco War exploded horizons and opened up new issues, they took up the question of the Bolivian Indians' civic responsibilities in wartime. Elizardo Pérez recalled how, "once war was declared, we gathered the population on the soccer field; present were men and women of all ages and condition, probably the entire community."[66] There, armed with their maps and notes, Warisata's teachers gave civics and history lessons, sketching Bolivia's borders with Paraguay, describing the Chaco region and its hostile lowland climate, along with its Guaraní population, products, and roads. Afterward, the men gathered to discuss their civic duty in this time of war. We have yet to know what sort of debate went on, or what sway (if any) Warisata's corps of teachers held over the council of amautas. But as Pérez later reported, the community voted unanimously to send a contingent of two hundred young men and their pack animals to the distant lowland battlefront, where they were plunged into a brutal border war with Paraguay, fighting against enemy Guaraní conscripts.[67]

Warisata's council of amautas conducted its weekly business, in traditional assembly style, in the Aymara language. But on some occasions, the Indigenous parliament called together the full community to discuss grave matters, or to receive visiting dignitaries. We can catch a rare glimpse of one such gathering in 1934. Bolivia's minister of education and a couple of foreign visitors traveled to Warisata to see for themselves what this school had accomplished. Tagging along was a curious journalist from *El Diario* who dispatched a vivid report on this encounter.[68] As it turned out, the dignitaries arrived late in the afternoon, their tour of the school was rushed, and the Indian assembly was cut short because, as the newspaper man explained, the nervous visitors wanted to return to the safety of the city before nightfall. Spending the frigid night in rustic accommodations, or even traveling by motorcar across the desolate plateau as night was falling, apparently was a frightening prospect. Yet even in their rush to leave, the visitors were momentarily arrested by the forceful eloquence of several Aymara orators. Wrote the newspaperman: "Gathered in the school's large salon for public events were the elders, men, and women of the community. It was poignant to behold this mass of Indians, whose severe but expectant expressions, and wrinkled faces, were deeply etched by lifetimes of betrayal. It was even more moving to watch the mass of Indians listening so intently to the speeches of the amautas."[69] Pérez and the amautas rose to speak before the Bolivian minister of education, who was flanked by visiting dignitaries from Mexico and Colombia. Pérez spoke at length about Warisata's difficult early history and its hard-won achievements. Then Avelino

Siñani took the podium and spoke "in a clear and expressive Aymara" about the meaning of the communal school for the Indian community and their children.[70] Judging by the reporter's reaction, the dignitaries were impressed. The spectacle seemed to puncture racial stereotypes of primitive Aymara people uttering an inferior, guttural language, allegedly impoverished of expressive syntax and intonation, their minds apparently devoid of abstract logic or the power of persuasion. To the visitors' astonishment, Siñani's art of oratory revealed him to be a man graced with the virtues of humility, dignity, and audacity. They beheld "the new Indian . . . a man profoundly preoccupied with the necessities of his race."

That impression was reinforced by Mariano Huanca's fierce indictment of Bolivia's centuries-long history of colonialism and oppression. In his speech, Huanca inverted the civilizing trope of backwardness to condemn the country's denial of education to its Indigenous masses and the plague of gamonal violence that now besieged the school. To stir their conscience, Huanca mixed sentiments of moral outrage with a dose of pathos. He pointed to an old man sitting in the audience, his back etched by the scars of a whip after years of imprisonment and persecution for having tried to bring a school into his rural community. Huanca's message was perfectly crafted for the occasion. Like Black abolitionists in nineteenth-century North America, whose fiery oratorical practice was persuasive yet prudent, Huanca was careful to condemn society's systemic racist oppression without directly accusing his listeners of complicity. Indeed, his challenge was to enlist their solidarity in the school's battle against landlord hostility and local aggressors. In closing, Huanca's performance reverted to the paternalist image of the *indio mansa* (humble Indian), thanking the delegates for the honor of their visit. No doubt relieved the assembly was over, the white men piled into their shiny black cars and hurried back to the safety of the city just as the sun was sinking below the edge of the Altiplano.

Meanwhile, that historic encounter left an indelible impression on the visitors, and soon enough, Warisata made the news. *El Diario*'s reporter praised the school for fashioning the "new Indian"—a human being capable of improving himself while also articulating society's historic injustices to the Indian race.[71]

Exercising the right to free speech, however, even in the courtyard of Warisata, was a dangerous proposition from the outset. As Warisata's amautas amplified their collective voice of moral protest, Omasuyo's provincial authorities and landlords grew more hostile. Meanwhile, with the army being mobilized for the Chaco War, military recruiters scoured the land for Aymara conscripts, and bounty hunters ripped open homes and villages in search of deserters.[72] In that jittery racial climate, Warisata went from being a beacon of the "new Indian" to an isolated enclave of restive Aymara men, increasingly under siege by surrounding landlords and their minions. In May 1934, just a few months after the eye-opening visit of government officials, Achacachi's corregidor invaded Warisata's courtyard looking for none other than the amauta and militant orator Mariano Huanca. Both Huanca and Pedro Rojas were accused of conspiracies, humiliated, and whipped in the school's courtyard; then the amautas were dragged off to prison by the hair.[73]

Under other circumstances, the local corregidor might have enjoyed immunity from such abusive acts. Indeed, Sixto Hernani counted on the support of prominent landlords and other authorities, who quickly dispatched a telegram proclaiming his "absolute innocence." Not only was Hernani one of their own, but the landlords also depended on Omasuyos' provincial authorities to keep the agrarian peace in the face of growing rural violence and wartime extraction.[74] But Hernani had clearly misjudged how regional power relations had shifted over the previous few years, or how effectively the amautas could mobilize counterattacks against the violence of provincial despots. This incident exploded into a national scandal, thanks to the efforts of Elizardo Pérez and the amautas, who quickly staged acts of protest in Bolivian courts and the public sphere. They turned the brutal incident into a scandal by gathering journalists, jurists, and politicians together in the school courtyard to denounce the whole edifice of "gamonal feudalism" (as they termed it). Present, too, were Achacachi officials and a few prominent landlords who had come to defend the corregidor against the treachery of the school, for they now considered the ayllu-school a seedbed of sedition. If any social group had imbibed the racial colonialist slogan "the lettered Indian = a rebellious Indian," it was this cabal of Omasuyos landlords, merchants, and their political lackeys. They feared the shifting alignment of rural and urban power relations in the postwar era, as Warisata's influence spread beyond the region into the city of La Paz.[75]

These sorts of incidents, sometimes captured by the passing news item, an impassioned essay, or newspaper editorial, were reverberating among a small group of young writers and political activists in the city of La Paz.[76] News of Warisata provoked racial fear and moral outrage, but it also kindled a spirit of revolutionary idealism among La Paz's progressive youth, which marked a radical departure from Bolivia's older, conservative brand of indigenismo (as embodied by the social Darwinist Bautista Saavedra and the Germanic idealist Franz Tamayo). The young writer Carlos Medinaceli wrote Elizardo Pérez a poignant letter that captured the radical tone of a few youthful idealists and intellectuals who were beginning to identify the "redemption of the Indian" with the larger left-wing causes of popular sovereignty, agrarian reform, and liquidation of the feudal hacienda. He excoriated the backward landlord and gamonal class: "Bolivia will never achieve the dignity of a sovereign nation, if her social masses (the vital nucleus and social cement that holds together the national edifice)—that is, the Indian—is reduced by uncomprehending authorities to the quality of a beast." In the name of the fatherland and civilization, he urged "all cultured Bolivians to resolutely protest the remains of feudal colonialism, which is so contrary to the constitution and other elementary democratic principles."[77] For conservatives, however, the 1934 incident signaled danger—the development of a "subversive communist" sect of militant Aymara men and radical teachers located in the very heartland of the Altiplano.[78] One newspaper, for instance, warned that the teachers did not have the right "to take away the law or the vigilance of provincial authorities in order to sustain a kind of 'republiqueta' which poses grave danger to the tranquility of both the region and nation."[79] Although still muted, rural tensions would eventually escalate, sentencing the escuela-ayllu to a precarious existence even as it flowered and its offshoots cropped up in other regions during the mid- to late 1930s—and even as a group of radical indigenistas in the city began to champion the cause of Warisata.

Origins of the Núcleo Escolar

At its height, Warisata functioned as a dynamic spatial and cultural hub. It became a regional symbol and site that thrived on transregional, interecological networks of people, goods, ideas, and loyalties. The núcleo escolar web was based on a geopolitical pattern of nested towns and communities whose local "satellite" primary schools were drawn into Warisata's radial orbit of influence.[80] Later institutionalized by Bolivian state authorities (and adapted by foreign educational aid workers in Bolivia and Peru during the 1940s), the original núcleo escolar sprang organically out of traditions of inter-ayllu reciprocity and Warisata's imperative to expand its radial influence into outlying regions, particularly into villages occupying distinct niches of the vertical landscape. In the mid- to late 1930s, Warisata's outreach activities stretched across parts of the Omasuyos province on the Altiplano and reached down into the eastern escarpment of Larecaja. In effect, the ideal configuration of the núcleo escolar was a reconstituted ethnic space governed by relations of hierarchy, reciprocity, and solidarity. As Carlos Salazar described it, Warisata projected the image of a realigned, latter-day *marka* (or cluster of ayllus and villages lying within the jurisdiction of the school center). This nucleated spatial arrangement rested, rather precariously, on a reimagined social world of communal autonomy and reciprocity.

How did the outlying "satellite" village schools gravitate toward the "center" in this incipient solar pattern of rural schooling?[81] Blunt material motives drove Warisata's early expansion into the eastern valley region of Sorata, for example. The Altiplano's hot noonday sun was perfect for adobe brick making, but the treeless plateau lacked the lumber needed for the school's beams, doors, window casings, and kiln. A school commission was dispatched to investigate the prospect of purchasing and hauling lumber from Sorata's eucalyptus groves. The trip to Sorata was productive in other ways too, for Elizardo Pérez and the traveling delegates perceived the "magnificent possibilities" of promoting a brisk interecological trade in the temperate region's vegetables and fruits. There was nothing novel in this plan: overland routes of barter, trade, and transhumance had long sustained this ancient interecological traffic pattern between the cold high plateau and warm intermontane valleys. The Warisata expedition sought to reconstruct it by harnessing exchange relations with Sorata peasants to their school enterprise. It was a matter of strategy: How to best establish the school's direct links to peasant producers in the valleys? And how to rearticulate relations of reciprocity so as to bring distant communities into this expanding school-oriented marka? These were the questions that the parliament took up once the commission had returned from Sorata. Pérez noted, "At our return to Warisata, we reported to the parliament all that we had seen and heard. Soon [the council] realized what needed to be done: it was necessary to establish a link with the communities of Sorata as an act of solidarity for the future."[82]

In hindsight, the solution seems rather obvious: Warisata would offer cultural capital (formal schooling, teachers, its own homegrown tribunal of justice, and moral support and alliance) in exchange for the material resources and food crops it needed to sustain its expanding school enterprise. It came down to the cultural produce that the escuela-ayllu could offer the surrounding regions: "It would be necessary to export primary schools [to those distant communities], which would depend on Warisata whenever

FIGURE 3.6. A peasant assembly, in 1934. The community of Chegje met with the Warisata amautas for the purpose of founding a "sectional" primary school in the village. Salazar Mostajo, *Gesta y fotografía*, photo no. 96.

[such] resources permitted."[83] This defined, writes Pérez, the foundational principle of the núcleo escolar: Warisata would sponsor multiple satellite (or "sectional") schools, all orbiting around the main escuela-ayllu, located on the Altiplano, in the fledgling town of Warisata. This reciprocal arrangement had an immediate economic and political significance for Warisata: it secured a source of vital material resources and, at the same time, extended its political-cultural reach into Indigenous communities of Larecaja. Soon they sent local delegates to Warisata to request that a teacher be dispatched to their tiny school establishments. Meanwhile, satellite village schools would send raw materials from their zones (lime, straw, clay, lumber, etc.) to the building site at Warisata. In return, the school center would dispatch a teacher or school supplies. On other occasions, Warisata sent doors and windows to help in the physical construction of the distant primary school (see fig. 3.6).

By the mid-1930s, Warisata's solar pattern radiated out to twenty-three outlying sectional schools, dispersed among the villages of Chegje (Sorata), Curupampa (Ilabaya), Pacacollo (Sorata), Atawallpani (a mountainous zone of Sorata), Turrini (Ancoraimes), Tajocachi (on the shores of the Lake Titicaca), and beyond. Fragile though it was, this sprawling web of Indigenous schools began to reconfigure an insurgent ethno-political space of communal governance, political voice, and education—an extraordinary achievement of self-determination that barely registered on the government radar during the early to mid-1930s, when the Chaco War (1932–35) was a major distraction. Later, the núcleo model of rural schooling would be institutionalized and adapted to official educational purposes; in other words, this largely improvised and empowering drive to reconstitute the geopolitical autonomy of the marka would be subverted and redirected toward various official government ends. Eventually, as we will see, Pérez would become central to that state-building effort in 1938 and 1939.[84]

In the meantime, the invention of the nuclear school network had wider political and economic ramifications. Might not Warisata, a potential axis of overland trade, become the motor of regional economic growth under this spatial, economic, and educational arrangement? In 1934, during his first major public speech on Warisata, Pérez began exploring the industrial potential of this emerging system of nuclear school networks.[85] Putting an economistic spin on his original nuclear school idea, Pérez argued that the establishment of satellite primary schools should be guided by Warisata's primary resource needs. Ideally, sectional schools would be planted in regions of densely populated Indian villages located near rich stands of forest or limestone quarries. Furthermore, he argued that the strategic location of *all* nucleo escolares would spur local economies and eventually displace primitive rural industries with modern agricultural farms and workshops. Imagining a scenario of regional development, Pérez began to recast the potential value of the núcleo escolar, not so much as a way of reconstructing the territorial domain of the marka but, instead, as a means of stimulating agricultural development in targeted regions. Pérez's bold vision of the Warisata model was rapidly evolving to suit Bolivia's postwar era of economic reconstruction.

For Warisata's council of amautas, however, the economic imperative of the núcleo escolar was a matter of securing their cultural power and institutional survival. Determined to break the monopoly of Achacachi's predatory mestizo merchants, Warisata's Indigenous authorities also wanted to create an open-air market, where peasants from surrounding provinces could peddle their livestock, crops, and vegetables (most of them hauled up from Sorata or the tropical Yungas). The parliament of amautas was determined to establish a peasant retail market (*feria*), to be held every Thursday.[86] The cluster of huts and storefronts that had sprung up along the roadside, adjacent to Warisata's main building, already hummed with the traffic of merchants, pack drivers, and Indigenous families, pupils, teachers, and assorted outside visitors going to and from the school. Indeed, Warisata was becoming a magnet for local peasants who converged on the school community to fulfill their labor obligations, attend council assemblies, participate in civic holidays, and engage in various trading, judicial, and bureaucratic matters related to the school. An ad hoc market already boomed as traders amassed in front of the school gate arches at dawn every Thursday to sell their crops and wares. Eventually, Aymara families began to parcel out small lots along the roadside for houses and stores. For the Indian parliament, organizing a market was an auspicious moment to petition the federal government for cantonal status, which would bring in federal revenue and bureaucracy to the area. With the official status of "pueblo," Warisata would gain the usual cantonal privileges (for example, the right to elect its own corregidor and alcalde).

Warisata's school director and teachers were skeptical, however. By establishing an official marketplace and municipality, they argued, Warisata would invite the onrush of greedy merchants, moneylenders, and corrupt power-mongers. It would mean the social death of the "pristine ayllu" that Pérez had once imagined he'd discovered. But the teachers' objection fell on deaf ears. The assembly of peasants saw no necessary contradiction in their pragmatic efforts to articulate the spatial meanings of inter-ayllu reciprocity *through* the medium of the núcleo escolar *and* the formation of an official municipality and regional market, lying immediately adjacent to the school complex.[87]

Letters or Plows? A Curricular Debate

As that debate simmered, Warisata's governing council and the teachers turned their attention to the school's official pedagogy. In their early encounters with Elizardo Pérez and his teachers, Avelino Siñani and other Aymara leaders were eager to promote the diffusion of popular literacy among their communities, so as to furnish adults and children with the cultural instruments of language and letters needed to participate in elections and confront dominant bureaucratic powers, particularly the court system, where Indigenous communities pressed their claims. Some parents hoped that schooling would open new opportunities for bootstrap mobility in distant towns and cities, where girls might bring in a meager income from their work as domestic servants, and boys might find wage work in an artisan workshop, day labor, or petty commerce. For many peasant families, sending their school-age children to the elementary school to learn their letters was as much a cultural aspiration as it was an investment strategy in the precarious household economy. By contrast, most rural adults saw little value in a work-oriented curriculum.

Consequently, Warisata's curricular goals became an early flash point of debate. Pérez was aware of the cultural fact that, to most Indigenous people, the promise of schooling was synonymous with the burning desire for literacy instruction. But he could not abide by such a "primitive" curriculum: "I did not go to Warisata to teach the alphabet or enclose students in a small room with a reader. I went to install the 'active school,' one filled with sunlight, oxygen, and wind; a school that alternated [academic] classes with practical training in the workshop, field, and construction site."[88] He never deviated from his original ideal of the hands-on rural work-school, adapted to the peasantry's natural milieu. In 1937, the year Pérez was promoted to serve as the DGEI's director of "Indigenal education," he broadcast his doctrinal position (by then reduced to a slogan): "I repeat that we do not want to build a school of letrados, but rather a school of workers [trabajadores]."[89] But grand designs for Warisata had depended on his power of persuasion over the school's Indian governing body. It was necessary, he later explained, "to make [the Indians] understand that literacy, alone, would solve nothing. Although we distorted reality a bit, we put to them the case of Avelino Siñani. [We explained that] Avelino, who knew how to read and write, was still subject to the same oppressions as that of Juan Quispe, who was illiterate."[90] His public message was that the mastery of literacy would not by itself bring material improvement or liberation, but his "hidden transcript" presumed that literacy training, by itself, could become a disruptive force in rural society if it unleashed migratory waves of newly literate youth. But this message was never delivered directly to the amautas; instead, Pérez pitched his pedagogy of work as the best and only pathway out of poverty. Education's purpose, he proclaimed before the amautas, would provide practical skills "so that you, your children, and grandchildren ... [can] improve your living conditions by inhabiting comfortable clean houses, sleeping on comfortable beds and mattresses, dressing in good clothes, eating better and more abundantly." All these signs of progress, he assured them, could be achieved "by working in agriculture, exploiting its abundant resources, using modern tools and techniques ... and by developing [rural] industries based on the region's natural wealth."[91]

How did this initial tension resolve itself? Pérez confessed that his passionate discourse may have "distorted reality a bit" to make the "Indians understand" the mandate of the schoolmaster. Gradually, as he imposed his tutelary authority, some Aymara authorities began to modify their preconceptions about what a school should teach the children. Literacy and civic knowledge were highly prized, but some on the governing council began to accept Pérez's work-oriented curriculum.[92] Or so Pérez avers. But his anecdote raises more questions than it answers. Were these tensions resolved? Did the amautas, and the padres de familia, really come around to Pérez's way of thinking, or did they simply "fall into line," given the unequal power equation that was developing between the director, his teaching corps, and the local body of Indian counselors? Did the institutionalization of the ayllu-school tip the interethnic balance in favor of the "professional" class of teachers, or did the growing hostility of outsiders tighten the intra- and intercultural webs of solidarity within the greater Warisata community? We can only speculate.

By the mid-1930s, Warisata's "integral curriculum" tried to balance the demands of classroom learning, artisan workshop, farmwork, and communal labor (supplied by students, teachers, and surrounding villages), but a growing rift developed along ethnic lines. Warisata's criollo director and many of the teachers enjoyed jurisdiction over the school's intellectual labor, boarding school routines, and curricular design. The Aymara parliament, by contrast, was in charge of the school's operations—its physical construction, agricultural production, and artisan workshops (each administered by a small commission composed of teachers, students, and one amauta). The interplay of self-governance, education, communal democracy, and the novel ways the ayllu-school extended its territorial reach and built reciprocal relations, all created a unique cultural phenomenon. The ayllu-school soon became a magnetic complex that drew rural people from surrounding rural communities and its outlying sectional schools. The ayllu school center tailored itself as a one-stop shop, or *escuela única*, in which the student had the luxury of continuing his or her studies through the different cycles of schooling, from elementary through vocational to professional classes. Warisata's elementary school offered the rudiments of Spanish speaking, reading, and writing, as well as arithmetic and civic lessons. Young boys and girls spent time in the fields and pastures, learning about plants and animals. Basic hygiene instruction took place, and eventually the schoolchildren were required to wear school uniforms. Day students and residential students in the work-oriented ("secondary") school had a tripartite course of study, moving from classroom to artisan workshop to planting field.[93] By 1939, the boarding school included a small normal school to train Indigenous teachers, one of whom was Tomasa, the daughter of Avelino Siñani.[94] At its peak, Warisata had developed an agro-industrial program that offered training in livestock and agriculture, including the experimental cultivation of wheat seed. There was also a plethora of workshops, where youth and adults apprenticed in the craft of spinning and weaving (producing blankets and carpets), carpentry (constructing desks and benches and other school furniture), mechanics and metalworking (repairing the school's trucks and manufacturing the boarding school's beds and mattresses), and tile making (producing, at one point, ten thousand bricks per year).[95] Within the walls of the primary classroom, many Warisata teachers gave lessons in Aymara, then gradually shifted over to Spanish-language lessons.[96] As the school evolved, its original work-oriented curriculum diversified, becoming richer, more varied, and more integrated across subject fields and disciplines. Its widening "integral curriculum" eventually offered classes in physical education and recreation, music and art, and hygiene.[97] By the late 1930s, Warisata incubated all forms of artistic and literary expression, and a few of its advanced Aymara students began to produce music, poetry, and essays in their own right (see fig. 3.7).[98]

By then, the school's reputation as a novel experiment in moral and instructional education, as well as the art of democratic self-rule, had transformed it into a shining beacon of cultural liberation. A stream of Indigenous delegations flooded the ayllu-school, and by the late 1930s the school regularly attracted hundreds of Aymara and Quechua pilgrims eager to celebrate civic celebrations, most notably the Day of the Indian (first designated as a national holiday in 1937 by President Germán Busch). Meanwhile, Warisata's fame was fast spreading beyond the Altiplano.

Arrival of Radical Teachers after the Chaco War

Warisata had a powerful allure for Bolivia's postwar generation of rebel youth. Having survived Bolivia's brutal war, humiliating defeat, and humanitarian crisis, Bolivia's youth were driven by a powerful revanchist motive. They called for revolutionary reform—the overthrow of the feudal bourgeoisie; the rehabilitation of the Indian race; and the liberation of the laboring classes. Once again, the "Indian question" loomed large in the national consciousness. Nationalists and leftists emerged from the Chaco War with one unifying

FIGURE 3.7. An early elementary school class, in 1939, where the children learned to read (through bilingual Aymara/Spanish instruction) and write (exclusively in Spanish). Older children passed through the "vocational" cycle of schooling in the school's artisan workshops and crop fields, and finally on to "professional" instruction, in what was supposed to be a seamless succession (*la escuela única*) in mental and manual ways of schooling. Salazar Mostajo, *Gesta y fotografía*, photo no. 207.

goal—the incorporation of the Indian into the national community. Nothing less than Bolivian sovereignty depended on it.

Bolivia's postwar generation of radicals, exiles, and antiwar dissidents now turned their gaze inward toward the country's deepest moral stain: the Indian question. A new generation of leftists sought a full-scale socialist revolution as the only solution. But while waiting for conditions to ripen, some youthful idealists seized on new developments in the field of Indigenous schooling as a pathway toward national recovery and moral vindication in the aftermath of the country's humiliating defeat in the war and brutal treatment of Indigenous conscripts. Indeed, rural Bolivia had sprouted several promising rural school experiments, all inspired by Warisata, in the early to mid-1930s. A network of Indigenous schools—not only the flagship school of Warisata, but now also Caquiaviri, Caiza D, Vacas, Llica, and a half dozen other communitarian schools—beckoned a youthful generation of social explorers anxious to abandon their bourgeois comforts to experience firsthand the "exotic" world of the Aymara and Quechua peasant. Warisata, of course, was still the main attraction. In 1936 and 1937, it became a mecca for Bolivia's postwar generation of leftists and bohemians. A steady stream of writers, teachers, and artists converged on the ayllu-school, many staying for long periods of time or becoming resident teachers, writers, and artists. Bolivia's most famous socialist writer and activist, Gustavo Navarro (né Tristan Marof), and his bohemian wife, Chocha Navarro, made the pilgrimage to Warisata, becoming great champions and frequent visitors. The young leftist activists Alipio Valencia and José Aguirre Gainsborg made the trek as well. As political exiles in Chile, they had dabbled in Marxist internationalism, thus fortifying their revolutionary credentials as they prepared to reenter Bolivia.[99] Once back in Bolivia, they wrote incendiary articles in *La Batalla*, *La Calle*, and *La semana gráfica* about the agrarian question and other revolutionary issues. Meanwhile, a group of progressive urban teachers, including several normal-trained women, also made their way to Warisata in the late 1930s. Many of the new teachers were not formally trained but were hired because they were master craftsmen, artists, writers, photographers, or musicians—all of them learning on the job and passionate about the greater cause of Indian liberation. Carlos Garibaldi was brought in from Arequipa, Peru, to install a weaving workshop (*taller*) of alpaca carpets, for example. The workshop was a resounding success for training and raising funds for the school, although this master weaver later studied in Warisata's normal school and threw himself into the political fight for Indian education in Bolivia.[100] Mario Alejandro Illanes was another formative artist-craftsman who arrived in Warisata to introduce the plastic arts into the curriculum by way of his striking woodcuts and brilliant mural art. Eight brilliantly colored murals—all folkloric scenes of the region—adorned the outside walls of Warisata's main pavilion. Lost in the pillaging of Warisata after 1940, the murals were reproduced in Carlos Salazar's stunningly beautiful, encyclopedic photographic album.[101]

Of this vibrant postwar generation of radicals, Salazar noted, "We were not normalistas [that is, teachers with formal training], but simply activists endowed with vision."[102] Many new teachers could not tolerate the harsh conditions or rural work requirements and left soon after they had arrived. But among those teachers who stayed in Warisata or other rural nuclear school centers, many eventually became important educational functionaries—school directors, inspectors, administrators, or public advocates on a national level. Toribio Claure, for example, emerged as a key intermediary for the fledgling communal school of Vacas in western Cochabamba, helping the peasants negotiate for the right to lease local agricultural fields from the corporate landowner, the municipality of Cochabamba. All the while, Claure helped local peasants found a labor union and school center in Vacas.[103] Rafael Reyeros (later a fierce rival of Pérez) was in charge of the Altiplano school of Caquiaviri; he later became a key lobbyist in the Office of Indian Affairs (Oficialía Mayor de Asuntos Campesinos), assigned to oversee the "special needs" of the Indian race while also handling the problem of peasant petitioners swamping the military socialist regime with bureaucratic paperwork.[104] And Elizardo Pérez's younger brother, Raúl, served as the founding director of the núcleo escolar in the Quechua-speaking valleys of Caiza D, in Potosí, before leaving for Warisata in 1938. His new assignment was to replace Elizardo (who had moved into the federal government) as Warisata's director.

But it was Carlos Salazar who best embodied the idealism of the postwar generation of activist-teachers who came of political age first in the battlefield of the Chaco, and later in the escuela-ayllu of Warisata. Indeed, it was the nightmare of war that initially propelled him to seek moral redemption in the work of Indian education during the war's horrific aftermath. Sent to guard the Bolivian border in the final phase of the Chaco War, Salazar bore witness to the endemic racial abuse that officers routinely inflicted on their own rank-and-file soldiers: "I soon realized that the Indian's real enemy was not the Paraguayan soldier, but the white Bolivian officers who treated him with brutality and contempt," he told me one day.

More subtle forms of racial and cultural discrimination also weighed on his conscience. Looking back across the expanse of half a century, Salazar still blanched at the memory of literate white and mestizo military officers profiting from the illiteracy of Indian soldiers who wanted to write letters home to their families. Unscrupulous soldiers, men who could read and write, sometimes fashioned a boilerplate letter designed for the "generic peasant." In exchange for a few centavos, the Indian could obtain a simulated letter made up of a few patriotic clichés and vague questions asking about the kids, the cow, and the crops. Armed with typewriters and carbon paper in their staff headquarters, white officers could produce multiple copies of the faux letter in what became a wholesale letter-writing operation. This practice might seem trivial when compared to the raw brutality and racial violence that permeated every facet of military life, but it gives us a glimpse of the predatory racism that fed off the Indian's "ignorance" and "illiteracy." For Salazar, it was a pivotal moment that helped shape his own political identity as a budding revolutionary socialist. While stationed in the Chaco, he had joined a small cadre of bilingual and educated comrades (some of them political activists

FIGURE 3.8. Carlos Salazar in the classroom, shortly after he arrived in Warisata, in 1936. His lecture on the Incas inspired students to think about the "problem of the land" as the deepest source of Indian oppression (an axiom of the left). Salazar Mostajo, *Gesta y fotografía*, photo no. 277.

sent to the front by the punitive Salamanca regime), who set themselves up in the field as cultural interlocutors and translators for Indigenous soldiers wanting to write home. His activism opened up channels of communication with his Indigenous comrades as he "learned about their families, hopes, and worries and so came to know the intimate inner world of the Indian."[105] War numbs the senses for a while, but wartime memories often mold the contours of political consciousness for a lifetime. So it happened with Salazar. In 1936, almost immediately following the war, Salazar packed his cameras and journal in his rucksack and set off across the Altiplano for Warisata. He hoped to find moral redemption in the work and solidarity he would offer to the fledgling ayllu-school (see fig. 3.8).

Salazar's gifts as teacher, artist, writer, photographer, journalist, and intellectual soon distinguished him, even among his peers. He became an essential member of the teaching staff, as well as a passionate advocate and emissary on behalf of Warisata's communitarian work/study model of pedagogy and cogovernance. Before long, he won recognition for his dedicated work in the field of Indigenous education. In 1938, under Germán Busch, Bolivia sent a small group of educators to study and tour Mexico (see chapter 4, fig. 4.1). Following in the footsteps of Bolivia's original pedagogical pilgrims (the civilizers who traveled to Europe in the early 1900s to study and bring back the latest fashions in educational reform), Salazar and his colleagues were on assignment to study Mexico's innovations in the field of rural education. And, indeed, President Lázaro Cárdenas's extraordinary apparatus of rural ("socialist") education had long been a source of intense curiosity and admiration among Bolivia's leading educators.[106] As the youngest member of this fact-finding delegation, Salazar spent an extraordinary year traveling through rural Mexico, stopping at designated rural schools to observe their pedagogic innovations that might be exported and adapted to Bolivia. The tour was an eye-opening experience, but not exactly in the way Salazar had anticipated. Certainly, the contrast between the two nations was stark: since the 1910 Revolution, Mexico's Secretariat of Public Education had channeled a fortune into rural schooling, eventually creating tens of thousands rural primary schools and thirty boarding schools for school-age children. Mexico's sprawling infrastructure of rural fiscal schools, and the state's bureaucratic and fiscal support, was on a scale far beyond what the Bolivians had seen.

But Salazar was most struck by the revolutionary loyalty and fervor of Mexican schoolteachers. He marveled at how rural schoolteachers managed to instill revolutionary ideals in their young charges, even before they drilled them in their ABCs. "We were living through a culminating moment of the revolution under Cárdenas, and we saw how the corporatist Mexican state used the Escuela Rural as an instrument to mobilize the rural masses.... It was the rural teachers who were the *portavoces de revolución* and who taught the Indians their rights." Salazar began to think about the Bolivian rural school in more instrumentalist terms. The critical task, he came to understand, was to inculcate a revolutionary political consciousness in Bolivia's rural teaching corps so that they, in turn, would instill that spirit in their students.[107]

But the longer he studied the "Mexican miracle," the more critical Salazar became. For one thing, he "was shocked at how armed the Mexican people were. Whites and blacks, Moors and Christians, everyone seemed to be armed ... and there was little respect for human life. The rural teacher was engaged in a dangerous mission, and we talked to women teachers who had suffered abominable abuses," he recalled.[108] Teachers needed more state protection, yet Salazar also harbored a deep distrust of Mexico's top-heavy corporatist state, which seemed to ignore the Indian altogether, except perhaps as the object of literate and practical instruction. "They delighted in showing us the marvels of the schools' organization, but I said to them: 'What does all this mean if the Indian doesn't participate?'"[109] He had similar reactions to the ejidos, which seemed to him to be agrarian enterprises imposed and run as cooperative enterprises by the central state. Thinking of the dynamics of cogovernance that had thrust Indigenous authorities into the very center of the communitarian school in Warisata, Salazar wondered whether the Mexico ejido enjoyed local legitimacy and the power of genuine cogovernance.[110] As his doubts gathered, Salazar finally began to realize that Bolivia's unique intercultural experiment in Indigenous schooling might well offer Mexican educators novel insights into communal forms of work, learning, and self-governance that had inspired the origins and workings of Warisata. Indeed, Salazar's transformation from scholarship student into expert lecturer, interpreter, and propagandist of Bolivia's communitarian schools went a long way toward disseminating news and excitement about the revolutionary indigenista project of Warisata in Mexico and, later, in the United States.[111] In late 1938, Salazar returned to Bolivia, where he released a stream of newspaper and magazine articles on the question of Indian education in both Mexico and Bolivia.[112]

Salazar's propaganda campaign amplified international interest in Warisata, especially in Mexico. By 1940, the ayllu-school was drawing educators, artists, and intellectuals from Peru, Argentina, Uruguay, Mexico, and the United States. Among the more famous of those pilgrims were the Argentine painter Ramón Subirats, who spent fifteen days observing daily life in the escuela-ayllu and sketching "Indian types"; the prominent Peruvian *indólogo* Uriel García, who had recently published his book *El nuevo indio* (1937); a Peruvian writer and educator and the former rector of the University of San Marcos, José Antonio Ensinas, who gave a course to Warisata's first group of normal students; and the Uruguayan journalist Lepanto García Fernández.[113] Indeed, visiting Warisata had become a rite of passage for leftist intellectuals and artists from near and far (see fig. 3.9).

From the United States came Frank Tannenbaum, a distinguished Columbia University sociologist, former anarchist, and labor organizer, whose visits helped bring international notoriety to Warisata. He visited three times

FIGURE 3.9. Warisata in 1939: a mecca of leftist indigenistas—educators, artists, writers, and poets—who gathered in solidarity with Warisata on the occasion of Carnaval. Salazar Mostajo, *Gesta y fotografía*, photo no. 55.

in 1938 and 1939, always accompanied by Elizardo Pérez, then the national director of Indigenous Education. The American sociologist became an enthusiastic publicist for the school. Interviewed in August 1938, he urged Bolivians to support the school, "because Warisata represents Bolivia's most authentic work [*obra*]" yet produced by the nation. Nowhere in Latin America, he said, had he seen any rural schools so deeply embedded in the local Indigenous culture as he had witnessed in Warisata. Using his visits as a bully pulpit, Tannenbaum urged the Bolivian government to establish and fund at least twenty more núcleos escolares (with their multitude of satellite primary schools) throughout the country and to disseminate news about Warisata throughout Latin America. Rather than dazzle Bolivian teachers by sending them to study in Mexico, he wanted Mexico to send delegations of teachers to study and observe the workings of Warisata. This ream of publicity began to take effect.[114] On the occasion of another trip to Warisata, in August 1939, Tannenbaum produced a copy of a letter he had written to Cárdenas, in which he praised "la obra educativa del señor Pérez."[115] By then, Mexican educators were already apprised of Bolivia's unique school experience, thanks to the publicity surrounding the 1937 tour of Bolivian schoolteachers. Soon enough, the Mexican Secretariat of Public Education sent its own delegation of educators to Bolivia to study "the education of the Indian, Bolivia's institutional type of school [embodied by] Warisata, in all its principal details."[116] Headed up by Adolfo Velasco, the delegates vowed to play a proactive role in Bolivia by "stimulating the Bolivian government" to multiply the núcleos de escuelas and throwing "public light [on] the atrocious social conditions under which Bolivian Indians lived."[117]

Here, then, was an international muckraking group, eager to expose Bolivia as a backward, unenlightened society with caste-like divisions. Disheartened by Bolivia's bleak feudal society, the Mexicans recovered a sense of hope and redemption during their visit to Warisata's fields, classrooms, and workshops. Velasco urged Bolivia's "military socialist" government to break the chains of the Indian, "converting [the indigene] from a slave into a socially liberated element."[118] While the Mexican comrades admired Warisata and venerated Pérez, however, they sincerely doubted that Bolivia's fragile program in Indigenal education would survive without the kind of agrarian change that Mexico had undergone, particularly under the Cárdenas regime. Their warning resonated among Bolivia's postwar youth. Indeed, a Weltanschauung of dissidence and pessimism had come to define the youthful left in Bolivia, just as it had for José Carlos Mariátegui years earlier, in Peru. As the socialist writer Tristan Marof warned his Bolivian compatriots, to try to liberate the Indian through an enlightened program of education without first instituting agrarian reform was to peddle "false sentimentalism." It was to mimic the "civilizer's charade," promising to improve the Indian without defeating the enemy.[119] Mariátegui, Marof's Peruvian mentor, could not have put it better.

Those cosmopolitan critics were certainly prescient, as the power of hindsight reveals, for no matter how impressive the communitarian school project, it was still subject to the gale forces of racial backlash and landlord gamonalismo, and the storm clouds were gathering across the northern Altiplano. By late 1938 and 1939, any lingering hope that *la educación indigenal* would unleash a revolution in the countryside had faded. Most progressive teacher-activists "realized that Mariátegui's position was essentially correct," as Salazar told me many years later. "Only revolution could change the system, and so [we] began to search for a new political vocabulary ... and for ways to improvise a radical pedagogy through ideology and struggle."[120]

Making Indigenal Education Official

Under the regime of military socialism, Bolivia's postwar state had other ideas. In its revanchist pursuit of national unity and social reform, the state seized on the vague ideal of Indigenal education as a nationalist and populist project. Bolivia's new military president, David Toro, was unequivocal in defining the postwar national agenda: "The incorporation of the autochthonous races into ... national life is the first duty of the state," he proclaimed on December 16, 1936. An earlier decree, issued on August 19, 1936, had reiterated the constitutional promise of obligatory primary education for all school-age Bolivian children. Like earlier government decrees, Toro called on "all rustic, industrial, or mining establishments with more than 30 children in residence" to establish free primary schools at their own expense. Smaller establishments were to send the children of their peasants, laborers, and "even domestic servants" to the nearest rural primary school, or "to provision them with the means of learning their letters, in accord with their conditions and economic faculties." The 1936 decree threatened to fine landlords and mine owners who defied the state order: "The maintenance of illiteracy in children of school age will be a public crime," punishable by fines of up to one thousand bolivianos, beginning January 1, 1937.[121]

But such fiats never work, if for no other reason than the fact that a weak state has no means to enforce its political will on an obdurate landlord class. All the same, both Toro and Busch were determined to hasten the acculturation and integration of the Indian into the nation, if only to prevent future debacles of war and unrest. There would be no land reform, but gradual reform would come in the form of unions, schools, and protective laws. Specifically, the Busch regime hoped to appropriate and institutionalize elements of the núcleo escolar by folding them into a new federal program of Indigenal Education. Why not speed up the diffusion of rural community-based schools through state sponsorship by recruiting Elizardo Pérez to serve as the new czar of Indian school reform? The plan was quickly executed: Pérez was appointed as the director of the DGEI, reporting directly to Busch's new minister of education. From the outset, he was faced with a mission impossible. The DGEI's stated goal was to establish fifteen thousand schools for the nation's 500,000 school-age children living in rural communities while also imposing federal authority over existing village schools, many of them still lying off the government radar. Nor could Pérez or the DGEI count on lavish state funding required to carry out this herculean project. It is a wonder that Pérez accepted the post at all!

Yet Pérez threw himself into the task. Driven almost beyond the limits of human endurance, Pérez traveled by truck, by horseback, and, in the lowlands, by river raft to visit all existing rural federal schools or to found new ones. He later chronicled his frenzied effort to "irradiate" the núcleo escolar model to Indigenous areas throughout the *entire country*. Perhaps he believed it was the chance of a lifetime to finally set in place the foundations of Bolivia's rural educational system and to project what he had accomplished in Warisata to Indigenous communities across the country. In any event, Pérez made a superhuman effort to establish or inspect Indian schools in far-flung corners of the nation: in the eastern lowlands of Beni (with the school of Casarabe); along the remote western border with Chile (the núcleo escolar of Llica); in the eastern valleys of Cochabamba (the schools of Cliza and Vacas) and Chuquisaca (the núcleo escolar of Caiza D); in the Guaraní semitropical lowlands (with Mojocoya); and on the northwestern Altiplano (with the núcleo of Jesús de Machaca).[122]

From an institutional standpoint, the educator's most daunting challenge was to mobilize and train a rural corps of teachers who could staff the new network of nuclear peasant complexes. Nothing much had changed since Georges Rouma had tried to solve the problem by establishing three rural normal schools in the 1910s. The postwar school campaign and government's ambitious language-assimilation policy would require a massive increase of trained hispanized teachers who were willing to live under difficult rural conditions. Max Bairon, the minister of education, recruited some 250 novice teachers, many of them Chaco War veterans; others were untrained instructors, some having had only two or three years of primary schooling. Short immersion courses (*cursos de capacitación*) were supposed to fill the gap, readying them for the job. In short order, rural instructors were dispatched to their posts with the promise of a paltry government wage of 140 bolivianos a month.[123] In the meantime, Pérez mounted a nationwide fund-raising campaign in the public sphere, much as Rouma had once tried to do. Letters of appeal went to mine owners, merchants, bankers, industrialists, and landowners; and the public sphere was saturated with press articles, radio addresses, public lectures, and exhibitions. The DGEI organized more visiting delegations to Warisata and other rural nuclear schools than ever before. And Salazar volunteered to write essays championing the national cause of Indigenal education for the progressive newspaper *La Calle*.[124]

But in the frenzied effort to expand and consolidate Indigenal education as an arm of the military socialist regime in 1937 and 1938, Warisata was inevitably evolving away from its foundational principles of communal autonomy, cogovernance, and emancipation. Despite his best intentions, Pérez's bureaucratic mission was turning the network of community schools into an instrument of political socialization under the military populist state. Apart from their partial support of agrarian unions and schools, Bolivia's twin military socialists (Toro and Busch) evinced little interest in confronting Bolivia's deeper "socioeconomic problems" (poverty, landlessness, caste hierarchy, feudal-like haciendas, and the unresolved issue of communal land claims). Instead, the education minister wanted rural teachers to spread patriotic sentiments, the national language, and practical skills to their young Indigenous charges. And under Busch's orders, there was to be no more talk of Indian emancipation or social revolution.

As he ascended into the ranks of government service, Elizardo Pérez's pedagogical ideas were also evolving. In 1937, by then a government functionary, Pérez had come to assess Warisata's success largely in economistic terms. He no longer framed the ideal of Warisata as a symbol of communal self-determination or Indian emancipation; rather, he celebrated the escuela-ayllu as a thriving vocational school and pole of regional economic integration. On that score, there was much to be proud of: the school enterprise was economically self-sufficient; it showcased its artisanal workshops to visitors from across the hemisphere; it had pulled surrounding villages into its orbit and become a magnet for Aymara people across the region; and its new normal program was training a new generation of Indigenous teachers.[125] In government circles, though, the question remained: Was Warisata compatible with the state's reformist goals of agrarian modernization, official unions, and patriotic loyalty to military socialism? Or was it becoming a nest of leftist teachers, flirting with socialist and communist doctrines?

For two short years, Pérez had a chance to disseminate and adapt the "Warisata model" to different regions across the country. As if he had been banished into internal exile, Pérez's quixotic mission took a heavy toll on his health and nearly cost him his life. But most of his frustration stemmed from the backroom partisan politics that threatened to sabotage his work in the field. Although his bold educational project had garnered praise among progressive delegates to Bolivia's 1938 Constitutional Convention, Pérez never won from the Congress the material support he needed to spread Indigenal education into the far reaches of Bolivia.[126] In the end, Pérez ran up against Bolivia's fortress wall of racist and reactionary landholders, on the one hand, and a weak and wavering populist government, on the other. Even before President Busch put a gun to his head in 1939, Pérez realized he was in deep political trouble. Warring partisan factions and political intrigue undercut his status and authority within the top echelons of state government. Even fellow indigenista educators, like Rafael Reyeros, began to turn the president's counselors against him. With Busch dead and buried, this maverick educator found himself cut off and isolated—and soon to become a social pariah among Bolivia's newly ascendant oligarchy.

Within a few months, a Conservative military regime that emboldened Bolivia's landed and mining oligarchy would sweep into power. By then, neither Warisata's official status nor its international fame could protect the escuela-ayllu from a tidal wave of reactionary violence. As 1939 was drawing to a close, the teacher-activist Carlos Salazar "felt in [his] bones that the whole historic experiment in Indigenal education was hanging by a thread."[127] Through the lens of hindsight, we can see that Salazar's insight was all too prescient.

4

Whose Indian School?
Revenge of the Oligarchy

The *Núcleos* of Indigenal Education ... preach hatred against the rest of ... the Bolivian family.... [We] proclaim that the ethnic end point for Bolivia will be *el mestizaje*.
—CONSEJO NACIONAL DE EDUCACIÓN (CNE), *El estado de la educación indigenal en el país*

The tragic suicide of Busch in 1939 opened the way for the oligarchy to grab the levers of state power, clamp down on the revolutionary left, and reassert its political agenda. For the first time since May 1936, Herbert Klein writes, "the now naked power of the oligarchy made itself profoundly felt" in all sectors of society.[1] In quick succession, two conservative military generals, Carlos Quintanilla (1939–40) and Enrique Peñaranda (1940–43), made common cause with Bolivia's traditional ruling elite (tin barons, powerful landowners, provincial political bosses, and a host of conservative politicians, journalists, and intellectuals) eager to stem the rising tide of political radicalism. The post–Chaco War years had brought about a political sea change in Bolivian state/society relations as groups of ex-combatants, dissident urban youth, teachers, miners, factory workers, and a host of new peasant unions began organizing themselves around the promises of populist and social reform under "military socialism." That wave of popular mobilization, in turn, prompted President Germán Busch to convene a Constitutional Convention in 1938 while also releasing a stream of official decrees and fiery rhetoric to consolidate its base of popular and nationalist support.

But the sputtering prospects of agrarian reform died suddenly along with Busch, exposing for all to see the precarity and vulnerability of incipient labor and leftist movements. Over the 1940s, the country was wracked by a series of internal political upheavals and social crises as it lurched between the power of right-wing oligarchic and military cliques and the growing left-wing political opposition. Around mid-decade, the interim rule of Col. Gualberto Villarroel (December 1943–July 1946) represented an anomalous political turn: Villarroel, the last of Bolivia's three postwar military socialists, pursued a platform of modest social reforms under the strictures of authoritarian rule. Government efforts to repair Bolivia's polarized polity and channel social unrest ultimately collapsed in the revolutionary fervor of the early 1950s. In the meantime, however, Bolivian politics would be continuously disrupted by powerful imperial intrusions and transnational forces, including World War II, Nazi penetration, the spread of communist ideologies, Standard Oil's encroachments in eastern Bolivia, the influx of US and multilateral foreign aid and development projects in the late 1940s and early 1950s, and the gradual onset of the Cold War. As Bolivia's internal fissures deepened, the country was swept into the vortex of global and hemispheric change over the 1940s.

Set against this tumultuous decade, the story of Indigenous schooling tends to get lost to view.[2] For the first time since the Montes era, intensive state initiatives in rural school reform moved into the purview of the ruling oligarchy as the new Consejo Nacional de Educación (CNE) tried to rebuild a centralized apparatus of public education after the conservative forces seized power in 1940. Run by Vicente Donoso Torres, the CNE launched a vigorous campaign to overhaul the program of Indigenal education, and a new generation took up the ideological project of constructing Bolivia's national pedagogy. But what, in this reactionary political climate, did it signify? The CNE ground out reams of paperwork, both within official circles and in the public sphere, that reevaluated and reorganized public education for Bolivia's rural children.³ Indeed, from his new headquarters in the CNE, Vicente Donoso and his colleagues launched an all-out assault on Warisata as they prepared to dismantle the whole edifice of educación indigenal.

Historical and ethnographic scholarship on the 1940s has brilliantly charted the insurrectionary political landscape that unfolded fitfully in rural Bolivia until a broad revolutionary coalition of peasants, laborers, and left-wing political activists seized the reins of power in 1952.⁴ Yet that scholarship tends to submerge the theme of rural school activism within the larger picture of Indigenous and popular insurgency. Read backward, the decade of the 1940s was an explosive decade that seemed to be hurtling toward the climax of national revolution in the early 1950s. But the 1940s also brought forth unforeseen developments in the field of rural schooling and popular education that were at the very center of Bolivia's escalating conflict between radical teachers, peasant activists, and the "feudal reaction" of Bolivia's conservative oligarchy.

From the outset, this chapter poses a simple question: Why did Warisata (and other núcleos escolares) unleash the fury of state violence in 1940? How and why did the government program of Indigenal education suddenly reverse course, turning it into an object of attack? The layered answers to those questions will emerge, I hope, in the course of this chapter. But the shorthand answer lies in the radical disjunctures of this postwar moment. First, there was a radical realignment of political power after Busch's suicide. With the conservative *rosca* swept back into power, Indigenal education (the proud product of the Busch years) became a convenient institutional scapegoat. Second, the landed oligarchy's "feudal reaction" unleashed a wave of fear and loathing toward the radical indigenista projects of Indian emancipation. International expressions of solidarity had turned the escuela-ayllu into a famous enclave of anticolonial and revolutionary aspirations. And that cultural development, in turn, threatened to upend Bolivia's (already weakened) neocolonial regime—hence the excited talk about agrarian reform, the liquidation of the latifundia, and liberation of the Indian that circulated in leftist newspapers, union conventions, and peasant congresses at the time. By 1939, Warisata had come to symbolize a bridgehead of anticolonialism, situated in the regional heartland of racism, latifundismo, and caste hierarchy. That Bolivia's pro-Indian school movement had finally garnered wide support among progressives, both at home and abroad, made it all the more urgent for the conservative oligarchy to take it down. While the danger to Warisata had once been confined to local incidents of hostility (an ongoing "low-intensity" ground war, to borrow James Scott's term), after

1940 it exploded into a campaign of aggression coordinated at the highest levels of state power.

In short, this chapter asks not only *why* but also *how* the oligarchic state organized and waged ideological warfare against Warisata, as it mobilized the tools of race-thinking, political propaganda, the law, backroom diplomacy, and government policy to bring the emancipatory school movement to an abrupt and ignominious end. More broadly, this chronicle of Warisata's destruction affords a close-up view of the intricate workings of neocolonial violence, right-wing nationalism, and state-building in this fraught political moment.

Diplomacy and Subterfuge

The year 1940 was a deeply paradoxical moment for Bolivia's elite cadre of indigenistas. Amid political flux and uncertainty at home, they were suddenly thrust into the international limelight, if only briefly, to present the results of their hard-fought achievements in the field of Indian education.

Their opportunity came in April 1940, at the First International Indigenista Congress, held in Pátzcuaro and hosted by Mexican president Lázaro Cárdenas. Along with hundreds of other delegates from across the Americas that converged on Pátzcuaro, six Bolivian delegates traveled from La Paz to the congress, where they spent ten days discussing "the Indian question" and formulating "continental-wide [indigenista] action in favor of the Indian." The prospect of touring the beautiful Tarascan countryside, hobnobbing with Mexican luminaries, engaging in dialogue and debate, delivering scholarly speeches, sharing field experiences, and enjoying folkloric spectacles promised to thrust the Bolivian delegates into this new Inter-American network of indigenista scholars, funders, and policy makers.[5]

Sentiments of sympathy and solidarity added to this heady mix. The Bolivians had come to participate in an international forum in which the challenges of Indian poverty, illiteracy, and landlessness throughout the hemisphere societies were openly discussed and native folkloric heritages celebrated.[6] For once, they need not have assumed a defensive posture or apologized for Bolivia's status as South America's "most Indian nation." On the contrary, the Bolivian team had traveled to Pátzcuaro to enlighten indigenistas and statesmen from across the Americas about Bolivia's Native peoples, their programs of social reform, and their novel efforts to educate, uplift, and manage the integration of its Aymara- and Quechua-speaking populations

FIGURE 4.1. The Bolivian teachers delegation to Mexico, 1938, including the young Carlos Salazar (*left, second row*) and his political rival, Rafael Reyeros (*middle, front row*). A second delegation of senior statesmen and intellectuals, including Elizardo Pérez, attended the 1940 International Congress of Indigenistas in Pátzcuaro, Mexico. Salazar Mostajo, *Gesta y fotografía*, photo no. 283.

into the nation. As it turned out, however, the delegation was riven by partisan rivalry and ideological conflict. In his opening address, Enrique Finot, Bolivia's new ambassador to Mexico, broached the colonialist "problem of the Indian" in Bolivia and elsewhere from a standard racialized perspective.[7] Tacking to the left, Eduardo Arze Loureiro, a socialist lawyer-activist and landlord from Cochabamba, delivered an impassioned speech about Bolivia's mandate to break up the feudal estates and open the countryside to peasant smallholding and rural wage labor. But it was Elizardo Pérez's exposition on Bolivia's "doctrine of *educación indigenal*" that momentarily electrified the congress. That is the way he wanted it, for as he later recalled, he had gone to Pátzcuaro for one reason alone: to drum up international solidarity for his cause and to bring glory to Bolivia (and, we might add, to himself, as the country's "apostle of Indian education").[8]

There was, by 1940, every reason to expect a cascade of accolades, thanks to Warisata's well-earned international reputation. More than a few of the delegates had made their own pilgrimages to the escuela-ayllu, and interest was intense among the delegates. Moreover, the tone of the conference seemed sympathetic to the "pluralist" (as opposed to "assimilationist") position among the indigenistas. The Mexican congress organizers, Moisés Sáenz and Luís Chávez Orozco, were both cultural pluralists who actively promoted the right of Indian cultures to self-determination and coexistence within modern nationalities—although that platform clashed head-on with President Cárdenas's corporatist, assimilationist, and *agrarianista* agendas.[9] Mexico's vigorous federal program of socialist education had promoted a brand of "rural schooling" designed to sweep Mexico's Indigenous peasants into the state's corporatist-syndicalist web and turn them into modern tool-wielding farmers living on state-sponsored ejidos. But the congress proved to be a big ideological tent, capable of accommodating alternative indigenista positions on Indian preservation, integration, and assimilation. In this ecumenical climate, Pérez had good reason to expect accolades, perhaps even a formal commendation, for the pedagogic work he had accomplished in Warisata and, later, as Bolivia's architect of Indigenal education under President Busch. When his turn came to speak, he delivered a passionate self-appraisal, presenting Warisata as the Americas' gold standard of communitarian schooling and, not immodestly, claiming it as his magnum opus. But to his astonishment, the formal commendation he sought from the Indigenista Congress never materialized. Not even the Bolivian delegation rallied behind him. In fact, a few of its leaders turned out to be saboteurs.

How and why had things gone so wrong? We can only surmise what went on in the smoky hallways and noisy salons of the hemisphere's first international indigenista forum. But evidence suggests that the nefarious work of backroom diplomacy and political subterfuge ultimately tipped the scales against Pérez. The nomination of Warisata for a "vote of applause" initially came from José Antonio Ensinas, Peru's distinguished educator and writer. One of many pilgrims to Warisata in the late 1930s, he wanted the Pátzcuaro congress to give formal recognition to the innovative pedagogical work of Bolivia's indigenistas. But he was blocked by Ambassador Finot, Bolivia's head delegate. Clearly complicit with the new military regime, Finot made it clear to Mexican authorities that any official commendation of Warisata would be in defiance of Bolivia's highest authorities.[10] Meanwhile, Pérez had other detractors—for example, a Mexican delegate representing the Pan-American Union who demanded to know why Bolivia's nuclear model of schooling should be singled out for praise when other American states (for example, the Cárdenas regime and its program of socialist education) had accomplished so much more. In the end, the First International Indigenista Congress withdrew its official endorsement of Bolivia's ten-year intercultural experiment in communitarian schooling.

There is an ironic backstory to Pérez's fall from grace in April 1940. That this congress was held in Pátzcuaro at all was indicative of his precarious status and influence in La Paz. Even at the height of his powers, in 1938, Pérez was unable to sway the Busch government to host the congress of indigenistas in La Paz. Pérez's proposal was shot down by Rafael Reyeros (already Pérez's most powerful rival within the Busch government), who urged Busch to oppose the idea. Reyeros, recently back in La Paz after almost a year touring rural schools in Mexico, believed that Bolivia had little to show for its efforts and that holding a congress in Bolivia in order to showcase its Indian schools would only bring embarrassment and shame to the country. At first the Bolivian government's plan was to postpone the congress for a year, but as the political situation deteriorated, Pérez found himself ever more isolated within the Busch government, even before the president took his own life in 1939. Once Busch was out of the picture, the new oligarchic regime had no sympathy for the likes of Elizardo Pérez and his brand of indigenismo.

The stealth campaign to deride Warisata and isolate Pérez continued in Pátzcuaro. A slanderous Bolivian pamphlet printed by the CNE circulated secretly among the congressional delegates. Titled *El estado actual de la educación en Bolivia*, it denounced the "sham" that Indigenal education had become under Pérez's DGEI administration during the Busch years.[11] A shot over the bow, this text launched the oligarchy's ideological war on the meaning and memory of Warisata—a propaganda smear campaign from which Bolivia's radical indigenista teachers and the Warisata school community would never fully recover. Using the Pátzcuaro conference to slander the "nefarious" doings of Pérez and discredit a decade of Indigenous school reform, the pamphlet rejected the pluralist ideal of Indigenous cultural autonomy in favor of the Mexicanist ideal of Indian assimilation through cultural mestizaje. Neither Luís Chávez Orozco nor even Moisés Sáenz felt compelled to take up the defense of Warisata, although they shared its basic pluralist tenets. And so the escuela-ayllu—an emerging international icon of progressive indigenista pedagogy just two years earlier—was recast by its detractors as the poster child of misguided Indianist utopianism or, worse yet, as the seedbed of racial agitation and communist sympathies.

The Bolivian oligarchy pursued a sly diplomatic strategy, using the Inter-American Congress of Indigenistas to sow divisions within the indigenista camp (widening the rift between pluralists and assimilationists), slandering the reputation of Pérez, discrediting Warisata's achievements, and trafficking in colonialist, anticommunist rhetoric. A lost opportunity, if ever there was one. Now the oligarchy's violent campaign against Indigenal education would have to run its course. And the metaphorical blood would be spilled not in the beautiful Tarascan countryside surrounding Pátzcuaro but in Aymara villages and schools across the Bolivian Altiplano.

The Government's Smear Campaign

The main battleground of this official war on Warisata was the capital of La Paz. In January 1940, Bolivia's new education minister and other education officials began mobilizing their battle plans to dismantle the program of Indigenal education, purge its teachers, and bring the network of núcleo schools under strict government control.[12] With Pérez's decision to remain in Mexico for several months after the Pátzcuaro congress (a short, self-imposed exile), Bolivia's new minister of education wasted no time in ordering the end of la educación indigenal. To execute his orders, the state created a new disciplinary organ, aptly named the Intervención General de Educación Indigenal. It was vested with the authority to displace the autonomous self-governing, communitarian schools with state administrators, beginning with the escuela-ayllu de Warisata. Rafael Reyeros, the new "Intervener," performed this demolition work by mobilizing inspectors and spies to monitor rural school activity and censure teachers. A warning went out that too many teachers had "assumed the authority of public officials, turning themselves into corregidores, judges, and even notaries." All indigenista teachers were forewarned: they were not to participate in the internal affairs of the Indian community, or spread "dangerous" ideas, or incite their Indian charges.[13]

This civil auto-da-fé was aimed at the "heretics" perpetrating their treacherous brand of Indian education. More ominously, the Intervener's method and message represented an institutional state assault on the escuela-ayllu's defining philosophy of communal autonomy and self-governance—the essence of communitarian schooling. An economic blockade was thrown up. State funding, already meager, dried up entirely. In early 1940, many of the original núcleo-styled boarding schools had trouble stocking staple supplies; students' scholarships disappeared, forcing them to return to their villages; rural teachers were furloughed; and rudimentary school supplies, tools, and machines could not be purchased or repaired.[14] A state-sponsored war of attrition was underway.

The blockade was bound to trigger a reaction—particularly among the throngs of Bolivian leftists, artists, and intellectuals who had visited Warisata, awakened to the cause of Indian liberation, and were now loosely associated with Bolivia's Indian school movement. Almost before the decree was issued and the DGEI suspended, the Quintanilla regime was engulfed by waves of protest. In late January 1940, prominent writers and activists protested the closure and accused the state of "false motives." They argued that the only real "danger" Indigenal education posed to the social order was to challenge society's entrenched neocolonial structures and racist attitudes, and called on the government to restore "this great civic project, the pride of Bolivia."[15] Expressions of outrage and solidarity flowed in from other quarters too: from organized labor, which pledged its allegiance to the cause of "our Indian compatriots"; from the núcleo school of Llica (located near the Chilean border in the western reaches of Potosí), which proclaimed its solidarity with Warisata; and from editorials on the pages of *La Calle* and other progressive newspapers.[16] "Why is this school program being demolished? Why unleash a new invasion of the barbarians?!," one editorial writer demanded to know. The Republican Party paper, *La Noche*, went on to repudiate the state for maligning the honor and work of Elizardo Pérez, calling him the nation's preeminent civilizer (!) and "intellectual heir of Bolivia's great founding educators—Tamayo and Bustamante."[17]

The January outcry of progressive intellectuals, journalists, and teachers made one thing clear to the new military regime: it needed to justify the policy decision to dismantle Indigenal education. The CNE's strategy was to show that Bolivia's original núcleo escolares were suffering from incurable social maladies—waste, corruption, ineptitude, sedition—that threatened to contaminate Bolivia's entire body politic.[18] Accordingly, the government launched a public investigation into the "state of Indigenal education," to be conducted by (none other than) the CNE, under the authority of Vicente Donoso Torres. In other words, the same government agency that had denounced Pérez and abolished DGEI was now put in charge of marshaling the evidence to defend and justify, ex post facto, its drastic actions.[19]

A secular inquisition quickly got underway in 1940. To gather incriminating evidence, Donoso Torres asked for detailed reports (*informes*) on the condition of the nation's sixteen núcleo school centers and their seventy-five outlying primary schools. Those inventories were to specify the pupil population, curricular programs, physical condition of the plant, quality of the teachers, and so on. On the surface, the questionnaire gathered useful data, but the CNE sought the collaboration of teachers and informants willing to supply the ugly facts needed to fuel its propaganda campaign against Indigenal education.[20] The extent to which these government reports on the state of rural schooling were filtered by partisan, pro-oligarchic interests is still difficult to tell—but the government's immediate political mandate was to gather evidence of crisis, scandal, and failure so as to justify its destructive policies toward Warisata and certain other núcleos escolares. On the other hand, there is no doubt that rural conditions *were* bleak and that many peasant school centers *did* show unmistakable signs of material deprivation and disarray. Report after report flowed into the government, building an irrefutable case that Indigenal education had been a disaster for the country. A quick inventory of those field reports tells the "official story" of Indigenal education as an unmitigated failure: Canasmoro (founded in 1936, in Tarija) was reported to have no medicines for its clinic and few notebooks or pencils for its pupils. More seriously, the school had never been able to mobilize labor from surrounding Indigenous communities; it seemed to have been poorly located amid hostile or indifferent Indians. Another inspector's report came in from the Department of Potosí. Its original núcleo escolar, Caiza D (hereafter called simply Caiza), still suffered from the "despotic rule" of its past directors, including Raúl Pérez (brother of Elizardo). It was said that Raúl had presided over Caiza as if it were "his own private property, a fiefdom." Caiza's "school council" pitched their report to the CNE, using it to plead for government aid and protection. The communal school of Vacas (Department of Cochabamba) was apparently in a sorrier state: according to the field report, its teachers were called lazy and corrupt; the school was apparently devoid of a teaching curriculum; and its Indian families were abandoning the school. The escuela escolar of Talina (Department of Potosí) still lacked a schoolhouse, since apparently it was impossible to solicit "free labor" from local communities.[21] The government's list of dysfunctional schools, apparently in need of closure or a state takeover, went on and on.

To cap off its official investigation into the dismal state of the núcleo school, the CNE organized a high-profile tour of Warisata, Caquiaviri, Cliza, and Vacas. With boots on the ground and notepad in hand, state officials set out to collect eyewitness testimony that would prove the government's case—that Indigenous people and their indigenista teachers had made a disastrous mess of things under military socialism. As he made the rounds, Vicente

Donoso singled out a teacher, one Julia Plaza, who had recently retired after a short stint of teaching Spanish to elementary school pupils in Warisata. Her express disenchantment with the school made her an ideal informant for Donoso's critical report (and he later used the interview, almost verbatim, as part of the state's official documentary record). She complained about her heavy workload, the substandard salary, her deficient Indian pupils, and the school's bogus curriculum and dismal pedagogical standards. As evidence of fraud, the teacher named several normal school students who had been granted diplomas in a hurry—before they had completed their course of study.[22] Trivial as this might sound, it was the kind of "smoking gun" Donoso needed to banish Warisata's director, Raúl Pérez, once and for all.

In those early months of 1940, suspicion, demoralization, and fear clouded Warisata's future and constricted the hearts and hopes of its teachers and students. Many teachers had already lost courage and fled; the few loyal indigenista teachers who persevered (including Carlos Salazar, who was sent by Raúl Pérez to bring discipline to Caiza, and Anita Pérez, daughter of Raúl, who stayed on in Warisata) were wary of the state's divide-and-conquer tactics. Salazar remembered the fear and dread they all felt under "the daily barrage of press attacks and rumors, calling us thieves and saying we had pillaged state property, or absconded with funds, or were communist agents trying to spark an uprising."[23] Who were the true indigenista loyalists, who the spies and informers? The state's incursions ripped the fragile webs of teachers' solidarity, communal participation, and the authority of the amautas that had supported, and insulated, the ayllu-schools during most of the 1930s.

As the state's propaganda war shifted into high gear, the CNE began using the back channels of rumor, innuendo, and news leaks to control the narrative and stir up public outrage against the "nest of communists." By March 1940, the tide of public opinion was turning in their favor. The Republican newspaper, *La Noche*—the same paper that had exalted Pérez as the nation's preeminent "civilizer" just two months earlier—now reversed its editorial position to lambast Warisata and everyone associated with it.[24] The state stirred up more trouble by accusing the ayllu-school of having perpetrated lies and betrayed the Indian race. Warisata's teachers were accused of arrogance and ostentation for having staged ethnic spectacles in the school's courtyard, and for falsely promising the Indians deliverance from feudalism and slavery while exploiting their labor. Even the school's ostentatious "monumental architecture" had supposedly tricked the Indian into believing in liberation, when in fact the ayllu-school had been run like a "feudal hacienda" for the benefit of the corrupt Pérez brothers. Everything that Warisata had claimed to be—an Indian teacher-training school; a voluntary communal endeavor; a showcase of truly progressive indigenista pedagogy—was demolished as a racist paternalist sham. To judge by *La Noche*'s slanted logic, its editors were in close touch with Vicente Donoso's office. And the new regime, in turn, had found an ideal ventriloquist, willing to amplify the slanderous attacks that would soon be appearing in print, on the pages of the CNE's 1940 investigative reports.

More importantly, *La Noche* played a crucial role in swaying the court of public opinion, as it helped frame Warisata's "crimes" against the nation and map out the prosecutorial argument. One is struck by the scope and viciousness of *La Noche*'s attack. It represented another order of magnitude from the social ills, petty venality, and administrative chaos that Donoso was anxious to document in his forthcoming report: here was an implicit indictment not just of Warisata but of the whole Chaco generation of indigenista activists, teachers, and intellectuals, for their alleged crime of perpetrating seditious lies and predations that simultaneously exploited and stirred up the Indians. Scandal and sensationalism sell copies, of course, and this newspaper's scoop was the apparent unmasking of "a decade of deception." In June 1940, *La Noche* proclaimed that Bolivia had been living in a fog of lies and delusions—Indian education was the nation's greatest "*bluff*"![25] Such was the new mantra of the conservative press, and it gave the government the perfect playbook for executing its own frontal assault on Indigenal education.

As we saw earlier, Donoso's report, *El estado actual de la educación indigenal*, was released to the public in early April 1940, just in time for the Indigenista Congress in Pátzcuaro.[26] The text was a dry bureaucratic document, but once published, it served as the regime's heavy artillery in its ongoing institutional and propaganda war. The report's biting polemical tone was reinforced by reams of data and documents. A pithy prologue (probably written by Rafael Reyeros) praised Donoso Torres as Bolivia's leading authority on "the social, political, and economic situation of the Indian in Bolivia[,] . . . the most intricate problem and the one that weighs most heavily on our nationality."[27] The report announced that the CNE's new mission of "Rural Education" (as opposed to "Indigenal Education") was the swift conversion of Indians into deracialized peasants and their total incorporation into Bolivian national culture. Repudiating the Indian's "false apostles and imitators," the report called for a new type of "rural school" (the word *Indian* was expunged in favor of *campesino*). The idea of rural education invoked an ideal of agrarian capitalism based on the principles of market-driven farming and private property (ideally, a tenure system devoid of ayllus and combining individual property units, including haciendas and peasant smallholding).[28] Thus, even if readers were unwilling to plow through Donoso's tedious empirical report, they would find the key conceptual framework defining the oligarchy's cultural and educative mission in the report's brief prologue: it outlined a uniform "rural pedagogy" of agricultural instruction, hygiene, piety, and behavioral management.

Although the CNE's twin 1940 reports targeted rural schooling, the new regime used its educators to cultivate a much grander vision of Bolivia's homogenizing racial future. Indeed, officialist race-thinking was redolent of the assimilationist rhetoric and civilizing sentiments of Bolivia's liberal oligarchy forty years earlier. But the return to the earlier liberalizing-civilizatory paradigm required, first of all, the extirpation of Warisata from the nationalist/indigenista narrative. The reports emphasized one note: Indigenal education was dangerous because it was "creating an Indian Republic within Bolivian nationality, [destroying] any sense of national unity."[29] Such incendiary words only occasionally enlivened Donoso's pedantic reportage, but the fundamental social stakes here involved no less than the future of Bolivian sovereignty and nationality. In the lingering aftermath of the Chaco War, this nationalist fearmongering resonated with statesmen, educators, and intellectuals across the political spectrum. Left activists embraced the new language of class, and they wanted to wash away the residue of colonial racism and Indianness. But for the landed aristocracy, Donoso's warning raised the specter of Indian rebellion and "race war" all over again. To help save Bolivia from that fate, the CNE trumpeted its mission against "racist" indigenistas and "communist" teachers. Instead, the CNE's new pedagogy would ready Bolivian Indians for assimilation into a homogenizing, modernizing national culture. In the meantime, the CNE's inquisition of "corrupt and seditious" educators played out on the public stage.

Dueling Tribunals

Lodged in the middle of Vicente Donoso's April 1940 report (*El estado actual de la educación indigenal*) was a signal that the government's war on Indigenal education was about to escalate. The ministry of government was ordered to establish a tribunal of judges to investigate the "grave irregularities" and impose "disciplinary measures" on the leaders of Indigenal education.[30] Thus began a new phase of the trial, in which the government inquisitors tried to wring exculpatory evidence from the reports and government informants so as to convict the accused. Vicente Donoso was authorized to set up the machinery of this administrative inquiry (*proceso administrativo*). Operating under the pretense of impartiality, he selected the tribunal's judges, furnished the evidence (the results of the 1940 field reports, etc.), issued recommendations to the judges, and then published the results of the tribunal's findings and its damning "verdict" in the later version of the CNE report.[31]

Why, one might wonder, would the Peñaranda regime (newly installed, as of the March 1940 elections) go to the trouble of ordering a tribunal of authorities to perform the same rituals of investigation and critique that Donoso had just enacted in the first 1940 report? Had Donoso's April report not documented in "minute detail" the crimes and heresies of the indigenistas? The new president must have felt compelled to justify the severity of the political reprisals that his regime was about to inflict on the Pérez brothers and their "accomplices."[32] A procedural rationale was also in play: once a guilty verdict was issued, the state could proceed with the *criminal prosecution* of school directors, teachers, and ideologues—a chain that led straight up to the principal "enemies" of the state—in the persons of Elizardo and Raúl Pérez. The political witch hunt that began in January 1940, with Rafael Reyero's directives to expel troublesome rural teachers, now targeted Elizardo, Bolivia's most famous indigenista educator. Behind this façade of judicial procedure and bureaucratic rationalism, then, the state would perform the public rituals of investigation, justice, and propaganda to hunt down its enemies in the field of rural schooling.

In August 1940, the tribunal issued the expected verdict of "guilty." Its final report condemned Indigenal education for becoming the vehicle for radical teachers to preach racial hatred, sow the seeds of race war, and prevent Bolivia from "imposing its patriotic imperative to homogenize the population and create an authentic nationality, a pure *bolivianismo*."[33] The Pérez brothers, in turn, were accused of committing various "heinous crimes"—corruption, despotism, nepotism, exploitation, paternalism, racism, sedition, duplicity, and betrayal.[34] In the end, the significance of the Indian school movement was denounced as a "colonial burden" imposed on the Indian, one more form of servitude disguised as Indian schooling.[35] The tribunal's self-appointed mission, therefore, was to banish Indigenal education (and purge all references to race, ethnicity, and Indianness).

As it turned out, Elizardo Pérez had one last public battle to fight. In July 1940, he finally returned home from Mexico, determined to clear his name of the scurrilous attacks. Even before the tribunal issued its verdict in August of that year, Pérez had decided that the best defense would be a strong counteroffensive. Repudiating the legitimacy of the government tribunal, he refused to appear before judges who had no legal or moral authority to rule over his fate. Thus began a brief legal skirmish to call out the real "scoundrels" and expose the "monstrous falsehoods" that had turned the CNE trial into "a travesty of justice." His irate letters to the press countered the tribunal's fiery rhetoric and criminal charges.[36] In reviling the CNE and its tribunal, Pérez took on the whole edifice of oligarchic neocolonialism: the conservative military regime, the reactionary ruling class, and their racist and exclusionary schemes of governance. His reputation at home and abroad probably saved him. Had the Peñaranda regime been foolish enough to put Pérez in chains, it might well have galvanized a coalition of peasant activists, unionized teachers, leftist organizations, and radical indigenistas in Bolivia and beyond.

But the tectonic plates under Bolivia's political landscape had shifted inalterably during Pérez's monthslong absence in Mexico. With regime change, the political odds were now stacked against the cofounder of the escuela-ayllu, and he had to face down the inquisitors and defend his honor in the public sphere. Decrying the bogus trial, Pérez demanded a fair hearing in a new tribunal, presided over by an impartial judge. For his part, the prodigal teacher promised to abide by the new tribunal's final verdict: "to repent [of my] errors and the harm done to the nation."[37] Uncharacteristically pessimistic, this old warrior seemed to believe that the golden age of insurgent indigeneity and liberatory education was irrevocably over: "Indigenal education is not for this time, [because] the men who fight it, or those who permit its assassination, are men whose mentality belongs to the past. . . . As Bolívar said, 'I have plowed the sea.' This epoch belongs to . . . Donoso Torres and his sycophants, and it is necessary to recognize that fact."[38] This self-designated "liberator of the Bolivian Indian" seemed to be preparing his own retreat into the quietude of scholarship.[39]

Yet before he retired, Elizardo Pérez hoped to restore the family honor and defend his monumental work in Indigenal education.[40] Over the next few weeks, the newly appointed tribunal conducted its own investigations, gathering testimonies about Warisata's history and administration from its ex-directors (Elizardo and Raúl Pérez) and Col. Alfredo Peñaranda (former minister of education under Busch, although no relation to President Peñaranda).[41] In October, the tribunal's counter-verdict came in: complete exoneration of Bolivia's leading lights of Indigenal education. Warisata was restored to a place of honor as the nation's "most noble mission of Indian redemption." Turning the tables, the judges lashed out at Donoso Torres and other conservative educators: the government's truly unpardonable crime, they argued, was to keep this program of Indigenal education in a state of suspension, rather than restore and improve it.[42]

For the moment, Bolivia's postwar generation of radical indigenista teachers and their progressive supporters had triumphed over the oligarchy's assault, and Pérez's honor was vindicated as the country's "great indigenal teacher; this apostle; the equal of Father Las Casas and Viceroy Toledo, of earlier ages!" wrote one effusive newspaper reporter.[43] But such public vindication could not tamp down the growing reactionary threat. Although this public battle was over, the oligarchy's ideological war on Warisata was about to escalate.

The Núcleos Escolares under Siege

By the turn of 1941, Elizardo Pérez and his indigenista allies had been vindicated by the second tribunal, but the bitter truth was that they were losing the larger propaganda and institutional war being waged by the right-wing oligarchy on the national, and even international, front. The state's armory of violent repression, the return of a virulent language of racism, brutal class conflicts in the mines and countryside, ideological schisms in the public sphere, and the growing imperial presence of the United States: all these forces were arrayed against Bolivia's insurgent popular and working-class movements, Indigenous and peasant activism, and the growing potential for radical politics and political alliances to bridge the geo-racial divide between city and country, Indigenous and mestizo laboring classes. With charges of sedition, communism, antiwhite racism, ineptitude, lack of orientation, and/or criminal malfeasance hanging over their heads, Bolivia's indigenista teachers and school activists became a focused target of state violence. The CNE's malevolent attacks on Warisata had opened the floodgates to all manner of pillage and persecution against rural Indigenous schools while providing the institutional rationale for dismantling the old school program, brick by adobe brick.

In this polarizing political climate, and as Donoso's secret tribunal rapidly devolved into raw racism and persecution, state authorities were preparing to turn its propaganda war into a ground operation. A methodical plan to dismantle Warisata (and, by extension, the whole program of Indigenal education) was in the works. First, the state would plant the seeds of chaos and decline, in the words of Carlos Salazar, by "starving Warisata [through economic embargoes], then by [partially] dismantling its operations."[44] As we saw, the reactionary CNE weaponized government policy by underfunding Warisata and the other original communario schools through economic blockades. Once the government's war by attrition was underway, it would send a commission to look into the deteriorated condition of the school, preparing the ground for censuring and even closing the original escuela-ayllu.

The principal target, of course, was Warisata. It was to be a surprise government visitation. One afternoon in late January 1941, a black motorcar carrying two nervous dignitaries from the Ministry of Education pulled into the patio outside Warisata's main pavilion. This inspection tour, which exuded a whiff of the dreaded sixteenth-century colonial visita, stood in stark contrast to the earlier wave of Indigenous and white pilgrims who had traveled to Warisata to pay tribute to the Indian school. Naturally, Warisata's amautas and teachers were alarmed by the arrival of powerful state officials dressed in their dark suits. Upon entering the large courtyard, the two inspectors (none other than Vicente Donoso Torres and Max Bairon) wasted no time in ordering Warisata's amautas to gather in the dining hall, the very space where, for years, this Indigenous "school board" had practiced the arts of self-governance, oratory, democratic assembly, and intellectual exchange. Like naughty schoolchildren, the elders were given a scolding for all the things the inspectors found wanting—the shoddy construction of the school buildings, and even the "audacity" of the amautas and teachers for having dared to build a two-story pavilion instead of a one-story schoolhouse, more "suitable" to the Indian's modest aspirations and humble station in life.[45]

This neocolonial performance was permeated by paternalist and racist contempt. Indeed, it is hard to overemphasize the symbolic violence that this visitation represented to Warisata's governing body of amautas. The very image of the black motorcar carrying hostile inspectors into the school's interior courtyard—the sacrosanct space of communal learning, celebrating, art, and self-governing—was itself an invasive act of transgression. But it was the arrogant tongue-lashing—the instantaneous "tribunal" of white authorities scolding the "inferior" Indian for having presumed they could build and cogovern this ambitious school community—that represented the deepest moral affront.

Years later, the young Tomasa Siñani, who was at her father's side, remembered this traumatic encounter:

We listened with indignation, and everything would have concluded then and there, had my father not been present and raised his voice in protest one last time. You know... that Avelino Siñani always spoke without fear, in ways that corresponded to the founder of the school. We could see him shivering feverishly from cholera, but he faced our enemies and pierced their lies with the bitterest truths, accusing them of Warisata's destruction.... It was the last time that such words were ever spoken by an Indian in that setting....

After the visit, my father had to leave hurriedly, and he was never the same again. A great disturbance seized his spirit, and in the refuge of our hut, he was haunted by memories of his ten years of struggle to maintain the school. The next day, on January 31, 1941, he was sad and debilitated, and at nightfall he called me to his side. The gravity of his words filled me with anguish: "Dear daughter," he said, "the Indians who have permitted the enemy to invade this school will repent when they see our work destroyed and pillaged. All the fruit of our labor will have been in vain, when the thieves and vandals carry away everything—up to the last piece of straw. But those who have come to accuse me will [someday] return to give speeches and put flowers on my grave."[46]

Cast as allegory, and bathed in pathos, Tomasa Siñani's oral memory eventually surfaced in print and various testimonial versions, long after the event happened. Her belated eulogy, later inscribed in Pérez's memoirs, cast Avelino as a martyr who died in the cause of Indian education and justice. It added a deep layer of authenticity to indigenista chronicles and debates about Warisata's manifest destruction at the hands of the oligarchy. Tomasa Siñani de Willka's testimony also secured her father's place of honor in the indigenista pantheon: she identified him as the authentic founder of Warisata (whereas Pérez's chronicle and nationalist historiography have taken pains to establish Avelino Siñani as the Indigenous "cofounder" who worked besides Elizardo Pérez, the Creole indigenista educator, activist, administrator, and ideologue who essentially put Warisata on the national map).

Avelino Siñani's death on January 31, 1941, cast a pall over the escuela-ayllu. The state's slander, threats, and economic embargo were powerful weapons, but with its founding amauta felled by fever, insult, and shock, how much longer could Warisata—the school, the symbol, the mecca of Indian education and emancipation—survive? For the moment, Avelino's sudden death went almost unnoticed outside the tight circle of Warisata students, teachers, padres de familia, a few trade union leaders, and some activists on the left. And the primordial role that Avelino had played in the origin of the escuela-ayllu would take a long time to surface—but surface it would, thanks to the lifelong activism and commemoration carried out by Pérez, Tomasa Siñani, Carlos Salazar, and a few other members of the original escuela-ayllu.[47] Oral tradition also encapsulated Warisata's brutal end. In many rural communities in Omasuyos, the inspectors' 1941 visitation was remembered as a symbolic act of war: "We had received the [visitors] in our parlamento, and there they told us that everything we had done was bad; that they had come to save us and make our work better. We were confused . . . and so the days, months, and years passed. How bitter we were to realize that their promise was converted into the destruction of our obra."[48]

The official visit to Warisata was but the dramatic beginning of a multifaceted *institutional assault* on the administration, curriculum, and integrity of the school community over the next three years. First, there were purges and persecution of Warisata's indigenista teachers. They were accused of being "imposters" who brandished the title of "teacher-defender of the Indian" (*maestro defensor del indio*). The last of Warisata's champions, including Carlos Salazar, Manuel Fuentes Lira, González Bravo, and Ana Pérez (Raúl's daughter), were expelled from Warisata in 1940 and 1941. To replace them, the CNE planned to recruit only loyalists, preferably teachers trained in a normal school, who were directly subordinate to the CNE's high command.[49]

The Indigenous parliament was next on the chopping block. The state's 1940 tribunal had pronounced the Indian incapable of self-governance. The council of amautas was mocked as "a decorative organization of 'amautas' who . . . have never fulfilled any responsible function, except to stir up certain racist passions."[50] The assembly—a sacred symbolic, political, and oratorical space of Indigenous self-representation—now had to be colonized by the civilizers, and so the 1941 inspectors finished the job by abolishing that autonomous council of self-governance.

Finally, the CNE revised the school curriculum, not just for Warisata but for all the rural núcleos escolares. The new regime would strive to introduce a strict agro-pastoral (vocational) curriculum, "fit" for Bolivia's natural farming class, much as Georges Rouma had advocated thirty years earlier. However, the CNE narrowed the scope of Rouma's earlier "farm-school" curriculum or Pérez's integrated curriculum. The teaching of rustic crafts, for example, was now forbidden. Specifically, Warisata's ceramics and weaving workshops were deemed "inappropriate" because they fostered social mobility and spurred the out-migration of newly skilled artisans (needed in the fields). Along with shuttering Warisata's artisan workshops, the CNE temporarily closed down Warisata's normal school. No need for teacher training in an institution tainted by an "exotic pedagogy" and socialist ideals.

Although the state probably did not intend this result, its hostility gave license to local vandalism and other forms of physical violence. Hair-raising stories told how vigilante groups and common thieves preyed on Warisata and many outlying sectional schools. In 1942, for instance, a mounted posse of armed vecinos from Combaya (province of Larecaja) stormed the peasant village of Milliraya, brandishing weapons and spraying bullets into the air, trampling the cornfields, and seizing livestock. Their motive was to appease the local landlord by intimidating villagers and destroying the village's new school. That, in any event, was how the Indian petitioners explained the bandits' motives: "They don't want our school to progress; whatever advance we make provokes their reaction."[51] Another report chronicled a carefully staged operation: the small village school of Pongohuyo, once a sectional school under Warisata's jurisdiction, was constantly harassed by neighboring landlords, but eventually they turned to local authorities to execute an attack. During the days of fiesta, police invaded the school grounds and hauled off three students, all members of a nearby comunidad. The youth were blacklisted by a local landowner (working through the police) for having assaulted some of the landlord's colono tenants (or perhaps for having urged the colonos to send their children to the local school).

News of deprivation and violence against Warisata, in particular, flooded newspaper columns and government reports. In early 1944, an agronomy teacher reported on the chronic "abnormalities and deficiencies" that had made it quite impossible for him to raise the next generation of modern field hands. Ravages of drought made things worse, but Warisata's most serious problems reflected three years of chronic scarcity and the ongoing problem of petty theft and pillage. Despite government promises, Warisata still had no modern farming equipment or functioning agricultural extension fields. Its stock of seeds was rotting, its herds of farm and draft animals were dwindling, and its outbuildings were in terrible disrepair.[52] A few weeks later, the CNE received another alarming report that showed Warisata to be in dire economic straits, unable to meet the payroll of its day laborers, purchase basic supplies, or invest in farm tools.[53] Warisata's sectional schools were vulnerable to the state's institutional neglect as well, for, once broken, the reciprocal bonds that had kept the satellite schools rotating within the regional orbit of the "solar" school center began to fray and disintegrate. Some village primary schools may have blinked out; others were cast off as tiny "unitary" schools—more isolated and vulnerable to gamonal violence. Still other village schools cropped up, having been planted by rural communities, or rural labor organizers, in the wake of the núcleo escolar collapse.

But this diffuse political landscape could not hide the overriding fact that the oligarchic state was presiding over the dramatic unraveling of the original núcleo escolar, including its sprawling web of outlying primary schools. A 1944 government report painted a bleak picture of this unraveling: some two-thirds (thirty-one) of Warisata's satellite schools had fallen into a state of anarchy or decay by that year. The presumed culprit, according to the CNE: Bolivia's legion of rustic, untrained, lazy, drunken, and/or incompetent rural teachers—compounded by the chronic racial condition of "peasant apathy."[54] The state's proclaimed effort to salvage rural schooling and to save the nation from "race war" had gradually destroyed the fragile network of nuclear schools while establishing a new top-down regime of administrative control over rural education. Meanwhile, in a shocking display of hypocrisy, the CNE's Vocalía de Educación Rural office set up a government program for aggrieved peasants to register their complaints about the abuses and deprivations that plagued rural life.

While Warisata garnered most public attention, other núcleos escolares were sucked into this wider ground war. Some schools were crunched in the CNE's centralizing bureaucratic machinery; others were dismantled, disaggregated, or relocated to places the government deemed more suitable or manageable. Still other núcleos escolares succumbed to state aggression, becoming micro-battlegrounds in the ongoing war that raged in the political sphere over the parameters and goals of Indigenous education and the racial fate of the Bolivian nation. The long-simmering núcleo escolar of Caiza erupted in a pitched battle in early 1940, to take but one example. Once the state's propaganda war began in earnest, Caiza—like its more famous counterpart, Warisata—became the poster child for all the crimes and misdemeanors ("criminal disorganization," "intrigue," teachers' "promiscuity," etc.) conjured up as pretexts for the CNE's impending seizure.[55] This official narrative, disseminated widely through government rhetoric, acts of symbolic violence, and print capitalism, went a long way toward reinvigorating a racist-colonial discourse that deflected the blame for Indian poverty and illiteracy, and for the decline of communitarian schools, onto the Indigenous and indigenista victims of state repression.

Guerrilla Schoolteachers

As the state proceeded to dismantle Indigenal education, an ersatz guerrilla operation surfaced in the Quechua-speaking region of Caiza, located some sixty kilometers from the old silver-mining town of Potosí. Fleeing the besieged Warisata, a small group of teachers took refuge there. The veteran teacher-activist Carlos Salazar led the way, on a mission to protect the original núcleo escolar project that had flourished under the direction of Raúl Pérez.[56] Upon arrival, he was shocked to find a school in rack and ruin; a cabal of hostile vecinos occupied the main schoolhouse. Driven into the countryside, Salazar spent five months organizing schools in the outlying Quechua-speaking villages.[57] He worked with local work parties to restore the fields and gardens, walls, and schoolrooms of rural Caiza. But by then Salazar was a marked man, and rural villagers were warned not to support this "rogue" and "dangerous" teacher. The núcleo escolar of Caiza, the CNE report warned, was being "converted into a revolutionary *foco* of dangerous agitation," and it ordered the expulsion of Salazar and his "cabal" of teachers and students.[58] They would not be banished quite so easily, however (see fig. 4.2).

It is perhaps difficult to imagine that this local tussle over school authority would trigger a wave of regional violence, blown all out of proportion to the supposed crime. But local incidents of racial or class defiance could easily trigger a political backlash, which in turn could set off a chain reaction of agrarian uprisings and government repression. Salazar's open defiance, and the seeds of "indiscipline" he was sowing in the Quechua communities, was viewed by provincial authorities as a naked act of sedition that "threatened the nation."[59] Shortly after the comptroller of Potosí sent an apocalyptic message about Bolivia's impending race war and warnings proliferated about the school's "revolutionary tendency," the government dispatched a new commission to investigate the trouble. Meanwhile, Salazar's cabal of teachers vanished into internal exile, while the CNE triumphantly installed the new school director. Rest assured, the new administrator told his superiors in La Paz: Caiza would no longer constitute "a kind of republic" of Indians carving out their own "patria in the ongoing war between the races."[60]

Uprooted and expelled from Caiza, Carlos Salazar eventually returned to the city of La Paz, where he embarked on a lifelong struggle to rescue and redeem the integrity of the núcleo school system and the public memory of Warisata. Over the years, Salazar became a prodigious public intellectual,

FIGURE 4.2. Carlos Salazar (*kneeling, fifth from the left*) poses with the normal students of Caiza D, shortly after he arrived there in 1940. Having fled Warisata, Salazar hoped to save the communitarian school. Salazar Mostajo, *Gesta y fotografía*, photo no. 326.

teacher, and artist, whose creative work combined visual imagery (painting, sketches, photography, etc.); written verse, novels, short stories, and autobiography; journalistic reports, news articles, and polemical debate; public testimonio; and studies in ethnography, pedagogy, and philosophy. But it was the crucible of violence in the field during the early 1940s that catalyzed his indefatigable career as warrior artist, teacher, and activist. Salazar operated almost as a one-man "truth commission," engaged in the dangerous work of unmasking the immoral and criminal acts of the "feudal bourgeois" elites while trying to rescue the true legacy of Warisata in the longer struggle for Indian justice and schooling.[61] In 1943 he launched his first literary grenade in the pages of *La Calle*. The first lines of his famous cri de coeur, "Warisata mía," set a combative yet plaintive tone: "The immense and prolonged fight has ended," he wrote dolefully, after having been driven into hiding and watching Warisata disintegrate under government siege. "I write this page, while the assassins dance around the still-warm corpse of my school.... Warisata cannot succumb without fighting, and here it falls, fighting. Because Warisata survives, not in the fancy places where malice lies, but in my own spirit and that of my few comrades.... Yes, I have [called Warisata] 'my school,' because today I am the last soldier of this lost cause."[62]

In fact, Salazar was not "the last soldier." The oligarchic state clearly was winning the institutional war, and its systemic demolition of Indigenal education was well underway by 1943. What Salazar's eloquent allegory signaled, however, was that the *symbolic struggle* over the meaning, memory, and legacy of Warisata was only just beginning (a theme reprised in the epilogue of this book). His passionate newspaper articles and essays would later catapult him into the unassailable ranks of Bolivia's heroic indigenista teacher/activists who had borne witness to, and participated in, the construction of the original escuela-ayllu. Throughout the late 1930s and early 1940s, Bolivia's radical youth debated the potentially revolutionary role that popular education, trade unions, and mass peasant organizing might play in the building of a militant peasant-worker coalition. As the tide turned against Indigenal education, Salazar (and later generations of radical teachers and activists) wondered aloud how they might revindicate the "lost cause" of Indigenous education by forging it into a potent tool of militant consciousness-raising and grassroots organizing. How might the longtime local struggles for lands, schools, and justice be hammered into a platform for social revolution and interclass coalition? In the early 1940s, these questions hung heavily over the heads and hearts of activist-teachers like Carlos Salazar, Alipio Valencia, Anita Pérez, and others being driven into self-exile or prison. Yet, as we shall see in chapter 5, that radicalizing process was already beginning to unfold in peasant villages and haciendas throughout the restive countryside.

Meanwhile, Warisata had generated a small but loyal group of Indigenous teachers who operated as the rank and file of the resistance movement, flooding the CNE with petitions expressing their outrage against gamonal forms of violence. One illustrative case is that of Juan Añawaya Poma, a Warisata alumnus who was a writer and rural teacher and had once been a prominent member of Warisata's parliament of amautas (see fig. 4.3). His formal schooling, and the lived experience of the political siege, had fortified his own "revolutionary consciousness." He sent letters of protest against military conscription (calling the barracks "the antechamber of prison"), and in a 1944 letter to the CNE, he called out the upsurge of violent crimes perpetrated by Bolivia's gamonal class against the Indigenous peasantry. Picking up the anticolonialist trope of earlier Indigenous protesters, this veteran of Warisata pinned the social cause of Indian illiteracy and ignorance not on "peasant apathy" but on the "criminal hatred that the masters of the land feel about the 'School of the Indian,' and [about] all Indians who receive the benefits of civilization, because they will no longer be the slaves or pariahs of those *señores latifundistas*."[63] Soon thereafter, Añawaya Poma was banished and his school was condemned on the official pretext that it was failing, supposedly due to a lack of students. It was reported that too many families were colonos, and therefore too burdened by their fieldwork to be willing to send their own children to the local elementary school. Accordingly, the CNE recommended that Añawaya Poma be transferred to somewhere else, although no mention was made as to where that might be.[64]

Rural teachers like Añawaya Poma were on the front lines of the oligarchy's internal war against Indigenous education, but they found potential support among a small group of radicalized youth—men like Salazar who had come of political age during the heyday of Indigenal education and grew more militant as they bore witness to the government's frontal attack on striking peasants and tin miners in the 1940s. Pouring gasoline on the embers, the oligarchy's brutal assault on peasants, miners, and middle-class dissidents inflamed Bolivia's alienated postwar generation. Its assault on Warisata was the last straw. Mobilizing revolutionary solidarity would prove difficult in those years, however. Not only did populist reformers and revolutionary activists turn against each other, but the revolutionary youth was also highly fractured. Salazar and many other radical indigenista teachers, for example, felt a strong aversion to the tenets of doctrinaire Marxism and its vanguardist approach to political orthodoxy and education under the party leadership. Eventually, Salazar openly repudiated the rigid strictures of Leninism and Stalinism and instead turned for inspiration to the Trotskyist ideal of permanent revolution and international solidarity work. During Salazar's study abroad in Mexico in 1937–38, he had come in contact with the writings of Leon Trotsky, the studious revolutionary scholar living in exile in Mexico at the time (until he was murdered in August 1940 by a local Stalinist wielding an ice pick). Trotskyism held great appeal for Carlos Salazar, and the old man himself had evinced great interest in the Warisata school when the young Salazar was visiting Mexico.[65] These swirling ideas and experiences, at home and abroad, forged Salazar's character and turned him into a tireless advocate for Indigenous justice and socialist transformation.

FIGURE 4.3. Juan Añawaya Poma, in 1940. An alumnus of Warisata, he also served on the parlamento de amautas. As a rural teacher, writer, and activist, he was persecuted by state authorities for spreading "dangerous" ideas. Salazar Mostajo, *Gesta y fotografía*, photo no. 47.

But an underlying tension suffused Salazar's struggle for political self-education. On the one hand, he believed fervently in the Trotskyist doctrine of continuous revolutionary struggle as the pathway to Indian emancipation (and toward socialism). On the other, inspired by the writings of the Peruvian Marxist José Carlos Mariátegui and the Bolivian activist and writer Tristan Marof, Salazar praised the escuela-ayllu as an Andean socialist project that was liberating the Indian through schooling, one pupil at a time. That is, the insurgent ayllu school *would have done so*, he believed, had the oligarchic wolves not been gathering at Warisata's gates all during the late 1930s. Thus, Salazar was caught on the horns of an ideological dilemma: while he defended the emancipatory indigenista ideals that the original Warisata symbolized, he had to confront the harsh reality that Bolivia's neocolonial conditions (specifically, Bolivia's feudal-agrarian regime on the Altiplano) had doomed the communitarian school project in the first place. Caught between the soaring hope of his own idealism and the bleak material reality he encountered on the ground, the young Salazar was thrust into the vortex of revolutionary political debate that would trouble Bolivian leftists over the next many years. But he never abandoned his lifelong mission of restoring Warisata's place of honor in the national narrative.[66]

Hay que mestizarnos: The Return of the Civilizers

The state's assault on Indigenal education left an institutional void that urgently needed to be filled. A cadre of statesmen—Gustavo Adolfo Otero (education minister); Vicente Donoso Torres (head of the Consejo Nacional de Educación); Rafael Reyeros (Departamento de Educación Rural); and Max Bairon (in charge of Bolivia's nascent "Cultural Brigade" program)—worked intensively over four years (1940–44) to forge a network of state-supervised ("fiscal") primary and secondary schools that spread "universal civilization" into the countryside.[67] The stakes, Otero reminded his colleagues, could not be higher: what we do with the Indian, he warned, will determine the "future of Bolivia."[68] Culture and civilization, no longer an adornment of Bolivia's urban letrado elites, would become the driving force, and the racial measure, of Bolivia's progress toward a unifying mestizo nationality and patriotic consciousness of *bolivianidad*. Otero believed that "our only objective [is] to forge the fatherland [*hacer patria*] ... to unify the will of all Bolivians ... their same ideals, identical aspirations, and analogous virtues, whose harmonious vitality forms the national soul."[69]

Behind those exalted nationalist ideals lurked a daunting set of institutional questions. Now that the oligarchy was intent on tearing down Warisata and other "renegade" communitarian school centers, how would they go about building a new kind of educational establishment for the Indian? What kind of national curriculum would generate a transracial "harmony of wills"? How might the power of scientific pedagogy accelerate the civilizing process, especially in those regions where "the Indian [had] not yet evolved in his customs, dress, language or culture" since the Spanish Conquest?[70] In short, how would the CNE rebuild a program of Indigenous schooling on the ruins of the old one?

On the level of racial ideology, the official answer was buried in the voluminous paperwork generated by Vicente Donoso's two devastating appraisals of the núcleo schools and the guilty verdict handed down by the handpicked tribunal of judges who sat in judgment of Warisata. The educators' "patriotic imperative," one of the 1940 reports proclaimed, was "to homogenize the population, to create a true nationality, a pure *Bolivianismo*, encouraged by similar ideals and sentiments."[71] In August 1940, the state's panel of jurists reinforced the conservatives' pro-mestizaje project: Bolivia's ethnic goal "will be el mestizaje and not the formation of racial groups, with their own languages, and without nationalist spirit, but only separated by hateful rivalries and mutual incomprehension."[72] "To forge the fatherland," proclaimed Donoso, "we have to become racially mixed [*mestizarnos*]."[73] A spiritualist paean to the patria by the new minister of education, Gustavo Adolfo Otero, also projected a strong assimilationist project. In his 1941 essay "Una política educacional," Otero called for education, immigration, and eugenic policies that would promote the process of de-Indianization through "ethnic symbiosis," and eventually through racial "miscegenation."[74] Furthermore, and this point was crucial: any program of racial assimilation must effect *gradual* socio-racial change, lest Bolivia become overwhelmed by a massive, semi-acculturated cholo population clamoring for suffrage and other civil rights. Donoso reminded his reader about Bolivia's "special problem"—"the racial majority" was neither white nor mestizo, but predominantly Indigenous. So the racial logics of whitening that made sense in the nation of Argentina and even Brazil—that is, absorbing "inferior" nonwhite races into the rapidly expanding population of white immigrants—was evolutionarily untenable for the Bolivian Andes. Its racial demographic skewed brown, and the prospect of massive European immigration had never materialized. Thus, Bolivia's "racial progress," it was reasoned, could easily go into evolutionary reverse if "the decadent culture of the aboriginal" were allowed to prevail.[75]

Two racial axioms—the civilizers' message (that "the endpoint of the Indian [race] in Bolivia must become el mestizaje") and the autochthonists' pragmatic/telluric trope (the presumption that, by nature, Indians' destiny was to work the land and feed the nation)—reinforced the official warning against the inherent dangers of popular enfranchisement and Indigenous citizenship to Bolivia's fragile social order. The belief that the Indian was temporally and culturally unfit for citizenship rights continued to frame the tutelary race-thinking of Bolivia's ruling elite well into the 1940s. Expanding suffrage was out of the question, at least until the assimilationist state had done its eugenic and cultural spadework. On this point, Donoso was emphatic: "We underline the need [of an individual or a race] to obtain a certain [level of] culture to understand and practice liberty. Because, among us Bolivians, *democracy is still far from being a reality*, given the great masses of illiterates (75 percent of the population) represented by the Indian and the mestizo."[76] Yet even if Bolivia's democracy was a distant dream, the educators believed they were caught in a pernicious race between education and revolution. In 1946, Donoso captured the nation's existential political dilemma: either Bolivia's elites must engineer "*a peaceful evolution*" or the country would be engulfed by "*a social revolution of the masses*."[77] No revolutionary agenda, no radical agrarian reform, and no opening of Bolivia's electoral system to the rural masses, he argued, would solve the Indian problem or eradicate the country's massive problem of rural poverty. Pushing against the mobilizing forces on the left, Donoso proclaimed that a government program of agrarian reform must be postponed: "It is not enough to dictate a law altering the feudal landholding regime, if the Indians are not prepared to enter the new property regime because of their ignorance, lack of initiative, and scarcity of resources."[78]

Thus did this tutelary paternalist, Bolivia's leading educational reformer between 1940 and 1944, emerge as Bolivia's primary ideologue of "racial progress" through the bio-cultural workings of "peaceful evolution." Donoso Torres's brand of cultural racism fashioned the ideal of cultural homogenization and harmony into a reactionary, anti-Indian project. The right-wing meaning of civilization, although now rebranded as mestizaje, aimed at *preempting*—not emulating—a Mexican-style revolutionary project (and particularly, its program of agrarian reform). Bolivia's reactionary elites would mobilize the tools of "soft eugenics" (to borrow Nancy Stepan's term) to engineer assimilation, viewed as the bio-cultural prerequisite for the expansion of citizenship rights.[79] Astute educational policy, he believed, could control the pace of cultural change and evolutionary outcomes, as long as it recognized the existence of "a hierarchy of difference in the level of intelligence, work, and aspiration" among individuals and races.[80]

Beneath the thin nationalist veneer of mestizaje, this oligarchy's neo-civilizing project had an uncanny resemblance to tutelary race-thinking of the early twentieth century (see chapter 1). Like their intellectual forebears, Bolivian intellectuals in the 1940s dabbled in the disciplines of anthropology, sociology, and psychology to buttress their diagnoses and prescriptions regarding the Indian problem. They trafficked in both biological and cultural determinisms, usually muddying the conceptual boundary between them. But strict doctrines of genetic determinism had no place in this strand of tutelary race-thinking (just as the currency of biological racism was dropping on the Western marketplace of ideas in the aftermath of World War II). Rather, Bolivian social reformers emphasized the enduring yet malleable role that culture, habit, and social environment played in explaining diversity and rationalizing inequality. Now, as in earlier decades, the racialized politics of culture provided a pseudoscientific scheme for rank-ordering Bolivia's regions, races, and ethnicities while leaving open the possibility of de-Indianizing the rural population through eugenic and educational policies. In his 1946 study, Vicente Donoso cautioned against noxious notions of "biology as destiny," yet he also reframed the fixity of racial hierarchy as a manifestation of man's place on the evolutionary scale.[81] The new "anthropological sciences," he pontificated, "teach us that there are no superior or inferior races and that [a race's] state of civilization and culture depends on the historical moment of its evolution, and on the favorable and deleterious influences in the physical environment." Biology, history, and the environment were the intermingled determinants of bio-cultural backwardness, he believed. But there was hope for swift progress: "Above all, education is the great force that elevates the cultural level of men and of a people."[82] On that point, Donoso still harped on education's ameliorative powers, and exhorted his public to promote rural schooling so as to quicken the assimilation of the Indian into a new mestizo Bolivia.[83]

Yet, like Franz Tamayo and the telluric indigenistas of yesteryear, this pedagogue pointed to select "racial virtues" that were worth preserving—either because they fortified the physiology of the Aymara as uniquely adapted to high-altitude agriculture, or because they lent folkloric authenticity to the national culture. Donoso's version of the essential Indian once again highlighted the Indian's "spirit of work, tenacity, love of fresh air, the discipline of daily life governed by the arc of the sun, his chastity, sobriety and lean diet, patience, and his boundedness to kinship, community, and the land."[84] By the 1940s, this essentialist profile of the Aymara had become a truism. Just as the foundational generation of indigenistas had proclaimed the Indian "irreplaceable" around 1920, so now did this new generation of neocolonial educators and letrados remind their readers that Bolivia's haciendas and ranches depended heavily on maintaining and upgrading the rural Indian workforce. The perpetuation of feudalistic forms of highland Indian exploitation rested on this bio-cultural premise. "What would Bolivia become if its Indians disappeared? Who would replace them as laborers in agriculture and the mines? What other races would adapt to the harsh climates of the

Altiplano or the ardent lands in the jungle?"[85] These rhetorical questions reverberated in the oligarchy's echo chamber and bridged partisan and ideological boundaries. Both leftist and conservative reformers subscribed to this incipient hegemonic mestizo doctrine, but they also insisted on anchoring the Indian in the rural Andean milieu. This contradictory impulse was captured by the indigenista writer Rafael Reyeros. A leftist admirer of Mexico's ideal of agrarianism and bio-cultural mestizaje, he called for a Bolivian national pedagogy that would simultaneously assimilate and rehabilitate the Indian by fashioning a hispanized campesino to fulfill his destiny as the nation's primordial agriculturalist.[86]

During the 1940s, then, a new cabal of pedagogic race-thinkers spanning the political spectrum, from right (Bairon and Finot) and moderate (Donoso Torres) to left (Reyeros), reworked the practical meanings of racial inequality and mestizaje to advance an "evolutionist" project that would eventually yield a nation of Spanish-speaking mestizos and whites, without disrupting the brittle agrarian order or unleashing migratory streams of would-be cholos into the city. As in other contexts, so here too: the malleable polysemic notion of mestizaje was a deep semantic reservoir from which multiple racial meanings and symbols, discourses and agendas, could be assembled for a variety of political and social engineering projects.[87] For the CNE officials trying to navigate a middle course toward national cohesion and harmony, the paradigm of cultural mestizaje offered an exit ramp from the dangers of radical indigenismo and educated Indians, capable of asserting their own revindicative agendas of sociocultural rights and citizenship.

Thus, the oligarchy's fractured discourse of mestizaje-cum-assimilation was inevitably filled with contradictions and discontinuities. To begin with, there was the conservative assault on the ideals and tenets of Indigenal education, a putative source of pro-Indian radicalism and antiwhite racism. That false premise was compounded by a recycled version of the civilizers' discourse, wrapped in a neo-Spencerian language of social evolution. Meanwhile, Reyeros and his colleagues envisioned a nationalist project of mestizaje as the answer to the country's so-called Indian problem—rural poverty and the race's putative evolutionary stagnation. Evidently, not much had changed since the early 1900s, according to this reconstructed matrix of race, nation, and education in the conservative elite imaginary. Various insurgent projects emanating from the Aymara-driven ethnic movement of the 1920s (including Eduardo

Nina Quispe's visionary discourse on Indian rights, the restitution of the commune, and the moral-cultural "renovation" of Bolivia) were not only long forgotten but were also virtually "unthinkable" in the early 1940s.[88] By then, the oligarchy was engaged in a multifaceted project of distortion and erasure. Its ideological and institutional war on Warisata was, at base, a neocolonial project to erase the true, albeit complex, significance of the ayllu-school from the national narrative. The tired trope of Indian backwardness had regained currency among this neocivilizing vanguard as it tried to mount a new set of pedagogic and policy interventions in rural La Paz. And as rural unrest flared, the timeworn "threat of race war" still served to rationalize government acts of military repression against rural disobedience, in particular the spread of agrarian labor strikes. In sum, Bolivia's recycled tutelary race-thinking still rationalized educative state policies of racial discrimination and structural inequality, on the one hand, and legitimated the civilizers' neocolonial trajectory of racial assimilation, on the other.

But the fervor of the neocolonial oligarchy reflected its collective sense of fear and precarious contingency as the sociopolitical ground began to shift under its feet. The scandal over Warisata was soon buried in the mass of alarming news about Bolivia's restive laboring and peasant classes. Newspapers blasted alarming reports about chronic labor shortages, rampant peasant itinerancy, organized peasant strikes on haciendas, and the infiltration of rural society by agents of radical leftist parties and trade unionism. The Catavi tin miners and their wives temporarily closed down that industrial pit before they were mowed down by government soldiers in late 1942. Meanwhile, that same year, the shocking outbreak of coordinated peasant colono sit-down strikes (called *huelgas de brazos caídos*, or "strikes of the fallen arms") cast shadows of fear and doubt across the oligarchy's program of Indian assimilation through rural education reform. And as it turned out, the oligarchy's assault on Warisata had only enflamed the Aymara countryside.

5

Instigators of New Ideas
Peasant Pedagogies of Praxis

The Indian is not capable of [stirring up] the countryside, nor is the miner responsible for the present situation. Who is? The instigator of movements, the revolutionary propagandist, the agitator of the peasant and laboring masses ... [men who are] not deterred for one moment by the grave consequences of their satanic labor.
—A. JÁUREGUI, "Reflexiones sobre la cuestión indígena"

In 1947, a troubling essay appeared on the pages of Sucre's Geographic Society magazine, warning its readers that Chuquisaca's once-tranquil countryside was aflame.[1] Casting himself as a telluric indigenista and benign paternalist, the author, A. Jáuregui, was quick to absolve the Indian. A passive peón bound to the hacienda, Jáuregui's "indio" was congenitally incapable of political agency, but all too susceptible to "ruinous vengeance" if provoked by outside agitators. "Beware!" he warned his readers: the Bolivian countryside was being infiltrated by roving labor and peasant organizers. Hardened by their experiences as soldiers, deserters, or political prisoners during the Chaco War years, those itinerant "troublemakers" would never again return to the tedium of servile labor on the hacienda or submit to random acts of racial violence. Warily, Jáuregui observed that a new type of "political agitator" (variously identified as "the instigator of movements," "the revolutionary propagandist," "the agitator of the peasant masses and laboring groups," or the "instigator of new ideas") was a lettered, and possibly even formally schooled, Indian (or a mestizo "disguised as an Indian") who was seeding the countryside with "seditious ideas" and "incendiary literature" for the purpose of inciting race war, labor unrest, and rural rebellion.

Read in hindsight, Jáuregui's apocalyptic warnings in the 1947 Geographic Society article would seem to presage the oligarchy's imminent collapse. Indeed, the rising threat of Indigenous and popular insurgency in Bolivia's cities, mines, and countryside during the 1940s was real enough, coming largely in response "to active pressures from below that had accumulated since the era of the Chaco war."[2] New political coalitions had crystallized, sometimes bringing groups of Aymara and Quechua peasants into alignment with the radical agendas of mining proletarians and dissident middle-class elements. In turn, Bolivia's militant labor unions and the left depended on the solidarity of peasant laborers in their growing offensive against the feudal bourgeoisie. Thus, by the late 1930s and 1940s, the "Indian question" had become a potent rallying cry for labor organizers, radical indigenistas, and leftist political parties, increasingly anxious to broaden their base of rural solidarity. In the 1939 congress of the Sindicato de Trabajadores Bolivianos, for example, delegates of working-class people (factory and railroad workers, miners and artisans, printers and schoolteachers, students and intellectuals, etc.) endorsed a platform of Indian labor rights and called on rural teachers and trade unionists to begin organizing peasant unions. An easy target of socialist parties was the perverse serf-like institution of *el pongueaje*, which required peones (both men and women) to perform unpaid labor services for their landlords on a regular basis, and render obligatory turns of corvée labor on public works (roads, irrigation ditches, mail carriage, etc.) for provincial authorities. Although long in decline, bonded forms of labor survived on many haciendas, rendering the image of the *indio pongo*—stooped under a huge pile of firewood, or hauling a jug of chichi to the landlord's city townhouse—as the noxious symbol of colonial slavery and oppression. Labor unions and the left called for "the abolition of Indian slavery" through piecemeal legislative reforms in the early 1940s; but the escalation of left/agrarian activism over the decade transformed that safe reformist slogan into a piercing revolutionary cry for Indian liberation from servitude, the breakup of the feudal hacienda, and overthrow of the old agrarian order.³

In this scenario, the older Liberal campaign for Indian education (disparaged by the Marxist left as merely ameliorative) seemed to play no essential role other than to camouflage the systemic nature of class oppression and defer the need for social revolution. Even the postwar generation of radical indigenista teachers, many of the men and women who had devoted their youth to working in the núcleos escolares, now pinned their hopes on social revolution. Nothing less than the overthrow of the ancien régime would unyoke the Indian from slavery and ignorance. Reading the work of the Peruvian indigenista and communist José Carlos Mariátegui, Bolivia's radicalized young teachers and intellectuals fastened on an axiom of historical materialism. "The problem of the Indian," Mariátegui had famously proclaimed, "is rooted in the land tenure system of our economy. Any attempt to solve it with administrative or policy measures, through education or by a road-building program, is superficial and secondary as long as the feudalism of the gamonales continues to exist.... Educators, I repeat, can *least* afford to ignore economic and social reality!"⁴ In Bolivia, this painful truth was playing out in real time on the Bolivian Altiplano as the feudal oligarchy laid siege to Warisata and other Indigenous schools beginning around 1940. Pedagogies of Indian liberation, proclaimed the young Marxists, were nothing but quixotic crusades against the structural determinants of class oppression and oligarchic violence. Or so it would seem in the wake of Warisata's destruction.

How, then, does the "problematic of Indigenous education" fit into this conjuncture of escalating rural unrest, peasant political organizing, and the deepening antagonism that set Bolivia's militant left (the dissident youth of the Chaco era) on a collision course with the repressive oligarchic state during the mid- to late 1940s? This chapter maps this wider terrain of organized peasant politics, which pried open microspaces for insurgent forms of literacy, critical political awareness, and citizenship practices to flourish in many highland regions.⁵ Although the rural school was often deployed, in consort with unions, as an organizing tool on haciendas, and while rural communities continued to lobby the government for schools, it was the broader conjuncture of rural syndicalism and the rise of peasant "pedagogies of praxis" (as I call it) that opened a new grassroots enterprise of political organizing, consciousness-raising, and insurgent citizenship practices—an organic form of popular education that animated a militant campesino movement among Aymara- and Quechua-speaking people in the regions of La Paz and Cochabamba, respectively.

In many ways, rural Bolivia offers a textbook case of the cultural entanglements of politics, knowledge, and popular education that reshaped Indigenous understandings of the nature of their own racial and class oppression. In the process, rural people expanded their repertoires of social protest (peasant strike actions, roadblocks, peasant congresses, worker-peasant confederations, networks of itinerant labor organizers, and fiery oratory and mass propaganda) and coalesced around radical political agendas that, taken together, threatened to overturn the neocolonial order of caste. The ubiquitous peasant assembly of the 1940s, more than the cacique archive of the 1920s, became the site of insurgent literacy and knowledge practices. While Bolivia's white lettered elites had once detested the spread of literacy, lawsuits, and suffrage among litigious caciques-apoderados or the semi-acculturated cholo plebe, now Jáuregui's postwar generation feared the specter of roving bands of peasant "agitators" carrying incendiary literature that urged "enslaved" peones to rise up against their masters.

Eventually, this cumulative social power of agrarian activism and strategic peasant innovation in the political sphere would produce an acute crisis of political hegemony. In its final sections, this chapter explores the reentry of the military populist state into this arena of rural mobilization for agrarian justice—namely, the right to land, labor rights, and basic education. Under the ephemeral rule of Col. Gualberto Villarroel (December 1943 to July 1946), grassroots political organizing and socialization culminated in the 1945 National Indian Congress. Briefly, I revisit that extraordinary moment of "contested hegemony"—in which a thousand Indian delegates brought their hopes and grievances to the proverbial table, in what became (as it later turned out) the last chance for populist redemption and interethnic compromise. Notwithstanding its political implosion, the 1945 Indian Congress may be read as a vivid display of Indigenous political knowledge, popular citizenship practices, and collective self-determination that converged on this ephemeral mass assembly as the delegates tried to insert the country's Indigenous majority into the national narrative under the banner of an inclusive and decolonizing nation-state.

The dramatic explosion of campesino politics on the national stage tends to submerge the older Aymara movement of caciques in the nationalist telos of revolutionary agrarian politics. Yet, as several historians have chronicled, the cacique movement did not wither away; it survived, resurfaced, and adapted its political rhetoric and strategies to meet the political threats and openings of the post-Chaco era. Some rural authorities (caciques, apoderados, alcaldes, teachers) continued to dabble in legal documents, seeking to restore their communal heritage, even while framing their demands in the fiery language of class oppression. Others resorted to older discursive tactics, invoking ancient lineages, colonial title deeds, nativist rituals, and ethnic identity to petition Bolivia's new political regime for the rights to communal lands, elementary schools, protection, and justice—just as their forebears had once done. This chapter begins therefore by exploring several offstage sites of everyday Indigenous activism that surfaced in the regions of La Paz and Oruro during the postwar era, for as we shall see, the cultural politics of indigeneity were overshadowed, but never swept away, by the bravado of rural syndicalism and peasant mobilizations. To bring the politics of indigeneity out of the proverbial shadows, it is worth pausing here to track the paper trail of several Aymara alcaldes and caciques on their quixotic mission to mobilize the nation's Indian population—almost as an ethnic nation-within-the-nation, bearing legitimate claims to self-governance and education.

Resurgence of the Caciques, Apoderados, and Alcaldes

In late 1941, two Aymara leaders from communities in Taraqu, bordering Lake Titicaca, packed three thick bundles of legal documents into their ponchos and set off for La Paz. Their destination was the Ministry of Education.[6] Not by chance, the caciques bypassed the offices of the CNE (the agency in charge of dismantling Warisata and turning the núcleo escolar into an arm of its assimilationist agenda) on their way to the stone monolith that housed the ministry's sprawling bureaucracy. Their destination hinted at the gravity of their mission. They carried a mass petition claiming to represent Bolivia's Indigenous citizens—the "caciques hailing from Oruro, Potosí, Chuquisaca, and Cochabamba"; "all caciques in the nine departments of the Republic"; and, finally, "all the Indians in Bolivia."[7] The claim of collective authorship was standard practice, but in this case Willka and Allca (the document's chief signatories) had collected an impressive list of names, signatures (including thumbprints), and titles, including (in this order) Rufino Willka, "cacique of Achacachi" and ex-comunario member of the ayllu Belén; Andrés Marka T'ula, "son of cacique of Curahuara-Pacajes"; José Santos Paticallisaya, cacique of Sicasica; Mateo Alfaro, cacique of Caquiaviri; Dionisio Paxipati, cacique of Tihuanaco; Santos Cornejo, cacique of Achocalla; Gregorio Titirico, cacique of Ancoraimes; and Antonio Quispe, cacique of Italaque. A few names stood out: Andrés Marka T'ula was the son and political heir of Santos Marka T'ula, while Willka, Paxsipati, Alfaro, Cornejo, Titirico, and others were veterans of the ayllu land-claims movement of the 1920s.[8] This list of names and provenances is illustrative: the cacique-apoderado network, although damaged by the Chaco War debacle, was still a political force to be reckoned with.

The petition's chief signatory, Rufino Willka, was a veteran cacique-apoderado whose wartime trajectory was emblematic of Indigenous men who had come of political age in the 1920s, only to be swept into the vortex of war and exile in the 1930s. Hailing from the embattled ayllus of Taquina, Willka's manifest legal skills had been honed over years of litigating the claims of divested ex-comunarios. In his youth, he had apprenticed with Santos Marka T'ula and other caciques, and eventually made a living by representing ayllus and ex-communities throughout the paceño countryside. Willka suffered the usual occupational hazards of the apoderado: he "traveled [the country] as a persecuted man, without land, and in bad condition," remembered Condori Chura (a fellow scribe) many years later.[9] With the Chaco War came a new menace: the risk of being rounded up and sent off to the desert trench war; conscripted for road work; or sent off to jail along with other troublemakers. Sure enough, Willka was arrested frequently and spent long spells in prison during the war years. He emerged from prison as a battle-scarred Aymara activist and legal agent, serving his comunario clients in their ongoing land disputes.[10] His work (usually in collaboration with other apoderados and caciques) required archival research, notary and legal protocol, and the submission of formal requests for land commissions to review colonial land titles, maps, and other old documents. Like two generations of caciques-apoderados, Rufino Willka fixed his hope on restoring communal land rights, in this case the "ayllu of Belen," located within the core of Omasuyo's moiety of Aransaya.[11]

Having accumulated experience and trust, Rufino Willka became a powerful interlocutor, a man able to patch together the cacique movement in the aftermath of war and repression. The 1941 petition signaled a tactical change, however. Having largely sidelined the communal land question, the caciques now focused on the issue of local control over schooling. They had designed an ingenious proposal that asserted the entwined principles of communal self-governance and control over local schooling. They laid out the plan: a traditional slate of councilmen (*alcaldes mayores, alcaldes menores, regidores*, etc.) was to be nominated and elected by their own peasant assemblies (a restored colonial right, recently ratified in the 1938 Constitution).[12] As tradition dictated, cabildo authorities were to be among the elders who had ascended the ranks of the local civil-religious hierarchy, thanks to years of service (fiesta sponsorship, etc.). Those Aymara council authorities (the alcaldes) would then be charged with overseeing the functioning of *las escuelas Yndígenas* in all the ayllus and communities throughout the republic. They wrote, "Indigenous authorities in the provinces and cantons ... [would be able] to fulfill their [civic] duties by founding indigenal schools in conformity with the anterior and superior decrees and [other] documents transcribed below."[13] In some places, cabildos would appoint men to take charge of local school affairs (variously named *alcalde escolar, amauta escolar*, or *alcalde de campo*). But the driving nativist motive behind this petition was to revitalize the institutions of self-governance and restore a measure of local autonomy to the community. A reinvigorated civil-religious hierarchy, in turn, would ensure "the free exercise" and "normal functioning" of village primary schools in "all the ayllus."[14] They argued that local ayllu schools were needed to be founded, funded, and administered under strong peasant councils, and their curriculum attuned to the values and traditions of ayllu life. Vernacular practices of local statecraft and schooling, in turn, would legitimate and revitalize the autonomy of the ayllu-community—theoretically, with the blessings of the state.

This bold ethno-political agenda—the harnessing of the community school to the restored *cabildo de indios*—was similar, in spirit at least, to the way Warisata was able to launch and govern itself under the parliament of amautas during the 1930s. Curiously, though, there is no reference in this petition to the ayllu-school or its communitarian ideals. This silence may have been tactical, for the caciques were appealing to the new oligarchic regime, a public enemy of Indigenal education. Indeed, the caciques' school plan was to fill the vacuum created by the state's destructive policies and institutional failures. And they would accomplish that feat through the reinvigoration of ethnic authority structures—a goal that contravened the CNE's efforts to centralize rural schooling under its assimilationist banner.

But there is another curious elision in this remarkable petition. The authors made no mention of Indian territorial rights; they maintained (what seems like) a studied silence on the land question. Instead, their laser focus was on defending the legality, customs, and values of comunario life. A spirit of civic democracy permeated their legal brief—for example, their invocation of the universal right to schooling; the image of *escuelas Yndigenas* flowering throughout the country's "cantons and provinces"; and their allusions to the Indians' deep patriotic reverence. Symbolically, the school was their rallying point, a way to bring far-flung and disparate groups of Indigenous people to claim their "civil right" to education under the new oligarchic ruling class. Yet the petitioners were not clamoring for government-supported schools, nor were they protesting the government's ongoing war against Indigenal education. Rather, as they patiently explained to government ministers, the spread of rural primary schools in Indian communities was perfectly compatible with the restoration of traditional Indigenous cabildos and their right to exercise authority over local justice and self-governance.

In keeping with elaborate judicial protocol, the caciques' mass petition contained its own modular archive of old papers, legal references, and evidentiary claims, all bundled into a *testimonio de obrados* and addressed to the minister of government and justice. This amalgam of auxiliary documents contained fragmented, run-on, and transcribed documents furnishing a corpus of legal precedents. Among them was a stream of prior petitions and other communications, signed and sent by Rufino Willka and other self-titled caciques and apoderados, to the highest Church and state authorities. The texts pleaded for aid and protection (amparo y garantías), so that native authorities might secure their local apparatuses of governance and rural schooling. The legal and rhetorical traditions of the earlier cacique-apoderado movement were on full display in this lengthy exposition. Legal precedence, and the invocation of inherited colonial-customary rights, framed the caciques' argument for the official recognition, revitalization, and protection of the local communal order. Once more, it was the magical power of the colonial archive (and its ancient colonial decrees dating from Viceroy Toledo's 1575 ordinances) that was invoked, not to defend their ancient lands, but to insist on their right to learn the Spanish language, be conversant in the scriptures, and thus "civilize themselves."[15] Willka's bundle of documents referenced Spanish colonial policies and discourses, but various papers also invoked Bolivia's republican promise of "universal obligatory education" for all school-age children. To press their point, the peasant petitioners noted how the 1938 Constitution had unleashed a torrent of petitions demanding "the free election of alcaldes," as well as the state's recognition of the Indian community and its traditional governing authorities (hilacatas, mallkus, etc.).[16] The nation's latest magna carta was doubtless what had fired up this bold proposal.

Beneath the sheen of legal erudition, the petition expressed the caciques' more immediate concerns. Willka and Allca wanted the minister of education to offer garantías to the alcaldes in charge of founding local village schools. There would be no "mestizo school director," dispatched by state authorities to take control of Taquina's local schools, for example, nor would the local corregidor be permitted to install a school functionary. They demanded that local unitary schools fall under the jurisdiction of the restored, and fortified, cabildos de indios. That meant, in turn, that the minister of education must safeguard the yearly tradition of chiefly investiture so the newly elected hilacatas and alcaldes could take up their staff of office and begin their year of communal obligations. The Indigenous petitioners wanted the education minister to wire certificates of safe passage to peasants traveling in from the outlying cantons to attend the investiture ceremony on the first day of the new year, in 1942. Official telegrams and notices were to litter the land, so the "Indians of Urinsaya and Arinsaya" (the inter-ayllu moieties of Omasuyos) might travel safely to Taquina without fear of landlord reprisal.[17] Omasuyos (the province most ravaged by latifundismo and violence) would be declared safe, by fiat, so rural communities could restore their governing councils, perform their rituals, and establish community-controlled village schools.

Hedging their bets, the caciques also directed their appeal to Bolivia's Catholic hierarchy in late 1939, when the Second Eucharist Congress was convened in La Paz to deal with Bolivia's "dispossessed indigenous class."[18] The Catholic Church's evangelical impulses were sparked, as well, by the very real competition that Protestant missions now posed in parts of the northern Altiplano.[19] With the oligarchy back in power after 1939, Church authorities found a strong ally in President Peñaranda, who lobbied vigorously for the reintroduction of Catholic teachings in the public school curriculum. Vicente Donoso Torres, in charge of the CNE, also embraced religious instruction, seeing it as the antidote to toxic secular doctrines (nihilism, Marxism, and other "internationalist" ideologies) contaminating the spirit of bolivianidad.[20] Yet, for their own strategic reasons, the caciques needed to secure the patrimony of the Catholic Church, and they drew on long precedence.[21] Bishop Macedonio Mercado was asked to support their campaign for special alcaldes in charge of schools so their children could learn "the first letters written in the national language and in the Christian doctrine."[22] The caciques were not lobbying for parish schools, because their project was to found their own autonomous community-based schools. Rather, they pleaded with the bishop to intercede on their behalf against their "ancient aggressors in the provinces and cantons." Invoking the image of Las Casas, their appeal kindled the flame of Christian charity and paternalism in a hostile world. Founding local alphabet schools for Indians was still a difficult and dangerous enterprise. This situation, they implied, revealed two deplorable truths about being Indian in neocolonial Bolivia: that "no justice was possible" and that the call to "civilize the Indian" was but a cruel hoax perpetuated by the modernizing elites.[23]

While Rufino Willka and his compañeros elaborated a formal project to restore cabildos and found schools, other pro-school activists performed the granular work of local organizing and proselytizing.[24] They worked on the sly, trying to evade the authorities as they moved across the highlands and into insular hacienda zones.[25] Toribio Miranda, for example, began his career by founding dispersed primary schools among the Uru people in the western parts of Oruro, but eventually he shifted his operation to the eastern valleys "to combat the abuses suffered by peones," according to Waskar Arí.[26] Over the late 1930s and 1940s, the eastern valley provinces of Campero and Mizque were seeded with "clandestine schools to educate Indians in literacy." There Miranda worked with primary school teachers who taught reading and writing with the aid of a phonetic Quechua-reader developed by Protestant missionaries. As Miranda and other bilingual teachers promoted literacy, they also preached Indian rights to colonos and, on occasion, advocated for direct labor action.[27] Meanwhile, Miranda offered moral lessons in the art of cultural revitalization, invoking the wisdom of the ancestors and local deities as the symbolic touchstones of indigeneity. Gregorio Titiriku, another leading alcalde mayor, traveled the countryside lecturing on various subjects and celebrating "Indians, the first peoples ... [whose] languages are Aymara and Quechua."[28] His lessons folded elements of Protestant evangelism into a blend of folk Catholicism and nativist rituals and beliefs—another variant of syncretic religiosity that saw nothing contradictory about listening to the occasional Protestant missionary while continuing to worship the Achachilas, the ancient deities of the mountains. Often he would keep his adult pupils after class to show them the proper way to worship the Achachilas or to prepare a traditional wedding ceremony. A nativist teacher and intellectual, Titiriku often crafted his lessons "so we can educate our people ... in the Indian laws: '*ama sua, ama llulla,* and *ama khella*' [do not rob, do not lie, and do not be lazy]."²⁹ Like Eduardo Nina Quispe's moral dream of a "renovated" Bolivia (which he sketched in a forgotten petition, penned on the eve of the Chaco War), Gregorio Titiriku's pedagogy of the 1940s offered a moral pathway forward by looking back toward the reimagined Inca heritage, embodied by the Republic of the Qullasuyu.

By the early 1940s, the land question had been largely eclipsed by the redemptive fight for schooling within these larger cacique and alcalde projects. In strategic and discursive ways, their pro-school campaigns—both the caciques' bold petition for communal self-governance and locally based schools and the alcaldes' clandestine teachings—contested the assimilationist state and helped fill the social vacuum left by its campaign of violence against Warisata. In different ways, they framed their quests as fundamentally Indianist projects of cultural empowerment and autonomy. But wider political circumstances conspired against those pro-school movements: ultimately, they proved too local, fragmented, and vulnerable to sustain themselves against the polarizing political forces at work in the Bolivian highlands.³⁰ Ironically, the same forces that crushed the educative politics of indigeneity in the early 1940s simultaneously opened spaces in which Bolivia's postwar generation of peasant organizers learned to harness the cultural power of Indigenous education to the insurrectionary potential of agrarian class politics.

Legacy of the Chaco War: The Peasant Dirigente

In the decade and a half following the Chaco War, the northern Altiplano and eastern valleys were infiltrated by a new breed of rural organizer, the likes of which traditional landholders had rarely seen. Most were Aymara- or Quechua-speakers with deep roots in rural society. But as survivors of the Chaco War, they also had acquired a patina of cosmopolitanism during their brutal experiences as military conscripts, in Paraguayan prison camps, or as exiles or deserters. This postwar generation of rural organizers—increasingly referred to as *dirigentes*—did not fit the usual Gramscian image of "organic intellectual," schooled in the art of political activism by the militant party, anarchist organization, or disciplined trade union.³¹ Nor did the local Andean notion resonate with Leninist notions of vanguard party operatives, carrying their orthodoxies into the countryside to indoctrinate the rural masses in the latest revolutionary ideas and strategies of class struggle. Rather, the label was deployed rather generically, much as it was in other rural contexts, such as in late nineteenth-century rural Andalusia in southern Spain.³² There, as in rural Bolivia after the Chaco War, the dirigente signified an itinerant and "politically conscious" rural organizer, one with deep roots in the countryside but whose cosmopolitan horizons, literacy, bilingualism, itinerancy, and associative networks (which often tied him to urban allies) were strategic cultural resources that could be deployed toward organizational, political, and educative ends.

In Bolivia, many rural dirigentes traveled the same circuits as the roving Indigenous alcaldes and caciques, who had long trafficked in legal resistance, grassroots school activity, and the defense of communal autonomy. But these roving newcomers pursued a starkly different agenda: to foment and spread an organized movement of rural laborers, namely, the underclass of service tenants (colonos, pongos, peones, etc.) living on haciendas. Rural dirigentes often identified themselves and their constituencies in trade unionist terms, infusing class identities with revolutionary overtones. Indeed, the rising currency of *campesinismo* flowed from revolutionary Mexico and its militant agrarian movements of the 1920s and 1930s. By the 1940s, the compounded category of *indio-campesino* was spreading among restive rural laborers living from, working on, and fighting for, the right to land and the freedom from "Indian slavery." In the Bolivian highlands, the rhetoric of *campesinización* provided rural organizers with tactical advantages: categorically, it repudiated the racial and cultural inferiority Bolivian elites still ascribed to *lo indio*; and instrumentally, it rallied a geographically dispersed population of Indigenous people to coalesce in mass opposition to their common enemy, the landowners, and eventually to overthrow the feudal-agrarian order. Not least, the popular designator *indio-campesino* implicitly challenged rural peoples to think and act from their historically compounded position of oppression—as both an internally colonized race and subaltern class of exploited laborers, alienated from their ancestral lands and heritage, and actively disenfranchised, humiliated, and oppressed.

If there was one major cohort that supplied the bulk of Bolivia's rural peasant organizers in the late 1930s and 1940s, it was the Chaco War veterans. The military had served as a painful political crucible for many Indigenous men, turning them into self-conscious soldiers and aspiring citizens: thousands of peasant recruits had come of political age, and some had even acquired intercultural organizing skills and a sense of patriotic self-pride during the Chaco War and its aftermath. The human cost of their political baptism by fire was almost unthinkable, however. Tens of thousands of Indian recruits had been torn from their lands and villages across northern Bolivia and dragooned into regiments to fight the "Guaraní Indian" soldiers of Paraguay, while other conscripts were marched off to dig trenches, build roads, and lay the dynamite and gas pipes for a hopeless border war that became Bolivia's greatest national debacle. Bolivian war stories and dissident literature tell how most conscripted Indians had little understanding of the patria that they were fighting and dying for. Equally shocking, the war's white officer caste, and many urban working-class men dragooned into the military, encountered their "Indian comrades" for the first time in their lives. A broken mirror of coloniality amid the ravages of the war, this shocking cross-cultural encounter reflected the misery and violence of wartime in the haggard faces of the mestizo and Indian soldier, forced to gaze on each other as victims or survivors. Bolivian soldiers who languished in Paraguayan prison camps, or escaped into Argentine exile, sometimes acquired useful networks of personal contacts—precious cultural capital they could tap as potential allies in their postwar organizational activities. In the meantime, many soldiers trudged homeward, half expecting that their patriotic sacrifices would translate into their rightful claims to labor freedom, schooling, and legal protections under Bolivian law.

But to many a landed patriarch, the image of the ragged Indian war veteran returning home (often still carrying his rusty weapons) represented a new source of imminent danger. As late as 1947, the lettered patriarch Jáuregui worried about how the northern Altiplano, unlike Bolivia's southern provinces, had uprooted and sent whole regiments of Indians to the front—Indigenous men who would no longer abide the quotidian violence, ignorance, tedium, and dependency of the semifeudal regime. Flooding back into Bolivia, the ex-combatants were seen as potential troublemakers, social pariahs unfit for pastoral life in their original villages or haciendas. As we saw earlier, Jáuregui captured the social anxiety of Bolivia's landed aristocracy suddenly faced with a new phenomenon—an uprooted class of Indigenous ex-combatants. Many had become bootstrap autodidacts in the field of political organizing and consciousness-raising:

> When the *repete* [pejorative slang for the monolingual Indian soldier, who quickly grasped the word he needed in order to ask for more grub] returned to ... his lands, hearth, and home, he was no longer the humble, silent, resigned aboriginal of past times. As an *ex-combatiente* or prisoner of war, he was ready to be sindicalized, or pressured by [the power of his numbers] to speak out against the bourgeoisie ... whom he now saw as inferior; now he

shouts for the equality of rights, the same as the educated and civilized man, but without knowing that, with equality, [also] come obligations.³³

By the late 1930s, then, war veterans were emerging as a new generation of intercultural brokers and pro-Indigenous advocates, channeling their skills into the founding of local schools and, on occasion, even peasant unions, on certain haciendas. These incipient rural labor activities and veteran initiatives first surfaced in 1936 in the Cochabamba valleys, then spread across the high plateau of Oruro and La Paz during the early to mid-1940s, before trickling down into the southern highlands of Chuquisaca and Potosí by 1946–47. The growing currency of agrarianist, ethnic, and *obrerista* discourses combined with veterans' invocation of patriotic honor to create a potent ideological alchemy—the sort of self-righteous "revolutionary propaganda" that Jáuregui warned about in his 1947 essay.

These political developments were not unidirectional (from the city to the country, or from vanguard parties to the mass of peasants). Nor, as I have argued, were rural dirigentes necessarily following the dictates of leftist parties or labor unions. Rather, those ersatz dirigentes performed the slow cultural spadework of the Indigenous activist, the Indian alcalde mayor, or the radical rural teacher—men who traced their own political formation to the painful experiences of wartime or to deeper traditions of Indigenous struggle for communal land and autonomy. Yet it is also true that Bolivia's postwar explosion of political dissension opened a historic opportunity for disparate groups and their associations to come together in broad, transregional networks and political coalitions. Across the Aymara Altiplano, this new flotilla of peasant dirigentes, buoyed by their associative links to militant labor activity in the cities, could also tap into the preexisting infrastructure and political experience of the older cacique movement.

Tracking Antonio Alvarez Mamani

The extraordinary memoir (published in 1987) of the trilingual *kallawaya* healer and activist Antonio Alvarez Mamani opens a window onto the political aspirations and activities of a rural dirigente forged in the burning sands of the Chaco War.³⁴ Like so many others of his generation, Alvarez was forced to come of political age in that war. A military recruit at age twenty, he served in the war before being captured and sent to a Paraguayan prison camp, where he worked in a gang digging ditches and roads. Thanks to lax security, he escaped after two months, fled across the Paraguayan border into Argentina, and traveled west across pampas and mountains into Chile, finally returning to Bolivia in 1934 by way of Peru. He soon reenlisted in the Regiment of Achacachi and was again dispatched to the front, although this time he was deployed to a hospital in the town of Tarija, where he could use his medicinal skills tending to wounded and ill soldiers. Thanks to his medical status as a kallawaya, along with his formal schooling and trilingualism (Aymara was his mother tongue, while Quechua and Spanish were acquired later on), Alvarez soon distinguished himself as an adept cultural broker and translator. Young officers no less than the likes of Col. Germán Busch and Col. Gualberto Villarroel came to rely on his intercultural dexterity, and Alvarez later exploited those connections to leverage his political capital as an emerging peasant leader (see fig. 5.1).[35]

But not before Alvarez was arrested, this time by military officials who accused him of falsifying a certificate of medical evacuation. Charged with desertion, he was imprisoned in a cell of *ex-combatientes*—an association that later served as Alvarez's first network of political activists and solidarity in his work as a peasant organizer:

> In prison, I saw the worst injustice, since so many prisoners were there because of starvation and the poverty that drove them to steal a hen, a sheep. Meanwhile, the great thieves were living in freedom. I saw the inhuman conditions that prisoners lived in, and I began to talk to them as I had once talked to the soldiers. And then I began taking notes, jotting down their names, where they lived, and I told them that someday I would visit them. That was why, after the war and once out of jail, I had an idea of where to begin the fight for the peasants and which persons I could contact, men who might be possible dirigentes or simply men who could help with lodging [effectively, safe houses] and food during my travels [*recorridos*].[36]

By 1936, as the country was beginning to heal its war wounds and government grants of political amnesty to thousands of prisoners began to empty Bolivian jails, Alvarez embarked on his new career as rural dirigente. At the front, and later in the hospital camp, Alvarez put his Spanish language and literacy skills at the service of Indian conscripts, men desperate to get word back to their families. He helped them write letters home and read aloud from the occasional scrap of newspaper reporting on the disastrous

FIGURE 5.1. Antonio Alvarez Mamani, in Punata (Cochabamba), five months after the April 1952 insurrection. As union leader and pro-MNR dirigente, Alvarez promoted the cause of agrarian reform (provisioning the peasantry with lands, unions, and schools) amid the escalation of rural unrest. Ranaboldo, *El camino perdido*, 185.

course of the war. It was as a forsaken young soldier, barely out of adolescence, that Alvarez learned how to mobilize his own cultural capital to transcend language barriers, quietly cultivate a natural political constituency, and begin building a transregional network of men he had come to know during the war and in prison camp.

As I have mentioned, Alvarez's story was emblematic of an astonishing group of pan-Andeanist peasant leaders thrust into the political arena in the aftermath of war. Like other veterans, Alvarez saw an opportunity in rural teaching and union organizing right after the war, and he ingeniously deployed the promise of schooling and the work of unionizing to build, step by step, an interethnic movement of Indigenous campesinos. The founding of a school, for example, was a crucial way of tapping the "fervent enthusiasm" that so many rural people felt toward the ideal of formal education and that political organizers quickly learned to exploit. Thus did the village school come to serve as a rural organizing tool (much as the network of caciques and alcaldes mayores were deploying it for their own nativist ends). More important, through the *process* of organizing a rural school—with nocturnal meetings devoted, in part, to reading aloud and discussing presidential decrees on the Indian's constitutional rights, or newspaper clippings, or a sample of "seditious propaganda" on the degradation of the pongo, and so on—local peasants were exposed to the subversive potential of political literacy even if they could not actually read or speak Spanish.

Alvarez seized on this strategy to penetrate the insular world of the hacienda, and at times he seemed to be everywhere at once. To blend into the rural communities he was traveling through, he would often switch the order of his surnames: in official circles and throughout the highlands, he used his hispanized paternal surname, "Alvarez"; while roaming the Quechua valleys of Cochabamba, he sometimes switched to "Mamani," his maternal surname.[37] Wherever he went, Alvarez toiled in the political vineyards of concientización: "I spent the majority of my time in Bolivia, before I was thinking about the organization of the peasantry, trying to begin [a project of] political socialization, above all with the peasant children, with the youth, so that they could improve themselves and occupy better stations in life than their parents."[38] Until 1942, he organized himself like a one-man *escuela ambulante*. Relying on his trusted circle of ex-soldiers and ex-prisoners from his time in the San Pedro prison, Alvarez spent years roaming the countryside "pursuing the concientización of peasants in a clandestine way."[39]

In those early years, he was like a lone traveling salesman, peddling radical ideas on the black market. Disguised in the distinctive homespun clothing of the region, he moved about the countryside, going from hut to hut on the edges of haciendas, to spread the good word. Sometimes small gatherings of men and women met in secret—in an abandoned parish church here, a hidden ravine there. Nocturnal meetings might be signaled by a mountainside bonfire or in other ways. Alvarez remembered how he often traveled with his dog, whipping him with a switch to signal his stealth arrival in a peasant hamlet. The pup's piercing bark, he later explained to his interviewer, functioned like the traditional conch, *el pututu*. (Since colonial times, the conch had served as a natural microphone for Indigenous authorities to summon people to secret meetings or rebel action.) These vignettes hint at the kind of tactics that rural dirigentes had to devise as they crossed provincial borders and sought out clusters of colono tenants living on haciendas. Like Santos Marka T'ula decades earlier, Alvarez made a point of traveling the back roads by night, always disguising his kallawaya identity, lest he draw attention as a "troublemaker."

Throughout his travels, Alvarez drew on a wide political and rhetorical repertoire to cultivate trust and cooperation among local alcaldes, hilacatas, amautas, and other civil-religious authority figures. But it was the prosaic village school—or, more broadly, the deep cultural aspiration in Andean society for the right to letters and schooling—that became Alvarez's most powerful (and portable) mobilizing device: "I spoke to them about the 1936 decree." Issued by President Toro, this order had stipulated the right of Indian children to primary schooling and reiterated the obligation of large landowners to provide schooling to the children of their colonos. "I told them it was a dead letter because it was never applied; that the Indians ought to have schools; and that the patrones had to feed the children while they learned."[40]

His message sometimes provoked doubt and hostility: "Many answered me: and knowing how to read and write, what is that going to do for our children? Not in the future, not in the past, not even when the patrón dies are they going to permit schools."[41] Apathy, fear, hopelessness—such potentially paralyzing sentiments were woven into the warp and woof of day-to-day campesino life under the boot of the patrón and the rapaciousness of local officials. The dirigente also had to fear the potential informant—that servile figure who might be inclined to denounce the interloper to his overlord, perhaps in return for a small favor.

Alvarez Mamani not only survived those long years of rural organizing but also managed to expand his radius of operation into hacienda zones throughout parts of Oruro, Potosí, western Cochabamba, and points south. Arguably, his effectiveness as a rural organizer depended on his ability to tap into the deep cultural vein of Aymara-based school activism and aspirations that ran through the comunario movement and was now spreading into hacienda zones. Alvarez tried to leverage the history and memory of earlier school movements: "Our thought was to found peasant schools in different communities, and to supply them with notebooks, pencils, books, and other materials," he later explained.[42] By 1945, he had transformed his years of grassroots educational activism into a fulcrum of Bolivia's emerging peasant movement, beginning with his own natural constituency—the country's Indian veterans: "My objective was to organize the ex-combatientes, not for the Agrarian Reform, but around the issue of peasant education."[43] They formed a loyal base of support in different parts of the country, and Alvarez eventually overcame the problem of communication by relying on Andean practices of sending verbal messages, letters, legal documents, and print material through the underground messenger system of chasquis.[44] "After I had been *'concientizando'* for a while," he remembered, "I faced the problem of how to dispatch [printed] notices, and how to inform the peasants in all the communities and haciendas. Then I realized I had to organize a network of chasquis, of messengers, who would traverse the country, with the proviso that they be trusted people who would not betray their comrades."[45]

Radical Print Networks and Rebel Communication

The practice of developing the back channels of rebel communication among unlettered peasants was commonplace to rural political movements that developed in different times and places. In his study of rural France on the eve of revolution, to take one of the more famous examples, Georges Lefebvre followed the tracings of rebel messengers who carried official decrees, newsprint, and hand-lettered posters into remote villages of unlettered peasants. During the revolution, he notes, "the rebels were rather tempted to support their claims by showing printed or hand-written posters to peasants who could not read."[46] In a strikingly different context, Ranajit Guha traced the veins of "rebel communication by means of . . . written messages, [which] was of course not widely prevalent in a county where illiteracy was high as in rural India under the Raj." But while "writing was socially privileged," Guha argues, "the production of verbal messages in graphic form for purposes of insurgency was feasible . . . when individuals of elite origin were induced by circumstance or conscience, or a combination of both, to make common cause with the peasantry, or when a few among the latter had managed, against all odds, to acquire the rudiments of literacy and put these at the service of an uprising."[47]

Seditious literature littered Bolivia's (supposedly) unlettered countryside during the mid- to late 1940s. The transmission of insurgent messages after the Chaco War often involved urban educated elites—the growing ranks of youthful radicals we encountered in earlier chapters of this book. But the cultural and material origins and infrastructure of rebel communication, in its multiplicity of oral and written forms, sprang from rural Indigenous activism. And vernacular literacy practices, tied to rural insurgency, had been around for a long time. Insurgent peasant moments, in turn, loosed a torrent of textual activities (circulating archival documents and print matter, forming clandestine reading groups, organizing legal or petition campaigns, etc.) that galvanized rural communities, as in the late eighteenth century, and again during the 1910s and 1920s (see chapter 2).[48] Subversive ideas gained currency again in the 1940s as Alvarez Mamani and other dirigentes blanketed the land with radical print matter and introduced new reading practices into their clandestine political repertoire.

From a distance, we can catch sight of these rebel circuits of communication through the surveillance of the Bolivian government and its allies in the US embassy in La Paz. In 1944 and 1945, a few government reports began to crackle with news about the "subversive dirigente" Luís Ramos Quevedo, for example. Hailing from the village of Sipesipe in the central valley of Cochabamba, his political formation was closely tied to organized union activity that surfaced on valley haciendas in 1936 and 1937. By the 1940s, Ramos Quevedo, a Quechua-speaking rural laborer, had acquired experience mediating tense colono-landlord relations on several local haciendas. Once Gualberto Villarroel was catapulted into the presidency (in late 1943), Ramos Quevedo expanded his radius of action and began associating with urban activists—progressive lawyers (such as Eduardo Arze Loureiro), labor leaders in Oruro, and tin miners in Oruro, Catavi, and elsewhere. He organized hacienda tenants and laborers in Cochabamba's western highland provinces (Tapacarí, Ayopaya, and Quillacollo) and Oruro's northeast corner. Ramos Quevedo was likely on the scene during Bolivia's first great sit-down strike of colonos in 1942.[49]

All these activities began to register on the official radar. A stream of US embassy dispatches in early 1945 warned that Ramos Quevedo and his roving cadre of agitators had been making trouble for more than two years, promising that "all the land would soon be returned to [the Indians] to hold as it was before the coming of the Spaniards."[50] Even the populist Villarroel regime considered him dangerous and devised a plot to destroy his reputation without triggering rural unrest. Ridiculed as delusional, Ramos Quevedo was accused of claiming to be the royal descendant of Viracocha, the supreme Inca lord and emperor. And when not posing as an Inca king, he was said to skulk about the countryside disguised as a miserable Indian, stirring up trouble on the haciendas and preying on Indians. Mad, stalking the Indian and yet posing as an imposter, this *dirigente* was ultimately attacked as a faux Indian, a "white agitator." Belittled as an ignoramus, he was also slandered for being a man of "grandiloquence to the extreme" and thus mentally "unbalanced."⁵¹ Trying to explain the "nature of the agitation among the Indians" and Ramos Quevedo's success as a prodigious grassroots organizer, the US embassy official Walter Thurston parroted the words of a Bolivian government authority. Ramos, it was said, was a conniving radical who had studied "the psychology of the Indian so as to be able to appeal and manipulate him."⁵² He did so not by appealing to socialism or communism but by casting himself as a radical nativist in the mold of "Tupac Amarú and other famous leaders of Indian revolts."⁵³ Having suffered the government's attempt at character assassination, he was now placed on the US embassy's counterinsurgency blacklist. As activity reached a feverish pitch in the lead-up to Bolivia's first National Indigenous Congress, Ramos Quevedo surfaced on the official radar screen as the most dangerous menace to the social order since the great rebellions of the late eighteenth century. Here, then, was yet another version of neocolonial race-thinking, another incident of the oligarchy broadcasting a warning about the "threat of race war" in preparation for a preemptive strike.

What accounted for Luís Ramos Quevedo's extraordinary influence among the so-called *indiada*? Officials suspected it had to do with something they were just beginning to perceive: first, the emergence of a sprawling Indigenous organization (converging in an "Indigenous Committee" charged with negotiating the terms and conditions of Indian rights and emancipation in the upcoming Indian Congress); and second, the *dirigente*'s underground network of oral and literate communication. In fact, he had built a sprawling system of relay messengers and letter carriers.⁵⁴ That cultural foot traffic was in the process of producing and circulating a bold political platform that the newly organized Bolivian Indigenous Committee planned to present at a historic national-level Indian Congress, originally set for February 2, 1945. The tangible result was a carefully crafted pamphlet (*boletín*) that framed the congress's unifying language of Indian rights and platform of revindication. Widely distributed through the channels of the Indigenous Committee, rural unions, rural teachers, and the chasqui network, that extraordinary document reached rural villages and haciendas far and wide. The sheer scale and efficiency of mass distribution of print matter to unlettered Indians simply astonished one US embassy official. His report attributed the feat to Ramos Quevedo's corrupt and deceitful behavior toward the ignorant Indians:

> [Ramos Quevedo] had perhaps as many as 25,000 copies run off, and [he] went out to the countryside again, showing the picture [of Villarroel on the cover of the pamphlet] to the Indians and telling them that Villarroel was the president of the Indians. He sold the paper for as much as he could get, and sometimes claimed that it was a deed to land, which would become valid when he and the Government had accomplished the reform in the whole political and land system of Bolivia.... He also printed alleged deeds to the land and sold them for as high a price as he could.[55]

Besides the diplomat's wide-eyed amazement, there were more surprises to come. Thurston told Washington how the Villarroel government (already anxious about the bold efforts of the Indigenous Committee to hold a massive congress in the first place) planned to send a commission to tour the countryside in order to assess the jittery state of rural affairs. Ramos Quevedo was invited to serve as the commission's guide and cultural translator. But the embassy and state had an ulterior motive—to spy on the dirigente, perhaps even ensnare Ramos so the government could take him out of the picture before the Indian Congress was convened. Privy to this primitive counterinsurgency plan, Thurston confided to the US State Department that several spooks would be involved in the inspection scheme: "Spies were also sent along to keep an eye on [Ramos's] activities while he was not close to the Ministerial party; they found out that... while with the Minister he would tell the Indians that the Government was with them; [but] whenever he could, he slipped off to the side and told them just the opposite."[56]

Among other things, this dragnet operation demonstrates the dawning awareness on the part of US embassy officials that Ramos and other rural organizers operated an underground system of rebel communication.

> The Embassy was amazed at the extent of the [Indian] organization, or at least at the movement which Ramos had been able to build up in a region as bereft of communications as the Bolivian Altiplano.... Mr. [Carlos] Morales said that he thought Ramos must use the *Chasqui*: the old Inca courier system. Because, he said, when Ramos was arrested in La Paz, within two days [a flood of] telegrams of protest poured in from Cochabamba and Potosí and, within three days, from as far away as Tarija. No communiqué was issued by the Government on the arrest [of Ramos] and the censorship would not have permitted any word of it to go out over the telegraph wires [in any event], so the Indians must have transmitted it from mouth to mouth.[57]

Exotic though it might seem today, the chasqui network had long been a crucial modality of transregional Andean communication as well as a mobile security apparatus. As we saw in chapter 2, cacique networks had circulated archival and legal documents through ad hoc messenger services (an ancient Andean institution) and dispatched *mensajeros indígenas* to Lima, hundreds of miles away, to conduct their long-distance business in the Peruvian National Archive. This oral/literate infrastructure had sustained Indigenous political activities and exchanges for decades and even centuries, and thus could be reactivated in times of political stress.[58] So it was in the lead-up to the 1945 Indian Congress. Some peasant dirigentes, like Alvarez Mamani in his early years as a rural organizer, traveled solo, but Ramos Quevedo tended to travel with vigilant bodyguards. Reported Thurston: "It was evident that Ramos always moved, watched at a distance by a number of Indians, so that were anything to happen to him, they could carry word immediately to his followers."[59] A group of Indian sentinels were posted to keep vigil and guide rebel organizers, like Ramos Quevedo and Alvarez Mamani, through the dangerous labyrinths of hostile landlords and provincial officials. President Villarroel promised to issue safe conduct passes to certain Indian delegates planning to travel from their rural villages to the Indian Congress in La Paz, even as the Ministry of Government plotted against Ramos and other "dangerous instigators." By April 1945, Ramos Quevedo was placed high on the government's blacklist of Indian conspirators, and the American embassy was informed that the Villarroel regime planned to arrest Ramos before the May 1945 Indian Congress convened. Indigenous leaders also saw the writing on the wall, according to Thurston's report: "Before his arrest, when he knew the Government was looking for him, Ramos moved about the country secretly, avoiding the main roads, cities or towns, and railroads, and being guided by the Indians through the mountains and over the Altiplano."[60]

This illicit sphere of Indigenous itinerancy and communication represented, in a metaphorical sense, Bolivia's own Underground Railroad. There was, of course, no North Star, no zone of freedom to which the semibonded colonos living and laboring on the lord's estate could flee—except perhaps into the cavernous tin mines or distant cities, where a threadbare living might be wrested from urban poverty. But in this distinctive Andean context, the incessant foot traffic of peasant dirigentes, alcaldes, caciques, union organizers, teachers, and leftist activists moving through the countryside—along with the diffusion of their revolutionary ideas and print matter—constituted the communicative apparatus of a modern social movement. Its primary goal, the "abolition of Indian slavery and ignorance," had roots in the earlier communal and school-based struggles, but its branches now reached into the mines and cities, where militant worker movements already flourished. That Ramos Quevedo's sudden arrest and imprisonment (coming on the eve of the 1945 Indian National Congress) could instantaneously light up a circuit of rural communication, and unleash a torrent of peasant telegrams, letters, and news, were telltale signs that rural Bolivia was harboring an insurgent peasant movement in the early to mid-1940s.

The Peasant Congress: Promises and Perils of Participatory Democracy

A signal development in the peasants' expanding political repertoire was the chain of Indian political assemblies that were convened in various sites during the mid-1940s (1942, 1943, 1944, 1945, and 1947). With the notable exception of the famous 1945 First National Indian Congress (NIC), those regionally based meetings were largely peasant affairs. As intercultural spaces, they functioned as hubs of ethnic and class activism and solidarity, microcosms of formal deliberation over ideas and plans of action, and experiential civic lessons in direct, participatory democracy.[61] Either directly or indirectly, peasant congresses were tied to strike actions spreading through various hacienda zones. The peasant assembly—much like any miners' or working-class congress—was a potential hotbed of peasant militancy, an arena of political consciousness-raising, a training ground for rural union and confederation leaders, and a launching pad for strike activity and other forms of protest.

But the peasant congresses of the 1940s were also vital sites of popular political education. Indians would gather in these rustic, polyphonic assemblies to find a collective voice as they deliberated over the injustices they endured or the rightful place of the Indian at the core of Bolivia's nationality. Assemblies functioned as incubators of political socialization in the art and craft of direct, participatory democracy—wherever delegates exercised their right to "vote and voice," in preparatory congressional committees that crafted agendas, and in preparing this new generation of peasant leaders in the art of coalitional politics. In the Quechua congress of 1942, for example, an elected slate of Indian delegates traveled to the city of Sucre, where they encountered hundreds of other Indigenous delegates (including several venerable old caciques, *alcaldes mayores particulares*, and other peasant authorities) hailing from villages and haciendas across southern and central Bolivia. Rural delegates also hobnobbed with trade unionists from the cities and mines.[62] Not only did the 1942 and 1943 regional Indian congresses coincide with spiraling strikes and other mass protests in the countryside; they also displayed unmistakable signs of *obrerismo* ("workerism"). Both regional peasant assemblies enjoyed support from labor, anarchist, and student confederations, which advocated for an "insurrectional" alliance of workers and peasants.[63] This heterodox constituency—with a mix of peasant dirigentes, colono delegates, comunario representatives, trade unionists, and leftists all jostling for leverage—hints at the scope and dynamism of Bolivia's escalating rural movement, one that was rapidly extending its reach across boundaries of geography, class, and ethnicity.[64] By August 1944, a vital interregional coalition was on full display in the third of those regional peasant congresses. The organizers included a committee of veteran labor leaders, along with traditional ayllu authorities from rural communities in Sucre, Oruro, Potosí, Cochabamba, and La Paz.[65] This eclectic group of congressional activists produced a radical and inclusive agenda. It combined traditional syndicalist demands (the right to organize unions on haciendas, the enforcement of the labor code, aid and protection for evicted peasants, etc.) with a creative blend of agrarianism and nativist demands (rural schools, the judicial protection of Indians, a general review of land titles in preparation for the return of stolen comunario lands, etc.). Here, then, was an unmistakable sign that a broad, interclass coalition of rural Indigenous activists and urban working-class groups was becoming a political force to be reckoned with.

Fired up by four years of grassroots political work, rural organizers began planning for a nationwide Indigenous congress that would draw its delegates from Quechua, Aymara, and Guaraní regions on a scale never before seen. Conditions for such a momentous event suddenly seemed ripe. In late 1943, Bolivia's political regime had reverted, once again, to military populism under Gualberto Villarroel. Neither famous for his exploits in the Chaco War nor a leader of much political influence, Villarroel cultivated his base from among military nationalists, many with crypto-fascist leanings. Once in office, he recruited several leaders from the young nationalist-reformist party, the Movimiento Nacional Revolucionario (MNR), into his coalitional government (partly to dilute the influence of Marxist and Trotskyist parties). That uneasy alliance between Villarroel and the MNR soon collapsed, under pressure from Washington. Though he tried to cast himself as the Andean version of Juan Domingo Perón, Villarroel's populist image suffered as he cracked down on dissident intellectuals, students, politicians, teachers, and labor leaders. Indeed, the regime would prove to be one of the most vicious in national history, notes Herbert Klein.[66] In the meantime, Villarroel tried to fashion an official populist-paternalist stance on the Indian problem. Much like his military socialist predecessors (Toro and Busch), he felt compelled to address the country's backward agrarian sector—its archaic hacienda regime, rural poverty, and the swelling wave of rural unrest—yet he avoided the issue of land reform.

Villarroel's populist gestures thus opened a rare hegemonic opportunity for rural Indian organizers to appeal directly for government support as they planned for a nationwide Indian peasant congress, to be held in the city of La Paz sometime in late 1944 or early 1945. Some two dozen members of the Bolivian Indigenous Committee (CIB) staged a highly ritualized meeting with the president in front of the doors of the government palace in September 1944. Their spokesman was the venerable Luís Ramos Quevedo. At the end of that staged encounter, the CIB obtained Villarroel's approval to hold Bolivia's first National Indian Congress. From the Ministry of Government came a circular instructing all provincial authorities to respect the right of "committees, agrarian unions, representatives, delegates, Apoderados and Alcaldes Escolares" to convene local planning meetings, travel across provinces, and eventually attend the full Indian Congress to be held in La Paz.[67] That the Villarroel regime was forced to guarantee those basic civil liberties (free assembly, speech, mobility, etc.) reveals the leverage the organized peasantry now wielded. But it also speaks to the depth of Indigenous political disenfranchisement and the daily risks they took whenever they traveled, gathered, organized, or spread propaganda in the course of their political work. But for a brief moment, a sense of political euphoria opened up new channels of intercultural negotiation. When, in October 1944, Ramos Quevedo publicly demanded the end to racial segregation in the city of La Paz (a decree leftover from the 1920s), Bolivia's lawmakers concurred.[68] And a stream of petitions demanding support for rural schools, and special laws of protection, flowed into the Villarroel administration from many parts of the country.

Meanwhile, in December 1944, the frenetic work of the CIB produced an extraordinary political document, an official eight-page bulletin titled "Congreso Indigenal Boliviano en la ciudad de La Paz, 2 de febrero de 1945."

As Laura Gotkowitz's insightful reading of this twenty-seven-item agenda reveals, the Indigenous Committee had created a bold "civil rights document" defining the moral and legal scope of Indigenous citizenship. A proclamation of liberty and equality, it demanded that the Indian "be free, secure in his life and work, and respected the same as everyone."[69] Yet the document also conjoined its leftist-agrarian project ("the land belongs to those who work it") to the older Aymara comunario project of lawful ayllu restoration ("the land belongs to the Indians" and must be "returned to the Community").[70] The text's patriotic flourishes could not camouflage its radical anticolonial and agrarian implications. Of immediate concern, however, was how to safeguard the Indian delegates planning to attend the congress. The CIB's bulletin even contained cut-out coupons that were supposedly safe conduct passes. In the meantime, it urged local peasant committees to put their own stamp on the congress's overall agenda, ensuring that the gathering would be truly representative. Local committees were to elect two representatives, draw up their own agendas, and plan their overland journeys to the city of La Paz.[71] By early 1945, grassroots organizing was well underway as Antonio Alvarez Mamani (head delegate for the CIB, in the Department of La Paz) worked with local peasant delegates to compose their own regional manifesto. Proclaiming "the revindication of the imminent rights of the humble class," this working document tried to sway the "sensible opinion of the Nation" while also preparing the delegates from Laja and Machacamarca for the forthcoming Indian Congress.[72]

This painstakingly democratic process, rooted in distinctive ethnic regions, indicates clearly that the CIB did not function as an iron-fisted vanguard political party but, rather, adapted itself to an astonishing variety of local conditions and heterogeneity of peasant concerns. The legitimacy of the Indian Congress would depend on its ability to translate local grievances into a unifying platform for structural change and to disseminate its organizing ideas, symbols, and strategies by using the tools of "print and association."[73] In short, the making of this nationwide representative body (an Indigenous counter-hegemonic congress) could not possibly have come about, or have accomplished what it did, through the vanguard-like imposition of Marxist party orthodoxies or strict trade union discipline. Here, then, was a fragile edifice of direct democracy, built from the bottom up, by rural people who might never before have experienced the exhilaration (or frustrations) of collective enfranchisement. Albeit short-lived, the Indigenous Committee's work represented an astonishing organizational feat: despite daunting logistical and political obstacles, the CIB managed to convene some 1,659 delegates, hailing from the far corners of the republic, for Bolivia's first National Indian Congress, held in La Paz in May 1945.

Race, Education, and the Tutelary Populism of Villarroel

From the outset, the Villarroel-MNR governing coalition turned out to be profoundly ambivalent about the proposed Indian Congress. The president's publicized meeting with the Indigenous Committee in September 1944 had burnished his populist credentials, but he was deeply worried about the peasant strikes engulfing certain hacienda zones in Oruro, La Paz, and Cochabamba. Furthermore, news of the impending Indian Congress provoked apocalyptic warnings about race war. Landowners warned of "outside agitators" sowing racial discord among the Indian race ("the unconscious element within Bolivian nationality").[74] More surprisingly, opposition came from populist-nationalist factions on the left. In February 1945, *La Calle* (a news outlet of the MNR) urged the president to suspend the meeting, or at least to postpone it. "The problem of our native races," the news article explained, "is not to be resolved with agitation... without proposing concrete solutions. Those [solutions] can only come from the fruit of study, from the disciplines of sociology and economics, and from drawing conclusions about how to incorporate the Indian into the active life of the nation." *La Calle* called on the Villarroel government "to assert its *tutelary role* and assume the direction of the indigenous movement... [since] agitation brings only harm to the nation's economy, and disorder would bring nothing good to the despised Indian race, which is so misunderstood by both Eurocentric 'civilizers' and Marxist demagogues."[75]

Taking *La Calle*'s editorial advice to heart, Villarroel would try to do just that—that is, reassert his "tutelary role" by working the levers of power and propaganda to remake the Indian Congress into a government-controlled, nationalist spectacle. To accomplish its takeover, the regime resorted to a series of tactical maneuvers. First, the government had to buy time, by postponing the proposed date of the National Indian Congress from late December, then to early February, and finally to early May 1945. A litany of official excuses was given, while the public sphere was saturated with racist warnings, black humor, and raw ridicule in the months leading up to the grand event.[76] Second, the state began purging the Indigenous Committee's leadership, beginning with the imprisonment of Ramos Quevedo in late March.[77] The arrest had a chilling effect on other Indigenous leaders. Alvarez Mamani later recalled that "many of the authentic dirigentes withdrew because of fear; others were arrested and accused of leftism. I too was accused of being a leftist because I defended Ramos Quevedo."[78] Thus were the "authentic dirigentes" expelled from their positions of authority even before the congress was convened. They were replaced by three spokesmen for Bolivia's Quechua, Aymara, and Guaraní peoples, all of them deemed loyal and malleable by government authorities.[79] To the Indigenous Committee, this maneuver represented a hostile act of state intervention, one that corrupted the integrity of the congress itself. Alvarez Mamani observed that the Aymara representative, Francisco Chipana (Ramos), "was always far outside of what the peasant was thinking, and he wanted to order [us] around like a property owner, never obeying the base."[80] Even US embassy officials knew that Villarroel's handpicked president of the congress was serving as "a government stooge."[81] Soon thereafter, Alvarez found himself on the government's blacklist. Slandered in the press as a "dangerous mestizo," he was denounced as a fraud, a bogus delegate of the Indians.[82] For such "crimes," this dirigente was arrested and sent to prison on the island of Coati on Lake Titicaca.[83] As it turned out, not even the government's handpicked Indian leaders were safe from harm. Both Chipana Ramos and Dionisio Miranda were arrested and imprisoned after the congress was over and they were no longer needed (see fig. 5.2).[84]

The transformation of the Indian Congress into a cultural arm of the populist state can perhaps best be viewed through the lens of the staged performance. The congress was transformed into a nationalist spectacle, designed to both inspire and humble the mass of delegates who converged on Bolivia's giant sports stadium in May 1945. For most campesinos, we can only imagine the visceral experience of marching through the streets of downtown La Paz (civic spaces historically off-limits to the Indian) in their sartorial splendor: hats, bright woven ponchos, silver staffs of office (the signifiers of their regional provenance, ethnic affiliation, noble heritage, pride, and dignity) glistening in the sunlight. From there, they entered the sports arena, where they joined over a thousand other delegates from around the country. This ritual act of convening the country's first nationwide Indian Congress, site and symbol of Bolivia's demographic majority, must have produced a potent mix of inspiration and intimidation among the delegates, many of whom had never traveled so far from home (see fig. 5.3).

FIGURE 5.2. Francisco Chipana Ramos, the government's handpicked Indigenous president of the 1945 Indigenous Congress. *La Razón*, May 11, 1945.

What the delegates heard and saw next was a dazzling performance of military populism, patriotism, and tutelary paternalism. After much pomp and circumstance (a city parade of the president's entourage, a military band and color guard inaugurating the four-day congress, a central stage showcasing "the nation's highest army officers, foreign military attachés, and other officers of the garrison," etc.), several high government officials used the occasion to lecture the peasant delegates on their solemn duty as patriotic and disciplined Indians. As a concession to wary elites, Villarroel made sure to offer seats on the stage to government ministers, prominent landlords, and several foreign dignitaries (including the US and Mexican ambassadors) so they could observe

FIGURE 5.3. Delegates gathered for Bolivia's first National Indian Congress, held in May 1945. *La Razón*, May 11, 1945.

and report on the proceedings. Over the week, the afternoon sessions were devoted to official speeches and lectures in which government authorities instructed the Indians in their moral, economic, and political responsibilities and promised to redeem government pledges of social reform.

Meanwhile, President Villarroel dazzled the crowd with a passionate inaugural speech full of ingratiating praise and stern warnings. In a classic populist maneuver, he used his speech to try to secure the loyalty and obedience of the Indian leadership and masses while also mollifying the landed elites and other skeptics (the same men who had urged the president to cancel the whole event). Thus, while the president heaped praise on the "peasant worker" and venerated the Indian's "natural" telluric virtues (the love of nature and the land, hard work, stoicism, self-sacrifice, etc.), he urged the Indian (as "a son of the flag") to fulfill his patriotic duty—to work the land incessantly for the good of the country. The president's tutelary message was clear: all manner of rural unrest (the colono strikes and comunario boycotts of their "labor obligations") must immediately cease; agrarian peace must be restored.

When you return to your villages as *principales* and caciques, you [must] execute your duty—to watch over the work and [guard] the peace of everyone [in your community]. In discharging this duty, you will be serving as my representative and will be answerable to me, just as I will keep vigil over you and your families, helping the good [ones] and punishing [the bad ones]. As caciques and principales, do not permit your neighbors to acquire vices; do not allow country lawyers [*tinterillos*] or other unscrupulous people to exploit or incite [the other Indians] with lies or deceit that will provoke violence; do not permit instigators or idlers [in your midst] so that I have to punish them. As caciques and principales, teach your people in the haciendas, communities, and ayllus to be good men, respectful of God and the authorities.... And have confidence that things will improve little by little; tell [your people] that the government will help them in what is good and just.[85]

Having crushed the movement's autonomous leadership, the Villarroel state now appealed directly to the mass of caciques, alcaldes, and other local authorities to serve as the arms, eyes, and ears of the populist state in the countryside. Not only would they root out the "instigators" and "idlers"; they were also instructed to teach obedience and loyalty to their people on the haciendas, communities, and ayllus. Ideally, the loyal Indian would also serve as the regime's spies in his home region. The other side of this grand tutelary bargain was not so clear: the government would offer the loyal peasant help in all things "good and just." A more transparent gesture of paternalistic race-thinking is hard to imagine.

This is not to say that throughout the Indian Congress, the traffic in ideas and communication flowed in only one direction, from the top down. Nor were the delegates reduced to passive recipients before the government's dazzling displays of nationalism and populism. At the margins of this meeting (during some of the morning sessions, off-site workshops, and multiple informal encounters), it was possible for Indigenous delegates to cultivate networks, acquire useful political knowledge and skills, and engage in the give-and-take of substantive exchange. Several historians have noted that two concurrent congresses occurred: an onstage official event, where political discourses and displays of power were exhibited for the public and press; and an offstage unofficial congregation of Indigenous people, where hidden transcripts circulated under the radar.[86] Furthermore, Indigenous delegates eventually forced the Villarroel government to use the final plenary session of the Congress to address the demand for social and agrarian reform that had been promised by Toro and Busch almost a decade earlier.

Educating the Indian was at the top of that list of demands. The issue had surfaced in the meeting sessions, various speeches, and circulating petitions all during the congress. That Indian schooling was a universal (constitutional) right was beyond dispute, but that it was not yet a reality was a source of bitter recrimination. Some delegates demanded the right to education so the Indian could be taught to read and write in Spanish, but "without neglecting to perfect his use of the native languages Quechua and Aymara."[87] For other delegates, bilingualism was valued largely as a pedagogical tool, a commonsense approach to teaching Native-speaking kids their letters. Writing against the state's ideal of castellanización, the delegates' interlocking demand for primary schools, literacy, and the preservation of Native languages was proposed as logical and compatible with Indigenous strivings for cultural empowerment and enfranchisement. But as we shall see, the language question would not soon be resolved.

Indeed, ever since the Chaco War (and before), strident linguistic nationalism had prevailed among statesmen, educators, and intellectuals on both the right and left ends of the political spectrum. Having suffered military defeat, Bolivian statesmen found it convenient to scapegoat the Indian soldier, blaming him for having failed to comprehend or obey the commands of their military officers at the front. But tens of thousands had shed blood for the patria, and more soldiers were needed to fill the lower ranks. Villarroel, like his predecessors, believed that the country's sovereignty depended on the swift and uncompromising *incorporación del indígena* through the cultural, behavioral, and linguistic rigors of assimilation. After 1940, the resurgent oligarchy pushed the assimilative agenda even further by urging a national program of cultural mestizaje. Villarroel's tutelary populism was a pathway toward Indian acculturation and integration through elementary education, workforce discipline, military service, and language assimilation.

Not surprisingly, therefore, the education of the Indian became a crucial plank in Villarroel's platform and a flash point of debate at the 1945 Congress. Among the congress's featured speakers was Toribio Claure, a veteran indigenista teacher, a critic of Warisata, and Villarroel's second minister of education.[88] Claure called for rural school reform to carry out two nation-building missions—both to uplift and integrate the Indigenous masses into the homogenizing Bolivian nation *and* to reorient the school curriculum (away from "mere alphabetization") to train up a modern agricultural workforce.

There was, of course, nothing novel about his proposal, although he embellished it with a devastating critique of Bolivia's history of failed school policies and racial exclusion of the Indian.[89] Claure proposed specific institutional reforms to enhance rural education (more technical and vocational training; more elementary schools; mobile brigades to bring hygiene, culture, and didactic films to rural communities; distribution of potable water, latrines, and other services, etc.). Much of this infrastructure was to be delivered by the Ministry of National Defense, and Claure was keen to use the military barracks for intensive literacy training as well as cultural "extension education." Indian recruits would take special courses in civic education and participate in programs like the Boy Scouts and Red Cross brigades, being developed and funded by the US aid program of SCIDE. Neither the pluralist principle of Indigenous self-determination nor the leftist call for land reform entered into this elaborate educational scheme.[90]

By the end of four days, the congress had assembled an impressive slate of social reforms. No matter how much Villarroel tried to control the gathering's outcome, he realized that the Indian delegates could not go home empty-handed. In the final session of the congress, Villarroel issued four decrees that he hoped would appease the delegates: (1) the right of colonos to paid labor (left intact, however, were the basic terms of servile tenancy); (2) the right of rural workers to a labor code; (3) the universal right of school-age children to basic education in primary schools; and (4) the right of all Indians to lawful protection against persecution and other forms of violence.[91] In essence, they were iterations of earlier promises made by Toro and Busch following the Chaco War.[92] Prospects for agrarian reform (whether the socialist variety, calling for "liquidation of the feudal hacienda" and "land to the tiller," or the older Indianist demand for the restitution of original communal lands) were virtually nil in 1945.[93]

In the end, the state's promise to provision rural communities with primary schools and hire an army of ten thousand schoolteachers was but cruel hyperbole. In 1945, a US embassy official confided to his bosses in Washington that in embassy circles, Villarroel's promise was considered a perverse joke. The Bolivian state had neither the material aid nor the administrative means to force landowners to establish schools on their estates. And the state lacked the resources to set up rural public schools in the provinces. The American diplomat had to confess that the Indian Congress was a spectacle of populist puffery. Villarroel's speeches and reforms, he noted rather smugly, were "not at all revolutionary." The upshot of this "First National

Indian Congress," Thurston told the State Department, was the president's "exhortation to the Indians to do their duty to the country."[94] Embassy officials no doubt breathed a collective sigh of relief.

Aftershocks

Many delegates trudged back to their villages and haciendas with high hopes, but with only the vaguest sense of how the regime might redeem its promises and enforce the president's four decrees. Under such circumstances, with the ex-delegates' inflated expectations crashing up against the bulwark of landlord intransigence, the "seeds of indiscipline and disobedience" germinated in the soil of an already restive countryside.[95] Even before the congress closed, American diplomats were bracing themselves for trouble. An embassy dispatch warned the State Department that "disappointment among the Indians and possible baleful consequences may reasonably be imagined."[96] News items of the day, and later oral testimonies, chronicled the cascade of violent incidents that befell the Indian delegates in the aftermath of the congress. Years later, campesinos from Ayopaya recalled those treacherous times: "When we returned home from the congress, they were waiting to grab us... so we communicated among ourselves, gathering people together bit by bit, telling them in this way and that. For this reason the patrones... were always watching us, waiting for a chance to seize us, and calling us 'these wandering ringleaders.'"[97] In 1952 and 1953, shortly after the MNR party seized power, peasant leaders unleashed a stream of retroactive grievances, detailing the hair-raising consequences of their participation in the 1945 Congress. One *político Villarroeista* recounted how, upon returning home from the congress, he found his lands, animals, and grain storage hut pillaged. Under death threats, and worried that his enemies would set fire to his hut, the man fled into the mountains, only to be later arrested in Potosí.[98] Meanwhile, a theater of the absurd cropped up: a few months after the Indian Congress, Bolivia's powerful cartel of landowners, the Sociedad Rural Boliviana (SRB), organized its own counter-congress (in September 1945) to express its "profound sense of unease" over the Indian Congress and Villarroel's dangerous concessions to the Indian race.[99]

Social historians have often viewed the spasm of rural violence that shook Bolivia in 1946 and 1947 as the onset of a longer, six-year cycle (*el sexenio*) of escalating political violence and a minor "civil war," which climaxed in the popular insurrection that swept the MNR into power in April 1952. That cycle of political contention saw the landed elite's firewall of defense crumble and the embers of peasant "indiscipline and disobedience" burst into flame.[100] After his public hanging (in July 1946), Villarroel's promised reforms turned into a dead letter. The political vacuum was filled by a succession of factionalized politicians who went up against a robust coalition of radical and popular forces—groups of organized tin miners, rural laborers and peasants, radical dissidents, and a handful of vanguard Marxist parties. Socialist slogans like "Mines to the state, lands to the people" ignited crowds in the city and countryside and conjured a sense of political possibility for justice and equality, come the revolution. Meanwhile, in late 1947 and early 1948, a vigorous alliance of anarcho-syndicalists based in La Paz began organizing village schools, labor unions, rural strikes, and other political activities in the provinces of Pacajes and Los Andes, where the hacienda regime of *colonaje* was deeply entrenched. The anarchists' liberationist project released a torrent of ephemeral print pieces (pamphlets, flyers, newspapers, etc.), introduced new ways of communal reading, and organized adult programs of radical popular education. New cells of political concientización among paceño artisans and peasants amplified the anarchist influence throughout the northern Altiplano during 1947 and 1948.[101]

A historic revolutionary conjuncture was unfolding, but not without unleashing a barbaric "feudal reaction" (in the phrase of the late Bolivian historian Josép Barnadas). By early 1947, Bolivia's pendulum of state power and militarized violence had swung back toward the ruling oligarchy (the mining and landholding *rosca*) and its American allies, all of whom were now aligned against the perceived threat of "communism," stoking the fires of popular discontent. Military assaults on striking peasants in the region of Ayopaya (in western Cochabamba) and striking miners and their wives in the tin-mining town of Catavi—covered copiously in the press—became sanguinary sites and symbols of the oligarchy's unrelenting counterattack on protesting laborers. Meanwhile, Washington's embassy in La Paz kept a wary eye on the volatile domestic situation while advising Enrique Herzog's regime (1947-49) about how to placate the rural masses while developing the country's agricultural economy. The Americans were vigilant in regard to escalating labor unrest, particularly the Trotskyist call for "permanent revolution."[102] By then, the MNR's exiled leaders had launched a propaganda campaign that called for the overthrow of the feudal oligarchy. From his safe haven in Buenos Aires, Augusto Céspedes (an MNR ideologue) published a shocking exposé. Titled *Una tiranía en Sudamérica*, the 1947 pamphlet depicted a brutal counterinsurgency operation, replete with aerial bombing, military executions, mass arrests of peasants, workers, and political dissidents, and their internal exile to the dreaded jungle prison of Ichilo.[103]

Looking back from the far side of the 1952 political insurrection, we can see how the military assault on striking laborers in 1947 would mark the oligarchy's last neocolonial defense against the gathering fury. North American officials watched anxiously as the explosive situation unfolded in the Bolivian mines and countryside, ever more convinced that the brittle oligarchy was incapable of bending before the inevitable. Surveying the Altiplano from their watchtower in the US embassy in La Paz, American officials had every reason to worry. The peasant upheavals marked a dangerous setback, a clear sign that Villarroel's brand of hegemonic populism was dead.

What this dramatic (and well-documented) conjuncture hides, however, is the slow, steady work that US aid officials had been performing in rural Bolivian schools and communities over the previous several years. Amid the agrarian turmoil, North Americans had quietly moved into the Bolivian Andes for the purpose of teaching the country how to modernize the countryside and, through the application of modern disciplinary techniques, how to pacify and acculturate its Indian inhabitants. Among their first assignments was to study the "Andean Indian" so as to chart the direction of rural development and redesign rural education in alignment with Western precepts of capitalist progress, cultural uplift, and racial assimilation. As rural unrest escalated and populist politics under Villarroel enjoyed a brief comeback, Bolivia seemed to offer itself up as an exotic experimental camp to US aid officers, educators, economists, and anthropologists, eager to show the country how to manage its unruly Indian population and develop the rural sector using the latest scientific and pedagogical tools.

6

Enclaves of Acculturation
The North American School Crusade

The U.S. staff was given the job of re-organizing... the Bolivian educational system—never an easy task for foreigners!
—ERNEST MAES, "An Experiment in Internationalism"

In the early 1940s, Bolivia moved to the center of Washington's strategic map of the Western Hemisphere, just as a small army of North American "technical experts" began streaming into Bolivia. Their fact-finding excursions to Bolivia's cities, mining camps, and rustic villages were one small but profoundly significant expression of Washington's larger ambition to strengthen its geopolitical reach, spread its political ideology and cultural values, and bring the hemisphere into strict alignment with the Allied cause during World War II.

Despite its small size on the geopolitical map of Latin America, Bolivia became the source of acute concern in Washington. German influences had long been pervasive in Bolivia's ruling economic and political circles, and it was not inconceivable that the Nazis were eyeing Bolivia as a possible inroad into the geographic interior of South America, the perfect springboard for its broader continental designs. Equally alarming was Bolivia's fertile political climate for local profascist sentiments to grow and flower. Since the late 1930s, but especially around the turn of the decade, Bolivia had become a hothouse of nationalist, Marxist, and fascist ideologies—united if only by their common hostility to the bankruptcy of Bolivian oligarchic liberalism and US incursions into Bolivia's mining and petroleum industries.[1] It is possible that, under other circumstances, those factors alone—Bolivia's German colony, its tradition of military nationalism, and the left's abiding hostility to *yanqui* imperialism—might not have registered so strongly on Washington's radar screen. But Washington's sudden obsession had an immediate material cause: Bolivia was sitting on the largest repository of tin reserves in the Western Hemisphere. Simón Patiño's Catavi mines contained some of the world's highest-grade tin, suitable for smelting in the great industrial furnaces of Texas, Holland, and England. Meanwhile, World War II had thrown all transatlantic shipping lanes into jeopardy, and by late 1941 Malaysia's tin-producing areas were in danger of falling to imperial Japan. Because tin was quickly becoming an essential material in weaponry and canning, there was good reason for Washington to worry. Once the Americans entered the war following the Japanese attack on Pearl Harbor in December 1941, it looked to highland Bolivia—an indispensable supplier of tin.

As might be expected of any commodity boom, particularly one driven by the contingencies of war, the US-Bolivian tin deal proved to be, at best, a mixed blessing for Bolivia. Not only did the tin boom cause massive social dislocations, hardships, and violence for mining communities; it also planted the seeds of its own demise. While Bolivian mines disgorged ore for the Texas smelter, the 1945 Allied victory spelled the end of its privileged status as a wartime trading partner. Bolivia was forced to cope with a postwar world economy that no longer had much need for its tin.

That dramatic episode in Bolivian-US relations drew attention away from America's deeper imperial incursions into the rural interior of the Bolivian Andes, far from the mining pits. In the early 1940s, Washington dispatched a group of diplomats, technical advisers, and social science experts to the Bolivian Andes for the purposes of investigating the country's social conditions, stabilizing its volatile working class, promoting economic development, and establishing social welfare programs targeted to the highland peasantry, particularly the Aymara. A quiet crusade was unfolding in certain rural areas, where a cadre of North American social scientists, technicians, educators, and aid workers were busy studying conditions on the ground and, by the mid-to-late 1940s, seeding parts of the Bolivian countryside with rural schools, hygiene and health stations, agro-industrial programs, and cultural missions.

Recent scholarship chronicles the smooth transition from World War II into the Cold War as North America positioned itself as global hegemon in the late 1940s.[2] As social scientists turned from wartime to peacetime work, their research priorities and strategies also shifted from staunching the spread of fascism to the containment of communism. Although Washington soon lost interest in Bolivian tin reserves, its postwar overseas agencies (including President Harry Truman's ambitious Point Four Program) looked at Bolivia through new Cold War lenses. What they saw was a volatile, impoverished, landlocked nation located in the heart of South America. Despite its small size, Bolivia loomed large in North America's imperial imaginary. America's foreign affairs establishment and overseas agencies (including the UN and the Carnegie and Rockefeller Foundations) hoped to get at the root causes of Bolivian poverty and labor unrest that threatened to push the working classes and peasantry into the arms of radical leftist parties and militant unions. During the 1940s, then, Bolivia went from being a giant tin supplier for the war effort to becoming a "natural laboratory" and practical testing ground for North American development schemes, ameliorative social programs, and soft diplomacy operations that would eventually converge on Cold War national security projects, including its military intelligence apparatus for "Communist Containment."[3]

This chapter examines North America's postwar aid programs to Bolivia in the field of rural education by tracing the pedagogical ideas and actions of US advisers, educators, and aid workers who ventured into highland Bolivia in the mid-1940s. There they blundered into a land aflame: a local oligarchy at war with Warisata; raging ideological debates over the causes of Bolivia's racial and cultural backwardness; escalating labor strife; a militant anti-imperialist left; and a daunting set of structural obstacles to capitalist progress and political stabilization. But the postwar era was also a time of Western exuberance and mega–development schemes, such as the Marshall Plan. Buoyed by the US's global ascendance and by the putative miracles of capitalist markets and modern agriculture, this on-site technocratic vanguard went to work diagnosing the Bolivia's socioeconomic and racial problems and then designing bold development schemes of various kinds that would bulldoze them away.

We begin this chapter by tracking Lloyd Hughes, an American school inspector sent to Bolivia in 1944. His critical on-site appraisal helped pave the way for Washington's postwar aid and investment in education, public health, and social welfare, as well as rural development programs in Bolivia (and in Latin America more generally). From there, the chapter chronicles the origins of the North Americans' ambitious postwar, bilateral program in rural Indian education. Its principal architect was Ernest Maes, a self-styled American indigenista boasting a long career in the US Bureau of Indian Affairs. Importing a holistic model of racial assimilation, Maes used his authority and generous funding to establish the forerunner to the Servicio Cooperativo Interamericano de Desarrollo Educativo (SCIDE), a bilateral "cooperative" program of rural schooling and cultural hygiene. Finally, we take a ground-up view to explore the ambivalent reception of the Americans' school program in specific local sites, as well as the profound skepticism that many Bolivian educators, including Elizardo Pérez, felt toward SCIDE's interventions in the field of Indigenous education.

Gazing at the Bolivian Andes from a distance, who might have imagined that a cadre of American aid officers and educational experts would stake the fate of American-Bolivian relations on the success of rural school reform? And that the US drive to uplift the Bolivian Indian and stabilize the country through its "rural extension" programs would eventually lead back to the ravaged battleground of Warisata?

The American Exposé of Failing Rural Schools

As World War II wound down, Washington's hemispheric policies turned back toward New Deal concerns with the underlying conditions of poverty, unrest, and myriad leftist and populist threats to US hegemony in the region. Newly formed inter-American extension services (the *servicios cooperativos*—SAI, SCISP, and SCIDE) provided the routes for channeling North American extension education and community organization programs into Bolivian mining camps and peasant villages,[4] and Washington was eager to begin raising living standards, disciplining the labor force, and stabilizing the country's political system. In early 1944, a US envoy arrived in La Paz to study the political situation and recommend a package of economic aid programs. The official report was encouraging: the Office of Inter-American Affairs was to establish two bilateral "cooperative service" programs in public health care and public schools (later, a third servicio would target the problem of agriculture). Very quickly, US aid officers identified rural ("Indian") education as central to Washington's larger goals of rural development, poverty reduction, and workforce training for Bolivia. Lloyd Hughes, the man in charge of negotiating the educational aid program, set out to investigate the present condition of rural schooling in Bolivia. What were the most pressing educational needs? How might the Americans deploy its modern pedagogical methods and tools to uplift and integrate the Indian masses into the modernizing economy? Hughes's mission was, first, to conduct rural site visits and gather official statistics (to the extent they existed) from the CNE's earlier reports on the state of rural education. He also depended on Bolivian officials to execute this inspection tour. It is ironic, but hardly surprising, that Hughes depended on Vicente Donoso Torres (the man most responsible for persecuting Pérez and destroying the escuela-ayllu) to oversee the field inspection of rural schools. Now, for a good salary, Donoso had no recourse but to reveal the dismal condition of public schools over which his own agency (the CNE) had presided during the previous four years.

Lloyd Hughes's initial typewritten report, "Education in Bolivia," furnished a shocking indictment of Bolivia's failed public school system in both urban and rural areas. Numbers told a dismal story: out of the total population of 3,412,600 people, only about 20 percent of its school-age population attended public schools regularly. A scandalous 80 percent of children were not matriculated in public schools. (How many attended local, community-based schools was off the government's radar, however.) The Hughes report also broke down rates of adult literacy by racial groups: the white race boasted the highest literacy rate (more than 65 percent of the total population), mestizos the second highest (about 25 percent), and Indians the lowest (merely 5 percent). Categories of race were correlated, in this scheme, to the functional ability to read and write, according to the state's dubious figures. The statistical report designated categories of "Indian" and "mestizo" to account for Bolivia's appalling illiteracy rate of 85 percent.[5] Erased from this public record was the long history of Indigenous struggle for access to elementary schools, the pervasive use of vernacular literacy practices, and prodigious documentary skills that Indigenous people had honed over the years. Instead, Hughes's simple matrix correlated race with illiteracy, then made illiteracy an official index of Indian backwardness (and government neglect) and thus the target of future US-funded operations.

Although Hughes's report circulated only in government policy-making circles, it charted the pathway for American involvement in Bolivian school reform. A small step was taken in September 1944, when the United States and Bolivia signed an agreement "to develop training projects for urban, rural and vocational teachers." Bolivia would send teachers to study abroad in teacher-training colleges in the United States, and the United States would send a team of specialists to help Bolivia train a corps of teachers under the auspices of SCIDE.[6] The Hughes team argued that teacher training offered an ideal venue for reaching the laboring poor and investing in Bolivia's future. Clearly, US aid to education should privilege the rural primary school, it reasoned, since Bolivia's future depended primarily on the development and assimilation of the Indigenous workforce into a Westernizing mestizo/white nation. And why not begin manpower training by targeting the next generation of rural schoolteachers? An earlier international commission had reported that some 70 percent of all rural schoolteachers lacked formal training; most had less than a six-year primary school education; and almost all of them engaged in old-fashioned rote methods, designed only to teach Indians the rudiments of literacy (a useless endeavor, in the eyes of most Bolivian and North American educators).[7] For his part, Lloyd Hughes urged Washington to funnel technical assistance into areas of public health and vocational education, and to begin by building primary and secondary schoolhouses and stocking them with supplies.[8] There were administrative problems to solve too. After four years of operation, the CNE's attempt to rationalize and centralize the educational bureaucracy had floundered.

In light of this disaster, Washington wanted to impose its own education czar, someone with the credentials, experience, and confidence needed to pressure the Bolivian government to "reorient" its national pedagogy. Its fledgling "cooperative bilateral programs" in public health, education, and agriculture were already earmarked for Bolivia, and aid money was beginning to flow. That was incentive enough for Bolivian government authorities to cooperate with the Americans, even if strident nationalists resented foreign meddling in Bolivian social institutions. For Washington, it was now an operational question of putting the right man in charge of SCIDE, someone who could accomplish what three generations of Bolivian school reformers had failed to do—establish rural school centers to train, discipline, and assimilate the peasantry. Of particular interest were the rural Aymara, still viewed as the most volatile and backward of the country's three major ethnic groups, and the new pedagogy of workforce training and behavioral reform was invoked as the solution to Bolivia's racial and agrarian backwardness.

Ernest Maes Sets Out to Redesign Public Education

In April 1945, Ernest Maes arrived in La Paz to take on the task of organizing a vocational school system especially targeted for rural highland peasants.[9] That Maes was appointed in the first place is a telling sign that Washington policy makers had taken to heart an earlier Smithsonian report and now were acutely aware of "Bolivian Indians" and their centrality to the country's workforce development in agriculture and mining.[10] Indeed, Maes had participated in the 1942 Yale conference as an expert scholar and administrator in US and Inter-American Indian affairs. Having also attended the 1940 indigenista conference in Pátzcuaro, he was well acquainted with the debates among Latin American anthropologists and social reformers, and he probably had already made contact with the quarreling Bolivian contingent of delegates to that conference. Thus, Maes brought to the Bolivian job a formidable mix of field experience, supreme confidence, and scientific authority, most of it accrued during his long career in Washington's Bureau of Indian Affairs. He was the archetypal imperial "extension agent," dispatched by Washington to transform Bolivia's Indian peasantry through the medium of "functional education" and community development programs in accordance with North American expansionary interests and racial assimilationist ideals.

Maes entered Bolivia at a delicate political moment and soon realized that he had to play his diplomatic cards carefully. The solicitous and conservative Peñaranda regime was now gone, forcing the United States to navigate a testy relationship with the new military populist regime. Maes quickly had to find ways to work with Villarroel and his ministers.[11] Meanwhile, the locus of racial and class anxiety seemed to be radiating out of the tin camps into rural villages. News of agitation and militancy among Aymara and Quechua peasants filled the pages of Bolivian newspapers, indigenista and leftist pamphlets, and US embassy reports, as we saw in chapter 5. Curiously, though, Maes seemed to turn a blind eye to the problem of chronic peasant unrest: the task of monitoring the threat to rural peace and political stability was left to US embassy officials. In the meantime, Maes's on-site introduction to the "Bolivian Indian" was carefully staged by the Bolivian government, as it turned out. As Villarroel's invited guest, the American educator attended the inaugural ceremony of the 1945 National Indigenous Congress (the first of its kind in Bolivia). Looking out from his perch on the stage, filled with other white dignitaries, Maes witnessed delegation after Indigenous delegation convene in the soccer stadium for the purpose of discussing and promoting their political demand for land reform, labor rights, legal equality, and access to schooling.

What impressions did that mass assembly make on this newly arrived gringo? What lessons might Maes have drawn from the May 1945 Indian Congress? One can only surmise, but to judge from Maes's later reports and actions, he was awestruck by the sheer scale of this historic congress of Indigenous delegates. Clearly, the timing of his arrival in Bolivia was fortuitous, he believed. Indigenous people had demonstrated a collective desire for rural schooling and other reforms; now it was up to the Americans to design and deliver a modern system of vocational schooling, tied closely to the US agricultural aid program (SAI) promoting modern family farms. With unbounded diplomatic ambition, Maes planned to use Bolivia as a springboard for launching an ambitious trilateral (US-Bolivia-Peru) program to confront the "Indian problem," simultaneously, on both sides of the Bolivia-Peru border.

But Maes's first task was to establish diplomatic rapport with key members of the Villarroel populist government, including Major Jorge Calero (newly appointed minister of education), Toribio Claure (head of the Department of Rural Education and ex-director of the núcleo school of Vacas), and the formidable Vicente Donoso Torres (the mastermind behind the state's earlier war on Warisata, who continued to operate offstage after the CNE was dismantled in 1944). Maes had to navigate among this fractious group of populists and nationalists, including the young leftist party of the MNR that was part of the Villarroel governing coalition. Watching how Maes operated, one Bolivian educator later reported that the naive American was caught in an echo chamber, where "Major Calero's opinions were nothing but a reflection of the [conservative] group that surrounded him . . . , and [thus] Mr. Maes was compelled to deal with this group and to gather information based on their opinions [and official reports]."[12] Aligning himself with the conservative faction within the Villarroel regime, Maes had blundered into a partisan sand trap, as it would later turn out.

Indeed, this preternaturally confident American quickly established himself as both expert and judge of Bolivian Indians and their rural schools.

Parroting the oligarchy's scabrous attacks, Maes singled out Elizardo Pérez for having created a monstrosity out of the escuela-ayllu of Warisata—what with its primitive communal practices, expansionist designs, and dangerous racist teachings. In one 1948 report, Maes explained why he felt compelled "to correct the excesses and errors" of Warisata, beginning with its "grandiose, monumental building housing a school [that was] ostentatious and dictatorial, designed to regiment the surrounding population through control of large land areas, and sentimentally designed to pay a kind of politically patriotic homage to the native sons of the land, its original owners, or 'indigenos' [sic]." This crusader thus associated himself with the enemies of Warisata and defined America's work as an effort to clean up Bolivia's "nuclear Indian schools," which were "decadent and in ill repute."[13] Maes had his own prescriptive pedagogy, one that would transform the Indian into a hardworking campesino through strict vocational training and resocialization in a regional school center, where carefully trained teachers (under American tutelage) applied the methods of "functional pedagogy."[14] Meanwhile, Maes told his colleagues and staff to refrain from addressing their Indigenous charges and clients as "indios." In keeping with the populist language of class, US officials were "to think of Indians as a distinct class in the rural population."[15]

On paper, Maes's comprehensive design for rural education dwarfed anything that had come before it. It was a classic example of mega–development planning emanating from the inflated global designs of postwar North America. SCIDE's blueprint for rural education reform in Bolivia identified seven ambitious goals: (1) the merger of all "Indian" and "rural" schools into one centralized bureaucratic system; (2) the creation of a "functional curriculum" centered around scientific agriculture, health and hygiene, and home economics; (3) the expansion of the normal school program, where technical instruction and supervision would be offered; (4) the development of "cultural services" to diffuse the practical instruction and modern values to rural communities, through cultural brigades and massive distribution of teaching materials (e.g., the "didactic guides" developed by US educators and the mimeographed pamphlets created by Bolivian educators); (5) a profusion of ethnographic studies of Aymara and Quechua communities; (6) a proposal for teacher salary increases; and (7) designs for a cooperative program involving the ministries of agriculture, health, and the Bolivian Development Corps.[16] To begin with, this imperial experiment would be applied to the most challenging of geo-cultural environments: the Aymara

Altiplano, where the pedagogy of Western progress could be tested against the half-millennium-long "persistence of native [Aymara] culture."[17]

Such a grand design had to be adapted to the local milieu, of course, so Maes decided to embark on his own field trip to gather impressions and information about the true state of Bolivia's rural schools. That trip allowed Maes to see beyond the ugly propaganda that had condemned Warisata and the other núcleo escolares as nefarious enclaves of communism and rebellion. Indeed, Maes had to admit there were things about the núcleo peasant school system that could be admired and elements that were worthy enough to appropriate and adapt to his grand pedagogic scheme. He was most impressed by the rural schools of Santiago de Huata and Vacas. Warisata, on the other hand, was still reeling from years of government neglect, slander, and pillage. What Maes was beginning to realize (no doubt encouraged by Vicente Donoso Torres) was that Bolivia's "núcleos" might be appropriated and transformed into a spatial-administrative arrangement for the purpose of centralizing and regulating rural school centers under SCIDE's control. Creating administrative "school districts" out of the núcleos escolares would allow SCIDE officials to stretch scarce resources, oversee the training of rural teachers, and standardize its work-oriented curriculum—all in the name of bureaucratic efficiency and technical oversight. Teacher training was Maes's immediate goal: "The núcleos [will] provide . . . the essential supervision needed by the rural schoolteachers . . . who require close supervision because of their inadequate training. . . . [This supervision] can be given with the least possible personnel" (see fig. 6.1).[18]

Under SCIDE, some forty-six new peasant school centers were officially created (up from eighteen at the height of Elizardo Pérez's time). On one level, this new landscape was a bureaucratic deceit: solar patterns were redrawn on a map; names of villages, their sectional schools, and the main school complex were listed on government inventories. As Maes mentioned in a revealing aside, it actually did not take much effort to draw lines on the Bolivian map, but putting real content into the bureaucratic numbers was an altogether different story. In a 1948 report titled "An Experiment in Internationalism," Maes claimed that SCIDE was administering a staggering number of rural núcleo schools—some forty-one peasant centers, including their nine-hundred-odd satellite primary schools located throughout the length and breadth of Bolivia. Judging by its official maps and numbers, SCIDE's influence had quickly spread far and wide.[19]

FIGURE 6.1. SCIDE's vision of the "núcleo" schools as a patchwork of farming properties (much like the US Midwest) and adjacent school districts. SCIDE, *Rural Education in Bolivia* (1955), 13.

Equally imperative to this endeavor was SCIDE's curricular efforts in the teacher-training schools. The 1944 Hughes report had found Bolivia's six normal schools for rural teachers in a deplorable state: fewer than 150 teachers graduated from normals each year; they were in a state of physical decay; and none offered training in agriculture, home economics, health education, or instructional teaching.[20] They would need wholesale reform: a "completely revised and reoriented curriculum"; teacher-training workshops (ironically, held in Warisata in 1945 and in other school sites in 1946);[21] and two rural normal schools (one for women, in Santiago de Huata, the other for men, in Vacas), where female and male teachers might be separately trained in gender-appropriate skills.[22] Under joint sponsorship of SCIDE and SCISP, the women normalistas would learn skills in "home visiting and social service," while male students were taught modern agricultural methods.[23] Later, other rural normal schools would be added to those under SCIDE-SCISP control, but this was a vigorous start for SCIDE officials. Meanwhile, Maes took advantage of American mass media, postwar propaganda, and Hollywood products to spread goodwill and secure alliances. Educational films, puppet shows, and folk theater were mobilized, and at the same time, American-trained health workers (many working for SCISP) began carrying out a massive vaccination campaign. In 1946, the Inter-American Education Foundation reported that an astonishing number of Bolivian children (an estimated ten thousand) were vaccinated for smallpox and typhoid fever.[24] This widely publicized campaign demonstrated the pharaonic power that postwar America seemed to exercise over the biomedical history of this Andean region. But such gross estimates also obscure the yawning gap between this US-driven public health campaign and the reality of poverty and ill health that still plagued Indigenous people in the countryside.[25]

Encouraged by his prodigious fieldwork in Bolivia, Ernest Maes dreamed of exporting his own semipatented version of the Bolivian núcleo escolar to other Latin American regions—starting with Peru, but eventually extending into Ecuador, Colombia, and even Guatemala. No doubt, the schoolmaster drew inspiration from the colony of Protestant missionaries who had been building schools, clinics, and churches on both sides of the Bolivia-Peru border since the early twentieth century. But in both scale and intensity, SCIDE's summer programs for immersive teacher-training among Bolivian and Peruvian rural teachers were beginning to dwarf the missionary enclaves. Encouraged, Maes's ambitions soared, and in 1945 he floated the idea that rural education should be developed for the whole Lake Titicaca basin, given that SCIDE extension workers already operated on both sides of the border. School techniques developed in Aymara villages on the Bolivian side of the border might just as easily be exported to Peruvian rural schools, and vice versa. A plan for teacher-training workshops was hatched with the venerable Peruvian education minister Luís Valcarcel. And in 1945, Peruvian and Bolivian teachers gathered in a summer workshop with SCIDE technicians with plans to develop a new "functional" curriculum specifically designed for the Aymara Indian.[26] These early field activities inflated Maes's ambitions for a transregional program of Indian education run by the Americans. In his 1948 report, "An Experiment in Internationalism," Maes outlined a grand scheme for "an Andean system of rural education," one that was capable of extending North America's cultural and pedagogical influences throughout the Andean peasant world of highland Peru and Ecuador, and beyond, into Guatemala.[27] Having just spent three grueling years in Bolivia, Maes had become the self-appointed architect of Indigenous education in Latin America. As ambitious as ever, Maes left his post in Bolivia for Guatemala (another troubled hot spot on Washington's hemispheric map) to expand his school reform mission throughout the Mayan highlands.

No less impressive, from Washington's point of view, was SCIDE's revised school curriculum—which later traveled to Peru, Ecuador, and Guatemala, largely thanks to Maes's efforts. At base, North American educators set out "to reorient [the] ways of thinking"—an epistemic and cultural revolution that would inculcate Western values, skills, habits, and practices in the Indigenous subject. Since then, postcolonial critics have unmasked the racial logic of coloniality that was, and continues to be, inherent in the politics and culture of informal empire and globally enacted in Western discourse, policy, and practice. Western epistemology (the very notion of social scientific knowledge and modern progress itself) came to be seen not merely as one way of knowing among others but as an imperial project that denigrated and displaced Indigenous forms of knowing, schooling, and learning.[28] That this cadre of educators went to the Indigenous Andes to "reorient ways of thinking" hints at the imperial implications of their educational reform project, as they themselves understood it. But forging consensus proved difficult. There were intraimperial tensions and contradictions about best practices: that is, *how best to "reorient"* local ways of thinking and knowing. Some anthropologists and pedagogues argued for a more nuanced approach (later labeled "inculturation") through the selective incorporation of Western elements of living and thinking into traditional Indian society. The Smithsonian anthropologists, hardly card-carrying "cultural pluralists," had argued that selected "virtues" of autochthony (coca-chewing and healing practices, for example) could be preserved without jeopardizing the West's acculturative project. In any event, the postwar mantra of progressive educators was that "Western civilization must adapt itself to the life of the Indian" if the Indian were to be culturally improved and integrated into modern life. Maes's pedagogical goals had little to do with empowering Indigenous people as political subjects, much less encouraging their integration into the nation as fully enfranchised citizens. Recognizing the Indian's contributions to "universal culture," he made sure to reprise a fundamental principle of Bolivia's conservative reformers: "The Indian should not be incorporated into the [political] life of the nation," at least not for the time being.[29] Citizenship still had no role to play in the educators' program of Indian assimilation.

Once in the field, Maes discarded the principle of "strategic cultural tolerance" that his Smithsonian Institution colleagues had recommended in their 1942 report.[30] Perhaps it was the realpolitik of the fieldwork experience, or the overweening influence of Vicente Donoso and other conservatives, or the fear or disgust he may have felt toward his Indigenous subjects. In any event, Maes's pedagogic orientation was formed by his long career in the Bureau of Indian Affairs—the leading hemispheric agency promoting racial assimilation through its boarding school and vocational programs, designed specifically for North America's "minority" Indian and Black populations. Envisioning a crude model of population management—vaguely resembling Michel Foucault's concept of "governmentality"—Maes directed his educators to burrow into the intimate corners of everyday rural life, so as to fundamentally reshape the contours of Indian social behavior and subjectivity.[31]

Intimate Modernity: Teaching Habits, Hygiene, and Homemaking

SCIDE's cultural mission initially came in the tangible form of massive manuals expressly written and published for rural teachers in Bolivia. SCIDE (in conjunction with the Ministry of Peasant Affairs, or MAC) put out three remarkable sets of pamphlets on functional pedagogy that appeared in 1946, 1947, and 1948.[32] Here was Ernest Maes's textual monument to the new program of rural education, produced over a two-year period. Preliminary drafts were written in the Warisata teacher-training workshop in December 1945 and circulated in mimeograph form during 1946. The final published version, the seven-part *Guías de instrucción para maestros rurales*, was published in 1948 with money from SCIDE. The first volume, *Guía didáctica de educación rural*, furnished an overview of the "functional curriculum," while the remaining six volumes were devoted to fields of rural vocational and community education, specifically agriculture, rural health, livestock raising, rural community and peasant school organizations, domestic economy, and rural pedagogy. To secure broad legitimacy, the textbooks garnered the names of almost one hundred Bolivian teachers, administrators, and government officials, as well as several foreign technicians (it was a textbook produced by a bilateral committee). To judge the book by its cover, it had the imprimatur of educational experts up and down the spine of the Andes, and especially prominent Bolivian educators. To judge the manual by its contents, however, Ernest Maes's imprint seemed to be stamped on every page (see fig. 6.2).

With four thousand of these published pamphlets circulating in 1948, SCIDE and the Bolivian education ministry felt they had turned a page in the

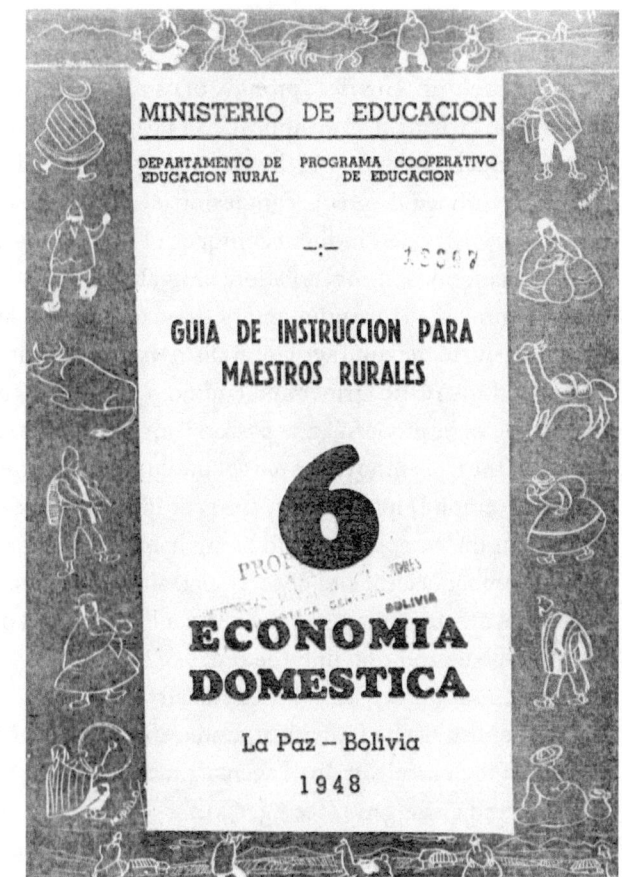

FIGURE 6.2. The rural teacher's manual specializing in home economics, published jointly by the Cooperative Education Program (later renamed the Servicio Cooperativo Interamericano de Desarrollo Educativo, or SCIDE) and Bolivia's Ministry of Education. Ministerio de Educación, *Guía de instrucción para maestros rurales*, vol. 6: *Economía doméstica* (1948).

long struggle to bring order and discipline to rural schooling. In 1949, the textbooks were made official by a ministerial decree and ordered to be sent to all fiscal rural schools. Finally, they hoped, Bolivia's village schoolteachers were going to discard their archaic ways of rote teaching and instruct their pupils in all kinds of practical matters, according to Maes's pedagogical gospel.[33] The reigning concept was to anchor formal schooling in the cultural context of the surrounding peasant community, by radiating the skills and values taught at the school out into the primitive countryside. The schoolchild would be the conduit. But in the last analysis, it was the campesino's community, home life, family, habits, beliefs, and body that were to become the terminal points of behavioral reform in SCIDE's "rural extension program."

On Body and Behavior

The allure of North America's promise of rural development and cultural progress was on vivid display on almost every page of the teacher's manual. Here was the textual production of the elusive icon of Bolivian modernizers—the skilled, disciplined, hygienic campesino. SCIDE's textbook campesino was thoroughly instructed in the techniques of modern agriculture, including the importance of soil conservation; animal domestication; house building; and he commanded the rudimentary language, literacy, and arithmetic skills deemed useful to the rural agriculturalist. Abstract learning was inappropriate to the lot of the rustic farmer and had no place in this curriculum, whereas the intricacies of modern agro-pastoralism were mapped out in exhaustive detail. But the truly innovative part of the curriculum extended the state (and its shadow empire) into the very heart of Indigenous communities in order "to form in the campesino good living habits with regard to diet, clothing, home, personal health, and civic, social, and religious practices." Taken together, these factors furnished the index and litmus test of racial ascendance from the subaltern indio into the ranks of campesino—"a good member of his family, community, as well as a socially useful citizen."[34] Moral and behavioral reform of the individual, under the tutelage of US rural extension agents and their locally trained agents, thus became the passport to eventual mestizaje and citizenship (see fig. 6.3).

It is worth taking a closer look at SCIDE's recipe for eradicating Indian culture through resocialization and moral regulation. First, there was the matter of improving the Indian's diet, which was devoid of healthy vegetables, milk, fruit, eggs, and meat. (Apparently, environmental factors—ecology, poverty, and scarcity—were not deemed causative factors; this dietary deficiency was primarily a matter of cultural ignorance.) The rural teacher must make the campesino family incorporate into the diet all the produce and animal products produced on the bustling family farm. Peasants would be taught the basics of nutrition for maintaining a healthy organism and optimistic spirit. Directives spilled off the manual's pages—every peasant household should plant a kitchen garden; peasant women should be taught how to turn garden vegetables into appetizing dishes; and dairy products should be a daily part of the family diet. Above all, the rural school must instruct peasants in the value of a hearty breakfast, replete with egg, meat, cereal grain, fruit, and milk.

Bodily cleanliness and proper dress were next in the list of "good habits" to be taught. As Marcia Stephenson has shown, Bolivian discourses on body management had long associated bodily filth and pollution with rustic *bayeta* clothing, the poncho, and other sartorial items of Indianness.³⁵ The textbook reverted to the old sartorial argument: "Body cleanliness is intimately linked to the use of clothing," and it pointed to the importance of bathing and the use of undergarments. The primary object of bodily rehabilitation was the prosperous campesino couple: peasant men who sometimes dressed in suits and wore shoes and their wives who draped their bodies in costly shawls (*mantas*), wore multiple skirts and petticoats (*polleras*), and hung ostentatious gold, pearl, and silver jewelry from their ears, necks, and shawls. But the original hygienic sin was going without underwear, and it was (implicitly) the Aymara and Quechua woman who were selected as the main culprit. Why? Because forgoing *ropa interior* was deemed a matter of cultural perversion, not material want or tradition: peasant and market (*cholita*) women who spent money on elaborate exterior clothing simply had to be taught, even pressured, to alter their bodily habits, embrace the virtues of cleanliness, and dress in "presentable, unostentatious clothing," just as women did everywhere in the West.³⁶

On Home and Family

Navigating outward from the site of the gendered body to the private sphere of home and family, the didactic guide became more elaborate in its diagnosis and prescription for cultural hygiene. Specifically, the architecture and arrangement of interior domestic space in the campesino home became another normalizing site. Regardless of the impoverished and precarious condition in which most village comunarios and hacienda-bound colonos lived, the *Digesto* called for a school campaign that would instruct campesino families in the craft of laying cement foundations, baking adobe bricks and roof tiles, and constructing modern rural homes. Glass windows, hinged doors, interior walls, outdoor cooking ovens, fenced corrals, and an outdoor latrine were indispensable to the remaking of the traditional Indigenous complex of hut and corral into a modern hygienic home. To advertise this makeover of the Indian's gloomy cave-like dwelling, it should be whitewashed—serving as a stark metaphor of enlightenment, purification, and cleanliness that Protestant missionaries had introduced to certain Altiplano villages in previous decades.

(It was, in Bolivia and elsewhere, standard missionary practice among Presbyterians and other Protestant sects to whitewash the clean, newly decorated homes of the converted, because bringing lightness, fresh air, and sunshine into the home was valued equally as a sign of both spiritual cleansing and sanitary improvement.) In the meantime, however, the campesino family had to "habituate itself to the daily use of basic furniture because only in that way could it conserve its cleanliness."[37] And the use of furniture would bestow a psychological benefit as well. For if it were "seated around the table, the family would acquire a dignity equal to that of families in the cities. And in this way, [the furniture] would help eliminate the inferiority complex that the Indian foments with his own submissive attitude." But the manual warned the normal-trained teacher not to be fooled by appearances, since the proof of the pudding lay in the habitual usage of furniture as a tangible signifier of family forms of sociability, Western style. A solid varnished table had to become the centerpiece of conjugal harmony and sociability, as well as the physical and metaphorical prop that lifted Indians up off the earthen floor and out of their own animal-like filth and humility. The kitchen table was to become the site of healthy and clean food, where utensils were used and conjugal conversation took place and domestic handiwork was performed between mealtimes.[38] Furthermore, houses must be swept clean, chickens kept outside, livestock corralled, and eventually latrines built. This profound transformation of the campesino's interior domestic spaces and intimate corporeal habits was to be affected by various means, as we shall see. But key to this whole process of hygienic and cultural policing was the trained rural normalista and an auxiliary team of parents and students, the Junta de Auxilio Escolar.

On Civic Morality and Masculinity

Ultimately, patriarchy dictated that enlightened civic, social, and religious values had to be inculcated in the male campesino. There were, of course, carefully delineated "civic and moral" lessons and routines built into the rural school curriculum. Public primary schools initiated their young charges into civic-national spaces through a variety of devices: a weekly "civic hour," commemorative ceremonies, introduction to the national flag, hymn, and coat of arms; lessons in the campesino's civic duties to his family, community, and nation. Yet the pathway to civic subjecthood, and the long road to a place in the nation, also passed through the thicket of quotidian forms and norms

FIGURE 6.3. Didactic images of the rural teacher as Western agent of acculturation. Ministerio de Asuntos Campesinos (MAC) and SCIDE, *Manual del maestro rural* (1956). Prepared by the Institute of Inter-American Affairs. Translated and "adapted" for Bolivia by Vicente Lema, architect of the MNR's rural education reform.

of civic-mindedness as defined by the new teacher manuals. The overriding civic duty of the peasant was articulated through the labor he invested in his land. Civic virtue was not the product of a liberal education; rather, it was bestowed on the rustic tiller simply for having taken up his duty—indeed, his destiny—as the nation's farmer. But the campesino's civic duties extended to his relationship to his own rural village. To enter the nation, the peasant must become an exemplar of progress and modernity by, for example, clearing stones from the road, fighting extortionists, rallying the community spirit, respecting individual thought, and replacing civic-religious traditions that still punctuated the village's ceremonial calendar with community-sponsored saints' day festivities, music, dance, and drink. The textbook warned the rural teacher not to meddle in religious matters, but the rural school was ordered to combat "alcoholism in religious fiestas."[39] Civic virtue and an ever-elusive citizenship came, therefore, not only through the power of the plow but also through the self-discipline of temperance—the cleansing of the body of racial vices (coca and alcohol) and superstitious beliefs.

Indeed, the aim was to define the special attributes that tailored a "socially useful citizen" out of the raw fabric of the Bolivian male campesino. Tutelary race-thinking now focused on instilling the virtues of patriarchy in the campesino. He would be taught how to treat his wife and children with paternal affection, respect, and tenderness. Accordingly, fatherly love would be expressed in the way he taught his own children the value of hard work, the desire to learn, the virtues of cleanliness, and abstention from alcohol and coca. Educating male virtue might begin in the rural school, but through the rural extension program, it would radiate outward to reposition the virtuous campesino within his larger community, the nation, and even the Inter-American sphere.[40] Ultimately, the pamphlet bestowed an englobalizing patina of "American citizenship" on Bolivia's "socially virtuous" campesino, inviting him to join the universal ranks of rural cultivators who were embracing the glories of agro-modernity up and down the Americas.[41]

Such grandiosity was, by then, common parlance among rural development agencies, but the discourse elided the social spaces usually associated with the construction of working-class masculinity and citizenship—the military, mines, unions, and politics.[42] What was implicitly at work here, then, was the ideological enclosure of the male campesino subject within the narrow confines of the rural economy and its pastoral life ways. US aid officers and their Bolivian partners were interested in socializing the peasant as a function of their larger modernization goals—increasing food production on the Altiplano, securing agrarian peace, and improving the eugenic reproduction of the campesino family as it assimilated into the dominant national culture. To define civic participation through other venues only distracted from those larger assimilationist and economistic goals. It is true, of course, that Bolivia had installed universal military service in the early years of the twentieth century, and Bolivia's Aymara, Quechua, and Guaraní conscripts had borne the brunt of the Chaco War. But the conscription of young Indian men into the army had also fired up controversies about the wisdom of putting peasants in uniform and handing them guns, for although the military was a powerful acculturating machine, and one that promised to domesticate its feral recruits, it was also incubating legions of semiliterate cholos swelling the ranks of transient laborers, migrants, and "racial misfits"—to the great consternation of Bolivian indigenista reformers. The landowning oligarchy, furthermore, was reticent to lose young male colonos to army recruiters and ever paranoid about the dangerous knowledge that Aymara conscripts might acquire about arms and militarism during their two years in the army. In neocolonial Bolivia, Indigenous access to guns and letters continued to be a perennial source of racial anxiety.[43]

Nor did the tin mine enter into hegemonic representations of masculinizing spaces. By the late 1940s, Washington's obsession with extracting tin ore from the Bolivian mines had subsided, and it no longer needed to dream up schemes about mobilizing peasant recruits for the mines. On the contrary: now that the tin mining boom was over, the problem was one of peasant labor retention and reabsorption. Stanching the flow of peasant labor migration out of Altiplano's villages into the cities and mines was becoming rather urgent, as was the need to clamp down on Bolivia's unruly countryside. And in 1947 and 1948, containment of rural unrest (and the supposed infiltration of international Marxist influences) in Bolivia and elsewhere in Latin America loomed ever larger on Washington's screen as global geopolitics rapidly shifted with the onset of the Cold War.

Under such circumstances, the idea of defining civic virtue, masculinity, and citizenship of the Bolivian campesino by encouraging participatory politics in trade unionism, political parties, or the ballot box was completely off the conceptual map of imperial education reformers. Rather, the implicit message here was that the Bolivian peasant must hew to the land, narrow his political horizons, and fulfill his destiny as the nation's natural cultivator within the existing structures of power and property. To be sure, this civilizatory message was not new; we have encountered it time and again in the discourses of Bolivian statesmen and indigenistas since the early 1900s. But now the ideal of the modern campesino was moored to deeper associations, binding masculinity, morality, race, and class to incipient civic virtues. Those gendered associations, in turn, were inscribed within a racial-modernist grammar, which simultaneously degraded the culture of the primitive Indian and redeemed him as the country's essential highland farm laborer. Strip away the modern textbook lingo, and not much had changed since Bolivia's telluric school of indigenismo had advanced this ambivalent racial assessment of the highland native in the early 1900s.

On Civic Morality and Femininity

We see this engendered civic ideal most sharply through the image of the ideal campesina, redressed in the guise of a modern housewife (*ama de casa*). The centrality of the campesina as both object and agent in the formation of "good habits of life" is inescapable. For the rural extension agent, the peasant woman was both the most difficult subject to mold *and* the most essential target to

FIGURE 6.4. Fashion tips for the rural housewife (*ama de casa*). Ministerio de Educación, *Guía de instrucción para maestros rurales*, vol. 6: *Economía doméstica* (1948), 86–87.

reach. On the one hand, Andean peasant women were viewed through the prism of Western paradigms of gender inequality: they were thought to be confined by gender and sexuality, race and geography, to the rural idyll and, more specifically, to the domestic domain of household and family (*el hogar campesino*).[44] The textbook campesina did not participate in the social life of the ayllu or village; she did not even share in the heavy tasks of agricultural modernization, for now that was portrayed as men's work. Nor did the campesina distance herself from the sheltered village to accompany her husband on long-distance trading trips, much less to engage in her own autonomous marketing activities. That untamed Aymara woman, the liminal figure that once inhabited the uneasy imaginings of earlier indigenista writers like María Frontaura, was nowhere to be seen.[45] Now the teacher manuals located the domesticated Aymara woman (shed of Indianness) in her putatively natural domain—the hearth and home. Thus, she had become the key agent in resocializing her kinsmen in the most intimate spaces of body, family, and domesticity.[46] Diet, dress, cleanliness, sociability, household spatial arrangements, and child-raising—these were the things that were going to secure the "vitality" of the Bolivian rural labor force, the reproductive health of the nation, and the racial-cultural process of homogenization. Bolivian nationalists and conservatives were marching to the same drumbeat during that decade, and their exaltation of the Bolivian woman (whether cast as Indian, chola, or white) carried strident nationalist and patriarchal overtones. But the game plan as to how best to effect the internalization of disciplinary norms of body management and moral self-regulation belonged, as we have seen, primarily to the North Americans (see fig. 6.4).

To fashion the modern Bolivian campesina, SCIDE commissioned Gladys Holden, a home economics expert working with the Institute of Inter-American Affairs. Working in collaboration with two other experts (both SCIDE employees), Holden parachuted into Bolivia, took a quick tour of the rural normal schools of Santiago de Huata and Vacas, and then wrote or edited the textbook on the subject of homemaking. Except for surface references to the rural Bolivian milieu and a couple of folkloric illustrations, the textbook might just as well been written for mothers and housewives of farming families in Illinois or Iowa. In fact, its original version probably was just that—a government-sponsored manual on the responsibilities of the good North American housewife on a big farm in the Midwest! And thus the modern Bolivian ama de casa was instructed in middle-class North American household routines and conventions defining the arts of domesticity in the late 1940s— when, in North America, postwar adjustments required the recalibration of gender inequalities and exaltation of domesticity as hundreds of thousands of US women streamed out of wartime factory production and farmwork back into the seclusion of the home and family, where they tended to their "essential duties" as housewives and mothers. This provided the template for SCIDE's textbook on home economics for peasant women, and needless to say, it now makes for somewhat hilarious reading. Recipes for peasant behavioral reform covered domestic and corporeal facets of bourgeois femininity, body management, child-raising, and housekeeping—from infant care, food preparation, home remedies, and vitamin supplements to techniques of ironing, setting the proper table, aesthetic combinations of colors, and the choice of sewing patterns that were "flattering to the slim figure." Funny, absurd, banal, and yet profoundly invasive: the home economics guide might seem to us today like a weird combination of Doctor Spock and Martha Stewart, 1940s style.[47] At some point, such an exercise in imperial arrogance is risible, but as we shall see toward the end of this chapter, SCIDE's project for fashioning the subject of the modernized gendered campesino(a) cast long shadows across Bolivia's landscape, even after the nationalists took power in 1952. In the short run, however, the home economics course could be used to train up a reserve labor force of young Aymara girls destined to be domestic servants for wealthy La Paz families.[48]

Working within the matrix of gender, race, and class, SCIDE's textbook and institutional makeover of rural schooling was an ingenious replica of a North American model of rural extension education, first developed for midwestern farming communities earlier in the century. Like many modernist utopias, this fantasy had little regard for the millennial history of Andean cultures, or even the recent history of conflict between Indigenous educational initiatives and the oligarchic counterassault. The deep history of Indigenous engagement in this saga never entered into the official North American narrative, other than to serve as a bleak backdrop against which to project Washington's bold imperial ambitions for Bolivian economic development.

The Spadework of Acculturation: Signs of Trouble

In the meantime, there was much work to be done in the dissemination of these new behavioral norms through teacher-training workshops. The newly trained rural corps of normal teachers worked with the Juntas de Auxilio Escolar, composed of "the most respected vecinos of the community." Modeled after the Protestant missionary program of house visits, their task was to pressure local families to attend to their bodily, clothing, and household hygiene; if there was resistance, or health infractions, the Auxilio was to resort to social pressure, even public reproach.[49] SCIDE also tried to get peasant school clubs (*clubes escolares campesinos*, the equivalent of the 4-H clubs in the United States) to perform "house-keeping campaigns in rural communities as part of the practical phase of the rural curriculum." Fourth-year normal students served as extension agents: their assignment was to instruct rural housewives and husbands in the art of "sweeping, cleaning and disinfecting the schools and homes, whitewashing and plastering walls, and manufacturing rabbit pens, etc."[50] SCIDE also organized a Rural Cultural Service to spread North American values and hasten the assimilation of Bolivian peasants into the universalizing "American culture." A portable movie theater, with its sound equipment and projection machine, bumped along in the back of a flatbed truck en route to highland villages, which turned out to see American cartoons and newsreels. For the literati in the cities, SCIDE advertised the "good work" it was doing in the countryside in a slick new magazine called *Bolivia Rural*.[51] That magazine and other glowing (and self-aggrandizing) reports displayed happy, grateful Bolivian campesinos eager to learn modern agricultural techniques, and robust campesina homemakers standing shyly on the threshold of their disinfected huts.

One surprise visit to the village of Batallas was designed to showcase SCIDE's wondrous work in the campo.[52] The magazine featured a local Aymara alcalde, who conducted the inspection tour so the American visitors might appreciate the school's "miraculous" effect on the material improvement of rural life. Much as North American Indian boarding school propaganda had famously featured "before and after" photographs of Native Americans to illustrate the school's impact on the physical/cultural transformation of the dirty "savage" Indian child into the clean "civilized" student, so now did the SCIDE tour display the contrast between dark, primitive huts and whitewashed homes to illustrate the program's efficacious beneficence. The first huts furnished startling demonstrations of the squalor, unsanitary, and primitive lifeways of the unschooled, untransformed Aymara Indian. Stepping out of the harsh Altiplano sunlight into a dark hut, the visitors slowly took in the squalid scene: a small rectangular room, bare of furniture and full of acrid fumes, where the family cooked and slept. Cooking equipment consisted of a blackened pot teetering on a pile of stones, and earthenware was stacked in a corner next to the family's store of potatoes and grains. A pile of woolen blankets marked the family's sleeping area, adjacent to the warm stones that kept the hut from freezing at night. Upon crossing the threshold, the men were startled by the family's chickens rushing noisily out of the hut. Even without commentary, these vivid descriptors defined the very meaning of Indian backwardness in the pages of the IIAA magazine.

The entourage then moved on to the next house, where they encountered an elderly woman who warned the men not to intrude in her life: "The old ways are best," she grumbled in Aymara to the local alcalde accompanying the gringos. By then, it was time to tour a "model home." Wilfred Mauck noted the material signs of improvement: the new windows cut into the adobe walls let in shafts of sunlight and ventilated the main room; the cooking fire had been banished to a lean-to shed out back; the chickens were penned; the hut's earthen floor was carefully swept and clothes neatly piled; and grain stocks were tucked away. And the pièce de résistance: a new sanitary latrine lying some distance from the house.

The Americans' rural extension program in Batallas must have impressed the visitors, but Mauck could not hide the fact that rural unrest was brewing in nearby villages. He worried that "the *colonos* on the nearby haciendas have taken to arms against the landowners," although he expressed relief that the comunario peasants of Batallas had refused to join the uprising.⁵³ There were other disquieting signs that SCIDE's program was floundering, however. Telltale signs began to surface in midlevel bureaucratic reports submitted by SCIDE's school inspectors themselves. For instance, SCIDE's showcase Indian boarding schools in both Vacas and Santiago de Huata were failing. Even more disturbing was the chilly reception that awaited SCIDE officials in many rural sites where they tried to establish schools. One inspector delicately noted that foreign aid workers enjoyed little authority and were dismissed by many Aymara village elders as "casual and not too welcome sightseers."⁵⁴ We get a sense here of gringos in sunglasses, and their local agents of modernization, rushing about the countryside trying to break through language and cultural barriers to spread the secular gospel to skeptical village authorities. But SCIDE headquarters would brook no resistance, either from local rural teachers or Aymara communities, in their campaign to spread the new rural extension program throughout the Altiplano. In 1948 and 1949, SCIDE decided to tighten up surveillance and control by sending inspectors out on field visits every single month of the year. Those monthly inspection reports were sent to both the Bolivian minister of education and SCIDE's Washington office. Ostensibly aimed at improving the administration and conditions of normal schools, SCIDE's rigorous inspections also provided a tool of surveillance during the rising tide of rural unrest.

On the ground, SCIDE inspectors tried to close the gap between pedagogy and practice by boring in on the quotidian routines and practices that were to discipline the student body (figuratively and literally). We get a strong sense how this local regime of surveillance, inspection, and regulation was supposed to operate: SCIDE inspections would visit, observe, and leave directives as to what, exactly, the school director and teachers should accomplish over the next month(s). On their return visit, the school inspectors might note small signs of progress before they left a new set of directives. On one inspection, in April 1949, the home economics technician instructed Vacas's normal school teachers on all "the work to be done." The directive read as follows:

> In the kitchen make a new stove, fix the chimney, build shelves or cupboards to keep utensils, build a working table, install running water[,] ... clean the

kerosene stove and teach [the students] to use it, make a place to keep fuel, make garbage cans, and buy the necessary utensils for the kitchen; in the dining room make a cupboard to keep china and silver, buy oil cloth for tables, arrange the tables in a convenient manner, buy the necessary chinaware and silverware and teach students how to clean them, and teach the students table manners.[55]

Other directives were equally daunting: teachers were commanded to prepare special vocational curricula under SCIDE's guidelines; launch a school lunch program; improve nutrition; beef up the stock-breeding program; build latrines; acquire new dormitory cots and mattresses; and instruct their own students into becoming agents of socialization and reform in their own families and in the surrounding peasant villages.[56]

When these directives were met with apathy or skepticism, SCIDE officials became frustrated that teachers were clinging to "the worthless principles of academic teaching" instead of embracing the new pedagogic norms.[57] On occasion, however, a social investigator would interview a group of normal students. To be sure, only on rare occasions would students be invited to voice their opinions, much less critique the pedagogy of behavioral reform being introduced by North American educators. But on one such occasion, a group of normal students in Santiago de Huata were asked their opinions about the school's acclaimed curriculum. To the inspector's surprise, the students mustered the courage to criticize the curriculum: they wanted "to acquire academic knowledge" and pleaded for more classes in language, arithmetic, history, and civics, with fewer classes in agriculture, latrine building, and sewing.[58]

In this disquieting exchange, the normal students were not simply lodging a complaint about the latrines they had to build. Implicitly, they were questioning the axiom that rural teachers-in-training should be taught mainly practical skills and moral rectitude, leaving the intellectual subjects (history, civics, mathematics) to the exclusive precinct of urban teacher-training institutes. Their critique was a coy allusion to the racially differentiated curriculum that continued to bifurcate Bolivia's public school system into rural and urban, Indian and white, and manual and mental categories of schooled knowledge. The anticolonialist implications of the students' request to study academic subjects did not seem to register with the inspector, however. In fact, Eduardo Arze Loureiro (a progressive lawyer, indigenista, and old friend of Elizardo Pérez) had little patience for such protestations, and he advised his SCIDE colleagues to stay the course. Santiago de Huata and SCIDE's other núcleo peasant centers should require their pupils to undergo "a severe phase of the so-called 'active school,'" he said, so they would be molded into industrious and skilled agriculturalists by the time they graduated.[59]

But imposing a regime of manual labor and behavioral discipline on rural normal schools was turning out to be a fretful process. Not only did North American school supervisors often encounter "scant welcome" in peasant communities, but SCIDE's presumptive authority to define the educated Indian subject, and in the process reorient Bolivia's national culture and "ways of thinking," was coming under intense public scrutiny during the late 1940s. In fact, North American advisers and educators were caught in the vortex of a dramatically changing political environment. With peasant labor strikes spreading into the hacienda zones, and articulated to radical working-class and left activities in the mining camps, Washington had much cause for alarm. Embassy communiqués warned of the growing anti-American sentiment and the need to shore up the US-Bolivian relationship with more economic, military, and humanitarian aid (see chapter 5). By contrast, most SCIDE officials had a blinkered view of rural Bolivia, and rarely registered social tremors across the Altiplano.[60]

The political situation abruptly changed in early 1947, a tumultuous year marked by escalating political violence, massive peasant upheaval, post–World War II cutbacks in tin production, mass firing of workers, and militant strike activity by powerful mine unions. Indeed, as the standard historiography plots, the year 1947 signaled the onset of a six-year cycle (el sexenio) of political insurgency and violence that lay the groundwork for the 1952 political victory of the MNR's national revolutionary movement. Amid this political turmoil, the eruption of public debate over Indian education—and the tutelary authority of North Americans—was bound to fire up leftist, nationalist, and anti-imperialist sentiments and raise larger questions about Bolivia's cultural sovereignty in the face of SCIDE's grand designs and feverish activity in the Altiplano zone.

Informal Empire and "the Delicate Question of Nationality"

Almost from the time Ernest Maes stepped onto the Altiplano, SCIDE's activities in the area of rural Indian schooling had touched a collective Bolivian nerve. Maes's cozy relationship with Vicente Donoso made him suspect to young Bolivian leftists. What Maes did not fully anticipate was that his tactical alliance with "the enemies of Warisata" would end up becoming a wedge issue, positioning Maes on one side of the deep divide while alienating leftist and indigenista teachers, rural normal students and teachers, and the partisans of Pérez on the other side. Maes misunderstood the cultural origins and significance of Warisata, and then blindly appropriated and transformed the núcleo escolar into an administrative school zone. At the time, Pérez was living as an exile in his own land, banished from power, his reputation in tatters among the CNE and SCIDE crowd. As long as SCIDE officials answered primarily to their own superiors in Washington and enjoyed the tacit respect of Villarroel's top educational authorities (Jorge Calero, the minister of education; and Toribio Claure, in charge of the Department of Rural Education), they were able to proceed rather blithely with their plan to "reorient the way of thinking," particularly in the field of Indigenous schooling. During the Villarroel-MNR years, SCIDE had burrowed deep into the interior of Claure's bureaucracy. Bolivian and North American officials seemed to act in seamless accord for a while, until Villarroel's murder in July 1946. That shocking event seemed to put SCIDE officials on notice that they were in for a rougher ride in the near future.

For a time, the North Americans were encouraged by Enrique Herzog's election in January 1947 (although it came at a moment of agrarian crisis in Ayopaya and across much of the Altiplano).[61] Herzog soon proved to be a weak leader, however, and in any event, his own education advisers were decidedly cool to Ernest Maes and SCIDE's ambitious plans for rural education reform. Furthermore, SCIDE's prestige took a beating from teachers unions and the left (particularly the Trotskyist party, the Partido Obrero Revolucionario) and from some of the rural normal schools (Santiago de Huata and Vacas, for example). Fierce criticism also came from university students, peasant leaders, rural teachers, and the displaced indigenista intellectuals and pedagogues long banished from the state's bureaucratic Rural Education offices. Taken together, these nodes of political opposition, together with a new wave of anti-imperialism, threatened the North American presence in rural Bolivia. Eduardo Arze Loureiro alluded to SCIDE's "scant welcome" from Bolivian teachers and educators, which was "threatening to derail the work of the Cooperative Educational Program [a.k.a. SCIDE]."[62]

That "scant welcome" flared into a partisan polemic over SCIDE's imperial presumption as the self-appointed vanguard of rural education reform in Bolivia. As the tumult of 1947 unfolded, the Bolivian legislature was plunged into a state of agitation over such themes as: the feudal regime on rural estates;

peasant uprisings in Ayopaya; land reform issues; the deepening crisis of the mining economy; and the outbreak of strikes and protest in the tin mines of Catavi and elsewhere. To make matters worse, acute food shortages were fanning the flames of unrest in the cities.[63] Set against this tableau of agrarian crisis, the politics of Indian education hardly seemed worthy of passionate public debate. Given SCIDE's symbolic and institutional presence in Bolivia, however, it played a singular role in galvanizing a growing coalition of anti-Americanism, just as the United States was becoming ever more invested in stamping out the embers of radicalism among Bolivia's mine unions, teachers, and university students. With SCIDE as the new driver of rural education, Bolivian critics began questioning Washington's political motives. And the congressman most responsible for targeting SCIDE was none other than Elizardo Pérez, a newly elected delegate to Congress from the western province of Nor Lipez, and just back from a long period of self-imposed exile.[64]

From early in 1947, then, Ernest Maes found himself up against Pérez, a formidable adversary operating from his new perch in the national Congress. Pérez was quick to seize the congressional bully pulpit and reclaim the mantle of Indian education. His timing was impeccable. In the face of growing anti-American sentiment, and a defensive Herzog regime trying to explain why SCIDE's contract had just been renewed, some Bolivian legislators demanded a report from the minister of education on the deficient state of rural schooling. They also demanded an official appraisal of SCIDE's track record since its arrival in Bolivia in 1944. A grand inspection tour was arranged under the new education minister, Armando Alba, and he invited the new deputy, Elizardo Pérez, to join him on that tour. At long last, Pérez had been granted a public platform from which he could inspect the condition of rural public schools and also condemn the oligarchy's war against Warisata carried out seven years early. This inspection tour, an event largely overlooked in Bolivian historiography, represented the best opportunity for Warisata's cofounders, teachers, and amautas to demand retribution in the Bolivian public sphere.

The first stop on the tour was Warisata, where the delegation bore witness to the ruins of a once-thriving ayllu school. In 1947, Warisata was not yet under SCIDE's supervision, nor was it well funded or supervised under Bolivia's Department of Rural Education. What these men found (to no one's surprise) was that in the seven years since the CNE's initial assault, the school had deteriorated almost beyond repair. The education minister was clearly shaken by what he saw and by the spontaneous testimonies of local people that the inspectors had gathered during their visit. Upon their return to La Paz, Alba took time to pay homage to Pérez's noble "socio-pedagogic experiment." Then he turned to describe the tragic remains of Warisata: "an experiment gone wrong, after having achieved great feats worthy of study and admiration."[65] In the hushed congressional chamber, the minister's requiem amounted to an implicit apology for the past crimes of the oligarchic state. One newspaper headline registered the minister's remorse at seeing Warisata's ruinous state: "With Historic Emotion, the Min. Alba Declares That Bolivia's Indigenal Education Has Been Destroyed."[66]

Such emotive proclamations provided the perfect prelude for Pérez to step back into the national arena to recover his integrity and restore the glory of the original Warisata in the public mind. Much as Carlos Salazar had tried to prick the national conscience with his own 1943 testimonial essay, "Warisata mía," so now did Pérez begin to shape a revindicative narrative of the lost utopia of la educación indigenal. Speaking before the Congress, he invoked the telluric indigenista ideals of his intellectual heir, Franz Tamayo. Bolivia, he proclaimed, must reclaim its unique national pedagogy (stolen and distorted by the gringos). This recycled genre of soil-and-soul nationalism ("the soul of Bolivia is in the land and... the heart of Bolivian children") provided the nationalist-indigenista counterpoint to Euro-American doctrines of cultural assimilation through education reform.[67] Almost fifty years after Tamayo had raged against the dangers of imported pedagogies, Pérez now trumpeted the threat of modern Occidentalism (this time in the guise of SCIDE educators, social workers, and agronomists). While the minister of education meekly defended the Herzog government's covenant with SCIDE, Pérez mobilized his authority as Bolivia's "apostle of Indian rights" to denounce SCIDE's rural vocational program as but a simulacrum of his own original doctrine of Indigenal education (based on a combined curriculum of field-workshop-classroom learning).[68]

Thus began, over the next weeks and years, Pérez's public disquisition on the state's ongoing "destruction of Bolivia's indigenal schools."[69] As national deputy, Pérez had found the perfect platform for reasserting his moral authority on the Indian question and for protesting the past crimes of the Bolivian state—first, for having laid waste to Bolivia's original communal-based program of Indian schooling and then, once the escuela-ayllu lay in ruins, for having divested itself of the entire mission by outsourcing the education of the Indian to the ethnocentric North Americans! Pérez railed, "What kind of training have the American experts acquired in the United States?" By what moral authority did they flock to Bolivia so as "to reorient the education of the [Bolivian] Indian, when [in fact] they know nothing about the Indian—neither his traditions, nor history, nor environment?!"[70] SCIDE's most egregious sin, he thundered, was the suppression of the Andean Indian's millennial cultural ecology to make way for Western technological progress. By the end of his impassioned speech, his indigenista rhetoric had caught fire. One enraged congressman demanded to know how US educators had the audacity to reorient Bolivia's rural school system, when they had "never once laid eyes on a núcleo indígena, except maybe one containing the celluloid Indians of Hollywood, or else maybe those strange núcleos created as reservations for North America's redskins!"[71] Another deputy railed against educators trying to cram American values down the throats of Bolivian schoolchildren by imposing their new pedagogy on Indian schools.[72] Delegate Saucedo Soriano took a more equivocal approach: he praised North America's public schools for educating artisans, the middle class, university students, and athletes. But he scolded the gringos for their racial biases and disparagement of Native cultures and languages.[73] This chorus of critics alarmed Herzog's minister of education, who warned against any further displays of xenophobic "ignorance, prejudice, and fear," lest they endanger Bolivia's access to US economic assistance.

But SCIDE's critics would not be silenced, and the battle was fast turning into a proxy war against the oligarchy's imperial dependence on North America. In a sly allusion to "the supremely delicate question of nationality," Pérez led the charge of imperial collusion, demanding answers: How had these foreigners insinuated themselves so deeply into this supposedly sovereign nation? How had the Bolivian state been led to surrender its autonomy to a foreign organism, responsible for recrafting Bolivia's national culture?[74] How, in short, had the *Programa Cooperativo* become a cultural and economic prop of the oligarchy through its monopoly control over the nation's educational funds, pedagogy, administration, spiritual values, and identity?[75] This troubling question was never resolved in the public mind.

Torn between Empire and Nation:
Warisata Restored?

Thus, Warisata—as an embattled symbol, nostalgic narrative, and sputtering rural school—was back in newspaper headlines during March and April 1948. As public debate simmered, an extraordinary document appeared in several leading newspapers. A long petition signed by five hundred "indígenas de Warisata" was addressed to the "president of the republic." The signatories included "amautas, campesinos, and indigenous teachers [*maestros indígenas*] del Núcleo Escolar de Warisata," who claimed to speak for thirty thousand peasants. This mass petition was the work of Indigenous community leaders and a few teachers who had met in assembly to discuss and compose their thoughts. One organizer was Carlos Garibaldi, a master craftsman who had instructed students in the art of carpet weaving at Warisata during its heyday. In March 1948, Garibaldi traveled in a cargo truck across the Altiplano, gathering the names (and thumbprints?) of more four hundred Indians during the course of one or two nights.[76] The petition gave collective voice to the men and women victimized by the early wave of state violence and institutional neglect of the original ayllu school.[77] The petitioners' defensive language ("our attitude is not subversive"; "we are the enemies of [peasant] rebellions") was, of course, a hedge against the political retaliation their actions were bound to provoke. The Indigenous petitioners put forward practical demands: they wanted the state to take inventory of the destruction and pillage that the school had suffered at the hands of earlier oligarchic regimes. They also asked the Herzog administration to place the school under the jurisdiction of the Ministry of Education (in effect ending the nation's long-standing administrative and curricular policy of segregating rural and urban schools); and they demanded the replacement of teachers and director with an indigenista teaching staff, under the proviso that the original parlamento de amautas be restored. If those basic demands were denied, then the petitioners wanted the school closed until a new staff could be hired and its local dispensary of liquor removed.

But the text's deeper significance lies in the fact that, after almost a decade of public assault, slander, and marginalization, the authors of Warisata's redemptive history and significance were Indigenous people themselves (including many of its original amautas and Indigenous teachers). Writing against the dominant narrative, the petitioners reframed Warisata as a monument to the memory, sacrifice, and aspirations of the school's founding generation.[78] It stood as a beacon of Indian self-emancipation: "The first Indian school raised in the heart of the ayllu and, on the basis of our collective effort, it [once] served as an example across the Americas."[79] The petition's message was reinforced by a student strike and lockout at Warisata, led by two founding amautas, Toribio Miranda and Serapio Mamani. That Warisata was suddenly back in the news, thanks to this spontaneous protest, was certainly not good publicity for the government. Alarmed at the potential for international fallout (and already besieged by rural unrest), President Enrique Herzog quickly arranged an official fact-finding tour of Warisata so that the strike might be settled and the school reopened. There, in the presence of several amautas and Elizardo Pérez, the president was given the ceremonial keys to the gates of the school complex. But that gesture of rapprochement between the amautas and the president only inflamed the racial anxieties of Achacachi's provincial authorities—the traditional enemies of the ayllu-school—for they too had assembled a mass petition of protest, warning federal authorities that the old Indian school was being taken over by radical *maestros educados*, a subversive act supposedly instigated by Pérez. Once again, the old educator was accused of trying to "subvert the [docile] spirit of the Indians of the region" to foment race war. And once again, Achacachi authorities used that perennial racist threat to rally townsmen and landlords to protect "a free, sovereign, and virile pueblo" against those professional indigenista and communist agitators.[80]

By 1949, when SCIDE's contract between Washington and La Paz came up again for renewal, the Americans felt that something drastic had to be done about Warisata, since the whole fate of their cooperative educational aid program seemed to hang in the balance. To buttress its case before its Bolivian critics, SCIDE claimed impressive policy achievements, including the vertiginous increase of núcleo peasant districts, in coordination with SCISP's rural campaign for public health. SCIDE's vocational school centers had provided manpower training and extension education programs that reached into the Indian hearth and home. In all, the Americans boasted that Washington's three integrated cooperative programs (SCIDE, SCISP, and SAI) had accomplished, in almost five years, what Bolivian educational policy makers had failed to do in the previous fifty! All the more frustrating to Maes and other aid officers, then, that their new farm-schools and other social programs had run up against local opposition and cultural mistrust, not to mention the new flare-up of public hostility in the Bolivian Congress and the press.

Undoubtedly, the most astute analyst of SCIDE's political problems, and the person best positioned to resolve them, was Eduardo Arze Loureiro, the progressive landowner, lawyer, and indigenista activist from Cochabamba. He quickly emerged as SCIDE's most effective cultural broker—a man who had the trust of most peasants yet also traveled comfortably in cosmopolitan circles. He could work both sides of the cultural divide.[81] By the late 1940s, however, Arze had moved squarely into the SCIDE camp as a paid consultant.

He joined other (well-paid) Bolivian foot soldiers assigned to carry the new vocational pedagogy and hygienic discipline into rural communities, and he showed little patience for the obstruction he found in many of the rural normal schools, where SCIDE continued to experience "a large degree of opposition." But it was Arze, perhaps more than any other individual, who realized the magnitude of SCIDE's political and bureaucratic opposition in Bolivia.

As SCIDE's local adviser, therefore, Arze worked hard to broker the tensions and restore the program's status in Bolivia, despite the rapidly deteriorating political climate. He knew he had to bring to the table several of Bolivia's leading indigenista authorities in the field of Indian education—men who were not so intransigent that they were unwilling to lend their expertise and authority to the common cause (if common ground could, in fact, be found). Tellingly, neither Aymara teachers nor community leaders were invited to the bargaining table. In a deeply ironic twist to this story, Eduardo Arze Loureiro sought to save SCIDE's work in Bolivia by turning to its most passionate critic—Elizardo Pérez.[82] If Congressman Pérez could be won over to the North American cause, then a historic rapprochement between Washington and Bolivia might well be in reach.

Reaching such an accord was a tricky maneuver, however. On the one hand, Arze Loureiro took it upon himself to provide a short reeducation course for the well-meaning but clueless North American educators. He tried to puncture their imperial arrogance and tear off their Eurocentric blinders so they might come to understand the deeper historical significance of Bolivia's once-celebrated núcleo peasant school.[83] On the other, Arze had to persuade Pérez that SCIDE's vocational program shared a fundamental premise with his own curricular orientation. Even if the gringos' scientific pedagogy clashed with Pérez's earlier indigenista ideals about the communitarian school, Arze averred, did they not agree that pedagogy should be designed and applied to address the material needs and local environment of the peasant community? Had not Georges Rouma, the venerable founder of Bolivia's first normal school in 1910 (of which Pérez himself was a proud graduate), proposed the farm-school to upgrade the agricultural workforce, improve the Indian's cultural hygiene, and prepare the rural masses for eventual integration into the nation? After all, Pérez's pedagogical priorities had evolved over the 1930s, and eventually he collaborated with the Busch regime to reorganize Indigenal education as an integrative arm of the populist state. It was a short-lived alliance, before Pérez was banished by the reactionary forces that rushed to power in 1940, but the indigenista had already shown himself to be pragmatic enough to adapt his pedagogical principles to shifting political opportunities. Here, then, was a second chance for Pérez to step up.

On the surface, Arze's diplomatic maneuver might be considered a resounding victory. With Pérez's ambivalent blessing, the North Americans finally won the right to extend their influence and actually "take charge of Warisata." Theoretically, that arrangement meant adhering to the school's communal values while also pursuing a rigorous vocational and hygienic curriculum; emphasizing school and extension lessons in nutrition, food production, animal husbandry, home economics, and sanitation; and generally "solving... problems related to rural life." SCIDE-trained rural teachers agreed to respect the ideal of community participation. They would be sure to "give community discussions the proper orientation by teaching [the Indians] the principles of self-government and strengthening the bonds of local cooperation, without resorting to a system of patriarchal authority." (No recognition was given here to the autonomy and achievements of Warisata's original escuela-ayllu and its parliamentary system of communal governance; rather, US educators still authorized themselves to demonstrate "the art of self-governance.") They would also "convert the peasants into intelligent citizens, interested in the progress of their community and school."[84]

Notwithstanding Arze's effort to resocialize SCIDE officials, most North Americans were still only dimly aware that they were addressing the heirs of parents and grandparents who had emerged out of clandestine school activism to fight for their legal rights to comunario lands, literacy, and schools since the 1910s and 1920s, and who had gone on to build a network of communitarian núcleo schools in the 1930s. But apparently generous American school aid was an offer that Pérez and his allies (including the Warisata petitioners) could hardly afford to refuse. Thus, in 1949, SCIDE secured its place in Bolivian society as the supreme tutelary authority of Indian school reform (and, as we shall see in the next chapter, it would be well positioned to weather the rocky transition to MNR revolutionary nationalism after 1952). In return, Bolivia delivered Warisata (the original crown jewel of intercultural and emancipatory Indian schooling) to the North American engineers of rural development and intimate modernity. The irony of this imperial bargain could not have escaped Bolivia's leftist teachers, intellectuals, and peasant activists, but the promise of material aid to rural schooling was irresistible. Warisata would obtain SCIDE funds to restore its pillaged buildings, withered crops, and stolen livestock and to acquire tools and tractors, school and dormitory supplies, and

FIGURE 6.5. The monumental "pavilion of México," built with communal labor, was still without a roof in 1939. Ten years later, Warisata became a North American showcase of Indian education and acculturation. US funds financed the physical completion of the pavilion. Salazar Mostajo, *Gesta y fotografía*, photo no. 90.

other essential things. And Pérez could now extract enough US aid to finish the construction of Warisata's main building, the *pabellón de México* (see fig. 6.5).[85] In 1949 Arze Loureiro accomplished the near impossible—he brought America's informal empire and the escuela-ayllu into strategic alignment so as to secure the future of the school and begin the material rehabilitation of Warisata after nine years of ruin and neglect. But there was no going back, of course. The original communitarian school complex was now going to be recast in SCIDE's image of the modern farm-school complex—North America's pedagogical solution to Bolivia's race problem and rural backwardness.

Wider political circumstances also conspired to transform Pérez from SCIDE's most vehement critic into its champion and enabler. In early 1949, just about the time Arze Loureiro wrote his secret memo to SCIDE's leadership, Pérez was appointed to serve as interim minister of education. He had long been angling for this government position, but his chance finally came in a moment of crisis. Shortly after Bolivia suffered a new wave of rural unrest, President Herzog fled Bolivia for Chile, where he stayed for several months of "sick leave." Pérez's tenure as interim minister of education was precarious (in fact, he was out of a job after only three months), but he was in a position to secure a Supreme Resolution (on April 23, 1949), which renewed

SCIDE's contract and gave the Americans supervisory control over Warisata (now officially designated as one of SCIDE's main "experimental núcleos"). For Arze Loureiro, Pérez, and the SCIDE program, there were immediate material benefits accruing from this new bilateral accord. The school was rescued from its state of material decay and placed under an indigenista director, Eufrasio Ibañez, who immediately hired a new teaching corps and tried to restore the "active school" curriculum (a reference to John Dewey's pragmatic child-oriented pedagogy). For his part, Pérez collaborated "with enthusiasm," by accompanying SCIDE officials on their first official tour of Warisata, where they began installing the new vocational curriculum. Apparently, Pérez gave the whole process his blessing.[86]

A happy ending to a tumultuous courtship, or simply a marriage of convenience bound to collapse in divorce? In this latest episode of the Warisata saga, the social dynamics of governance and education, power and pedagogy, were fraught with irony and ambiguity. In 1945, toward the end of the oligarchy's war on Warisata, Ernest Maes had charged through rural Bolivia, determined to sweep away the decrepit rural school system. Like the earlier Protestant missionaries, Maes had strong convictions about how to construct an assimilationist project (inspired by his earlier work in the US Bureau of Indian Affairs). Setting out to "reorient a way of thinking," Maes planned to export his rural education paradigm to other Indigenous regions of Latin America. After Maes's swift departure for friendlier political climes, the veteran indigenista and lawyer Eduardo Arze Loureiro entered the scene to rescue SCIDE's reputation and secure its long-term place in Bolivia just as the Cold War was intensifying. And the lawyer was certainly not averse to leveraging Washington's growing political anxieties about "red extremism" infiltrating Bolivia's teacher unions to bargain for more US aid and influence in Bolivia's public schools, particularly its rural Indian school programs and urban vocational schools. With the playbook of Cold War diplomacy in hand, Arze told his SCIDE employers that the education of the Bolivian Indian under "North American guidance" was now feasible: he assured them that the oligarchy—Bolivia's bastion of neocolonial obstruction and violence—was finally starting to buckle before the "current of rebellion . . . that may someday overthrow the established system through forcible or anarchic methods." The *yanquis* could rest assured, he wrote, that the landlord class now wanted SCIDE to take charge of Indian schooling (presumably to become an enlightened agent of rural pacification and assimilation). For their part, Bolivia's feudal landlords and gamonal authorities would no longer put the torch to rural schoolhouses, threaten rural teachers, or prevent children from learning how to read and write. This tenuous class truce, then, was the bargaining chip that Arze Loureiro put before SCIDE officials: they would be able to educate the Bolivian Indian without worrying about the disruptive effects of landlord violence or the dangerous influence of anarcho-syndicalism.[87] Thus, Arze played his cards carefully, betting that progressive American reformers would stay the course if they thought they could win hearts and minds in the ongoing battle between Bolivia's reactionary feudal oligarchy and growing leftist and communist influences. Even as he composed his secret 1949 memo, however, Arze Loureiro must have realized that a strong "current of rebellion" was engulfing many parts of rural Bolivia and that, in the end, its brittle labor regime of feudalism and racial hierarchy of caste would have to be swept away by the tsunami of popular revolution in the cities, mines, and countryside. Indeed, glancing ahead, we well know that the 1952 revolutionary coup lay but three years down the road.

There is, finally, one more ironic twist to this story. When Elizardo Pérez changed stripes in early 1949 to defend SCIDE's program in its hour of need, he virtually rescued the American program from its staunchest anti-American critics. Why this about-face? Years later, with some anguish, Pérez tried to explain how he had come to admire the North Americans' "honesty and efficiency," the technical expertise they brought to the teaching profession, and the material resources they poured into the núcleo schools under their close supervision (including Warisata, after 1949). When set against the appalling record of underfinanced rural schooling in Bolivia, and the state's long history of institutional failure, the SCIDE program seemed to promise the long-awaited solution to the country's Indian education problem. Forced to choose between the allure of modern pedagogical methods, material aid, and hands-on technical expertise and Bolivia's history of institutional failure, poverty, and racial violence, Pérez chose to compromise his indigenista principles and align himself with the ideals of Western progress and assimilation. The immediate payoff was to secure American funding to complete the physical construction of Warisata's grand pavilion, but at what cultural or moral cost?[88] Those questions haunted this venerable educator into his old age. Years later, looking back from the vantage point of old age and foreign self-exile, Pérez found it almost incomprehensible that Bolivia, with its rich vernacular traditions and innovations in the field of Indian education, could have fallen into the "extreme position of contracting foreign services so that [North Americans] would come to teach us the very same thing we invented."[89]

In Cold War lingo, Arze's secret warning to SCIDE officials about "red extremism" reflected the rising tide of unrest in the late 1940s. By then, Bolivia's rigid caste hierarchy and its feudal order of haciendas and colonos were crumbling. As it turned out, North America's rural extension programs in Bolivia were incapable of pacifying the Indian countryside or preempting the spread of popular mobilization over the late 1940s.

But even as rural unrest escalated, US educators were slowly laying the groundwork for a new rural education system that promised, with time, money, and patience, to domesticate a class of acculturated farmers in the miracles of agrarian modernization. Through pedagogic manuals and discourses, teacher training, overseas scholarships, curricular reform, rural extension programs, and massive propaganda, the modern Bolivian peasantry was conjured by North American development officers as an ideal agrarian class, assembled from the ethnic fragments of primitive Indianness and precapitalist agrarian practices. In just a decade or so, the North Americans had provided Bolivia with a modern assimilative template for rural education that would persist into the 1950s and 1960s, laying the foundations of its Alliance for Progress (an ambitious Cold War program in rural development, labor discipline, and communist containment). Ironically, the North Americans also inspired, guided, and partially funded the MNR's plans for rural education reform under the banner of revolutionary nationalism. But neither Bolivian social reformers nor North American engineers of rural development could stem the flood tide of social revolution around the turn of the 1950s.

7

The Hour of Vindication

Rural Literacy and Schooling in the Age of Revolution

[In this] hour of social vindications [*revindicaciónes sociales*] ... we ask His Excellency for the multiplication of schools in all the Ayllus, Communities, Haciendas, and Cantons. A revolution in the alphabetization of the Indian!
—LOS PRINCIPALES CACIQUES DE LA REPÚBLICA, September 4, 1952

Among the "soldiers of the revolution" who converged on the presidential palace in the weeks and months following the April 1952 insurrection was a delegation of caciques, carrying their staffs of office and a mass petition. Speaking for all the "principal caciques of the republic," and representing Bolivia's "Indigenous Race" at large, the petitioners presented themselves as warriors engaged in an ongoing struggle for the emancipation of the Indian. As their wartime reparation, they demanded that the new president, Victor Paz Estenssoro, provide basic literacy instruction for children and adults in the nation's Indian communities, thus redeeming the republic's constitutional promise. Their appeal was not couched in a civic language of citizenship rights, however, but framed as an anticolonialist vindication for having been denied their basic right to schooling. True revolution, they implied, would come in the form of the lettered Indian.

That literacy and the school would become potent symbols of revolutionary change was the cultural outcome of half a century of Aymara and Quechua struggle in rural communities, as well as in Bolivia's political and public spheres. As traced in earlier chapters of this book, the roots of that ethnopolitical genealogy first surfaced around the turn of the twentieth century as the escalating defense of communal traditions and lands nurtured a cultural reverence for literacy and schooling, particularly among Aymara caciques. Those early cacique-driven school petitions and various forms of local activism also paved the way toward Bolivia's first experiments in intercultural community schooling, later made famous by Warisata and a few other núcleo escolares in the early to mid-1930s. The political landscape shifted again in the late 1930s and early 1940s, when returning Chaco War soldiers applied their newly acquired skills in intercultural communication, bilingualism, and literacy in the burgeoning postwar occupations of rural teaching, labor organizing, and urban wage work. What Bolivian elites did not fully anticipate, however, was how vernacular literacy practices could be forged into instruments of radical agrarian organizing and popular-front politics. In the 1940s, a roving group of rural dirigentes cast themselves as proselytizing teachers and activists ("instigators of the new ideas") working to liberate Bolivia's underclasses. As plotted in chapter 5, postwar political activists developed an innovative repertory of popular education, communal reading practices, participatory peasant democracy, trade union kinds of consciousness-raising, and other forms of rural mobilization and resistance. Over that decade, interregional groups of peasant activists built tenuous alliances with militant miners and other urban allies, well before the MNR mounted its final insurrectionary push in early 1952. Building on the tradition of Indian land and school politics from the 1920s, and propelled by the insurgent political currents from the 1940s, the Taraqu delegation of petitioners seized this pivotal moment to proclaim their long-sought right to basic schooling. Their collective aspiration, captured in the epigraph above, was defined by what they perceived as the essence of revolutionary justice—"the alphabetization of the Indian!"[1]

This revolutionary hope seemed to flower in the months following the April 1952 insurgency. Less than two years later, in 1954, a roving UNESCO official reported that, to his surprise, the popular revolution had unleashed an effervescent school movement in the Aymara provinces. Recently arrived from Quito, Gonzalo Rubio Orbe was conducting investigative fieldwork to prepare for establishing a UN-funded pilot program in rural education and adult literacy. Conditions on the ground seemed surprisingly favorable, he reported. Some of that impetus came from the work of Canadian Baptists, whose missionary schools had flourished in the Huatajata region, near Lake Titicaca. But the main source of his optimism came from the profusion of peasant groups soliciting material resources for their local primary schools. A flurry of local initiatives astonished the Ecuadorian: "Everywhere they ask for the opening of schools; and the same groups build local schoolhouses and pay teachers. And they ask for help with their agricultural activities, with [building] latrines; and with all kinds of other things."[2] Once again, a visiting white dignitary had to make a mental adjustment: his racial stereotypes of congenital Indian lethargy and indifference evaporated in the light of face-to-face experience. Although Rubio Orbe's ethnohistorical knowledge of Bolivia was limited, he could appreciate how a functional command of Spanish, both written and spoken, was vital to Indigenous communities—if only so they could decipher government decrees flowing out of La Paz, or deal with the mass of legal paperwork (*trámites*) required by the new agrarian reform bureaucracy. Before his very eyes, Bolivia's somnolent Indian race seemed to be "awakening" to the value of literacy and schooling in "this new historical stage in the life of Bolivia."[3]

Anchored in ethnography of Indigenous politics and peasant schooling, this chapter revisits this effervescent political moment by recasting it, analytically and narratively, as a dynamic field of encounter and conflict over the rural school, as both site and symbol of Indigenous liberation from the indignity of illiteracy. To encompass the multiple social groups that jockeyed for a stake in opening formal education to the rural masses, the chapter toggles between the resurgent peasant movement; the MNR's historic efforts to rebuild a system of public education, with a focus on schooling the rural masses; and North America's growing influence in the bourgeoning field of rural development, an outgrowth of SCIDE's cumulative impact on rural school reform over the 1940s (discussed in chapter 6). In the course of this discussion, I explore how the early revolutionary euphoria, upheaval, and transformation created fertile terrain for Indigenous literacy, peasant school activism, and "social vindication" to flower under the MNR's shaky ruling coalition. Predictably enough, Bolivia's popular revolution unleashed a slew of powerful counterforces of repression, reform, and cooptation, designed to clamp down and channel the political fervor of Bolivia's rural masses. In an ironic twist to this familiar dialectic of revolution and reaction, the MNR hardened its disciplinary institutions and sought new sources of support from Washington to sustain its growing institutional and cultural intervention in the field of rural education. Forging *el nuevo campesino*—viewed as the modern disciplinary solution to Bolivia's Indian problem and history of endemic rural poverty—became a strategic point of convergence in the contested process of taming the Bolivian revolution. Part one critically revisits Bolivia's terrain of revolutionary fervor in order to capture the empowering explosion of popular expectations, vernacular literacy practices, and rural school activism during the early 1950s. Part two shifts the focus to the MNR's historic state-building efforts, as it tried to engineer, codify, and channel the direction of rural education for its own political and institutional purposes.

PART ONE

The Revolutionary Public Sphere

Largely overshadowed by the unruly process of agrarian unrest and reform, the Aymara Altiplano was quietly undergoing a civic revolution of its own making in the early to mid-1950s. Eighteen months of rural agitation (between the April 1952 insurrection and the proclamation of agrarian reform in August 1953) gave rise to a new surge of Indian school activism, spreading beyond the locality of one community and even beyond the caciques' networks into "all the Ayllus, Communities, Haciendas, and Cantons" of the republic. The 1952 mass petition, led by caciques from Taraqu, eloquently translated the liberal right to universal education into a strident demand for Indian schools, civic knowledge, and letters under the protection of the new revolutionary regime.[4]

The cacique petitioners were in good company. With the insurrection, the proverbial dam had burst, and MNR authorities suddenly found themselves drowning in a torrent of peasant-authored petitions flowing in from rural communities across the country. Over several months in 1952, thousands of peasant messengers, delegates, and petitioners traveled down into the urban canyon of La Paz to conduct the bureaucratic work involved in advancing their communities' long-standing claims, or securing specific favors, or seeking new kinds of revolutionary concessions. People and their paperwork came from many different sources: aggrieved or hopeful individuals simply congratulating the new president or asking for a personal favor; regional cacique networks seeking the restitution of their ethnic rights; *sindicato* leaders advancing progressive class agendas; rural representatives of the triumphant revolutionary coalition trading on their sacrifices and support for the MNR; and so on. Addressed to the new revolutionary "comrade-president," Victor Paz Estenssoro, the letters and petitions were often funneled to the Ministry of Peasant Affairs (Ministerio de Asuntos Campesinos, or MAC), where they were transcribed and typed by an army of secretaries, and presumably filed deep in the ministry's archives.[5] Most probably never reached the eyes of Ñunflo Chávez Ortíz, the MAC's powerful new minister. But read in bunches, and laterally across region and topic, they provide the scholar with a crude inventory of both the soaring hopes and long-held grievances that drove many rural people to mobilize in the immediate aftermath of the April 1952 insurrection. The bolder petitions offered decolonial proposals and political agendas. For instance, some letters recycled the five-decade-long campaign for communal land restitution; others asked for the restoration of the original núcleo escolar centers, destroyed or left to decay by the oligarchic regimes. There were proposals asking for state aid to found peasant cooperatives in the shells of old haciendas; others pleaded for amnesty for Indigenous political prisoners caught and jailed during the brutal sexenio period, leading up to the 1952 insurrection; still other petitions demanded the enforcement of Villarroel's famous four decrees, including rural schools and a labor code, issued at the close of the 1945 Indian Congress. One proposal asked the state to keep the illiterate masses informed about their rights and obligations under the new regime. Just as often, mundane matters surfaced: various requests for tax relief, or farm tools, or for the transfer of a federal teacher or the assignment of a veterinarian to the village. Other petitions catalogued the miseries of everyday life: the burden of rural poverty, labor exploitation, and racial violence that had plagued colono and comunario peoples down through the ages.[6]

This moment of euphoria turned La Paz's downtown streets into a dusty labyrinth of miners, peasants, and factories workers. MNRista revelers celebrated with raucous victory rallies where their leaders delivered incendiary speeches and the crowd pledged fealty to the new regime. Such street scenes signaled the geopolitical opening of public space that was virtually unthinkable under oligarchic rule: the revolution had broken the landlords' neocolonial siege, making it possible for mass congregations of peasants to spring up across the land—in city streets, town squares, and union headquarters; in the shadows of government palaces and courthouses; and, most dramatically, in the antechamber of the semifeudal estate, where the patron and his overseer now, astonishingly, had to answer to peasant spokesmen. A new climate of coalitional politics and its democratizing ethos of civil liberty brought the state, the pueblo, and the Indian peasantry into one discursive field of intensive interaction. Spontaneous and planned assemblies—"peasant concentrations," they were called—suddenly burst onto the political scene, becoming a ubiquitous feature of the rural landscape over the next two or three years. A first, spontaneous expression of Indian emancipation, then, was simply to define a legitimate place for Indigenous representation in Bolivia's political public without fear of unleashing gamonal fury or a violent military reaction. Most dramatically, large and small bodies of peasants came together to publicly air their grievances and demand retribution. "Thousands of peasants gathered in all the rural districts ... in absolute liberty to deliberate over their problems and defend themselves" against the reign of violence and abuse, wrote Luís Antezana Ergueta, a fervent MNRista and advocate for agrarian reform.[7] The ancient sound of the conch (*el pututu*)—once forbidden by terrified landlords as the sound that signaled the onset of Indian rebellion—now pierced the thin air, heralding peasants to leave their fields and gather in assembly. It came to symbolize the freedom of the Indian people to gather, deliberate, and act collectively under the "guarantees" of the new regime.[8]

The cityscape of racial hierarchy and transgression, too, was dramatically transformed after the 1952 coup. Of course, La Paz already boasted a sprawling Aymara populace, made up of laborers, artisans, transporters, traders, and shopkeepers; and a stream of women now serviced wealthy families as their domestic servants. The city's retail and wholesale markets had always been a vibrant center of Indigenous and popular commerce. Yet, as we discussed in earlier chapters, race and caste were deeply etched into the city's physiognomy, carving out segregated public spaces where Indians were forbidden to walk, much less to rest or congregate. Into most of the twentieth century, civic space and civil liberties were proscribed, particularly to the legions of litigious cholos and Indians, roving peasant organizers, and itinerant rustics converging on the capital. Before the revolution, transient Indians traveling to the city of La Paz—pongos driving their mule trains loaded with llama dung to serve as fuel in their masters' town houses; itinerant day laborers coming to the city to carry sacks of flour from truck to warehouse; or aggrieved petition-bearing men and women seeking an audience with a minister or trafficking in bureaucratic paperwork—would slip through the city's back alleys, congregate in Indigenous barrios, and try to avoid segregated public spaces and conveyances (trains and streetcars, lobbies and elevators, public squares and downtown street corners) where they were once forbidden to tread. In the words of one United Nations official who witnessed the revolutionary turmoil, before 1952 the Indians were "ciphers in the city"—a floating subclass of human beings with no importance, there to do the bidding of others.[9]

The explosion of popular politics—and particularly the massive influx of peasants and workers into downtown La Paz in the aftermath of the April coup—quickly transformed the city's plazas and streets into political theaters of revolutionary euphoria. The walls of the Ministry of Peasant Affairs were plastered with graffiti and posters proclaiming the liberation of the Indian after four centuries of conquest and servitude, and the building was soon ringed by Indian delegations hoping to deliver their petitions to MAC authorities or registering under the new government crusade against illiteracy. Almost overnight, the spatial politics of La Paz—once the white metropole of the Liberal landholding oligarchy—had been turned upside down. The revolution's political pilgrims now flooded into the city from the surrounding provinces.

Standing offstage was a growing crowd of Indigenous delegates who began amassing outside the heavy wooden doors of government ministries and the presidential palace between April and September 1952. Hundreds, sometimes thousands, of itinerant petitioners waited patiently—often for days and weeks—for a chance to deliver their messages and petitions to their new leaders. The line of supplicants and petitioners that snaked around the Ministry of Peasant Affairs only grew longer as government decrees multiplied, the paperwork ballooned, and the bureaucracy got ever more bogged down. By late 1953, peasant "loiterers" had become an indelible part of the urban landscape. The minister of the MAC described the scene: "Every day about a thousand peasants come to the ministry to wait in interminable lines. Many do not say what their objective is. They ask for money for their return journey. But the ministry has neither the money to give, nor the authority to order the railroads to reduce the fare for their return journey." And so it had become routine and expected that MAC officials would have to wade through a crowd of ragged men and women waiting "interminably" for something to happen.[10]

A Revolutionary Brigade of Peasant Petitioners

A signal index of this organic civic revolution was peasant insistence on their right to information about the country's political norms and decrees—both an emblem of political inclusion and a potential instrument of mobilization. The April 1952 insurrection unleashed a stream of print matter—manifestos, texts, newsletters, broadsides, and decrees inundated places of public assembly in and around rural towns and villages. In the flush of revolution, the MNR's earliest supreme decrees were propagated by word of mouth and by leaflet in the mass victory rallies, but peasant leaders began insisting on their access to civic knowledge and intercultural communication as a civil right. For them, Indian political enfranchisement was less about the universal vote per se, and more about their right to be informed about the government's new laws, policies, and decrees promising a better future.

In August 1952, peasant delegates from Potosí, Chuquisaca, and Cochabamba raised this very concern before the MNR government. The Bolivian peasantry, they said, was widely aware that the revolution had happened and that the new government was promising immediate benefits. But word was not yet reaching Indigenous hamlets; many were unaware of the state's latest decrees. Their demand was for the new president to close the communication gap, "to make known in the Indigenous settlements the conquests the current Government of the Nation has achieved for them."[11] The petitioners translated their revolutionary aspirations into a specific demand: the right to be informed of their social rights under the new governing regime; the right to civic knowledge, information, and awareness. They demanded to know the scope and content of their newly endowed liberties: What were the latest supreme decrees? How might the peasantry protect itself against the escalation of gamonal violence? Would the MNR honor its promise of amnesty to peasants still locked up for their political activities before the April insurrection? And what about fulfilling populist and leftist agendas that had long promised Indians the right to rural schooling for their children, release from coerced labor regimes, and some kind of land reform program?

In the winter of 1952 (June through September), the immediate challenge was to open bilingual and trilingual (Spanish, Aymara, and Quechua) circuits of social communication. "Illiteracy impedes the power of diffusion through the circulation of newspapers in the country," wrote the petitioners. News rarely breached the wall of ignorance, and most colonos were trapped in isolation on feudalistic haciendas. Illiteracy was the scourge of racial oppression and greatest impediment to revolutionary change, those petitioners believed. Compounding the problem was the absence of radio transmitters (*radiodifusoras*)—modern technology that might breach language barriers. How, then, to shatter the physical and cultural isolation of the rural population? The petitioners offered a "modest" proposal: to mobilize a roving band of communication workers to visit rural school centers, organizing rustic teach-ins to inform students and their parents about the new government's laws/conquests. They wanted to establish a Casa del Indio in every provincial capital of the country, where peasants could obtain free legal advice and information about the new laws. Meanwhile, the same petitioners demanded that the MNR address the crimes of landlords who were purging their own hacienda workforce of peasant troublemakers.[12] Here, then, was a bold scheme for dismantling the caste structure of isolation, ignorance, and illiteracy so that Bolivia's Indigenous people might freely participate in civil society and the public sphere under the new regime.

Much of the traffic in peasant paperwork concerned the new protocol of agrarian reform (or what Minister Ñunflo Chávez called "los trámites de revindicación de tierras"), promulgated in August 1953. Historians of the agrarian reform have long acknowledged its confounding mix of policy achievements and failures, its slow and cumbersome bureaucracy, the uneven and unfinished process of land redistribution, and its built-in institutional biases, which tended to favor the colonos over the comunarios, and Cochabamba valley smallholding over Altiplano communal tenure.[13] Two regions, the Lake Titicaca district of the Altiplano and the central valleys of Cochabamba, experienced agrarian transformations in the aftermath of the Agrarian Reform Decree. In the northern Altiplano, the new law provided legal leverage to those ayllu-communities only recently dispossessed of their ancestral lands. For example, Indigenous claims to communal lands in Taraqu and other regions were honored in the courts under the new law, as long as the claimants could prove their dispossession happened after the year 1900.[14] Such lawsuits sometimes devolved into internal land disputes, pitting comunario claims against colonos and sharecropping populations, all scrambling for pieces of the expropriated estate.[15] This feverish activity flooded government ministries, the courts, and the Servicio Nacional de Reforma Agrarian with peasant paperwork. The surge of land invasions (including transplanted groups of miners); the endless chain of legal claims and counterclaims that gummed up the works of judicial administration; and the chronic state of confusion and conflict over the legitimacy and legality of new landholding practices turned parts of the northern Altiplano (and other regions) into zones of intense agrarian conflict, competition, and flux during the 1950s.

In short, the MNR's Agrarian Reform Law seemed to spawn a new version of the official lettered city—peasants trekking into the city to process documents and to find officials to help them register or litigate their land claims under the new rules. Just as their forebears had waged a legal defense of communal (*originario*) lands, or rallied for "a general title and boundary review" of usurped hacienda lands during the early 1900s, so now did a small army of peasant researchers and litigators dig into colonial, provincial, and national archives in search of colonial land titles to "original" lands. The Ecuadorian visitor, Rubio Orbe, was astonished to see how the MNR's Agrarian Reform Law had triggered peasant *trámites* and turned legalism and literacy into indispensable tools for legions of paper-clutching Indian petitioners.

In the first two or three years of MNR rule, the political gravity of rural unrest pivoted on collective demands to abolish Bolivia's semifeudal landholding and labor regime. That agrarian agenda, which the MNR party had tried to avoid until the last possible moment, became the sine qua non of the MNR's revolutionary promise to the peasantry (and to leftist groups) in the early months of 1953.[16] By that point, there was no hope of stuffing the genie back into the chicha jug. In fact, agrarian reform was almost a foreordained project once several peasant leagues had sealed a tactical "pact of alliance" with the MNR leadership in a desperate political moment in 1951.[17] That tenuous alliance rode on the promise that, once in power, the MNR would follow through with fundamental land reform. Nonetheless, the new revolutionary leadership stalled until peasants took matters into their own hands and began invading and occupying private estates in late 1952 and early 1953. This process, historians have argued, produced a de facto agrarian reform, *avant la lettre,* until the MNR's urgent need to stem the tide of "rural anarchy" forced its institutional hand.

For the MNR leadership, the 1953 Agrarian Reform Law and the dramatic spectacle the party presented to the public were designed to pacify the countryside and sweep the peasantry into the party, as its largest and most crucial popular constituency. When the day finally arrived, delegations of peasants, estimated to have ballooned to some 100,000 people, flooded into the Cochabamba valley town of Ucureña, the site of the event.[18] They came by foot, mule, train, truck, and bus from all parts of the country in anticipation of the Day of the Indian, the ceremonial day (established by government decree under Busch in 1937) chosen to honor the country's Indian heritage. Progressive news headlines celebrated this "transcendental decree" as Bolivia's version of the Emancipation Proclamation, ending four centuries of Indigenous slavery.[19] Surrounded by his ministers and a color guard of loyal peasant dirigentes decked out in their finest ponchos and silver staffs of office, Paz Estenssoro finally rose to speak. Gazing down at the excited faces of tens of thousands of hopeful men, women, and children, the new president raised his voice to proclaim the dawn of a new epoch: "Today, the 2nd of August 1953, there ends a long period of more than four centuries of oppression for the peasants of Bolivia. The government of the National Revolution has dictated a Decree of Agrarian Reform that gives the land to those who work it.... Today, more than 2½ million peasants are being incorporated into the national life, with a new economic situation that will permit them to develop all the qualities of the human personality."[20]

This heroic narrative cast the MNR leader as the true liberator, having freed Indians from the landlord's whip and set them on the pathway toward progress and redemption. From that day forward, the oppressed "indio" of the feudal-colonial past was banished by the revolutionary state (as would be the very nomenclature of Indianness in public discourse). Paz Estenssoro framed this epochal moment for his fervent listeners: "Ever since the Spanish arrival," he explained, "the peasants were subjugated under a servile regime. Upon losing their land, they lost their liberty. Today, we return their land and, with it, we return their liberty. We grant them the possibility to educate themselves, improve their living conditions, and send their children to high school and the university. Thus, we have laid the foundation for Bolivia to become a great Nation."[21]

But deliverance from slavery did not come without conditions. The Indian's liberation brought with it civic obligations, tailored to the country's need for a modern rural workforce. What Paz Estenssoro had in mind, in fact, was a grand bargain that offered liberation in exchange for hard work. The national revolution granted the peasant the right to enfranchisement on condition that he fulfill his destiny as the nation's food producer: "We desperately need to increase agricultural production; there are food shortages among the workers of our mines and factories; and so, I exhort everyone [in this crowd] to make the Agrarian Reform bear the fruits that it must yield.... The Government... has fulfilled its obligation with you; now it is you who have to also fulfill your obligation to the National Revolution, by producing more and more."[22] The grand bargain would be sealed, Paz made clear, only with the immediate restoration of calm and obedience among the rural populace.

While Bolivia's historic agrarian reform has captured most public (and historiographical) attention, the revolution simultaneously unleashed a powerful undercurrent of rural school activism, as we have already seen (but that has attracted woefully little scholarly attention by comparison). It first broke the surface of political consciousness when streams of political pilgrims, wielding petitions and lobbying government officials, demanded their right to literacy and education in the immediate aftermath of the April 1952 insurrection. Their appeals or indignation were often couched in the righteous language of an aspiring Indian citizenry, denied their fundamental rights by colonialist elites and gamonal thugs. Straightforward requests for the establishment of a federal school, such as that forwarded by the village of Toledo (Oruro), were rare.[23] More often, pro-school demands were wrapped in rationalizing stories or reciprocal proposals. A mass petition from Chuquisaca, for example, mounted a protest against the jailing of their own leader, but tacked on to the end of their petition was a plaintive request to the president "to issue the papers that give legal guarantees so that 'we, the comunarios del Ayllu Uruguay,' can found a school, which would not cost a single centavo for the state, because our efforts have put us in a condition to hire teachers and provision the school with the supplies necessary for the education of our children." They asked for a simple presidential document, a "resolution," that would "free us from many difficulties."[24] Here the imprimatur of the state (a documentary "resolution") was to serve as the bulwark against the threat of landlord violence or pillage.

A more elaborate proposal, cast as an assembly resolution, came in from the ayllu-community of "Phina" (in Pacajes, La Paz) in August 1952. In return for pledging allegiance to the new constitutional president and head of the National Revolution, the assembly expected the new regime to "sustain two schools by funding normal-trained teachers." The document also called on the new government to create a rural union, granting it "a quota of consumer goods of the first necessity" for all the comunarios. It also threw a flagpole into the proposition, to be used on patriotic days in commemoration of the surviving veterans who had served in the Chaco War. With material aid from the state, their schoolhouse could be furnished with benches, blackboards, a national flag, and even a shield imprinted with the republic's coat of arms. The peasant assembly clearly envisioned a more robust reciprocal relationship between state and the rural community: it pressured the revolutionary regime to deliver basic material subsidies to the rural school, turning the village school into a font of patriotism. The state would no longer simply mandate the founding of schools, or promise protection, but would also take institutional responsibility for provisioning elementary schools with basic material support. In return, the compact promised steadfast peasant loyalty to the MNR.[25] Meanwhile, another group of petitioners hoped the new revolutionary regime would resurrect the old núcleo peasant center of Caquingora-Sewencani. The letter writers begged for an emergency infusion of state aid. Having erected the school with the labor of local padres de familia, the community could no longer sustain the original núcleo network of schools on its own. Conditions were deplorable: the schoolhouse lacked seats and workbenches, so children sat on piles of mud. Supplies were scarce, and parents were unable to continue subsidizing the cost of educating their children. Here was a plaintive appeal to the new regime to help their rural community salvage the schools they had built up over the years with their own labor and meager subsidies. Revolution, to them, meant a modern system of schooling subsidized by a modicum of state funding.[26] Other letters took the opposite approach: soliciting state aid for their own local schools on the basis of the success achieved thus far. Pitching an appeal for state aid and protection, the five ayllus of Caiza D (province of Linares, Potosí) wanted their rural normal school and its outlying primary schools to be fully state-subsidized and federalized, and they asked that trained teachers be sent into their region.[27]

What is striking about most of these petitions is their proactive appeal to the new revolutionary state for material aid. Rather than demanding legal protection for local schools against the threat of landlord prohibition or violence, these petitioners expected the state to redeem the broken promise that Villarroel had delivered to the Indigenous delegates at the end of the 1945 Indian Congress: to provide all Indigenous children with rural elementary schools. In this moment of soaring expectation, many petitioners tried to negotiate a hegemonic populist pact. Ideally, Indigenous expressions of fealty to the MNR in exchange for lands and schools would reciprocally define the terms of this new revolutionary populist order.

Imagining the Postrevolutionary Order:
Two Aymara Proposals

Among the dozens of peasant petitions that flowed into the Ministry of Education in the two or three months following the April 1952 insurrection, two petitions (one from the ayllus and communities of Taraqu, the other from the ex-ayllus of Huarina) stand out: first, because of their elaborated visions of what the postrevolutionary world might look like; and second, because they charted different pathways toward a utopia of Indian emancipation. In this fluid transition, the prospects of revolutionary change were fraught with uncertainty, tension, and promise. Although both petitions asserted the basic proposition that Bolivia's Indigenous majority must be allowed to join the nation on its own terms, exactly what those terms should be, and how they were to be achieved, remained points of uncertainty and contention. Implicitly, the Taraqu utopia was framed as a nativist project of ayllu restoration, while the Huarina project invoked a narrative of Indigenous educational ambition and partial acculturation into a welcoming pluralist nation-state. It is worth pausing briefly to take a closer look at these activist texts, as they seemed to represent two aspects of Indigenous political thinking at the outset of the MNR revolution—when the Indian's place in the new regime was not yet fixed, the national future was still to be molded, and social expectations were unbounded.

Speaking for all the "caciques of the republic," the Taraqu petitioners demanded restitution of their lands, traditions, and autonomy that were stolen around the turn of the twentieth century.[28] The authors advanced their case by the logic of precedence (their colonial entitlements, etc.) as well as through partisan expressions of revolutionary solidarity. The caciques self-identified as Paz Estenssoro's loyal "soldiers of the revolution fighting for social revindications and the liberation of our pueblo." Their revolutionary agenda came down to three fundamental reforms. First, they pleaded for education, the "multiplication of schools in all the Ayllus, Communities, Haciendas, and Cantones," so as to launch a mass literacy campaign—"a revolution in the alphabetization of the Indian." Second, they called on the state to carry out a massive review of the Indians' old land titles and boundary lines so that they could, at long last, restore their legitimate claims to ancestral territories.[29] Third, they pledged solidarity to the MNR in exchange for those reforms, and in the expectation that Paz Estenssoro would dictate laws favorable to their race, finally incorporating "their humble sons [into the military] in the defense of national sovereignty."

Here, then, was the caciques' agenda for revolutionary solidarity and "resurrection of the pueblo of Bolivia"—the articulation of an "ethnic project" (the wholesale restoration of ayllu-communal territoriality and official recognition of the caciques as legitimate representatives "of the race") and an ambitious civic program of universal education and literacy, which would open new channels of communication, litigation, and negotiation for the nation's subaltern majority. Taraqu's petitioners did not stake out a simple "autonomist" or "restorationist" position; rather, they inscribed the principle of ethnic identity and diversity within the MNR's larger national-popular project ("the resurrection of the pueblo"). Perhaps more than envisioning a just future, the power of their words captured, in testimonial form, the moral memory of colonial and racial violence perpetrated against Bolivia's Indian peoples in times past. For the "hour of social revindications" also meant the unveiling of neocolonial history, which had reduced the Indian race to a state of subhumanity: "Mr. President... we have fought for the emancipation of the Indian until this very day, asking for Schools for our children though we were never listened to, because that was not in the interest of the usurper landlords who took our land; on the contrary, they treated us as slaves, renting or selling us, making us work without pay in the *pongueajes* and other services of the cruel tyrants [*verdugos*] ... who took away our sight of knowledge and plunged us into [the darkness of] total ignorance."[30]

Clamoring for "a revolution in the alphabetization of the Indian" was tantamount to overthrowing Bolivia's landlord regime in 1952, even before the MNR was ready to announce its (reluctant) assent to a radical plan of agrarian reform. Along with the restoration of ancestral lands, then, would come the light of schooling and knowledge, bringing an end to the enforced state of Indigenous unschooling and unseeing. To the elders, the time of the patrons was symbolized not only by the whip but also by the Indian's "ignorance" of the letter that rendered him powerless before the lettered lords of the land. Bringing this testimony into the political sphere in early September 1952 leveraged the caciques' authority to advocate for liberating the Indigenous peasantry. From the landlord's whip to the alphabet reader: such were the material artifacts of an agrarian regime being turned upside down—or so it was envisioned by the Taraqu petitioners.

The coming of popular literacy was the symbolic touchstone of Indian liberation for this revolutionary generation of peasant adults across the

Altiplano. It marked the first time village elders felt able not only to claim their legal-citizenship right to universal education but also, more profoundly, to reclaim their freedom, dignity, and personhood that emanated, symbolically and technologically, from their ability to read and write in the dominant national language. Across three or four decades, literacy had become indissolubly tied to the struggle for self-determination and representation, for voice and justice, in the face of colonial-racial violence and marginality. The national revolution promised to change all that—or so, for the moment, this group of petitioners fervently believed.

In August 1952, an alternative Aymara proposal came in from the canton of Huarina, over the main signature of Mariano Mayta. Paying their "fervent respects" to the revolutionary party, these petitioners had fashioned their own ambivalent meaning of social integration: their proposal for a just social order was progressive, nativist, and opportunistic all at once.[31] No doubt, this syncretic mix reflected the shaping influence of their immediate social environment. Inhabiting a network of thirteen ayllus and ex-communities, Huarina was a region of robust peasant union activity, bustling trade, and Protestant missionary activity. Communal landholding had diminished over the years, and their petition addressed a host of social maladies of neocolonialism, such as racial discrimination, poverty, and marginality. The authors envisioned a postrevolutionary world that would remedy "the poorly named problem of the Indian" and inaugurate an "epoch of true recuperation of the Indian," thus remaking the spirit of Bolivian "nationality."[32] Their postrevolutionary utopia was founded on the premise that Indian liberation would come from a just program of land reform, closely administered by local leaders. In this imagined social world, protective laws would prohibit all forms of land fragmentation or alienation either by Indigenous people or by outsiders. Thus, their agrarian utopia would bind communal preservation to the ideals of economic progress and the state's benign authority. Wily advocates, the Indians wanted the minister of agriculture to jump-start the region's agro-industrial revolution (playing into the MNR acute concern over rural productivity trends) while also guaranteeing monthly provisions of imported wheat, potato, and other crops (to be used as seeds to diversify their crop yields).

The Huarina petition also tapped the vein of revolutionary euphoria. It beseeched the new government to invest in the education of Indigenous youth—but in a way that would stem the flow of youth abandoning the countryside for the city. Rural education, they argued, should be tailored to the practical needs of the peasant, training him to improve his agricultural methods. On that point, the petitioners coincided with the North Americans' and MNR's pedagogical priority of practical knowledge to upgrade the rural labor force. But there was a democratic twist to this position on rural education, for Huarina petitioners also demanded that the new government throw open the country's secondary schools and universities to a select group of talented Indian youth, between fifteen and twenty years old. This concrete demand was tantamount to the democratization of Bolivia's public educational system, which would involve desegregating the higher echelons of learning and funneling a steady stream of Indians (much like W. E. B. Du Bois's "talented tenth" of Black youth being recruited and encouraged to attend colleges and universities) into Bolivia's liberal and technical professions.[33] Many years earlier, Eduardo Nina Quispe had fought for the right of Indigenous youth to gain advancement through secondary schooling, before his life was cut short by state repression during the Chaco War years (see chapter 2). From night to day, from the dark days of the Chaco War to the bright horizons of revolutionary promise: Huarina's authors reimagined a postcolonial nation brimming with educated professionals in which Indigenous engineers would advance the country's material progress, Indigenous medical doctors would heal the sick and teach their patients to shed "their vices and illnesses," and Indigenous lawyers would help their Indian "brothers" leave the temptations of the city and return to their ancestral lands.[34] In this scenario, Aymara and Quechua professionals would have a moral and disciplinary role to play as the nation's learned cultural brokers, teachers, civilizers, and counselors to their less fortunate and less cultivated kinsmen. Over the long term, they would become the agents of acculturation. Yet this reimagined postrevolutionary order would also preserve civic spaces for the communal (ayllu) tradition to flourish, and Huarina's leaders vigorously advocated for the restitution of communal landholding rights. Building on the bedrock of the communal Indigenous past but charting a pathway forward into the modernizing nation, the petitioners who spoke for Huarina's thirteen communities tried to harness the logic of ethnic rights and communal autonomy to the nationalist ideals of public education, cultural integration, and upward social mobility. In different ways, then, both the Taraqu and Huarina petitioners interwove strands of nativism and nationalism into whole cloth, and then displayed their textual tapestries of postrevolutionary justice to the ascendant MNR authorities.

But as it turned out, state officials were scarcely listening, and those two Aymara petitions (along with most others) ended up being transcribed, forgotten, and filed away in a cabinet (eventually landing in Bolivia's national archive of "presidential papers"). Meanwhile, however, the locus of rural school activism was shifting from the fervor of mass petitioning to the upsurge of local school initiatives, while government authorities and educators deliberated among themselves about the problems and prospects of Indian education reform.

Building Rural Schools, Sinking Flagpoles

As never before, the revolutionary field of force opened spaces for local school initiatives to flourish and spread in regions across the northern Altiplano in the years leading up to the MNR's 1955 Code of Education Reform. In 1952, the prospect of revolutionary reform had put the landholding elite on notice that its days were numbered while emboldening the radical coalition of laborers and peasant organizations to align with the MNR political vanguard and its allies in the Confederación de Obreros Bolivianos (COB). Organizing rural unions and schools often worked in tandem. Deploying union tactics and leverage to organize local school campaigns or, alternatively, using school organizing to jump-start a rural union had been intertwined efforts since the late 1930s and 1940s. But in the flush of insurrection, the alchemy of pro-union and pro-school activism suddenly became explosive, raising expectations among colonos that "the hour of social revindications" had finally arrived.[35] The quickening spread of unions (in many cases encouraged and sanctioned by the Agrarian Reform Law after August 1953) was a boon to the spontaneous village school movement. In tactical terms, the Agrarian Reform Law accelerated that trend by requiring peasants to allocate specific parcels of ex-hacienda land for the purpose of founding schoolhouses. New schools sprang up in the husks of expropriated haciendas, partly thanks to the collaboration of union leaders, teachers, and state authorities. Meanwhile, as noted earlier, as literacy's currency rose, the number of rural schools multiplied, and the demand for rural teachers grew accordingly. Many teachers, in turn, helped the still largely unlettered population cope with the avalanche of laws, protocols, and paperwork unleashed by the agrarian reform program.[36]

It is difficult to quantify this explosive growth of rural schools during the first few years of MNR governance. Chaos, improvisation, inefficiency, and the haphazard transition from local to federal schooling all tended to inhibit good government record-keeping.[37] But preliminary figures gathered by Marcelo Sangines Uriarte plot a steady (though hardly spectacular) increase in

FIGURE 7.1. The rural school: symbol of revolution, hope of the nation. Dirección National de Informaciones, *Bolivia: 10 años de revolución*, 83.

the number of registered fiscal schools between 1952 and 1956.[38] He notes that after a steady increase, school matriculation leveled off to about 34 percent in the second half of the 1950s (still shockingly low by the standards of Bolivia's neighboring countries to the south). On the other hand, Robert Alexander (having interviewed several MNR officials) described an impressive wave of school activity unfolding on the Altiplano and praised the government for promoting it.[39] By the early 1960s, the MNR regime would take full credit for having launched a veritable revolution in rural education. According to the MNR's ten-year anniversary album, education reform represented the MNR revolution's "gift to the Bolivian Indian" (see fig. 7.1).[40]

If reliable government data was lacking, however, a growing number of field reports provided vivid impressions of ground-up (often hidden) school initiatives that were transforming the agrarian landscape. A host of international visitors described the fervor of rural people capitalizing on the favorable turn of events. Rubio Orbe, the Ecuadorian indigenista we met earlier, was one of the first visiting dignitaries to recognize that the expansion of rural schooling on the Bolivian Altiplano in the early 1950s was largely driven by peasants, not by state authorities or policies.[41] That impression was reinforced by an American envoy, Jeffrey Rens, who went to Bolivia in the late 1950s and early 1960s to invest UN and International Labour Office money and expertise in a sprawling network of rural clinics, schools, workshops, cooperatives, roads, and other kinds of infrastructure. When pressed, he conceded that the program's 150 rural schools were largely the product of "voluntary" work brigades. Peasant communities had catalyzed the whole project of school-building and provided the labor "free of charge" (in exchange for which the UN program helped villages petition the Bolivian state for licenses, subsidies, and teachers).[42] While he recognized the proactive role that local communities had played in underwriting the cost of this rural development project, Rens shared the vainglorious view of the typical international development officer wandering the backlands of the Cold War's "Third World" during the late 1950s and 1960s. His NGO program, he boasted, had arrested the long evolutionary decline of the Andean Indian. For the first time in five hundred years, the long-term effects of the Spanish Conquest had actually been reversed!

On a more somber note, the Colombian economist Antonio García described how he spent months traveling through Bolivia as part of a UN project to evaluate the MNR's "agrarian reform and social development." He was not terribly impressed by what he saw, and was especially critical of the MNR's embrace of (inappropriate) Western agro-technology to fast-forward the development of Bolivia's traditional highland regions. The one policy achievement that García did single out for praise was the simmering activity in rural schooling. The MNR government was pressured into investing state funds in rural schools because of the demographic surge in Bolivia's school-age population, he noted. But the main impetus behind the feverish burst of school-building had come not from the government or from Western development agencies but from community-based initiatives building elementary schoolhouses where none had existed before.[43]

Such fleeting impressions were confirmed and contextualized by a group of American anthropologists and other social scientists who worked in Bolivia during the mid- to late 1950s. Through their ethnographic field reports, they furnished eyewitness reports of hollowed-out ex-haciendas honeycombed with new peasant smallholders, school collectives, and union associations. That the grassroots surge in schooling was indissolubly linked to the shifting agrarian circumstances seemed crystal clear to the American economist Melvin Burke, for example. His intensive fieldwork in haciendas on both sides of the Bolivia/Peru border demonstrated the positive aftereffects of the MNR-led revolution. On the Bolivian side, rural schools had proliferated and literacy spread over the 1950s, while schools were scarce and illiteracy rates hovered around 90 percent on Peru's feudalistic estates.[44] Meanwhile, the American anthropologist William Carter was impressed at how "formal education [had] permeated the Aymara territory," spreading across the northern Altiplano with lightning speed.[45] Years later, Carter elaborated on this initial impression: over the 1950s and 1960s Bolivia had experienced a fivefold growth in the number of rural schools and student enrollments—thanks in part to the MNR's commitment to agrarian reform and formal schooling for the children of rural dwellers. Carter also registered the unabashed peasant enthusiasm for school learning, and the willingness on the part of rural communities and families to make material sacrifices to achieve their goals:

> Education has become a highly valued good for rural dwellers. They see it as enabling their offspring to move into Bolivia's urban centers ... and they [also] look at education as an important defense of community rights. Because the central government places a premium on local representatives who are Spanish-speaking and literate, only through the dissemination of educational skills can there be any assurance that a community's legal rights will be honored. [And thus] because of these convictions, most of today's rural schools were constructed with locally donated materials and labor and with a minimum of dependence on state aid.[46]

In this passage, Carter captures the shifting symbolic and practical values of education in rural society. For many rural people, the arrival of the schoolhouse expanded their aspirational horizons and opened pathways for individual mobility, labor migration, and wage work in the city, if only for the next generation of kinsmen. The cultural technology of legal writing—the ability to wield the language, laws, and archival knowledge in defense of individual and communal rights—was held in high regard as the most effective weapon in the Andean peasants' cultural armory under the new hegemonic order. Yet times were inevitably changing. Working on the sloping mountainsides and valleys of the Nor Yungas, another American anthropologist, Dwight Heath, filed a report on the robust civic activities of the local self-governing councils (*cabildos abiertos*, he called them) that were springing up in the ruins of the old haciendas.[47] Many ex-haciendas were being transformed into integrated networks of rural towns, defined by the nexus of a locally enfranchised union, a functioning primary school, a traditional cabildo, and a weekly peasant market, and perhaps with the newly designated status of canton.

This patchwork picture affords glimpses of the subterranean school movement as it was becoming an integral component of the hegemonic bargaining process. This agrarian development in schooling was gradual and uneven and could easily turn into a source of local discord, as it did among a later generation of Indigenous youth in the 1970s (many of whom, ironically, were among the first generation of educated Aymara intellectuals and activists). But we would be remiss, as historians, to leap ahead to a retrospective critique of the MNR era of school reform without recognizing this landmark political moment, when certain Aymara people seized their "hour of vindication" to demand literacy and schooling as a fundamental right. In their moral reckonings, the rural school symbolized emancipation from the tyranny of isolation, ignorance, and illiteracy. While living and working in an Aymara community several years ago, anthropologist Andrew Canessa tapped into the paradoxical meanings and memories that village elders attached to the functional power of Spanish literacy—its double-sided significance as both a traditional weapon of neocolonial domination and potential tool of Indigenous empowerment and resistance. His village interlocutors shared a fundamental premise about the contradictory nature of alphabetic literacy in the rural Andean world: that the "power of literacy ... [could] be used to dominate people and, as a consequence, to liberate them." But by that measure, the *denial or absence of reading and writing among the rural poor* had served as a device of neocolonial disenfranchisement, racism, and marginality. And while the racial stereotype of the *indio iletrado* had stigmatized and excluded the rural majority, so too had the "reading Indian" (indio letrado, or *indio leído*) been feared, suppressed, or persecuted by the conservative oligarchy in prerevolutionary times. Canessa translates the words of one elderly man from the Aymara-speaking village he studied: "The Spanish came to abuse our people.... Our ancestors did not speak or read Spanish, and that is why they treated our ancestors like animals."[48] Filtered through moral memory, the coloniality of knowledge and power was manifested, simultaneously, through the systemic denial of Indigenous literacy and the racial stigmatization of illiteracy. Another Aymara elder remembered how "the *q'aras* [white people] did not want us to learn to read.... The *patrón* would say that if the Indians knew how to write then they could contradict us; that is [how] they took away our lands.... In those days, the patrón was not afraid to whip us or insult us."[49] As these interlocutors would seem to suggest, Indigenous literacy (and its negation) was a flexible idiom used to mark the passage from colonialism, servitude, and racial oppression in the dark ages of prerevolutionary times to the euphoria of postrevolutionary promise. "After the Agrarian Reform we learned how to read... [and it] gave us new laws," the old man explained.[50] So long denied or forbidden, the once subversive act of "learning to read" Spanish script most clearly defined what the revolution had come to mean for many Indigenous people.

The Reading Indian: A Civic Revolution from Below

The robust expansion of rural schooling reflected not only the currency of formal education, but also the profusion of print culture and the improvisation of new forms of communal reading. In both rhetorical and practical ways, popular technologies of literacy and print broke through the neocolonial wall of cultural isolation, an enormous (but still little-studied) transformation that swept through the northern Altiplano during the 1950s and early 1960s. Reporting from the villages in the northern Altiplano, anthropologist Olen Leonard sometimes encountered ad hoc reading groups—a latter-day version of Aymara textual communities collectively deciphering their colonial land titles in the 1920s, or the rural dirigentes' revolutionary print communities and other forms of rebel communication that helped articulate a modern peasant movement in the 1940s. Now, in the flush of agrarian change, Leonard bore witness to ad hoc peasant study groups being organized "in many small villages and rural communities, [where] a teacher or some other literate person [would] regularly divulge the most important content of the occasional newspaper among a group of friends and vecinos." Those considered formally literate, who could independently decipher Spanish print, constituted a small minority among the northern Altiplano villages Leonard visited, and the number of peasants who had regular access to newspapers was almost nil.[51] Newsprint was still an article of privilege limited largely to urban readers. Yet the rise of syndicalism and spread of rural insurgency in the prerevolutionary years had unleashed a torrent of popular print, channeling news and propaganda, as well as decrees and laws, into the rural domain. Once the MNR's agrarian reform laws began dismantling the power of the landed oligarchy and opening up spaces for village school initiatives, more rural men began acquiring the rudiments of literacy and schooling. By then, the MNR had abolished the country's literacy requirement, which had once excluded the vast majority of Indigenous men (and all women) from enfranchised citizenship. Starting in 1952, universal suffrage delivered voting rights to the mass of "illiterate" adults, both women and men. For those who could not read or write, an initial of their name or thumbprint was good enough to register in the voter rolls. But while literacy was no longer a requirement of suffrage, its symbolic and functional value was more transcendent than ever before. Reading conferred status and dignity, along with a sense of national belonging; without the terror of landlord reprisal, reading printed materials aloud became a common pastime in many rural communities. The sociologist Luís Antezana Ergueta described streams of peasants traveling from their villages into the city of La Paz, where they stocked up on "magazines, pamphlets, periodicals, notebooks, etc. Whatever pamphlet was given them became a valuable means of instruction," he told the American labor historian Robert Alexander.[52]

Along with the variety of reading practices, communal writing flourished. The long tradition of collaboration and coauthorship of written political tracts could still be found in rural localities, where peasant assemblies composed and circulated a corpus of petitions, letters, manifestos, testimonies, and legal documents—the documentary ammunition supporting peasant demands for justice and reform in the first months after the coup. Once again, mass petitions were the common currency; rural society was saturated with official paper; cacique archives were dusted off for purposes of conducting business with the offices managing agrarian reform; and people were riveted to news articles and notices about all facets of the MNR revolution. It was not unusual for the roving anthropologist to come upon nocturnal peasant "listening bees." Villagers gathered around the rare and precious transistor radio, an iconic artifact of modernity. As the metaphorical watering hole for village gossip, news, and other forms of sociability, the transistor radio drew small crowds—families who gathered to hear the news or listen to didactic programs on animal breeding, crops, or homemaking that were beamed to listeners during evening hours when the farm chores were done and radio reception was best. On occasion, the radio was turned into an adult literacy classroom for "listening comprehension lessons" in the Spanish language. One of Olen Leonard's informants told him that "for the elders, we would like to learn Spanish. When they elect us to go to La Paz to represent our community before the government, there the functionaries do not speak Aymara, so it is difficult for them to understand us."[53] It was the officials' lack of understanding, their inability to speak native languages, or to engage in bilingual discussion, that motivated alcaldes, dirigentes, and caciques to bridge the communication divide, just as the caciques-apoderados had struggled to do in the early 1900s.

There was also a keen sense that to understand spoken Spanish was the proverbial ticket to exit the insular world of the hacienda; cross the threshold of the geo-racial divide; open the sluice gates of economic opportunity and social mobility; shield the self, family, and community from the ubiquitous predation of local landlords and merchants; and chart an intergenerational pathway toward a better future. A village elder explained to the American anthropologist how revolution and the new technology had widened their horizons: "We are interested in knowing what happens outside our community, and the radios are the only means we have to inform ourselves of those things. And that makes us appear more civilized in the eyes of the rest of Bolivia."[54] Radio, newspaper, or pamphlet—those were the tools that could bestow a measure of cosmopolitanism on a rural village, without necessarily erasing the rituals and routines of Indigenous ways of living, working, and knowing in the changing world around them (see fig. 7.2).

All these spoken and written messages, along with the mundane work involved in setting up rural primary schools in the immediate aftermath of the 1952–53 revolutionary reforms, turned the village school into an anticolonialist/antiracist instrument and symbol of social empowerment and political integration. Naive foreign aid workers and government officials still expressed shock and surprise at the overwhelming "enthusiasm" and "desire" for schooling that defied their stereotypes of stupefied Indian peasants awaiting the arrival of state teachers or NGO officials to rescue them. Even MNR officials conceded in their commemorative album of 1962 that "the peasant did not remain passive before the [progressive revolutionary] force of the government. With their own resources, innumerable peasant communities constructed their own schools, across the length and breadth of the territory of the Republic."[55] In this telling comment, the MNR government revealed that even at the height of government funding for education, the burden of establishing and funding a rural school still fell largely to rural communities themselves. Rural poverty, agrarian frictions, and the work rhythms of the peasant household still imposed enormous obstacles for local educational projects. With remarkable speed, though, the new political culture revolved around the rural school, union, and land entitlement, making it possible for rural people to gain access to political literacy and to exercise their franchise, even if most village elders still could neither read nor write. Without fear of landlord violence, rural communities could send their children to a local elementary school, and perhaps even send their sons off to the city to acquire

Cualquier lugar es bueno para aprender a leer

FIGURE 7.2. Literacy acquisition represented a revolutionary act. The child, clutching a notebook and using a makeshift desk, is studying his letters. Or could it be that the child is helping his father learn to read? Rural literacy became an intergenerational endeavor in the 1950s. Dirección Nacional de Informaciones, *Bolivia: 10 años de revolución*, 82.

formal training in a trade school or to acquire a professional degree from the public university. Building on the cumulative political experience of the 1940s and securing the advantages of formal education in the early 1950s was as much about cultural dignity and collective emancipation as about individual mobility and opportunity. The upsurge of peasant school activity and mass petitioning expressed a nearly universal ideal that, at base, Bolivia's unfolding civic revolution would finally settle on the mud-baked foundation of the rural village school.

PART TWO

The MNR's Architecture of Rural Education Reform

As noted, the 1952 insurrection catapulted an unruly popular coalition into power under the party leadership of Victor Paz Estenssoro and Hernán Siles Suazo. Middle-class social reformers, they hoped to harness the exuberance of the COB (Bolivia's militant labor confederation), Bolivia's dissident leftist youth, and the rural masses in ways that would secure a peaceful transition to popular-democratic rule. During the first eighteen months of rule, Bolivia's popular coalition fought for fundamental social and economic change, just as the Huarina and Taraqu petitioners were drawing up their own blueprints for revolutionary justice. The new MNR leadership had to manage the explosion of popular expectations and political agendas that had long been brewing. As Laurence Whitehead notes, "The revolution expressed a clash of ideas about fundamental issues of national identity and collective direction. The ideas motivating the revolution gained early expression... [in the late 1930s] and extended their popular appeal through the 1940s. After 1952, prior constraints on the application of these ideas were abruptly lifted, and a variety of rival interpretations of the meaning of the revolution competed for ascendance."[56] In just a few years, this revolutionary ferment would lose its fizz, but in the meantime, there was a mad scramble within the revolutionary coalition to seize the moment and redirect the process of state-building and institutional change.

Education reform quickly soared to the top of the state's priorities. It was widely acknowledged among the new ruling elite that Bolivia desperately needed an overhaul of its public schools, technical institutes, and public universities. But most of all, the Bolivian state wanted to spread public primary schools into the countryside, in much the same way the Church had once extended a chain of parish churches in rural towns and villages. Deploying the public school to nationalize ("bolivianize") the Indian masses, ideally within the short span of a generation, would become the driving pedagogical motif of MNR cultural nationalism.

The MNR's Comisión de la Reforma de la Educación (CRE) began its deliberations in June 1953.[57] Inaugurated around the same time as the agrarian reform, the CRE's work was soon eclipsed by the MNR's urgent need to break up the hacienda, allocate smallholdings to the restive peasantry, and pacify rural areas. The education commission was also hindered by its own cumbersome organization, painful internal deliberations, and copious research efforts.[58] But after twenty months, in January 1955, the commission finally unveiled its massive plan for the bureaucratic overhaul of Bolivia's cumbersome system of public education. On paper, the CRE's 1955 *Código de la educación boliviana* represented a remarkable institutional feat of state-building. Its overall administrative goal was to sweep the functions of governance, education, and integration under one bureaucratic umbrella.[59] On that score, the Education Code (as I will refer to it) represented Bolivia's first serious institutional attempt to centralize, standardize, discipline, and democratize Bolivia's public school system. As historians of Bolivian education often point out, the MNR's education reform represented a high-water mark in Bolivia's fifty-year-long history of attempted public school reforms, beginning with the Liberal reforms of the Montes years.[60] Rhetorically, the CRE's blueprint of public school reform was presented as both a symbol and an arm of Bolivia's cultural and democratic revolution: education's moral purpose, declared CRE's president, was to promote "the harmonious development of the Bolivian man, oriented toward an ideal and practical goal of collective advancement."[61] A party slogan—"Instead of an education of the castas, an education of the masses!"—would become the MNR's new mantra.

Along with an "education of the masses" came the cultural imperative to instill in the ideal "Bolivian man" a deep spirit of patriotic duty and habits of hard work. Several clauses of the Education Code called for "the spiritual orientation of the pueblo and that of the future generations."[62] Education reform would instill "the attitudes, ideals, and conduct" defining the subject and subjectivity of Bolivia's patriotic citizen. But for the popular classes, the express purpose of public schooling was inextricably tied to work skills and self-discipline. Henceforth, according to the Education Code, classroom pedagogy would be "active, vitalist, and work-oriented." It closely followed the curricular prescription of both UNESCO (defined as "fundamental education") and SCIDE ("functional education"). At last, rural education was to raise up the country's first generation of efficient agricultural producers and consumers. Along with the government's program of land reform, the new rural public school was to advance "the economic emancipation of the Nation," dissolving the lingering "forms of feudal exploitation in the countryside."[63]

Presided over by Fernando Diez de Medina, Bolivia's most prominent literary scholar and coeditor of the new indigenista periodical *Inti Karka*,[64] the CRE's most revealing discussions about Indian education took place within several of its subcommittees. The CRE's "Seminar on Fundamental Education" (and its Mechanization and Agrarian Technology subcommittee) designed a new vocational training program that would encourage Indians to give up their "primitive farming methods." New farm-schools, it was hoped, would also stem the hemorrhaging of peasant migrants to La Paz and other cities. Anxious officials warned that without modern agricultural establishments, the countryside would be emptied out within a generation, leaving "an impending dearth of agricultural laborers [*falta de brazos*]!" To reverse the "exodus of the campesinos toward the urban centers," the new pedagogy would diffuse "basic and technical knowledge" to induce the young campesino to stay on his land and thus become "a positive factor of production."[65] The heroic rural teacher would "pay... his pedagogic debt, of great importance to the future of la Patria," by following this prescription: "THE CHILD OF THE COUNTRYSIDE [*NIÑO DEL CAMPO*] SHOULD BE EDUCATED AS A CHILD OF THE COUNTRYSIDE, SO AS TO LIVE IN THE COUNTRYSIDE AND FEEL HIMSELF CONTENT WITH LIFE IN THE COUNTRYSIDE."[66] How? The new technical curriculum would "tear off the blinders of ignorance," "shake the peasant child out his stupor of lethargy," "forge a personality" within the unformed Indian child, and convert him into a "useful, positive, and effective being." Tutelary racism and the mystique of pedagogical power still permeated elite deliberations about Indian education—although national-populist idioms of agrarianism, class, and mestizaje now began to reframe public discussion. Catapulting the campesino into the modern age became synonymous with "saving our agricultural economy, synonymous with our national economy": the stakes could not be higher. Education reform now pivoted on the transformation of the *niño del campo* into the "archetypal Bolivian campesino—sober, clean, disciplined, producer and consumer, endowed with all his inherent rights and obligations."[67]

The man most responsible for shaping the CRE's rural education program was Vicente Lema. Appointed as a liaison to the all-important Ministry of Peasant Affairs (MAC), Lema was a man pulled in two ideological directions. Closely allied with the teachers union, he supported Bolivia's militant, anti-imperialist worker confederation (COB), but he also greatly admired North America's rural extension programs in Bolivia. Lema's strong support of SCIDE turned out to be crucial to the CRE's deliberations about Indigenous education. Just months after the MNR victory, the first issue of its official indigenista magazine, *Inti Karka*, carried a searing (and anonymous) critique of US infiltration of Bolivia's núcleo campesino schools: "We consider it necessary to make known... that some núcleos escolares still depend on the Yanqui intervention, whose bureaucratic organism of 'technicians' spends millions of bolivarianos [sic] in tourist trips and the propagandistic simulacra of our Indians, [whose images] are exclusively manufactured for the screens of photographic cameras, with ends anathema to the true purveyors of education." The editorial blasted SCIDE, specifically, for having exploited the history and image of Warisata, for its exoticism, and for having distorted the organic relationship between school and community.[68] That inaugural issue of *Inti Karka* also displayed the iconic photograph of Franz Tamayo, invoking the image of Bolivia's most famous literary indigenista to reclaim the mantle of national pedagogy from the North Americans, who were corroding Bolivia's cultural sovereignty.[69] On the left side of the political ledger, Alipio Valencia Vega's article in the same issue invoked the symbol of Warisata as an ideological foil. Liberating the Indian through enlightened school reform was a dead letter, he proclaimed, and the Yankees' miracle of rural modernity was but another prop of the old feudal order.[70] Caught up in that bitter debate, Vicente Lema (the man in charge of the CRE's rural education plan) had to tread carefully, but he had no intention of expelling the North Americans from Bolivia. And SCIDE's new director, Thomas Hart, used a later issue of *Inti Karka* to launch a vigorous defense of SCIDE's achievements to date.[71] In the end, the MNR's blueprint for rural education, as designed by Lema, looked suspiciously like the North American model.

Thus, Vicente Lema rallied to the defense of SCIDE at a moment when its fate hung in the balance. Enamored of its functional work-oriented pedagogy and totalizing acculturative programs, Lema's reforms were driven by two major goals: first, to foster modern skills, habits, and attitudes toward agricultural work; and second, to improve basic living conditions in the countryside.[72] Utopian in both vision and scale, Lema's scheme would depend on massive public investment from both domestic and foreign sources. Equally, it would depend on bureaucratic competency. That is to say, in retrospect, Lema's grandiose design was almost doomed from the start, given Congress's skimpy budget and the built-in competition among government branches (and in the fierce rivalry between urban and rural schooling, administered and funded by separate ministries). Having little faith that the Ministry of Peasant Affairs could actually commandeer the necessary funding for rural schools, Lema proposed that the state require subsidies from rural communities, cooperatives, or unions, with the proviso that all local school establishments (except private, missionary, and parish schools) would fall under supervisory control of the federal government. Although he was acutely aware of the impoverished condition of most local schools (their "enormous deprivation"; the "absolute absence of teaching materials in many cases"), he apparently saw no alternative but to throw the burden of school funding back onto the rural community. Harnessing the peasant desire for alphabet schools, he argued, might provide just the hidden resource the MNR needed to launch its rural school revolution in the absence of adequate state funding:

> In the last few years, the evidence shows that an appreciable number of children and their parents are not only personally *disposed* to pay for the cost of indispensable school supplies for their little ones, but that they have actually been able to do so; that is to say, they have actually begun to acquire that material with their own money. This is, without a doubt, a precious sign that shows us the great possibility of [promoting] education in the campo, slowly eroding the myth that the Indian cannot pay for the education of his own children.... It is the peasant dirigentes who, little by little, are recognizing the social, practical, and cultural value of the school. When they see the schoolhouse needs a door, a new classroom, roof repair, or the purchase of a flag, they meet and work out how they can raise the funds they need for the school that the state cannot afford to give them.[73]

Hoping to close the gap between soaring rhetoric and harsh conditions, Lema figured the only way "to improve and revitalize the education of the peasantry" was to make rural communities pay for it. In return, the state would impose its authority by "routinizing this practical form of mutual aid between the school and the community it serves."[74] Needless to say, this arrangement only institutionalized the burden that rural communities had carried in the prerevolutionary era.

Rural Schooling under the MNR: A Rebirth of Inequality

Vicente Lema's blueprint for rural education reform passed, almost unaltered, into Bolivia's 1955 Education Code.[75] As such, it represented a sly example of the MNR's double standard of schooling and citizenship and its recycled logic of racial caste inequality. On the one hand, the MNR trumpeted its democratic slogan: "from an education of the castes to an education of the masses." Political discourse and the press, along with key articles of the 1955 Education Code, celebrated the revolution's platform of universal rights and social equality. On the other hand, the CRE argued that rural and urban education must be hierarchical and segmented, each tailored to fit the different needs and characteristics of the geography and population it was serving.

Spelled out in black and white, the 1955 Education Code (chap. 3, art. XVI) mandated the (re-)creation of two spheres—"the urban school system" and the "peasant school system"—the latter targeted to rural hamlets, haciendas, communities, and cooperatives. They were to have two sets of standards, a different curriculum, unequal funding, and different administrative rules, under the Ministry of Peasant Affairs (for rural schools) and the Ministry of Education (for urban establishments). Urban schoolchildren would benefit from a six-year elementary school curriculum, while the rural elementary school would offer a rudimentary education in a two- or three-year cycle (usually in a one-room schoolhouse). Students wishing to continue their formal schooling would have to travel or resettle in a town or city. Meanwhile, if local communities were lucky, they might win a modicum of state aid to pay their local teachers. Most likely, however, the rural schoolteacher would have had no formal training, perhaps not even a full cycle of primary school education (unless, perhaps, recruited for summer teacher-training programs with SCIDE). To be sure, reinstating the old geo-colonialist logic of separate and unequal schooling caused unease among a few members of the CRE, including Vicente Lema himself. Confiding in Robert Alexander, a visiting historian from Rutgers University, he expressed doubts about the MAC's capacity to fund and administer the nation's rural primary schools. He believed the Ministry of Education, a much more robust and well-funded ministry, would be better suited to administer *both* urban and rural branches of public education.[76] In the end, however, the CRE decided to lodge *Educación Rural* within the jurisdiction of the MAC, the government's "one-stop shop" for all Indian affairs.

Thus, education reform revealed the deep contradictions between the MNR's egalitarian populist ideals and its discriminatory policies that perpetuated racial and class inequities.[77] Yet on the surface, the unveiling of the 1955 Education Code was a public occasion to herald the MNR's integrative revolution. Newspaper headlines gloried in the belated arrival of "universal education," long ago promised by the 1874 Constitution. Education reform would also serve as the vector of cultural amalgamation and radical egalitarianism. In early January 1955, *La Nación* articles proclaimed that "the Educational

Reform will be for all the people of our country"; "education will no longer be a monopoly of a minority"; and "reading and writing will be taught in the cities, the towns, the factories, the mines, and the countryside."

But ineffectual educational policy, meager government budgets, and dismal field reports soon punctured this euphoric balloon.[78] The lion's share of state revenue earmarked for education and culture, for example, went to the Ministry of Education, in charge of urban public schools, public institutions of higher education, and a host of new cultural institutes. Preliminary evidence reveals this shocking urban/rural discrepancy. In 1963, when overall government spending on education was rising again (thanks in part to US economic assistance), Cristóbal Suárez estimated that some 98 percent of the national budget for public education flowed to the urban sector, while only 2 percent of state funding for all schools actually went to rural schools.[79] This grotesque institutional inequality persisted well into the 1960s and beyond. In 1968, Marcelo Sangines's research, for example, revealed that over the first eight years of the 1960s (a period flush with foreign aid to the MNR and, after 1964, to the Barrientos regime), the MAC's budget increased significantly, surpassing the annual rate of population growth. Presumably, more state aid flowed into rural schooling, increasing the net expenditure per school-age child. In 1967, though, government aid to urban education and culture represented 20.6 percent of total government expenditures, whereas state aid to rural schools amounted to 8.6 percent. Scant funding supported rural teachers (whose salaries were dismal), leaving little revenue to cover the cost of publications, schoolroom supplies, school construction, or repairs. Such infrastructural costs were expected to be covered by local communities.[80] Around the same time, this urban/rural gap was exposed by James Wilkie's 1969 study of Bolivian government revenue and US aid: between 1953 and 1964, the MAC subsisted on a fraction (between one-half and one-third) of the Ministry of Education's budget (which was strictly earmarked for urban institutions).[81] Even without the aid of reliable government data, preliminary research reveals the systemic deprivation of state funding for Bolivia's rural school sector.[82]

Concrete signs of rural school poverty and inequity surfaced almost immediately. A disquieting 1958 report revealed that Bolivia's seven rural normal schools were in such disrepair that the state had decided to shut down several of them (despite the acute shortage of trained rural teachers).[83] Growing US pressure on Bolivia to "stabilize its currency," tamp down inflation, and slash government spending only made things worse and punctured the public morale and momentum of the early revolutionary years. No less an MNR luminary than Fernando Diez de Medina (who presided over the CRE between 1953 and 1955) despaired of ever improving the quality of rural schooling. In 1962 he lambasted the "government's stagnation" and estimated that, in technical terms, the country's rate of illiteracy had fallen by only about 5 percent over a decade.[84] Other critics decried the lavish state support that flowed into Bolivia's "archaic and dysfunctional system of university education," which still produced legions of lawyers, journalists, and poets, but too few useful professionals (agronomists, engineers, veterinarians, and the like).[85]

As the MNR's loyalists and critics argued over whether rural education reform was a resounding nationalist success or an abysmal state failure, a few foreign researchers began to weigh in. William Carter, working in Aymara villages near Lake Titicaca, was among the first visiting anthropologists to cast aspersion on the MNR's claims of having liberated the Indigenous peasantry through educational reform. "The school system set up by the revolutionary government to implement universal education," he wrote, "became dichotomized between urban and rural, and thus tended to institutionalize traditional caste boundaries."[86] But no one exposed the chasm between official rhetoric and harsh reality more starkly than Carter's North American colleague Lambos Comitas. He assembled a collection of ethnographic snapshots, looking at various indices of progress, including rural schools, in each place he visited.[87] Releasing his composite findings in 1968, Comitas painted an ugly picture: nearly 90 percent of the rural schools he had toured had "no adequate school desks, benches or other furniture; no laboratories; no libraries." Most "núcleo escolar" centers still lacked artisan workshops, cultivable fields, and farm machinery, and rural elementary schools did not go beyond the "basic cycle," forcing those few children who hoped to continue their schooling to travel by foot or bicycle to schools in distant towns.

But perhaps the MNR's gravest institutional error was its decision to "balkanize the educational system, disperse responsibility to multiple sites, and impose different educational standards for [a hierarchy] of different socioeconomic groups." A blatant betrayal of the MNR's egalitarian ethos and integrative revolution, Bolivia's heralded 1955–56 education reform policies represented the rebirth of racial and class inequality, for the urban/rural divide "corresponded intimately with the old social divisions of Bolivian society; and [thus] the rural segment was virtually impeded from participating in the secondary and university levels." The sorry outcome, Comitas argued, was "the institutionalization of the [entrenched] patterns of stratification.... Given the structure of education, there is no opportunity for the peasant, in his physical relocation and cultural transformation, to receive the level of training that would permit him, with some luck, to compete for advantageous positions in society."[88]

Nor was that all. Equally toxic was the state's "pathological obsession" to extirpate "all elements considered dysfunctional in peasant life," but not to replace them with "anything better." Here Comitas was concerned about the perpetuation of rural poverty and isolation, while the state tried to cleanse the Indian of "dysfunctional elements" that might be blocking his passage into the modern campesino class. The stakes in this critique were enormous, for the MNR's campaign of Indian acculturation was tantamount to remaking the national culture through the mystique of mestizo homogeneity. But this anthropologist was more concerned with structural problems of racial discrimination and marginality than with upholding the principle of ethnic diversity and cultural pluralism. All too aware of North America's insidious system of racial apartheid (after all, he arrived in Bolivia about the same time the civil rights movement was exploding in the United States), Comitas laid bare the MNR's racially bifurcated system of public schooling.[89]

Despite the MNR's deeply flawed and discriminatory educational policies, rural schools continued to proliferate during the 1950s and early 1960s. As we have seen, the driving impetus came from below, as rural alphabet schools mushroomed in villages and former haciendas across the Altiplano (a ubiquitous sign that the oligarchic landholding regime was in freefall). In later years, the MNR oversaw (and institutionalized) a growing number of *núcleos educativos*. Perpetuating the earlier bureaucratic policies of the CNE, the MNR state tried to regulate local Indigenous schools, the *escuelas unitarias particulares* that had managed to elude state control (and gamonal violence) in the prerevolutionary era. Certainly, the MAC encouraged the proliferation of núcleo schools, although they had already been multiplying during the 1940s under the authority of the CNE and SCIDE. But scholars today still argue over the scale, intensity, nature, and timing of educational changes in rural Bolivia during and after the MNR revolution.[90] Be that as it may, there is little disagreement that, for a variety of reasons, rates of popular literacy and formal education enjoyed a sustained increase after 1950. Tracing secular trends, Herbert Klein, for example, compares national census records of 1950 and 1985 to reveal a dramatic overall increase in Bolivia's matriculated students (from 25 to 84 percent of the total school-age population between those two census years).⁹¹ Official literacy rates rose too: from 31 percent in 1950 to 67 percent in 1976.⁹² These rough global estimates, extracted from flawed government records, say little about the prevailing geo-racial and class discrepancies that still sentenced Indigenous people, and particularly rural women, to higher rates of illiteracy and threw up barriers to formal education. Arguably, the reinscription of endemic poverty and racial inequity into the body politic was as much a legacy of the MNR national revolution as the dramatic integration of the Bolivia's popular classes into its dominant national culture and language.

In the meantime, the MNR government translated "the education of the Indian" into a fervent rallying cry, aimed at winning hearts and minds at home and attracting foreign aid from abroad. In 1962, on the occasion of the revolution's tenth anniversary, the MNR leadership published a glossy commemorative album that took stock of the regime's monumental achievements. Foremost among them was the revolution's stunning success in "overcoming illiteracy, [the] heavy inheritance of the past." According to government claims, the proof was in the numbers. In 1950, with 726,158 Indigenous adults officially categorized as "illiterate" (and estimated to make up 84.1 percent of the total population), Bolivia could not yet claim to be an integrated modern nation-state (or so the leading nationalists argued). Thus, the national revolution had set out to dismantle the elite's "monopoly" over the cultural assets of knowledge, power, and education. Ten years later, the MNR claimed a resounding victory. It had revamped the national pedagogy, democratized the educational system, and built an infrastructure of rural schools: the number of schoolhouses had been increased by 91 percent (from 2,495 in 1952 to 4,767 in 1962); the number of teachers by 87 percent (9,498 to 17,782); and the number of matriculated students by an eye-popping 135 percent (226,931 to 532,238).⁹³ On the surface: it was a monumental achievement that belied the persistence of structural racism and endemic inequity in the very design of the MNR's educational reform policies.

At the height of the MNR's propaganda campaign, Victor Paz Estenssoro (by then in his second term) was busily courting Washington for massive economic and military to help underwrite the regime's authoritarian model of economic development and political consolidation. As the politics of Bolivia's governing elite pivoted to the right, the regime consolidated its rural education project under the bilateral cosponsorship of the MAC and SCIDE. By the early 1960s, the two agencies had become extricable, and SCIDE's influ-

FIGURE 7.3. The MNR's tenth-anniversary "album of the revolution" unveiled the *nuevo campesino*, embodied agent of agro-industrial modernity. The campesino as the MNR's new *Homo economicus* is captured by the image and accompanying text: "The campesino today: a new attitude toward life." The long caption elaborates: "The agrarian reform has changed life in the countryside.... The peasant no longer goes barefoot; they build houses with windows, raise and administer their own schools, and go to the market where they buy and sell. Now, time is valued by the peasant. The bicycle and truck have replaced the llama and donkey. Men and merchandise are transported more rapidly in the general economy [thanks to] more trucks and better roads. The Indian is the one who most uses bicycles, sewing machines, and radio receptors, a sure sign of his greater capacity as a consumer." Dirección Nacional de Informaciones, *Bolivia: 10 años de revolución*, 71.

ence (even as its funding for Bolivian education declined) was more visible than ever before. Overcoming rural illiteracy and educating the peasantry now centered on the agency's twin rural development goals: "the technification of agriculture" and the resocialization of the *nuevo campesino*.[94] SCIDE's earlier infiltration of Bolivia's núcleo escolares, its rural extension program, and its intensive work in the field of behavioral reform had laid the essential groundwork needed to inflate and normalize its influence within the Bolivian government. Toward the end of the MNR era, Bolivia had mobilized its foot soldiers, trained to carry out this dual agrarian agenda. Armed with textbooks, pamphlets, posters, and radio programs, a bilateral group of trained agronomists, hygienists, and rural teachers would now work with local unions and community leaders to raise up Bolivia's first postrevolutionary generation of loyal, hardworking, market-friendly campesinos (see fig. 7.3). Finally, it would seem, the modern solution to the country's Indian problem was in reach!

Crafting Cultural Hegemony

To advance the MNR's nation-building project, the MNR plowed the symbolic terrain of popular culture while using mass media to construct a unifying national culture out of the fragments of ethnicity and vestiges of the colonial past.[95] Although only a pale reflection of Mexico's state-funded cultural revolution in folklore, archaeology, and mural art (which the MNR regime ardently admired),[96] the Bolivian state began assembling a repertory of cultural, academic, and aesthetic programs to foster the nationalist mystique of bolivianidad. The Ministry of Education and its subsidiary offices encouraged the popularization of history, literature, and mythology, and inserted the "folk" into the core of national revolutionary culture (through folklore, popular civic fiestas, and an iconography of Bolivia's miners, peasants, and revolutionary martyrs). A neo-indigenista movement also flourished for a short time: the inaugural 1952 issue of *Inti Karka*, for example, featured a paean to the literary legacy of Franz Tamayo (Diez de Medina was probably the author of this anonymous essay). On another front, the archaeological site of Tihuanaku was celebrated (once again) as a nationalist icon of Bolivia's native heritage; and an exuberant revolutionary aesthetics (permeating mural art, symbols, and rituals) celebrated the dawn of a new era. *Forjando patria*, Bolivian style, called for the infusion of state funds into the production of a national "cultural pedagogy," as it was designated in the 1955 Education

Code.⁹⁷ Reimagining the civic nation, inventing el pueblo, homogenizing the nation's mestizo identity, and crafting a national pedagogy of popular unity and integration: through this strategy, the MNR made a vigorous effort to fashion a triumphalist nationalist narrative, which proclaimed to the world that the "end to four centuries of slavery" was finally at hand.

The task of crafting a "cultural pedagogy" for revolutionary times largely fell to Fernando Diez de Medina, an eminent intellectual and the CRE president. He called for a renovated national pedagogy (much as his mentor, Franz Tamayo, had done some forty years earlier): "The first imperative of the Bolivian pueblo," he told the Congress in 1953, must be "the formation of the [national] character." Not only formal schooling but also a vibrant "popular culture" must instruct the masses "to improve their moral and cultural [way of] life, perfecting their capacity for work and forming desirable civic and democratic attitudes."⁹⁸ A year later, he translated his lofty rhetoric into a short, practical training manual for educators.⁹⁹ Significantly, Diez de Medina's pamphlet framed the MNR's integrative revolution in racial terms: "In terms of the Indians and mestizos . . . who constitute a considerable majority of our total population, the [Education] Commission has expressed the criterion that all Bolivians should inculcate in themselves the pride of the *indo-mestizo* [people], the value of our long historical tradition, and the singularly rich and original [quality] of our artistic folklore in the present day."¹⁰⁰

Cultural recognition and pride in Bolivia's amalgamated "indo-mestizo" race opened a parallel symbolic pathway to the myth of national unity at the very moment the MNR's left-leaning unions and agrarianists were vigorously trying to expunge explicit race-thinking, including the label *indio*, from the public transcript. Although this hybrid formulation would later be collapsed into the official trope of bio-cultural mestizaje, Diez de Medina's neo-indigenista formulation left open a narrow intercultural space within which Bolivia's Indigenous and mestizo cultures might (theoretically) blend, harmonize, and/or coexist in a pluralist framework.

But CRE's hardline cultural assimilationists paid scant attention to this hybrid neo-indigenista formulation. Vicente Lema (the main architect of rural education reform) was an unrelenting advocate of cultural assimilation, a program to be orchestrated under a strict policy of castellanización. All Indigenous children, he argued, must be subject to language immersion through the "direct method" (of Spanish only), except in those regions where "Spanish has no appreciable function." Only then, he added, might teachers introduce the occasional word or phrase in the child's native language so as to clarify the reading lesson. This draconian policy of language assimilation sparked fiery debate and sharp criticism among a few advocates of bilingual methods of schooling in later years (as we shall see in the epilogue). But among his CRE colleagues, Lema carried the day at the very moment the MNR was overhauling its national educational policy. The Education Code mandated "the immediate apprenticeship of castellano as a necessary factor of national linguistic integration" (although it conceded the tactical value of using "the native vernacular" when teachers faced the utter incomprehension of monolingual native school children).[101]

The vexed "language question" reveals how thoroughly cultural racism still saturated the attitudes and ideas of statesmen and educators in the formative years of revolutionary reform. A good illustration of endemic racism surfaced in the CRE's Literacy and Adult Education subcommittee. One member defined its mission as an attack on the Indian's "ancestral prejudices and superstitions... still the basis of the autochthonous culture, itself a vestige of primitivism, by all lights.... The cultural evolution of the Bolivian aboriginal," he explained, "depends only on the *grade of culture* that is acquired through the medium of [Spanish] literacy, the precise instrument that will expand the intellect of the individual and condition him to adapt to *the evolution of world civilization*; [it is] *a daily process of conquest*."[102] Such race-thinking still framed the neocolonial trope of the civilizing crusader: the teacher as conquistador, waging a "daily process of conquest" in the schoolhouse and the wider rural community. Reduced to a crude slogan, the teacher-cum-conquistador sometimes surfaced in a popular ditty:

> The [Education] Reform must be fulfilled
> And a new pueblo forged
> Once again to conquer the Indian
> By a legion of teachers![103]

The MNR's obsession with language assimilation reveals little about what was happening on the ground, of course. As we have seen throughout this book, Andean peasants' aspirations to wield the letter and the law, and their novel uses of documentary culture, were embedded features of Aymara society and politics throughout the first half of the early twentieth century. In the aftermath of the Chaco War and the debacle of Warisata, the rise of radical agrarian syndicalism had rediscovered the insurgent value of literacy, print culture, and networked communication in the process of building militant, transregional coalitions to confront their neocolonial class oppressors. These everyday forms of subversive literacy practices constituted a crucial cultural resource that Indigenous communities could mobilize in times of political crisis or opportunity as they did (once again) in the immediate aftermath of the April 1952 insurrection. How else to explain the outpouring of hundreds of peasant petitions and lawsuits, the spontaneous wave of peasant land seizures, the clamor for communal land restoration, and the creation of hundreds of local unions and schools during the early years of MNR rule?[104]

As this chapter has chronicled, the historic thaw in Bolivia's political climate after April 1952 precipitated an outpouring of local Indigenous activism around the right to land, unions, and schools. As both the circulating medium of intercultural communication and symbolic capital, the value of popular literacy soared in those pivotal years. To read or write, or to found a village school, no longer carried the risk of landlord violence, and the state's promotion of rural education spurred rural mobilization to tap the populist fervor and promises of the MNR leadership for a "civic movement of national transcendence." Revolutionary effervescence, and the soaring social expectations it kindled, helped catalyze a wave of rural literacy practices, village schooling, and print culture as never before.

Thus, agrarian and education reform had a recursive effect, by inflating the functional and symbolic currency of literacy, on the one hand, and by opening new venues for acquiring the rudiments of written and spoken Spanish, on the other. In short order, the revolutionary era and new opportunities to engage with the state had created an urgent social need for rural peoples to master their letters, and the spread of elementary alphabet schools fed and helped satisfy that need—even in regions where Aymara and Quechua were still the prevailing means of oral and ritual communication. Now, the ubiquitous elementary school, the barracks, and the rapid spread of peasant unions, cooperatives, and confederations actively incentivized peasant men (and some women) to acquire, practice, teach, or share their literacy skills. A "dramatic and continuing increase in bilingualism," notes Herbert Klein, came out of the revolutionary period. Significantly, the spread of Spanish into Aymara- and Quechua-speaking areas did not signal the onset of racial and language assimilation, or castellanización, as many educational reforms had hoped and predicted. Years later, many rural inhabitants and urban migrants (often categorized in everyday parlance as "cholos") were registered as "bilingual" in the censuses of 1976 and 1992 because they still spoke their native languages at home, in the peasant market, and in the campo.[105] Furthermore, unequal access to literacy and print culture created new tensions and inequities within rural society (which often ran along gendered and generational lines). Women and girls enjoyed much less access to formal schooling (although trading activities and domestic servitude demanded rudimentary bilingualism and literacy), while socially mobile young men had more exposure to spoken and written Spanish in schools, sindicatos, barracks, and the cities. Indeed, the ability to transact official community or union business in Spanish became a gendered signifier of status and manhood in many places. Meanwhile, the functional value of literacy was rapidly evolving as peasant/state interaction intensified and rural syndicalism spread. Earlier forms of vernacular literacy (assembling a legal dossier, tracing ancestral lineages, naming caciques, and other exegetical approaches to the archival document) still prevailed, and mass petition and judicial campaigns still flooded the MNR bureaucracy. But they were giving way to a wider range and function of social texts and more functional and critical ways of reading and writing. Dissident print culture, one legacy of militant peasant movements, had turned into an arm of postrevolutionary state propaganda and the state's growing influence in the syndicalist movement.

As we saw earlier, this effervescence of literacy and print culture represented a real and interpretive break with neocolonialism. All during the first half of the twentieth century, oligarchic rule and racial anxiety had underwritten Bolivia's culture of violence—virtually barring rural peoples from claiming basic citizenship rights, contesting the injustices of everyday life, organizing communitarian schools, or mobilizing for collective action and representation. Even members of the "enlightened" oligarchy, from Franz Tamayo to Vicente Donoso, had worried about the political side effects of diffusing literacy to litigating Indians and transgressive cholos. Philosophical essays, pedagogical plans, partisan warnings, and indigenista literature had warned against promoting "merely" alphabet schools, or diffusing literacy among Aymara Indians, lest they turn into political mischief-making cholos (thus corrupting the electoral system and infiltrating the white lettered metropolis), litigious caciques, subversive rural teachers, or peasant dirigentes. Even in the late 1950s, La Paz's indigenista elite, just like their forebears, continued to embrace a practical brand of Indian essentialism, predicated on the idea that special rural schools must breed hard-working farmers, not lettered and litigious Indians moving off the land to make mischief in the cities. On the other hand, the MNR's corporatist project of Indian acculturation compelled the state to enforce the hispanized resocialization of the Indian peasantry, loyal to both party and patria, and motivated to produce food crops for the cities and improve local living standards in the countryside.

Under the revolution, that neocolonial logic of geo-racial exclusion was partially ruptured. Universal rights to suffrage, passed in July 1952, meant that literacy and property barriers were no longer needed to shield the white lettered metropole from the rabble. The revolution had thrown the electoral system open to the nation's Indigenous majority. Consequently, the state's political imperative was not to bar Indigenous people from gaining access to literacy, mobility, or suffrage but to create a state apparatus of civic culture, social institutions, and mass communication capable of disciplining the newly enfranchised rural masses while also winning "hearts and minds" for the MNR's patriotic and partisan causes.

As early as 1952 and 1953, the MNR state sprang into action. It began assembling an apparatus of political propaganda under the new Ministry of Press, Propaganda, and Information. Its outreach office, the Subsecretaría de Prensa, Informaciones y Cultura (SPIC), was charged with mobilizing mass media (print, radio, photography, folklore, didactic literature, civic performance, mural art, etc.) to disseminate the state's official messages, monitor local concerns, stir up nationalist pride, and secure the loyalty of the working class and peasantry.[106] Print and association were now harnessed to state-building under the populist wing of the party, and its official messages were blasted into the precincts of rural life as never before. Radio Illimani, for example, beamed a variety of moral and informational messages, as well as advice, and disseminated practical lessons in health, hygiene, and self-improvement through the now-ubiquitous transistor radio.[107] Meanwhile, didactic forms of print matter circulated through official sindicato channels. Already by 1953, widely circulating union posters propagated the schoolhouse as the beacon of the National Revolution. A SPIC manual pitched to rural teachers instructed them to use graphic print media in classrooms where Spanish was not yet spoken or understood.[108] A few years later, the MAC circulated a morality tale in which a goofy-looking campesino illustrated the slogan "Education, production, and work: the best arms to defend the revolution and your land!" (see figs. 7.4–7.6).[109]

Thus, the MNR's integrative political culture tried (and largely failed) to harness the power of mass literacy, the rural school, and official propaganda to the wave of grassroots civic activism flowing out of the villages, mining

FIGURES 7.4–7.6. This adult reader promotes rural schooling as a cultural arm of the MNR government: specifically, to secure a loyal peasant clientele, promote agricultural development, and defend the party from reactionary threats. Three sample pages illustrate. *Top image/message*: "Education of your children should be your main preoccupation, because they are the future of the Patria and the best defense against your most bitter enemy: THE ROSCA!" *Middle image/message*: "Education, work, and production are the best arms with which to defend your land and to secure a happy future for your home and the Patria." *Lower image/message*: "When your house is built, the land is plowed and bearing fruit, your children are healthy and educated in schools, then you will...feel the pride of being a useful citizen to the Patria and to the M.N.R." Ministerio de Asuntos Campesinos and Dirección Nacional de Informaciones, *Educacion, producción, y trabajo* (n.d.). (I thank Matt Gildner for bringing this source to my attention.)

camps, and working-class barrios during the age of revolution. To judge by what several contemporary observers reported, novel ways of rural reading were taking root in the revolutionary era. Recall Olen Leonard's discovery of community reading and listening circles, in which people gathered to read newspapers or listen to the crackly sounds of the Illimani radio station in order to understand, debate, and act on the government new decrees or bits of national news. Or consider Luís Antezana's indelible image of peasants traveling into the city to conduct their trámites, and then returning homeward, their pack animals loaded with bundles of newspapers, magazines, pamphlets, and books.[110] The empowering symbol of the "lettered Indian" ran deep in everyday cultural practice and memory of the Aymara peasant community. Whereas the caciques had invented the "walking archive" during the heights of the ayllu-repatriation movement in the 1920s, and peasant dirigentes had dabbled in popular political education and participatory citizenship practices in the 1940s, peasant authorities and rural teachers now trafficked in new forms of print matter, land reform documents, newspapers, pamphlets, graphics, and other ephemera of the revolutionary regime. It was commonplace for them to wield pen and paper and then to walk their legal documents between village, courthouse, and government ministry in relative safety. Rural literacy flourished and paperwork circulated for all kinds of strategic purposes—to swear fealty to the MNR; ask for special favors; demand social and/or citizenship rights; register grievances or demand retribution for past crimes; solicit state protection; request permission to found a school or hire a teacher; establish cantonal status; and—more grandiosely—propose the parameters of a reimagined, genuinely multiracial, and inclusive national culture.[111] Oral memory and archival power still mattered, especially among Aymara communities trying to recover their ancestral land rights under the 1954 "restitution clause" of the MNR's agrarian reform.[112] But the signal cultural achievement of Bolivia's larger "civic revolution from below" was the collective right of rural peoples to freely organize schools and, as literate peasants, to write themselves into the national narrative as vital citizen-subjects and, projecting ahead to the late twentieth century, *to rewrite the national narrative itself* from the position of resurgent indigeneity (see the epilogue).

At the end of his long inspection tour of rural Bolivia, the Colombian economist Antonio García marveled that the agrarian reform had assumed "the character of an *irreversible fact*, whatever the [political] outcome of the revolutionary process might be." (Ironically, García's 1964 article appeared in print the same year the MNR was deposed by a military coup.)[113] The same might be said about the MNR's program of education reform, fundamentally flawed as it was. As with agrarian reform (and partly because of it), the redistribution of this cultural asset (and the new laws that legitimated basic education for all children) bestowed a powerful sense of *irreversibility* about schooling—a civil liberty that Bolivia's newly enfranchised rural people had fought long and hard for and would not ever relinquish.

This sea change came about not because the MNR state promoted rural education (since equity was never a government priority, and the yawning gap between official rhetoric and reality opened soon enough). It came about because because the political winds had shifted direction, tearing asunder the decaying edifice of oligarchic neocolonialism, and opening channels for rural communities to bring the practical and symbolic benefits of literacy, schooling, and communication into their isolated social world with little fear of violent reprisal from local bosses. The very existence of that political possibility stemmed, in part, from fifty long years of an unquiet cultural revolution in rural literacy and school activism that had unfolded across the Bolivian Altiplano.

Epilogue

Silences, Remembrances, and Reckonings

On a cold windy night in August 1954, as the *surazo* swept out of the Antarctic South and scoured the arid Altiplano, Antonio Alvarez Mamani, the country's venerable old peasant dirigente, scrambled onto the nightly freight train as it rumbled through the outskirts of Oruro en route to La Paz. Once the nine o'clock police check was over (for he had become, by then, a "troublemaker" to be watched under the government's surveillance regime), the coast was clear enough for Alvarez to make this stealth journey to the capital. His destination was the government palace, where an international conference on the hemisphere's "Indian Question" was being hosted by Bolivia's vice president, Hernán Siles Suazo, and other high MNR officials.

With distinguished delegates streaming into La Paz from all corners of the hemisphere, the Third International Indigenista Congress provided a unique venue for the MNR government to display a progressive "indigenista face" to the wider world. After all, the MNR could rightly claim to represent, after Mexico, the hemisphere's most progressive political regime, to judge by its slate of agrarian, political, and civic reforms. For their part, the conference's foreign delegates were eager to discuss the array of problems that burdened the hemisphere's estimated 30 million native peoples and to learn how Bolivia's revolutionary state was planning to deal with what Siles Suazo publicly referred to as the country's "greatest problem": the Indian.

The MNR engineered the weeklong conference, a spectacular public relations opportunity. There were flowery speeches by Bolivia's highest officials, folkloric pageantry to showcase the country's ethnic diversity, and a thick meeting agenda to occupy the foreign visitors. The city's streets were patrolled to safeguard the dignitaries and prevent unruly street demonstrations. Although hosted by Bolivia, the conference was sponsored by the Mexico-based Institute of Interamerican Indigenistas (III) and presided over by the renowned Mexican anthropologist Mario Gamio (although he did not attend). Like the III's two earlier congresses (held in 1940 in Mexico, and in 1949 in Cuzco), the Bolivia-based meeting was the most important forum for Latin American social scientists, intellectuals, and reformers (authorized by their respective governments or representing NGOs) to speak about, and for, the Indigenous masses. The heirs of the tutelary indigenista elites of the early 1900s, this modern generation wielded the scientific authority as experts in the fields of rural sociology, anthropology, linguistics, and development economics. Others were NGO officials and country experts in humanitarian aid, education, and development programs. Otherwise, not much had changed since Bolivia's first generation of indigenistas had tackled the so-called Indian problem. Their object, the generic Indian, was still the mute object of diagnostic assessment and subject to all kinds of development, disciplinary, and acculturative schemes. Except for the decorous presence of a few Indians chosen and credentialed by the MNR, the public Indian voice was barely audible in this congress. Bolivia's three major language groups—the Aymara, Quechua, and Guaraní—were represented, respectively, by Francisco Chipana Ramos (a loyal MNRista since he had served as state-authorized president of the 1945 National Indian Congress); José Rojas (a veteran campesino leader from Cochabamba); and Santos Arreyo (assigned to stand in for the Guaraní and tribal groups living in Bolivia's eastern lowlands). All were MNRistas: they could be counted on to toe the party line.[1]

This carefully choreographed congress had no room for the likes of Antonio Alvarez Mamani. No longer the heralded peasant leader, he was now under government surveillance—a troubling indicator of how rapidly a peasant leader could fall from grace, now that the Jacobin phase of the 1952 revolution was ceding to the imperatives of state consolidation, US pressures, and problems of "internal security." From an MNRista *campesino dirigente*, featured at the agrarian reform jubilee in August 1953, to political pariah just a year later, Alvarez Mamani was spurned for being too independent, too untrustworthy, to represent Bolivia's campesino masses at the indigenista congress.

The distrust was mutual. Alvarez Mamani's disenchantment with the official leadership of the COB (still cogoverning within the MNR coalition) surfaced in 1953.[2] By the end of that year, he had withdrawn from official party politics and its apparatus of rural sindicalismo. Having retreated to Oruro, he turned to the local work of forming a peasant cooperative in Humahuaracta. But what made him so dangerous to the regime was his call for amnesty for political prisoners. Dozens, perhaps hundreds, of political prisoners, many of them peasants accused of being "communists," still languished in jail or in exile at the same time that the MNR (under Washington's influence) was ramping up its effort to purge leftist influences from the party, as well as from the worker/peasant confederation, the COB.[3] Calling for political amnesty was viewed as an incendiary act in light of the MNR's promise to Washington that it would purge all insurgent or communist elements. Placed on the watch list, Alvarez Mamani was effectively banished from politics and, more immediately, barred from mingling with the gray eminences attending the III's Congreso de Indigenistas. If he were going to crash the congress, it would have to be through subterfuge. Waiting until just before midnight, he slipped past his minders and hopped the train to La Paz. The next morning, he made his way to the Colombian embassy, where the ambassador, an old acquaintance of his father (a distinguished kallawaya healer), agreed to provide the credentials he needed to enter the conference. Once inside, he managed to upgrade his status from persona non grata to that of "independent" peasant delegate. As such, he would infiltrate this congregation of white indigenistas, "none of them ... genuinely Indian."[4]

Thus credentialed as a free agent, Alvarez Mamani attended committee sessions on a variety of burning subjects—human rights, agrarian reform, folklore, language and literacy, and rural education. Education, in particular, was a vital topic of discussion.[5] Moving among those sessions, and sometimes speaking up, Alvarez Mamani gained visibility and accrued respect among the delegates. By the end of the week, he had garnered enough support to win a place on the roster of "distinguished speakers" for the congress's closing session. This leap—from censured figure to persona non grata to plenary speaker—represented an extraordinary (though ephemeral) achievement. The dirigente seized his moment at the podium to broadcast an emancipatory message not just to the delegates but also, *through them*, to Native peoples across the Americas. Although mediated and muffled, his message tried to inspire revolutionary acts of solidarity and self-determination among the hemisphere's Indigenous peoples:

> On this solemn occasion, we cannot silence the voice of the Indian, representing those who have felt the crack of the landlord's whip on their backs and endured the most shameful [system of] exploitation for over 400 years.... Señores delegados, I ask you to carry home to your own countries a salute from the *indio boliviano* who, armed with his gun and plow, stands guard over the revolution... FOR THE UNITY OF THE PEASANTRY OF AMERICA! A CENTRAL INDIGENOUS ORGANIZATION OF AMERICA IS IMPERATIVE FOR THE FUTURE! FOR THE REVOLUTION![6]

No pastoral Indian, he! Alvarez Mamani projected an image of an insurgent sentinel, standing guard with "gun and plow," calling for Indigenous and peasant revolution throughout the continent. But his fiery rhetoric enclosed an eminently practical plan (and, no doubt, a veiled appeal to progressive NGOs): he urged the establishment of an international Indian confederation to promote programs of cultural and educational exchange. It would bring together Indigenous delegates, students, and leaders to represent the hemisphere's diaspora of colonized peoples of Indigenous descent, from the Inuit of the far North to the Mapuche of the far South.[7] An autonomous *unión americana indígena*—a precocious "Fourth World" in the emerging Cold War era—would serve as the hub of this sprawling transnational network. As imagined here, Indigenous peasants, armed with guns and plows, would rise up to demand their "rights to land, life, and liberty," and especially their rights to "the universal vote." His immediate agenda was to decolonize the white indigenista congress. Future congresses should not be forums of white social scientists, policy makers, and NGO funders monopolizing the conversation about the Indian; rather, they should be platforms for the hemisphere's ethnic groups to come together to determine their own destiny. Under the aegis of the American Indian union, "we peasants will be able to mobilize an authentically agrarian *Indian bloc*, operating under the norm of [Indian] nationalism, for the next Congress. There, we will be able to debate conference papers in Aymara and Quechua; and they will be translated and interpreted in other Indigenous languages, thanks to the standardized alphabet that was approved by this Congress."[8]

Of course, the staid Pan-American organ of white indigenistas was not about to allow an "Indian bloc" to superimpose its revolutionary agenda on the technicians' agenda of racial integration and rural development. But Alvarez Mamani's proposal was not so farfetched in the case of revolutionary Bolivia, where the Indigenous majority was suddenly in possession of "vote and voice," thanks to the 1952 decree of universal suffrage. It was only a matter of time, he expected, before Bolivia's Aymara-, Quechua-, and Guaraní-speaking peoples would begin translating their social aspirations into concrete political actions, party platforms, and government policies. How much longer would it take for the Bolivian congress to become a marvelous tower of Babel, where elected delegates proudly delivered speeches and conducted negotiations in their native languages?

But this urgent appeal to the pluriethnic ideal of nationhood and transnational native solidarity came at the very moment that the new MNR governing coalition was building the architecture of Indian acculturation and rural modernization. Already by 1954, the MNR was avidly courting Washington for large amounts of economic aid to propel its plan for agro-capitalist development. And in the field of rural education, government reformers were bedazzled by the prospects of creating modern, tractor-driving campesinos (later crystallized in the *nuevo campesino*) under the aegis of SCIDE and various NGOs promoting assimilation-oriented programs of "rural extension." Clearly, there was little ideological space in the MNR's Occidentalist model of nationalism for a decolonizing agenda driving forward pluralist ideals, much less imagining a democratic polity based on majoritarian Indigenous rule.

The official published transcript of the Inter-American Indigenista Congress made sure of that. Reading the 1954 Indigenista Congress's published report today, one is struck by the text's sly semantics of racial silencing. In both tone and content, Alvarez Mamani's liberatory message of indigeneity was diminished and distorted in the conference's final resolutions. In a striking inversion of meaning, article XX issued a call for more contacts, bridges, and networks—in particular, "cultural contacts between Indians and non-Indians in order *to extend the acculturation process* and incorporate the Indian masses into the cultural and economic life of the modern world."[9] This resolution was attributed to Alvarez Mamani, whose imprimatur presumably gave it legitimacy as an "authentic" Indian proposal. In the margins, Siles Suazo made "special mention of the fact that this resolution was originally presented by the Bolivian Indian leader, Antonio Mamani Alvarez."[10]

Thus, Alvarez Mamani's articulated vision for a continent-wide Indigenous rights movement—one that blended agrarian, civic, and ethno-political rights—was buried and forgotten in a patronizing footnote amid the congress's long list of final resolutions. What was lost in translation, as it were, was the dissenting view of a leading Aymara peasant intellectual and a veteran of the peasant wars of the 1940s. His speech represented a virtual call to arms across the Americas. A breach of protocol, Alvarez Mamani's performance had reframed the racist trope of the putative Indian problem, turning it into a burning civil rights issue about ethnic autonomy and self-determination. Arguably, his vision anticipated an Indian rights movement that would flower in Bolivia and across parts of Latin America in the last three decades of the twentieth century.

Hegemonic processes of negotiation and coercion have insidious means and methods of silencing subaltern nativist voices, as historians and anthropologists have long argued. Historically, Western civilizing projects of whatever stripe have aspired to a telos of racial progress and assimilation (or, more modestly, to selective modes of acculturation) as engineered through state institutions (schools, clinics, barracks, etc.), the workings of capitalist labor discipline, and self-regulatory citizenship regimes. Political, philosophical, and scientific discourses that propound the innate or demonstrative racial superiority of Anglo-Europeans (or criollo people of Spanish descent) actively "unimagine" the inherent rights of nonwhite (colonized) peoples struggling for social equality, citizenship, and self-determination. While the MNR had tried to repudiate public discourses of racial inequality and expunge race-thinking from the public transcript, it had inherited a racist-neocolonialist ontology that would prove difficult to shed. As we saw in chapter 7, its 1955 Education Reform program was structured on the premise that the Indian race (a product of the feudal order being dissolved) was unfit for Bolivia's modernizing economy and polity without a full sociocultural makeover in modern rural schools (and other institutions).

Furthermore, the MNR had an immediate tactical motive for pushing forward the goal of Indian assimilation at the Indigenista Congress. In 1954, Vice President Siles Suazo was eager to demonstrate before the US and other delegates that the new revolutionary state had an iron grip on Bolivia's famously restive peasantry and was in the process of engineering a solution to the country's "Indian problem" through a peaceful transition to agrarian capitalism (while also staving off the threat of communism in the countryside and mining camps). Siles used his platform to cast the agrarian reform as the result of an orderly government program pushing the feudal countryside into the modern market economy.

> Feudalism has been liquidated!
>
> The granting of land to the farmers, including the large Indian population, becomes an element of stability in the political field.... Up to the present, the liquidation of feudalism has been conducted like a short but effective trial. We believe this experience has hemispheric importance because of the contrast of methods it offers with other countries. In Bolivia, it has been carried out in all places legally and peacefully by the Central Government. Compared with the bloody struggle to give the worker land in Mexico or to give the slaves in North America [their] freedom, we must respect the steps taken by Bolivia, which have led to equally positive results without tragedy or anarchy.[11]

In this technocratic fantasy, Indians were being transformed into "farmers" under the benign tutelage of the MNR, thus demonstrating that "the liquidation of feudalism" could be effected by enlightened state policy without unleashing a Mexican-style revolution or a protracted civil (race) war. A magnificent case of nationalist propaganda designed to placate Washington, Siles's address spoke for the muted Indian, silencing subaltern voices of dissent and dismissing the spirit of Indigenous self-determination. In microcosm, Alvarez Mamani's experience at the Indigenista Congress is an example of the subtle power of semantics silencing dissent in a very public setting. It reveals how the MNR's public transcript reduced the peasant leader's spontaneous revolutionary message to a footnote (quite literally) and twisted its fiery exhortation into an apparent endorsement of the MNR's official indigenista position on Indian acculturation, both at home and across the Western Hemisphere.

The mobilization of a collective Indigenous voice to challenge the assimilationist state and rewrite the national narrative—that is, the emergence of a cultural politics of dissident indigeneity—would have to wait until a new generation of Aymara activists and intellectuals breached the wall of silence as they came of political age during the late 1960s and 1970s.

The Self-Education of Aymara Rebel Youth

Perhaps more than any other postrevolutionary institution, the rural school emerged as a multivalent symbol for the "children of the 1952 revolution." While the arrival of a rural schoolteacher, or the construction of a schoolhouse, represented a hard-fought achievement to the older generation, the men and women who bore the scars of neocolonial violence, the *lived experiences and painful memories* of formal schooling could be a traumatic experience for many Aymara- and Quechua-speaking children in the postrevolutionary era. Years later, Luciano Tapia recounted his school experience as a pressure cooker of "acculturation" that caused him years of psychological problems.[12] The rigid language barrier and the pervasive effects of everyday racism in the classroom made the school experience particularly challenging for the rural monolingual child.

Two sides of the postrevolutionary coin: the cruel "tyranny of the classroom" could also, at times, serve as an intercultural springboard for striving Indigenous students and their families.[13] Indeed, the 1952 revolution, and its agrarian impact, unleashed a wave of rural migration from the hinterland into the city of La Paz. Driven in part by the quest for education, rural youth headed for the city to attend trade schools, high schools (*colegios*), and even, for a fortunate few, the public university. La Paz's Universidad Mayor de San Andrés (UMSA) saw a trickle of Aymara students begin to occupy and integrate this Hispanic bastion of lettered elites. If the blended cities of La Paz / El Alto had long been an urban refuge of Aymara people fleeing rural poverty and oppression or seeking political and legal justice, by the 1960s it was becoming a haven for upwardly mobile Aymara youth—men and (many fewer) women who wanted a chance to advance their formal schooling, escape rural poverty, and expand their radius of economic opportunity, union activity, and political solidarity work.

Once the white lettered metropole, La Paz thus rapidly became the site of a sprawling literary underground of Aymara writers, teachers, students, and intellectuals, many of them involved in crafting new forms of collective identity, insurgent forms of anticolonial thinking, and sociocultural activity. Capturing their rebel spirit, Silvia Rivera describes how this new generation of Kataristas saw themselves as "'foreigners in their own land,' despite their [formal] inclusion in the citizenry."[14] It was the lived reality of racist oppression that put the lie to the egalitarian promises of revolutionary nationalism and ignited the flames of ethnic revindication and Indian-peasant solidarity among this vanguard youth movement. The cultural politics of indigeneity permeated sectors of La Paz's urban popular and bohemian student cultures, lending an Indigenous tonality and solidarity to the performance of local music, dance, and street festivals in the city's working-class barrios. Bolivia's explosive mining towns and university culture, in turn, helped turn the martyred Ernesto (Ché) Guevara (murdered in 1967 by military men and their US advisers) into the apotheosis of Latin America's continental youth movement. As they acclimated to urban life, many Aymara activists sought a decolonizing knowledge and praxis based on the cultural revitalization of indigeneity, popular education, and social activism.[15]

Tangible signs of Indigenous resurgence cropped up across La Paz during the late 1960s and early 1970s. The Centro Campesino Túpac Katari (CCTK), for example, became a vital hub of campesino activity, support, and popular education surviving in the shadows of Col. Hugo Banzer's military regime (1971–78). Operating under the protective cover of several progressive church groups and NGOs, the CCTK managed to disseminate bilingual textbooks, broadcast radio programs, establish a night school, and create an informal marketing guild for peasant women—all of which opened new channels for political networking, education, and association.[16] When local elections came around, its nocturnal radio programs would urge rural listeners to vote for slates of candidates running on platforms of economic justice, democratization, and cultural rights.[17] The Centro Campesino's urban counterpart, the collective MINK'A, was another Aymara hub of decolonized thinking and action. It became known for its stream of polemical essays on the structural and historical nature of racial and class oppression in Bolivia and beyond.[18] On occasion, MINK'A activists linked their local struggles to the work of progressive NGOs, liberation theology activists, and other international organizations variously involved in legal and institutional battles for Indian rights (broadly defined)—a growing transnational movement that the peasant leader Antonio Alvarez Mamani could only imagine in 1954, the year he crashed the white man's Indigenista Congress in La Paz.

Amid this urban Aymara effervescence, the politics of formal education loomed large in the purview of many student activists. A small cohort of Aymara youth, most of them from the provinces of Aroma and Omasuyos, was determined to crash the city's gates of higher education. Much as the racial politics of school (de)segregation in the US South was becoming a battleground in the 1950s and early 1960s, so now Bolivia's segregated rural/urban school system was being breached by Bolivia's first postrevolutionary generation of Aymara students.[19] In Bolivia's volatile political climate, the Universidad Mayor de San Andrés was turning into an armed camp of military soldiers carrying machine guns and tear gas canisters.

Amid the political and militarized violence that engulfed Bolivian civil society during Bolivia's long era of modern military rule (1964–82), this generation of katarista intellectuals, teachers, and activists began to confront Bolivia's history of institutional racism, neglect, and inequality that had plagued the country's public school system for almost a century. Not surprisingly, a prime target of katarista critics was the MNR's 1955 Education Code, which had shaped the school experience of Aymara youth, particularly the children of peasants. In 1973, the "Tiwanaku" cadre of Aymara activists developed the most pointed critique of the MNR's rural school policies.[20] At the outset, their *Manifiesto de Tiahuanacu* (its spelling often varied) offered this observation: "We see two extremely grave problems in rural education: the first concerns [educational] programs; the second relates to the grave deficiencies of resources." The authors' concise critique exposed the systemic problems of institutional racism and social inequity that still structured Bolivia's public education system: "It is no secret that Bolivia's rural school system does not impart our cultural values ... [but tries] to convert the Indian into a kind of mestizo without definition or personality, ... and [who is] assimilated into the culture of Western capitalism."[21] On an operational level, they argued, Bolivia's rural school system was "a NATIONAL CATASTROPHE" of the state's making. Institutional racism, they argued, had deprived the countryside of its fair share of elementary and secondary schools, abandoning 51 percent of rural children who did not yet have access to local schooling. By that measure alone, they said, "the revolution in the countryside has not taken place; and it is time to make it!"[22]

More fundamentally, MINK'A intellectuals condemned the *ethnocidal implications* of Bolivia's history of educational policy. In an ironic twist, though, the MINK'A critique of educational policy also underscored its historic failure to conquer, cleanse, marginalize, or assimilate the country's native Andean peasantry into a homogenizing Western culture of modernity and whiteness. Aymara historical revisionism challenged Occidentalist teleologies by invoking the countervailing forces of colonial oppression and resistance (captured by Rivera's famous phrase "oprimidos pero no vencidos") that had shaped Andean social formations over the four centuries. This revisionist narrative had implications for Bolivia's racist system of schooling: "If education is the formation of the human character, and if it functions in the service of society," the MINK'A authors argued, "then it follows that for the *pueblo indio*, the prevailing educational system in these [Andean] countries, with its Anglo-American origins, signifies a brain washing [*un lavaje cerebral*], a domestication, and [thus] abject servility to European culture."[23] In lyrical Orientalist language, the authors invoked the telluric power of Nature, History, and Indigeneity as millennial forces that had defied five hundred years of ethnocidal forms of Western imperialism: "Thanks to traditions, authentically lived and passed down from generation to generation; thanks to the language of petroglyph monuments; thanks to the mute testimony of our snowcapped mountain peaks; and [to our resistance] against all ethnocidal superimpositions, 'we proclaim the survival of our languages and cultures beyond the empire of death.'"[24] Taken together, MINK'A and Tiwanaku authors elaborated scripts that raised anticolonialist questions about the complex matrix of race, nation, and Indigenous education that would wrack Bolivian society and cultural politics during the final years of the twentieth century.

More broadly, the kataristas' piercing critique of Bolivia's history of institutional racism and discrimination reverberated among Indigenous school activists across the Americas. By the 1970s and 1980s, the physical and cultural violence imposed by Indian boarding school culture in Canada, Australia, and the United States (both in the present and the past) was becoming a flash point of moral debate within the hemisphere's emerging Indian rights movement. Transnational solidarity networks flourished, bringing Indigenous actors, activists in liberation theology, and literacy workers into close collaboration with progressive NGOs, many of them based in western Europe.[25] Closer to home, Bolivia's political climate under eighteen years of US-supported military dictatorship (1964–82) turned grassroots activism into dangerous enterprises, often creating life-and-death dilemmas for Bolivia's militant miners, certain sectors of the peasantry, university students, teachers unions, and leftist party leaders. A new cycle of political contention unfolded across the Altiplano as young katarista organizers (the new "apostles" of Indian liberation) visited rural communities and towns throughout this radically transformed, post–agrarian reform landscape. The most difficult work of political organizing and popular education was performed under the military's radar during the 1970s and the beginning of the 1980s. The genius of the kataristas' underground operation lay in its improvisational and diffuse character: they carried on "the work of the ant in resistance" (in the apt phrase of Javier Hurtado).[26] The work of the ant in resistance was often hidden in plain sight. Remembering back to those painful years, Jesuit scholar and activist Xavier Albó recalled how the kataristas mixed and adapted their communicative and educational strategies in the shadow of state terror. Katarismo's radical pedagogies, he noted, were practiced "on the quiet, [spreading ideas] from community to community, through almost the entire Aymara Altiplano."[27]

Warisata Rediscovered

On another front, Bolivia's popular resistance movement opened the possibility for a new generation to rediscover the origins and legacy of Warisata. Public interest in the original escuela-ayllu resurfaced in the 1970 pedagogic conference of public school teachers (convened during the final days of the leftist/populist regime of General Juan José Torres [1970–71]). Desperate for alternative schools and progressive pedagogies that might displace the deadly "academicism" that prevailed in most Bolivian public schools, progressive teachers lit upon a published study of Warisata that was circulating among the delegates. There was much curiosity about Elizardo Pérez's model "active" curriculum, which had sent its pupils from classroom to workshop to planting fields in order to afford them a balanced "integral" education. Here was, the teachers hoped, a clear pathway out of the quagmire of the MNR's failed education reform policies.[28] But in August 1971, as General Hugo Banzer swept into power, the political winds suddenly shifted against progressive educators. Civil society crumbled, dissidents went underground, and the new right-wing dictatorship descended like a dark fog on Bolivian society. There would be no national public gatherings of schoolteachers for another eight years.

But political censorship and repression failed to obliterate the early history of Warisata or to silence its original champions. Years later, as Pérez lay dying in his home in Buenos Aires, the 1979 Teacher's Congress used this historic occasion to pay homage to his novel contributions and personal sacrifices in the field of Indian schooling. One delegate was Carlos Salazar, the veteran Warisata teacher, writer, journalist, and artist. Elected as the president of the Congress's Evaluative Committee for the Department of La Paz, he inspired this new generation of rural activist-teachers, students, and intellectuals to take up the cause of Indigenous education as Bolivian social movements struggled to restore democratic rule.[29]

As it turned out, Warisata—with its contested meaning and memory—erupted in public debate once again. In August 1978, the polemic exploded on the pages of *Presencia*. This time Warisata's critics were not the usual right-wing suspects; rather, they were leftist educators, and their withering critique was argued along the axes of Marxian ideology and pedagogy.[30] Their polemical pamphlet *The Reason behind a Failure* (*El por qué de un fracaso*) scolded Warisata's founders for their naive belief in the power of a "philanthropic school" to raise up the Indian, especially given that the escuela-ayllu was located in hostile territory of feudal-like haciendas and gamonal violence. The second reason for failure, they argued, was the school's relationship to the "anachronistic" ayllu that was "in the process of extinction." But the study's coup de grâce was its critique of Warisata's "communitarian anarcho-pedagogy"—an ad hoc, unscientific, anything-goes approach to teaching (if it could be so dignified). Here, then, was a tragic episode of messianism, paternal love, and iron tenacity—all sacrificed on the altar of misguided do-gooding in a feudalist society, where the forces of latifundismo and gamonal violence were already arrayed against Indian schooling.

Erasure, distortion, critique: this partisan attack on Warisata from a progressive Jesuit NGO sprang from the false premise that Indian education reform was a philanthropic white man's project that was doomed from the start, given Bolivia's underlying feudal order. A half century of Indigenous agency—its hard-fought battles, bitter setbacks, and moments of vindication—were obliterated by the Marxian premise that Indian peasants could not possibly be agents of progressive change in a fundamentally backward rural society. To be sure, this familiar Marxist critique (echoing the Peruvian intellectual Mariátegui) contained certain inevitable truths about the oppressive powers of neocolonialism. As we saw in chapters 3 and 4, Warisata's decade-long history of achievement in the 1930s had unleashed a powerful reactionary wave of landlord violence, petty partisan rivalry, and organized state repression in the early 1940s, making the original ayllu-school virtually unsustainable under the Conservative oligarchy. Yet as this book has shown, this overly determined narrative of institutional failure (which prevails in some circles to this day) does discursive violence to Warisata's deep connections to the earlier cacique movement; its intercultural origins and collaborations; and the ayllu school's novel structures of Indigenous self-governance and emancipatory forms of collective self-empowerment. Its formative decade of interethnic innovation and struggle was reduced, almost obliterated, behind (what these authors saw as) the tragic folly of Elizardo Pérez's hubris and naïveté. Aymara people were largely written out of this narrative critique, as if their participation had been induced, or marginal, to this interethnic community enterprise. A glaring omission, it reminds us how often official history and memory, including Marxian critique, disappear Indigenous subjects from master narratives as agents of social transformation or as the progenitors of their own emancipatory projects.[31]

Today one is tempted to mock this hackneyed study, but such a dismissal would profoundly underestimate the firestorm it sparked in 1978 and 1979, and the pseudoscientific authority it bestowed on Warisata's fierce critics on both the right and left sides of the ideological spectrum.[32] Moreover, this devastating critique had the longer-term effect of catalyzing another cycle of national debate about the ayllu-school. A new generation of rural teachers and educators struggled over the moral politics of memory in their ongoing search for ways to confront the enduring problems of structural racism and inequality that plagued Bolivia's educational system.

Yet the quandary remained: How to sort out the contending paradigms and contested symbols inscribed within the ayllu-school? To reprise the question posed in chapter 4, who owned the meaning and legacy of Warisata anyway? That is, who might rightfully claim the authority to craft the narrative, interpret its legacy, and reflect on the wider meanings of Warisata in a moment of resurgent indigeneity, rising popular expectations, and continuing military repression during the 1970s and 1980s? Who would emerge as the legitimate interlocutors, shaping the public memory of Warisata and its deeper implications for reconstructing Indigenous forms of knowledge, pedagogy, autonomy, and citizenship in a more just and inclusionary nation?

There were, as always, many old champions (and the usual critics) of Warisata, all of whom participated in this chorus of debate. But no one individual took up the cause of Warisata's rehabilitation in the public memory with more passion and tenacity than Carlos Salazar did. Allying himself with Bolivia's beleaguered rural teachers, and positioning himself as Warisata's veteran indigenista teacher, Salazar took up the weapons of pen and ink, painting and speech, print and association, to interpret the communitarian school's originality to a new generation of teachers, activists, and students. Combining emotion and analysis, narrative and polemic, Salazar produced two powerful and complementary essays in the pages of *Presencia* in 1978 that tried to recast the terms of the national debate.[33]

Thus, just as Bolivia was plunged into civic struggle to restore the semblance of democratic rule, Salazar took up the cause of restoring the honored memory and history of Warisata as a symbol of Indigenous emancipation through radical educational activism. In defiance of Warisata's parade of enemies, charlatans, and critics, Salazar's mission was not to put Pérez on a national pedestal but to highlight Warisata's achievements as one of Latin America's most novel experiments in Indigenous education.

In spite of Warisata's symbolic return (confirmed by the new edition of Salazar's *Warisata mía* in 1983), it remained a highly contested symbol—even among its champions. At home and abroad, the ayllu-school has often been viewed as a unique intercultural endeavor, founded on Aymara forms of community, self-governance, and reciprocity. Both Pérez and Salazar placed great emphasis on the principle of "Indian self-determination," giving due respect to the role that the parlamento de amautas played in cogoverning the school during the difficult 1930s. By the 1980s, however, many young Aymara students and teachers had a disquieting sense that the more nationalist homage was paid to Elizardo Pérez's obra, the more Warisata's Aymara protagonists and their sacrifices slipped from public view.

That situation began to change in 1986, when the daughter of Avelino Siñani, a strong Aymara activist in her own right, entered the fray. Along with Carlos Salazar, Tomasa Siñani de Willka reaffirmed the foundational role that Aymara peasants had played in the original struggle to build an Indigenous school in the middle of "gamonal country." Siñani, a graduate of Warisata's original normal school, groomed herself to become a feminist activist and popular educator, and later a proselytizer of Warisata's early history and long memory. Eventually, she published her testimony so that "the new generations would gain knowledge about the promoters and defenders of our own people, who supported [the cause], adding a grain of sand in the history of education in Latin America."[34] More than that, she wanted to rescue her father's honor and enshrine his memory alongside that of Elizardo Pérez.[35] She stepped forward, in other words, to project an autonomous Aymara voice and to tell "the Aymara side of the story." Her intent, it seems, was to gently dethrone the indigenista master narrative by foregrounding the formative role and terrible sacrifices that her father (and the other amautas) had brought to the school enterprise both before and after Pérez appeared on the scene. It was Avelino Siñani—a humble, uncredentialed teacher of literacy, not the great white educator Pérez—who deserved most credit for having cofounded Warisata, she averred. Her testimonio helped create a subject position of social and moral equivalency for her father in Bolivia's pantheon of national heroes. Just as Carlos Salazar chronicled the wounds they had collectively suffered at the hands of the gamonal state, Tomasa narrated the "agony" of her father's death, turning it into an allegory of martyrdom for the cause of Indian liberation.

Tomasa Siñani's life mission was to re-create the epic story of Warisata and honor the sacrifices that her father and uncle had made in the struggle for the right to Indigenous schools and justice. But in our extended conversations, it became clear that her subtext was to write herself—and by extension, the women of the community—into this revisionist, Aymara-centric narrative. Not only had she lived through the formative years of Warisata and endured the racist humiliations and threats that her family had suffered at the hands of Achacachi's landlords and political authorities; she was also a proud alumna of Warisata's "escuela única." Growing up amid the school's early trials, Tomasa graduated from Warisata's normal school just before the state launched its assault in 1940. She went on to become a lifelong teacher, community organizer, and feminist activist in the fight against the burdens of racism, poverty, illiteracy, and patriarchy that weighed on the backs of rural Indigenous women.[36]

During the bleakest years of dictatorship and repression, Warisata constituted a vehicle for dialogic struggle and political dissent among disparate groups of rebels. For katarista activists, the history of Warisata belonged to a much longer horizon of struggle against the violence of neocolonialism, land annexation, and the ethnocidal impulses of the civilizing state. For Bolivia's post–Chaco War generation of radical teachers and intellectuals, Warisata represented a utopian project of emancipation that sprang from the deep well of Aymara forms of self-governance, communal labor, and the work and sacrifice of progressive teachers. Writing against Warisata's warped denigration as a "lost cause," or worse, as merely a "vanity project" of a few self-important indigenistas, Carlos Salazar opened a new dialogue on Warisata's memory and legacy at the 1979 teacher's conference. As we saw, his Warisata became a vehicle of revindication in the ongoing battle "to ratify greatness in one of the [nation's] most disturbing episodes of struggle... among its protagonists—not technicians but artisans, not specialists but revolutionaries, not professionals but critics."[37] For him, the seeds of revolution had germinated in Warisata's fields, workshops, and classrooms, long before it was consummated by the MNR's grand programs of agrarian and education reform. In the 1980s and 1990s, Tomasa Siñani entered into this public dialogue by reworking the meaning and legacy of Warisata into a gendered instrument of Indigenous women's liberation. Once again, Warisata's contested history and disputed memory opened spaces for critical dialogues on race, schooling, and citizenship within the public sphere, once Bolivia's electoral democracy and civil society were reassembled in the aftermath of dictatorship.

On Indigenous Education: Toward Decolonization?

All this cultural ferment and political disquiet, particularly in the field of rural schooling, eventually unleashed a wave of critical pedagogy and decolonial historiography in Bolivia, beginning in the 1980s. The turn from Aymara history to historiography, and from an earthbound Indigenous movement to a new intellectual school of Aymara historicism, was registered in manifold ways. The Tiwanaku Manifesto produced a through line running from the violence of the Incas' defeat in the Spanish Conquest to the epic 1781 uprising of Túpac Katari; and from there to the 1899 revolt of Zárate Willka and the rise of the cacique-apoderado movement in the early 1900s; and finally to the contemporary Aymara youth movement.[38] This long-term history of oppression and resistance, survival and vindication, formed the driving narrative shaping contemporary identity politics and moral memory among radical Aymara youth. Meanwhile, the prodigious intellectual output of MINK'A indianistas challenged the authority, and reversed the direction, of the Western civilizing paradigm and its transmutation into tutelary race-thinking and practices of castellanización in Bolivia.[39] Writing against the coloniality of Occidentalism, the Aymara interpretive rediscovery of Warisata's original significance marked another epistemic turning point in the decolonization of Bolivia's history/historiography of education.

This revisionist turn in the scholarly field of education was perhaps best embodied in the lived experiences and lifework of the late Roberto Choque Canqui (1942–2020), a prolific research historian and archivist who first plowed the furrows of an Indian-centered history of education in Bolivia.[40] Born in the provincial town of Caquiaviri (province of Pacajes), Choque represented the quintessential "child of '52." He came of age in the swirl of revolutionary reform, when colonos were released from servitude and granted the civil liberty to send their school-age children to the local elementary school. Anxious to break free of his father's restricted rural world, Choque apprenticed with a local woman, who taught him his "first letters" in her home. Eventually he got his father's blessings to strike out for La Paz, where he mastered the craft of shoemaking under his uncle's guidance. But the benchwork of a cobbler was just a way station en route to formal education. Choque eventually enrolled in La Paz's sprawling Universidad Mayor de San Andrés. Long shunned for his Indigenous roots and rustic Spanish (for he now had to read and write in academic Spanish at the university level), Choque went on to study history and in time became Bolivia's first professionally trained Aymara historian and archivist. But for years he labored in relative isolation, at best serving as the "token" Indigenous historian on the occasional scholarly panel, where (it appeared to me at the time) his presence was only politely tolerated by some criollo academics. By the mid-1980s, however, Choque had gained a reputation for challenging prevailing nationalist narratives. Seared by the living memory of his father's life of poverty and oppression during "the time of *colonaje*," he plumbed archival repositories and gathered oral testimonies to lay bare the structural violence of internal colonialism.[41] Meanwhile, Choque and other Bolivian historians gathered documents from prefectural archives in the outlying provinces, including from the District Supreme Court. Over time, they turned the Archivo de La Paz (ALP) into a magnificent vault of provincial and national records, including Indigenous lawsuits, petitions, title deeds, and myriad other documents—all inscribed with the muffled and mediated voices of Aymara protagonists seeking their rights to lands, schools, justice, protection, or relief. In a metaphorical sense, Bolivia's ALP became the ultimate caciques' archive (see chapter 2).[42]

There was, and still is, a strong moral and political compass orienting Aymara historiography, methodology, and the politics of knowledge.[43] The early 1980s saw the formation of a collective project of Aymara university students and graduates, the Taller de Historia Oral Andina (THOA). In 1983, a group of first-generation university students, working with sociologist Silvia Rivera Cusicanqui, created THOA's archive of photocopied archival and printed documents and generated a library of oral testimonies. Here, then, was another astonishing archival creation, much like the caciques' walking archives of the 1910s and 1920s. While the caciques had once used archival power to defend their right to ayllu land and the logic of restorative justice, so now did THOA historians and social scientists generate a treasury of oral memory and documentary gems to advance their own epistemic projects to rethink, rewrite, and reteach the history of Indigenous peoples, all set within a moral framework of ethnic revindication and anticolonial critique.[44] At the outset, THOA's intellectual agenda was "to reconstitute the autonomous meaning of the comunario struggle [*la lucha comunaria*] in all its complexity and reality."[45] Mining government archives for the ancient artifacts of lettered Indians, this foundational school of Aymara historiography developed a documentary bank and decolonizing epistemology from below.[46] Their revisionist work inevitably raised critical questions about educational reform under Bolivia's recently restored democracy: What was the best way to define the instrumentalities of public and popular education in the context of ethnic diversity, social inequality, and racial stratification? How might a revitalized democratic state (or progressive NGOs) exploit the transformative potential of Freire's pedagogy of critical consciousness and revolutionary praxis? How might Bolivia finally redeem the MNR's revolutionary promise to launch an adult literacy campaign, much as Cuba had done in its massive literacy crusade in the early 1960s? Indeed, the continent's escalating Indian rights programs and their progressive NGO donors were raising similar pedagogical questions across much of late twentieth-century Latin America.[47]

As this book has mapped across the twentieth century, Bolivia's contentious journey toward a decolonized political culture of diversity (and the redefinition of the national community as "pluriethnic," "multilingual," and today "plurinational") surged out of the paradoxes of the 1952 revolution, then escalated during the Aymara-led katarista/indianista movements of the 1970s, and finally broke into the political sphere during Bolivia's transition to civilian rule after 1982. But that political transition was fraught with contradictions and setbacks. Eighteen long years of military dictatorship had destroyed the MNR's civic spirit of universal education, reversed its steady institutional gains (a fourfold increase in student matriculation, for example), and dismantled its powerful teachers union (driving many urban teachers into exile or underground). When electoral democracy finally returned in the early 1980s, propelling the old MNR leaders (Siles Suazo and Paz Estenssoro) back into state power, the country faced a new debilitating crisis. This time, its market economy was in free fall: hyperinflation, the crash of the tin market, spiraling external debt, endemic corruption, and chronic social unrest destabilized the fragile neoliberal political order and plunged the rural population (in particular) back into deep poverty during a period of severe drought. Bolivia's international donors, in turn, imposed severe austerity measures, which resulted in soaring rates of economic destitution and labor migration, the explosion of the informal sector, the rise of child labor, and plunging rates of school matriculation. Moreover, Bolivia's economic crisis, and its clientelist dependence on foreign aid, provided the context within which the neoliberal regime privatized the tin mines, imposed fiscal austerity measures, and dismantled other social policies introduced many years earlier by the original MNR revolutionary regime. Public schooling and the state's adult literacy campaign became the prime targets of massive government cutbacks.

A "lost decade" due to Bolivia's foreign debt and economic austerity, the 1980s also became a lost decade of educational reform.[48]

But the confluence of NGO pressures, the continental Indian rights movement, and the ethnic resurgence of Aymara, Quechua, and Guaraní peoples across Bolivia propelled the politics of Indigenous education back into the political limelight. By the late 1980s, bilingual nativism had seeped into educational politics and practices of lowland Guaraní peoples, prominent activists in the campaign to introduce Indigenous languages, alongside Spanish, in public elementary schools. Radical Aymara activists went further, arguing for the decolonization of the public school curriculum. In 1991, Bolivia's sprawling confederation of rural laborers (the Confederación Sindical Única de Trabajadores Bolivianos, or CSUTCB) crafted an anticolonialist/antiracist platform of educational reform that would displace Bolivia's neo-civilizing goal of Indian assimilationism with the politics of *interculturalidad*.[49] The confederation sought "to leave a legacy to our sons and daughters: an education born of our cultures, languages, and history . . . [so that they would] not suffer as we have."[50]

Then came a long-sought political breakthrough. Spurred by pressures from Indigenous intellectuals and activists, including his own Aymara vice president, Victor Hugo Cárdenas, as well as incentives from the World Bank and various NGOs, in 1994 President Gonzalo Sánchez de Losada (Goni) presided over the founding of a pluralist, bilingual mode of national pedagogy called Educación Intercultural Bilingüe (EIB). For the first time in Bolivia's history, the state linked the liberal-nationalist ideals of universal education and citizenship to new bilingual intercultural ideals and curricula in public schools, particularly in rural elementary schools located in Indigenous regions. Not all students, teachers, parents, or communities embraced the bilingual program. Teachers unions balked at the extra, unpaid effort the new curriculum would demand of them; many rural padres de familia worried that teaching children to speak and read in Spanish would be sacrificed on the altar of neo-indigenismo. Still other rural teachers and administrators resented the managerial intrusion of state authorities in their classrooms. On the ground, the EIB was a neoliberal instrument of nation-building involving a multiplicity of contentious stakeholders in a highly stratified society. In the larger scheme of things, however, this "multicultural" paradigm of education reform was the product of fifty years of struggle and represented a partial break with Bolivia's entrenched nationalist project of Indigenous assimilation.

There was, as yet, no way of knowing how transformative the EIB project might turn out to be, but there was good reason for optimism. By the early 1990s, the transnational tide of ethno-education and native-language rights was rising across the Americas. In 1994, the Mexican region of Chiapas exploded in rebellion, triggered by Indigenous resistance to the North American Free Trade Agreement (NAFTA)—the symbol and arm of rampant neoliberalism and globalization. Out of that uprising was born neo-Zapatismo and a spate of grassroots experiments in liberatory forms of self-governance and popular education (some of which survive to this day). Since then, other experiments in popular education have flowered in the fertile soil of Indigenous and peasant movements, including in southern Colombia and rural Brazil.[51]

Once again, the Bolivian state was trying to catch up to events on the ground. Popular disenchantment with neoliberalism deepened, and the reaction to Goni's belt-tightening economic policies and faux populism turned ugly in the early 2000s. Popular mobilizations escalated across Bolivia, Guaraní protesters launched a hunger strike, and Aymara people mounted roadblocks outside the city of La Paz. In September 2003, military violence erupted in the interior patio of Warisata—sacred ground in the collective memory of progressive teachers, students, and Indigenous communities across the highlands. Gunshots ricocheted off the school's walls, killing two soldiers, a teacher, a student, and three other civilians. This shocking turn of events transformed Warisata, yet again, into a bloodstained battleground. Played out on that historic stage, the state's assault on the Warisata community was emblematic of Bolivia's long internal colonial warfare over "the problem of Indigenous education" that had raged for most of the twentieth century. The 2003 incident was but the latest and most dramatic violent encounter between insurgent Aymara activists and an authoritarian state, but it marked a point of no return for Bolivia's failed experiment in neoliberal multiculturalism.

Since then, Bolivia has lived through tumultuous cycles of popular insurrection, along with dramatic reforms in the politics of governance and education (to reprise Kant's twin pillars of modernity). The overthrow of Goni's regime coincided with mass protests over the sovereign control of strategic resources, and against the ravages of globalization, between 1999 and 2003. Then, in a dramatic turn of events, the citizenry elected Evo Morales in late 2005. A coca union leader of Aymara descent, Morales was the hemisphere's first Indigenous president—an electrifying political symbol of ascendant indigeneity that he played to when it suited his political agendas at home and abroad.[52] Following Morales's landslide election, Bolivia embarked on a challenging state-building experiment, along the way rewriting the political scientists' script on governance, capitalist development, democracy, cultural inclusion, and social equality under the reconstituted parameters of the Estado Plurinacional (Plurinational State).[53]

The political will to wrestle with these ethical and institutional questions and to renegotiate the ethno-political terms of robust NGO support was certainly evident in the early 2000s. Once more, the entangled politics of race, nation, and Indigenous education surfaced in public policy and discourse. In 2006, the Ministry of Education redefined the country's educational values as "decolonizing, liberating, anti-imperialist, revolutionary and transformative ... [and] oriented toward self-determination and the reaffirmation of the originary indigenous agro-Bolivian nations and of Bolivian nationality." Those ideals were to guide the state's plan for education reform, later codified in the 2010 Nueva Ley de Educación "Avelino Siñani y Elizardo Pérez."[54] Set in historical context, this symbolic recovery of Siñani and Pérez as Bolivia's founding fathers of emancipatory, pro-Indigenous school reform represents a culminating moment in the hard-fought battles, and partial victories, that four generations of Indigenous people and progressive educators had achieved over the course of a century.[55] A stunning offshoot, almost unthinkable during the neocolonial twentieth century, is the "pop-up" Indigenous university recently founded to redress the marginality of Indigenous people in higher education. In 2008, the Morales regime launched UNIBOL (the Indigenous University of Bolivia), with sites in three ethnolinguistic regions (Aymara, Quechua, and Guaraní). Although still largely symbolic in scale, its educative mission was to advance the pluriethnic ideal of "inclusion within diversity" by offering a chance for subsidized higher education to Bolivia's millennial generation of Indigenous students. Just as Warisata once represented a vibrant experiment in the pedagogy of liberation and self-determination in the 1930s, so now the old escuela-ayllu was transformed into sacred ground for the purpose of redressing endemic problems of poverty, racism, and marginality in the present while also "rethinking the territorial and ideological order of the state itself."[56] This liberatory tradition has planted itself firmly in the terrain of Bolivia's Indigenous university—a lived, built, and unfolding symbol of decolonization if ever there was one.

In short, Bolivia's millennial turn toward pluriethnic nationhood opened new civic, educative, and institutional pathways toward political inclusion, social equity, and Indigenous cultural enfranchisement. It has been a fitful process, troubled by terrible setbacks, inherent policy contradictions, escalating social conflicts, and monumental mistakes on the part of the Morales government, which in 2019 was dramatically swept from power.[57] As is all too evident today, the tangled roots of cultural racism grow thick and deep, and manifold challenges to the conflict-riven process of "decolonization" still lie ahead. Arguably, however, there is perceptible change on many fronts, especially in Bolivia's recent efforts to reckon with its history of structural racism and cyclical battles over rural peoples' equitable access to land, schools, citizenship, and identity.

Since 2000, Bolivia has reinvented itself as an Indigenous-majority nation, arguably the only one in Latin America. To be sure, the ethnic question cuts both ways: it is used for political purposes of inclusion *and* exclusion. In recent years, the ethnic question has devolved to many lowland groups—not only the old warrior nation of the Guaraní but also the confederation of eastern lowland indigenous people (known collectively as the TIPNIS) that have surfaced as militant critics of the dominant governing party (Movement toward Socialism, or MAS) and its predominantly highland Aymara constituency. But it is also crystal clear that the social ecology of indigeneity has been irrevocably altered by the sovereign, often unruly, presence of a vitally engaged citizenry—the heirs of four generations of Aymara educational activists and their Quechua and Guaraní allies, not to mention the teachers and comrades who joined their struggles. Whereas the "lettered Indian" used to be viewed by the oligarchy as a danger to the neocolonial order, Bolivia's educated Indigenous people, armed with strategic knowledge, power, and governing skills, are now shaping the content of their own social subjectivities and political destinies. When set against the long horizon of twentieth-century history, contemporary Bolivian society appears to have moved far beyond the oppressive constraints of racial violence and neocolonial modernity in ways that are halting, contradictory, and sometimes exasperating, but also unexpectedly hopeful and inspiring.

ACKNOWLEDGMENTS

My deepest intellectual debt belongs to the generation of scholar-activists, teachers, and intellectuals who were involved in the cause of Indigenous education during the 1930s and 1940s. Even before I was truly ready to launch a full-scale research project, I suddenly realized in 1990 that time was of the essence if I wanted to meet and interview several foundational figures involved in the formative history of Warisata. I honor the memory and generosity of four extraordinary "veterans" of the original Warisata experiment. Jaél Oropeza de Pérez, a former teacher and the widow of Elizardo, shared her remembrances of the triumphs and travails of her late husband's work and opened his collection of newspaper clippings for me to peruse. Shortly after we met, a freak street accident cut short the life of this vibrant woman. I am also indebted to the late Ana Pérez, daughter of Raúl Pérez (and niece of Elizardo). She spent part of her youth in Warisata, and in later years worked to redeem the public memory of her father's work, first in the communitarian school of Caiza D and later in the epic struggle to defend the escuela-ayllu against hostile political forces. I am grateful for the precious time I spent with the late Tomasa Siñani de Willka, daughter of Avelino Siñani, the Aymara literacy teacher who cofounded Warisata in 1931. Tomasa became a feminist-activist and teacher in her own day. Her daughter, Lola Willka de Apasa, and granddaughter, Tomasita Willka, were also generous interlocutors in the early stages of my research. Above all, the late Carlos Salazar Mostajo, a lifelong teacher, journalist, writer, artist, photographer, and passionate champion of the original escuela-ayllu, took me into his confidence during my initial fieldwork in Bolivia. Over the years, he generously shared his oral memories, personal archives, published work, photographic collection, and broad-ranging ideas about Bolivian history. Were he still with us, I would have had the privilege of testing my ideas and findings against his wisdom and understandings of the past.

Some years before I touched down in Bolivia to mount this research project, a new generation of Bolivian activists and intellectuals was already engaged in "decentering" and "decolonizing" the dominant nationalist pedagogies. Those scholars moored their research to the oral testimonios, communal memories, local knowledges and emotions, lived historical experiences of the past, and buried paper trails that their elders and ancestors had generated during the early 1900s. I am especially indebted to the members of the Taller de Historia Oral Andina (THOA), both individually and as a collective, for the scholarship they produced and for sharing their work and insights with me. I thank María Eugenia Choque for believing in the value of this project and allowing me to work with THOA's collection of photocopied documents (most of them Indigenous petitions and published *boletines* gathered from provincial archives and the Archivo de La Paz). I am also grateful for the conversations, encouragement, and scholarship of Silvia Rivera Cusicanqui, the late Xavier Albó, the late Roberto Choque Canqui, Esteban Ticona Alejo, Carlos Mamani, Karen Claure, Ramón Conde Mamani, Humberto Mamani Capchiri, and Vitaliano Soria Choque, along with other members of the THOA collective. I also thank my Aymara tutor, Román Crespo Titirico, for trying to pound the complexities of Aymara syntax and grammar into my head.

This long journey would not have been possible without the constancy of friendship, solidarity, and intellectual exchange with several lifelong *compañeras del campo*. My heartfelt thanks goes to Rosario León for her abiding friendship, for our collaborative work in Cochabamba, and later for encouraging me to study the history of Warisata. I also owe a heartfelt debt to Cecilia Salazar de la Torre for introducing me to her father, Carlos Salazar Mostajo, and for generously sharing her own passion, knowledge, and information about the escuela-ayllu. I cannot possibly thank Rossana Barragán enough for her generous hospitality during my early fieldwork in La Paz, when she helped me settle in, with two small children in tow. The astonishing range and depth of her historical work, as well as her directorship of Bolivia's Archivo de la Paz and (many years later) the International Institute of Social History in Amsterdam, have inspired a new generation of Bolivian historians. I also thank Carmen Medeiros for her wonderful friendship in New York, when we were both writing about Cochabamba; for sheltering me in her La Paz home during later phases of this research project; and for challenging me to think more deeply about contemporary Bolivian politics and history. Not least, I am grateful to María Lagos, Silvia Rivera, and Pamela Calla for their scholarship, friendship, and solidarity. This support network made it possible to keep the embers burning and to make my periodic return to Bolivia a time of joyful reunion.

There is no adequate way to thank all the colleagues, friends, and graduate students who have contributed to this study, even if their input is unbeknownst to them. But I would be remiss if I didn't single out several colleagues for their scholarly contributions, fellowship letters, and/or moral support. I thank Sinclair Thomson for years of dialogue, critique, and support, as well as Laura Gotkowitz, with whom I have shared many deep conversations about Bolivian history. Thanks also go to Carmen Soliz, Sarah Hines, Kevin Young, Marcia Stephenson, Andrew Ehrinpreis, and Waskar Ari (all Bolivianists working in the United States, whose work has inspired and informed parts of this book). This project was supported over the years, at least indirectly, by a community of wonderful scholars and friends, including April Masten (my local "writing pal"), the late Elizabeth Dore, Ann Zulawski, Temma Kaplan, Nancy Tomes, Mary Kay Vaughn, Barbara Weinstein, Elizabeth Monasterios, Joanne Rappaport, Carmen Ramos Escandón, Marisol de la Cadena, the late Olivia Harris, Seemin Qayuum, Kevin Healy, Christine Hunefeldt, Thomas Klubock, Huascar Rodríguez, Eric Langer, Jorge Hidalgo, José Gordillo, Françoise Martínez, Ramiro Molina, Cassandra Torrico, Giovanni Bello, Benjamin Dangl, Manuel Contreras, Herbert Klein, Linda Farthing, Kevin Healy, Robert Smale, and other colleagues who have participated in shared panels and seminars. I am also grateful to my History Department colleagues at Stony Brook University for years of warm collegiality and support, and to three cohorts of brilliant Latin American(ist) graduate students with whom I have had the privilege to work. Special thanks go to several colleagues and research assistants in La Paz, including Luís Reinaldo Gómez, Moisés Gutiérrez Rojas, Mary Money, and Marina Murillo Ari. For years of wonderful conversation, strategic advice about Bolivian archives, and for sharing ideas and documents, I thank both Hernán Prudén and Matthew Gildner, two formidable young *bolivianista* historians. More recently, the young Peruvian historian José Miguel Munive has been a wonderful sounding board for rethinking the comparative history of rural education in Peru and Bolivia. In addition, I owe much appreciation to Matthew Ford, an accomplished young historian of Ecuador, for years of fruitful discussion and for the editorial work he did on an earlier version of this manuscript. And I will never forget how Julie Franks, then a young graduate student working on the rural history of the Dominican Republic but eager to see the high Andes, accompanied me for a month of camaraderie in Bolivia as my two very young children and I settled in to life in La Paz.

Several fellowship programs provided generous financial support during various stages of research and writing, including the William J. Fulbright Travel Fellowship; a Social Science Research Council fellowship; the ACLS/NEH International Research Fellowship; the Woodrow Wilson International Center for Scholars; Harvard University's David Rockefeller Center on Latin American Studies; and the John Simon Guggenheim Memorial Foundation Fellowship.

I also toast the many unsung heroes of research projects like my own. In particular, I owe a great debt to the dedicated men and women who staff Bolivian repositories and patiently serve the public, particularly foreign researchers, often pressed for time and short of patience. In this day of digitalization, collecting has become relatively quick and easy (although not necessarily better), but there is no substitute for on-site research or the guidance of seasoned archivists (often research historians in their own right). I am grateful to Luís Oporto and the professional staff of the Archivo Histórico del Honorable Congreso Nacional (AHHCN), as well as to the colleagues and archivists who staff Bolivia's Archivo de la Paz (ALP); Archivo Nacional de Bolivia (ANB); the periodical library (Heremoteca) of the Universidad Mayor de San Andrés (UMSA); the library of the Comisión de Investigación y Promoción del Campesinado (CIPCA); the Centro Boliviano de Investigación y Acción Educativa (CEBIAE); and the Biblioteca Arturo Costa de la Torre. Not least, I thank Stony Brook's Interlibrary Loan staff for searching the world for obscure books and articles.

Working with the editors at Duke University Press through three books (including this one) has always been a privilege. The late Valerie Millholland championed this book project at its inception, and Gisela Fosado has been her worthy successor, a brilliant editor, a source of constant support, and a wise friend. I thank Duke's two anonymous reviewers for their invaluable commentary and critique and Alejandra Mejía, Liz Smith, and freelancer Christi Stanforth for shepherding the manuscript through the editorial process. Duke's art, production and design teams, including A. Mattson Gallagher, also deserve my sincere thanks for the talent and care they invested in the final work. I also thank Victoria Pilates, Digital Librarian of Stony Brook University, for helping me to scan, edit, and file the book's illustrations.

Oddly, authors usually save their most heartfelt gratitude for last, perhaps because there seems to be no adequate way to express it on the pages of an academic book. But to those loved ones closest to me, know that, in fundamental ways, this book belongs to you (even if you never read a word of it!). In particular, I am grateful to my loving mother, Barbara—my greatest listener and cheerleader until her final years of decline (just as I was finishing this book). I also thank my sister Jodie Larson for her unflagging support. To Josh and Devon, who have brought love, joy, and compassion into my life in incalculable ways: I will be forever grateful. Finally, I thank Carter Bancroft. It was my great luck to have teamed up with him, just in time, for a lifetime of loving companionship and the shared joys and unforeseen challenges of family life. Carter's generosity of spirit, love and affection, moral compass, and abiding patience (not to mention his essential technical skills!) have sustained me in this long journey through the seasons of life.

NOTES

Preface

1. In 1967, within months of our encounter, Foster would publish his best-known book, *Tzintzuntzan: Mexican Peasants in a Changing World*.
2. Our illustrated literacy readers included *Nunca es demasiado tarde*; *Hacia el progreso por la unión*; and *Miguel el pescador*.
3. As I later learned, rural Michoacán was an epicenter of conflict over the expansion of secular school programs under the Cárdenas administration. See Becker, *Setting the Virgin on Fire*; and Boyer, *Becoming Campesinos*.

Introduction

1. Rousseau, *Émile ou de l'education*, cited and discussed in Donald, *Sentimental Education*, 4–7. Rousseau's complexity of ideas about education is best captured by reading *Émile* against *The Social Contract*, in which he concerns himself with the socialization of the citizen-subject under an enlightened social order.
2. Kant, *Thoughts on Education*, 4. A man of the Enlightenment, Kant believed that "proper education," if applied early in life, could instill in society and the individual the virtues of civilization. But if neglected or denied, "undisciplined men are apt to follow every caprice," he warned. This same reasoning was projected to the nonwhite world beyond western Europe. There the problem was not only the denial of education or discipline but also the nature of character and culture in "savage nations." Kant elaborates: "We see this [lack

of discipline] also among savage nations, who, though they may discharge functions for some time like Europeans, yet can never become accustomed to European manners. With them, however, it is not the noble love of freedom which Rousseau and others imagine, but a kind of barbarism—a kind of animal, so to speak, not having yet developed its human nature" (4).

3 Beyond his abstract musings, Kant's words seem to register Europe's quickening tempo of social change, the profusion of new education schemes, and the intense uncertainty about people's capacity to be educated for the purpose of social integration and self-governance. Indeed, Britain and the Continent were on the threshold of modernizing the arts of government and education. With the accelerated pace of industrialization, explosive growth of the laboring classes, rise of cultural nationalism, and imperial expansion, "the whole educational system was under new pressures, which would eventually transform it," writes Raymond Williams (*The Long Revolution*, 164).

4 Rama, *The Lettered City*, 42 (emphasis in the original).

5 Hobsbawm, *The Age of Revolution*, 166, quoted in B. Anderson, *Imagined Communities*, 69–70.

6 See Puiggrós, *Imaginación y crisis en la educación latinoamericana*, 17. Her seminal work explores formal and informal modes of education as an ongoing crisis and unresolved ideological battle, or *campo problemático*, throughout twentieth-century Latin America.

7 Rama, *The Lettered City*, 44–49; Puiggrós, *Imaginación y crisis en la educación latinoamericana*, 18.

8 Szuchman, "In Search of Deference," 9.

9 See Hooker, *Theorizing Race in the Americas*; Schwarcz, *The Spectacle of the Races*; and Stepan, "The Hour of Eugenics."

10 Hale, "Political and Social Ideas," 255. Arthur de Gobineau's "notorious racist views" and Gustave Le Bon's ideas about racial psychology projected a gloomy outlook, which cropped up in several famous Latin American works in the early twentieth century, such as Alcides Arguedas's *Pueblo enfermo* and Carlos Octavio Bunge's *Nuestra América*.

11 See Sarmiento's *Conflicto y armonías de las razas en América*, a social Darwinian treatise "rife with virulent anti-indigenous racism," notes Hooker (*Theorizing Race in the Americas*, 106).

12 Hooker, *Theorizing Race in the Americas*, 70–79, 81, 98, 103, 106–7.

13 These themes are explored in my book *Trials of Nation Making*. See also Mallon, *Peasant and Nation*; de la Cadena, *Indigenous Mestizos*; Rojas, *Civilization and Violence*; and Rappaport, *The Politics of Memory*.

14 A note on the racialized terms, phrases, labels, stereotypes, and categories that continually crop up in this study: To capture the sentiments

and thoughts of the age, I often use contemporary "keywords" (the term from Raymond Williams), thoughts, and slogans that embody the racist-colonialist, radical agrarian, or national-populist language and tenor of the times under discussion. Given that these offensive categories and discourses are woven into the narrative and contextualized, I hope and presume that I do not always have to use "scare quotes" around them to distance myself from racialized references. By that criteria, the racial-colonial term "Indian" was often used, or invoked, to designate the racialized subalternity of Aymara- and Quechua-speaking peoples living under neocolonial rule; likewise, that self-same category of *indio* was repurposed by Indigenous interlocutors to project a collective voice, vision, or claim into the dominant public sphere. Where the rubric Indian (*indio*) is used in discussion, it references the contemporary racial category and various connotations deployed by different groups of protagonists in this story. Indigenous people often self-identified as members of the "Indian race" (*la raza de indios*, or *la raza indigenal*) in their legal documents. Of course, racial slippage, intensive boundary crossings, differentiation of geography, ethnicity, and language, along with social mobility and class stratification, all complicated the racialized nomenclature of social identity, alterity, and hierarchy. More discrete categories (*originario, comunario, colono,* etc.) were used by contemporaries (and are referenced in this book) to differentiate the landholding status of Indigenous people; urban Aymara people carried (often pejorative) mixed-race labels (*chutas,* cholos, mestizos, etc.). Aymara and Quechua people were sometimes distinguished by ethnicity, language, and region, but more often were lumped together as *los indios* in the eyes of criollo elites (i.e., Hispanized people of Spanish American descent). By midcentury, agrarian class designations (campesino, *obrero, agricultor,* etc.) adhered to rural people in the rhetoric of populist, leftist, and syndicalist movements. The symbolic violence of race, ethnicity, and caste categories, as well as the discursive turn toward gendered forms of campesino self-identification and state-driven forms of peasant subject-making, are recurring themes in this book.

15 In Bolivia, the subject of rural education has been the object of social scientific research, much of it critical of the MNR's historic 1955 Education Reform. Since the 1980s and 1990s, critical ethnography has focused on the role of state policy and rural school practices in Andean peasant communities, often with an emphasis on the state's long entrenched "Spanish-only" curriculum. The turn toward "bilingual and intercultural" educational reform, prompted by Bolivia's Indian rights movements and progressive NGO policies, was finally consecrated in the Bolivian Education Reform Law of July 7, 1994. Bolivia's new EIB (from the Spanish *educación intercultural bilingüe*) was inspired by this pedagogical sea change, which finally recognized the moral and functional value of cultural and linguistic pluralism as a more equitable and effective way to educate Bolivia's rural population. In the past three decades,

ethnographers have explored various aspects of schooling within local Indigenous contexts. See, for example, the work of Xavier Albó, Aurolyn Luykx, R. Howard-Malverde and A. Canessa, Andrew Canessa, Denise Arnold with Juan de Dios Yapita, Bret Gustafson, Patricia Oliart, Mario Yapu and Cassandra Torrico, and Marcelo Sarzuri-Lima (all listed in the bibliography). Historical studies include M. Contreras, "Educación" and "A Comparative Perspective on Education Reforms in Bolivia"; Cajías, *Continuidades y rupturas*; F. Martínez, *"Régénérer la race"*; Choque Canqui and Quisbert Quispe, *Educación indigenal en Bolivia*; Sangines Uriarte, *Educación rural y desarrollo en Bolivia*; Brienen, "The Clamor for Schools"; and Rodríguez García, "Caciques, escuelas, y sindicatos rurales."

16   This chapter draws inspiration, ideas, and secondary sources from the body of work that came out of the Taller de Historia Oral Andina, including the lifelong body of scholarship produced by the late Roberto Choque Canqui (listed in the bibliography).

17   On the Peruvian Andes, see Alberti and Cotler, *Aspectos sociales de la educación rural en el Perú*; Oliart, *Políticas educativas y la cultura del sistema escolar en el Perú* and "Education, Power, and Distinctions"; Wilson, "In the Name of the State?"; and de la Cadena, *Indigenous Mestizos*.

18   Adorno, *Guaman Poma*.

19   See Steve Stern's classic study of judicial politics, *Peru's Indian Peoples and the Challenge of Spanish Conquest*; Ramos and Yannakakis, *Indigenous Intellectuals*; Salomon, "Testimonies"; and Penry, *The People Are King*.

20   Salomon and Niño-Murcia, *The Lettered Mountain*. They write, "A major aim of village literacy-learning from the start was to defend village interests by presenting cases before authorities in Lima" (58). "Strong literacy is [also] associated with self-defense against fraud and abuse. Writing is even spoken of as the *arma* ('weapon') of the community" (25). However, their community-based ethnohistory is primarily concerned with the "internal" cultural meanings and uses of writing and reading as contextualized within the matrix of rural village life, its ancestral rituals, and traditions of self-governance.

21   See Rappaport's body of scholarship on the Cauca region of Colombia, including her coauthored book with Tom Cummins, *Beyond the Lettered City*; Wogan, *Magical Writing in Salasaca*; Lund, "On the Margin"; and Salomon and Chambi Apaza, "Vernacular Literacy on the Lake Titicaca High Plains." As ethnographers have shown, the tactical use of literacy among non-Spanish-speaking people of the Andean countryside was embedded in fundamentally oral cultures.

22   The caciques (Indigenous peasant authorities) and their bilingual representatives (apoderados) represented rural communities' legal land fights as the "title bearers." In charge of finding, safeguarding, and litigating colonial title

deeds, they used this paper currency to negotiate Indigenous claims in the courts and ministries.

23 Pratt, *Imperial Eyes*, 7.

24 According to de la Cadena, the Peruvian slang word *gamonal* probably originated in the mid-nineteenth century, when urban elites began referring to Peru's semifeudal landholders as *gamonales*. Later, José Carlos Mariátegui and other Marxists used the phenomenon of *gamonalismo* to signify a system of provincial tyranny under the neocolonial trinity of priest, lawyer, and landowner, all of whom exploited the Indigenous underclass (*Indigenous Mestizos*, 78–84). Bolivian leftists applied the label to their own class enemies, the landowning oligarchy and provincial elites, during the buildup to the 1952 national revolution.

25 Although my narrative sidesteps contemporary theory about colonization, decolonization, internal colonialism, and "the coloniality of power," I draw inspiration from that scholarly literature, including the works of Silvia Rivera (see especially "La raíz" and *Ch'ixinakax utxiwa*); Anibal Quijano ("Coloniality of Power, Eurocentrism, and Latin America"); and Mary Louise Pratt (*Planetary Longings*, chap. 14).

26 See Gramsci's seminal essay "On Education" for insight into the relationship between education (broadly defined) and organized class struggle. For Gramsci, "critical understanding of self takes place . . . through a struggle of political 'hegemonies' and of opposing directions, first in the ethical field and then in that of politics proper, in order to arrive at . . . a higher level of one's conception of reality." *Selections from the Prison Notebooks*, 333; and cited in Coben, *Radical Heroes*, 37.

27 Activist consciousness-raising (*concientización*) was theorized and practiced by the educator and philosopher Paulo Freire, whose pedagogic work also informed liberation theology. By the late 1960s, his ideas about an alternative "dialogic" approach to education-for-liberation had swept across Latin America and beyond. See Freire, *Education for a Critical Consciousness* and the classic work *Pedagogy of the Oppressed*.

28 This chapter draws inspiration from Guha, *Elementary Aspects of Peasant Insurgency in Colonial India*; Scott, *Domination and the Arts of Resistance*; and Tarrow, *Power in Movement*.

29 Critically reappraised by several generations of scholars, Bolivia's epic "national revolution" (1952–64) is still the subject of intense political and historiographical debate. If there is any historiographical consensus, it is that the Bolivian revolutionary regime passed through an early radical ("Jacobinist") stage in which the MNR issued a series of groundbreaking social reforms (universal suffrage, nationalization of the largest tin mines, a massive agrarian reform, and the overhaul of public education). But as domestic and transnational

circumstances shifted, the MNR regime (or the "'52 state," as critics call it) began to reinstitutionalize state power, pull back on its redistributive social policies, and yield to US-imposed economic austerity pressures and Cold War policies. After 1960, Bolivia's clientele status was reinforced by the new Alliance for Progress package of US economic and military aid. In his classic 1970 book *Bolivia: The Uncompleted Revolution*, political scientist James Malloy characterized it as a protracted and unfinished political process. For a set of recent historical reflections and social scientific appraisals, see Grindle and Domingo, *Proclaiming Revolution*.

30 Corrigan and Sayer, *The Great Arch*. For classic sociocultural approaches to education, nationalism, and state formation, see B. Anderson, *Imagined Communities*; Hobsbawm, *Nations and Nationalism since 1780*; Gellner, *Nations and Nationalism*; and Green, *Education and State Formation*.

31 Hobsbawm, *Nations and Nationalism since 1780*, 267.

32 See Vaughn, *Cultural Politics in Revolution*; Dawson, *Indian and Nation in Revolutionary Mexico*; Knight, "Racism, Revolution, and Indigenism"; Gutiérrez, *Nationalist Myths and Ethnic Identities*; and R. A. López, *Crafting Mexico*.

33 Siles Suazo, "Speech Delivered by Dr. Hernán Siles Suazo."

1. To Civilize the Indian

1 The multivocal concept of national pedagogy accommodated a variety of positivist, nationalist, and traditionalist impulses. In Argentina and Chile, the idea was associated with the spirit of democracy, popular clamor for schools, and university reform movements. During the centennial celebrations around 1910, the Argentine intellectuals Ricardo Rojas and José María Ramos Mejía deployed the ideal to exalt the authentic nation, including its folkloric traditions. See Helg, "Race in Argentina and Cuba," 45, 64. While Rojas was advocating for a nationalist pedagogy for Argentina, Franz Tamayo championed the idea of a Bolivian national pedagogy in 1910 in a series of newspaper essays. This theme comes up later in the chapter.

2 Klein, *Bolivia*, 166–67.

3 This unabashed enthusiasm comes from Benjamín Fernández, a lawyer, writer, and early advocate of positivist thinking (he was known by some as "the Comte of Bolivia"). A champion of education reform, Fernández followed in the footprints of other Latin American criollo modernizers, by touring and living in Europe, where he studied their advanced systems of public instruction. See Francovich, *La filosofía en Bolivia*, chap. 28; quotation, 199.

4 I. Calderón, "Dreams of the Railroad."

5 ONI, *Censo general* (1900), 2, lxxvi, lxxvii.

6   Arguedas, *Pueblo enfermo* (3rd ed., 1995), 54; for an ample, insightful analysis of Arguedian race-thinking, see Salmón, *El espejo indígena*, 61–75.

7   Arguedas, *Pueblo enfermo* (2nd ed., 1936), 46–47. The myth of the Indian's antimarket mentality—yet another marker of the Indian as a human anachronism—has been roundly disputed by historians and anthropologists (see, for example, Rivera, "Rebelión e ideología," 89–92; and various contributions to Larson, Harris, and Tandeter, *Ethnicity, Markets, and Migration*). On the other hand, Andean traditions of trade and transportation did face competition, not only with the arrival of railroads but with the influx of imported wheat from Chile. Technology and commerce disrupted traditional agriculture and supply chains. Real estate and divestiture laws further threatened rural ways of life, and many rural peoples did turn hostile, displaying a learned aversion to the peddlers (and swindlers) of Western progress.

8   I. Calderón, "Dreams of the Railroad," 193 (emphasis added).

9   J. Sanjinés, *Mestizaje Upside-Down*, 33.

10 Alcide D'Orbigny, a French zoologist, was commissioned by his government to map the linguistic and physiological groupings of South America (later reported in his published work, *L'homme américain* [1839]). He spent eight years traveling through the South American continent, collecting enough material and impressions to fill nine volumes of travel memoirs (*Voyage dans l'Amérique Méridionale*, 9 vols. [1835–47]). I have drawn my material from an abbreviated (four-volume) Spanish-language version of D'Orbigny's travelog (*Viaje a la América Meridional*, republished in 1945; citation, 3:970). On his enduring influence on Bolivian geographers and writers, see Qayum, "Creole Imaginings," chap. 2; and Piñeiro Iñíguez, *Desde el corazón de América*, 48–49.

11 D'Orbigny, *Viaje a la América Meridional*, 3:984.

12 On Alto Peruvian Indigenous trade and transport, see Glave, *Trajinantes*; and on the late eighteenth-century Aymara siege of the city, see Thomson, *We Alone Will Rule*; and Serulnikov, *Revolution in the Andes*, chaps. 14–15.

13 D'Orbigny, *Viaje a la América Meridional*, 3:982–93. See Barragán, *Espacio urbano y dinámica étnica*; Soruco, *La ciudad de los cholos*; and Stephenson, *Gender and Modernity in Andean Bolivia*.

14 On the tale of these intertwined cities, see Albó, Greaves, and Sandoval, *Chukiyawu*; Barnadas et al., *Los Aymaras dentro de la sociedad boliviana*; and Barragán, *Espacio urbano y dinámica étnica*.

15 Demographically, La Paz was Bolivia's most Indigenous department: an estimated 75 percent of its population was categorized as Indigenous. The historian Fellman Velarde estimated that around 1900 the city of La Paz counted, at most, some sixty thousand inhabitants. The rural population was

composed of "*comunarios* (ayllu- and community-based Indians) and *siervos* (peones attached to haciendas)." Thus, he noted, Bolivia in 1900 "was not [yet] a Nation" (*Historia de Bolivia*, 3:18). To "civilize the Indian" was no less than to forge the nation.

16 ONI, *Censo general* (1900), 2:37.
17 ONI, *Censo general* (1900), 2:36.
18 ONI, *Censo general* (1900), 2:36.
19 ONI, *Censo general* (1900), 2:36.
20 For historians' analysis of the 1900 census document, and other contemporaneous texts, as representing the Bolivian literary apogee of social Darwinism, see Demelas, *Nationalisme sans nation?* and "Darwinismo a la criolla"; and Irurozqui, *La armonía de las desigualdades*.
21 ONI, *Censo general* (1900), 2:37.
22 ONI, *Censo general* (1900), 1:155–56. On the politicized blind spots of the "seeing state" (to borrow James Scott's term), see the candid report of Bolivian census takers on the "difficulties" and "flaws" that marred the 1901 population report on the Department of La Paz. Census takers recalled their failed efforts to enumerate the Indian population living on "fincas, comunidades, and estancias." Their mission was obstructed, they noted, by "the invincible ignorance and ingenuous and sneaky mistrust of the Indian race, which has always seen in such administrative procedures a motive for [the state] imposing higher land taxes or military service, [and] which is looked upon today with true horror—all this motivates the Indian to avoid . . . giving personal or family information for the census." Provincial authorities found it necessary to compensate for these gaping holes by adding "a maximum of 8 percent" to the population count. That brought the number of Indian inhabitants to 423,587. (By contrast, the census's urban population estimate was inflated by 4 percent to an estimated total of 56,901, to compensate for the undercount in the city and immediate surroundings of La Paz.)
23 ONI, *Censo general* (1900), 2:36–37.
24 Pratt, *Imperial Eyes*, 152.
25 On the technologies of social and spatial order, and modern modes of population management, see Barragán, "The Census and the Making of a Social 'Order'"; Radcliffe, "Imagining the State as a Space"; and Gupta, "Governing Population."
26 *El Heraldo*, January 27, 1899, quoted in Torrez, *El indio en la prensa*, 40.
27 *El Heraldo*, January 27, 1899, quoted in Torrez, *El indio en la prensa*, 42.
28 Bautista Saavedra's public defense of the Aymara rebels invoked positivist social sciences (criminology, psychology, sociology, etc.) to argue that the

Indians, as a degenerate race, had committed a "collective crime" and thus could not be tried as individuals under the law. He relied on Gustave Le Bon's idea of "crowd psychology" to build his "scientific case" against Indians' racial depravity. Saavedra, "Proceso Mohoza," in his collection *El ayllu*.

29 Rivera, *"Oprimidos pero no vencidos"* (1986), 29. See also Mendieta, *Indígenas en política*, 13; and Irurozqui, "The Sound of the Pututos."

30 "Insistimos," *El Heraldo*, March 2, 1899, quoted in Torrez, *El indio en la prensa*, 58 (emphasis added). The "Yankee" imperial slogan of "civilization or extinction" began circulating in the 1830s and 1840s. Pontificating on the country's westward colonizing campaigns, one US senator proclaimed in 1846 that the apocalyptic choice of "civilization, or extinction, has [always] been the fate of all people who have found themselves in the track of the advancing Whites, and [that] civilization, always the preference of the Whites, has been pressed as an object, while extinction has followed as a consequence of resistance." Pearce, *Savagism and Civilization*, 240.

31 ONI, *Censo general* (1900), 1:162; M. Contreras, "Educación," 483.

32 R. J. Calderón, "La 'deuda social' de los liberales," 69–70.

33 Suárez Arnez, *Historia de la educación en Bolivia*, 242.

34 R. J. Calderón, "La 'deuda social' de los liberales," 58–59.

35 Paredes, *Provincia de Inquisivi*, 121–22. R. I. Calderón ("Paradojas de la modernización," 113–14) confirms the 1906 report.

36 R. J. Calderón, "La 'deuda social' de los liberales," 70.

37 F. Martínez, *"Régénérer la race,"* 191–92.

38 Under the Liberals' watch, the Protestant missionary influence spread rapidly across parts of the northern Altiplano, crossing the Bolivian/Peruvian border. By and large, Bolivian modernizers warmly welcomed the new wave of Adventists, Baptists, and other Protestant sects from the United States and Canada. They were admired for introducing good habits of industry, cleanliness, and piety among Aymara communities—a theme we return to later in this book. See Strobele-Gregro, *Indios de piel blanca*, 119–30; Alvaréz Calderón Gerbolini, *En búsqueda de la ciudadanía indígena*; and Hazen, "The Awakening of Puno" (on the Peruvian side of the border).

39 R. J. Calderón, "La 'deuda social' de los liberales," 56.

40 R. J. Calderón, "La 'deuda social' de los liberales," 55–57, 58–59.

41 Saracho served as minister of education between 1903 and 1908. Bolivian historiography credits him with having launched the first institutional cycle of modern education reform.

42 Quoted in F. Martínez, *Qu'ils soient nos semblables, pas nos égaux*, 137 (my translation).

43 Misael Saracho, *Ley del Presupuesto y Plan General de Instrucción Pública*, February 11, 1905, 1, Ministerio de Justicia e Instrucción Pública, ALP.

44 Saracho, *Ley del Presupuesto y Plan General de Instrucción Pública*, 7–8.

45 Saracho, *Ley del Presupuesto y Plan General de Instrucción Pública*, 1.

46 *Memoria del Ministro de Justicia e Instrucción Pública al Congreso Ordinario* (1904), 52–53, AHHCN; Saracho, *Memoria 1904*, quoted in R. J. Calderón, "La 'deuda social' de los liberales," 56. The minister pleaded for 300,000 bolivianos for sixty elementary school establishments, and to cover the cost of school supplies imported from the United States.

47 *Memoria del Ministro de Justicia e Instrucción Pública al Congreso ordinario*, March 1, 1905.

48 *Memoria del Ministro de Justicia e Instrucción Pública al Congreso ordinario*, March 1, 1905, 63.

49 *Memoria del Ministro de Justicia e Instrucción Pública al Congreso ordinario*, March 1, 1905, 64.

50 *Memoria del Ministro de Justicia e Instrucción Pública al Congreso ordinario*, March 1, 1905. Saracho begged the Congress to allocate twenty thousand bolivianos for the program—a modest budget request for financing the infrastructure of rural elementary schools. Frustrated by Congress, he resorted to this fly-by-night pilot project.

51 Ministro de Justicia e Instrucción Pública al Señor Rector, "Los maestros ambulantes de aillos y comunidades de indígenas," March 1, 1905 (circular no. 37), 211, ALP.

52 Finot, *Historia de la pedagogía boliviana*, 32. Montes had another education scheme in mind, elaborated in a presidential decree in late 1905. Impatient with Saracho's formal educational scheme, he created a simple fee-for-literacy program that would pay a per capita rate (twenty bolivianos) for each Indian instructed in speaking, reading, and writing the Spanish language. Indians would be certified as "literate" by town and political authorities in each locale (a kind of state "accreditation") before the instructor was to be recompensed, and there would be fines for instructors who rounded up lettered Indians and claimed them as their pupils. Those who taught literacy to at least ten Indian pupils (of whatever age or gender) over the course of a school-year cycle would receive a certificate of "preceptor" and a few school supplies. Bypassing institutional norms, this ad hoc arrangement turned literacy instruction into a commercial enterprise for the (unwritten) purpose of creating Indigenous electors for the Liberal Party. Ley de 11 de Diciembre de 1905 ... en que se dediquen a la instrucción y educación de los indígenas por cuenta particular, May 15, 1906, ALP. The decree became law in 1906.

53 F. Martínez, *"Régénérer la race,"* 200–201.

54 Martínez cites a teacher's letter: "The hilacatas ordered my students from the communities of Chiarkahua, Sibicani, and Totorani, in the name of the corregidor, to get to work [on the hacienda] ... by threatening to send them into the armed forces if they didn't obey." F. Martínez, *"Régénérer la race,"* 201.

55 F. Martínez, *"Régénérer la race,"* 201.

56 R. J. Calderón, "Paradojas de la modernización," 118.

57 Ministerio de Justicia e Instrucción Pública, *Memoria del Ministro ... Dr. Juan Misael Saracho al Congreso Ordinario de 1908*, lxxxvi, ALP.

58 Ministerio de Justicia e Instrucción Pública, *Memoria del Ministro ... Dr. Juan Misael Saracho al Congreso Ordinario de 1908*, lxxxvi.

59 Ministerio de Justicia e Instrucción Pública, *Memoria del Ministro ... Dr. Juan Misael Saracho al Congreso Ordinario de 1908*, lxxxvii.

60 Ministerio de Justicia e Instrucción Pública, *Memoria del Ministro ... Dr. Juan Misael Saracho al Congreso Ordinario de 1908*, lxxxvii.

61 See Saavedra, *Memoria de justicia e instrucción pública* and *La democracia en nuestra historia*.

62 Study abroad—the administrative, political, and educational pilgrimages to the Old World, together with the diffusion of ideas through the circulation of printed materials—became a feature of criollo elite formation in late eighteenth- and nineteenth-century Latin America. See B. Anderson, *Imagined Communities*, chap. 4.

63 Sarmiento's six-hundred-page travel journal, *Viajes en Europa, Africa, y América*, appeared in 1849. See Pratt, *Imperial Eyes*, 190–93.

64 Patton, *Sarmiento in the United States*, 32. See Sarmiento, *Memoria sobre educación común* and *Ideas pedagógicas*.

65 Protestantism, Sunday schools, and Bible study furnished the socioreligious context within which popular literacy spread in both seventeenth-century northern Europe and New England. Layered onto that template was New England's flourishing culture of town councils, incipient industrialization, and technology of print capitalism—all factors that spurred the region's early elementary school movement.

66 By contrast, Sarmiento paid scant attention to the US South, where laws criminalized enslaved people for attending schools or for learning how to read and write on their own.

67 Hale, "Political and Social Ideas," 242–43; Zea, *The Latin American Mind*, 145–49.

68 In exchange for receiving sixty pensioners (funded by the Bolivian government), Chile sent only five normal instructors, contracted to stay for a year. F. Martínez, *Qu'ils soient nos semblables, pas nos égaux*, 261–68.

69 In 1908, Daniel Sánchez Bustamante was appointed to the ministry of education to succeed his mentor, Misael Saracho. See Francovich, *La filosofía en Bolivia*, chap. 30.

70 He published a stream of letters and reports in Bolivia's *Revista de Instrucción Pública* in 1907 and 1908. See F. Martínez, *Qu'ils soient nos semblables, pas nos égaux*, 268–70.

71 F. Martínez, *Qu'ils soient nos semblables, pas nos égaux*, 268–70.

72 Weber, *Peasants into Frenchmen*; B. Anderson, *Imagined Communities*, chap. 5; and Muller, Ringer, and Simon, *The Rise of the Modern Educational System*.

73 Hobsbawm, *Nations and Nationalism since 1780*, 115.

74 F. S. Guzmán, *El problema pedagógico*, 156–62.

75 Published in *Revista de instrucción pública* (1908), 37, cited and quoted in F. Martínez, "'Que nuestros indios se conviertan en pequeños suecos!,'" 372.

76 F. Martínez, "'Que nuestros indios se conviertan en pequeños suecos!,'" 372.

77 The spirit of Lamarckism (the idea that acquired characteristics were inheritable) permeated this brand of tutelary race-thinking in Europe and Latin America. It offered an escape from the trap of biological determinism by arguing that evolution could be tempered by enlightened state policies. Neo-Lamarckian ideas framed the idea of racial progress (vis-à-vis whitening) and underwrote a whole range of educational, hygienic, moral, charitable, and social reforms targeted at the underclasses in early twentieth-century Latin America. See Stepan, *"The Hour of Eugenics"*; Schwarcz, *The Spectacle of the Races*; and Rosemblatt, *The Science and Politics of Race in Mexico and the United States, 1910–1950*.

78 F. S. Guzmán, *El problema pedagógico*, 73–74.

79 While Guzmán's essays circulated Darwinian notions of whitening in the public sphere, Alcides Arguedas published his widely read book *Pueblo enfermo* (1909). Bringing a mass of descriptive and diagnostic material together to analyze myriad sectors of Bolivian society, Arguedas quickly emerged as another Darwinian prognosticator on the "laws of evolution." Josefa Salmón writes that "for Arguedas racial homogenization (or, 'whitening') is the entry to 'civilization' and to universal 'culture,' as well as the model of progress and modernity of the industrialized nations.... [Yet] Arguedas does not plant a proposal for such a homogenization, since race mixing [*el mestizaje*] is considered to be a negative force due to racial incompatibility. In this sense, he followed the theories of Le Bon regarding the impossibility of a racial and cultural homogenization." Salmón, *El espejo indígena*, 76 (my translation). Though they shared basic evolutionary premises, Guzmán and Arguedas read the evolutionary tea leaves differently.

80 F. S. Guzmán, *El problema pedagógico*, 72 (emphasis added).

81 F. S. Guzmán, *El problema pedagógico*, 72.
82 F. S. Guzmán, *El problema pedagógico*, 44.
83 F. S. Guzmán, *El problema pedagógico*, 78.
84 F. Martínez, "Régénérer la race," 316–19.
85 F. S. Guzmán, "La educación de la raza indígena boliviana," October 21, 1922, 2, typescript copy from the APEP.
86 Irurozqui, *La armonía de las desigualdades*, chap. 4.
87 J. Sanjinés, *Mestizaje Upside-Down*, 35. See also Albarracín, *Sociología indigenal y antropología telurista*; Salmón, *El espejo indígena*; García Pabón, *La patria íntima*, chaps. 5 and 6; and Larson, "Redeemed Indians, Barbarianized Cholos." Sample tellurist works include Arguedas, *Raza de bronce*; J. Mendoza, *El macizo boliviano*; and Paredes, *La altiplanicie*.
88 J. Sanjinés, *Mestizaje Upside-Down*, 35.
89 Halconruy, *Georges Rouma*, 31–32; F. Martínez, "Régénérer la race," 232n129. See also F. Martínez, *Qu'ils soient nos semblables, pas nos égaux*, 286–90.
90 See Rouma, *Las bases científicas de la educación* and *Pedagogie sociologique*.
91 Quotation in F. Martínez, "Régénérer la race," 237. See also Talavera, *Formaciones y transformaciones*, 64–67.
92 F. Martínez, "Régénérer la race," 247.
93 Quoted in Halconruy, *Georges Rouma*, 29. Soon after this disheartening realization, Rouma began recruiting Belgian colleagues to work in Bolivia's normal institute and in the education ministry.
94 Rouma got cooperation from some of Bolivia's most notorious and powerful latifundistas, men who relied on dozens, if not hundreds, of semibonded servile tenants to work their land, pasture their flocks, haul their crops to market and bundles of firewood to their townhouses, etc. The hacendados were often direct beneficiaries of Bolivia's liberal land policies, having carved out estate lands from ex-communal territory. One of Rouma's research sites, for example, was the hacienda Pillapi, located in the rich belt near Lake Titicaca and owned by Benedicto Goitia, then the president of the Bolivian Senate.
95 Rouma, *Les indiens Quitchouas et Aymaras des Hauts Plateaux de la Bolivie*, 10–11. See also Rouma, *Quitchouas et Aymaras*, chap. 11.
96 Rouma, *Les indiens Quitchouas et Aymaras des Hauts Plateaux de la Bolivie*, 62.
97 Rouma, *Les indiens Quitchouas et Aymaras des Hauts Plateaux de la Bolivie*.
98 Rouma, *Les indiens Quitchouas et Aymaras des Hauts Plateaux de la Bolivie*, 66 (emphasis added).
99 Rouma, *Les indiens Quitchouas et Aymaras des Hauts Plateaux de la Bolivie*, 67.
100 Suárez Arnez, *Historia de la educación en Bolivia*, 244.

101 Suárez Arnez, *Historia de la educación en Bolivia*, 244–45. See the revealing 1918 field report by two rural normal-school teachers: Mariaca and Peñaranda, *Proyecto de organización de una escuela normal agrícola de indígenas en el altiplano*; and Ministerio de Instrucción Pública y Agricultura, "Informe de la Dirección General de Educación Indígena," 254–56.

102 Suárez Arnez, *Historia de la educación en Bolivia*, 244–45.

103 Ballivián, "El problema del indio," ix–x (emphasis added). This argument was not unique to Bolivia. It circulated in Peru around the same time. Indigenista writers, men like Fernando García Calderón and José de la Riva-Aguero, viewed Indians as permanent obstacles to progress. But they also extolled the race as an indispensable rural workforce. By the 1930s and 1940s, naturalizing the indio as the agrarian labor force came fully clothed in the language of class, a semantic shift toward *campesinización* that was thinly layered over embedded stereotypes of race and rurality. See de la Cadena, *Indigenous Mestizos*; Drinot, *The Allure of Labor*; and Alvaréz Calderón Gerbolini, *En búsqueda de la ciudadanía indígena*.

104 Paredes, "La altiplanicie," 596.

105 Quoted and cited in J. Sanjinés, *Mestizaje Upside-Down*, 85.

106 J. Mendoza, *El factor geográfico en la nacionalidad boliviana*, 84. Taking a page from Franz Tamayo's sentimental indigenismo, Mendoza added the luster of geographic determinism to the indigenista quest for national identity. Around the same time Mendoza was writing, the Congress took up the Indian labor question, linking it to a series of other policy subjects (land reform, protectionist laws for the Indians, and the idea of technical training for the rural Indian). The wide-ranging discussion among the delegates reiterated the prevailing racial trope: the Indian was irreplaceable. Octavio Salamanca's 1931 essay reinforced the indigenistas' skepticism about the possibility of colonizing rural Bolivia with white farmers from Europe. Bolivia's high altitude and climate posed immediate dangers: mountain madness, shortness of breath, high infant mortality rates, and the "melancholic effects" of the barren, treeless landscape of the Altiplano. Only the Indian, through millennia of adaptation, could endure the rigors of the high plateau. There was no alternative, he argued, but to preserve Bolivia's Indian workforce. See Salamanca, *El socialismo en Bolivia*.

107 Guillén Pinto, *La educación del indio*, 85. See the epigraph.

108 Hoxie, *A Final Promise*, 86–87; and Fear-Segal, *White Man's Club*.

109 Pearce, *Savagism and Civilization*, 49. See also Pearce, *The Savages of America*. On negotiating US imperial power and education reforms in Puerto Rico, Cuba, and the Philippines, see McCoy and Scarano, *Colonial Crucible*, part 3; and for racial and ethnic minorities located within the continental United States, see Stratton, *Education for Empire*.

110 Saracho made rhetorical capital out of this simplistic notion. In fact, the US government administered a variety of school programs for its native minorities, including day schools, agency boarding schools on reservations, and large, off-reservation, barracks-like boarding schools, such as the famous Carlisle Indian Industrial School in Pennsylvania. Furthermore, as Hoxie argues, US educational thinking and policy underwent a dramatic reorientation, shifting the pedagogic methodology and goal from racial assimilation (toward citizenship) to a more segmented form of vocational schooling (tailored to a permanent underclass of Indian and Black laboring people) during the crucial Jim Crow years between the 1880s and 1920s.

111 Szasz, *Education and the American Indian*; Fear-Segal, *White Man's Club*; and Adams, *Education for Extinction*.

112 J. D. Anderson, *The Education of Blacks in the South, 1860–1935*; Hall, *Black Vocational, Technical, and Industrial Arts Education*; Smock, *Booker T. Washington*; and Washington, *Up from Slavery*.

113 Guillén Pinto, *La educación del indio*, 99–100.

114 Finot, *La reforma educacional en Bolivia*, 188. They served a double orientation, he explained: first, to stimulate "new needs and desires" in the rural masses (i.e., new habits of clothing, sleeping, diet, living arrangements, and hygiene); and second, "to give them, by means of apprenticeship in a trade, a solid moral formation, a love of work, and a facility to obtain the economic resources necessary to satisfy those new needs." In that way, 1.5 million people—Bolivia's great mass of Indians—would participate in the benefits of civilization and promote the nation's progress (188).

115 Ignacio Prudencio Bustillo, *Ensayo de filosofía jurídica* (1923), quoted in Zea, *The Latin American Mind*, 203. Enthusiasm for Booker T. Washington's pedagogical model of cultural uplift and bootstrap mobility permeated Bolivia's early historiography of education, from Finot (*Historia de la pedagogía boliviana* and *La reforma educacional en Bolivia*) to Suárez Arnez (*Historia de la educación en Bolivia*).

116 F. S. Guzmán, "La educación de la raza indigena boliviana," October 21, 1922.

117 See Hahn, *A Nation under Our Feet*; J. D. Anderson, *The Education of Blacks in the South*.

2. Lettered Aymara

1 *La Razón*, September 14, 1929.

2 The office of corregidor, inherited from colonial times, housed the highest official at the cantonal level. In colonial times, the official was supposed to oversee local judicial proceedings, public works labor, and tribute collection.

3   Although I have drawn widely on Bolivian scholarship (including THOA-sponsored research and its archive of photocopies) throughout this study, here I want to acknowledge several works that helped guide my thinking in chapter 2: Mamani, *Taraqu, 1866–1935*; Condori Chura and Ticona Alejo, *El escribano de los caciques apoderados*; Rivera, "'Pedimos la revisión de límites'"; Soria Choque, "Los caciques-apoderados y la lucha por la escuela"; K. Claure, *Las escuelas indígenas*; Choque Canqui, "La problemática de la educación indigenal" and *Historia de una lucha desigual*; and Choque Canqui and Quisbert Quispe, *Líderes indígenas aymaras* and *Educación indigenal en Bolivia*. See also THOA's pamphlet history of Santos Marka T'ula. Combining bilingual (Aymara-Spanish) oral testimony, context, and narrative based on archival research and illustrated by Cecilia Salazar, the text catapulted this forgotten, silenced history into the public sphere—as well as restoring this historical memory in written form to rural village elders, many of whom were interviewed in the course of THOA-sponsored research into the cacique movement. THOA, *El indio Santos Marka T'ula*; and an English version of the pamphlet published in 1992: THOA, "The Indian Santos Marka T'ula, Chief of the *Ayllus* of Qallapa and General Representative of the Indian Communities of Bolivia." For an insightful study of the THOA project and achievements, see Dangl, *The Five Hundred Year Rebellion*, chaps. 4 and 5.

4   Street, *Cross-Cultural Approaches to Literacy*, 9.

5   Rappaport and Cummins, *Beyond the Lettered City*, 19.

6   Rappaport and Cummins, *Beyond the Lettered City*, 22. To this point, see also Justice, *Writing and Rebellion*, 55; Stock, *Listening for the Text*; Castiglione, "Adversarial Literacy"; Guha, *Elementary Aspects of Peasant Insurgency in Colonial India*; and Graff, *The Legacies of Literacy*.

7   Rivera, "La expansión del latifundio en el altiplano boliviano."

8   Platt, *Estado boliviano y ayllu andino*; Mendieta, *Entre la alianza y la confrontación*, 95–109.

9   Aside from the Quechua ayllus of Chayanta (in the Department of Northern Potosí), the bastion of propertied communalism was concentrated on the Altiplano across the western swath of the high plateau in the Departments of La Paz and Oruro. While many Aymara communities accrued populations of peasant renters and sharecroppers, they continued to hold and claim swaths of territory throughout the highlands, and sometimes even held on to ancient "islands" of coca and maize land, tucked into the mountainous slopes of the Cordillera Oriental. The persistence of Aymara forms and norms of territoriality, even a full century after Bolivia's independence, astounded the roving American anthropologist George McBride. Following his tour of highland Indian communities around 1920, McBride estimated that some 500,000 people—about 67 percent of the country's Aymara and Quechua

population—still lived in rural communities of one kind or another. McBride, *The Agrarian Indians of Highland Bolivia*.

10 Albó, "Andean People in the Twentieth Century," 769.

11 See Mendieta, *Entre la alianza y la confrontación*.

12 Abercrombie, *Pathways of Memory and Power*, 306. Just three years later, the nascent comunitario movement won a major concession. An 1883 government decree ruled that if the claimants could ratify ancient title deeds, preferably the Crown's seventeenth-century land deeds (*títulos de composición y venta*), proving their ancestors had duly purchased titles to their community lands under contract from the colonial state, and if those lands were still held corporately as communal-ayllu lands (*pro-indiviso*), the Bolivian government would consider granting "absolute property rights" to those *tierras de origen* in question.

13 Abercrombie, *Pathways of Memory and Power*, 306.

14 Mamani, *Taraqu, 1866–1935*, 56–57.

15 Solicitud de Patricio Mamani por los indígenas del Cantón Ayoayo sobre la Revisita de tierras originales, 1904, box 281, no. 52, AHHCN.

16 Stern, *Peru's Indian Peoples and the Challenge of Spanish Conquest*, 123–24.

17 General Mariano Melgarejo presided over the first neocolonial wave of dispossession in rural La Paz during the 1860s.

18 Choque Canqui and Quisbert Quispe, *Líderes indígenas aymaras*, 27, 200. This estimate is based on the signatories of official paperwork (*gestiones*). For a brief moment, the designated leader of the cacique association was Martín Vázquez, an originario from the province of Pacajes. His appointment as leading cacique-apoderado was cut short in 1915 by scandal and repression, as we shall see in the pages below. Banished, Vázquez's authority was superseded by Santos Marka T'ula, a self-proclaimed *cacique de sangre*.

19 Gotkowitz, *A Revolution for Our Rights*, 77–87. She traces the dissemination of ancient land titles, communiqués, and print materials through a vital network of *kurakas*, caciques, alcaldes, and hilacatas of communities and haciendas, mostly in Cochabamba's western highland regions of Vacas and Tapacarí, where the ragged vestiges of communal landholding were still being defended in the courts. Gotkowitz, *A Revolution for Our Rights*, 96.

20 Ari, *Earth Politics*, 43–46.

21 This point is developed in Mendieta, "En defensa del pacto tributario," 133–34; and Irurozqui, "A bala, piedra, y palo."

22 The archive was part of Spain's vast imperial infrastructure that extended the legal, administrative, and symbolic authority of the Spanish patrimonial state into the lettered cities and colonial hinterlands across Spanish America. A hierarchy of archives and the heavy traffic in official documents created a

baroque edifice of legalism and mediation—the Spanish system of justice that kept the machinery of colonial domination humming for some three centuries. In the Andes, the first massive state inventories of Indigenous populations and their territories were created under Viceroy Francisco de Toledo. In the seventeenth century, colonial archives became the repository of royal land titles, voluminous lawsuits, and thus the destination of Indigenous people seeking justice under the Laws of the Indies.

23 See Stern, *Peru's Indian Peoples and the Challenge of Spanish Conquest*; Thomson, *We Alone Will Rule*; Serulnikov, *Subverting Colonial Authority* and *Revolution in the Andes*; Penry, *The People Are King*; and Burns, *Into the Archive* and "Making Indigenous Archives."

24 Serulnikov, *Subverting Colonial Authority*, 119, and *Revolution in the Andes*, 25.

25 Vázquez's documentary collection probably included a mix of genres, from colonial title deeds to tribute records to legal dossiers pertaining to earlier land disputes. Presumably, he did not carry home original documents, unless they were smuggled out, or bribes were transacted. Standard notarial procedure was to pay a public notary to draw up affidavits (on official, stamped paper) for the purpose of proving in court the legal authenticity of the document(s). Notaries made a good living from this work, and their Indigenous clients had to pay hefty fees (or *derramas*, often collected regularly, or as a special assessment, from rural communities involved in the case).

26 THOA, *El indio Santos Marka T'ula*, 22.

27 "Obrados sobre los reclamos de Marka Tola, cacique principal del ayllu Ilata del cantón Callapa y Curaguara de Pacajes" (hereafter cited as "Obrados sobre los reclamos de Marka Tola"), 1913–1925, ALP-P, E. (Note the variation in spelling, Marka Tola/T'ula, in the primary and secondary texts.) The 1915 trial document, inserted in this massive dossier of documents, is cited as "Testimonio de varias piezas del proceso criminal contra Julio Monroy, Martín Vázquez, y demás cómplices por los delitos de subversión, tumulto, y otros, a mérito de las denuncias pasadas por el Señor Prefecto del Departamento de La Paz y por el Ministro Público," ff. 9–16. The late Roberto Choque first discovered this patrimonial document in the Archivo de La Paz, and was generous to allow me to consult it. THOA investigators used this long, rich document to bring into public awareness Marka T'ula's extraordinary lifework as an Aymara activist. See THOA, *El indio Santos Marka T'ula*.

28 "Obrados sobre los reclamos de Marka Tola."

29 "Obrados sobre los reclamos de Marka Tola," ff. 9–9v.

30 "Obrados sobre los reclamos de Marka Tola," f. 19v.

31 "Obrados sobre los reclamos de Marka Tola," ff. 14v–15; Choque Canqui and Quisbert Quispe, *Líderes indígenas aymaras*, 203–15.

32 Mamani, *Taraqu, 1866–1935*, 63–69.

33 "Obrados sobre los reclamos de Marka Tola," f. 15.

34 "Obrados sobre los reclamos de Marka Tola," ff. 9v–10, 15. In 1919, just four years after the trial, the cacique movement drafted a manifesto (*memorial*) that carried the signature of more than fifty Indigenous people from different regions. By then, their demand had escalated into a radical call for annulling the private property claims of all hacendados and the restoration of territory to its rightful owners: "We make known to this Honorable Congress that the señores hacendados tell us that they are the entitled owners, whereas we are the legitimate and absolute owners [of ayllu lands] since the time of the Inca and the Spanish crown in the year 1585 . . . [and thus] we unanimously request of this congress a general review of property boundaries, by special decree, since there . . . is no justice to be found in the ordinary tribunals." Quoted in Ticona Alejo and Albó, *La lucha por el poder comunal*, 102.

35 "Obrados sobre los reclamos de Marka Tola," f. 14.

36 *El Norte*, March 25, 1914; Rivera, "'Pedimos la revisión de límites,'" 621.

37 Condori Chura and Ticona Alejo, *El escribano de los caciques apoderados*, 80.

38 THOA, *El indio Santos Marka T'ula*, 25, 27.

39 See Salomon and Niño-Murcia, *The Lettered Mountain*; Wogan, *Magical Writing in Salasaca*; Lund, "On the Margin"; and Salomon and Chambi Apaza, "Vernacular Literacy on the Lake Titicaca High Plains."

40 Ari, *Earth Politics*, 103. Caciques' documentary bundles were sacrosanct ritual objects embodying "Indian law," according to Ari. He notes how caciques interpellated "Indian law" to establish ethnic rights, legitimize the practice of religious rituals, and dress in Indigenous clothes, in violation of some municipal laws.

41 See the bilingual oral testimonies in THOA, *El indio Santos Marka T'ula*; and Ticona Alejo, *Memoria, política, y antropología en los Andes bolivianos*.

42 Elusive to the Western imperial eye, communal (or cacique) archives are located at the core of community life and memory, safeguarding a bank of communal knowledge and memory. Anthropologist Tristan Platt had the privilege of consulting the archive of a moiety chief of the Quechua-speaking Macha people in northern Potosí. There he found a variety of documents bundled together by rope under sheepskin covers, including copies of a seventeenth-century boundary inspection of all the communities of Macha, drawn up in 1646; lists of all Indian tributaries, regularly updated; various lawsuits over many years regarding a disputed boundary with a neighboring hacienda; receipts for payments in kind (potatoes, chuño, and barley) to the Bolivian national army during the Chaco War in the 1930s; and sundry other items recording more contemporary transactions with the state. Indeed, the

contents of this communal archive probably served local ayllu authorities in legal suits and petition campaigns over the ages—whenever it became necessary to marshal documentary proof to press a claim, defend a boundary, or document the contributions the ayllu had rendered to the state. But as Platt showed, the Macha endowed these textual treasures with ritual and shamanistic powers as well. In the hands of village spiritual leaders (*los yatiris*), the Macha's "papers of the grandfathers and grandmothers" became the medium for communicating to both the Christian saint of miracles, Santiago, and the ancient vernacular deities. Platt, "Writing, Shamanism and Identity or Voices from Abya-Yala," 137, 139. (That particular field visit took place in the 1970s.) See also the astonishing ethnographic work of de la Cadena, especially "Story 4: Mariano's Archive," in *Earth Beings*, 117–51.

43 Harris, "'Knowing the Past,'" 118.

44 Abercrombie, *Pathways of Memory and Power*, 286–91.

45 Condori Chura and Ticona Alejo, *El escribano de los caciques apoderados*, 97–98.

46 Andeanists Denise Arnold and Juan de Dios Yapita have observed how many Western researchers are held in contempt by traditional peasant authorities because they are seen as disrespecting and misunderstanding the cultural value of their old papers. *The Metamorphosis of Heads*, 286, 292.

47 On the peregrinations of caciques in Sucre and their search for (or safekeeping of) colonial land titles and other documents, see THOA, *El indio Santos Marka T'ula*, 29–32. The quintessential lettered city, Sucre houses both the Supreme Court and National Archive (ANB). To the present day, its archive has drawn a stream of Indigenous people in search of documentary ammunition for their ongoing litigious battles. (Personal communication, the late Gunnar Mendoza, longtime director of the ANB and cataloguer of the documentary collection, Tierras e Indios.)

48 This extraordinary oral history was conducted primarily by Esteban Ticona Alejo during the 1980s. Copious interviews were published, side by side, in the original Aymara and its Spanish translation. (Here, translated excerpts in English are from the Spanish.) See Condori Chura and Ticona Alejo, *El escribano de los caciques apoderados*, 32–33.

49 María Frontaura Argandoña estimated that some four thousand Indians were recruited for military service every year. She criticized the brutal military training they received, and particularly the fact that military training did not integrate the fundamentals of literacy, civics, morality, or hygiene into the curriculum. The state was urged to provide basic instruction for rural recruits, since the future depended on alphabetizing the Indian and converting him into a rural smallholder. Frontaura Argandoña, *Hacia el futuro Indio*, 30.

50 Mamani Capchiri, "La educación en la visión de la sociedad criolla," 86–87.

51 Faustino and Marcelino Llanqui played crucial roles as "instigators" of Jesús de Machaca's 1921 rebellion, and most studies revolve around the drama, and the trauma, of that horrific event. See Choque Canqui and Ticona Alejo, *Jesús de Machaqa*; and Ticona Alejo and Albó, *Jesús de Machaqa en el tiempo*. The 1921 Machaca rebellion, led by Marcelino and Faustino Llanqui, has been richly chronicled by the historians Roberto Choque and Esteban Ticona. Here my interest is in tracking Marcelino Faustino's circular pathway to literacy and political activism against the broader canvas of peasant schooling and political unrest.

52 Choque Canqui and Ticona Alejo, *Jesús de Machaqa*, 45.

53 Petición de los "Víctimas de Machaca," April 15, 1921 (emphasis added), box 311, AHHCN.

54 Cámara de Diputados, 1921, vol. 3, 73rd Sesión Ordinaria, April 1, 1921, AHHCN, reprinted in Choque Canqui and Ticona Alejo, *Jesús de Machaqa*, 193.

55 Choque Canqui and Ticona Alejo, *Jesús de Machaqa*, 319.

56 Choque Canqui and Ticona Alejo, *Jesús de Machaqa*, 317.

57 Soria Choque, "Los caciques-apoderados y la lucha por la escuela," 62.

58 Soria Choque, "Los caciques-apoderados y la lucha por la escuela."

59 "Informe de la inspección," 1931, 5, ALP-P, C.

60 Soria Choque, "Los caciques-apoderados y la lucha por la escuela," 62.

61 "Denuncian los hechos mencionan y pide el cambio del preceptor que se indica," February 21, 1929, box 75-22, AHHCN. See also chapter 4, below, for a discussion of the social grievances and demands that flowed in from rural communities to the government's rural education bureaucracy during the early 1940s.

62 Rosendo Cosme "Los indios de Jesús de Machaca piden conmiseración ofreciendo regenerarse," *La Razón*, February 22, 1930.

63 See Llanos, "El rito de uqhart'akuy escolar en el ayllu Chari (Charazani)."

64 See Arnold and de Dios Yapita, *The Metamorphosis of Heads*.

65 Arnold and de Dios Yapita, *The Metamorphosis of Heads*, 138.

66 Arnold and de Dios Yapita, *The Metamorphosis of Heads*, 144.

67 Llanos, "El rito de uqhart'akuy escolar en el ayllu Chari (Charazani)," 156, 159–60.

68 In this context, the term *originario* refers to Indigenous people claiming ayllu lands and ancestral lineages, often tracing back to early colonial times. Along with *agregados* (relative newcomers whose ancestors had acquired land from the original inhabitants), they comprised the comunario population of ayllu-communities.

69 "Obrados sobre los reclamos de Santos Marka T'ula," f. 91. In 1923, in response to the growing pressure of schooling, Bautista Saavedra ordered elementary schools to be built in larger haciendas, mining enterprises, and large Indian communities. The decree, while responsive to grassroots demands, was also designed to fill the vacuum left by the state's failure to set up rural schools as it once promised to do. Not for the first time, this government decree represented an empty gesture, since the state had no capacity to enforce it. Rhetorically, it shifted the responsibility for administering rural school reform from the state to the local enterprise.

70 "Varios indígenas representantes pidiendo amparo y garantías," June 12, 1924, ALP-P, E.

71 Carter and Mamani, *Irpa Chico*, 371.

72 See Hahn, *A Nation under Our Feet*.

73 "Piden que se cumplan todos los decretos y resoluciones... para la instrucción y que su justiciera autoridad haya cumplido," March 10, 1928, box 75-3, AHHCN.

74 Ministerio de Gobierno y Justicia, *Cuestiones indigenales*, 172 (emphasis added).

75 The term "wild literacy" (as seen by state authorities) comes from Eklof, *Russian Peasant Schools*. To curb this undergrowth, the Bolivian government began to get back into the game of rural educational reform. In 1928, the minister of public education and agriculture issued a thick government pamphlet, *La reforma de nuestras escuelas rurales*. Devoid of data, it was an instruction manual for administrators and teachers to regulate what was a barely existent system of rural public schools.

76 "Informe de la Inspección Técnica Departamental de la Educación Indigenal," July 25, 1931, 1–2, and *Memoria de la Instrucción Pública y Agricultura... de 1931* (1932), ALP-P, C.

77 "Informe de la Inspección Técnica Departamental de la Educación Indigenal," July 25, 1931, 1–2, and *Memoria de la Instrucción Pública y Agricultura... de 1931* (1932).

78 *Memoria de la Instrucción Pública y Agricultura... de 1931* (1932), 2.

79 Frontaura, *Hacia el futuro indio*, 27.

80 Frontaura, *Hacia el futuro indio*, 29.

81 "Informe de la Inspección Técnica Departamental de la Educación Indigenal," 6–7.

82 "Informe de la Inspección Técnica Departamental de la Educación Indigenal," 6–7.

83 "Informe de la Inspección Técnica Departamental de la Educación Indigenal," 6–7 (emphasis in the original).

84 "Informe de la Inspección Técnica Departamental de la Educación Indigenal," 7.

85 The classic study of this region is Mamani, *Taraqu, 1866–1935*. See also Choque Canqui and Quisbert Quispe, *Líderes indígenas aymaras*, 48–60.

86 Cited in Mamani, *Taraqu, 1866–1935*, 128. See also Ticona Alejo, "Education and Decolonization in the Work of Aymara Activist Eduardo Leandro Nina Qhispi"; Gotkowitz, *A Revolution for Our Rights*, 48–51; and Wahren, *Encarnaciones de lo autóctono*, 137–65.

87 Ticona Alejo, "Education and Decolonization in the Work of Aymara Activist Eduardo Leandro Nina Qhispi."

88 "Una entrevista a Nina Quispe: El maestro indio que sostiene una escuela...a costa de sus propios esfuerzos," *El Norte*, October 28, 1928.

89 "Una entrevista a Nina Quispe," 4.

90 "Una entrevista a Nina Quispe."

91 Nina Quispe, "Solicitudes de Eduardo L. Nina Quispe para la orientación técnica de la educación indigenal en Bolivia" (1933), 1, Ministero de Gobierno, ALP-P, C (hereafter cited as "Solicitudes").

92 Quotation in Nina Quispe, "Solicitudes," 4.

93 "El 16 de Julio próximo se reunirá un gran congreso de maestros indígenas," *El Universal*, June 10, 1930; Mamani, *Taraqu, 1866–1935*, 133.

94 Nina Quispe, "Solicitudes," 7.

95 Bolivia had several modest Catholic Church and lay charities dedicated to promoting Indian education, most notably the Centro Católico de Aborígenes "Bartolomé de Las Casas." The Centro was the result of a collaborative effort of the caciques-apoderados and progressive churchmen to promote Indian schooling. In 1931, it was presided over by Anselmo Choque under the cloak of the archbishop of La Plata, in Sucre. See Soria Choque, "Los caciques-apoderados y la lucha por la escuela," 66.

96 In 1932 and 1933, Nina Quispe published two boletines consisting of an assemblage of legal and notarial documents, much like the legal portfolios that rural caciques presented in court or occasionally published in newspapers to support a land claim, or register a grievance, or simply to make a documentary claim to lands long ago stolen or contested. Nina Quispe's only extant writings to date, they represent a powerful synthesis of the ideas brewing within the evolving comunario movement of the late 1920s.

Nina Quispe's embrace of the territorial issue comes to light in his lengthy 1932 pamphlet titled *De los títulos de composición de la Corona de España; composición a título de usufructo como se entiende la excensión revisitaria; venta y composición de tierras de origen con la corona de España; títulos de las comunidades de la República; renovación de Bolivia; años 1536, 1617, 1777, y 1925* (1932), Gaveta 29, ALP (hereafter cited as *De los títulos de composición*).

An eleven-page textual tapestry made up of transcribed letters, petitions, lawsuits, and government circulars, the pamphlet turns the Bolivian nation itself into the object of reform and "renovation." Its primary objective was to advance the comunario agenda for the restoration of colonial boundaries and jurisdictions (*un deslinde general*) by implementing colonial title deeds. That goal was most clearly enunciated in a letter, written in 1931, from Nina Quispe to President Salamanca: "The Society [of the Collasuyu] that I have the honor of presiding over, respectfully requests that ... you proceed with the recognition of Indian land possession on the basis of the colonial titles acquired through the *composición* [granted by] the Spanish crown, in that almost the totality of those lands have been violently expropriated from their owners." This brief document, transcribed and buried in the middle of his 1932 published pamphlet, brings clarity to Nina Quispe's bold agenda of communal restitution. See also the analysis in Mamani, *Taraqu, 1866–1935*, 139–53; Ticona Alejo, "Education and Decolonization in the Work of Aymara Activist Eduardo Leandro Nina Qhispi"; Choque Canqui, "Sociedad República del Collasuyu (1930)" and "De la defensa del ayllu a la creación de la República del Qullasuyu"; and Gotkowitz, *A Revolution for Our Rights*, 48–51, 56, 63, 71.

97 Nina Quispe, *De los títulos de composición*, 1.

98 Nina Quispe, *De los títulos de composición*, 1.

99 Condori Chura and Ticona Alejo, *El escribano de los caciques apoderados*, 118–19. See Laura Gotkowitz's insightful discussion of Nina Quispe and Marka T'ula as activists and intellectuals in *A Revolution for Our Rights*, 48–51.

100 "Existe en el altiplano ... una curiosa república ... ," *La Razón*, March 10, 1933; "Sobre la República comunista indígena," *La Razón*, March 14, 1933.

101 In jail, he received visitors and continued to produce all sorts of petitions and manifestos on behalf of the comunario movement. But his health failed, and Nina Quispe died in the mid-1930s, not long after his release from prison. Mamani, *Taraqu, 1866–1935*, 136–37; Choque Canqui and Quisbert Quispe, *Líderes indígenas aymaras*, 83–89; and Wahren, *Encarnaciones de lo autóctono*, 162–64.

3. Warisata

1 I use several interchangeable terms in both English and Spanish to refer to the Warisata school project, depending on the time and context, including the ayllu-school (or *la escuela-ayllu*); the núcleo school (or *el núcleo escolar*); the indigenal school (or *la escuela indigenal*); and the communal, community, or communitarian school. In the late 1930s, Elizardo Pérez and other indigenistas began to codify pedagogic goals and practices, drawn from the Warisata experience, to define their larger educational orientation, rooted in ayllu-communities but geared toward practical agrarian life, as "Indigenous education" (or *educación indigenal*).

2   Today Warisata is celebrated as a national icon and commemorated on the official date of its founding (August 2, 1931). The holiday is now shared with two other civic holidays: the Day of the Indian (designated in 1937 by President Busch) and the Day of Agrarian Reform (decreed by the new revolutionary nationalist regime of the MNR in 1953). A cottage industry has produced the official history, social memory, and telluric mystique of Warisata—thanks to many decades worth of scholarly articles, testimonial histories, journalistic articles, photographic exhibitions, pedagogic studies, and university theses in Bolivia, along with a few studies by foreign scholars. During the revolutionary decade of the 1950s and early 1960s, Indigenous people injected their own voices into the oral and written history of Warisata. Oral history studies, and the activist voices of Warisata's educated children (the heirs of the Aymara founders), added another layer of meaning and perspective to what was becoming an intercultural, dialogic history of Warisata. Meanwhile, critical counternarratives and revisionist studies—from critics and rivals on both the left and the right of the political spectrum—have never let up. Most recently, an iconoclastic Dutch doctoral dissertation (Brienen, "The Clamor for Schools") has attempted to "unmask" the true nature of the escuela-ayllu, much as its right-wing critics did in the 1940s. But for acolytes and critics alike, Elizardo Pérez's extraordinary 1962 book, *Warisata: La escuela-ayllu* (combining the genres of chronicle, memoir, ethnography, history, polemic, romance, and didacticism), secured Warisata's place in Bolivia's nationalist literary canon, even as they argued over its significance. In addition to Elizardo Pérez's memoir and his other writings, this chapter owes an intellectual debt to the written and oral testimony of two other protagonists, Carlos Salazar Mostajo (teacher, journalist, artist, and activist) and Tomasa Siñani de Willka, the daughter of Avelino Siñani, an Aymara teacher, amauta, and the preeminent cofounder of Warisata.

3   The 1930s saw the flowering of multiple and varied community-based Indigenous schools, adapted to different regional and ethnic contexts. The field is ripe for in-depth, interregional research projects.

4   Halconruy, *Georges Rouma*.

5   Rouma, *Les indiens Quitchouas et Aymaras des Hauts Plateaux de la Bolivie*, 66.

6   Jaél Oropeza de Pérez, interview with author, September 25, 1990.

7   Pérez, *Warisata*, 73.

8   Pérez, *Warisata*, 34.

9   Pérez, *Warisata*, 75.

10 Pérez, *Warisata*, 83.

11 Pérez, *Warisata*, 62.

12 Pérez, *Warisata*.

13 See the classic work on this uprising: Choque Canqui and Ticona Alejo, *Jesús de Machaqa*.

14 Pérez, *Warista*, 64–66.

15 Pérez, *Warista*.

16 Pérez, *Warista*, 70–71.

17 Pérez, *Warista*, 71.

18 Pérez, *Warista*, 71.

19 Pérez, *Warista*, 72.

20 Pérez, *Warista*, 73.

21 Pérez, *Warista*, 73.

22 Carmelo y Melchor Miranda contra Manuel y Mariano Nachoy Ancelmo Ramos, sobre despojo de terrenos, 1940, AJA.

23 On the mortgaging of fragments of *sayañas* and *tupus*, see Pérez, *Warisata*, 43–44.

24 Decreto Supremo de Presidente José Luís Tejada Sórzano . . . sobre la dotación de tierras para el cumplimiento de los fines de educación e instrucción indigenal, March 14, 1936, box 6, no. 9, ALP-LML. The decree was reprinted in Pérez, *Warisata*, 150.

25 Pérez, *Warisata*, 150.

26 Pérez, *Warisata*, 77; Carlos Salazar, interview with author, September 27, 1990. Eventually President Germán Busch appropriated forty hectares for Warisata, but that land annexation was never consolidated.

27 Pérez, *Warisata*, 73. (*Q'ara* is a derogatory Aymara term for white, or "peeled," people.)

28 Pérez, *Warisata*, 74.

29 Pérez, *Warisata*, 73–74.

30 Pérez, *Warisata*, 74.

31 Salazar, *Gesta y fotografía*. I am grateful to Carlos Salazar and Cecilia Salazar for permission to reproduce a small sample of those collected photographs from that book.

32 Andean-colonial practices of ayni (or mink'a) channeled streams of labor tribute for state-directed public works projects (irrigation, road-building, mail-dispatching, etc.); ayni work parties were also allocated for specific collective tasks, such as planting or harvesting potato fields on communal lands, crushing potatoes for chuño, or thatching or raising a roof for a family hut in the ayllu.

33 Velasco, *La escuela indigenal de Warisata*, 20–21.

34 Velasco, *La escuela indigenal de Warisata*, 82.

35 Velasco, *La escuela indigenal de Warisata*, 76–77.

36 Velasco, *La escuela indigenal de Warisata*, 75.

37 Tomasa Siñani de Willka, interviews with author, August 25, 1990, and September 5, 1990; Siñani de Willka, "Breve biografía de Avelino Siñani."

38 In the 1910s, the Liberal Party congressional deputy, Ramón González, recruited Avelino as an electoral client who would deliver "literate" Indian voters in exchange for two billetes a head. As his daughter tells it, this corrupt but commonplace proposition plunged Siñani into a difficult moral dilemma, but eventually he decided to use the opportunity to promote the lettering of the fifty "voters" he delivered to the Liberal candidate. It established an immediate economic motive for peasants to learn their letters under Avelino Siñani's tutelage. He also saw it as a chance for leveraging Indigenous influences on the Liberal Party in the region under President Montes and, not least, of campaigning for public primary schools throughout Omasuyos.

39 Tomasa Siñani de Willka, interview with author, August 25, 1990; Siñani de Willka, "Breve biografía de Avelino Siñani," 129–30.

40 Choque et al., *Educación indigena*, 129–30.

41 "Piden garantías y escuelas y otros obrados," 1924, box 263, ALP-P, E.

42 "Piden garantías y escuelas y otros obrados," 1924, 6. Julián Siñani traced his lineage to colonial caciques and at one point asked religious authorities to review the ancient parish records of baptism and marriage to verify his claim and to determine who figured in the records as ancient chiefs in the provinces of Omasuyos. His use of the past was to restore the lineage of these chiefly authorities, so they might preside over "the advancement of schooling [*la instrucción*], which is the main thing we should work for to advance our race." Cited and quoted in Albó, *Achacachi*, 20–21.

43 Interview with Tomasa Siñani de Willka, August 25, 1990: see Siñani de Willka, "Breve biografía de Avelino Siñani," 130.

44 In the late 1920s, other local authorities were also pulled into the community's struggle for rural schooling. Specifically, men like Apolinar Rojas, Carlos Quispe, and Valentín Choque launched a local campaign to pressure the federal government to intervene in local affairs and fire the abusive "mestizo" teacher, one Dionisio Molinedo. He was accused of reenacting gamonal-styled abuses (physical assaults, alcoholism, and verbal abuse) within the confines of the school. This recently established "fiscal" school, which was supposed to serve Warisata's children, was turning into a travesty of moral education and was emblematic of the state's indifferent, or ineffectual, educational apparatus. "Informe de la solicitud de los comunarios del cantón Huarizata," 1928–29, AHHCN.

45 The parliament was sometimes referred to as a council (*consejo*) of village leaders, or amautas. *Amauta* is a Quechua-hispano term used in the early colonial chronicles to refer to "official intellectual authorities" under the Inca

state. It connoted the work they did: "to conjecture and bring out in speech what will be good and turn out well and what will not." Their wisdom was a repository of both prophecy and memory. Salomon, "Testimonies," vol. 3, part 1, 24.

46 Pérez, *Warisata*, 82–83.

47 Pérez, *Warisata*, 82–83.

48 Carlos Salazar, interview with author, September 27, 1990.

49 Pérez, a graduate of Sucre's normal school, was channeling Georges Rouma's advocacy for coeducation in Bolivia's rural schools. There is no evidence to suggest that the school hired Siñani or other (formally untrained) Aymara teachers, but its normal program did train a few local young women, including Avelino Siñani's daughter, Tomasa.

50 Over time, the number of school commissions grew. By 1940, Warisata was organized into subcommittees on government, outreach, finance, justice, sports, education, supplies, agriculture and irrigation, construction, hygiene, industry, potable water, and gardening. Those commissions were composed of teachers, students, and at least one amauta, or community representative). They, too, had become more regulatory and instrumentalist. *Boletín de Warisata* 1, no. 7, January 21, 1940, 4.

51 Carlos Salazar, interview with author, October 11, 1990.

52 Pérez, *Warisata*, 81–83.

53 Pérez, *Warisata*, 92.

54 Carlos Salazar, interview with author, September 20, 1990; Pérez, *Warisata*, 29.

55 Velasco, *La escuela indigenal de Warisata*, 20–21.

56 Pérez's report to the Ministerio de Educación, May 13, 1937, quoted in Pérez, *Orientación agrícola de las escuelas indigenales*, 16–17. Running short on money and supplies, the main building's second story was not finished until sometime in the late 1940s.

57 Carlos Salazar, interview with author, September 27, 1990.

58 Carlos Salazar, interview with author, September 20, 1990; Velasco, *La escuela indigenal de Warisata*, 58.

59 The most explosive incident came in 1934, when the local corregidor entered the school and flogged Mariano Huanca. The incident catalyzed a criminal suit and a flurry of telegrams and press releases; it also provided the council of amautas with its first national exposure as a forum on justice (see below). In later years, Indigenous council members sometimes used sympathetic newspapers to denounce particular landlords or gamonales in the region. One spectacular example comes from *La Noche*, in August 1938, when the parlamento's "secretary," Rufino Sosa, used that newspaper to publicize his denunciations of the prominent landowner, Carlos Hanhart, for slandering

him, and for closing down the local school on his rented hacienda, Chúa. See Sosa, "Un indígena professor de la escuela de Warisata hace Declaraciones," *La Noche*, August 8, 1938. Hanhart, in turn, directed a propaganda campaign against Warisata in July and August 1938, which eventually drew in the prestigious landowners' organization La Sociedad Rural Boliviana (SRB), of which Hanhart was the titular head in 1938. See Hanhart, "Warisata no es un Centro Educacional sino Especie de Tribunal Supremo," *La Razón*, August 5, 1938, and "Comunicado de la Sociedad Rural Boliviana," *La Razón*, August 14, 1938.

60 Carlos Salazar, interview with author, September 20, 1990.

61 Carlos Salazar, interview with author, September 27, 1990. The situation became so dangerous by 1935 and 1936 that the parlamento eventually forbade any teacher from participating in their expeditions to investigate and mediate disputes with local landlords. Nor, of course, did students participate on that commission, though they did work on the other commissions. So these dangerous forays into rural zones of conflict became the sole prerogative of the community's amautas.

62 Pérez, *Warisata*, 240–41; see, for example, the story of Rufino Sosa's expeditions to various haciendas in the region in 1938 as reported in *La Noche*, August 10, 1938.

63 Carlos Salazar, interview with author, September 12, 1990.

64 Salazar noted that Elizardo Pérez attended the council sessions and occasionally addressed the Indians, sometimes instructing them on their right to speak out on issues that concerned them, and to take up their responsibilities in the cogovernance of the school. A great admirer of Pérez, Salazar nonetheless noted the tone of paternalism that permeated Pérez's authoritative pronouncements, as well as the way many of the other teachers (himself included) addressed the Indigenous audience. But he was convinced that the best way to guard against paternalism was to buttress the Aymara council and allow it to operate as a representative body of decision-making and discourse. Ultimately, Salazar saw the parlamento as "the locus of indigenous self-determination." Carlos Salazar, interview with author, September 20, 1990.

65 Carlos Salazar, interview with author, September 12, 1990.

66 Pérez, *Warisata*, 127–28.

67 Like the compulsory labor allocation of colonial Indians, tapped by the mita to serve for a year of obligatory labor in the distant silver mines of Potosí, Warisata's ayllus and school amassed food supplies, loaded onto caravans of mules and donkeys, to help sustain their contingent of troops during the long overland journey southward, toward the lowland battlefields of the Chaco. They were honored as patriotic recruits, representing the school's commitment to the defense of the *Patria*. Pérez, *Warisata*, 128.

68 "Un parlamento Amauta," *El Diario*, February 1, 1934.

69 "Un parlamento Amauta," *El Diario*, February 1, 1934.

70 The translator, Professor Ibañez, confirmed these first impressions.

71 "Un parlamento Amauta," *El Diario*, February 1, 1934. See also "La voz de la Raza," *El Diario*, February 3, 1934.

72 On the violence and oppression that created a hidden "internal front" during the Chaco War, see Arze Aguirre, *Guerra y conflictos sociales*; Mamani, *Taraqu, 1866–1935*; and Shesko, "'Our Sons Who Defend the Honor and Integrity of the Patria.'"

73 Proceso administrativo contra el corregidor, Sixto Hernani, 1934, ALP-P, E; Pérez, *Warisata*, 138–40.

74 Telegrama de Mendoza et al. al Min. Gobierno, Prefecto, Notaría, Amigos Ciudad, May 15, 1934, Omasuyos, 1934, ALP-P, C.

75 Proceso administrativo contra el corregidor, Sixto Hernani, 1934; Pérez, *Warisata*, 138–40.

76 *El Diario* and *La Razón*, for example, published various editorials and articles during May and June 1934, which chronicled the violent incident and demanded justice for Huanca, Rojas, and the school; see Pérez, *Warisata*, 139. For the file inserted into the criminal trial record, see Proceso administrativo contra el corregidor, Sixto Hernani, 1934.

77 Letter from Medinaceli to Pérez, July 9, 1934, APEP. The letter, dated July 9, 1934, is on *La Gaceta de Bolivia* stationery. (I am grateful to Elizardo Pérez's widow, the late Jaél Oropeza de Pérez, for allowing me to read part of this documentary collection.)

78 *La Patria* and other newspapers provided the editorial mouthpiece for the conservative voice. They defended the vecinos of Achacachi and tended to direct their attack against the radical teachers of Warisata (presuming, I suppose, that Aymara leaders were incapable of autonomous acts except under the influence of those "agitators").

79 "Omasuyos y la Escuela Indigenal de Huarizata," *La Patria*, July 7, 1934; "El Diputado por Omasuyos Hizo una Representación ante la Prefectura," *La Patria*, June 10, 1934.

80 Pérez writes (*Warisata*, 144), "The ancient plans to revitalize *la marca* were realized in the course of 1934, with the foundation of four elementary schools, situated along the valley floor leading to Sorata. We are talking of a region of great resources and a relatively easy way of life. Those heads of valleys yielded up to four annual harvests of potatoes, because of constant irrigation from the purest waters of Illampu and the land, black and rich, was not thin like that of the altiplano."

81 "Omasuyos y la Escuela de Huarizata," *La Patria*, June 7, 1934.

82 Pérez, *Warisata*, 95.

83 Pérez, *Warisata*.

84 That the spatial and administrative arrangement of the "nuclear school system" grew out of Warisata's spontaneous and planned outreach activities seems clear from much of the evidence; see Pérez, *Warisata*, 144–47; Velasco, *La escuela indigenal de Warisata*, 66–71; Carlos Salazar, interview with author, September 20, 1990. But it is equally evident that the two Pérez brothers, Elizardo and Raúl, shared ideas and experiences about this configuration. And, in fact, during his administration of Caiza D (a school located in the Department of Potosí), Raúl Pérez made important innovations, including the establishment of tiny primary schools in distant outlying villages that were placed under the aegis of the central ("mother") school, Caiza D. Carlos Salazar and Anita Pérez, Raúl's daughter, noted that it was Raúl Pérez who formalized the idea of the "núcleo" school district by trying to extend the jurisdiction of his own central boarding school into outlying Quechua communities.

85 Pérez, *Mensaje de la escuela indigenal de Warisata en el Día de las Américas* (the first document relating the social-economic character of the "Indian Program," from which was later extracted Pérez's paper on the "principles of the Peasant School"). It was presented at Bolivia's first national Congress of Indigenist Teachers in 1936. Excerpts are published in Pérez, *Warisata*, 168n2.

86 Pérez, *Warisata*, 108–9.

87 Carlos Salazar, interview with author, September 27, 1990.

88 Pérez, *Warisata*, 86–87.

89 Elizardo Pérez, "La doctrina pedagógica social del Indian," *La Calle*, August 24, 1937.

90 Pérez, *Warisata*, 86–87.

91 Pérez, *Warisata*, 87. Elizardo Pérez truly believed in the redemption of the "pure Aymara" as the nation's virtuous rural laborer. Unlike most other indigenista reformers, however, he turned pedagogical theories into innovative programs and practical action, by working collaboratively at the community level, at great personal risk.

92 Pérez, *Warisata*, 88.

93 In 1939, the boarding school had 180 pupils. The school never succeeded in enrolling many girls, however. Many families were resistant to the prospect of sending their girls off to board. On occasion, their mothers accompanied their own daughters to the boarding school, and simply staked out their living space in a corner of the school complex so they could be watchful mothers.

94 Warisata's normal section was not established until late in the decade, under the directorship of Elizardo's younger brother, Raúl Pérez. The first class of

fifteen *maestros normales titulados* graduated in 1939. The male *titulados* were required to enroll in the military to complete their obligatory two-year service. There they were to be assigned as literacy teachers for the other conscripts. See "La escuela Warisata y los primeros indigenistas," *La Noche*, October 19, 1939; Pérez, *Warisata*, 221.

95 The year 1937 was a peak time for Warisata's harvests, and the school hoped to triple its agro-industrial output once it acquired more lands. Optimistic about its productive prospects, Pérez ordered the school to increase its boarding school population to a hundred children (already fifty boarders were subsidized by the income from the school's harvest yields). He also urged the school to recruit twenty to thirty girls, including those orphaned by the Chaco War (*Warisata*, 189–91). The school's abundant agricultural yields was reported by several visitors, including the agricultural minister (under the "military socialist" president Germán Busch), who described the Warisata region as having turned into a rich "Altiplano valley" that had even surpassed the hacienda zone of Achacachi. See "La granja agrícola de Achacachi pasa a depender de Warisata," *El Debate*, March 30, 1939.

96 Carlos Salazar noted that many teachers spoke to their pupils in Aymara but did not pretend to formalize or teach Aymara as a written language. Others taught children the alphabet in Spanish, later translating some familiar Spanish words (for "cow," "sheep," "road," "house," etc.) into Aymara. Very few teachers read Aymara fluently, however. Carlos Salazar, interview with author, October 4, 1990.

97 The idea of "integral curriculum" grew out of the liberal reaction to the limited economistic view that mass education should promote the formation (through apprenticeship-styled training) of the laboring class. Educational reformers such as Horace Mann and John Dewey promoted a more integrated curriculum, in which humanistic values, "active" and community-oriented forms of learning, as well as democratic ideals were inculcated. See the abundant scholarship on the US movement of Progressive Education. Warisata's ideal curriculum was "integral" but clearly pitched to the value of "practical" skills and "useful" knowledge, adapted to the rural Bolivian environment.

98 One of the most accomplished students was Máximo Wañuco, who wrote copious Aymara poetry and often put it to song. His most famous composition, *Illampu*, became the school hymn (Pérez, *Warisata*, 229–31); see especially Carlos Salazar's public celebration of Warisata's other gifted students, such as Eusebio Karlo, who wrote for and edited the *Boletín de Warisata*, and Juan Poma Añawaya, who wrote "La historia de la escuela de Turrini" in *La Calle*, February 17, 1939, reprinted in Salazar's influential book, *Warisata mía*, 31.

99 John, *Bolivia's Radical Tradition*, 54–65. Those postwar leftists gravitated toward Trotskyism, either the militant vanguard party—the POR (Partido Obrero

Revolucionario)—or the more moderate PSOB (Partido Socialista Obrero de Bolivia). Many Warisata teachers became affiliates of the latter.

100 Salazar, *Gesta y fotografía*, photograph no. 44, caption (no pagination).

101 Salazar, *Gesta y fotografía*, photograph no. 44, caption (no pagination); see the reproduction of Illanes's murals in Salazar, *Gesta y fotografía*, photograph nos. 257–65.

102 Carlos Salazar, interview with author, September 20, 1990.

103 T. Claure, *Una escuela rural en Vacas*, 132–33.

104 Reyeros, *Caquiaviri* and "Caquiaviri"; Gotkowitz, *A Revolution for Our Rights*, 197, 213, 216.

105 Carlos Salazar, interview with author, September 20, 1990.

106 See Vaughn, *Cultural Politics in Revolution*; Rockwell, "Schools of the Revolution"; and the influential 1928 essay by the preeminent Mexican indigenista, Moisés Sáenz, *La educación rural en México*.

107 Carlos Salazar, interview with author, October 11, 1990. See also Vilchis Cedillo, "La escuela-ayllu de Warisata, Bolivia, y sus relaciones con México."

108 He remembered a horrible incident in 1938, when the conservative *Cristero* peasant movement had incinerated a contingent of government soldiers riding inside a wagon. Carlos Salazar, interview with author, October 11, 1990.

109 "We wanted to learn how they organized rural education, but the only thing we found there were dispersed schools without [pedagogic] programs or any sense of purpose, except perhaps one—to teach the revolution in political terms. That was the failure of successive [Mexican] states." For him, Mexico's rural education was too traditionalist, too bureaucratized, and itself too much of an instrument of state power. Carlos Salazar, interview with author, October 11, 1990.

110 Carlos Salazar, interview with author, October 11, 1990.

111 Salazar was invited by the Organization of American States to give conferences in Washington, New York, and Oklahoma on Bolivia's innovative *Educación indigenal*. He remembered that by the end of his tour, Bolivia was known in US government circles for "its tin and for Warisata." Carlos Salazar, interview with author, September 20, 1990.

112 And, as we shall see in chapter 4, he found himself plunged into the middle of a high-level debate over Bolivia's rural school reforms and the racial identity of the whole nation. For a sample of Salazar's extraordinary journalistic work at the time of his reentry into Bolivia, see "Las lecciones de México fijadas por el maestro indigenista, Carlos Salazar," *La Calle*, January 8, 1939; "Escuelas indigenales y rurales," *La Calle*, January 31, 1939; "La escuela rural mexicana y nuestros programas de educación indigenal," *La Noche*, February 2, 1939;

"El internado indígena mejicano y nuestros núcleos," *La Noche*, February 4, 1939; "La escuela indígenal mexicana," *La Noche*, February 9, 1939. In all these pieces, Salazar offers critical appraisals of the rural Mexican school system and then goes on to extol the virtues of Warisata's model of Indigenous integration and participation in the school, along with its pedagogical integration in what they now labeled "la escuela única."

113 "La obra de Subirats en Warisata," *La Noche*, March 15, 1940; Pérez, *Warisata*, 234–35; Salazar, *Gesta y fotografía*, part II, on "the role of the intellectual and artist in Warisata" in photographs. In addition to the traffic in radical educators, activists, and artists, a stream of local political pilgrims, including groups of university students and trade unionists, and groups of Indigenous delegations hailing from distant communities and other rural schools, streamed into Warisata on special occasions.

114 Fernando Loaíza, "Declaraciones del profesor Sr. Frank Tannenbaum sobre tópicos indigenistas," *El Diario*, August 20, 1938; and another version of the interview in *El Diario*, August 29, 1938, which is partially reprinted in Pérez, *Warisata*, 242–43. See Fernando Loaíza, "'No se puede hacer patria en Bolivia sin el Indio,' dice Frank Tannenbaum," *La Nación*, August 15, 1939.

115 It is telling that in August 1939 Tannenbaum presented a carbon copy of the letter to Elizardo Pérez, who desperately needed to shore up the legitimacy of Warisata in the face of gathering criticism and attacks on the school itself.

116 For the delegation's report, see Velasco, *La escuela indigenal de Warisata*.

117 Velasco, *La escuela indigenal de Warisata*, i–iii.

118 Velasco, *La escuela indigenal de Warisata*.

119 Marof, *La tragedia del altiplano*, 42–43.

120 Carlos Salazar, interviews with author, September 12 and 20, 1990.

121 "Supreme Decree of August 19, 1936," in Montero Justiniano and Villegas, *Nuevo digesto de legislación educacional*, 160–63.

122 Pérez, *Warisata*, 178–81.

123 The 250 recruits fell far short of the ministry's goal to mobilize and train one thousand rural teachers. The Sociedad Rural Boliviana mocked the government effort to impose "universal obligatory" education in the rural areas. It estimated that the Department of La Paz alone needed eight thousand trained rural normal graduates to staff rural schools on some of the department's seven thousand or so haciendas. See Republic of Bolivia, Ministerio de Educación 1937, no. 5; SRB to Ministerio de Educación y Asuntos Campesinjos, August 2, 1937.

124 Pérez, *Warisata*, 182–83.

125 Pérez, *Mensaje de la escuela indigenal de Warisata en el Día de las Américas*.

126 Gotkowitz, *A Revolution for Our Rights*, 127.

127 Carlos Salazar, interview with author, September 20, 1990.

4. Whose Indian School?

1 Klein, *Parties and Political Change in Bolivia*, 323.

2 Certainly, in standard nationalist historiography, the topic of Indigenous schooling is almost an afterthought, if it is mentioned at all. Notable exceptions include Sangines Uriarte, *Educación rural y desarrollo en Bolivia*; the many studies of Roberto Choque Canqui, including his book (coauthored with Cristina Quisbert Quispe) *Educación indigenal en Bolivia*; Ari, *Earth Politics*; Cajías, *Continuidades y rupturas*; Brienen, "The Clamor for Schools"; and Larson, "Capturing Indian Bodies, Hearths, and Minds."

3 Much official documentation, including CNE reports, various correspondence, and petitions for rural communities, can be found in the ALP. Vocalía indio y rural: oficios recibidos [and] procesos between the years 1942 and 1944.

4 See, for example, Antezana Ergueta, *La revolución campesina en Bolivia*; Calderón and Dandler, *Bolivia*; Choque Canqui, *Historia de una lucha desigual*; Dandler and Torrico, "From the National Indian Congress to the Ayopaya Rebellion"; Gotkowitz, *A Revolution for Our Rights*; and Kohl, *Indigenous Struggle and the Bolivian National Revolution*.

5 The team was composed of two conservatives (Enrique Finot, Bolivia's ambassador to Mexico and the normal teacher we met in chapter 1, and Antonio Díaz Villamil, vice president of the Consejo Nacional de Educación, both serving under the conservative new president, Col. Enrique Peñaranda); two leftist intellectuals (the writer Alipio Valencia and the lawyer Eduardo Arze Loureiro); and Bolivia's most prominent indigenista educator, Elizardo Pérez, and his wife and former teacher in Warisata, Jaél Oropeza de Pérez.

6 One tangible outcome of the conference was the creation of the Instituto Indigenista Interamericano (III). It was a new international organ based in Mexico and designed to promote indigenista scholarship, networking, and advocacy under the Inter-American system.

7 Finot, in the first cohort of Sucre's normal school graduates, was an early critic of President Monte's liberal education reforms. (See chap. 1.)

8 Pérez, *Warisata*, 250.

9 Dawson, *Indian and Nation in Revolutionary Mexico*, 83.

10 Pérez, *Warisata*, 253.

11 A rough internal report, or *informe*, published by the CNE in April 1940 was titled *El estado actual de la educación indigenal en Bolivia: Informe del Vice-Presidente del Consejo Nacional* (hereafter cited as CNE, *El estado actual*

de la educación indigenal en Bolivia) to distinguish it from "the definitive" CNE report with a similar title, *El estado de la educación indigenal en el país*. Significantly, a copy of the informe is located in the archive of the Instituto Indigenista Interamericano (Mexico City) among the papers of the Primer Congreso Indigenista Internacional. The document's location in that archive supports Pérez's claim that his enemies were circulating a "slanderous report" during the congressional sessions. I will return to these important government reports later in this chapter to examine the texts, their circumstances, and their significance.

12 Two men took charge of that task. One was Dr. Vicente Donoso Torres (a conservative normal school graduate who was briefly in charge of Umala, one of Bolivia's first rural normal schools), newly appointed as head (or *vocal*) of Bolivia's primary, normal, and rural Indigenous schools. Eventually, Donoso assumed control of the CNE and launched an administrative overhaul of the rural education program. The other appointee was Rafael Reyeros, a moderate socialist, strident critic of indigenismo, and great admirer of Mexican social reformism. He was put in charge of a new Bureau of Asuntos Campesinos, which he hoped would be the launching pad for a Mexican-inspired program of "peasant action brigades."

13 In late 1939, under the new Quintanilla regime, a government order forbade all public employees to engage in any kind of political action. The CNE used it to censure or punish preceptors and teachers for meddling in politics. "Fórmula denuncia contra los preceptores," March 19, 1942, ALP-CNE, V; Carta de Donoso Torres al Vocal de Educación Rural, January 29, 1942, ALP-CNE, V. See also Pérez, *Warisata*, 280.

14 Pérez, *Warisata*, 279.

15 The letter, dated January 24, 1940, was addressed to Bolivia's "Provisional President of the Republic, Quintanilla" and signed by twenty prominent intellectuals, including Felix Eguino Zaballa, Raúl Botelho Gonsálvez, Yolanda Bedregal, Gustavo Adolfo Navarro, Victor Paz Estenssoro, and Eduardo Arze Loureiro. They spoke in the name of "the writers and professionals who protest the cancellation of the DGEI" by the new regime. An excerpt of the letter is published in Pérez, *Warisata*, 278–79.

16 Letter to Minister of Education from the Confederación Sindical de Trabajadores de Bolivia, no. 297, January 22, 1940, ANB-P, C.

17 *La Noche* editors demanded to know how "an enlightened logic, educated mentality, patriotic spirit [could] deny the reality of *una obra* [Indigenal education] like this one; how it could not but gain the admiration, pride and gratitude of all Bolivian hearts. Only the hatred of races could explain the suicidal motive behind the [government's] destruction of [Indigenal education]." See "La obra de educación indigenal es el más vigoroso esfuerzo civilizador," *La Noche*, February 1, 1940.

18 Arguedas, the consummate pessimist of early twentieth-century tutelary race-thinking, presented his racial diagnosis of social illness in Bolivia in his 1909 (and recently reedited) book, *Pueblo enfermo*. The elderly Arguedas was still a prominent political and intellectual figure around 1940.

19 Of course, mobilizing "evidence" after the fact in order to legitimize a violent act of conquest or colonization that went against Spanish law or protocol was commonplace in colonial Spanish America. A famous incident occurred under Church authority in the Yucatán Peninsula in the early 1560s, when the zealous Franciscan friar, Diego de Landa, had to mobilize a mountain of evidence of idolatry among his native charges to prove to his superiors that his brutal Inquisition against "the heretics" had been necessary and justified. A classic account of this ex post facto punitive tactic is examined in Clendinnen's *Ambivalent Conquests*.

20 Donoso claimed that the field reports filled five thick folders, but some of them were excerpted and published in two government reports published in 1940 on the state of Indigenous education: CNE, *El estado actual de la educación indigenal en Bolivia*; and a slightly later version, *El estado de la educación indigenal en el país*. Both versions contain appendices and inserts of field reports and letters, generated by the CNE, to provide documentary evidence of (what the government declared was) the "disastrous state" of Indigenous education.

21 Those four reports were included in CNE, *El estado de la educación indigenal en el país*, 54–59, 62–69; and CNE, *El estado actual de la educación indigenal en Bolivia*, 12–20.

22 CNE, *El estado actual de la educación indigenal en Bolivia*, 60–61.

23 Carlos Salazar, interview with author, September 20, 1990.

24 "En 10 años de vida la Escuela Huarizata [sic] graduó 1 normalista," *La Noche*, March 10, 1940. The blatant inaccuracy of this claim was amended in Vicente Donoso's report, which slammed Warisata for producing only "fourteen semi-literate graduates in a ridiculous folkloric ceremony!" CNE, *El estado actual de la educación indigenal en Bolivia*, 28.

25 "El País ha vivido por diez años engañado con el 'bluff' de la educación indigenal," *La Noche*, June 4, 1940.

26 CNE, *El estado actual de la educación indigenal en Bolivia*.

27 Anonymous, "Prólogo," in CNE, *El estado actual de la educación indigenal en Bolivia*, 3.

28 Anonymous, "Prólogo," in CNE, *El estado actual de la educación indigenal en Bolivia*, 3–7.

29 Anonymous, "Prólogo," in CNE, *El estado actual de la educación indigenal en Bolivia*, 14, 16.

30 CNE, *El estado actual de la educación indigenal en Bolivia*, 49–50.

31 All but one of the judges were prominent critics of Indigenal education: Rafael Reyeros (president of the tribunal), V. Fernández, Arturo Posnasky, Alfonso Claros, Walberto Llanos, and Max Bairon.

32 As mentioned earlier, *La Calle* and other leftist outlets released messages of solidarity with Elizardo Pérez, who was in Mexico getting ready to attend the International Indigenista Congress in Pátzcuaro: "Responde al Vocal de primaria Doctor Donoso Torres el Jefe del Departamento Indigenal Señor Raúl Pérez," *Crónica*, April 2, 1940; "Intelectuales Bolivianos envían a Elizardo Pérez un mensaje de solidaridad," *La Calle*, April 2, 1940.

33 CNE, *El estado de la educación indigenal en el país*, 3–4.

34 For a summary of the tribunal report, see Sangines Uriarte, *Educación rural y desarrollo en Bolivia*, 57–63. See also Pérez, *Warisata*, 282–84.

35 At an earlier moment, the problem of Indian labor—and whether to categorize it as voluntary or conscripted labor, and whether school construction should be funded by the state or through communal donations of labor and supplies, emerged as a legitimate focus of debate in the mid-1930s, sharpening the distinction between Pérez's pluralist-Indianist faction (which argued in favor of mobilizing communal work parties as the very essence of the ayllu-school) and Claure, Reyeros, and Guillén Pinto, who advocated for a state-sponsored integrationist program, designed to train an Indian workforce (though not necessarily wage laborers). Toribio Claure, for example, promoted President Toro's 1936–37 postwar policy of conscript Indian labor. The policy forced rural men accused of military desertion to perform a year of gang labor building rural schools, roads, and other public works in exchange for an official pardon and identity card. See Claure, *Una escuela rural en Vacas*.

36 See, for example, Pérez's published letter of protest, sent to the minister of education: "Grave recusación a los enemigos," *Inti*, July 20, 1940, and "El crímen Americano es destruir escuelas de Indios," *La Razón*, July 22, 1940. Two months later, Pérez delivered a major university address elaborating his ideas about Indigenal education. The September 24, 1940, conference paper was later published, as an appendix, in Pérez, *Warisata*, 333–49.

37 "Intelectualidad boliviana goza en México del aprecio de la crítica," interview with a reporter from *La Calle*, July 23, 1940.

38 "Intelectualidad boliviana goza en México del aprecio de la crítica."

39 By then, Pérez was already organizing his personal archive and planning to write a redemptive memoir so that the truth about his lifework in Indigenal education would be brought to light. *Warisata* was Pérez's magnum opus. Published in 1962 (and republished with a new introduction by Carlos Salazar

40 See the rapid series of exchanges in *La Razón*: "Recusación de Comisiones," July 20, 1940; "El crimen Americano destruir escuelas de Indios," July 22, 1940; "Debate sobre educación indígena," July 24, 1940.

41 "Ante el Nuevo Tribunal asumirá E. Pérez la Defensa de su obra," *La Calle*, September 4, 1940. The judges were Vicente Mendoz López, Roberto Zapata, and Col. José Capriles, all admirers of Pérez and his work.

42 Long excerpts of the tribunal's findings appear in Pérez's book *Warisata*, 286–89. Indeed, Pérez relied heavily on this document in his memoir to buttress his claims and secure an honorable legacy in Bolivian historical memory. See also "Veredicto del Jurado Revisor de Educación Indigenal," *La Calle*, October 25, 1940.

43 "Intelectualidad boliviana goza en México del aprecio de la crítica," *La Calle*, July 23, 1940.

44 Salazar, *Warisata mía*, 26.

45 Pérez, *Warisata*, 289–90.

46 Tomasa Siñani de Willka, quoted in Pérez, *Warisata*, 289–90. In 1990, in her home in La Paz, Tomasa de Siñani recounted the circumstances of her father's death in a tearful interview.

47 See Pérez, *Warisata*, 289–90; Siñani de Willka, "Breve biografía de Avelino Siñani"; and Salazar, *Warisata mía*.

48 In April 1947, some thirty amautas from communities surrounding Warisata sent a petition to the minister of education, Armando Alba. Reprinted in Pérez, *Warisata*, 291.

49 CNE, *El estado de la educación indigenal en el país*, 131–32.

50 CNE, *El estado de la educación indigenal en el país*, 132.

51 Carta del Ministerio de Educación al Prefecto, 1942, ALP-CNE, V. This denunciation, submitted by two Indigenous authors, was transcribed in full in the minister's letter to the prefecto.

52 Carta del profesor de agricultura de Warisata, April 9, 1944, ALP-CNE, V. Other letters were sent by a group of amautas, asking for seeds and tools, and from the newly appointed director, Lino Fuentes. Carta del director Lino Fuentes al Sr. Vocal, January 21, 1944, ALP-CNE, V.

53 Carta de Eufrasio Ibañez al Sr. Vocal, June 22, 1944, ALP-CNE, V.

54 Informe respecto a las escuelas seccionales de Warisata, November 28, 1944, ALP-CNE, V.

55 CNE, *El estado de la educación indigenal en el país*, 23–29, 50–66.

56　Caiza became a source of ideological rancor between two indigenista schools of thought, embodied by Raúl Pérez (the Indianist school director) and Toribio Claure (the assimilationist director). Internal disputes, frequent staff turnover, lack of funding, and tensions between the town and surrounding Indigenous villages added to its organizational troubles. Carlos Salazar took over directorship in 1940 and produced one of the mandatory evaluations that went into the CNE's 1940 damning report on the decay of Indigenal education. See CNE, *El estado de la educación indigenal en el país*, 23–29, 50ff.

57　The network of sectional schools included Caltapi, Questuchi, Chajnacaya, Pancochi, Calila, Alckatuyo, Nohata, Tuctapari, and Sepoltoras.

58　CNE, *El estado de la educación indigenal en el país*, 65.

59　CNE, *El estado de la educación indigenal en el país*, 64.

60　CNE, *El estado de la educación indigenal en el país*.

61　Salazar went on to become Bolivia's indefatigable "memory entrepreneur" for Warisata and a culture warrior fighting for Indigenous justice and the right to education over the next few decades.

62　Salazar, "Warisata mía" (1943), in the 1997 compilation of essays titled *Warisata mía*, 17.

63　Juan Añawaya Poma al Sr. Vocal, September 22, 1944, ALP-CNE, V; Salazar, *Gesta y fotografía*, legend to photograph no. 47 (no page number).

64　Juan Añawaya Poma al Sr. Vocal, September 22, 1944.

65　Salazar was drawn to the writings and activism of Marof, and eventually helped form the Partido Socialista Obrero de Bolivia. Sandor John notes that, while small in comparison to the more militant Trotskyist Partido Obrero Revolucionario, the party had a foothold in the labor movement, gained access to congressional seats, and put out the newspaper *La Batalla*, for which Salazar often wrote. The larger Trotskyist party of POR became a major force within the teachers union in later years. See John, *Bolivia's Radical Tradition*, 63–67.

66　This interpretive rendering of Salazar's "idéological dilemma" is my own. It derives from the series of oral interviews and conversations we held, as well as from Salazar's prodigious writings and photographic work. I am also grateful to Cecilia Salazar de la Torre for sharing her own ideas, writings, and research on Warisata.

67　Otero, *Una política educacional*; Donoso, *Filosofía de la educación boliviana*, 179.

68　Otero, *Una política educacional*, 12.

69　Bellas Artes, y Asuntos Indigenas, Discurso del Ministro de Educación, August 6, 1940, ALP-P, C, ME.

70 This evolutionist stance belonged to the diplomat and educator Max Bairon. Carta del Max Bairon al Jefe del Dept. de Antropología, Mexico, September 30, 1941, ALP-CNE, V.

71 CNE, *El estado de la educación indigenal en el país*, 4.

72 CNE, *El estado de la educación indigenal en el país*, 137.

73 CNE, *El estado actual de la educación indigenal en Bolivia*, 15.

74 Otero, *Una política educacional*, 26.

75 CNE, *El estado actual de la educación indigenal en Bolivia*, 105.

76 Donoso, *Filosofía de la educación boliviana*, 32 (emphasis added).

77 Donoso, *Filosofía de la educación boliviana*, 181 (emphasis added).

78 Donoso, *Filosofía de la educación boliviana*, 180.

79 See Stepan, "The Hour of Eugenics." As we will see in chapter 6, Donoso Torres was deeply involved in North American aid programs of cultural hygiene and rural education that entered Bolivia in the early to mid-1940s.

80 Donoso, *Filosofía de la educación boliviana*, 181. As it turned out, the educators' immediate challenge was in the mundane bureaucratic realm of policy and administration. The CNE's Vocalía de Educación Rural y Indígena (variously named) became the main vehicle for this centralizing effort between 1940 and 1944. Ideally, the primary school was to represent the terminal point in the CNE's newly established bureaucratic chain of command. Rural school directors were vested with the authority to intervene in the civil life of Indigenous communities, effectively marginalizing the councils of amautas that had exercised authority during the early communitarian phase of nuclear schooling. The CNE generated mountains of paperwork (school inventories, inspection reports, directors' reports, curricular plans, and correspondence of all kinds)—tangible testimony to the state's frenzied effort to impose a top-down hierarchy of administrators and teachers and to standardize the national curriculum for Indigenous children.

81 Donoso, *Filosofía de la educación boliviana*, 176.

82 Like Bolivia's early twentieth-century race thinkers, Donoso was influenced by Spencerian notions of human evolution, but he also put great faith in the potential of the state's disciplinary interventions to turn the trajectory of racial decline, or stagnation, into cultural progress.

83 Donoso, *Filosofía de la educación boliviana*, 176.

84 Donoso, *Filosofía de la educación boliviana*, 177.

85 Donoso, *Filosofía de la educación boliviana*, 176; Otero, *Una política educacional*, 17–18.

86 Reyeros, *Caquiaviri*, 265, 276.

87 The 1940s also saw the flowering of mestizaje as a bio-cultural metaphor of nationalist unity in the literary work of postwar bohemian and leftist writers and activists. Illustrative is Carlos Medinaceli's costumbrista novel *La Chaskañawi: Novelas de costumbres bolivianas*, which celebrated (and sexualized) "la chola" as a gendered symbol of Bolivia's authentic national culture. According to Ximena Soruco, Medinaceli, a young writer and activist from Cochabamba, was the "only Bolivian novelist that fashioned la chola as symbol of the nation without requiring her racial assimilation" (*La ciudad de los cholos*, 161).

88 On the active cultural power of Western imperialism to silence and marginalize subaltern history, ideas, and agency, see Trouillot, *Silencing the Past*.

5. Instigators of New Ideas

1 Jáuregui's provocative title, "Reflexiones sobre la cuestión indígena: Sublevaciones y levantamientos," set the panicky tone for his sociological "reflections." He furnished a synoptic historical framework for understanding the most recent events in 1946 and 1947, casting them as "the final chapter of this long tragedy of the Bolivian Indian" (530). He called for a combined state strategy of repression and reform.

2 Hylton and Thomson, *Revolutionary Horizons*, 77. The 1938 Constitutional Convention represents a political benchmark of this postwar era of reformism. There, progressive, populist, and nationalist delegates had negotiated a new charter for the nation. Key subjects of debate included the "Agrarian Question," universal rights to education and citizenship, and thus the very boundaries of political inclusion/exclusion in this Indigenous-majority nation. See Gotkowitz, *A Revolution for Our Rights*, chap. 4.

3 *La Calle* published a series of editorial pieces calling for the "abolition" of the institution, and a few senators tried to legislate it out of existence. See, for example, "Proyecto en el senado para abolir el pongueaje," August 19, 1942, and "La abolición del pongueaje y otras gabelas extorsivas," August 22, 1942.

4 Mariátegui, *Seven Interpretive Essays on Peruvian Reality*, 22, 28 (emphasis added).

5 Interpretive ideas in this chapter draw from Antonio Gramsci's work on the interplay between collective mobilization and popular education, on the one hand, and the radical notion of pedagogy, theorized and practiced by the Brazilian educator Paulo Freire in the late 1960s and 1970s, on the other. For an insightful analysis of the politics of education in the work of both Gramsci and Freire, see Coben, *Radical Heroes*. For a broad discussion of popular

education in Latin America, see Puiggrós, *La educación popular en América Latina* and *Imperialismo y educación en América Latina*.

6   Rufino Willka et al. to Sr. Ministro de Educación y Asuntos Indígenas, November 26, 1941, "Pide se ordene los nombramientos... de los alcaldes mayores y menores para su colaboración para sus funciones en las escuelas Yndígenas," ALP-P, E (hereafter cited as "Pide se ordene los nombramientos"; the petition's auxiliary documentation is cited as "Testimonio").

7   "Testimonio," ff. 1–1v.

8   Choque Canqui and Quisbert Quispe, *Educación indigenal en Bolivia*, 196–97.

9   Quoted in Condori Chura and Ticona Alejo, *El escribano de los caciques apoderados*, 102.

10 Condori Chura and Ticona Alejo, *El escribano de los caciques apoderados*, and "Piden se me devuelva los obrados por telegráficamente que indica," ANB-P, ca. July 26, 1933. See Choque Canqui and Quisbert Quispe, *Educación indigenal en Bolivia*, 287–90.

11 Condori Chura and Ticona Alejo, *El escribano de los caciques apoderados*, 289.

12 The 1938 Constitution ratified the jurisdiction of "the Indian community" but did not recognize its right to elect its own alcaldes, nor did it grant territorial rights or accede to the long-standing demands of comunario authorities for a legal review of original colonial title deeds or the remapping of ayllu territorial claims. In short, this constitutional clause was symbolic, at best. See Gotkowitz, *A Revolution for Our Rights*, 152.

13 "Testimonio," ff. 3, 4v.

14 "Pide se ordene los nombramientos," f. 13v.

15 The institution of the *cabildo comunal* traces its lineage back to early colonial times, when Viceroy Francisco de Toledo mandated the establishment of local governing organs, based loosely on the peninsular model, as a site of intercultural mediation and indirect rule under a heavy apparatus of colonial dominance and extraction. As historians have shown, that colonial institution fragmented and devolved into an Andean-colonial form of governance, with its variant mixes of participatory and tributary norms (including the annual election of local-level Indian authorities to perform their "service turns" to the community as they moved up the ritual-political ladder of hierarchy and prestige). See Thomson, *We Alone Will Rule*, 45–46; Abercrombie, *Pathways of Memory and Power*; and Fernández, *La ley del ayllu*.

16 "Testimonio," ff. 2–2v.

17 "Testimonio," f. 1v. Under Viceroy Toledo, colonial law imposed strict requirements to encourage the dissemination of royal ordinances through written and oral channels of communication throughout the Indian repartimientos of the viceroyalty.

18 "Testimonio," ff. 7v–8.

19 Indeed, by the early 1940s, evangelical Protestantism was running rampant across the Altiplano, and Omasuyos had become ground zero in the contest for native believers. The order of the Seventh-Day Adventists, alone, had established some fifty Indigenous schools in highland Bolivia, and the Methodists were not far behind them by the 1940s. On the other hand, Catholic missionary schools in Indigenous areas had much deeper roots in rural Bolivia, especially in northern Potosí. Father José Zampa, a pioneer in teaching literacy and scriptures to Indians in the Church's Escuelas de Cristo, had been active since Bolivia's first ambulatory schools were established in the 1910s and 1920s. By 1928, the Escuelas de Cristo numbered 120 across all four provinces of Potosí. Much later, in the 1940s, the Escuelas de Cristo assumed control of various núcleos escolares in Potosí, including Caiza (often called Caiza D), when neither the Bolivian government nor the US-Bolivian "cooperative" school program (SCIDE) was able to administer those schools. Meanwhile, the Catholic Church intensified its charitable work under the National Pro-Indian Crusade (Cruzada Nacional Pro-Indio), founded in 1926. On the growth of Protestant missionary schools in rural Bolivia, particularly La Paz, see Choque Canqui and Quisbert Quispe, *Educación indigenal en Bolivia*, 140–41.

20 Donoso *Filosofía de la educación boliviana*, 105–9. Under President Peñaranda, the Supreme Decree of January 10, 1942, reintroduced religious instruction into the public school curriculum.

21 "Testimonio," ff. 10v–11. Elements of the Catholic establishment had a long history of involvement in rural schooling, not only in their own parish schools but also in a few collaborative efforts with Indigenous authorities. Most notably, church authorities forged a tenuous alliance with Santos Marka T'ula and Eduardo Nina Quispe in 1928 and 1929, when they founded a rudimentary organization to aid the caciques' rural school efforts. An improvised mutual aid society, the Centro Católico de Aborígenes Bartolomé de las Casas aided Indigenous authorities seeking justice, lands, and schools. Soria Choque, "Los caciques-apoderados y la lucha por la escuela," 66–67.

22 "Testimonio," ff. 2, 8, 10–10v.

23 "Testimonio," ff. 10v–11.

24 See Ari's *Earth Politics*, which establishes the historical context and then profiles the prominent activist-teachers, Quechua- and Aymara-speaking men and women who associated with the *alcaldes mayores particulares*.

25 Oral interview with Lucas Miranda Mamani, talking about his father, the alcalde mayor and teacher Toribio Miranda. Quotation in Conde, "Lucas Miranda Mamani," 116–17.

26   Ari, *Earth Politics*, 68.

27   Ari, *Earth Politics*, 70, 73–77; Conde, "Lucas Miranda Mamani"; Gotkowitz, *A Revolution for Our Rights*, 244–45.

28   Ari, *Earth Politics*, 99.

29   Quoted in Ari, *Earth Politics*, 108. This Quechua code of ethics was invoked to distinguish the moral integrity and self-governing ethos of Andean society from the debased violence and corruption of Western colonialism. Reclaiming the utopian past, or invoking a moral "time before," was a common discursive tool used by Indigenous people to contest the racial project of domination or advance decolonizing proposals. On the politics of moral memory, see Rivera, *"Oprimidos pero no vencidos"* (1986); Hylton et al., *Ya es otro tiempo el presente*; and J. Sanjinés, *Embers of the Past*.

30   Neither the cacique movement nor the network of alcaldes mayores disappeared altogether, as we will see in chapter 7. But, arguably, they were swept into the larger historical currents of peasant mobilization and agrarian conflict that escalated during the mid-1940s.

31   *Dirigente*, a hispanization of the Italian word *dirigenti*, referred to vanguard political leaders, often union or party leaders, who often were self-educated activists and "organic intellectuals." See Gramsci, *Selections from the Prison Notebooks*, 5.

32   See Hobsbawm, *Primitive Rebels*, 83–84. He studies a subset of rural organizers loosely aligned with anarcho-syndicalism in Andalusia.

33   Jáuregui, "Reflexiones sobre la cuestión indígena," 529.

34   Ranaboldo, *El camino perdido*. The kallawaya were known for their specialized knowledge and skills as bodily and spiritual healers, and some of the leading kallawaya doctors, such as Antonio Alvarez Mamani's father, traveled and practiced medicine in places far beyond Bolivia. Although Antonio was born into this specialized guild and enjoyed the status of the kallawaya in the eyes of many peasants, he pursued a career as a political organizer and teacher.

His life story, as told to Claudia Ranaboldo, appears in narrative form, organized around themes and episodes in his life, spanning his early years of apprenticeship with his father to his rise as a nationwide peasant leader, his ambivalent alliance with the MNR, and his postrevolutionary retreat from political work when he returned to his roots and worked with Indigenous peasants to build a modern rural cooperative in Oruro. This extraordinary text is layered: it supplements Alvarez's oral testimony with editorial side comments and context, and also provides relevant documents, mostly leaflets and newspapers that comment on, or complement, Alvarez Mamani's testimony. Although I use the conventional mode of citing Ranaboldo's name as the work's editor and publisher, this book was truly authored by Alvarez

Mamani, whose life story winds through this extraordinary text. The book is enriched with newspaper articles and other documents that Alvarez gave to his interlocutor, many of which she included in the book.

35 Ranaboldo, *El camino perdido*, 61–66; Blanco, *Antonio Alvarez Mamani*, 3–4. Alvarez later made a point of saying that, for all the services he had rendered Villarroel during the war years, the colonel never reciprocated those favors with patronage—the offer of a political post in his government, for example. Alvarez was enlisted, however, to help the Villarroel regime organize the government-sponsored 1945 National Indian Congress—that is, until he became suspect because of his independence and growing base of peasant support.

36 Ranaboldo, *El camino perdido*, 72.

37 Gordillo, "Modernity, Politics, and Identity," 249. Alvarez Mamani (or Mamani Alvarez) was fluent in Quechua, Aymara, and Spanish, and his status and skills helped open channels into rural communities wherever he worked. He was intensely engaged in rural organizing in the region of Ayopaya, but may have come up against a more entrenched culture of smallholding and sindicalismo in the Cliza region of Cochabamba. On that point, Gordillo notes that Alvarez never had much success with valley peasants. See also Ranaboldo, *El camino perdido*, 249.

38 Ranaboldo, *El camino perdido*, 78–79.

39 Ranaboldo, *El camino perdido*, 79.

40 Ranaboldo, *El camino perdido*, 79. See also Dandler and Torrico, "From the National Indian Congress to the Ayopaya Rebellion," 342–44; and Gotkowitz, *A Revolution for Our Rights*, chap. 8.

41 Ranaboldo, *El camino perdido*, 79.

42 Ranaboldo, *El camino perdido*, 88.

43 Ranaboldo, *El camino perdido*, 88.

44 The chasqui (Quechua for "messenger") was a runner who served the Incas by transmitting vital information, verbally and through the quipus, along thousands of miles of stone roads across the sprawling empire of Tawantinsuyu. Under Spanish colonial rule, the chasqui became a more organic messenger, plying the roads between villages, and between country and city, in service of the caciques or other Indian authorities. The colonial state created its own official system of mail carriers, by imposing this rotative labor service on its tributary villages. As late as the 1940s, provincial authorities still made highland communities in Potosí and La Paz send men to "take their turn" staffing the inns (tambos) and carrying the mail in their provinces.

45 Ranaboldo, *El camino perdido*, 81–82. The plan turned into a costly operation, since chasquis' travels and food had to be subsidized, a cost that Alvarez Mamani had to sustain with the savings from his own small inheritance. He was

frequently accused by political officials of imposing fees (*ramas*) on Indian peasants, something he vehemently denied.

46 Lefebvre, *The Great Fear*, 96, cited and quoted in Guha, *Elementary Aspects of Peasant Insurgency in Colonial India*, 248. My discussion is also inspired by Hahn, *A Nation under Our Feet* (chap. 4), for his analysis of the informal networks and practices that freed Black communities established in rural North America before abolition and the Civil War; and Tarrow's *Power in Movement*, for his suggestive analysis of horizontal networking through subaltern modes of "association and print" in the building of early modern social movements in Europe and elsewhere.

47 Guha, *Elementary Aspects of Peasant Insurgency in Colonial India*, 247.

48 On the late eighteenth century, see Serulnikov, *Subverting Colonial Authority*; Thomson, *We Alone Will Rule*; and Penry, *The People Are King*.

49 Bromley Smith, "Economic Background Report," September 7, 1942, box 48, RG 166, NARA.

50 Adam to US Secretary of State, March 1, 1945, box 824, RG 59, NARA.

51 Adam to US Secretary of State, March 1, 1945.

52 Thurston to US Secretary of State, May 5, 1945, box 824, RG 59, NARA.

53 Thurston to US Secretary of State, May 3, 1945, box 824, RG 59, NARA.

54 For a detailed discussion of the original Indigenous Committee, its social makeup, political priorities, meeting agenda, and relations with Villarroel in the lead-up to the (postponed) Indian Congress of May 1945, see Gotkowitz, *A Revolution for Our Rights*, 197–212; Dandler and Torrico, "From the National Indian Congress to the Ayopaya Rebellion."

55 Thurston to US Secretary of State, May 3, 1945.

56 Thurston to US Secretary of State, May 3, 1945, f. 2.

57 Thurston to US Secretary of State, May 3, 1945, f. 2. Morales was head of the Ministry of Government and, representing the government, a leading member of the congressional planning committee.

58 On the role of *mensajeros indígenas* in early twentieth-century Peru, see especially Alvaréz Calderón Gerbolini, *En búsqueda de la ciudadanía indígena*, chap. 2.

59 Thurston to US Secretary of State, May 3, 1945.

60 Thurston to US Secretary of State, May 3, 1945.

61 Dandler and Torrico, "From the National Indian Congress to the Ayopaya Rebellion," 339–48; Gotkowitz, *A Revolution for Our Rights*, 206–8.

62 See Ari, *Earth Politics*, chap. 5, on the organizing role that Melitón Gallardo, a prominent alcalde mayor, had in mobilizing Quechua and Aymara interest and participation in the 1942 congress.

63 Antezana Ergueta, *La revolución campesina en Bolivia*, 46–47; Gotkowitz, *A Revolution for Our Rights*, 161.

64 Very little has yet been written about the regional congresses. Most attention has focused on the May 1945 National Indigenous Congress, because it was the first nationwide assembly of Indians. As such, it generated much publicity. More importantly, the NIC was eventually appropriated by the Villarroel regime and transformed into an official, government-sponsored event. On the regional and national congresses, see Antezana and Romero, *Historia de los sindicatos campesinos*; Antezana Ergueta, *La revolución campesina en Bolivia*; Dandler and Torrico, "From the National Indian Congress to the Ayopaya Rebellion"; Shesko, "Hijos del Inca y de la patria"; and Gotkowitz, *A Revolution for Our Rights*, chap. 7. By comparison, Mexico's "regional" congresses organized in the Cárdenas era were more protected (if not manipulated) by Mexico's postrevolutionary corporatist regime. See Dawson, *Indian and Nation in Revolutionary Mexico*, chap. 4.

65 Gotkowitz, *A Revolution for Our Rights*, 161.

66 Klein, *A Concise History of Bolivia*, 202, and *Parties and Political Change in Bolivia*, 369–82; Dunkerley, *Rebellion in the Veins*, 32–33.

67 Gotkowitz, *A Revolution for Our Rights*, 199.

68 Gotkowitz, *A Revolution for Our Rights*, 201.

69 Gotkowitz, *A Revolution for Our Rights*, 207. For Gotkowitz's extended discussion of the CIB's work leading up to the official Indian Congress, see 197–212. See also Choque Canqui, *Historia de una lucha desigual*, 110–11; and Dandler and Torrico, "From the National Indian Congress to the Ayopaya Rebellion," 344–45.

70 Quoted in Gotkowitz, *A Revolution for Our Rights*, 207. See also Soliz, *Fields of Revolution*, chaps. 2 and 3.

71 Dandler and Torrico, "From the National Indian Congress to the Ayopaya Rebellion," 345.

72 "Manifiesto del Delegado General por el Departamento de La Paz al Primer Congreso Indigenal de Bolivia," March 1945, in Ranaboldo, *El camino perdido*, 98–101.

73 See Tarrow, *Power in Movement*, 50–52.

74 "Sugieren que se suspenda el anunciado congreso indígena," *El Diario*, February 5, 1945. Anxious about a recurrence of the 1942 peasant strikes, the landowner association of Oruro (Sociedad Rural de Oruro) pressured the state to crack down on any and all signs of agrarian unrest. Provincial authorities, in turn, were urged to arrest all "transients" traveling without government authorization. See Antezana and Romero, *Historia de los sindicatos campesinos*, 89–90.

75 "Propaganda sin Sentido," *La Calle*, February 4, 1945 (emphasis added).

76 Thurston to US Secretary of State, February 15, 1945, box 824, RG 59, NARA; "Sugieren que se suspenda el anunciado congreso indígena," *El Diario*, February 5, 1945; "Se atienden las reclamaciones de los indígenas que visitan la ciudad," *La Razón*, February 1, 1945; "Extraña sensación puso la presencia de multitud de Indios en La Paz," *Ultima Hora*, February 3, 1945.

77 Dandler and Torrico, "From the National Indian Congress to the Ayopaya Rebellion," 349.

78 Ranaboldo, *El camino perdido*, 104.

79 A young Aymara man, Francisco Chipana Ramos, was appointed by the government as president of the National Indian Congress; Dionisio Miranda, an elderly man from Cochabamba, represented the Quechua people; and Desiderio Chilina stood in for the Guaraní and tribal groups in the eastern lowlands. Gotkowitz (*A Revolution for Our Rights*, 214–15) notes that Chipana Ramos's credentials included his service in the Chaco War, a close working relationship with Busch, and collaboration with the MNR.

80 Ranaboldo, *El camino perdido*, 104.

81 Zengotita to US Secretary of State, September 20, 1945, 2, box 824, RG 59, NARA.

82 "Mestizo peligroso actúa como delegado de los Indígenas al Congreso de Estos," *El Diario*, May 16, 1945, in Ranaboldo, *El camino perdido*, 110.

83 Ranaboldo, *El camino perdido*, 109–10; Dandler and Torrico, "From the National Indian Congress to the Ayopaya Rebellion," 350.

84 Gotkowitz, *A Revolution for Our Rights*, 111–12, 216; Choque Canqui, *Historia de una lucha desigual*, 118–20; Antezana Ergueta, *La revolución campesina en Bolivia*, 52–55.

85 This speech is quoted at length in "Ayer inauguró sus labores en el Primer Congreso Indigenal," *La Razón*, May 11, 1945. See also the embassy report: Thurston to US Secretary of State, May 29, 1945, box 824, RG 59, NARA.

86 Dandler and Torrico, "From the National Indian Congress to the Ayopaya Rebellion," 349–51; Gotkowitz, *A Revolution for Our Rights*, 206–7.

87 Gotkowitz, *A Revolution for Our Rights*, 207–8.

88 A strong advocate of Indian integration and mestizaje, Claure was a prominent educator under the military populist regimes of Toro and Busch, having served as director of the núcleo escolar of Vacas, in Cochabamba. (See his memoir and monograph, *Una escuela rural en Vacas*.) He was a leading rival and critic of Elizardo Pérez and apologist, if not enabler, of the CNE's assault on Warisata in the early 1940s.

89 Claure prefaced his grand vision for rural education by denouncing the republic's abject failure—from its foundation in 1825 to the founding of

Warisata in 1930—in providing "concrete" and "positive" educational reform. He blamed ineffectual state policies but also denounced the "lethal attitudes toward indigenous concerns, more generally." He scolded "the whites and mestizos [who] disavow their involvement in the moral and material improvement of the aboriginals, whom they treat with indolence and disdain" (15). Toribio Claure, "Educación indígena," 15–19, in *Primer Congreso Indígena Boliviano: Principales ponencias*, May 10–15, 1945, box 824, RG 59, NARA.

90 Claure, "Educación indígena," 15–19.

91 Claure, "Educación indígena," 15–19. On these government decrees, see "Fue Clausurado el Primer Congreso Indigenal Nacional," *La Razón*, May 16, 1945.

92 Thurston to US Secretary of State, May 29, 1945, 3, box 824, RG 59, NARA.

93 Laura Gotkowitz (*A Revolution for Our Rights*, 221) cites a fiery speech by a young Siles Suazo (an MNR party member, the future vice president and president, and at the time closely allied with the Villarroel regime) in which he called for a radical agenda of agrarian reform. He was censured for his rash action because the leadership of his own political party (the Movimiento Nacional Revolucionario, or MNR) remained profoundly ambivalent toward the radical agenda of land reform. Villarroel himself was adverse to any promise of land reform. In July 1945, he stated unequivocally that "the Indian problem is not actually about land, but about [the work] regime... what is lacking is [a disciplinary regime] of the Indian... since the Indian has no clear concept of property... and has never been a [private] property owner" (quoted in Antezana and Romero, *Historia de los sindicatos campesinos*, 115). In other words, the Indian must be educated and disciplined in good habits of work and agricultural production before he was to be entrusted with a parcel of titled land, and—most certainly—before the state intervened in society with an agrarian reform program. On the recurring debates and tensions over the question of land reform, see Soliz, *Fields of Revolution*.

94 Thurston to US Secretary of State, May 29, 1945, 9. In July of that year, the Ministry of Labor tried to dispel the embassy's doubts by reporting that some four hundred schools were established on haciendas for colono children. The embassy remained skeptical. See Zengotita to US Secretary of State, August 11, 1945, box 824, RG 59, NARA.

95 *La Razón*, September 7, 1945, quoted in Antezana and Romero, *Historia de los sindicatos campesinos*, 122.

96 Zengotita to US Secretary of State, August 11, 1945.

97 Oral testimony of Ayopaya peasants recorded by Dandler and Torrico, "From the National Indian Congress to the Ayopaya Rebellion," 357.

98 Ministerio de Asuntos Campesinos, no. 765, Nicolás Mamani Colque to President, August 15, 1952, ANB-P, C.

99 *La Rázon*, September 7, 1945, quoted in Antezana and Romero, *Historia de los sindicatos campesinos*, 122.

100 René Zavaleta called the sexenio a "prolonged civil war" that culminated in the 1952 revolution. Zavaleta's Marxian sociological focus on the mining proletariat, as both the vanguard of revolution and victims of oligarchic violence, tended to downplay, if not erase, the role of rural mobilizations, except as an offshoot of militant worker unionism. Cited in John, *Bolivia's Radical Tradition*, 97.

101 See the pathbreaking study by Lehm and Rivera, *Los artesanos libertarios y la ética de trabajo*. Drawing on oral history and archival documents, they trace the evolution of the anarcho-syndicalist movement from its urban origins in the early 1900s through its escalation into a transregional agrarian coalition in 1947 and 1948. Operating in the Province of Los Andes, rural anarchists invaded haciendas, organized colonos, and called for a general strike of all agrarian laborers. Anarchist intellectuals also produced potent manifestos depicting the nature of internal colonialism and racism that buttressed the feudal oligarchic regime. Besides the Lehm and Rivera book, see also Young, "The Making of an Interethnic Coalition"; Antezana Ergueta, *La revolución campesina en Bolivia*; Antezana and Romero, *Historia de los sindicatos campesinos*; and Gotkowitz, *A Revolution for Our Rights*, 247–53.

102 The 1946 Thesis of Pulacayo represented "a landmark of Latin American Trotskyism," according to John, *Bolivia's Radical Tradition*, 91. Bolivia's Trotskyist party, the POR, was the author of the thesis, on behalf of the Miners Federation. See also Lora, *A History of the Bolivian Labour Movement*, 435–38, 439.

103 Reported in *La Razón*, February 14, 1947. Quoted in Antezana Ergueta, *La revolución campesina en Bolivia*, 69; and Antezana and Romero, *Historia de los sindicatos campesinos*, 131–32. The pamphlet described Indian prisoners filling up jails in La Paz and then being transported to the tropical labor camp, where the peasant political prisoners were deprived of food and basic medical care in their dank cells. Herzog, by contrast, told the Congress that the confinement of Indian ringleaders in the tropics was a government "measure aimed at the colonization of eastern lands." Herzog, *Mensaje al Congreso Ordinario de 1947*, quoted in Antezana Ergueta, *La revolución campesina en Bolivia*, 69.

Whether, or how, the United States contributed to the government's military campaign against rural uprisings and union organizing in 1947 is still an open question. US economic aid, developmentalist expertise, and strategic interest in Bolivia began in 1942, thanks to the Americans' military war needs for Bolivian tin. For that reason the volatility of Bolivia's mineworkers became a major security concern, which in turn implicated rural labor unrest and the so-called Indian problem. The postwar years (though described by some scholars as a brief "democratic opening" in some parts of Latin America) quickly faded in the face of Washington's Cold War anxieties about nationalist, anti-imperialist, populist, syndicalist, socialist, and communist threats to Western free-trade capitalism and democratic rule. Bolivia, by 1947, was back on Washington's hemispheric radar, as a source of growing diplomatic concern and recipient of US economic and military aid. See Siekmeier, *The Bolivian Revolution*, 24–33.

6. Enclaves of Acculturation

1. The US State Department wanted to break the close ties between Bolivia and Germany, "which included everything from military missions and support for the national air lines to the subsidization of the MNR newspaper *La Calle*." See Klein, *A Concise History of Bolivia*, 199. Even before World War II, the military socialist regime of Germán Busch set off alarm bells in Washington, first with its 1937 nationalization of Standard Oil, and then with various authoritarian mandates and its protofascist leanings.

2. See especially Price, *Anthropological Intelligence*.

3. Lehman, *Bolivia and the United States*, 94.

4. Eventually the acronyms SAI, SCISP, and SCIDE stood for, respectively, Servicio Agrícola Interamericano; Servicio Cooperativo Interamericano de Salúd Pública; and Servicio Cooperativo Interamericano de Desarrollo Educativo. On SCISP's evolving program in Bolivia, particularly after the 1952 revolution, see the work of Nicole Pacino (listed in the bibliography).

5. Hughes, "Education in Bolivia," July 11, 1944, 20, box 1175, RG 229, NARA. Hughes attributed the source of mass illiteracy to three primary factors: first, Bolivia's material lack of public schools and trained teachers (particularly in the rural sector); second, the psychology of the Indian, specifically the widespread fear that male schoolchildren would be picked off for obligatory service in the military, or that schooling would "make the Indian children dissatisfied with life in their own communities and villages"; and third, Bolivia's adverse economic conditions, particularly rural poverty and scarce government revenue (21–22). An abbreviated version of Hughes's report was published in 1946 by the Office of Inter-American Affair in its *Bulletin of the Pan American Union*.

6. SCIDE, "Narrative Report of the Inter-American Educational Foundation," September 7, 1944–June 30, 1946, 1, box 1175, RG 229, NARA.

7. ILO, *Los problemas del trabajo en Bolivia*, 13–14. Known as the Magruder report, it was conducted by an international commission of fact-finders. Their mission was to look into the circumstances surrounding the Catavi miners' strike, followed by the government's massacre in late 1942. The Allies' con-

8   Hughes, "Education in Bolivia," July 11, 1944, 22–23.

9   SCIDE's vocational training programs were also designed for urban workers, but Maes invested most effort in the area of rural schooling (which caused some measure of controversy within US embassy circles).

10 The Smithsonian-sponsored conference on the Indian problem in Bolivia derived, broadly, from the Inter-American project of indigenistas, who had recently met in Pátzcuaro, Mexico, to deliberate on the intractable problems of rural poverty and marginality among Native peoples across the Americas. More immediately, the conference was part of the generative effort of American anthropologists to provide useful (government-funded) "foreign area studies" that would help guide Washington's wartime (and later postwar) aid and diplomacy in Latin America and elsewhere. But the most urgent motive driving the Yale meeting was to generate ethnographic context and policy recommendations for the purpose of improving the living standards and work ethic of Bolivian tin miners (most of whom had Indigenous roots). Smithsonian Institution Archives, Ethnogeographic Board, Conference on Bolivian Indians, Yale University, September 20, 1942.

11 The Ministry of Education, in particular, was under control of a young officer, Major Jorge Calero, who tacitly supported North American reformers. The Villarroel regime wanted to quietly secure US material aid and technical support without tarnishing its nationalist/populist image. This observation came later, in a report by the indigenista lawyer and reformer Eduardo Arze Loureiro. Memorandum from Eduardo Arze Loureiro to George Greco, Director of SCIDE, March 30, 1949, 4, box 1175, RG 229, NARA.

12 Memorandum from Eduardo Arze Loureiro to George Greco, Director of SCIDE, March 30, 1949, 4. Eduardo Arze Loureiro furnishes this observation about Maes's alliance with Warisata's "enemies" and his contempt for Elizardo Pérez—a rigid ideological stance that Maes later had to abandon.

13 Education Division, Conference on Rural Education, Quito, Ecuador, November 4–9, 1948, 4, box 1175, RG 229, NARA.

14 In the war and postwar era, the "functionalist" concept of popular education, with its economistic emphasis on skilling and disciplining the future farmers and workers of the nation, entered the lexicon of modernization and rural development programs (replacing, or complicating, the positivist emphasis on educating technocratic elites). See Puiggrós, *Imperialismo y educación en América Latina*, 16–19.

15 Education Division, Conference on Rural Education, Quito, Ecuador, November 4–9, 1948, 6.

16 SCIDE, "Narrative Report of the Inter-American Educational Foundation," September 7, 1944–June 30, 1946, 1, box 1175, RG 229, NARA.

17 SCIDE, "Narrative Report of the Inter-American Educational Foundation," 3, 7–8.

18 SCIDE, "Narrative Report of the Inter-American Educational Foundation," 3.

19 Ernest Maes, "An Experiment in Internationalism," 1948, 8, box 1175, RG 229, NARA. Although SCIDE's plans were impressive on paper, there is still little research on its regional impacts in Bolivia. After SCIDE's pedagogical orientation was implanted in Bolivia in the late 1940s, Washington slowly began to scale back funding. By 1955, SCIDE operated only a half dozen or so "demonstration schools." Beginning around 1961, and in the aftermath of the Cuban revolution, a fresh infusion of US economic and military aid (and counterinsurgency propaganda) flowed into Bolivia under Washington's hemispheric "Alliance for Progress" program.

20 SCIDE, "Narrative Report of the Inter-American Educational Foundation," 3.

21 Teacher-training workshops included subjects like "Civic and Moral Education," "Community-School Relations," "Personal Hygiene," "The School Lunch," "Hygiene and the Improvement of the School," "Hygiene and the Community," "Prevention of Common Communicable Diseases," "Recreation and Educational Games," etc. Many of these workshop topics were later included in the seven-volume *Guía de instrucción para maestros rurales*, published jointly by the Bolivian Ministry of Education and the Programa Cooperativo de Educación (later called SCIDE) in 1948.

22 The training workshops in health and agriculture had produced some sixty *técnicos*, many of them sent to disseminate their newly acquired knowledge and skills at the Peasant School Centers; others joined roving teams of teachers and health workers.

23 The Vacas school was one of the original *núcleos escolares*, established with great fanfare by peasants, syndicalists, and teachers in the aftermath of the Chaco War.

24 SCIDE, "Narrative Report of the Inter-American Educational Foundation," 6.

25 See Zulawski, *Unequal Cures*.

26 SCIDE, "Narrative Report of the Inter-American Educational Foundation," 9.

27 Maes, *An Experiment in Internationalism*, 10. Maes's pedagogic model (itself a perversion of the original núcleo escolar) was adapted to those distinctive locales and thus took on particular cultural and political characteristics and significance. Maes himself was reassigned by Washington to Guatemala in 1948 (another region known for its political turmoil and dense Indigenous population), but that later episode of imperial school reform lies beyond the scope of this story.

28 On the epistemological ambitions of Western society abroad, see Mignolo, *Local Histories / Global Designs*; Seth, *Subject Lessons*; and Escobar, *Encountering Development*.

29 SCIDE, "Narrative Report of the Inter-American Educational Foundation," 9.

30 As mentioned earlier, Ernest Maes was one of the coauthors of that 1942 Smithsonian report.

31 Loosely defined, "governmentality" refers to the power of dominant discourses and routines to permeate the normative order of postindustrial Western society and culture. Theoretically, they operate through key social institutions (the school, clinic, prison, barracks, etc.), to inculcate behavioral norms and knowledge that routinely define identities, reinforce gender and class hierarchies, and govern the self-regulation of individual subjects. See Foucault, *Discipline and Punish*.

32 A typed, mimeographed version titled *Guía de instrucción para maestros rurales* circulated in 1946; in January 1947, Bolivia's Ministry of Education and Department of Rural Education put out another mimeographed version, titled *Guía didáctica de educación rural*. These documents were put together by Bolivian and Peruvian social scientists and educators, many of whom had deep ethnographic knowledge of rural Indigenous communities. Those booklets were supplanted in 1948, when the Programa Cooperativo de Educación (SCIDE's earlier and local designation) furnished funds to publish a series of seven pamphlets, (again) titled *Guía de instrucción para maestros rurales*. Written mainly by North Americans with local collaboration, they furnished local school directors and teachers with practical instructions that derived, generally, from earlier North American programs of extension education. The first pamphlet in that series of teacher manuals laid out "the objectives of rural education." It circulated widely at the time, and is most often cited in scholarly studies. For purposes of the discussion that follows, I have concentrated on that 1947 mimeograph and on three of the published 1948 *Guías de instrucción* (no. 1, on objectives of rural education; no. 2, on agro-vocational instruction; and no. 6, on home economics).

33 "Report on Activities of Health and Sanitation Division and Education Division of the IIAA in Bolivia," 1949, 17, 21, box 1175, RG 229, NARA.

34 Ministerio de Educación, Departamento de Educación Rural, and Programa Cooperativo de Educación, *Guía de instrucción para maestros rurales*, vol. 1: *Los objetivos de la educación rural*, 5.

35 See Stephenson, *Gender and Modernity in Andean Bolivia*.

36 Ministerio de Educación, Departamento de Educación Rural, and Programa Cooperativo de Educación, *Guía de instrucción para maestros rurales*, vol. 6: *Economía doméstica*.

37 Ministerio de Educación, Departamento de Educación Rural, and Programa Cooperativo de Educación, *Guía de instrucción para maestros rurales*, vol. 1: *Los objetivos de la educación rural*, 6–7; Ministerio de Educación and Departamento de Educación Rural, *Guía didáctica de educación rural* (1947), 4–6.

38 Ministerio de Educación, Departamento de Educación Rural, and Programa Cooperativo de Educación, *Guía de instrucción para maestros rurales*, vol. 1: *Los objetivos de la educación rural*, 7–8. For a discussion of hegemonic intrusions across the threshold of house and home, see Stephenson, *Gender and Modernity in Andean Bolivia*, chap. 3. For an ethnographic reading of the "space-time" meanings of the rural K'ulta home and its gendered domestic arrangements in the context of everyday work and ceremonial routines, see Abercrombie, *Pathways of Memory and Power*, 332–35.

39 Ministerio de Educación, Departamento de Educación Rural, and Programa Cooperativo de Educación, *Guía de instrucción para maestros rurales*, vol. 1: *Los objetivos de la educación rural*, 9.

40 US hygienic campaigns were long anticipated by the Bolivia's Ministry of Education, which had harbored official anxieties about the body politic in the aftermath of the Chaco War. One 1938 government pamphlet, for example, took aim at the degenerate male citizenry. Using the narrative voice of a schoolboy, the pamphlet scolded the father for his drunkenness and neglect. The moral message engendered a nationalist call to fatherhood: "Father: your social debt is enormous. Remember that you will live on in future generations. If you deliver to society a degenerate, ignorant and miserly oaf, he [your son] will embody all your base passions like hatred, envy, regionalism, etc." To redeem the honor of the nation, fathers must "ask of [their] children the maximum of effort, valor without limit, a strict conscience, and vigorous character." The pamphlet then warned the father that he must be prepared to sacrifice his sons to the greater good of the nation in times of war. A regenerated patriarchy was fundamental to Bolivia's ability to defend its territorial sovereignty in the next war. What is striking here is the government effort to define masculine norms as patriotic virtues (sobriety, discipline and hard work, self-sacrifice, family nurturing, etc.) in ways that cut across racial divides and bound the nation into an organic whole. Ministry of Education, *Propaganda moralizadora del Ministerio de Educación*. See also Tarifa Ascarrunz, *Programas de instrucción para escuelas indigenales*.

41 Ministerio de Educación, Departamento de Educación Rural, and Programa Cooperativo de Educación, *Guía de instrucción para maestros rurales*, vol. 1: *Los objetivos de la educación rural*, 12.

42 Canessa, *Intimate Indigeneities*, 220–28.

43 On the army and the mines as "masculinizing spaces," see Canessa *Intimate Indigeneities*, 220–28; Canessa, "The Indian Within, the Indian Without," 136–42; Gill, *Teetering on the Rim*, chap. 6; Gill, "Creating Citizens, Making Men."

44 Foreign aid officers displayed an appalling unawareness of traditional Andean norms of gender complementarity, which bestowed status on the woman, defined the married couple as the organic whole of male-female (the *chachawarmi*, or "manwoman"), and conferred social personhood (*jaqichasiña*) to both partners of the married couple. Although Western aid workers might have glimpsed a village assembly meeting, where the men deliberated and their womenfolk observed from the sidelines, they might not have understood that, in vital ways, women were considered household heads and took part in all important decisions, even though men traditionally represented the household in local assemblies and in their engagement with political authorities.

45 Frontaura Argandoña, *Hacia el futuro indio*.

46 See Larson, "Capturing Indian Bodies, Hearths, and Minds."

47 Ministerio de Educación, Departamento de Educación Rural, and Programa Cooperativo de Educación, *Guía de instrucción para maestros rurales*, vol. 6: *Economía doméstica*.

48 Female domestic service was a crucial means of economic survival for many peasant households, of course, and most prosperous, urban La Paz households imported young Aymara women to perform the menial labor of house cleaning, laundry, cooking, childcare, etc. Indeed, the very definition of ideal white womanhood resided, at least partly, in the señora's social distance from sweat labor and its displacement to the domestic servant. To the extent the new rural school curriculum might furnish country girls with a veneer of urban civilization, it was performing a vital function in the modernization and reproduction of domestic servitude. See Gill, *Precarious Dependencies*, chap. 1.

49 Ministerio de Educación, Departamento de Educación Rural, and Programa Cooperativo de Educación, *Guía de instrucción para maestros rurales*, vol. 1: *Los objetivos de la educación rural*, 8.

50 Report on Activities of Health and Sanitation Division and the Education Division of the IIAA in Bolivia, 1949, 18, box 1175, RG 229, NARA.

51 Report on Activities of Health and Sanitation Division and the Education Division of the IIAA in Bolivia, 1949, 18–19.

52 The dignitary was Wilfred Mauck, director of the Education Division of the IIAA. In 1956, he published his report, "More Than ABCs," in the IIAA's *Americas Magazine*. At least one prominent US anthropologist, Carlton Beals, criticized Washington's propaganda campaign as reeking with "power, wealth, and arrogance," cited in Lehman, *Bolivia and the United States*, 89.

53 Mauck, "More Than ABCs," 4.

54 Memorandum from Eduardo Arze Loureiro to George Greco, Director of SCIDE, March 30, 1949, 1, 6.

55 Memorandum from Dolores Morales Díaz, Home Economics Technician, to George Grego, Director of SCIDE, "Monthly Report for April, 1949," 3, box 1175, RG 229, NARA.

56 See various inspectors' reports under April–November 1949, box 1175, RG 229, NARA.

57 Memorandum from Eduardo Arze Loureiro to George Greco, Director of SCIDE, March 30, 1949, 6.

58 Memorandum from Eduardo Arze Loureiro to George Greco, Director of SCIDE, March 30, 1949, 6. The school inspector and interlocutor at Santiago de Huata was the venerable old Cochabamba lawyer and sociologist Eduardo Arze Loureiro. The students Arze Loureiro interviewed were, in fact, voicing the opinion of the school's director and faculty, who objected to the SCIDE's imposed curriculum of Health and Agriculture, and Arze noted that the faculty studiously ignored SCIDE's pedagogical directives and thus "came to repeat . . . a curriculum which bears no relation whatsoever with the peasants' life."

59 Memorandum from Eduardo Arze Loureiro to George Greco, Director of SCIDE, March 30, 1949, 6; Memorandum from Eduardo Arze Loureiro to George Greco, Director of SCIDE, "Monthly Report for April, 1949," April 29, 1949, 4–5, box 1175, RG 229, NARA.

60 This was characteristic of many newly arrived American aid workers and envoys performing shorts stints of fieldwork in Bolivia or elsewhere in the Andes. Marc Becker (personal communication) found that US State Department officials working in highland Ecuador during the early Cold War, although attuned to the growing "communist threat," were almost clueless when it came to apprehending the nature and scope of Indigenous and peasant activism.

61 The return to civilian government under a coalition of recently reunited Republican parties (known as the Partido Unión Republicana Socialista) brought together middle-class reformers and nationalists. But the specter of agrarian violence and rural unrest pushed the Herzog regime into alliance with Bolivia's landholding oligarchy and the US embassy. In early 1947, the Herzog regime launched a military assault, complete with airpower, on striking peasants in Ayopaya and other regions.

62 Memorandum from Eduardo Arze Loureiro to George Greco, Director of SCIDE, March 30, 1949, 1.

63 *Redactor de la H. Cámara de Diputados* (hereafter cited as *Redactor de Diputados*), AHHCN. See the redacted interpellations in various congressional sessions (both Ordinary and Extraordinary) between March and August 1947.

64 In Nor Lipez, Pérez had quietly assembled a base of support among Aymara farmers and pastoralists who were integrated into the rural nuclear school of Llica. It was, in Pérez's estimate, the only authentic *escuela-ayllu* that had survived the Bolivian state's campaign of destruction, begun in 1940, under the

auspices of the CNE. The western region's severe high-altitude climate, sparse population, and geographic isolation (wedged, as the village school of Llica was, between the vast salt lakes to the east and the international Chilean-Bolivian border to the west) seemed to have shielded it from repressive state policies. As a result, Llica quietly emerged as a refuge for many of Warisata's exiled students and teachers during the early 1940s. Pérez, too, eventually made his way there, where he reinvented himself as a congressional delegate from the region. Pérez, *Warisata*, 312–13.

65 *Redactor de Diputados*, Congreso Extraordinario, 46th sess., May 20, 1947, 83–91, AHHCN.

66 *Patria Libre*, April 9, 1947.

67 Pérez, *Warisata*, 80.

68 See chapter 3 for a discussion of Pérez's evolving pedagogical ideas during Warisata's heyday.

69 The debates, including Pérez's long orations, took place mostly on the days of May 22, August 23, 27, and 29 in "extraordinary" (i.e., extra) legislative sessions. See *Redactor de Diputados*, Congreso Extraordinario, 47th sess., May 22, 1947, 3:107; 7th sess., August 23, 1947, 1:79–88; 8th sess., August 27, 1947, 97–107; and 10th sess., August 29, 1947, 143–73, AHHCN.

70 *Redactor de Diputados*, Congreso Ordinario, 8th sess., August 27, 1947, 104.

71 *Redactor de Diputados*, Congreso Ordinario, 8th sess., August 27, 1947, 163.

72 *Redactor de Diputados*, Congreso Ordinario, 10th sess., August 29, 1947, 161.

73 *Redactor de Diputados*, Congreso Ordinario, 10th sess., August 29, 1947, 162–64.

74 *Redactor de Diputados*, Congreso Extraordinario, 8th sess., August 27, 1947, 103–4.

75 *Redactor de Diputados*, Congreso Ordinario, 10th sess., August 29, 1947, 148. This trope reverberated through the public sphere over many months. By mid-1948, when a flurry of activities thrust Warisata back into the limelight, newspaper editorials registered "grave concern" that Bolivia had compromised its cultural sovereignty by allowing SCIDE to impose its didactic orthodoxies on Bolivia's rural teachers. See, for example, "El Programa Cooperative Educacional," *El Diario*, April 29, 1948.

76 Pérez, *Warisata*, 294. Garibaldi also organized a local school sit-down strike against the corrupt administration and led a delegation of (impeccably groomed) Warisata students to meet with the Bolivian president.

77 "500 indígenas de Warisata reclamaron ayer por su Escuela al Presidente de la República," *Ultima Hora*, March 12, 1948; "Memorial presentado al Jefe de Estado por los Campesinos de la Escuela de Warisata," *El Diario*, April 5, 1948.

78 Picking up the threads of the emerging subaltern narrative of state violence against Warisata, the press elaborated and circulated an allegorical rendering, by tracing Warisata's founding (often attributed by journalists to the sole

"founding father," Elizardo Pérez), glory days, and fall at the greedy hands of the feudal oligarchy and gamonal state. See, for example, "Desde muchos años ha venido destruyéndose la Escuela Indigenal de Warizata: La visita del Primer Mandatario," *El Diario*, April 4, 1948.

79 "500 indígenas de Warisata reclamaron ayer por su escuela al presidente de la República," *Ultima Hora*, March 12, 1948; "Memorial presentado al jefe del estado por los campesinos de la escuela de Warisata," *El Diario*, April 5, 1948.

80 Reported and quoted in Pérez, *Warisata*, 295.

81 Arze Loureiro was a veteran of the Chaco generation and a public indigenista who also defended rural union leaders in the Cochabamba region. He also spent time in Warisata and understood its significance to Aymara peasant communities in the region, and later became a partisan of Warisata's defenders during the culture wars in the early 1940s. On the other hand, Arze Loureiro was also the beneficiary of US higher education thanks to a scholarship to study at the University of Minnesota, and he became a consultant to SCIDE sometime in the late 1940s.

82 Memorandum from Eduardo Arze Loureiro to George Greco, Director of SCIDE, March 30, 1949, box 1175, RG 229, NARA.

83 Memorandum from Eduardo Arze Loureiro to George Greco, Director of SCIDE, March 30, 1949, 4.

84 Memorandum from Eduardo Arze Loureiro to George Greco, Director of SCIDE, March 30, 1949, 7–8.

85 Memorandum from Eduardo Arze Loureiro to George Greco, Director of SCIDE, March 30, 1949.

86 Memorandum from Eduardo Arze Loureiro to George Greco, Director of SCIDE, March 30, 1949, 16–17.

87 Memorandum from Eduardo Arze Loureiro to George Greco, Director of SCIDE, March 30, 1949, 8.

88 Pérez said as much in his 1962 memoir, *Warisata*, 311.

89 Pérez, *Warisata*, 311. A few years later, SCIDE turned Warisata into a "demonstration" núcleo escolar. A glossy English-language brochure heralded Warisata as a microcosm of "technical cooperation" and agrarian modernization, deploying the pedagogic guidelines set forth in the series *Guía de instrucción para maestros rurales*. See SCIDE, *Rural Education in Bolivia*.

7. The Hour of Vindication

1 Los principales caciques de la República, en representación de la Raza Indígena, September 4, 1952, ANB-P, C, MAC. The petition's principal signatories were Santos Cornejo, cacique principal of La Paz; Mariano Acarapi, repre-

senting Cochabamba: Romualdo Chañi, Oruro; Juan Moraja, Potosí; Simón Omachoque, Sucre; Mariano Cussi, Tarija; and Julio Gutiérrez, Santa Cruz.

2   Rubio Orbe, *Educación fundamental*, 32.

3   Rubio Orbe, *Educación fundamental*, 32; Rubio Orbe, "Aculturaciones de Indígenas de los Andes," 33, 51.

4   Los principales caciques de la República, en representación de la Raza Indígena, September 4, 1952.

5   Kohl, "Peasants and Revolution in Bolivia," 248; Soliz, *Fields of Revolution*. Many such petitions (housed in the Archivo Nacional de Bolivia) went in the form of letters to the president, which were transcribed and sent to the MAC.

6   See the cache of petitions in the ANB's Presidencia documentary collection of correspondence. Kohl discovered that many such petitions were published in newspapers at the time, too. His survey shows the kind of demands bubbling up from the base of rural society in Cochabamba. See Kohl, "Peasants and Revolution in Bolivia," 248. The peasant union of Cliza, for example, sent a letter demanding the abolition of coercive labor practices (pongueaje, thinly disguised as a mule-driving service) and the return of usurped lands on the monastic estate of Santa Clara. No. 765, September 22, 1952, ANB-P, C, MAC.

7   Antezana Ergueta, *Resultados de la reforma agrarian*, 2.

8   Antezana Ergueta, *Resultados de la reforma agrarian*, 4.

9   Goodrich, "Bolivia in Time of Revolution," 19.

10 No. 803, October 21, 1953, ANB-P, C, MAC.

11 No. 765, September 1, 1952, ANB-P, C, MAC. The petition was signed by various peasants on August 8, 1952.

12 No. 765, September 1, 1952, 1–2.

13 See Kohl, "Peasants and Revolution in Bolivia"; Soliz, *Fields of Revolution* and "'Land to the Original Owners'"; Malloy, *Bolivia*, chap. 10; and Carter, "Revolution and the Agrarian Sector."

14 Soliz, *Fields of Revolution*. Soliz analyzes the whole corpus of peasant petitions, emanating mainly from ex-comunarios, colonos, and smallholders.

15 A. García, "Agrarian Reform and Social Development in Bolivia," 315–26.

16 Kohl notes that "the MNR's position towards the rural question reflected the national leadership's middle-class attitudes and values—fear of violence, emphasis on stability and moderation, respect for private property (except, of course, large estates)." See "Peasants and Revolution in Bolivia," 248. The imperatives of political insurgency overrode those bourgeois landowning habits of mind, opening the way for drastic agrarian reforms within eighteen months of MNR rule. When agrarian reform was promulgated in August 1953, the law tried to impose government control over the ad hoc

process of agrarian transformation happening on the ground in many parts of Cochabamba and La Paz.

17 Prior to the MNR's 1951 electoral victory, the party had been pressured into a tacit agreement with peasant leagues to honor their "thesis of Caranguillas," which had set forth their demand for agrarian reform in the peasant congress of 1947. That "thesis" (sometimes referred to as the "thesis of Pachamama") forced the MNR to adopt the land reform agenda (the keystone of the socialist left too) in its electoral platform. By 1951, both land reform and universal suffrage were major planks in the platform of the insurgent coalition that was swept into power on April 9, 1952. Alvarez Mamani, in Ranaboldo, *El camino perdido*, 261–63; Antezana Ergueta, *La revolución campesina en Bolivia*, 74.

18 Ucureña was the hub of radical peasant unions and school activism in the Valle Bajo of Cochabamba. This was the heart of agrarian syndicalism, where displaced (or repatriated) mining settlements, Quechua-Spanish bilingualism, and a strong tradition of *clasist* and *sindicalista* sentiments had long pervaded local peasant politics. See Gordillo, *Campesinos revolucionarios en Bolivia*; and Dandler, *El sindicalismo campesino en Bolivia*.

19 This jubilant tone resurfaced in the MNR's ten-year anniversary photographic commemoration as it looked back on that most historic of days. Dirección Nacional de Informaciones, *Bolivia*, 55.

20 Paz Estenssoro, *El pensamiento revolucionario*, 61.

21 Paz Estenssoro, *El pensamiento revolucionario*, 65.

22 Paz Estenssoro, *El pensamiento revolucionario*, 64.

23 No. 765, June 27, 1952, ANB-P, C, MAC.

24 No. 765, September 22, 1952, ANB-P, C, MAC.

25 No. 765, August 21, 1952, ANB-P, C, MAC.

26 No. 765, August 22, 1952, ANB-P, C, MAC.

27 No. 765, September 8, 1952, ANB-P, C, MAC.

28 No. 765, Los principales caciques de la República, en representación de la Raza Indígena, September 4, 1952, ANB-P, C, MAC. See the chapter's epigraph.

29 Weeks later, a more frustrated Santos Cornejo, principal cacique of La Paz, pressed the MNR government to "solve the great problems that affect the majority classes [and] to make social justice with nationalism," including revisiting the country's *tierras de origen* and conducting an official review of land claims and boundaries. This age-old quest of the country's comunarios was proposed here as the litmus test of a true agrarian reform plan because it would annul the property claims and hacienda boundaries of the white usurpers since the time of the (illegitimate) 1874 Liberal Land Reform. Only through the restitution of communal lands would true "social revindication" be achieved, ending the "misery and disgrace" of the Indian race.

The Taraqu-led campaign may well have had an impact on MNR policy. In 1954, the government reiterated the earlier Liberal oligarchic law of 1883, granting the right of colonial title-holding ayllus to defend their communal claims in courts of law. This modern iteration of the 1881 communal exception offered some communities the chance to defend their claims to ayllu lands, usurped or alienated through duplicitous land sales after the year 1900, pursuant to the official examination of their legal colonial documents and deeds. Significantly, this decree actually favored the twelve Taraqu communities and other lakeshore ayllu-communities that had suffered from the Liberal oligarchy's ruthless land-grab campaign around the turn of the twentieth century (see chap. 2).

30 No. 765, Los principales caciques de la República en representación de la Raza Indígena, September 4, 1952, 1, ANB-P, C, MAC.

31 No. 765, Mariano Mayta..., August 12, 1952, ANB-P, C, MAC. The petition itself was dated July 18, 1952. It was addressed to the new president and recorded and filed with the Ministerio de Asuntos Campesinos on August 12. Signed by Mariano Mayta and other (unidentified) signatories, the petition represented thirteen "ex-comunidades" (that is, expropriated ayllu-communities) throughout the canton of Huarina. A longtime dirigente working with the MNR party, Mayta and his comrades seized the political moment to lay out a collective revolutionary agenda on behalf of Bolivia's Indigenous majority.

32 No. 765, Mariano Mayta..., August 12, 1952, 1.

33 See Du Bois, *The Souls of Black Folks*, chap. 6.

34 No. 765, Mariano Mayta..., August 12, 1952, 3. Mariano Mayta, a longtime MNRista organizer, spoke as an Indigenous leader on behalf of the mass of Huarina community leaders.

35 No. 65, August 24, 1952, ANB-P, C, MAC; Sangines Uriarte, *Educación rural y desarrollo en Bolivia*, 96.

36 Many local community schools eventually passed into government hands, at least on paper, as the MNR's educational reform program got underway in the later 1950s and early 1960s. See Carter, *Aymara Communities and the Bolivian Agrarian Reform*; D. Heath, "The Aymara Indian and Bolivia's Revolution," 35; Heath, Erasmus, and Buechler, *Land Reform and Social Revolution*, 227–28, 233; Lagos, *Autonomy and Power*, 60; Arnold and Yapita, *The Metamorphosis of Heads*, 75–78.

37 In 1954, Vicente Lema (a delegate of the MAC and the MNR's main architect of rural education reform) noted in an unpublished report, "There is no reliable information about the number or condition of the private rural schools (escuelas rurales particulares)—neither with reference to the teachers and administrators, nor with reference to the number of matriculated students

and attendees, nor to the [schools'] budgets." He was a member of the Commission on Education Reform, which spent almost two years gathering information for a massive blueprint for reorganizing public education (including "peasant education") in Bolivia.

38 According to the findings of sociologist Marcelo Sangines Uriarte, the recorded number of fiscal schools in rural Bolivia increased steadily, if not spectacularly, from 79 (in 1952) to 106 (in 1953); from 136 (in 1954) to 143 (in 1955); and finally to 162 (in 1956), the year the government's education reform became law. The rate of student matriculation rose, correspondingly. According to government records, some 15.6 percent of children were formally registered as pupils in those school units in 1952. The rural primary school population inched up over the next three or four years: to 19.2 percent (in 1953), 24.2 percent (in 1954), and 30.3 percent (in 1955), before leveling off. Sangines Uriarte, *Educación rural y desarrollo en Bolivia*, 81, appendix 1.

39 Alexander, *The Bolivian National Revolution*, 91–92. By contrast, Elizardo Pérez, while recognizing the proliferation of núcleo school centers under the MNR, felt only scorn for the way the original núcleo escolar had become corrupted by conservative educators in the 1940s and, now again, by the new nationalist party (*Warisata*, 308–9).

40 In its ten-year anniversary album, the MNR gave itself a stunningly good report card. It claimed that more federal schools were created and more money was plowed into public education than at any time since the founding of the Republic. It cast itself as the savior of the illiterate peasant, having mobilized "all its resources to combat illiteracy and carry out a national campaign that has reached into the most remote places of the Republic." This theme resurfaces later in this chapter. See Dirección Nacional de Informaciones, *Bolivia*, 8; and A. Guzmán, *Historia de Bolivia*, 429.

41 Rubio Orbe, *Educación fundamental*, 32.

42 Rens, "The Andean Programme," 441, 444.

43 A. García, "Agrarian Reform and Social Development in Bolivia," 328.

44 Burke, "Land Reform in the Lake Titicaca Region," 330.

45 Carter, *Aymara Communities and the Bolivian Agrarian Reform*, 88. Arriving in Bolivia for field research in 1960, Carter worked extensively in the province of Ingavi, anchoring his fieldwork in the village of Irpa Chico and in two nearby ex-haciendas.

46 Carter, *Bolivia*, 145.

47 D. Heath, "The Aymara Indian and Bolivia's Revolution," 35–37.

48 Canessa, *Intimate Indigeneities*, 86.

49 Canessa, *Intimate Indigeneities*, 85.

50 Canessa, *Intimate Indigeneities*, 85.

51 Leonard, *El cambio económico y social*, 37–38.
52 Alexander, *The Bolivian National Revolution*, 92.
53 Leonard, *El cambio económico y social*, 39.
54 Leonard, *El cambio económico y social*, 39. On the MNR's obsessive use of political propaganda, see Cajías, *Así fue la Revolución*, 249; Gildner, "Indomestizo Modernism," 189–96.
55 Dirección Nacional de Informaciones, *Bolivia*, 84.
56 Whitehead, "The Bolivian National Revolution," 42.
57 The MNR appointed Fernando Diez de Medina to preside over the CRE, along with several other representatives: one to serve as interlocutor to Paz Estenssoro, and two representatives each from the Ministries of Education and Peasant Affairs. The CRE's eight other members were drawn from the "popular sector"—representing the COB, the nation's seven universities, and the directors of private secondary schools. Its social makeup skewed the distribution of power in favor of higher education and urban private schools—the precinct of a tiny minority of urban elites. Only two commissioners were responsible for designing a new program in rural education to serve two-thirds of the country's school-age children, the most underserved and needy segment of the population. Only one commissioner, representing the COB, gave voice and vote to the country's mass of laboring and peasant people. No peasant leader sat on this planning committee. See Alexander, *The Bolivian National Revolution*, 85; and Gildner, "Indomestizo Modernism," 65.
58 By 1954, the CRE had created an archive (most unpublished and still to be thoroughly studied by scholars) consisting of some four hundred documents—including ethnographic and other "scientific studies" of educational policies; a historical overview of Bolivia's educational reforms since the republic was founded; statistical compilations; and diagnostic field studies on the current state of public education, particularly in the rural sector. The result was a massive encyclopedia of rules and regulations, norms and orientations, which tried to resurrect and impose a centralizing bureaucratic logic on the helter-skelter nature of federal schooling. To my knowledge, no historian has yet plumbed the depth of CRE's ad hoc archive, housed in the APJRA. Besides this brief discussion, see also Gildner, "Indomestizo Modernism," 162–71.
59 A sprawling, top-heavy bureaucracy was erected, spanning two ministries (Education and Peasant Affairs). Those ministries oversaw the workings of the Consejo de Coordinacion Educativa; Dirección General de Educación; Dirección de Educación Fundamental Campesina; and the Instituto de Investigaciones Pedagógicas. Those institutes, in turn, administered a hierarchy of directors and teachers, teachers unions, the school calendar, disciplinary rules, pedagogical materials and methods, the cooperation of the padres de

familia, etc. One administrative hierarchy pertained to the urban sphere, the other to the drastically underfunded rural sphere.

60 See, for example, Sangines Uriarte, *Educación rural y desarrollo en Bolivia*; M. Contreras, "Educación"; Talavera Simoni, *Formaciones y transformaciones*; F. Martínez, "Pour une nation blanche, 'metisse,' ou pluriethnique et multiculturelle?"; and Cajías, *Continuidades y rupturas*.

61 Diez de Medina, "Discurso de Don Fernando Diez de Medina al asumir la Presidencia de la CRE," 32.

62 The 1955 Education Code is reprinted in Valois Arce, *Bolivia*; see chap. 1, art. I, 128–29.

63 Valois Arce, *Bolivia*, chap. 1, art. I, 129.

64 On the intellectual and political influence of Diez de Medina, see J. Sanjinés, *Mestizaje Upside-Down*, 89–92.

65 *Gaceta Campesina*, "Conclusiones de la Primera Comisión de Mecanización y Técnica Agraria de Educación Fundamental."

66 Flores Rodríguez, "La educación fundamental y la agricultura," 38 (emphasis in the original).

67 Forging the modern campesino subject was the key to "'the progress and grandeur of the Bolivia of tomorrow.'" See Flores Rodríguez, "La educación fundamental y la agricultura," 39.

68 *Inti Karka*, "El Servicio Cooperativo Interamericano de Educación y la Educación Indigenal."

69 Anonymous, "Don Franz Tamayo," *Inti Karka* 1, no. 1 (1952): 57–68.

70 Valencia Vega, "Revolución agrarian y educación indígena."

71 Hart, "Cooperación educacional."

72 In November 1953, Lema produced his unwieldy typewritten report for the CRE. It hammered out a broad platform of administrative and curricular goals for rural education reform, both inside and beyond the classroom. It may be summarized as follows (1) to professionalize the rural teachers (following the program set up by SCIDE, beginning in 1945); (2) to develop mechanisms of oversight, testing, and supervision of students; or to professionalize the administration of public schools as advocated by the central office of SCIDE; (3) to distribute modern didactic materials and school furniture, some of it purchased with SCIDE money; (4) to enhance classroom teaching methods, with a "technical orientation"; (5) to mobilize an adult literacy campaign, using all kinds of readers and other self-help materials; (6) to crack down on partisan politics (particularly leftist and anti-imperialist influences) among all teachers, especially in the rural normal schools; and (7) to enforce an "integral curriculum," using SCIDE's comprehensive (and assimilative) teachers manuals. Lema, *Conferencia Informativa sobre: La edu-*

cación campesina en Bolivia (hereafter cited as Lema, *La educación campesina en Bolivia*). The report consisted of twenty-eight typewritten pages. It was included in the 1954 volume of Conferencias of the CRE (Comisión de Reforma de Educación, sometimes cited as the Comisión de Reforma Educativa), 278–305, APJRA.

73 Lema, *La educación campesina en Bolivia*, 293–94.

74 Lema, *La educación campesina en Bolivia*, 293–94.

75 The phrase in this section's subheading is borrowed from Kelley and Klein's *Revolution and the Rebirth of Inequality*.

76 Alexander, *The Bolivian National Revolution*, 89.

77 On the basis of his own research, M. Contreras notes: "The widely held claim that the revolution changed education from the 'elites to the masses' is hollow." See his "A Comparative Perspective on Education Reforms in Bolivia," 282.

78 For insightful discussion and critique of the 1955 Code's bifurcation of rural and urban schooling, see Talavera, *Formaciones y transformaciones*, 112–14. She notes that the MNR education reform drew heavily from the assimilative norms and bureaucratic blueprint established by conservative educators in the Consejo Nacional de Educación (under Vicente Donoso Torres), rather than from the Warisata experience. Indeed, Donoso's rhetoric of mestizaje and castellanización dovetailed with the left-leaning integrationist (pro-mestizaje) ideal of the MNR party, newly founded in 1942 (see chap. 4).

79 Cristóbal Suárez, *Desarrollo de la educación boliviana*; cited in Gómez Martínez, *Bolivia*, 338. He compared revenue for education in the two ministries: Education (for the urban sector) and Peasant Affairs (for the rural).

80 Sangines Uriarte, *Educación rural y desarrollo en Bolivia*, 105.

81 Wilkie, *The Bolivian Revolution and U.S. Aid since 1952*, appendix nos. 70, 72.

82 M. Contreras has also noted the paucity of reliable government data on rural schooling in the MNR era ("A Comparative Perspective on Education Reforms in Bolivia," 264). But it is also true that, to date, few scholars have examined the CRE's corpus of documents.

83 Ministerio de Asuntos Campesinos and SCIDE, *Informe*. Defying logic, the 1958 report offered iterations of the tired refrain: "The lack of good teachers constitutes the gravest problem, and impacts directly on the normal progress of the schools."

84 Diez de Medina, *Bolivia y su destino*, 31. This critique of schooling reflected Diez de Medina's disenchantment with the corrupt revolutionary process at "this hour of darkness and confusion" (83). Still the lofty moralist, he rebuked Bolivia's young leftist intelligentsia for failing to grapple with the deeper spiritual malaise of the country. He also decried the lack of progress of his own

"cultural pedagogic movement," initiated in 1956–57. "Nothing exceptional has been produced in the last few years," he wrote in 1962 (87).

85 Baptista Gumucio, *Salvemos a Bolivia de la escuela*, 98. By contrast, the MNR's propaganda album of 1962 issued a glowing report card. Using statistics, slogans, and graphics, the MNR lauded its education reform program for having "liberated the campesino class." See Dirección Nacional de Informaciones, *Bolivia*, 77–86.

86 Carter, "Revolution and the Agrarian Sector," 266. See also M. Contreras, "A Comparative Perspective on Education Reforms in Bolivia," 282.

87 See Comitas, "Educación y estratificación social en Bolivia." An American anthropologist from Columbia University, Comitas went on assignment to rural Bolivia in the early 1960s. His mission was to conduct a preliminary study of agrarian reform, in conjunction with the United States' newly established Alliance for Progress (and its nascent Peace Corps program). The project yielded a massive body of data, based on the six community case studies. Funded by the Research Institute for the Study of Man, the data was later used by Kelley and Klein to critique the revolution. See their 1981 book, *Revolution and the Rebirth of Inequality*. Ironically, the authors pointed to rural education as the proverbial exception to prove the rule, but argued that increased rates of schooling were more a function of shifting socioeconomic circumstances than government policy reform.

88 Comitas, "Educación y estratificación social en Bolivia," 648.

89 Comitas, "Educación y estratificación social en Bolivia," 649.

90 See, for example, Kelley and Klein's *Revolution and the Rebirth of Inequality*, which, despite its title, argues that the rural school system expanded at over six times the prerevolutionary rate and, equally significant, was *perceived* in rural society as being the most valuable conquest of the popular revolution (131). By contrast, Manuel Contreras ("A Comparative Perspective on Education Reforms in Bolivia," 264–65) argues that the expansion of núcleos escolares was less the outcome of deliberate state policy than the cumulative impact of many factors over two decades (the 1940s through the 1960s). To the extent that the rate of rural primary education increased dramatically in the 1950s, it owed more to the agrarian reform, increased peasant migration, and other circumstances on the ground than it did to government education policy.

91 Klein, "Social Change in Bolivia since 1952," 245. See M. Contreras, "A Comparative Perspective on Education Reforms in Bolivia," for a more critical approach.

92 Klein noted: "Given Bolivia's extraordinary language [diversity], [together] with the fact that in 1950 the majority of the population did not even speak Spanish, let alone were literate in the language, the rapid reduction of illiteracy in Bolivia is truly impressive." Klein, "Social Change in Bolivia since 1952," 248.

93 Dirección Nacional de Informaciones, *Bolivia*, 81. To bolster its claims, the MNR issued another comprehensive report card in 1963 that summed up its decade of achievements in the areas of governance, agrarian development, and social integration—including its distribution of land reform entitlements; the tax on rustic properties; the development of peasant cooperatives; the exponential expansion of schools and teachers; the curriculum of "fundamental education"; and its adult literacy programs. Produced (again) for propaganda purposes (with its UNESCO and US funders in mind), the MAC reported that 2,172 new rural schools were established over eight years (1952–60, an average of 271 schools each year). The pace accelerated in the final years of the regime, 1960–63: 443 schools were created each year—the main accelerant being foreign aid (though the report makes no mention of that factor). Over twelve remarkable years, student matriculation in rural schools shot up by an astronomical 359 percent, according to this report. Ministerio de Asuntos Campesinos (La Paz, n.d.), *Educación fundamental*.

94 On the fashioning of the "Third World" modern "campesino" (and the role of anthropology) in the age of rural development, see Kearny, *Reconceptualizing the Peasantry*. On the work of Western rural development projects in Bolivia during the Cold War, see Healy, *Llamas, Weavings, and Organic Chocolate*, chaps. 1–3; and Field, *From Development to Dictatorship*.

95 See Gildner, "Indomestizo Modernism."

96 Invited by Paz, Diego Rivera paid a visit to Bolivia in May 1953. He wanted to see the Bolivian revolution for himself and express solidarity in honor of Latin America's only "two pueblos" in revolutionary struggle. "Diego Rivera habló de la lucha de nuestros pueblos," *El Diario*, May 21, 1953; cited in Gildner, "Indomestizo Modernism," 228n491.

97 The state's propaganda campaign, broadly conceived, permeated a host of new institutions, projects, and forms of expression. A variety of new institutions, together, operated on a grand scale to diffuse the "cultural revolution" among the bourgeois and popular classes. See Dirección Nacional de Informaciones, *Bolivia*, 211–22; Bridikhina, *Fiesta cívica*, 60–69; and Gildner, "Indomestizo Modernism," chap. 3.

98 Diez de Medina, "Planteamiento filosófico y humanista."

99 Presidencia de la CRE, "Explicación popular de las labores realizadas por la CRE," 6–7, APJRA.

100 Presidencia de la CRE, "Explicación popular de las labores realizadas por la CRE," 6 (emphasis added).

101 Alexander, *The Bolivian National Revolution*, 85; Lema, *La educación campesina en Bolivia*, 291; and Bolivian Education Code, chap. 10, art. 115, in Valois Arce, *Bolivia*, 154.

102 *Gaceta Campesina*, "Primer Seminario de Educación Fundamental en Bolivia," 40–41 (emphasis in the original).

103 *El Pueblo*, February 12, 1955. I thank José Gordillo for bringing this verse to my attention.

104 For a ground-up study of spontaneous *sindicalista* activism, see Soliz, *Fields of Revolution*; and the foundational study of Antezana Ergueta, *La revolución campesina en Bolivia*.

105 Klein, "Social Change in Bolivia since 1952," 250.

106 The MNR adapted the craft of mass media and political propaganda from Mexico, but more directly from the United States' Office of Wartime Propaganda. According to Matthew Gildner, SPIC's purpose was "to create ideological cohesion among party and government officials, manage the flow of information from state to society, and mold public opinion" ("Indomestizo Modernism," 193, 220).

107 Gildner, "Indomestizo Modernism," 198–99; Coronel, *En un estado de coma*; Cajías, *Así fue la Revolución*, 248–51. The radio had long been a fixture of mass communication in Bolivia's mining towns; its airwaves often became a cultural combat zone between mine companies, the state, and militant miners unions alike. Meanwhile, American missionaries, particularly the Mary Knoll priests in northern Bolivia, turned to the radio for evangelical and instructional purposes.

108 Gildner, "Indomestizo Modernism," 218.

109 Ministerio de Asuntos Campesinos and Dirección Nacional de Informaciones, *Educación, producción, y trabajo*. Thanks to Matthew Gildner for bringing this source to my attention.

110 Leonard, *El cambio económico y social*, 390; Luís Antzana Ergueta's observation, as told to Alexander, *The Bolivian National Revolution*, 92.

111 This is not to suggest that the MNR state tolerated manifest expressions of political dissent. To the contrary: political prisoners were a permanent feature of MNR rule, especially when the party leadership ruptured its alliance with the militant sectors of the COB, purged certain peasant leaders (for example, Antonio Alvarez Mamani), and consolidated its one-party rule in the late 1950s. (This theme comes up in the book's epilogue.)

112 See Soliz, *Fields of Revolution*, chap. 5.

113 A. García, "Agrarian Reform and Social Development in Bolivia," 315 (emphasis in the original). In *Fields of Revolution*, Soliz illuminates the *failure* of successive right-wing regimes to roll back or diminish the country's massive agrarian reform program after the end of the MNR regime.

Epilogue

1. *Boletín Indígena*, "Número Especial dedicado al III Congreso Indigenista Interamericano, La Paz, Bolivia, 2–13 August, 1954."
2. Alvarez Mamani later recalled his alienation. "At the end of 1952 I still thought about joining the MNR sindicalista movement to create a strong organization. But already by then, I had suffered abusive treatment by the POR and other parties, and from the leaders of COB, and then I realized that the peasants were going to be exploited in the name of [official] sindicalismo, and I became totally disillusioned." Alvarez Mamani in Ranaboldo, *El camino perdido*, 240. His fall from grace is all the more startling when we consider the political leadership roles he played in the 1940s (see chap. 6) and at the outset of the MNR revolution.
3. The MNR's anticommunist rhetoric and actions played to the MNR's strategy to win over the Cold War Eisenhower regime to its cause and to secure more economic aid. See Siekmeier, *The Bolivian Revolution*, chap. 1.
4. Alvarez Mamani in Ranaboldo, *El camino perdido*, 247–48.
5. Through the Inter-American system, Washington played a prominent role in manipulating this Mexican-based transnational body of diplomats, philanthropists, development agents, and social scientists.
6. "Discurso de [Alvarez] Mamani," in Ranaboldo, *El camino perdido*, 249 (emphasis in the original).
7. "Discurso de [Alvarez] Mamani," 248–49.
8. "Discurso de [Alvarez] Mamani," 249.
9. Siles Suazo, "Speech Delivered by Dr. Hernán Siles Suazo," 222 (emphasis added).
10. Siles Suazo, "Speech Delivered by Dr. Hernán Siles Suazo," 222. The order of Antonio's surnames (Alvarez Mamani) was switched in the transcript, a reflection of the fact that Antonio preferred to use his maternal surname, Mamani, among Quechua-speaking regions.
11. Siles Suazo, "Speech Delivered by Dr. Hernán Siles Suazo," 211.
12. Tapia, *Ukhamawa Jakawisaxa*, 124. On Tapia's early encounters with life in the city, see 63–69.
13. Rivera, "La raíz"; Healy, *Llamas, Weavings, and Organic Chocolate*, 15; and Dangl, *The Five Hundred Year Rebellion*, 27, 95.
14. Rivera, *"Oprimidos pero no vencidos"* (1984), 124–34. See also Hurtado, *El katarismo*; and Alvizuri, *La construcción de la aymaridad*, chaps. 3 and 4. A rich secondary literature explores this rebel youth movement: its strands of ideology, modes of operation, internal tensions, and adaptations to the shifting political climate under dictatorship. In the early years, some Aymara

activists gravitated toward "katarismo" (a wide ethnic banner, but many early katarista activists had roots in rural villages and forged strong links to independent peasant unions). By contrast, an urban, more literary faction of kataristas (often self-identified as "indianistas") studied with the philosopher and writer Fausto Reinaga and produced a stream of dissident intellectual texts. (On Reinaga, see his major work, *La revolución india*; and "Iconoclast and Prophet: Fausto Reinaga," in Thomson et al., *The Bolivia Reader*.) Those wings of the katarista/indianista movement gave flight to the most potent ethno-political movement in the Andes at the time, according to Xavier Albó ("Andean People in the Twentieth Century," 826).

15 On the identity politics of indigeneity that flourished among Aymara students, activists, and intellectuals, see Alvizuri, *La construcción de la aymaridad*. The emerging katarista movement first came to light in the wider reading public in the early 1980s, largely thanks to Silvia Rivera's *"Oprimidos pero no vencidos"* (1984 ed.), 163–71. In that seminal work, she argued that Aymara dissidents were building an ethnic liberation movement that drew force and cohesion from a reconstructed "long-term" memory of the eighteenth-century rebel hero, Tupac Katari. Born in the Aymara region of Ayo Ayo (the province of many Katarista activists in the 1970s), Katari emerged in the 1780s as the apotheosis of anticolonial struggle against racial and class oppression, both then and in the contemporary present. See Thomson, *We Alone Will Rule*.

16 Rivera, *"Oprimidos pero no vencidos"* (2003 ed.), 151, 153.

17 Healy, *Llamas, Weavings, and Organic Chocolate*, 196.

18 Founded in 1969, MINK'A (whose name evokes the Andean tradition of communal labor and reciprocity) was organized by "peasants who had had the opportunity to become professionals," according to Albó ("From MNRistas to Kataristas to Katari," 393). Their workshop churned out radical pamphlets and papers, some of which were presented at local and international conferences and later collected and published in Guillermo Bonfil Batalla's edited volume, *Utopía y revolución*.

19 This extraordinary educational achievement was first brought to light by scholars studying the roots of the katarista movement, which emerged in the late 1960s and early 1970s. See Rivera, *"Oprimidos pero no vencidos"*; Hurtado, *El katarismo*; Albó, "From MNRistas to Kataristas to Katari"; and J. Sanjinés, *Mestizaje Upside-Down*.

20 The Tihuanaku group, including many members of MINK'A, held a secret meeting at the site of the archaeological ruins to hammer out a "magna carta" defining the principles and strategies of the katarista movement.

21 MINK'A et al., "Manifiesto de Tiwanaku," 217.

22 MINK'A et al., "Manifiesto de Tiwanaku," 222–23 (emphasis in the original).

23 MINK'A, "La liberación del indio en Bolivia," 232–33. This language was inspired by the "Declaration of Barbados," a 1971 UN-sponsored gathering of Indigenous peoples.

24 MINK'A, "La liberación del indio en Bolivia," 232.

25 Ronald Neizen (*The Origins of Indigenism*, 71–72) makes this point in comparing the conditions and trajectories of modern Indigenist movements in the Northern Hemisphere and in the global NGO sphere, where an Indian rights movement was beginning to flourish. By comparison, military dictatorships in Bolivia, Chile, Argentina, Uruguay, and Brazil created life-and-death circumstances, not only for Indigenous activists, but for dissident and oppositional activists of all stripes.

26 See Hurtado, *El katarismo*.

27 Albó, "Andean People in the Twentieth Century," 842.

28 Cajías, *Continuidades y rupturas*, 40–41.

29 Salazar, *Warisata mía*, 11–12.

30 The study carried the authoritative stamp of the NGO (Centro Boliviano de Investigación y Acción Educativa, or CEBIAE) that funded the researchers and published the study, and it circulated widely. Subirats, Mamani, and Huancani, *Warisata "escuela-ayllu."* Excerpts were published in *Presencia*, August 13, 1978.

31 The body of the study is a sprawling compilation of field notes, data, and interviews. It surveys the history of Warisata through several stages of evolution, bringing the study up through the 1970s. Its appendices of transcribed interviews with Aymara people, including several surviving amautas, offers potentially valuable ethnographic material for future studies. But this unwieldy study was ultimately reduced to its terse polemical conclusion, in the service of its materialist premise: Bolivia's dystopian feudal society had reduced the original Warisata to a pile of paternalist gestures and futile utopian dreams.

32 As mentioned, the study was sponsored by the CEBIAE, a Jesuit initiative that was newly established at that time but has since become an important institution and research center in the educational field.

33 In 1978, Salazar explained that, much to his surprise, the CEBIAE's devastating critique of Warisata soon backfired, because it "awakened considerable interest" in the school's history. To counterattack the "calumny" in that report, Salazar retraced the events leading to Warisata's demise at the hands of the oligarchy and the state ("El por qué de una destrucción," *Presencia*, August 27, 1978). More importantly, he was intent on clarifying and redeeming the integrity of Pérez's pedagogic ideas and norms, oriented around Aymara communitarian traditions and practices. See "La escuela ayllu y las

concepciones educativas de Elizardo Pérez," published in *Presencia*, December 10 and 17, 1978. These and other essays were reprinted in multiple editions of Salazar's edited volume, *Warisata mía*, beginning in 1983. Cecilia Salazar, interview with the author, 1999.

34 Siñani de Willka, "Breve biografía de Avelino Siñani," 126. (This testimony also appeared as "Testimonio sobre Avelino Siñani," in *Presencia*, February 16, 1992. The original testimonial appeared in mimeograph form in 1986.) This discussion is also based on my two interviews with the author, August 25, 1990, and September 5, 1990. I am grateful to Silvia Rivera for putting me in touch with Tomasa Siñani's granddaughter, Tomasita, who in turn reached out to her grandmother on my behalf.

35 Tomasa Siñani was instrumental in having Bolivian officials agree to bring the remains of Elizardo Pérez from Buenos Aires to Bolivia, to be buried in a grave site alongside that of her father. Both graves are located in the courtyard of Warisata's "Mexico" pavilion. Siñani de Willka, "Breve biografía de Avelino Siñani," 134.

36 Tomasa Siñani's activism anticipated, by a decade or two, the influx of NGOs focusing on Indigenous people, particularly Indigenous women. To take but one example: the 1993 World Bank report underscored the persistent deficiencies in Bolivia's educational system: scant public funding and material resources, especially for primary education, inadequate teacher training; the alienation and exclusion of children and their parents from decision-making; and indifference to the needs of monolingual native students and their families. The 1993 report is summarized in M. Contreras, "A Comparative Perspective on Education Reforms in Bolivia," 272.

37 Salazar, *Warisata mía*, back of book jacket.

38 See Rivera, "Horizons of Memory," for her original thesis of the "long horizon" of Indigenous memory, tracing back to the centuries of colonial oppression and resistance, versus the "short horizon" of campesino memory, grounded in the revolutionary era of agrarian reform and class politics (and anchored in the Quechua-speaking regions of Cochabamba); and Albó's brilliant essay "From MNRistas to Kataristas to Katari."

39 As noted earlier, many early MINK'A essays were published in Bonfil Batalla, *Utopía y revolución*.

40 This synopsis is based on González Apaza, "Biographical Sketch of Roberto Choque Canqui"; and on personal communication with Roberto Choque on numerous occasions in La Paz, between 1983 and 2017. See Healy, *Llamas, Weavings, and Organic Chocolate*, 86–87; also Dangl, *The Five Hundred Year Rebellion*, 48–49. As Dangl mentions (49), Choque often discussed his historical research with katarista leaders.

41 Among his pioneering studies, see Choque Canqui, "La problemática de la educación indigenal"; *Educación indigenal en Bolivia* (coauthored with Cristina Quisbert Quispe); *Líderes indígenas aymaras* (coauthored with Cristina Quisbert Quispe); and *Historia de una lucha desigual*. One of Choque's magisterial projects, combining archival research with oral history, was the three-volume, coauthored study of Jesús de Machaca—its Indigenous society, history of oppression and violence, and the 1921 rebellion. See the citations of Choque Canqui; Choque Canqui and Ticona Alejo; and Ticona Alejo and Albó in the bibliography.

42 The ALP has been directed by many distinguished historians over the years. It is closely aligned with UMSA's History Department, which in turn has trained hundreds of university students in the craft of archive-based history. Bolivia's Museo de Etnografía y Folklore (MUSEF) houses a rich repository of documents related to contemporary Indigenous issues.

43 See Stephenson, "Forging an Indigenous Counterpublic Sphere"; Larson, "Revisiting Bolivian Studies"; Rivera and Aillón, *Antología del pensamiento crítico boliviano contemporaneo*; and various essays in Thomson et al., *The Bolivia Reader*.

44 Rivera's seminal book, *"Oprimidos pero no vencidos,"* still stands as the touchstone work of this Indigenist revisionism, although in recent years Rivera's intellectual and activist trajectory has moved in many different directions, using a variety of genres and media. For insightful analysis of THOA's scholarship, woven into his interviews with THOA members, see Dangl, *The Five Hundred Year Rebellion*, chap. 4; and Healy, *Llamas, Weavings, and Organic Chocolate*, 86–87.

45 Rivera, "Taller de historia oral andina," mimeograph.

46 In the symbolically fraught year 1992, Aymara historians published a critical volume titled *Educación indígena: Ciudadanía o colonización?* See Choque Canqui et al., *Educación indígena*.

47 See, for example, Puiggrós, *Imaginación y crisis en la educación latinoamericana*; Torres, *Democracy, Education, and Multiculturalism* and *The Politics of Nonformal Education in Latin America*; and Reimers, *Unequal Schools, Unequal Chances*; as well as the rich body of work by (or inspired by) Paulo Freire.

48 Talavera, *Formaciones y transformaciones*, 191.

49 Gustafson (*New Languages of the State*, 7) argues that the idea of "interculturalism" gained political currency in the early 1990s. It was more compatible with the neoliberal state's reformist orientation than was the militant politics of indigeneity, particularly on the Altiplano. See also M. E. García, "Encounters with *Interculturalidad*." For a grassroots look at the workings of "intercultural" dialogue and activism in rural Colombia, see Rappaport, *Intercultural*

Utopias. For a ground-up study of "interculturalism" as improvised pedagogy and practice in a rural Aymara region, long before it was ever coined by progressive educators in the 1990s, see chapter 3 above.

50 CSUTCB, *Hacia una educación intercultural bilingüe*, 1–2, quoted in Gustafson, *New Languages of the State*, 158–59.

51 For comparative reference to Chiapas and other contemporary political-pedagogical movements in Latin America, see Mora, *Kuxlejal Politics*; Pinheiro Barbosa, *Educación, resistencia, y movimientos sociales*; Medina Melgarejo, *Pedagogías insumisas*; Mallon, *Decolonizing Native Histories*; Rappaport, *Intercultural Utopias*; and Gustafson, *New Languages of the State*.

52 This tumultuous era is studied and analyzed in a sprawling scholarly literature. See, for example, Dangl, *The Price of Fire*; Hylton and Thomson, *Revolutionary Horizons*, part 3; Mamani Ramírez, *El estado neocolonial*; Kohl and Farthing, *Impasse in Bolivia*; Postero, *Now We Are Citizens*; Gutiérrez Aguilar, *Rhythms of the Pachakuti*; and García Linera, *La potencia plebeya*.

53 Arguably, Bolivia's plurinational constitution (approved by popular referendum in 2009) was the fruit of a century-long struggle to reconcile Western notions of nationality and citizenship with Bolivia's heritage of ethnic and linguistic pluralism. It defines Bolivian nationhood as being "plurinational, communitarian, sovereign, democratic, intercultural, and with [ethnic] autonomies." As such, the nation's Indigenous people were redefined as full citizen-subjects, endowed with social and cultural rights, and thus no longer inscribed in the polity as "minorities." Along with the state language of Spanish, the Plurinational State recognizes thirty-six Indigenous languages.

54 Ministerio de Educación y Cultura, *Ante proyecto: Nueva Ley de Educación "Avelino Siñani y Elizardo Pérez"* (2006), cited and quoted in Howard, "Education Reform, Indigenous Politics, and Decolonisation in the Bolivia of Evo Morales," 587. On the "politics of decolonization and educational practices," see Yapu, *Modernidad y pensamiento descolonizador* (2006); the 2004 Indigenous Congress Statement, *Por una educación indígena originaria*; and the government's 2011 planning document for curricular reform: Ministerio de Educación, *Curriculo base del sistema educativo plurinacional*. See also the critique of official educational policies over the years in Patzi, *Etnofagia estatal*. NGOs working on these issues include the influential Centro para la Investigación y Promoción del Campesino (CIPCA), established in Bolivia in the early 1970s and operating, until recently, the ambitious, six-country Training Program for Intercultural Bilingual Education for Andean Countries (PROEIBANDES), funded mostly by Germany.

55 A widely inclusive educational congress was held in 2006, with the aim of drafting a new law. It soon ran into opposition from the Catholic Church, the teachers unions, and the traditional universities. Thereafter, the Ministry of Education attempted to draft a new educational blueprint in consultation

with newly formed Indigenous Education Councils. Its guiding ethos was both intra- and intercultural: to revitalize knowledge and cultures within Indigenous communities and between Indigenous and Western cultures. See Cajías, *Continuidades y rupturas*, 88–109.

56 Mandepora, "Bolivia's Indigenous Universities"; Farthing and Kohl, *Evo's Bolivia*, 103–8.

57 See the insightful ethnographic studies on educational reforms in contemporary Bolivia: Regalsky and Laurie, "The School, Whose Place Is This?"; Canessa, "Reproducing Racism"; Howard-Malverde and Canessa, "The School in the Quechua and Aymara Communities of Highland Bolivia"; and Howard, "Education Reform, Indigenous Politics, and Decolonisation in the Bolivia of Evo Morales."

BIBLIOGRAPHY

Archival Holdings

AHHCN: Archivo Histórico del Honorable Congreso Nacional de Bolivia (Note: On January 22, 2010 the official designation of this archive was changed to Biblioteca y Archivo Histórico de la Asamblea Legislativa Plurinacional. My citations and notes reference the original name of this archive.)

AJA: Archivo del Juzgado de Achacachi (Achacachi)

ALP: Archivo de La Paz
    ALP-C: Archivo de La Paz, Correspondencia
    ALP-CNE, V: Archivo de La Paz, Consejo Nacional de Educación, Vocalía de Educación Indígena y Rural
    ALP-LML: Archivo de La Paz, Colección León M. Loza
    ALP-P: Archivo de La Paz, Prefectura
    ALP-P, C: Archivo de La Paz, Prefectura, Correspondencia
    ALP-P, C, ME: Archivo de La Paz, Prefectura, Correspondencia, Ministerio de Educación
    ALP-P, E: Archivo de La Paz, Prefectura, Expedientes

ANB: Archivo Nacional de Bolivia (Sucre)
    ANB-P: Archivo Nacional de Bolivia, Presidencia
    ANB-P, C: Archivo Nacional de Bolivia, Presidencia, Correspondencia
    ANB-P, C, MAC: Archivo Nacional de Bolivia, Presidencia, Correspondencia, Ministerio de Asuntos Campesinos

APCSM: Archivo privado de Carlos Salazar Mostajo (La Paz)
APEP: Archivo privado de Elizardo Pérez (La Paz)

APJM: Archivo privado de Jaime Mendoza (Sucre)
APJRA: Archivo privado de José Roberto Arze (La Paz)
ATHOA: Archivo del Taller de Historia Oral Andina (La Paz)
CBIAE: Centro Boliviano de Investigación e Acción Educativo (La Paz)
FT: Fondo de la Torre, Casa de la Cultura (La Paz)
NARA: National Archives and Records Administration, College Park, MD
    RG (Record Group) 59: State Department
    RG 84: Foreign Service, Consular Reports
    RG 166: Foreign Agricultural Service
    RG 229: Institute of Inter-American Affairs

Published Primary and Literary Sources

Aliaga Suarez, Ernesto. *Planes para orientar la educación*. La Paz: n.p., 1940.
Alurralde, Enrique. "La castellanización del Indio." *Indiología boliviana: Revista mensual de educación del indio boliviano* 1 (1918): 23–29.
Amauta: Revista pedagógica. "Hacia una nueva educación en Bolivia." 7, no. 4 (1937).
Anonymous. *La cruzada nacional pro-Indio*. La Paz: Salesiana, 1926.
Anonymous. "Don Franz Tamayo." *Inti Karka* 1, no. 1 (1952): 57–68.
Anonymous. "A Rural Taylor System for the Indian." *Boletín indigenista* 3 (1943): 2–13.
Arguedas, Alcides. *Pueblo enfermo*. 1909. 2nd ed., La Paz: Puerta del Sol, 1936. 3rd ed., La Paz: Puerta del Sol, 1995.
Arguedas, Alcides. *Raza de bronce*. 1919. Reprint, La Paz: Gisbert y Cía, 1976.
Bairon, Max. "La educación del indio en Bolivia." *América indígena* 2 (1942): 7–10.
Bairon, Max. "La educación en las selvas de Bolivia." *América indígena* 12 (1952): 141–47.
Baliaga Suarez, Ernesto. *Planes para orientar la educación*. La Paz: n.p., 1940.
Ballivián, Manuel V. "El problema del indio." *Boletín de la sociedad geográfica de La Paz* 47 (1918): i–x.
Beaglehold, Ernest. "A Technical Mission in the Andes." *International Labour Review* 67, no. 6 (June 1953): 520–34.
Beltrán, Teodomiro. *Instrucciones pedagógicas*. Cochabamba: El Heraldo, 1912.
Bohan, Merwin. *A Report of the Economic Mission of the United States to Bolivia*. Washington, DC: US State Department, 1942.
Boletín Indígena. "The Andean Indians and Technical Assistance of the United Nations." 15 (1955): 7–9.
Boletín Indígena. "Editorial." 3 (1943): 2–13.
Boletín Indígena. "Número especial dedicado al III Congreso Indigenista Interamericano. La Paz, Bolivia, 2–13 August, 1954." 14 (1954): 199–227.
Bustos, Romualdo. "Indios semi-instruidos atentan la propiedad privada." *Cuestión social jurídica* (1924): 1–26.
Calderón, Ignacio. "Dreams of the Railroad." In Thomson et al., *The Bolivia Reader*, 193–94.
Canelas, Demetrio. *Aspectos de la Revolución Boliviana: La reforma agraria y temas anexos*. La Paz: n.p., 1958.

Cárdenas, Ángel. *Instrucción y educación de la raza indígena: Informe presentado al ilustrísimo Sr. Vicario Capitular*. La Paz: Tipografía La Unión, 1911.

Castro, Martín. *La civilización del indio: Escrita por el cura párroco de Macha, Dr. Martín Castro*. Colquechaca: Imprenta del Pueblo, 1897.

Chávez Ruíz, Ángel. "La escuela normal rural." *Indiología boliviana: Revista mensual de educación del indio boliviano* 1 (1918): 1–23.

Chervin, Arthur. *Anthropologie bolivienne*. Vol. 1. Paris: Imprimerie Nationale, 1908.

Claure, Toribio. *Una escuela rural en Vacas*. La Paz: Editorial Universo, 1949.

Claure, Toribio. "¿Seguimos en Bolivia los principios de la educación fundamental?" *América indígena* 13 (1953): 65–72.

CNE (Consejo Nacional de Educación). *El estado actual de la educación indigenal en Bolivia: Informe del Vicepresidente del Consejo Nacional de Educación*. La Paz: n.p., 1940.

CNE (Consejo Nacional de Educación). *El estado de la educación indigenal en el país*. La Paz: n.p., 1940.

Comitas, Lambros. "Educación y estratificación social en Bolivia." *América indígena* 28 (1968): 631–51.

Convención Nacional de 1938. *Proyectos de ley*. La Paz: Editorial Trabajo, 1938.

CSUTCB (Confederación Sindical Única de Trabajadores Campesinos en Bolivia). *Hacia una educación intercultural bilingüe*. La Paz: Jaima, 1991.

Dewey, John. *Democracy and Education*. 1916. Reprint, New York: Free Press, 1944.

"El día del indio." *América indígena* 3 (1943): 3–8.

Díaz Vera, Humberto. "La educación física en Bolivia." *Boletín de Educación Física* (1936).

Diez de Medina, Fernando. *Bolivia y su destino*. La Paz: n.p., 1962.

Diez de Medina, Fernando. "Discurso... al asumir la Presidencia de la Comisión de la Reforma Educacional [CRE]" (June 30, 1953). In *Código de la Educación Boliviana*, 27–41. La Paz: Departamento de Publicaciones y Difusión Cultural, 1956.

Diez de Medina, Fernando. "Planteamiento filosófico y humanista de la Reforma: 'La formación del hombre integral boliviano'" (October 30, 1953). In *Código de la Educación Boliviana*, 101–4. La Paz: Departamento de Publicaciones y Difusión Cultural, 1956.

Dirección Nacional de Informaciones. *Bolivia: 10 años de revolución*. La Paz: Editorial Industrial Gráfica Burillo y Cía, 1962.

Donoso Torres, Vicente. *El estado actual de la educación en Bolivia: Informe a la Misión Magruder*. La Paz: Consejo Nacional de la Educación, 1943.

Donoso Torres, Vicente. *Filosofía de la educación boliviana*. Buenos Aires: Editorial Atlántida, 1946.

Donoso Torres, Vicente. *Proyecto de estatuto para la organización de la facultad de ciencias pedagógicas*. Sucre: Escuela Tipográfica Saleciana, 1930.

Donoso Torres, Vicente. *La sección de maestros rurales en la escuela normal*. Sucre: Imprenta Bolivar, 1933.

D'Orbigny, Alcide. *Viaje a la América Meridional*. 4 vols. Buenos Aires: Editorial Futuro, 1945.

Du Bois, W. E. B. *The Souls of Black Folk*. 1903. Reprint, New York: Dover, 1994.

Eder, George Jackson. *Inflation and Development in Latin America: A Case History of Inflation and Stabilization in Bolivia*. Ann Arbor: University of Michigan, 1968.

Escuela Normal de la Florida. *Educación indígena*. Cochabamba: n.p., 1941.

Escuela Normal de la Florida. *Educación indígena: Informe que el Director de la Escuela Normal Rural de la Florida (Sacaba) presenta a la ilustrada consideración del señor Presidente del Consejo Universitario del Distrito*. Cochabamba: n.p., 1921.

Fellman Velarde, José, ed. *El album de la Revolución*. La Paz: Subsecretaría de Prensa, Informaciones, y Cultura, 1954.

Finot, Enrique. *Historia de la pedagogía boliviana*. La Paz: n.p., 1917.

Finot, Enrique. *La reforma educacional en Bolivia*. La Paz: n.p., 1917.

Finot, Enrique. *Sobre el problema del indio*. Mexico City: n.p., 1940.

Flores Moncayo, José. *Legislación boliviana del indio: Recopilación. 1825–1953*. La Paz: Editorial Zenix, 1953.

Flores Rodríguez, Carlos. "La educación fundamental y la agricultura." *Gaceta Campesina* 2, no. 2 (April 1953): 36–39.

Francovich, Guillermo. *La filosofía en Bolivia*. Buenos Aires: Editorial Losada, 1945.

Francovich, Guillermo. "Las ideas nacionalistas de Jaime Mendoza." *Revista de la Universidad de Chuquisaca* 2 (1928): 31–40.

Frontaura Argandoña, María. *Hacia el futuro indio*. La Paz: Editorial América, 1932.

Gaceta Campesina. "Conclusiones de la Primera Comisión de Mecanización y Técnica Agraria de Educación Fundamental." 2, no. 3 (August 1953): 163.

Gaceta Campesina. "Primer Seminario de Educación Fundamental en Bolivia: Alfabetización y educación de adultos." 2, no. 2 (April 1953): 40–41.

Guillén Pinto, Alfredo. "Confraternidad pedagógica perú-boliviana." *Educación: Revista mensual de pedagogía y letras* 2 (1918): 1–2.

Guillén Pinto, Alfredo. *La educación del indio: Contribución a la pedagogía nacional*. La Paz: González y Medina, 1919.

Guillén Pinto, Alfredo. "La educación indigenal." *Educación: Revista mensual de pedagogía y letras* 2 (1918): 2–4.

Guillén Pinto, Alfredo. *Nuestro problema educacional: Algunos apuntes relativos a la educación del indio*. La Paz: n.p., 1929.

Guillén Pinto, Alfredo, and Natty Peñaranda de Guillén Pinto. *Utama: Novela vivida en cuatro años*. La Paz: Gisbert y Casanovas, 1945.

Guzmán, Benjamín. *La educación de la raza indígena*. La Paz: n.p., 1917.

Guzmán, Felipe Segundo. "La educación de la raza indígena." Unpublished manuscript, 1922. Mimeograph.

Guzmán, Felipe Segundo. *El problema pedagógico en Bolivia*. La Paz: n.p., 1910.

Hart, Thomas A. "The Bolivian Nucleos." *Education for Better Living: The Role of the School in Community Improvement. Office of Education Bulletin* 9 (1956): 7–23.

Hart, Thomas A. "Cooperación educacional." *Inti Karka* 4 (1954): 89–107.

Huacani, Carlos, Elías Mamani, and José Subirats. *Warisata "Escuela-Ayllu": El por qué de un fracaso*. La Paz: Centro Boliviano de Investigación y Acción Educativa (CEBIAE), 1978. Mimeograph.

Hughes, Lloyd H. "Rural Education Program in Bolivia." *Bulletin of the Pan American Union* 80 (1946): 267–71.
Ichaso Vásquez, Raquel. *La enseñanza nacional femenina*. La Paz: Imp. Intendencia de Guerra, 1927.
ILO (International Labour Office). *Los problemas del trabajo en Bolivia: Labour Problems in Bolivia*. Montreal: ILO, 1943.
INDICEP (Instituto de Investigación Cultural para Educación Popular). *Dinamización cultural: Método para la educación popular*. La Paz: INDICEP [ca. 1971].
Inti Karka. "El Servicio Cooperativo Interamericano de Educación y la Educación Indigenal." 1, no. 1 (1952): 71–76.
Iturricha, Agustín. *¿Es posible llevar la civilización al indio?* Sucre: Imprenta Bolivar, 1932.
Jáuregui Rosquellas, Alfredo. "Reflexiones sobre la cuestión indígena: Sublevaciones y levantamientos." *Boletín de la Sociedad Geográfica de Sucre* 62 (1947): 522–32.
Kant, Immanuel. *Thoughts on Education*. 1803. Reprint, Ann Arbor: University of Michigan Press, 1960.
Lema, Vicente. *Conferencia Informativa sobre: La educación campesina en Bolivia*. La Paz: Comisión de Reforma Educacional, 1953.
Lewis, Oscar, and Ernest Maes. "Base para una nueva definición práctica del indio." *América Indígena* 5 (1945): 107–18.
Mariaca, Juvenal, and Arturo Peñaranda. *Proyecto de organización de una escuela normal agrícola de indígenas en el altiplano*. La Paz: Boliviana, 1918.
Mariaca, Manuel Ernesto. "La educación indigenal." *El Altiplano* 24 (1937): 279–83.
Mariátegui, José Carlos. *Seven Interpretive Essays on the Reality of Peru*. 1928. Reprint, Austin: University of Texas Press, 1971.
Mariátegui, José Carlos. *Temas de educación*. Lima: Amauta, 1970.
Marof, Tristan. *La justicia del Inca*. Brussels: La Edición Latino Americana, 1926.
Marof, Tristan. *La tragedia del altiplano*. Buenos Aires: Colección Claridad, n.d. [1934?].
Martí, José. *Escritos sobre educación*. Havana: Instituto Cubano del Libro, 1976.
Mauck, Wilfred. "More than ABCs: Point 4 in Action." *Americas Magazine*, no. 16 (1956): 3–7.
McBride, George. *The Agrarian Indians of Highland Bolivia*. New York: Oxford University Press, 1921.
Medinaceli, Carlos. *El chaskañawi*. 1947. Reprint, La Paz: Los Amigos del Libro, 1982.
Medinaceli, Carlos. *Estudios críticos*. 1938. 2nd ed., La Paz: Los Amigos del Libro, 1969.
Mendoza, Jaime. "El comunismo." *Revista de Federación de Estudiantes de Chuquisaca* 2 (1930): 113–30.
Mendoza, Jaime. *El factor geográfico en la nacionalidad boliviana*. Sucre: Imprenta Bolívar, 1925.
Mendoza, Jaime. *El macizo boliviano*. 1935. Reprint, La Paz: Ediciones Juventud, 1986.
Mendoza, Jaime. "El niño boliviano." *Universidad de San Francisco Xavier* 7 (1939): 115–77.
Mendoza, Jaime. "Notas sobre la educación del Indio." In *Antología pedagógica de Bolivia*, edited by Mariano Baptista Gumucio. 1939. Reprint, La Paz–Cochabamba: Los Amigos del Libro, 1979.

Mendoza, Saúl. "La industria nacional indígena." *Indiología boliviana: Revista mensual de educación del indio boliviano* 1 (1918): 29–38.

Mercado, Joaquín. "Hacia la educación económica de Bolivia." *Revista boliviana de instrucción pública* 2 (1922): 254–71.

Ministerio de Asuntos Campesinos. *Educación fundamental*. La Paz, n.d.

Ministerio de Asuntos Campesinos. *Orientación agrícola de las escuelas indigenales: Respuesta a las observaciones de la Sociedad Rural Boliviana*. La Paz: n.p., 1937.

Ministerio de Asuntos Campesinos. *Plan y programas de educación rural, no. 1*. La Paz: n.p., 1963.

Ministerio de Asuntos Campesinos and Dirección Nacional de Ministerio de Educación. *Curriculo base del sistema educativo plurinacional*. Sucre, 2011.

Ministerio de Asuntos Campesinos and Dirección Nacional de Informaciones. *Educación, producción, y trabajo*. Sucre, n.d.

Ministerio de Asuntos Campesinos and SCIDE (Servicio Cooperativo Interamericano de Desarrollo Educativo). *Curso para directores y profesores de escuelas normales rurales*. La Paz: n.p., 1961.

Ministerio de Asuntos Campesinos and SCIDE (Servicio Cooperativo Interamericano de Desarrollo Educativo). *Informe: Escuelas normales rurales de Bolivia*. La Paz: Comision de Reestructuración, 1958.

Ministerio de Asuntos Campesinos and SCIDE (Servicio Cooperativo Interamericano de Desarrollo Educativo). *Manual del maestro rural*. La Paz, 1956.

Ministerio de Educación. *Propaganda moralizadora del Ministerio de Educación*. La Paz, 1938.

Ministerio de Educación. *Proyecto de Código de la educación boliviana*. La Paz, 1954.

Ministerio de Educación and Departamento de Educación Rural. *Guía didáctica de educación rural*. Mimeograph. La Paz, 1947. Mimeograph.

Ministerio de Educación, Departamento de Educación Rural, and Programa Cooperativo de Educación. *Guía de instrucción para maestros rurales*. 7 vols. Vol. 1, *Los objetivos de la educación rural*; vol. 2, *Agricultura*; vol. 6, *Economía doméstica*. La Paz: Prensa del Estado, 1948.

Ministerio de Educación y Bellas Artes. *Código de la educación boliviana*. La Paz: Editorial Industrial Gráfica Burillo y Cía, 1956.

Ministerio de Educación y Bellas Artes. *Plan de fomento de la educación nacional*. La Paz: Ministerio de Educación, 1958.

Ministerio de Gobierno y Justicia. *Cuestiones indigenales*. La Paz, 1954.

Ministerio de Instrucción Pública. *Memoria*. La Paz: Editorial Eléctrica, 1931.

Ministerio de Instrucción Pública y Agricultura. "Informe de la Dirección General de Educación Indígena." In *Memoria y Anexos*. La Paz: Moderna, 1919.

MINK'A. "La liberación del Indio en Bolivia." In Bonfil Batalla, *Utopía y revolución*, 226–34.

MINK'A. "MINK'A y la oficialización del Aymara y el Quechua." In Bonfil Batalla, *Utopía y revolución*, 240–45.

MINK'A et al. "Manifiesto de Tiwanaku." In Bonfil Batalla, *Utopía y revolución*, 216–23.

Molina Campero, Lionel. *Contenido orgánico de nuestra educación pública.* La Paz: Editorial Universo, 1944.

Montenegro, Carlos. *Nacionalismo y coloniaje.* 1943. Reprint, La Paz: Editorial Juventud, 1994.

Montero Justiniano, José, and J. Alfredo Villegas, eds. *Nuevo digesto de legislación educacional.* La Paz: Ministerio de Educación, Bellas Artes, y Asuntos Indígenas, 1941.

Morales Guillén, Carlos. "Ponencia sobre supresión de servicios gratuitos." Unpublished manuscript presented at Primer Congreso Indígena Boliviano, La Paz, 1945. Mimeograph.

Moscoso, Octavio. "Informe que presenta el inspector de instrucción primaria fiscal del Departamento de Chuquisaca." Sucre: Tipografía Ligera, 1913.

Mujía, Ricardo. *Manual de instrucción primaria.* 4th ed. Sucre: Imprenta Bolívar, 1911.

Muñoz Reyes, V. *El problema del indio.* La Paz: Sociedad Geográfica de la Paz, 1927.

Nelson, Ernesto. "Aspectos de la crisis actual de educación." *Revista boliviana de instrucción pública* 3 (1922): 410–23.

Nelson, Raymond. *Education in Bolivia.* Washington: US Government Printing Office, 1949.

Nina Quispe, Eduardo. *De los títulos de composición de la Corona de España: Composición a título de usufructo, como se entiende la exención revisitaria. Venta y composición de tierras de orígen con la corona de España. Títulos de las comunidades de la Républica. Renovación de Bolivia.* La Paz: n.p., 1932. (Housed in the ALP-EP, box 346, 1933.)

Nina Quispe, Eduardo. *Solicitudes de Eduardo L. Nina Quispe para la orientación técnica de la educación indigenal en Bolivia.* La Paz: n.p., 1933. (Housed in the ALP, Ministerio de Gobierno, Correspondencia.)

Ondarza León, Joaquín. "La educación de la postguerra." *Revista educación* (1937): 6–8.

ONI (Oficina Nacional de Inmigración, Estadística y Propaganda Geográfica). *Censo general de la población de la República de Bolivia según el empadronamiento de 1 Septiembre de 1900.* Tomos 1–3. 1900. Reprint, Cochabamba: Editorial Canelas, 1973.

Otero, Gustavo Adolfo. *Figura y carácter del indio: Los andes bolivianos.* 1941. 4th ed., La Paz: Editorial Juventud, 1981.

Otero, Gustavo Adolfo. *Una política educacional: Ensayos y discursos.* La Paz: Editorial del Estado, 1941.

Pardo Uzeda, Alfonso. *Núcleo de la recuperación campesina de Caiza "D."* Sucre: Editorial Indoamericana, 1942.

Paredes, Manuel Rigoberto. *La altiplanicie: Anotaciones etnográficas, geográficas y sociales de la comunindad aymara.* 1914. Reprint, La Paz: Ediciones Isla, 1965.

Paredes, Manuel Rigoberto. "La altiplanicie: Rasgos psicológicos de sus moradores." *Revista boliviana de instrucción pública* 4 (1922–23): 584–602.

Paredes, Manuel Rigoberto. *La Paz y la provincia El Cercado.* Ca. 1910s. Reprint, La Paz: Ediciones Isla, 1955.

Paredes, Manuel Rigoberto. *Política parlamentaria de Bolivia: Estudio de psicología colectiva.* 1907. Reprint, La Paz: Velarde, 1911.

Paredes, Manuel Rigoberto. *Provincia de Inquisivi: Estudios geográficos, estadísticos y sociales.* La Paz: Gamarra, 1906.

Paredes, Manuel Rigoberto. *La provincia de Omasuyos.* Ca. 1910s. Reprint, La Paz: Ediciones Isla, 1955.

Paredes, Manuel Rigoberto. *Tiahuanacu y la Provincia de Ingavi.* Ca. 1910s. Reprint, La Paz: Ediciones Isla, 1955.

Paz Estenssoro, Victor. *Discursos y mensajes.* La Paz: Ediciones Meridiano, 1953.

Paz Estenssoro, Victor. *Mensaje al pueblo.* La Paz: Subsecretaría de Prensa, 1955.

Paz Estenssoro, Victor. *El pensamiento revolucionario de Paz Estenssoro.* La Paz: Burillo y Cía, 1954.

Pérez, Elizardo. *Mensaje de la escuela indigenal de Warisata en el Día de las Américas.* La Paz: Semana Gráfica, 1934.

Pérez, Elizardo. *Orientación agrícola de las escuelas indigenales: Respuesta a las observaciones de la Sociedad Rural Boliviana.* La Paz: Ministerio de Educación y Asuntos Indígenas, 1937.

Pérez, Elizardo. *Warisata: La escuela-ayllu.* 1962. Reprint, La Paz: HISBOL/Ceres, 1992.

Pérez, Raúl. "Refutación a fondo del fallo del Tribunal de E. indígena." *Inti,* August 31, 1940.

Pérez Velasco, Daniel. *La mentalidad chola en Bolivia: Al través de un siglo de vida democrática.* La Paz: López, 1928.

Piérola, Raúl Alberto. *Educación nacional.* Buenos Aires: Editorial Nora, 1955.

Pinto Escalier, Arturo. "La educación pública en el último período." *Estudios sociales* 3 (1941): 27–35.

Pizarro, Felipe. *El alfabetizador del indio.* La Paz: Cervantes, 1929.

Posnasky, Arturo. "Los dos tipos indigenales en Bolivia y su educación." *América indígena* 3 (1943): 55–60.

Posnasky, Arturo. "Opinión autorizada sobre la instrucción indigenal." *El Altiplano* 25–26 (1937): 343–55.

Primer Congreso Interamericano de Indigenistas. *Reglamento, temario y agendas.* La Paz: Editorial Fénix, 1939.

Prudencio, Ernesto. "La instrucción cívica." *Indiología boliviana: Revista mensual de educación del indio boliviano* 1 (1918): 42–45.

Ramírez, Juan. "La reforma integral de la educación en Bolivia." *Revista boliviana de instrucción pública* 1 (1922): 80–92.

Reinaga, Fausto. *Franz Tamayo y la Revolución boliviana.* La Paz: Editorial Casegural, 1956.

Reinaga, Fausto. *La revolución india.* La Paz: Cooperativa de Artes Gráficos, 1969.

Rens, Jef. "The Andean Programme." *International Labour Review* 84 (1961): 423–61.

Retamoso, Abel. *Civilización y cultura indígena.* La Paz: La Prensa, 1927.

Retamoso, Ramón. *Estudio sociológico y psicológico del niño boliviano.* La Paz: Escuela Municipal de Artes, 1930.

Reyeros, Rafael. *Caquiaviri: Escuelas para los indígenas bolivianos.* La Paz: Editorial Universo, 1937.

Reyeros, Rafael. "Caquiaviri: Informe de una visita." *Revista educación* 1 (1937): 2–3.

Reyeros, Rafael. *El pongueaje: La servidumbre personal de los indios bolivianos*. La Paz: n.p., 1949.

Rodríguez, Saturnino. "Warisata, una escuela en la vida del indio." In *De mi tierra*, 41–48. Buenos Aires: Delta, 1942.

Romero, Carlos. *Las taras de nuestra democracia*. La Paz: ARNO, 1919.

Rouma, Georges. *Las bases científicas de la educación: Resúmenes*. Sucre: Bolívar, 1911.

Rouma, Georges. *El desarrollo físico del escolar boliviano*. La Paz: Editorial Universo, 1938.

Rouma, Georges. *Les indiens Quitchouas et Aymaras des Hauts Plateaux de la Bolivie*. Brussels: Société d'Antropologie de Bruxelles, 1913.

Rouma, Georges. *Informe presentando a la consideración del supremo gobierno por el comisionado Dr. Georges Rouma*. La Paz: Imprenta Artística Ayacucho, 1931.

Rouma, Georges. *Una página de la historia educacional boliviana*. Sucre: Editorial López, 1928.

Rouma, Georges. *Pedagogie sociologique: Les influences des milieux en éducacion*. Brussels: Neuchatel Editerus, 1914.

Rouma, Georges. *Quitchouas et Aymaras: Etude des populations autochtones des Andes bolivienne*. Brussels: Société Royale Belge d'Anthropologie et de Préhistoire, 1933.

Rousseau, Jean-Jacques. *Émile ou de l'éducation*. 1762. Reprint, Paris: Garnier-Flammarion, 1966.

Rubio Orbe, Gonzalo. "Aculturaciones de Indígenas de los Andes." *América Indígena* 13 (1953): 187–222.

Rubio Orbe, Gonzalo. *Educación fundamental*. Quito: Casa de la Cultura Ecuatoriana, 1954.

Saavedra, Bautista. *El ayllu: Estudios sociológicos*. 1901. Reprint, La Paz: Juventud, 1987.

Saavedra, Bautista. *La democracia en nuestra historia*. La Paz: González y Medina, 1921.

Saavedra, Bautista. *Memoria de justicia e instrucción pública*. La Paz: Imprenta Artística, 1910.

Saavedra, Bautista. "Proceso Mohoza: Defensa del abogado Bautista Saavedra." In *El ayllu: Estudios sociológicos*. 1901. Reprint, La Paz: Juventud, 1987.

Sachetti, Alfredo. "Second Trip of the Argentine Mission of Anthropological Studies to the Aymara Region." *Boletín indigenista* 13 (1953): 327–35.

Sáenz, Moisés. *La educación rural en México*. Mexico City: Talleres Gráficos de la Nación, 1928.

Salamanca, Octavio. *El socialismo en Bolivia: Los indios de la Altiplanicie*. Cochabamba: Imprenta Rojas, 1931.

Salazar, Rufino. *Recordando nuestros deberes*. Sucre: Imprenta Bolívar, 1932.

Salazar Mostajo, Carlos. *La cueva*. 1946. Reprint, La Paz: Editora Urquizo, 1992.

Salazar Mostajo, Carlos. *Gesta y fotografía: Historia de Warisata en imágenes*. La Paz: Ediciones Lazarsa, 2005.

Salazar Mostajo, Carlos. *La taika: Teoría y práctica de la escuela ayllu*. 1986. Reprint, La Paz: Universidad Mayor de San Andrés, 1992.

Salazar Mostajo, Carlos. *Warisata mía*. 1983. 3rd ed., La Paz: Juventud, 1997.

Salinas, Flora. *Lecturas infantiles no. 1*. La Paz: Gilbert y Casanovas, 1942.

Salinas López, Alberto. "El patriota." *Revista de educación* (1937): 5.
Salmón Ballivián, José. *Ideario aimara*. La Paz: Escuela Tipográfica Salesiana, 1926.
Salmón Ballivián, José. *El indio escribirá mañana la historia de Bolivia*. La Paz: Impresora Atenea, 1931.
Salmón Ballivián, José. "El indio íntimo: Contribución al estudio biológico social del indio." In *Ideario aimara*, 105–63. La Paz: Salesiana, 1926.
Sánchez Bustamante, Daniel. *Programa político: Problemas de Bolivia en 1918*. La Paz: Imprenta Velardo, 1918.
Sanjinés, Alfredo. *La reforma agraria en Bolivia*. La Paz: Editorial Renacimiento, 1932.
Sarmiento, Domingo F. *Ideas pedagógicas de Domingo F. Sarmiento*. Buenos Aires: Talleres Gráficos del Consejo de Educación, 1938.
Sarmiento, Domingo F. *Memoria sobre educación común*. Santiago: Impr. del Ferrocarril, 1856.
Saturnino, Rodrigo. "Revolución de veras." *Educación: Revista del Ministerio de Educación y Asuntos Indígenas* 1 (1937): 1–4.
Schweng, Lorand. "An Indian Community Development Project in Bolivia." In *A Casebook of Social Change*, edited by Arthur H. Niehoff, 42–57. Chicago: Aldine, 1966.
SCIDE (Servicio Cooperativo Interamericano de Desarrollo Educativo). *Rural Education in Bolivia: A Study in Technical Cooperation*. La Paz: Institute of Inter-American Affairs, 1955.
Siles Suazo, Hernán. "Speech Delivered by Dr. Hernán Siles Suazo... at the Closing Session of the Inter-American Indian Congress (August 12)." *Boletín indigenista* 14, no. 3 (September 1954).
Smithsonian Institution. "Conference on Bolivian Indians." *Ethnographic Board*, September 20, 1942.
Soria Galvarro, Carlos. "Warisata: Un insólito experimento pedagógico." *Bases* 1 (1982): 148–68.
Spencer, Herbert. *Education: Intellectual, Moral, and Physical*. 1860. Reprint, New York: Appleton and Co., 1927.
SPIC (Subsecretaría de Prensa, Informaciones y Cultura). *Albúm de la Revolución: 128 años de lucha por la independencia de Bolivia*. La Paz: SPIC, 1954.
SRB (Sociedad Rural Boliviana). "Sobre la educación de Indio." *El altiplano* 2 (1937): 435–45.
Stahl, F. A. *In the Land of the Incas*. Mountain View, CA: Pacific Press, 1920.
Suárez Arnez, Faustino. *Hacia la nueva educación nacional*. La Paz: Editorial Universo, 1953.
Suárez Arnez, Faustino. *Historia de la educación en Bolivia*. La Paz: n.p., 1958.
Subirats, José, E. Mamani, and C. Huacani. *Warisata "escuela-ayllu": El por qué de un fracaso. Estudio de caso: Una experiencia de escuela comunitaria*. La Paz: CEBIAE, 1978.
Tamayo, Franz. *Creación de la pedagogía nacional*. 1910. Reprint, La Paz: Librería Editorial "Juventud," 1988.
Tamayo, Franz. *Creación de una pedagogía nacional*. La Paz: Puerta del Sol, 1910.

Tapia, Luciano. *Ukhamawa Jakawisaxa (Asi es nuestra vida): Autobiografía de un aymara*. La Paz: HISBOL, 1995.
Tarifa Ascarrunz, Erasmo. *Programas de instrucción para escuelas indigenales*. La Paz: Imprenta Intendencia, 1938.
Uranga, Javier. "¿Qué es indigenismo?" *America indígena* 1 (1941): 51–53.
Valencia Vega, Alipio. "Revolución agrarian y educación indígena." *Inti Karka* 1, no. 1 (1952): 21–26.
Valois Arce, Daniel. *Bolivia: Realidad y destino*. Bogotá: Antares, 1955.
Vázquez, Emilio. "Panorama de la educación rural en los países andinos." *América Indígena* 14, no. 3 (1954): 253–70.
Velasco, Adolfo. *La escuela indigenal de Warisata, Bolivia*. Mexico City: Departamento de Asuntos Indígenas, 1940.
Villaroel Claure, Rigoberto. *Educación indígena: Informe que el director de la Escuela Normal de la Florida... presenta al... Consejo Universitario del distrito*. Cochabamba: n.p., 1921.
Wayar, Luis S. *El problema social del niño boliviano*. Sucre: Editorial Indoamericana, 1942.
Zenobia Valderrama, M. "Necesidad de preparar a la madre indígena." *Indiología boliviana: Revista mensual de educación del indio boliviano* 1 (1918): 38–42.

Secondary Sources

Abercrombie, Thomas. *Pathways of Memory and Power: Ethnography and History among an Andean People*. Madison: University of Wisconsin Press, 1998.
Adams, David Wallace. *Education for Extinction: American Indians and the Boarding School Experience, 1875–1928*. Lawrence: University of Kansas Press, 1995.
Adorno, Rolena. *Guaman Poma: Writing as Resistance in Colonial Peru*. Austin: University of Texas Press, 1988.
Adorno, Rolena. "Images of *Indios Ladinos* in Early Colonial Peru." In *Transatlantic Encounters: Europeans and Andeans in the Sixteenth Century*, edited by Kenneth J. Andrien and Rolena Adorno, 232–70. Berkeley: University of California Press, 1991.
Aimes, Patricia. *Para ser iguales, para ser distintos: Educación, escritura, y poder en el Perú*. Lima: IEP, 2002.
Albarracín Millán, Juan. *El gran debate: Positivismo e irracionalismo en el estudio de la sociedad boliviana*. La Paz: Editorial Universo, 1978.
Albarracín Millán, Juan. *Sociología indigenal y antropología telurista*. La Paz: Editora Universo, 1982.
Alberti, Giorgio, and Julio Cotler, eds. *Aspectos sociales de la educación rural en el Perú*. Lima: IEP, 1972.
Albó, Xavier. *Achacachi, medio siglo de luchas campesinas*. Cuaderno de Investigación 19. La Paz: CIPCA, 1979.
Albó, Xavier. "Andean People in the Twentieth Century." In *The Cambridge History of the Native Peoples of the Americas: South America*, edited by Frank Salomon and Stuart B. Schwartz, 765–871. Cambridge: Cambridge University Press, 1999.

Albó, Xavier. "From MNRistas to Kataristas to Katari." In *Resistance, Rebellion and Consciousness in the Andean Peasant World, 18th to 20th Centuries*, edited by Steve J. Stern, 379–419. Madison: University of Wisconsin Press, 1987.

Albó, Xavier. *Idiomas, escuelas, y radios en Bolivia*. La Paz: ACLO-UNITAS, 1981.

Albó, Xavier. "The 'Long Memory' of Ethnicity in Bolivia and Some Temporary Oscillations." In *Unresolved Tensions: Bolivia, Past and Present*, edited by John Crabtree and Laurence Whitehead, 13–34. Pittsburgh: University of Pittsburgh Press, 2008.

Albó, Xavier. "Making the Leap from Local Mobilization to National Politics." NACLA *(North American Congress on Latin America) Report* 29, no. 5 (1996): 15–32.

Albó, Xavier. "Our Identity Starting from Pluralism in the Base." In *The Postmodernism Debate in Latin America*, edited by John Beverley, José Oviedo, and Michael Aronna, 18–33. Durham, NC: Duke University Press, 1995.

Albó, Xavier. *Pueblos indios en la política*. La Paz: CIPCA, 2002.

Albó, Xavier, ed. *Raíces de América: El mundo aymara*. Madrid: Alianza Editorial, 1988.

Albó, Xavier, and Josep Barnadas. *La cara campesina de nuestra historia*. La Paz: Alenkar, 1984.

Albó, Xavier, Thomas Greaves, and Godofredo Sandoval. *Chukiyawu, la cara aymara de La Paz: Cabalgando entre dos mundos*. La Paz: CIPCA, 1983.

Alexander, Robert. *The Bolivian National Revolution*. New Brunswick, NJ: Rutgers University Press, 1958.

Almaráz Paz, Sergio. *Bolivia: Requiem para una república*. 1967. 5th ed., La Paz: Universidad Mayor de San Andrés, 1988.

Alvaréz, Sonia, Evelina Dagnino, and Arturo Escobar, eds. *Cultures of Politics, Politics of Cultures: Re-visioning Latin American Social Movements*. Boulder, CO: Westview, 1998.

Alvaréz Calderón Gerbolini, Annalyda. *En búsqueda de la ciudadanía indígena: Puno, 1900–1930*. Lima: Fundación Bustamante–De la Fuente, 2021.

Alvizuri, Verushka. *La construcción de la aymaridad: Una historia de la etnicidad en Bolivia (1952–2006)*. Santa Cruz: El País, 2009.

Anderson, Benedict. *Imagined Communities: Reflections on the Origins and Spread of Nationalism*. London: Verso, 1986.

Anderson, James D. *The Education of Blacks in the South, 1860–1935*. Chapel Hill: University of North Carolina Press, 1988.

Andolina, Robert, Nina Laurie, and Sarah Radcliffe. *Indigenous Development in the Andes: Culture, Power, and Transnationalism*. Durham, NC: Duke University Press, 2009.

Antezana Ergueta, Luís. *La revolución campesina en Bolivia: Historia del sindicalismo campesino*. La Paz: Editora Siglo, 1982.

Antezana Ergueta, Luís. *Resultados de la reforma agrarian en Bolivia*. Cochabamba: Imp. F. O. Guenca, 1955.

Antezana Ergueta, Luís, and Hugo Romero. *Historia de los sindicatos campesinos*. La Paz: CNRA, 1973.

Apffel-Marglin, Frédérique, ed. *Decolonizing Knowledge: From Development to Dialogue*. Oxford: Clarendon, 1996.

Apffel-Marglin, Frédérique, ed. *The Spirit of Regeneration: Andean Culture Confronting Western Notions of Development*. London: Zed Books, 1998.

Appelbaum, Nancy, A. Macpherson, and K. A. Rosemblatt, eds. "Introduction." In *Race and Nation in Modern Latin America*, edited by Appelbaum, Macpherson, and Rosemblatt, 1–31. Chapel Hill: University of North Carolina Press, 2003.

Appelbaum, Nancy, A. Macpherson, and K. A. Rosemblatt, eds. *Race and Nation in Modern Latin America*. Chapel Hill: University of North Carolina Press, 2003.

Ari, Waskar T. *Earth Politics: Religion, Decolonization, and Bolivia's Indigenous Intellectuals*. Durham, NC: Duke University Press, 2014.

Arias, José. *La educación del indio y las bases para su organización*. La Paz: Escuela Salesiana, 1994.

Arnold, Denise Y., with Juan de Dios Yapita. *The Metamorphosis of Heads: Textual Struggles, Education, and Land in the Andes*. Pittsburgh: University of Pittsburgh Press, 2006.

Arnold, Denise, Juan de Dios Yapita, and Ricardo López. "Leer y escribir en aymara bajo La Reforma." *Tinkazos* 3 (1999): 103–15.

Arze Aguirre, René. *Guerra y conflictos sociales: El caso rural boliviano durante la campaña del Chaco*. La Paz: CERES, 1987.

Baker, Lee. *Anthropology and the Racial Politics of Culture*. Durham, NC: Duke University Press, 2010.

Balibar, Etienne, and I. Wallerstein. *Race, Nation, and Class: Ambiguous Identities*. London: Verso, 1991.

Baptista Gumucio, Mariano. *La educación como forma de suicidio nacional*. La Paz: Ediciones Camarlinghi, 1973.

Baptista Gumucio, Mariano. *Salvemos a Bolivia de la escuela*. La Paz: Los Amigos del Libro, 1987.

Barnadas, Josep. *Apuntes para una historia agraria*. Cuaderno de investigación 6. La Paz: CIPCA, 1976.

Barnadas, Josep, et al. *Los Aymaras dentro de la sociedad boliviana*. La Paz: CIPCA, 1976.

Barragán, Rossana. "Bolivia: Bridges and Chasms." In *A Companion to Latin American Anthropology*, edited by Deborah Poole, 32–55. Oxford: Blackwell, 2008.

Barragán, Rossana. "The Census and the Making of a Social 'Order' in Nineteenth-Century Bolivia." In *Histories of Race and Racism: The Andes and Mesoamerica from Colonial Times to the Present*, edited by Laura Gotkowitz, 113–33. Durham, NC: Duke University Press, 2011.

Barragán, Rossana. "Entre polleras, lliqllas y nañacas: Los mestizos y la emergencia de la tercera república." In *Etnicidad, economía y simbolismo en los Andes*, edited by Silvia Arze and Ana María Lorandi, 85–128. La Paz: HISBOL, 1992.

Barragán, Rossana. *Espacio urbano y dinámica étnica: La Paz en el siglo XIX*. La Paz: HISBOL, 1990.

Barragán, Rossana. "The 'Spirit of Bolivian Laws': Citizenship, Patriarchy, and Infamy." In *Honor, Status, and Law in Modern Latin America*, edited by Sueann Caulfield and Sarah C. Chambers, 66–86. Durham, NC: Duke University Press, 2005.

Barton, David, M. Hamilton, and R. Ivanic, eds. *Situated Literacies: Reading and Writing in Context*. London: Routledge, 2000.

Bastien, Joseph W. *Healers of the Andes: Kallawaya Herbalists and Their Medicinal Medicines*. Salt Lake City: University of Utah Press, 1987.

Bastos, Isabel. "El indigenismo en la transición hacia el imaginario populista." *Estudios Bolivianos* 2 (1996): 19–47.

Becker, Marc. *Indians and Leftists in the Making of Ecuador's Modern Indigenous Movements*. Durham, NC: Duke University Press, 2008.

Becker, Marjorie. *Setting the Virgin on Fire: Lázaro Cárdenas, Michoacán Peasants, and the Redemption of the Mexican Revolution*. Berkeley: University of California Press, 1995.

Blanco, J. *Antonio Alvarez Mamani: Historia de un dirigente campesino*. La Paz: n.p., 1969.

Blanco Esteban, María Cecilia. "Warisata: Proyecto de transformación integral." Tésis de bachillerato. La Paz: Universidad de San Andrés, 1999.

Blasier, Cole. "The United States and the Revolution." In Malloy and Thorn, *Beyond the Revolution*, 53–109.

Bonfil Batalla, Guillermo, ed. *Utopía y revolución: El pensamiento político contemporaneo de los indios en América Latina*. 1979. Reprint, Mexico City: Editorial Nueva Imagen, 1981.

Bonfil Batalla, Guillermo. "Utopía y revolución: El pensamiento político de los indios en América Latina." In Bonfil Batalla, *Utopía y revolución*, 11–53.

Boone, Elizabeth Hill, and Walter Mignolo, eds. *Writing without Words: Alternative Literacies in Mesoamerica and the Andes*. Durham, NC: Duke University Press, 1994.

Bourdieu, Pierre, and Jean-Claude Passeron. *Reproduction in Education, Society and Culture*. London: Sage, 1977.

Boyer, Christopher. *Becoming Campesinos: Politics, Identity, and Agrarian Struggle in Postrevolutionary Michoacán, 1920–1935*. Stanford, CA: Stanford University Press, 2003.

Bridikhina, Eugenia. *Fiesta cívica: Construcción de lo cívico y políticas festivas*. La Paz: Instituto de Estudios Bolivianos, 2009.

Brienen, Marten. "The Clamor for Schools: Indigenous Communities, the State, and the Development of Indigenous Education in Bolivia, 1900–1952." PhD diss., University of Amsterdam, 2011.

Brienen, Marten. "The Clamor for Schools: Rural Education and the Development of State-Community Contact in Highland Bolivia, 1930–1952." *Revista de Indias* 62 (2001): 615–50.

Brienen, Marten. "Por qué Warisata no es lo que parece: La escuela-ayllu y el establecimiento del control estatal en la educación indígena." In *Cambio y continuidad en Bolivia, Etnicidad, culura, e identidad*, edited by Nicholas Robins, 133–50. La Paz: Plural Editores, 2005.

Britton, John, ed. *Molding the Hearts and Minds: Education, Communications, and Social Change in Latin America*. Wilmington, DE: Scholarly Resources Books, 1994.

Burke, Melvin. "Land Reform in the Lake Titicaca Region." In Malloy and Thorn, *Beyond the Revolution*, 301–39.

Burns, Kathryn. *Into the Archive: Writing and Power in Colonial Peru*. Durham, NC: Duke University Press, 2010.

Burns, Kathryn. "Making Indigenous Archives: The Quilcaycamayoc of Colonial Cuzco." *Hispanic American Historical Review* 91, no. 4 (November 2011): 665–89.

Cajías, Magdalena. *Así fue la Revolución: Cincuentenario de la Revolución del 9 de abril de 1952.* Vol. 1. La Paz: Fundación Cultural Huáscar Cajías K, 2002.

Cajías, Magdalena. *Continuidades y rupturas: El proceso histórico de la formación docente rural y urbana en Bolivia.* La Paz: PIEB, 2011.

Calderón, Fernando, and Jorge Dandler, eds. *Bolivia: La fuerza histórica del campesinado.* Geneva: UNRISD-CERES, 1986.

Calderón, Raúl J. "La 'dueda social' de los liberales de principios de siglo: Una aproximación a la educación elemental entre 1900 y 1910." *Data: Revista del Instituto de Estudios Andinos y Amazónicos* 5 (1994): 53–83.

Calderón, Raúl J. "Paradojas de la modernización: Escuelas provinciales y escuelas comunales en el Altiplano de La Paz (1899–1911)." *Estudios bolivianos* 2 (1996): 111–24.

Canelas, Amado. *Bolivia: Un caso de reforma agraria.* Havana, Cuba: CASA, 1967.

Canessa, Andrew. "The Indian Within, the Indian Without: Citizenship, Race, and Sex in a Bolivian Hamlet." In *Natives Making Nation: Gender, Indigeneity, and the State in the Andes*, edited by Canessa, 130–55. Tucson: University of Arizona Press, 2005.

Canessa, Andrew. *Intimate Indigeneities: Race, Sex, and History in the Small Spaces of Andean Life.* Durham, NC: Duke University Press, 2012.

Canessa, Andrew, ed. *Natives Making Nation: Gender, Indigeneity, and the State in the Andes.* Tucson: University of Arizona Press, 2005.

Canessa, Andrew. "Reproducing Racism: Schooling and Race in Highland Bolivia." *Race, Ethnicity and Education* 7, no. 2 (2004): 185–204.

Cárdenas, Victor Hugo. "La lucha de un pueblo." In *Raíces de América: El mundo aymara*, edited by Xavier Albó, 495–534. Madrid: Editorial Alianza, 1988.

Cárdenas, Victor Hugo. "Prologue." In Choque Canqui et al., *Educación indígena*, 5–15.

Carnoy, Martin. *Education as Cultural Imperialism.* New York: McKay, 1974.

Carter, William. *Aymara Communities and the Bolivian Agrarian Reform.* Gainesville: University of Florida Press, 1964.

Carter, William. *Bolivia: A Profile.* New York: Praeger, 1971.

Carter, William. "Revolution and the Agrarian Sector." In Malloy and Thorn, *Beyond the Revolution*, 233–68.

Carter, William, and Xavier Albó. "La comunidad Aymara: Un mini-estado en conflicto." In *Raíces de América: El mundo Aymara*, edited by Xavier Albó, 451–94. Madrid: Alianza Editorial, 1988.

Carter, William E., and Mauricio Mamani P. *Irpa Chico: Individuo y comunidad en la cultura aymara.* La Paz: Librería Editorial "Juventud," 1982.

Castiglione, Caroline. "Adversarial Literacy: How Peasant Politics Influenced Noble Governing of the Roman Countryside during the Early Modern Period." *American Historical Review* 109, no. 3 (2004): 783–804.

Centro de Estudios Sociales. *La alfabetización en Bolivia: Situación actual y perspectivas.* La Paz: ILDIS, 1994.

Chadwick, Allen. *Blood Narrative: Indigenous Identity in American Indian and Maori Literary and Activist Texts.* Durham, NC: Duke University Press, 2002.

Chartier, Roger. *The Cultural Origins of the French Revolution.* Durham, NC: Duke University Press, 1991.

Chatterjee, Partha. *The Nation and Its Fragments: Colonial and Postcolonial Histories.* Princeton, NJ: Princeton University Press, 1983.

Child, Brenda, and Brian Klopotek, eds. *Indian Subjects: Hemispheric Perspectives on the History of Indian Education.* Santa Fe: School for Advanced Research Press, 2014.

Chiodi, Francesco, ed. *La educación indígena en América Latina.* Quito: Abya-Yala; Santiago: UNESCO/OREALC, 1990.

Choque Canqui, Roberto. "De la defensa del ayllu a la creación de la República del Qullasuyu: Historia del movimiento indígena en Bolivia (1912–1935)." Paper presented at Encuentro de Estudios Bolivianos, La Paz, Bolivia, 1986.

Choque Canqui, Roberto. "La educación indígena boliviana: El proceso educativo indígena-rural." *Estudios bolivianos* 2 (1996): 125–82.

Choque Canqui, Roberto. "La escuela indigenal: La Paz (1905–1938)." In Choque Canqui et al., *Educación indígena*, 19–40.

Choque Canqui, Roberto. *Historia de una lucha desigual: Los contenidos ideológicos y políticos de las rebeliones indígenas de la pre-revolución nacional.* La Paz: UNIH-Pakaxa, 2005.

Choque Canqui, Roberto. *La masacre de Jesús de Machaca.* La Paz: Chitakolla, 1986.

Choque Canqui, Roberto. "La problemática de la educación indigenal." *Data: Revista del Instituto de Estudios Andinos y Amazónicos* 5 (1994): 9–34.

Choque Canqui, Roberto. "Sociedad República del Collasuyu (1930)." *Boletín Chitakolla* 25 (1985): 5–10.

Choque Canqui, Roberto, et al. *Educación indígena: ¿Ciudadanía o colonización?* La Paz: Ediciones Aruwiyiri, 1992.

Choque Canqui, Roberto, and Cristina Quisbert Quispe. *Educación indigenal en Bolivia: Un siglo de ensayos educativos y resistencia patronales.* La Paz: Unidad Investigaciones Históricas, 2006.

Choque Canqui, Roberto, and Cristina Quisbert Quispe. *Líderes indígenas aymaras: Lucha por la defensa de tierras comunitarias de origen.* La Paz: Unidad Investigaciones Históricas, 2010.

Choque Canqui, Roberto, and Esteban Ticona Alejo. *Jesús de Machaqa, la marka rebelde: Sublevación y masacre de 1921.* La Paz: CIPCA/CEDOIN, 1996.

Claure, Karen. *Las escuelas indígenas: Otra forma de resistencia comunaria.* La Paz: HISBOL, 1989.

Clendinnen, Inga. *Ambivalent Conquests: Maya and Spaniard in Yucatan, 1517–1570.* 2nd ed. Cambridge: Cambridge University Press, 2003.

Coben, Diana. *Radical Heroes: Gramsci, Freire and the Politics of Adult Education.* New York: Garland, 1998.

Comaroff, Jean, and John Comaroff. *Ethnography and the Historical Imagination.* Boulder, CO: Westview, 1992.

Comboni Salinas, Sonia, and José Manuel Juárez Núñez. "Education, Culture, and Indigenous Rights: The Case of Education Reform in Bolivia." *Prospects* 30, no. 1 (2000): 3–22.

Condarco Morales, Ramiro. *Zárate, el "temible" willka: Historia de una rebelión indígena de 1899*. La Paz: Talleres Gráficos Bolivianos, 1966.

Conde Mamani, Ramón. "Lucas Miranda Mamani: Maestro indio Uru-Murato." In Choque Canqui et al., *Educación indígena*, 109–22.

Conde Mamani, Ramón. "Lucha por la educación indígena, 1900–1945." *Data: Revista del Instituto de Estudios Andinos y Amazónicos* 5 (1994): 85–95.

Condori Chura, Leandro, and Esteban Ticona Alejo. *El escribano de los caciques apoderados: Kasikinakan purirarunakan qillqiripa*. La Paz: HISBOL/THOA, 1992.

Contreras, Carlos. *Maestros, mistis, y campesinos en el Perú rural del siglo XX*. Lima: IEP, 1996.

Contreras, Manuel. "A Comparative Perspective on Education Reforms in Bolivia: 1950–2000." In Grindle and Domingo, *Proclaiming Revolution*, 259–88.

Contreras, Manuel. "Educación: Reformas y desafíos de la educación." In *Bolivia en el siglo XX: La formación de la Bolivia contemporánea*, edited by Fernando Campero Prudencio, 483–507. La Paz: Harvard Club de Bolivia, 1999.

Contreras, Manuel. "Políticas y reformas educativas en Bolivia, 1900–2000." In *Un amor desenfrenado por la libertad: Antología de la historia política de Bolivia, 1825–2020*, vol. 2, edited by Lupe Cajías and Iván Velásquez-Castellanos, 115–44. La Paz: Konrad Adenauer Stiftung, 2021.

Cook-Gumperz, Jenny, and Deborah Keller-Cohen. "Alternative Literacies in School and Beyond: Multiple Literacies of Speaking and Writing." *Anthropology and Education Quarterly* 24, no. 4 (1993): 283–307.

Copana Yapita, Pedro. "Linguistics and Education in Rural Schools among the Aymara." In *The Aymara Language in Its Social and Cultural Context*, edited by Martha J. Hardman, 255–61. Gainesville: University Presses of Florida, 1981.

Coronado, Jorge. *The Andes Imagined: Indigenismo, Society, and Modernity*. Pittsburgh: University of Pittsburgh Press, 2009.

Coronel Quisbert, Cristóbal. *En un estado de coma: Radio Illimani 1950–1964*. Sucre: Universidad Andina Simón Bolívar, 2003.

Corrigan, Phillip, and Derek Sayer. *The Great Arch: English State Formation as Cultural Revolution*. Oxford: Basil Blackwell, 1985.

Crehan, Kate. *Gramsci, Culture and Anthropology*. Berkeley: University of California Press, 2002.

Cummings, Richard, and Donald Lemke. *Educational Innovations in Latin America*. Metuchen, NJ: Scarecrow, 1973.

Dandler, Jorge. "Local Group, Community, and Nation: A Study of Changing Structures in Ucureña, Bolivia (1935–1952)." MA thesis, University of Wisconsin, 1967.

Dandler, Jorge. *El sindicalismo campesino en Bolivia: Los cambios estructurales en Ucureña*. Mexico City: Instituto Indigenista Interamericano, 1969.

Dandler, Jorge, and Juan Torrico. "From the National Indian Congress to the Ayopaya Rebellion: Bolivia, 1945–1947." In *Resistance, Rebellion and Consciousness in the*

Andean Peasant World: 18th to 20th Centuries, edited by Steve Stern, 334–78. Madison: University of Wisconsin Press, 1997.

Dangl, Benjamin. *The Five Hundred Year Rebellion: Indigenous Movements and the Power of History in Bolivia*. Chico, CA: AK Press, 2019.

Dangl, Benjamin. *The Price of Fire: Resource Wars and Social Movements in Bolivia*. Oakland, CA: AK Press, 2007.

Davis, Natalie Zemon. "Printing and the People." In *Society and Culture in Early Modern France*, 189–226. Stanford, CA: Stanford University Press, 1975.

Dawson, Alexander. "Histories and Memories of the Indian Boarding Schools in Mexico, Canada, and the United States." *Latin American Perspectives* 39, no. 5 (2012): 80–99.

Dawson, Alexander. *Indian and Nation in Revolutionary Mexico*. Tucson: University of Arizona Press, 2004.

De Certeau, Michel. "The Scriptural Economy." In *The Certeau Reader*, edited by Graham Ward, 158–76. Oxford: Blackwell, 2000.

De la Cadena, Marisol. "Are *Mestizos* Hybrid? The Conceptual Politics of Andean Identities." *Journal of Latin American Studies* 37, no. 2 (2005): 259–84.

De la Cadena, Marisol. *Earth Beings: Ecologies of Practice across Andean Worlds*. Durham, NC: Duke University Press, 2015.

De la Cadena, Marisol. *Indigenous Mestizos: The Politics of Race and Culture in Cuzco, Peru, 1919–1991*. Durham, NC: Duke University Press, 2000.

Demelas, Marie-Danielle. "Darwinismo a la criolla: El Darwinismo social en Bolivia, 1880–1910." *Historia Boliviana* 1–2 (1981): 55–82.

Demelas, Marie-Danielle. *Nationalisme sans nation? La Bolivie aux XIXe–XXe siècles*. Paris: Editions du CNRS, 1980.

D'Emilio, Lucia. *Voices and Processes toward Pluralism: Indigenous Education in Bolivia*. Stockholm: SIDA, 2001.

Denton, Virginia Lantz. *Booker T. Washington and the Adult Education Movement*. Gainesville: University Presses of Florida, 1993.

Devine, Tracy Lynne. "Indigenous Identity and Identification in Peru: *Indigenismo*, Education, and Contradictions in State Discourses." *Journal of Latin American Cultural Studies* 8, no. 1 (1999): 63–74.

Díaz Polanco, Héctor. *Indigenous Peoples in Latin America: The Quest for Self-Determination*. Boulder, CO: Westview, 1997.

Diez de Medina, Fernando. *Franz Tamayo: Hechicero del Ande*. 1942. Reprint, La Paz: Editorial Juventud, 1968.

Diez de Medina, Fernando. *Literatura boliviana*. Madrid: Aguilar, 1954.

Digges, Diana, and Joanne Rappaport. "Literary, Orality, and Ritual Practice in Highland Colombia." In *The Ethnography of Reading*, edited by Jonathan Boyarin, 139–57. Berkeley: University of California Press, 1992.

Donald, James. *Sentimental Education: Schooling, Popular Culture and the Regulation of Liberty*. London: Verso, 1992.

Dore, Elizabeth. "The Holy Family: Imagined Households in Latin American History." In *Gender Politics in Latin America: Debates in Theory and Practice*, edited by Elizabeth Dore, 101–17. New York: Monthly Review Press, 1997.

Dore, Elizabeth, and Maxine Molyneux, eds. *Hidden Histories of Gender and the State in Latin America*. Durham, NC: Duke University Press, 2000.

Dorn, Glenn. *The Truman Administration and Bolivia: Making the World Safe for Liberal Constitutional Oligarchy*. University Park: Pennsylvania State University Press, 2011.

Dover, Robert, Katharine E. Seibold, and John Holmes McDowell, eds. *Andean Cosmologies through Time*. Bloomington: Indiana University Press, 1992.

Drino, Paulo. *The Allure of Labor: Workers, Race, and the Making of the Peruvian State*. Durham, NC: Duke University Press, 2011.

Dunkerley, James. *Orígenes del poder militar en Bolivia: Historia del ejército, 1879–1935*. La Paz: Quipus, 1987.

Dunkerley, James. "Origins of the Bolivian Revolution in the Twentieth Century: Some Reflections." In Grindle and Domingo, *Proclaiming Revolution*, 135–63.

Dunkerley, James. *Rebellion in the Veins: Political Struggle in Bolivia, 1952–1982*. London: Verso, 1984.

Eckstein, Susan. *The Impact of Revolution: A Comparative Analysis of Mexico and Bolivia*. London: Sage, 1976.

Ehrinpreis, Andrew. "Green Gold, Green Hell: Coca, Caste, and Class in the Chaco War, 1932–1935." *The Americas* 77, no. 2 (2020): 217–45.

Eklof, Ben. *Russian Peasant Schools: Officialdom, Village Culture, and Popular Pedagogy, 1861–1914*. Berkeley: University of California Press, 1986.

Eley, Geoff. "Nations, Publics, and Political Cultures: Placing Habermas in the Nineteenth Century." In *Habermas and the Public Sphere*, edited by Craig Calhoun, 289–339. Cambridge, MA: MIT Press, 1996.

Elias, Norbert. *On Civilization, Power, and Knowledge: Selected Writings*. Edited by Stephen Mennell and Johan Goudsblom. Chicago: University of Chicago Press, 1998.

Eriksen, Thomas H. *Ethnicity and Nationalism: Anthropological Perspectives*. London: Pluto, 1993.

Escobar, Arturo. *Encountering Development: The Making and Unmaking of the Third World*. Princeton, NJ: Princeton University Press, 1995.

Espinoza, G. Antonio. "The Origins of the *Núcleos Escolares Campesinos* or Clustered Schools for Peasants in Peru, 1945–1952." *Naveg@mérica: Revista electrónica de la Asociación Española de Americanistas*, no. 4 (2010).

Farcau, Bruce. *The Chaco War: Bolivia and Paraguay, 1932–1935*. Westport, CT: Praeger, 1996.

Farthing, Linda, and Benjamin Kohl. *Evo's Bolivia: Continuity and Change*. Austin: University of Texas Press, 2014.

Fear-Segal, Jacqueline. *White Man's Club: Schools, Race, and the Struggle of Indian Acculturation*. Lincoln: University of Nebraska Press, 2007.

Fell, Eva-Marie. "Warisata y la irradiación del núcleo escolar campesino en los Andes, 1930–1960." In *Educación rural e indígena en Iberoamérica*, edited by Pilar Gonzalbo Aizpuru, 209–23. Mexico City: Colegio de México, 1996.

Fellman Velarde, José. *Historia de Bolivia*. 3 vols. Cochabamba: Los Amigos del Libro, 1970.

Fernández, Marcelo. *La ley del ayllu: Práctica de jach'a y jisk'a justicia (Justicia Mayor y Justicia Menor) en comunidades aymaras*. La Paz: PIEB, 2000.

Field, Thomas. *From Development to Dictatorship: Bolivia and Alliance for Progress in the Kennedy Era*. Ithaca, NY: Cornell University Press, 2014.

Fifer, J. Valerie. *Bolivia: Land, Location, and Politics since 1952*. Cambridge: Cambridge University Press, 1972.

Findji, María Teresa. "From Resistance to Social Movement: The Indigenous Authorities Movement in Colombia." In *The Making of Social Movements in Latin America: Identity, Strategy, and Democracy*, edited by Arturo Escobar and Sonia Alvaréz, 112–33. Boulder, CO: Westview, 1992.

Flores Galindo, Alberto. *In Search of an Inca: Identity and Utopia in the Andes*. New York: Cambridge University Press, 2010.

Foley, Douglas. "Rethinking School: Ethnographies of Colonial Settings. A Performance Perspective of Reproduction and Resistance." *Comparative Education Review* 35, no. 3 (1991): 532–51.

Foster, George M. *Tzintzuntzan: Mexican Peasants in a Changing World*. New York: Little, Brown, 1967.

Foucault, Michel. *The Archaeology of Knowledge*. New York: Pantheon, 1972.

Foucault, Michel. *Discipline and Punish*. Harmondsworth, UK: Penguin, 1979.

Fraser, Nancy. "Rethinking the Public Sphere: A Contribution to the Critique of Actually Existing Democracy." In *Habermas and the Public Sphere*, edited by Craig Calhoun, 109–42. Cambridge, MA: MIT Press, 1992.

Freire, Paulo. *Education for Critical Consciousness*. New York: Seabury, 1973.

Freire, Paulo. *Pedagogy of the Oppressed*. 1970. Reprint, New York: Continuum, 1993.

Garcés V., Fernando. "Quechua Knowledge, Orality, and Writings: The Newspaper Conosur Ñawpagman." In *Decolonizing Native Histories: Collaboration, Knowledge, and Language in the Americas*, edited by Florencia E. Mallon, 85–121. Durham, NC: Duke University Press, 2012.

García, Antonio. "Agrarian Reform and Social Development in Bolivia." In *Agrarian Problems and Peasant Movements in Latin America*, edited by Rudolfo Stavenhagen, 301–46. New York: Anchor Books, 1970.

García, María Elena. "Encounters with *Interculturalidad*: Education and the Politics of Knowledge in the Andes." In *Indian Subjects: Hemispheric Perspectives on the History of Indigenous Education*, edited by Brenda Child and Brian Klopotek, 177–99. Santa Fe: School for Advanced Research Press, 2014.

García, María Elena. *Making Indigenous Citizens: Identities, Education, and Multicultural Development in Peru*. Stanford, CA: Stanford University Press, 2005.

García Liendo, Javier. "Teachers, Folklore, and the Crafting of *Serrano* Cultural Identity in Peru." *Latin American Research Review* 52, no. 3 (2017): 378–92.

García Linera, Álvaro. *La potencia plebeya: Acción colectiva e identidades indígenas, obreras, y populares en Bolivia*. Buenos Aires: CLACSO, 2008.

García Pabón, Leonardo. *La patria íntima: Alegorías nacionales en la literatura y el cine de Bolivia*. La Paz: CESU/Plural, 1998.

Geertz, Clifford. *The Interpretation of Cultures: Selected Essays*. New York: Basic Books, 1973.

Gelino Gonseco, Elena. "Bolivia: Influencia de las transformaciones socio-políticas en la educación." PhD diss., Universidad Autónoma de Barcelona, 1989.

Gellner, Ernst. *Nations and Nationalism*. 1983. Reprint, Ithaca, NY: Cornell University Press, 2006.

Gildner, R. Matthew. "Indomestizo Modernism: National Development and Indigenous Integration in Postrevolutionary Bolivia, 1952–1964." PhD diss., University of Texas at Austin, 2012.

Gill, Leslie. "Creating Citizens, Making Men: The Military and Masculinity in Bolivia." *Cultural Anthropology* 12, no. 4 (1997): 527–50.

Gill, Leslie. *Precarious Dependencies: Gender, Class and Domestic Service in Bolivia*. New York: Columbia University Press, 1994.

Gill, Leslie. *Teetering on the Rim: Global Restructuring, Daily Life, and the Armed Retreat of the Bolivian State*. New York: Columbia University Press, 2000.

Gilly, Adolfo. "Prologue: The Spirit of Revolt." In Forrest Hylton and Sinclair Thomson, *Revolutionary Horizons: Past and Present in Bolivian Politics*, xiii–xix. London: Verso, 2007.

Giraudo, Laura. "De la ciudad mestiza al campo indígena: Internados en el México y en Bolivia." *Anuario de Estudios Americanos* 67, no. 2 (2010): 519–47.

Giroux, Henry A. *Pedagogy and the Politics of Hope: Theory, Culture, and Schooling*. Boulder, CO: Westview, 1997.

Giroux, Henry A. *Schooling and the Struggle for Public Life: Critical Pedagogy in the Modern Age*. Minneapolis: University of Minnesota Press, 1988.

Glauert, Earl. "Ricardo Rojas and the Emergence of Argentine Cultural Nationalism." *Hispanic American Historical Review* 43, no. 1 (1963): 1–13.

Glave Testino, Luis Miguel. *Trajinantes: Caminos indígenas en la sociedad colonial, siglos XVI/XVII*. Lima: Instituto de Apoyo Agrario, 1989.

Goldberg, David Theo. *The Racial State*. London: Blackwell, 2002.

Gómez Martínez, José Luís. *Bolivia: Un pueblo en busca de su identidad*. La Paz: Los Amigos del Libro, 1988.

Gonzalbo Aizpuru, Pilar, ed. *Educación rural e indígena en Iberoamérica*. Mexico City: Colegio de México, 1999.

González, Gilbert. *Progressive Education: A Marxist Interpretation*. Minneapolis: Marxist Education Press, 1982.

González Apaza, Reina Jeanet. "Biographical Sketch of Roberto Choque Canqui." Unpublished manuscript, 2014.

González Echevarría, Roberto. *Myth and Archive: A Theory of Latin American Narrative*. Cambridge: Cambridge University Press, 1990.

Goodale, Mark. *A Revolution in Fragments: Traversing Scales of Justice, Ideology, and Practice in Bolivia*. Durham, NC: Duke University Press, 2019.

Goodrich, Carter. "Bolivia in Time of Revolution." In Malloy and Thorn, *Beyond the Revolution*, 3–24.

Gordillo, José M. *Campesinos revolucionarios en Bolivia: Identidad, territorio, y sexualidad en el Valle Alto de Cochabamba, 1952–1964*. La Paz: Plural, 2000.

Gordillo, José M. "Modernity, Politics, and Identity: Post-revolutionary Peasant Struggles in the Upper Valley of Cochabamba (Bolivia), 1952–1964." PhD diss., Stony Brook University, 1999.

Gordillo, José M. *Peasant Wars in Bolivia: Making, Thinking, and Living the Revolution in Cochabamba (1952–1964)*. Calgary, Canada: University of Calgary Press, 2022.

Gotkowitz, Laura, ed. *Histories of Race and Racism: The Andes and Mesoamerica from Colonial Times to the Present*. Durham, NC: Duke University Press, 2011.

Gotkowitz, Laura. "Race and Education in Early Twentieth Century Bolivia." Unpublished manuscript, 1991.

Gotkowitz, Laura. "Revisiting the Roots of the Revolution." In Grindle and Domingo, *Proclaiming Revolution*, 164–82.

Gotkowitz, Laura. *A Revolution for Our Rights: Indigenous Struggles for Land and Justice in Bolivia, 1880–1952*. Durham, NC: Duke University Press, 2007.

Gow, David, and Joanne Rappaport. "The Indigenous Public Voice: The Multiple Idioms of Modernity in Native Cauca." In *Indigenous Movements, Self-Representation, and the State in Latin America*, edited by Kay Warren and Jean Jackson, 47–80. Austin: University of Texas Press, 2003.

Graff, Harvey J. *The Legacies of Literacy: Continuities and Contradictions in Western Culture and Society*. Bloomington: Indiana University Press, 1991.

Graham, Richard, ed. *The Idea of Race in Latin America, 1870–1940*. Austin: University of Texas Press, 1990.

Gramsci, Antonio. *Selections from the Prison Notebooks*. Edited and translated by Quintin Hoare and Geoffrey Nowell Smith. New York: International Publishers, 1971.

Green, Andy. *Education and State Formation: The Rise of Education Systems in England, France, and the United States*. London: Macmillan, 1990.

Grieshaber, Erwin. "Fluctuaciones en la definición del Indio: Comparación de los censos de 1900–1950." *Historia Boliviana* 5 (1985): 45–65.

Grieshaber, Erwin. "Resistencia indígena a la venta de tierras comunales en le departamento de La Paz, 1881–1920." *Data* 1 (1991): 113–44.

Grieshaber, Erwin. "Survival of Indian Communities in Nineteenth-Century Bolivia: A Regional Comparison." *Journal of Latin American Studies* 12, no. 2 (1980): 223–69.

Grindle, Merilee S. *Despite the Odds: The Contentious Politics of Education Reform*. Princeton, NJ: Princeton University Press, 2004.

Grindle, Merilee S. "1952 and All That: The Bolivian Revolution in Comparative Perspective." In Grindle and Domingo, *Proclaiming Revolution*, 1–21.

Grindle, Merilee, and Pilar Domingo, eds. *Proclaiming Revolution: Bolivia in Comparative Perspective*. London: Institute of Latin American Studies, University of London;

Cambridge, MA: Harvard University Press for David Rockefeller Center for Latin American Studies, 2003.

Gruner, Wolf. *Parias de la Patria: El mito de la liberación de los indígenas en la República de Bolivia, 1825–1890*. La Paz: Plural Editores, 2015.

Guha, Ranajit. *Elementary Aspects of Peasant Insurgency in Colonial India*. Durham, NC: Duke University Press, 1999.

Guiteras Mombiola, Anna. *Warisata en la Selva: El núcleo escolar selvícola de Casarabe entre los Sirionó, 1937–1948*. Barcelona: Universtat de Barcelona Ediciones, 2020.

Gupta, Akhil. "Governing Population: The Integrated Child Development Services Program in India." In *States of Imagination: Ethnographic Explorations of the Postcolonial State*, edited by Thomas B. Hansen and Finn Stepputat, 65–96. Durham, NC: Duke University Press, 2001.

Gustafson, Bret. *New Languages of the State: Indigenous Resurgence and the Politics of Knowledge in Bolivia*. Durham, NC: Duke University Press, 2009.

Gutek, Gerald Lee. *Pestalozzi and Education*. New York: Random House, 1968.

Gutiérrez, Natividad. *Nationalist Myths and Ethnic Identities: Indigenous Intellectuals and the Mexican State*. Lincoln: University of Nebraska Press, 1999.

Gutiérrez Aguilar, Raquel. *Rhythms of the Pachakuti: Indigenous Uprisings and State Power in Bolivia*. Durham, NC: Duke University Press, 2014.

Guzmán, Augusto. *Historia de Bolivia*. La Paz: Los Amigos del Libro, 1976.

Hahn, Steven. *A Nation under Our Feet: Black Political Struggles in the Rural South from Slavery to the Great Migration*. Cambridge, MA: Harvard University Press, 2003.

Halconruy, René. *Georges Rouma, pionero de las relaciones pedagógicas belgo-bolivianas*. Sucre: Imprenta Offset Universitaria, 1980.

Hale, Charles. "Political and Social Ideas." In *Latin America: Economy and Society, 1870–1930*, edited by Leslie Bethell, 225–300. Cambridge: Cambridge University Press, 1989.

Hall, Clyde W. *Black Vocational, Technical, and Industrial Arts Education: Development and History*. Chicago: American Technical Society, 1973.

Hansen, Thomas B., and Finn Stepputat, eds. *States of Imagination: Ethnographic Explorations of the Postcolonial State*. Durham, NC: Duke University Press, 2001.

Hardman, Martha, ed. *The Aymara Language in Its Social and Cultural Context*. Gainesville: University Presses of Florida, 1981.

Harris, Olivia. "Ethnic Identity and Market Relation: Indians and Mestizos in the Andes." In *Ethnicity, Markets and Migration in the Andes: At the Crossroads of History and Anthropology*, edited by Brooke Larson, Olivia Harris, and Enrique Tandeter, 351–90. Durham, NC: Duke University Press, 1995.

Harris, Olivia. "'Knowing the Past': Managing the Diversity of Knowledge." In *Counterworks: Managing the Diversity of Knowledge*, edited by Richard Fardon, 105–22. London: Routledge.

Harrison, Regina. *Signs, Songs, and Memory in the Andes: Translating Quechua Language and Culture*. Austin: University of Texas Press, 1989.

Hazen, Dan. "The Awakening of Puno: Government Policy and the Indian Problem in Southern Peru, 1900–1955." PhD diss., Yale University, 1974.

Healy, Kevin. *Llamas, Weavings, and Organic Chocolate: Multicultural Grassroots Development in the Andes and Amazon of Bolivia*. Notre Dame, IN: University of Notre Dame Press, 2001.

Heath, Dwight. "The Aymara Indian and Bolivia's Revolution." *Inter-American Economic Affairs* 18 (1966): 31–40.

Heath, Dwight B., Charles J. Erasmus, and Hans C. Buechler. *Land Reform and Social Revolution in Bolivia*. New York: Praeger, 1969.

Heath, Shirley Brice. *Telling Tongues: Language Policy in Mexico, Colony to Nation*. New York: Teachers College Press, Columbia University, 1972.

Heilman, Lawrence. "U.S. Development Assistance to Rural Bolivia, 1941–1974: The Search for Development Strategy." PhD diss., American University, 1982.

Helg, Aline. *La educación en Colombia, 1918–1957*. Bogotá: Maza y James, 2001.

Helg, Aline. "Race in Argentina and Cuba, 1880–1930: Theory, Policies and Popular Reaction." In *The Idea of Race in Latin America, 1870–1940*, edited by Richard Graham, 37–70. Austin: University of Texas Press, 1990.

Herman, Rebecca. "An Army of Educators: Gender, Revolution, and the Cuban Literacy Campaign of 1961." *Gender and History* 24, no. 1 (2012): 93–111.

Hines, Sarah T. *Water for All: Community, Property, and Revolution in Modern Bolivia*. Oakland: University of California Press, 2022.

Hobsbawm, Eric J. *Nations and Nationalism since 1780: Programme, Myth, Reality*. Cambridge, UK: Canto, 1990.

Hobsbawm, Eric J. *Primitive Rebels: Studies in Archaic Forms of Social Movement in the 19th and 20th Centuries*. New York: Norton, 1965.

Hooker, Juliet. *Theorizing Race in the Americas: Douglass, Sarmiento, Du Bois, and Vasconcelos*. Oxford: Oxford University Press, 2017.

Howard, Rosaleen. "Education Reform, Indigenous Politics, and Decolonisation in the Bolivia of Evo Morales." *International Journal of Educational Development* 29 (2009): 583–93.

Howard-Malverde, R., and Andrew Canessa. "The School in the Quechua and Aymara Communities of Highland Bolivia." *International Journal of Educational Development* 15 (1995): 231–43.

Howe, James. *Chiefs, Scribes, and Ethnographers: Kuna Culture from the Inside and Out*. Austin: University of Texas Press, 2009.

Hoxie, Frederick. *A Final Promise: The Campaign to Assimilate the Indians, 1880–1920*. Lincoln: University of Nebraska Press, 1984.

Huanca, Tomás. "Los procesos de desestructuración en las comunidades andinas a fines del siglo XIX: Altiplano lacustre." In *Coloquio estado y región en los Andes*, 45–86. Cuzco: Centro de Estudios Rurales Andinos Bartolomé de las Casas, 1987.

Hurtado, Javier. *El katarismo*. La Paz: HISBOL, 1986.

Hylton, Forrest, and Sinclair Thomson. *Revolutionary Horizons: Past and Present in Bolivian Politics*. London: Verso, 2007.

Hylton, Forrest, Sinclair Thomson, Félix Patzi, and Sergio Serulnikov. *Ya es otro tiempo el presente: Cuatro momentos de insurgencia indígena*. La Paz: Muela del Diablo, 2003.

Illich, Ivan. "Bolivia y la revolución cultural." In *Antología pedagógico de Bolivia*, edited by Mariano Baptista Gumucio, 197–210. 1970. Reprint, La Paz: Los Amigos del Libro, 1979.

INDICEP (Instituto de Investigación Cultural para Educación Popular). "INDICEP y la educación popular en América Latina—grandes corrientes ideológicas." *Educación popular para el desarrollo* 2 (1971): 45–54.

Irurozqui, Marta. *"A bala, piedra y palo": La construcción de la ciudadanía política en Bolivia, 1826–1952*. Sevilla: Diputación de Sevilla, 2000.

Irurozqui, Marta. "La amenaza chola: La participación popular en las elecciones bolivianas, 1900–1930." *Revista andina* 13 (1995): 357–86.

Irurozqui, Marta. *La armonía de las desigualdades: Élites y conflictos de poder en Bolivia, 1880–1920*. Cuzco: Centro Bartolomé de las Casas, 1994.

Irurozqui, Marta. "The Sound of the Pututos: Politicisation and Indigenous Rebellions in Bolivia, 1826–1921." *Journal of Latin American Studies* 32, no. 1 (2000): 85–114.

Jacobsen, Nils, and Cristóbal Aljovín de Losada, eds. *Political Cultures in the Andes, 1750–1950*. Durham, NC: Duke University Press, 2005.

Jelin, Elizabeth. *State Repression and the Struggles for Memory*. New York: Social Science Research Council, 2003.

John, S. Sándor. *Bolivia's Radical Tradition: Permanent Revolution in the Andes*. Tucson: University of Arizona Press, 2009.

Joseph, Gilbert, C. Legrand, and R. Salvatore, eds. *Close Encounters of Empire: Writing the Cultural History of U.S.-Latin American Relations*. Durham, NC: Duke University Press, 1998.

Joseph, Gilbert, and Daniel Nugent, eds. *Everyday Forms of State Formation: Revolution and Negotiation of Rule in Modern Mexico*. Durham, NC: Duke University Press, 1994.

Joseph, Gilbert M., and Daniela Spenser, eds. *In from the Cold: Latin America's New Encounter with the Cold War*. Durham, NC: Duke University Press, 2008.

Justice, Steven. *Writing and Rebellion: England in 1381*. Berkeley: University of California Press, 1994.

Kane, Liam. "Community Development: Learning from Popular Education in Latin America." *Community Development Journal* 45, no. 3 (2010): 276–86.

Kearney, Michael. *Reconceptualizing the Peasantry: Anthropology in Global Perspective*. Boulder, CO: Westview, 1996.

Kelley, Jonathan, and Herbert S. Klein. *Revolution and the Rebirth of Inequality: A Theory Applied to the National Revolution in Bolivia*. Berkeley: University of California Press, 1981.

Kirkendall, Andrew J. *Paulo Freire and the Cold War Politics of Literacy*. Chapel Hill: University of North Carolina Press, 2010.

Klein, Herbert S. *Bolivia: The Evolution of a Multi-ethnic Society*. Oxford: Oxford University Press, 1982.

Klein, Herbert S. *A Concise History of Bolivia*. Cambridge: Cambridge University Press, 2003.

Klein, Herbert S. *Parties and Political Change in Bolivia, 1880–1952*. Cambridge: Cambridge University Press, 1969.

Klein, Herbert S. "Prelude to Revolution." In Malloy and Thorn, *Beyond the Revolution*, 25–52.

Klein, Herbert S. "Social Change in Bolivia since 1952." In Grindle and Domingo, *Proclaiming Revolution*, 232–58.

Knight, Alan. "The Domestic Dynamics of the Mexican and Bolivian Revolutions." In Grindle and Domingo, *Proclaiming Revolution*, 54–90.

Knight, Alan. "Racism, Revolution, and Indigenism: Mexico, 1910–1940." In *The Problem of Race in Latin America*, edited by Richard Graham, 71–114. Austin: University of Texas Press, 1990.

Knippenberg, Joseph M. "Moving beyond Fear: Rousseau and Kant on Cosmopolitan Education." *Journal of Politics* 51, no. 4 (1989): 809–27.

Knudson, Jerry W. *Bolivia, Press and Revolution, 1932–1964*. Lanham, MD: University Press of America, 1986.

Kohl, Benjamin, and Linda Farthing. *Impasse in Bolivia: Neoliberal Hegemony and Political Resistance*. London: Zed Books, 2006.

Kohl, James. *Indigenous Struggle and the Bolivian National Revolution: Land and Liberty!* New York: Routledge, 2021.

Kohl, James. "Peasants and Revolution in Bolivia: April 9, 1952–August 2, 1953." *Hispanic American Historical Review* 58, no. 2 (1978): 238–59.

Kuenzli, E. Gabrielle. *Acting Inca: Identity and National Belonging in Early Twentieth-Century Bolivia*. Pittsburgh: University of Pittsburgh Press, 2013.

La Belle, Thomas J., ed. *Educational Alternatives in Latin America: Social Change and Social Stratification*. Los Angeles: University of California Press, 1975.

La Belle, Thomas J., ed. *Nonformal Education and Social Change in Latin America*. Los Angeles: University of California Press, 1976.

Lagos, Maria L. *Autonomy and Power: The Dynamics of Class and Culture in Rural Bolivia*. Philadelphia: University of Pennsylvania Press, 1994.

Langer, Erick. *Economic Change and Rural Resistance in Southern Bolivia, 1880–1930*. Stanford, CA: Stanford University Press, 1989.

Langer, Erick. "El liberalismo y la abolición de la comunidad indígena en el siglo XIX." *Historia y cultura* 14 (1988): 59–95.

Laqueur, Thomas W. "Working-Class Demand and Growth of English Elementary Education, 1750–1850." In *Schooling and Society: Studies in the History of Education*, edited by Lawrence Stone, 192–205. Baltimore: Johns Hopkins University Press, 1976.

Larson, Brooke. "Capturing Indian Bodies, Hearths, and Minds: 'El hogar campesino' and Rural School Reform in Bolivia, 1920s–1940s." In Grindle and Domingo, *Proclaiming Revolution*, 183–212.

Larson, Brooke. *Cochabamba, 1550–1900: Colonialism and Agrarian Transformation in Bolivia*. Expanded ed. Durham, NC: Duke University Press, 1998.

Larson, Brooke. "Forging the Unlettered Indian: The Pedagogy of Race in the Bolivian Andes." In *Histories of Race and Racism: The Andes and Mesoamerica from Colonial Times to the Present*, edited by Laura Gotkowitz, 134–56. Durham, NC: Duke University Press, 2011.

Larson, Brooke. "Redeemed Indians, Barbarianized Cholos: Crafting Neocolonial Modernity in Liberal Bolivia, 1900–1910." In *Political Cultures in the Andes, 1750–1950*, edited by Nils Jacobsen and Cristóbal Aljovín de Losada, 230–52. Durham, NC: Duke University Press, 2005.

Larson, Brooke. "Revisiting Bolivian Studies: Reflections on Theory, Scholarship, and Activism since 1980." *Latin American History Review* 54 (2019): 294–309.

Larson, Brooke. *Trials of Nation Making: Liberalism, Race, and Ethnicity in the Andes, 1810–1910*. Cambridge: Cambridge University Press, 2004.

Larson, Brooke. "Warisata: A Historical Footnote." *ReVista: Harvard Review of Latin America* 11, no. 1 (2011): 65–67.

Larson, Brooke, and Olivia Harris, with Enrique Tandeter, eds. *Ethnicity, Markets, and Migration in the Andes: At the Crossroads of History and Anthropology*. Durham, NC: Duke University Press, 1995.

Lazar, Sian. *El Alto, Rebel City: Self and Citizenship in Andean Bolivia*. Durham, NC: Duke University Press, 2008.

Lefebvre, Georges. *The Great Fear of 1789: Rural Panic in Revolutionary France*. New York: Schocken Books, 1973.

Lehm, Zulema A., and Silvia Rivera Cusicanqui. *Los artesanos libertarios y la ética del trabajo*. La Paz: Gramma / Ediciones THOA, 1988.

Lehman, Kenneth D. *Bolivia and the United States: A Limited Partnership*. Athens: University of Georgia Press, 1999.

Lehman, Kenneth D. "Completing the Revolution? The United States and Bolivia's Long Revolution." *Bolivian Studies Journal / Revista de Estudios Bolivianos* 22 (2016): 4–35.

Leonard, Olen E. *El cambio económico y social en cuatro comunidades del Altiplano de Bolivia*. Mexico City: Instituto Indigenista Interamericano, 1966.

L'Estoile, Benoit de, Federico Neiburg, and Lygia Maria Sigaud, eds. *Empires, Nations, and Natives: Anthropology and State-Making*. Durham, NC: Duke University Press, 2005.

L'Estoile, Benoit de, Federico Neiburg, and Lygia Maria Sigaud, eds. "Introduction: Anthropology and the Government of 'Natives,' a Comparative Approach." In *Empires, Nations, and Natives: Anthropology and State-Making*, edited by L'Estoile, Neiburg, and Sigaud, 1–29. Durham, NC: Duke University Press, 2005.

Levinson, Bradley, Douglas E. Foley, and Dorothy C. Holland, eds. *The Cultural Production of the Educated Person: Critical Ethnographies of Schooling and Local Practice*. Albany: SUNY Press, 1996.

Levinson, Bradley, and Dorothy C. Holland. "The Cultural Production of the Educated Person: An Introduction." In Levinson, Foley, and Holland, *The Cultural Production of the Educated Person*, 1–53.

Lewis, Stephen. "The Nation, Education, and the 'Indian Problem' in Mexico, 1920–1940." In *The Eagle and the Virgin: Nation and Cultural Revolution in Mexico, 1920–1940*, edited by Mary Kay Vaughn and Stephen Lewis, 176–95. Durham, NC: Duke University Press, 2006.

Llanos, David. "El rito de uqhart'akuy escolar en el ayllu Chari (Charazani)." In Choque Canqui et al., *Educación indígena*, 153–60.

Lomawaima, K. Tsianina. "'All Our People Are Building Houses': The Civilization of Architecture and Space in Federal Indian Boarding Schools." In *Indian Subjects: Hemispheric Perspectives on the History of Indigenous Education*, edited by Brenda Child and Brian Klopotek, 148–76. Santa Fe: School for Advanced Research Press, 2014.

Lomawaima, K. Tsianina, and T. McCarty, eds. *To Remain an Indian: Lessons in Democracy from a Century of Native American Education*. New York: Teachers College Press, 2006.

Lomnitz, Claudio. *Deep Mexico, Silent Mexico: An Anthropology of Nationalism*. Minneapolis: University of Minnesota Press, 2001.

Long, Norman, and Ann Long, eds. *Battlefields of Knowledge: The Interlocking of Theory and Practice in Social Research and Development*. London: Routledge, 1992.

López, Luís Enrique, and Ruth Moya, eds. *Pueblos indios, estados, y educación*. Lima: PEB-EBI-ERA, 1989.

López, Rick A. *Crafting Mexico: Intellectuals, Artisans, and the State after the Revolution*. Durham, NC: Duke University Press, 2010.

López Beltrán, Clara. "Lo que se escribe y lo que se entiende: El lenguaje escrito en la sociedad colonial de Charcas (hoy Bolivia)." In *Usos del documento y cambios sociales en la historia de Bolivia*, edited by C. López Beltrán and A. Saito, 9–26. Osaka: National Museum of Ethnology, 2005.

Lora, Guillermo. *A History of the Bolivian Labour Movement, 1848–1971*. Cambridge: Cambridge University Press, 1977.

Lora, Guillermo, Juan Pablo Bacherer, Elena Gentino, and Vilma Plata. *Sindicalismo del magisterio (1825–1932): La escuela y los campesinos; reforma universitaria (1908–1932)*. La Paz: Ediciones Masas, 1979.

Loza, León. *Historia de la educación boliviana*. Unpublished manuscript, 1942.

Loza, León. "Los partidos políticos y la educación indígena." *Estudios Sociales* 1 (1941): 19–30.

Lucero, José Antonio. *Struggles of Voice: The Politics of Indigenous Representation in the Andes*. Pittsburgh: University of Pittsburgh Press, 2008.

Lund, Sarah. "On the Margin: Letter Exchange among Andean Non-literates." In *Creating Context in Andean Cultures*, edited by Rosaleen Howard Malverde, 185–95. Oxford: Oxford University Press, 1997.

Luykx, Aurolyn. *The Citizen Factory: Schooling and Cultural Production in Bolivia*. Albany: SUNY Press, 1999.

Luykx, Aurolyn. "De *Indios* to *Profesionales*: Stereotypes and Student Resistance in Bolivian Teacher Training." In Levinson, Foley, and Holland, *The Cultural Production of the Educated Person*, 239–77.

Macera dall'Orso, Pablo. *Bolivia: Tierra y población, 1825–1936*. Lima: Biblioteca Andina, 1978.

MacLeod, Murdo J. "Bolivia and Its Social Literature before and after the Chaco War: A Historical Study of Social and Literary Revolution." PhD diss., University of Florida, 1962.

Malik, Kenan. *The Meaning of Race: Race, History and Culture in Western Society*. New York: New York University Press, 1996.

Mallon, Florencia. *Courage Tastes of Blood: The Mapuche Community of Nicolás Ailío and the Chilean State, 1906-2001*. Durham, NC: Duke University Press, 2005.

Mallon, Florencia, ed. *Decolonizing Native Histories: Collaboration, Knowledge, and Language in the Americas*. Durham, NC: Duke University Press, 2012.

Mallon, Florencia. "Indian Communities: Political Cultures, and the State in Latin America, 1780-1990." *Journal of Latin American Studies* 24, no. 1 (1992): 35-53.

Mallon, Florencia. *Peasant and Nation: The Making of Postcolonial Mexico and Peru*. Berkeley: University of California Press, 1995.

Malloy, James M. *Bolivia: The Uncompleted Revolution*. Pittsburgh: University of Pittsburgh Press, 1970.

Malloy, James M. "Revolutionary Politics." In Malloy and Thorn, *Beyond the Revolution*, 111-56.

Malloy, James, and Richard S. Thorn, eds. *Beyond the Revolution: Bolivia since 1952*. Pittsburgh: University of Pittsburgh Press, 1971.

Mamani Capchiri, Humberto. "La educación en la vision de la sociedad criolla: 1920-1943." In Choque Canqui et al., *Educación indígena*, 79-98.

Mamani Condori, Carlos. *Los Aymaras frente a la historia: Dos ensayos metodológicos*. La Paz: Ediciones Aruwiyiri, 1992.

Mamani Condori, Carlos. *Metodología de la historia oral*. Chukiyawu: Ediciones del THOA, 1989.

Mamani Condori, Carlos. *Taraqu, 1866-1935: Masacre, guerra, y "renovación" en la biografía de Eduardo L. Nina Qhispi*. La Paz: Ediciones Aruwiyiri, 1991.

Mamani Ramírez, Pablo. *El estado neocolonial: Una mirada al proceso de la lucha por el poder y sus contradicciones en Bolivia*. La Paz: Rincón Ediciones, 2017.

Mandepora, Marcia. "Bolivia's Indigenous Universities: Building Community." *ReVista: Harvard Review of Latin America* 11, no. 1 (2011): 68-69.

Martínez, Françoise. "La création des 'escuelas ambulantes' en Bolivie (1905): Instruction, éducation ou déculturation des masses indigènes?" *Cahiers de l'UFR d'études Ibérique et Latino-américains* 11 (1997): 161-71.

Martínez, Françoise. "La peur blanche: Un moteur de la politique éducative libérale en Bolivie (1899-1920)." *Bulletin de l'Institut Francaise d'études andines* 2 (1998): 265-83.

Martínez, Françoise. "Pour une nation blanche, 'metisse,' ou pluriethnique et multiculturelle? Les trois grandes reformes educatives du XXe siecle." In *Pour comprendre la Bolivie d' Evo Morales*, edited by Rolland Denis and Joelle Chassin, 188-206. Paris: L'Harmattan, 2007.

Martínez, Françoise. "'Que nuestros indios se conviertan en pequeños suecos!': La introducción de la Gimnasia en las Escuelas Bolivianas." *Bulletin de l'Institut Francais d'Etudes Andines* 28 (1999): 361-86.

Martínez, Françoise. *Qu'ils soient nos semblables, pas nos égaux: L'école bolivienne dans la politique libérale de "régénération nationale" (1898-1920)*. Tours: Université François Rabelais de Tours, 2000.

Martínez, Françoise. *"Régénérer la race": Politique educative en Bolivie, 1891–1920*. Paris: Editions de l'IHEAL, 2010.

Martínez, Juan Luís. *Algunas experiencias de la educación popular en Bolivia*. La Paz: Ediciones Garza Azul, 1991.

Mayo, Peter. "Critical Literacy and Emancipatory Politics: The Work of Paulo Freire." *International Journal of Development* 15, no. 4 (1995): 363–79.

Mbembe, Achille. "The Power of the Archive and Its Limits." In *Refiguring the Archive*, edited by C. Hamilton, 19–26. New York: Springer, 2002.

McCoy, Alfred, and Francisco Scarano, eds. *Colonial Crucible: Empire in the Making of the Modern American State*. Madison: University of Wisconsin Press, 2009.

McEwen, William, ed. *Changing Rural Bolivia*. 1969. Reprint, New York: Oxford University Press, 1975.

Medina, Javier, ed. *Tres reflexiones sobre el pensamiento andino*. La Paz: HISBOL, 1987.

Medina Melgarejo, Patricia. *Pedagogías insumisas: Movimientos politico-pedagógicos y memorias colectivas de "educaciones otras" en América Latina*. Chiapas: Universidad de Ciencias y Artes de Chiapas, 2015.

Mendieta Parada, Pilar. "En defensa del pacto tributario: Los indígenas bolivianos frente al proyecto liberal: S. XIX." *Revista andina* 41 (2005): 131–54.

Mendieta Parada, Pilar. *Entre la alianza y la confrontación: Pablo Zárate Willka y la rebelión indígena de 1899 en Bolivia*. La Paz: Plural-PIEB, 2010.

Mendieta Parada, Pilar. *Indígenas en política: Una mirada desde la historia*. La Paz: Instituto de Estudios Bolivianos, 2008.

Mignolo, Walter. "Coloniality, Power, and Subalternity." In *The Latin American Subaltern Studies Reader*, edited by Ileana Rodríguez, 424–44. Durham, NC: Duke University Press, 2001.

Mignolo, Walter. *Local Histories / Global Designs: Coloniality, Subaltern Knowledges, and Border Thinking*. Princeton, NJ: Princeton University Press, 2000.

Miller, Nicola. *In the Shadow of the State: Intellectuals and the Quest for National Identity in Twentieth-Century Spanish America*. London: Verso, 1999.

Miller, Valerie. *Between Struggle and Hope: The Nicaraguan Literacy Crusade*. Boulder, CO: Westview, 1985.

Miracle, Andrew W., and Juan de Dios Yapita Moya. "Time and Space in Aymara." In *The Aymara Language in Its Social and Cultural Context*, edited by Martha James Hardman, 33–56. Gainesville: University Presses of Florida, 1981.

Monasterios, Elizabeth. *La vanguardia plebeya del Titikaka: Gamaliel Churata y otras beligerancias estéticas en los Andes*. La Paz: IFEA/Plural, 2015.

Montoya M., Víctor. *Gabriel María Laudini: Paladín de la educación en Bolivia*. La Paz: Ediciones Fray Giuseppe Rossi, 1993.

Mora, Mariana. *Kuxlejal Politics: Indigenous Autonomy, Race, and Decolonizing Research in Zapatista Communities*. Austin: University of Texas Press, 2017.

Morales, Juan Antonio. "The National Revolution and Its Legacy." In Grindle and Domingo, *Proclaiming Revolution*, 213–31.

Morrow, Raymond, and Carlos Alberto Torres. "Education and the Reproduction of Class, Gender, and Race: Responding to the Postmodern Challenge." *Educational Theory* 44, no. 1 (1994): 43–59.

Muller, Detlef, Fritz Ringer, and Brian Simon. *The Rise of the Modern Educational System: Structural Change and Social Reproduction, 1870–1920*. New York: Cambridge University Press, 1987.

Neizen, Ronald. *The Origins of Indigenism: Human Rights and the Politics of Identity*. Berkeley: University of California Press, 2003.

Niño-Murcia, Mercedes. "'Papelito Manda': La literacidad en una comunidad de Huarochirí." In *Escritura y sociedad: Nuevas perspectivas teóricas y etnográficas*, edited by Virginia Zavala, Mercedes Niño Murcia, and Patricia Ames, 347–65. Lima: Red para el Desarrollo de las Ciencias Sociales en el Perú, 2004.

Niño-Murcia, Mercedes. "Paper Rules: Vernacular Literacy in an Andean Village." *International Accents* 2, no. 2 (2002): 6–7.

Nye, Robert A. *The Origins of Crowd Psychology: Gustave LeBon and the Crisis of Mass Democracy in the Third Republic*. London: Sage, 1975.

O'Cadiz, Maria del Pilar, Pia Lindquist Wong, and Carlos Alberto Torres. *Education and Democracy: Paulo Freire, Social Movements, and Educational Reform in São Paulo*. Boulder, CO: Westview, 2001.

Oliart, Patricia. "Education, Power, and Distinctions." In *The Andean World*, edited by Linda Seligman and K. Fine-Dare, 539–51. New York: Routledge, 2019.

Oliart, Patricia. *Políticas educativas y la cultura del sistema escolar en el Perú*. Lima: Instituto de Estudios Peruanos, 2001.

Ong, Walter J. *Orality and Literacy: The Technologizing of the World*. London: Methuen, 1982.

Oropesa, Ruy. *La educación rural boliviana: Warisata. Una contradicción superestructural*. Licenciatura thesis, Universidad Mayor de San Andrés, 1977.

Orta, Andrew. *Catechizing Culture: Missionaries, Aymara, and the "New Evangelization."* New York: Columbia University Press, 2004.

Osborn, Harold. *Bolivia, a Land Divided*. London: Oxford University Press, 1955.

Osuna, Carmen. "Educación intercultural y Revolución Educativa en Bolivia: Un análisis de procesos de (re)esencialización cultural." *Revista española de antropología americana* 43, no. 2 (2013): 451–70.

Pacheco, Diego. *El indianismo y los indios contemporáneos de Bolivia*. La Paz: HISBOL-MUSEF, 1992.

Pacino, Nicole. "Constructing a New Bolivian Society: Public Health Reforms and the Consolidation of the Bolivian National Revolution." *Latin Americanist* 57 (2013): 25–56.

Pacino, Nicole. "Creating Madres Campesinas: Revolutionary Motherhood and the Gendered Politics of Nation Building in 1950s Bolivia." *Journal of Women's History* 27 (2015): 62–87.

Pacino, Nicole. "Liberating the People from Their 'Loathsome Practices': Public Health and 'Silent Racism' in Post-revolutionary Bolivia." *História, Ciencias, Saúdade—Manguinos* 24 (2017): 1107–24.

Pacino, Nicole. "Stimulating a Cooperative Spirit? Public Health and U.S.-Bolivia Relations in the 1950s." *Diplomatic History* 41 (2017): 305–35.

Padilla, Tamalís. *Unintended Consequences of Revolution: Student-Teachers and Political Radicalism in Twentieth-Century Mexico*. Durham, NC: Duke University Press, 2021.

Patch, Richard. "The Bolivian Revolution: United States Assistance in a Revolutionary Setting." In *Latin American Politics: Studies of the Contemporary Scene*, edited by Robert D. Tomasek, 310–46. 1960. Reprint, Garden City, NY: Doubleday, 1966.

Patterson, Orlando. *Slavery and Social Death: A Comparative Study*. Cambridge, MA: Harvard University Press, 1992.

Patton, Elda Clayton. *Sarmiento in the United States*. Evansville, IN: University of Evansville Press, 1976.

Patzi, Félix. *Etnofagia estatal: Modernas formas de violencia simbólica*. La Paz: Recop, 2000.

Pearce, Roy Harvey. *The Savages of America: A Study of Indians and the Idea of Civilization*. Baltimore: Johns Hopkins University Press, 1965.

Pearce, Roy Harvey. *Savagism and Civilization: A Study of the Indian and the American Mind*. Baltimore: Johns Hopkins University Press, 1953.

Penry, S. Elizabeth. *The People Are King: The Making of an Indigenous Andean Politics*. Oxford: Oxford University Press, 2019.

Pérez Oropeza, María Victoria. *Elizardo Pérez, el despertar de las conciencias*. La Paz: Plural Editores, 2017.

Pike, Frederick B. *The United States and the Andean Republics: Peru, Bolivia, and Ecuador*. Cambridge, MA: Harvard University Press, 1977.

Piñeiro Iñíguez, Carlos. *Desde el corazón de América: El pensamiento boliviano en el siglo XX*. La Paz: Plural, 2004.

Pinheiro Barbosa, Lia. *Educación, resistencia, y movimientos sociales: La praxis educativo-política de los Sin Tierra y de los Zapatistas*. Mexico City: Universidad Nacional Autónoma de México, 2015.

Platt, Tristan. "The Andean Experience of Bolivian Liberalism, 1825–1900: Roots of Rebellion in 19th Century Chayanta (Potosí)." In *Resistance, Rebellion, and Consciousness in the Andean Peasant World: 18th and 20th Centuries*, edited by Steve Stern, 280–326. Madison: University of Wisconsin Press, 1987.

Platt, Tristan. *Estado boliviano y ayllu andino: Tierra y tributo en el norte de Potosí*. Lima: Instituto de Estudios Peruanos, 1982.

Platt, Tristan. "Liberalism and Ethnocide in the Southern Andes." *History Workshop* 17 (1984): 3–18.

Platt, Tristan. "Simón Bolivar the Son of Justice and Amerindian Virgin: Andean Conceptions of the *Patria* in Nineteenth-Century Potosí." *Journal of Latin American Studies* 25, no. 1 (1993): 150–85.

Platt, Tristan. "Writing, Shamanism and Identity or Voices from Abya-Yala." *History Workshop Journal* 34, no. 1 (1992): 132–47.

Postero, Nancy. "Andean Utopias in Evo Morales' Bolivia." *Latin American and Caribbean Ethnic Studies* 2, no. 1 (2007): 1–28.

Postero, Nancy. *Now We Are Citizens: Indigenous Politics in Postmulticultural Bolivia*. Stanford, CA: Stanford University Press, 2007.

Postero, Nancy, and Leon Zamosc, eds. *The Struggle for Indigenous Rights in Latin America*. Brighton, UK: Sussex Academic Press, 2004.

Prakash, Gyan. *After Colonialism: Imperial Histories and Postcolonial Displacements*. Princeton, NJ: Princeton University Press, 1995.

Pratt, Mary Louise. *Imperial Eyes: Studies in Travel, Writing and Transculturation*. New York: Routledge, 1992.

Pratt, Mary Louise. *Planetary Longings*. Durham, NC: Duke University Press, 2022.

Preston, David. *Farmers and Towns: Urban-Rural Relations in Highland Bolivia*. Norwich, UK: Geo Abstracts, 1978.

Price, David H. *Anthropological Intelligence: The Deployment and Neglect of Anthropology in the Second World War*. Durham, NC: Duke University Press, 2008.

Puiggrós, Adriana. *La educación popular en América Latina: Orígenes, polémicas, y perspectivas*. Mexico City: Editorial Nueva Imagen, 1984.

Puiggrós, Adriana. *Imaginación y crisis en la educación latinoamericana*. Mexico City: Alianza Editorial Mexicana, 1990.

Puiggrós, Adriana. *Imperialismo y educación en América Latina*. Mexico City: Editorial Nueva Imagen, 1989.

Qayum, Seemin. "Creole Imaginings: Race, Space, and Gender in the Making of Bolivia." PhD diss., Goldsmith's College, University of London, 2002.

Quijano, Anibal. "Coloniality of Power, Eurocentrism, and Latin America." *Nepantla* 1 (2000): 533–80.

Radcliffe, Sarah A. "Imagining the State as a Space: Territoriality and the Formation of the State in Ecuador." In *States of Imagination: Ethnographic Explorations of the Postcolonial State*, edited by Thomas Blom Hansen and Finn Stepputat, 123–46. Durham, NC: Duke University Press, 2001.

Rama, Angel. "El área cultural andina: Hispanismo, misticismo, indigenismo." *Cuadernos americanos* 33 (1974): 136–73.

Rama, Angel. *The Lettered City*. Durham, NC: Duke University Press, 1996.

Ramos, Gabriela, and Yanna Yannakakis, eds. *Indigenous Intellectuals: Knowledge, Power, and Colonial Culture in Mexico and the Andes*. Durham, NC: Duke University Press, 2014.

Ramos Flores, Marcelo. "Santos Marka T'ula y las demandas de los caciques apoderados en la primera parte del siglo XX." *Fuentes: Revista de la Biblioteca y Archivo Histórico de la Asamblea Legislativa Plurinacional* 10 (2016): 24–42.

Ranaboldo, Claudia, ed. *El camino perdido: Chinkasqa ñan Armat thakhi. Biografía del dirigente campesino kallawaya, Antonio Alvarez Mamani*. La Paz: Semta, 1987.

Rappaport, Joanne. "Alternative Knowledge Producers in Indigenous Latin America." *Forum* 36 (2005): 11–13.

Rappaport, Joanne. *Cumbe Reborn: An Andean Ethnography of History*. Chicago: University of Chicago Press, 1994.

Rappaport, Joanne. *Intercultural Utopias: Public Intellectuals, Cultural Experimentation, and Ethnic Pluralism in Colombia*. Durham, NC: Duke University Press, 2005.

Rappaport, Joanne. *The Politics of Memory: Native Historical Interpretation in the Colombian Andes*. Cambridge: Cambridge University Press, 1990.

Rappaport, Joanne. "Reinvented Traditions: The Heraldry of Ethnic Militancy in the Colombian Andes." In *Andean Cosmologies through Time: Persistence and Emergences*, edited by Robert Dover, Katherine Seibolt, and John McDowell, 202–28. Bloomington: Indiana University Press, 1992.

Rappaport, Joanne, and Tom Cummins. *Beyond the Lettered City: Indigenous Literacies in the Andes*. Durham, NC: Duke University Press, 2012.

Regalsky, Pablo, and Nina Laurie. "'The School, Whose Place Is This?': The Deep Structures of the Hidden Curriculum in Indigenous Education in Bolivia." *Comparative Education* 43, no. 2 (2007): 231–51.

Reimers, Fernando. "Perspective in the Study of Educational Opportunity." In *Unequal Schools, Unequal Chances: The Challenge to Equal Opportunity in the Americas*, edited by Fernando Reimers, 25–39. Cambridge, MA: Harvard University Press, 2000.

Reimers, Fernando, ed. *Unequal Schools, Unequal Chances: The Challenge to Equal Opportunity in the Americas*. Cambridge, MA: Harvard University Press, 2000.

Rengifo Vásquez, Grimaldo. "Education in the Modern West and in the Andean Culture." In *The Spirit of Regeneration: Andean Culture Confronting Western Notions of Development*, edited by Frédérique Apffel-Marglin, 172–92. London: Zed Books, 1998.

Reyeros, Rafael. *Historia de la educación en Bolivia: De la independencia a la revolución federal*. La Paz: Editorial Universo, 1952.

Reyeros, Rafael. *Historia social del indio boliviano*. La Paz: Editorial Fénix, 1963.

Rivera Cusicanqui, Silvia. *Ch'ixinakax utxiwa: Una reflexión sobre prácticas y discursos descolonizadores*. Buenos Aires: Tina Limón, 2010.

Rivera Cusicanqui, Silvia. "La expansión del latifundio en el altiplano boliviano: Elementos para la caracterización de una oligarquía regional." *Avances* 2 (1978): 95–118.

Rivera Cusicanqui, Silvia. "Horizons of Memory." In Thomson et al., *The Bolivia Reader*, 494–98.

Rivera Cusicanqui, Silvia. "*Oppressed but Not Defeated*": Peasant Struggles among the Aymara and Qhechwa in Bolivia, 1900–1980. 1984. Reprint, Geneva: UNRISD, 1987.

Rivera Cusicanqui, Silvia. "*Oprimidos pero no vencidos*": Luchas del campesinado aymara y qhechwa, 1900–1980. 1984. Reprint, La Paz: HISBOL, 1986; Ediciones Yachaywasi, 2003.

Rivera Cusicanqui, Silvia. "'Pedimos la revisión de límites': Un episodio de incomunicación de castas en el movimiento de caciques-apoderados de los andes bolivianos, 1919–1921." In *Reproducción y transformación de las sociedades andinas, siglos XVI–XX*, edited by Segundo Moreno Yáñez and Frank Salomon, 603–52. Quito: Abya-Yala, 1991.

Rivera Cusicanqui, Silvia. "El potencial epistemológico y teórico de la historia oral: De la lógica instrumental a la descolonización de historia." *Voces recobradas: Revista de historia oral* 8 (2006): 12–22.

Rivera Cusicanqui, Silvia. "La raíz: Colonizadores y colonizados." In *Violencias encubiertas en Bolivia: Cultura y política*, edited by Xavier Albó and Raúl Barrios Morón, 25–139. La Paz: CIPCA-Aruwiyiri, 1993.

Rivera Cusicanqui, Silvia. "Rebelión e ideología: Luchas del campesinado aymara del altiplano boliviano, 1910–1920." *Historia Boliviana* 1 (1981): 83–99.

Rivera Cusicanqui, Silvia. *Taller de histora oral andina*. Mimeograph.

Rivera Cusicanqui, Silvia, and Virginia Aillón, eds. *Antología del pensamiento crítico boliviano contemporaneo*. Buenos Aires: CLACSO, 2015.

Robins, Nicholas, ed. *Cambio y continuidad en Bolivia: Etnicidad, cultural, e identidad*. La Paz: Plural Editores, 2005.

Rockwell, Elsie. "Keys to Appropriation: Rural Schooling in Mexico." In Levinson, Foley, and Holland, *The Cultural Production of the Educated Person*, 301–24.

Rockwell, Elsie. "Schools of the Revolution: Enacting and Contesting State Forms in Tlaxcala, 1910–1930." In *Everyday Forms of State Formation: Revolution and the Negotiation of Rule in Modern Mexico*, edited by Gilbert M. Joseph and Daniel Nugent, 170–208. Durham, NC: Duke University Press, 1994.

Rodríguez Alfaro, Leslye. "La educación artística como componente cultural de la educación de las masas, en la pintura muralista de la Revolución Nacional de 1952." *Historia: Revista de la Carrera de History, Universidad Mayor de San Andrés* 30 (2007): 357–72.

Rodríguez García, Huascar. "Caciques, escuelas, y sindicatos rurales: Una cartografía de las luchas y organizaciones del campesinado indígena durante la primera mitad del siglo XX." In *Un amor desenfrenado por la libertad: Antología de la historia política de Bolivia (1825–2020)*, vol. 1, edited by Lupe Cajías and Iván Velásquez-Castellanos, 603–52. La Paz: Konrad Adenauer Stiftung / Plural, 2021.

Rojas, Christina. *Civilization and Violence: Regimes of Representation in Nineteenth-Century Colombia*. Minneapolis: University of Minnesota Press, 2002.

Roseberry, William. "Hegemony and the Language of Contention." In *Everyday Forms of State Formation: Revolution and the Negotiation of Rule in Modern Mexico*, edited by Gilbert M. Joseph and Daniel Nugent, 355–66. Durham, NC: Duke University Press, 1994.

Rosemblatt, Karin. *The Science and Politics of Race in Mexico and the United States, 1910–1950*. Durham, NC: Duke University Press, 2018.

Safford, Frank. *The Ideal of the Practical: Colombia's Struggle to Form a Technical Elite*. Austin: University of Texas Press, 1976.

Salazar de la Torre, Cecilia. *El problema del indio: Nación e inmovilismo social en Bolivia*. La Paz: CIDES-UMSA, 2015.

Saldaña-Portillo, María. *The Revolutionary Imagination in the Americas and the Age of Development*. Durham, NC: Duke University Press, 2003.

Salmón, Josefa. *El espejo indígena: El discurso indigenista en Bolivia, 1900–1956*. La Paz: Plural/UMSA, 1997.

Salomon, Frank. "Testimonies: The Making and Reading of Native South American Historical Sources." In *The Cambridge History of the Native Peoples of the Americas*, vol. 3, edited by Frank Salomon and Stuart Schwartz, 19–95. Cambridge: Cambridge University Press, 1999.

Salomon, Frank, and Emilio Chambi Apaza. "Vernacular Literacy on the Lake Titicaca High Plains." *Reading Research Quarterly* 41, no. 3 (2006): 304–26.

Salomon, Frank, and Mercedes Niño-Murcia. *The Lettered Mountain: A Peruvian Village's Way with Writing*. Durham, NC: Duke University Press, 2011.

Salvatore, Ricardo D. *Disciplinary Conquest: U.S. Scholars in South America, 1900–1945.* Durham, NC: Duke University Press, 2016.

Sanders, G. Earl. "The Quiet Experiment in American Diplomacy: An Interpretive Essay on U.S. Aid to Bolivia." *The Americas* 33, no. 1 (1976): 25–49.

Sangines Uriarte, Marcelo. *Educación rural y desarrollo en Bolivia.* La Paz: Don Bosco, 1968.

Sanjinés, Javier. *Embers of the Past: Essays in Times of Decolonization.* Durham, NC: Duke University Press, 2013.

Sanjinés, Javier. *Mestizaje Upside-Down: Aesthetic Politics in Modern Bolivia.* Pittsburgh: University of Pittsburgh Press, 2004.

Sarzuri-Lima, Marcelo. "La Lucha por 'comunitizar' la educación: Construcciones desde el subsuelo político." *Foro de educación* 12, no. 16 (2014): 169–90.

Schivelbusch, Wolfgang. *The Culture of Defeat: On National Trauma, Mourning, and Recovery.* New York: Metropolitan Books, 2003.

Schroeder, Joachim. *Modelos pedagógicos latinoamericanos: De la Yachay Wasi Inca a Cuernavaca.* La Paz: CEBIAE, 1994.

Schwarcz, Lilia Moritz. *The Spectacle of the Races: Scientists, Institutions, and the Race Question in Brazil.* New York: Hill and Wang, 1993.

Scott, James C. *Domination and the Arts of Resistance: Hidden Transcripts.* New Haven, CT: Yale University Press, 1990.

Scott, James C. *Seeing like a State: How Certain Schemes to Improve the Human Condition Have Failed.* New Haven, CT: Yale University Press, 1998.

Seligmann, Linda, and Kathleen Fine-Dare, eds. *The Andean World.* New York: Routledge, 2019.

Serulnikov, Sergio. *Revolution in the Andes: The Age of Túpac Amaru.* Durham, NC: Duke University Press, 2013.

Serulnikov, Sergio. *Subverting Colonial Authority: Challenges to Spanish Rule in Eighteenth-Century Southern Andes.* Durham, NC: Duke University Press, 2003.

Seth, Sanjay. *Subject Lessons: The Western Education of Colonial India.* Durham, NC: Duke University Press, 2007.

Shesko, Elizabeth. *Conscript Nation: Coercion and Citizenship in the Bolivian Barracks.* Pittsburgh: University of Pittsburgh Press, 2020.

Shesko, Elizabeth. "Constructing Roads, Washing Feet, and Cutting Cane for the Patria: Building Bolivia with Military Labor, 1900–1975." *International Labor and Working-Class History* 80, no. 1 (2011): 6–28.

Shesko, Elizabeth. "Hijos del Inca y de la patria: Representaciones del indígena durante el Congreso Indigenal de 1945." *Fuentes: Revista de la Biblioteca y Archivo Histórico de la Asamblea Legislativa Plurinacional* 4, no. 6 (2010): 5–10.

Shesko, Elizabeth. "Negotiating Authority and Belonging in Bolivian Barracks, 1900–1950." PhD diss., Duke University, 2012.

Shesko, Elizabeth. "'Our Sons Who Defend the Honor and Integrity of the Patria': Using Military Sources to Rethink the 'Indian Problem.'" Paper presented at the American Historical Association meeting, Boston, January 9, 2011.

Siekmeier, James. *The Bolivian Revolution and the United States, 1952 to the Present.* University Park: Pennsylvania State University Press, 2011.

Simon, Brian. *Studies in the History of Education, 1780–1870.* London: Lawrence and Wishart, 1960.

Siñani de Willka, Tomasa. "Breve biografía de Avelino Siñani, fundador de la 'escuela-ayllu.'" In Choque Canqui et al., *Educación indígena*, 125–34.

Skrabut, Kristin. "Documents, Law, and the State." In *The Andean World*, edited by Linda Seligman and K. Fine-Dare, 524–38. New York: Routledge, 2019.

Smale, Robert. *"I Sweat the Flavor of Tin": Labor Activism in Early Twentieth-Century Bolivia.* Pittsburgh: University of Pittsburgh Press, 2010.

Smock, Raymond. *Booker T. Washington: Black Leadership in the Age of Jim Crow.* Chicago: Ivan Dee, 2009.

Soliz, Carmen. *Fields of Revolution: Agrarian Reform and Rural State Formation in Bolivia, 1935–1964.* Pittsburgh: University of Pittsburgh Press, 2021.

Soliz Urrutia, Carmen. "'Land to the Original Owners': Rethinking the Indigenous Politics of the Bolivian Agrarian Reform." *Hispanic American Historical Review* 97 (2017): 259–96.

Soliz Urrutia, Carmen. "La modernidad esquiva: Debates políticos e intelectuales sobre la reforma agraria en Bolivia, 1935–1952." *Ciencia y cultura* 29 (2012): 23–49.

Soria Choque, Vialiano. "Los caciques-apoderados y la lucha por la escuela (1900–1925)." In Choque Canqui et al., *Educación indígena*, 41–78.

Soruco Sologuren, Ximena. *La ciudad de los cholos: Mestizaje y colonialidad en Bolivia, siglos XIX y XX.* La Paz: PIEB, 2011.

Soux, Maria Luisa. "Jueces pedáneos, jilacatas, apoderados y otros articuladores de la justicia local entre colonia y república." Paper presented at the Fourth Congress of the Asociación de Estudios Bolivianos, Sucre, Bolivia, 2006.

Spivey, Donald. *Schooling for the New Slavery: Black Industrial Education, 1868–1915.* Westport, CT: Greenwood, 1978.

Stefanoni, Pablo. *"Qué hacer con los Indios...": Y otros traumas irresueltos de la colonialidad.* La Paz: Plural Editores, 2010.

Stepan, Nancy Leys. *"The Hour of Eugenics": Race, Gender, and Nation in Latin America.* Ithaca, NY: Cornell University Press, 1994.

Stephenson, Marcia. "The Architectural Relationship between Gender, Race, and the Bolivian State." In *The Latin American Subaltern Studies Reader*, edited by Ileana Rodríguez, 367–82. Durham, NC: Duke University Press, 2001.

Stephenson, Marcia. "Forging an Indigenous Counterpublic Sphere: The Taller de Historia Andina in Bolivia." *Latin American Research Review* 37, no. 2 (2002): 99–118.

Stephenson, Marcia. *Gender and Modernity in Andean Bolivia.* Austin: University of Texas Press, 1999.

Stern, Steve J. "New Approaches to the Study of Peasant Rebellion and Consciousness: Implications of the Andean Experience." In *Resistance, Rebellion, and Consciousness in the Andean Peasant World: 18th and 20th Centuries*, edited by Steve Stern, 3–28. Madison: University of Wisconsin Press, 1987.

Stern, Steve J. *Peru's Indian Peoples and the Challenge of Spanish Conquest: Huamanga to 1640*. Madison: University of Wisconsin Press, 1982.

Stobart, Henry, and Rosaleen Howard, eds. *Knowledge and Learning in the Andes*. Liverpool: Liverpool University Press, 2002.

Stock, Brian. *Listening for the Text: On the Uses of the Past*. Baltimore: Johns Hopkins University Press, 1990.

Stoler, Ann Laura. *Carnal Knowledge and Imperial Power: Race and the Intimate in Colonial Rule*. Berkeley: University of California Press, 2002.

Stoler, Ann Laura. *Race and the Education of Desire: Foucault's History of Sexuality and the Colonial Order of Things*. Durham, NC: Duke University Press, 1995.

Stratton, Clif. *Education for Empire: American Schools, Race, and the Paths of Good Citizenship*. Berkeley: University of California Press, 2016.

Street, Brian V. *Cross-Cultural Approaches to Literacy*. Cambridge: Cambridge University Press, 1993.

Street, Brian V. *Literacy in Theory and Practice*. Cambridge: Cambridge University Press, 1984.

Strobele-Gregor, Juliana. *Indios de piel blanca: Evangelistas fundamentalistas en Chuquiyawu*. La Paz: HISBOL, 1989.

Stutzman, Ronald. "El Mestizaje: An All-Inclusive Ideology of Exclusion." In *Cultural Transformations and Ethnicity in Modern Ecuador*, edited by Norman Whitten, 45–94. Urbana: University of Illinois Press, 1981.

Szasz, Margaret. *Education and the American Indian: The Road to Self-Determination, 1928–1973*. Albuquerque: University of New Mexico Press, 1974.

Szuchman, Mark. "In Search of Deference: Education and Civic Formation in Nineteenth-Century Buenos Aires." In *Education, Communications, and Social Change in Latin America*, edited by John Britton, 1–18. Wilmington, DE: Scholarly Resources, 1994.

Talavera Simoni, María Luisa. *Formaciones y transformaciones: Educación pública y culturas magisteriales en Bolivia, 1899–2010*. La Paz: CIDES-UMSA-PIEB, 2011.

Tarrow, Sidney. *Power in Movement: Social Movements and Contentious Politics*. Cambridge: Cambridge University Press, 1998.

Taylor, Solange B. "Intercultural and Bilingual Education in Bolivia: The Challenge of Ethnic Diversity and National Identity." *Documento de Trabajo* 01/04. Instituto de Investigaciones Socio-económicas. Universidad Católica Boliviana, 2004.

Teel, Charles, Jr. "Las raíces radicales del adventismo en el Altiplano peruano." *Allpanchis* 21 (1989): 209–48.

THOA (Taller de Historia Oral Andina). *Ayllus y proyectos de desarrollo en el Norte de Potosí*. La Paz: Ediciones Aruwiyiri, 1993.

THOA (Taller de Historia Oral Andina). "The Indian Santos Marka T'ula, Chief of the Ayllus of Qallapa and General Representative of the Indian Communities of Bolivia." *History Workshop Journal* 34, no. 1 (1992): 101–18.

THOA (Taller de Historia Oral Andina). "Indigenous Women and Community Resistance: History and Memory." In *Women and Social Change in Latin America*, edited by Elizabeth Jelin, 151–83. London: Zed Books, 1994.

THOA (Taller de Historia Oral Andina). *El indio Santos Marka T'ula, cacique principal de los ayllus de Qallapa y Apoderado General de la Comunidades Originarios de la República*. 1984. Reprint, La Paz: Ediciones THOA, 1988.

THOA (Taller de Historia Oral Andina). *Mujer y resistencia comunaria: Historia y memoria*. La Paz: HISBOL, 1986.

Thomson, Sinclair. "La cuestión India en Bolivia a principios del siglo: El caso de Rigoberto Paredes." *Autodeterminación* 2, no. 4 (1987–88): 83–116.

Thomson, Sinclair. "Iconoclast and Prophet: Fausto Reinaga." In Thomson et al., *The Bolivia Reader*, 399–406.

Thomson, Sinclair. "Indian Perceptions of Collective Identity in the Late-Colonial and Insurgent Andes." Unpublished manuscript, 2002.

Thomson, Sinclair. "Revolutionary Memory in Bolivia: Anticolonial and National Projects from 1781 to 1952." In Grindle and Domingo, *Proclaiming Revolution*, 117–34.

Thomson, Sinclair. "El vuelco de los tiempos: La rupture indianista de Fausto Reinaga." In *La Revolución India: Edición 50 Aniversario*. La Paz: Fundación Amaútico Fausto Reinaga / La Miradad Salvaje, 2020.

Thomson, Sinclair. *We Alone Will Rule: Native Andean Politics in the Age of Insurgency*. Madison: University of Wisconsin Press, 2002.

Thomson, Sinclair, Rossana Barragán, Xavier Albó, Seemin Qayum, and Mark Goodale, eds. *The Bolivia Reader: History, Culture, Politics*. Durham, NC: Duke University Press, 2018.

Thorn, Richard S. "The Economic Transformation." In Malloy and Thorn, *Beyond the Revolution*, 157–216.

Ticona Alejo, Esteban. "Conceptualización de la educación y alfabetización en Eduardo Leandro Nina Qhispi." In *Educación indigenal: Ciudadanía o colonización?*, 99–108. La Paz: Ediciones Aruwiyiri, 1992.

Ticona Alejo, Esteban. "Education and Decolonization in the Work of Aymara Activist Eduardo Leandro Nina Qhispi." In *Histories of Race and Racism in the Andes and Mesoamerica since Colonial Times to the Present*, edited by Laura Gotkowitz, 240–53. Durham, NC: Duke University Press, 2011.

Ticona Alejo, Esteban. *Lecturas para la descolonización: Taqpachani qhispiyasipxañani*. La Paz: Plural/AGRUCO, 2005.

Ticona Alejo, Esteban. *Memoria, política, y antropología en los Andes bolivianos: Historia oral y sabers locales*. La Paz: Plural/AGRUCO, 2002.

Ticona Alejo, Esteban. *Organización y liderazgo aymara, 1979-1996*. La Paz: Universidad de la Cordillera / AGRUCO, 1992.

Ticona Alejo, Esteban, and Xavier Albó. *Jesus de Machaqa en el tiempo*. La Paz: Fundación Diálogo, 1998.

Ticona Alejo, Esteban, and Xavier Albó. *La lucha por el poder communal*. La Paz: CEDOIN/CIPA, 1997.

Tilly, Charles, and Lesley J. Wood. *Social Movements, 1786-2008*. Boulder, CO: Paradigm, 2009.

Torres, Carlos Alberto. *Democracy, Education, and Multiculturalism: Dilemmas of Citizenship in a Global World*. Lanham, MD: Rowman and Littlefield, 1998.

Torres, Carlos Alberto. "Education and the Archaeology of Consciousness: Freire and Hegel." *Educational Theory* 44, no. 4 (1994): 429–45.

Torres, Carlos Alberto. *The Politics of Nonformal Education in Latin America*. Westport, CT: Praeger, 1990.

Torres, Carlos Alberto, and Theodore Mitchell, eds. *Sociology of Education: Emerging Perspectives*. Albany: SUNY Press, 1998.

Torrez, Yuri. *El indio en la prensa: Representación racial de la prensa boliviana con respecto a los levantamientos indígenas/campesinas (1899–2003)*. La Paz: Centro Cuarto Intermedio, 2010.

Trouillot, Michel-Rolph. *Silencing the Past: Power and the Production of History*. Boston: Beacon, 1995.

Trovia Alejo, Esteban. "La revolución boliviana y los pueblos indígenas." In *Tenemos pechos de bronce... pero no sabemos nada*, 282–96. La Paz: Plural Editores, 2003.

Urioste, Miguel. "Educación popular en el Altiplano: El program ECORA." *América Indígena* 42 (1982): 253–68.

Urquidi, Arturo. *Bolivia y su reforma agraria*. Cochabamba: Editorial Universitaria, 1969.

Urquidi, Arturo. *El feudalismo en América y la reforma agraria boliviana*. Cochabamba: Los Amigos del Libro, 1966.

Valcarcel, Luís. *La educación del campesino*. Lima: Universidad Nacional Mayor de San Marcos, 1954.

Van Cott, Donna Lee. *The Friendly Liquidation of the Past: The Politics of Diversity in Latin America*. Pittsburgh: University of Pittsburgh Press, 2000.

Van Cott, Donna Lee. "Indigenous Struggle." *Latin American Research Review* 38, no. 2 (2003): 220–33.

Vanderstraeten, Raf. "The Historical Triangulation of Education, Politics, and Economy." *Sociology* 40, no. 1 (2006): 125–42.

Vargas Machaca, Casimiro. *Surikiña: Historia y educación*. La Paz: Ediciones Aruwiyiri, 1994.

Vaughn, Mary Kay. *Cultural Politics in Revolution: Teachers, Peasants, and Schools in Mexico, 1930–1940*. Tucson: University of Arizona Press, 1997.

Vaughn, Mary Kay. "The Educational Project of the Mexican Revolution: The Response of Local Societies (1934–1940)." In *Molding the Hearts and Minds: Education, Communications, and Social Changes in Latin America*, edited by John A. Britton, 105–26. Wilmington, DE: Scholarly Resources Books, 1994.

Vaughn, Mary Kay. "Modernizing Patriarchy: State Policies, Rural Households, and Women in Mexico, 1930–1940." In *Hidden Histories of Gender and the State in Latin America*, edited by Elizabeth Dore and Maxine Molyneux, 194–214. Durham, NC: Duke University Press, 2000.

Vaughn, Mary Kay. *The State, Education, and Social Class in Mexico, 1880–1928*. DeKalb: Northern Illinois University Press, 1982.

Vaughn, Michalina, and Margaret S. Archer. *Social Conflict and Educational Change in England and France, 1789–1848*. Cambridge: Cambridge University Press, 1971.

Vázquez, Josefina Zoraida. *Nacionalismo y educacíon en México*. 1970. Reprint, Mexico City: El Colegio de México, 2000.

Vilchis Cedillo, Arturo. "La escuela-ayllu de Warisata, Bolivia, y sus relaciones con México." *De raíz diversa* 1 (April–September 2014): 145–70.

Vom Hau, Matthias. "Unpacking the School: Textbooks, Teachers, and the Construction of Nationhood in Mexico, Argentina, and Peru." *Latin American Research Review* 44, no. 3 (2009): 127–54.

Wade, Peter. *Race and Ethnicity in Latin America*. London: Pluto, 1997.

Wahren, Cecilia. *Encarnaciones de lo autóctono: Prácticas y políticas en torno a la indianidad de Bolivia a comienzos del siglo XX*. Buenos Aires: Teseo / Universidad de San Andrés, n.d.

Walsh, Catherine, ed. *Pedagogías decoloniales: Prácticas insurgentes de resistir, (re)existir y (re)vivir*. Quito: Abya-Yala, 2013.

Walsh, Catherine. *Pedagogy and the Struggle for Voice: Issues of Language, Power, and Schooling for Puerto Ricans*. New York: Bergen and Garvey, 1991.

Ward, Graham, ed. *The Certeau Reader*. Oxford: Blackwell, 2000.

Warren, Kay B. "Indigenous Movements as a Challenge to the Unified Social Movement Paradigm for Guatemala." In *Cultures of Politics, Politics of Cultures: Re-visioning Latin American Social Movements*, edited by Sonia Alvaréz, Evelina Dagnino, and Arturo Escobar, 165–95. Boulder, CO: Westview, 1998.

Warren, Kay, and Jean E. Jackson, eds. *Indigenous Movements, Self-Representation, and the State in Latin America*. Austin: University of Texas Press, 2002.

Washburn, Wilcomb. *The Indian in America*. New York: Harper and Row, 1975.

Washburn, Wilcomb. *Red Man's Land and White Man's Law*. Norman: University of Oklahoma Press, 1995.

Washington, Booker T. *Up from Slavery: An Autobiography*. Garden City, NY: Doubleday and Company, 1901.

Weber, Eugen. *Peasants into Frenchmen: The Modernization of Rural France, 1870–1914*. Stanford, CA: Stanford University Press, 1976.

Whitehead, Laurence. "Bolivia." In *Latin America between the Second World War and the Cold War, 1944–1948*, edited by Leslie Bethell and Ian Roxborough, 120–46. Cambridge: Cambridge University Press, 1992.

Whitehead, Laurence. "The Bolivian National Revolution: A Comparison." In Grindle and Domingo, *Proclaiming Revolution*, 25–53.

Whitehead, Laurence. *The United States and Bolivia: A Case of Neocolonialism*. Oxford: Haslemere Group, 1969.

Wilkie, James W. *The Bolivian Revolution and U.S. Aid since 1952: Financial Background and Context of Political Decisions*. Los Angeles: University of California Press, 1969.

Williams, Raymond. *The Country and the City*. New York: Oxford University Press, 1973.

Williams, Raymond. *Keywords: A Vocabulary of Culture and Society*. New York: Oxford University Press, 1983.

Williams, Raymond. *The Long Revolution*. New York: Penguin Press, 1965.

Wilson, Fiona. "In the Name of the State? Schools and Teachers in an Andean Province." In *States of Imagination: Ethnographic Explorations of the Postcolonial State*, edited by Thomas Blom Hansen and Finn Stepputat, 313–44. Durham, NC: Duke University Press, 2001.

Wilson, Fiona. "Transcending Race? Schoolteachers and Political Militancy in Andean Peru, 1970–2000." *Journal of Latin American Studies* 39, no. 4 (2007): 719–46.

Wise, David. "Indigenismo de izquierda y de derecha: Dos planteamientos de los años 1920." *Revista iberoamericana* 122 (1983): 159–69.

Wogan, Peter. *Magical Writing in Salasaca: Literacy and Power in Highland Ecuador.* Boulder, CO: Westview, 2003.

Wood, Robert. *"Teach Them Good Customs": Colonial Indian Education and Acculturation in the Andes.* Culver City, CA: Labyrinthos, 1986.

Yapu, Mario, ed. *Modernidad y pensamiento descolonizador: Memoria del Seminario Internacional.* La Paz: U-PIEB and IFEA, 2006.

Yapu, Mario, and Cassandra Torrico. *En tiempos de reforma educativa: Escuelas primarias y formación docente.* 2 vols. La Paz: PIEB, 2003.

Yashar, Deborah J. *Contesting Citizenship in Latin America: The Rise of Indigenous Movements and the Postliberal Challenge.* Cambridge: Cambridge University Press, 2005.

Young, Kevin. *Blood of the Earth: Natural Resources, Revolution, and Empire in Bolivia.* Austin: University of Texas Press, 2017.

Young, Kevin. "The Making of an Interethnic Coalition: Urban and Rural Anarchists in La Paz, 1946–1947." *Latin American and Caribbean Ethnic Studies* 11, no. 2 (2016): 163–88.

Zavala, Virginia, Mercedes Niño-Murcia, and Patricia Ames, eds. *Escritura y sociedad: Nuevas perspectivas teóricas y etnográficas.* Lima: Red para el Desarrollo de las Ciencias Sociales en el Perú, 2004.

Zavaleta Mercado, René. *Lo nacional-popular en Bolivia.* Mexico City: Siglo Veintiuno, 1986.

Zea, Leopoldo. *The Latin American Mind.* Norman: University of Oklahoma Press, 1963.

Zevallos Aguilar, Ulises Juan. *Indigenismo y nación: Los retos a la representación de la subalternidad aymara y quechua en el Boletín Titikaka, 1826–1930.* Lima: IFEA/BCRP, 2002.

Zook, David. *The Conduct of the Chaco War.* New Haven, CT: Bookman Associates, 1960.

Zulawski, Ann. *Unequal Cures: Public Health and Political Change in Bolivia, 1900–1950.* Durham, NC: Duke University Press, 2007.

Zunes, Stephen. "The United States and Bolivia: The Taming of a Revolution, 1952–1957." *Latin American Perspectives* 28 (2001): 33–49.

Zuñiga, Madelein, Juan Ansion, and Luis Cueva, eds. *Educación en poblaciones indígenas: Politicas y estrategias en América Latina.* Santiago: Instituto Indigenista Interamericano, 1987.

INDEX

achachilas (Aymara, ancestral spirits), 95
Adorno, Rolena, 11
Agrarian Reform Decree (1953), 277–80
Aguirre Gainsborg, José, 149
Alba, Armando, 258–59
Albó, Xavier, 74, 325
alcalde escolar (in charge of ayllu's school activities), 198
alcalde mayor (Indigenous authority), 198, 200; as activist teacher, 201–5
Alexander, Robert, 287, 292, 300
Alliance for Progress, 349–50n29, 374n80, 398n19, 412n87
Altiplano: ancient Aymara settlement of, 55; climate and topography of, 73–75, 121–22; land conflicts in, 10, 12, 74–80, 102–3, 106–8; metropole vs. hinterland, 26–29; racial violence throughout, 13, 96, 139, 266, 274, 327, 329; telluric mystique of, 55–56, 113
Alvarez Mamani, Antonio: in Chaco War, 205–7; as delegate to 1954 Indigenista congress, 315–21; as kallawaya, 389–90n34; and rural labor activism, 206–10, 214, 217, 220, 315–21, 390–91nn44–45

ama de casa (housewife), textbook lessons in the domestication of, 249–52
amauta (wise elder), 124, 131, 139, 146, 196, 371–72n45. *See also* parliament of *amautas*
anarchism, 389n31, 395n101
Añawaya Poma, Juan, 183–85
Antezana Ergueta, Luís, 274, 292
anthropology and anthropologists: foreign fieldworkers in rural Bolivia, 58–63, 97, 289, 291–92, 302–3, 307, 311, 408n45, 412n87, 413n94; involvement in international congresses, 396n7, 397n10; 1942 Smithsonian conference of, 341
apoderado (legal representative of an Indian community), 75. See also *caciques*
archive: Archivo de La Paz, 88, 332; Archivo Nacional de Bolivia, 88; as artifact of communal memory, 331–32; cacique archives, 87–88, 363–64n42; Indigenous research in, 12, 81–88, 278, 292; as repository of colonial title deeds, 83–85, 87; Spanish America's documentary culture and, 361–62n22, 362n25; subaltern archives, 85–88, 364n46; THOA archives, 332; "walking archive," 313

Argentina: Conquest of the Desert, 5; disappearance of Indian races in, 62; idea of national pedagogy in, 24, 350n1; policies of education and immigration in, 40; positivist educational reforms in, 4–5; teacher scholarships to, 65. *See also* Sarmiento, Domingo Faustino

Arguedas, Alcides, 27–28, 113, 351n7, 381n18

Ari, Waskar, 87, 201

Arnold, Denise, 95–96

Arreyo, Santos, 36

Arze Loureiro, Eduardo, 164, 211, 255–57, 262–68, 402n58, 404n81

ayllus (networks of Andean landholding communities). *See comunarios*; land and landholding

Aymara people (*Jaqi*, in Aymara): alleged degeneration of, 33–34; in defense of land, 12, 74–80, 106–8; ethnic resurgence of, 321–25; historiography of, 324–25, 331–33; racial stereotypes of, 7–9, 55–56, 62, 113, 189; social ecology of, 5–7, 73–75, 121–22; as targets of racial violence, 77–79; transregional networks among, 75–80, 210–17. *See also* peasants; Quechua people

Aymara school activism, 71–73, 80, 88–93, 97–98; role of caciques-apoderados, 12, 80, 88–89, 91, 96; clandestine nature of, 88–93; comunarios as driving force behind, 10–12, 80, 89, 100; literacy, legal struggles, and the politics of, 10–12, 80, 91–92; Nina Quispe as educator, advocate, and visionary, 102–9, 367–68n96, 368n101; oral remembrances of, 92–93, 95–96; racialized violence perpetrated against, 96–97; village school as ritual space, 93–97

Aymara women and girls: crafting the ideal homemaker, 249–52; patriarchal resistance to girls' education, 133, 310, 375n93; prospect of domestic servitude of, 144, 252, 401n48; Warisata's matriculation of girls, 133, 146, 376n95

Bairon, Max, 157, 186–87

Ballivián, Manuel Vicente, 34–35, 64

Banzer, Hugo, 323, 326

Barnadas, Josép, 217

Belgium mission: Bolivian field research by, 59–61; Indian education reforms promoted by, 63–64; origins of, 57–58; scientific pedagogy introduced by, 58. *See also* Rouma, Georges

Bolivia, topographic map of, 29

Burke, Melvin, 288

Busch, Germán, 14, 11, 147, 161; E. Pérez's relationship with, 152, 156–58, 165–66; populist reforms under, 225, 279, 396n1; suicide of, 162

cabildo de indios (Indigenous council for purpose of discussing political, economic, and educational matters): cacique petition for restitution of, 197–99, 200, 289; colonial origins of, 387n15

cacique-apoderado movement: archival pilgrimages of, 12, 81–88, 278, 292, 363n42; authorities of, 75, 77, 361n18; communal lands defended by, 74–75, 81–88; epicenter of, 79; insurgent literacy practices among, 81–88, 91–93, 363n34, 365n51; litigation, literacy, and paper trails of, 75–88; S. Marka T'ula as leader of, 85, 88; persecution of, 82–86, 91–92; petition campaigns of, 77–80, 88–93, 198–202, 282–86; post–Chaco War resurgence of, 196–202; scribal tradition of, 83–87; transregional networks of, 75–79, 361n19. *See also* archive; Aymara school activism; land and landholding

cacique de sangre (person claiming direct descent from colonial caciques, or *mallkus*), 78–79

caciques: colonial lineages of, 78–79; as cultural brokers, 77–79; La Paz's leading circle of, 79. *See also* cacique-apoderado movement

Caiza D: núcleo escolar in, 148, 150, 157, 375n84; as target of state repression, 169–70, 180–82, 281, 384n56

Calderón, Ignacio, 26–27

Calero, Jorge, 236, 397n11

Callisaya, Prudencio, 79
campesino. *See* peasants
Canessa, Andrew, 290
Caquiaviri, núcleo escolar in, 98, 148, 150, 169, 197, 331
Cárdenas, Lázaro, 152, 163, 165
Carlisle Indian Industrial School, 66, 359n110
Carter, William, 97, 289, 307, 408n45
castellanización: arm of MNR's assimilationist project, 22, 307–9; critics of, 224, 331, 334; pedagogies of, 53, 91, 224, 411n78. *See also* language
caste system: and Bolivia's neocolonial order, 25, 33, 34, 64, 162; persistence of, 43, 69, 74, 56; and racial segregation, 9, 24–25, 26–28, 32, 35–38, 113, 217, 274; reinforced by educational policy, 41–42, 67; resistance to, 81, 195, 267, 277. *See also* Indigenous laborers; neocolonialism; racial ideology; violence
Catholic Church: and the cacique-apoderado movement, 199, 200–201, 367n95, 388n2, 420n55; church-state relations, 2, 39, 40, 54, 59, 200, 295, 420n55; Escuelas de Cristo, 388n19; liberation theology, 323, 325, 349; parish and mission schools, 39, 45, 388n19; progressive forces within, 74, 323, 325, 327, 367n95, 388n19, 414n107, 417n32
CCTK (Centro Campesino Túpac Katari), 323
CEBIAE (Centro Boliviano de Investgación y Acción Educativa), 417n30
census data: literacy and school matriculation rates, 286, 303–4, 309, 408n38, 412–13nn92–93; 1900 population census and race-thinking, 32–38, 351–52n15, 352n20, 352n22; 1920 Indian population estimate, 360–61n9
Centro Católico de Aborígenes Bartolomé de las Casas, 367n95, 388n21
Céspedes, Augusto, 227
chachawarmi (Aymara, ethos of gender complementarity), 401n44
Chaco War (1932–35), 15, 73, 98, 107, 109, 147–48, 192–94, 197, 202–5
chasqui (messenger), 83, 210, 213, 390n44, 391n58

Chávez Orozco, Luís, 165–66
Chávez Ortiz, Ñunflo, 273, 277
Chervin, Arthur, 60
Chile: border tensions with, 107; educational diplomacy with, 48–49, 65, 355–56n68; exiled Bolivians in, 149, 206, 265; positivism and educational reforms in, 4, 24, 350n1; racial whitening and immigration in, 34, 40, 63
Chipana Ramos, Francisco, 220–21, 316, 393n79
cholo and *chola* people: in the city of La Paz, 29, 32, 52; elite hostility toward, 129, 187, 195; gender stereotypes of, 251, 386n87; race and class categories of, 32, 51–52, 90. *See also* mestizo and mestiza people
Choque Canqui, Roberto, 79, 331–32
Chukiyawu, 32, 351n14
CIB (Comité Indígena Boliviano), 212, 215, 217–19, 391n54
CIPCA (Centro para Investigación y Promoción del Campesinado), 420n54
citizenship: agrarian mobilization and grassroots practices of, 7, 16, 194–95, 215–19; CIB manifesto of Indian rights to, 217–18; enduring barriers to, 7, 46, 54, 187–88, 310; E. Nina Quispe's vision of communal restitution as integral to, 105–7; 1952 decree of universal suffrage and, 20, 291, 319, 349–50n29, 406n17; postrevolutionary Aymara visions and demands for, 8, 269–71, 272–81, 282–86
Claure, Toribio, 149, 224–25, 257, 382n35, 384n56, 393n88
Cliza, núcleo escolar in, 15, 157, 169, 399n37, 405n6
CNE (Consejo Nacional de Educación): as arm of the Conservative oligarchy, 161–62; bureaucratic centralization under, 119, 180, 380n12; Indigenal education dismantled by, 161–63; pedagogy of Indian assimilation of, 186–91; persecution of rural teachers by, 181–86; policy, pillage, and propaganda war waged by, 167–80, 380n17, 382n36; reports on school conditions by, 168–72, 379–80n11, 381n20. *See also* Donoso Torres, Vicente

INDEX 467

COB (Confederación de Obreros Bolivianos), 286, 295, 297, 317, 409n57, 414n111
coca, 27, 31, 61, 104, 241, 247, 248, 335, 360–61n9
Cochabamba, 15, 16; agrarian reform in, 277–78, 418n38; cacique networks in, 79–80, 196; Indigenous schools in, 63, 149, 157, 169, 393n88; peasant labor organizing throughout, 15, 80, 195, 205, 207–9, 211, 213, 216, 219, 227, 390n37, 405n6
Cold War, 17, 161, 231, 249, 266, 268, 318, 349–50n29, 395–96n103, 398n19, 402n60, 413n94, 415n3
Colla (Aymara and Quechua peoples of the Altiplano region), 55, 62
Collasuyo (ancient homeland of Aymara and Quechua peoples), 55, 105–6, 108–9
Colombia, 11, 22, 348n21
colonialism (Spanish): and the archive, 81–82, 361–62n22; and the caste regime, 5, 27, 73–75, 121–22, 370n32; inherited institutions of, 74, 387n15, 390n44; land titles as legal artifacts of, 77–78, 80–81, 291, 348–49n22, 362n25, 367–68n96, 406–7n29; racial categories of, 346–47n14. *See also* neocolonialism
colonos (hacienda tenants): servile labor conditions of, 28, 45, 103, 126, 179, 357n94; labor and school activism among, 191, 209, 211, 216, 222; schools established by, 394n94
Comitas, Lambros, 302–3, 412n87
comunario movement. *See* cacique-apoderado movement
comunarios (members of an ayllu-community): categories of originario and agregrado, 365n68; ex-comunarios as servile colonos, 44, 77; mobilized in defense of communal lands, 75–76, 77, 103, 197
concientización (political consciousness-raising): concept of, 15, 349nn26–27; peasant activists as agents of, 115–17, 162, 183, 205–10, 227, 270; urban anarchism as locus of, 227, 395n101. *See also* peasants; popular education

Condori Chura, Leandro, 85–87, 89, 103, 107–8, 197
Cornejo, Santos, 98, 197, 406–7n29
corregidor (highest government official at cantonal level), 44, 139, 144, 200, 355n54, 359–60n2, 372–73n59
CRE (Comisión de Reforma Educativa), 21–22, 295–300, 302, 307, 409nn57–58, 410–11n72. *See also* MNR education reforms; 1955 Education Code
criollo (person claiming Spanish descent), 5, 7–8, 28–29, 31–32, 41, 108
CSUTCB (Confederación Sindical Única de Trabajadores Bolivianos), 334
cultural eugenics, 51, 188, 385n79
cultural hygiene: domesticating the ama de casa, 249–52, 400n40; instructions in nutrition, gardening, and personal hygiene, 244–45; lessons in modern homemaking, 245–46; resocialization of the male campesino, 246–48
cultural nationalism, 19, 56, 186–89, 295, 306–7, 346n3. *See also* National Revolution
cultural pedagogy, 306–7. *See also* national pedagogy
cultural racism, 188, 308, 337. *See also* racial ideology
Cummins, Thomas, 22
curricular reform: CNE's assimilationist program of, 169–70, 178–79, 186, 200; debates over, 56–57, 64–65, 67–68; geo-racial segregation as basis of, 41, 42, 67; Indigenal education and, 114, 119, 127, 134, 145; influence of foreign pedagogies on, 37, 47–48, 51, 58, 63, 65–68; *instrucción* vs. *educación*, 40; Mexico's influence on, 151–53; under US program of functional education, 235–52; Warisata and the internal debate over, 127, 144–47. *See also* educational policy

decolonization/recolonization, ethno-historical approach to, 5–7, 11–12, 290–91, 315–37, 349n25. *See also* emancipation; moral memory; neocolonialism
Dewey, John, 266, 376n97

DGEI (Dirección General de Educación Indigenal), 98, 99, 119, 156–57, 166, 168, 380n15

Diez de Medina, Fernando, 296, 302, 306–7, 409n75, 411n84

dirigente campesino (peasant organizer with syndicalist ties), 16, 202–15

Donoso Torres, Vicente: assault on Indigenal education under, 161–62, 168, 171–76, 379–80n11; conservative philosophy of, 171–73; educational background of, 63, 380n12; tutelary race-thinking and, 186–91; and US extension program, 233, 236, 238, 256. *See also* CNE

D'Orbigny, Alcide, 31–32, 34, 351n10

educational policy: alleged Indian problem as target of, 9, 18, 21, 25, 36, 65, 113, 256, 272, 306, 354n52; as arena of debate, 56–57, 64–65, 67–69; as arm of modern state-building, 3–5, 36–47, 156–59, 186–91, 224–26, 307–9; neocolonial logic of, 9, 21, 41–44, 299–303; North American influence on, 65–69. *See also* Liberal oligarchy; MNR education reforms; rural schools and schooling

EIB (Educación Intercultural Bilingüe), 33–35, 347–48n15

1874 Law of Divestiture (Ley de Ex-vinculación), 74, 78, 122; 1883 pro-indiviso decree, 361n12

emancipation: Aymara ideas about, 282–83, 294; literacy and schooling as instruments of, 1, 6, 14, 16, 162, 177; nativist and popular struggles for, 108, 269, 274; self-education as pathway to, 261; from slavery and ignorance, 81; village school as symbol of, 290; Warisata as Indigenous school of, 328, 335

Enlightenment, 1–4, 7–10

Ensinas, José Antonio, 153, 165

escuelas ambulantes (government-run mobile schools; itinerant instructors), 42, 44–46. *See also* rural schools and schooling

escuelita particular (autonomous school, built by the community and run by local teacher; outside state jurisdiction), 116–17

ethnicity: Aymara geo-politics of, 73–88, 105–9, 196–202; nationalism, folklore, and, 316; political resurgence of, 321–25; postrevolutionary politics of, 282–86; racial, class, and regional notions of, 9, 56, 346–47n14

ethnography: as discipline, 6–7; at the interface of literacy and orality, 11–12, 71–72, 87, 95–96, 348nn20–21, 363n42, 366n75; and study of Indigenous schools, 92–97

Europe: the Belgian mission to Bolivia, 57–64; grand tours and pedagogic pilgrimages in, 47–51, 65, 350n3; ideas about race, nation, and educational reform in, 1–3, 20, 50, 345–46n2, 346n3

Fernández, Benjamin, 350n3
Finot, Enrique, 67, 164–65, 190, 359n114
Flores Galindo, Alberto, 24
Foucault, Michel, 242, 399n31
Freire, Paulo, 333, 349n27, 386–87n5
Frontaura Argandoña, María, 91, 100, 364n49
Fuentes Lira, Manuel, 178

Gallardo, Melitón, 391n62
Gamio, Mario, 316
gamonalismo (state of predatory violence): Achacachi, provincial site of, 116, 122, 131, 134, 136, 138, 262; concept discussed, 349n24; protest against, 140, 183, 276, 280; rural schools assaulted by, 53, 138, 180, 274, 303, 327; rural terror and violence perpetuated by, 13, 96, 139, 266, 274, 327, 329; Warisata as target of, 138–39, 140, 183–84

García, Antonio, 288, 313
García, Uriel, 153
Garibaldi, Carlos, 149, 261, 403n76
gender: Aymara feminist activism, 329–30; Aymara norms of, 133, 401n44; differential rates of bilingualism, literacy, and schooling by, 304, 309–10, 322; female labor and domestic servitude, 274, 401n48; female political enfranchisement, 291; US imposition of female/male behavioral norms, 242–52; women's role in Warisata, 125–26, 133, 137

Gobineau, Arthur de, 346n10
González Bravo, Antonio, 178
Gotkowitz, Laura, 218, 361n19
governmentality, 399n31
Gramsci, Antonio, 15, 202–3, 349n26, 386–87n5
Guaraní people, 137, 157, 204, 216, 248; ethnic resurgence of, 334–35; and fight for bilingual education, 336–37
Guevara, Ernesto (Ché), 323
Guha, Ranajit, 210
Guías de instrucción para maestros rurales, 242, 398n21, 399n32, 400n38
Guillén Pinto, Alfredo, 23, 25, 38, 65, 382n35
Guzmán, Felipe Segundo, 49–54, 56–57, 67–68

Hampton Institute, 66, 67–68
Harris, Olivia, 87
Hart, Thomas, 298
Hernani, Sixto, 139
Herzog, Enrique, 227, 257, 259–62, 265, 395–96n103, 402n61
hilacatas (Aymara; local indigenous leaders within the ayllu, escuela-ayllu, or hacienda), 44, 131, 132, 133, 135, 200, 209, 355n54, 361n19
historiography: Aymara revisionist school of, 331–33; of Bolivian education, 347–48n15, 353n41, 379n2; of the THOA collective, 360n5; on the Warisata experiment, 112, 177, 258. *See also* ethnography
Hobsbawm, Eric, 3, 20, 50
Holden, Gladys, 251–2
Home Economics, 237, 239, 243, 251–52, 254, 264, 399n32
Huanca, Mariano, 138–39, 372–73n59
Huarina, 98, 129, 282, 284–85, 295
Hughes, Lloyd, 232–35
Hurtado, Javier, 325

Ibañez, Eufrasio, 266
ideology. *See* racial ideology; tutelary race-thinking
IIAA (Institute of Inter-American Affairs), 247, 251, 253, 401n52
III (Instituto Indigenista Interamericano), 316, 317, 379n6
Illampu, 374n80
Illanes, Mario Alejandro, 149
illiteracy: census data on, 233, 304, 330; discourse on racial inequality and, 180–81; government ban on, 156; Indian oppression as underlying cause of, 20, 116, 233–34, 277, 290; Indigenous struggle for emancipation from, 290–91; MNR plans to eradicate, 275, 408n40, 412n92
Inca moral code, 201–2, 389n29
Indian (racialized colonial category), 346–47n14. *See also* Aymara people; peasants; Quechua people; racial ideology
Indian problem: as colonialist trope, 5, 54, 65–66, 320; contested notions of national pedagogy and, 24–25, 55–56, 68–69; literary and scientific diagnoses of, 23–26, 33–38, 54–65, 113, 187–91; MNR's rhetorical uses of, 306, 316; populist spin on, 217, 394n93; proposed educative solutions to, 23–26, 55–56, 64–66, 113, 236, 272, 306; US strategic interests in, 26, 395n103, 396–97n10. *See also* racial ideology; tutelary race-thinking
Indian rights movement, 320, 325, 335
Indigenal education: curricular debates within, 144–47; as indigenista pedagogy, 114, 116, 119–20, 127; institutionalization of, 156–57, 368n1; oligarchy's political opposition to, 161–72
indigeneity: contemporary ethnic mobilizations around, 319, 321–24, 334–35, 415–16n14, 416n15, 416nn18–20; Inter-American solidarity under banner of, 318–20; and intercultural education reforms, 326–27; and the Plurinational State, 335–37; regional Aymara politics of, 12, 73–88, 196–202
indigenismo (field of inquiry into the alleged Indian problem): the Aymara Indian as literary and diagnostic object of, 27–28, 58–62, 64–65, 106, 189–90, 358; cultural mestizaje as strand of, 186–89, 306–7, 356n79; international circuits of,

149–55, 163–67, 315–21; Liberal civilizing mission as anathema to, 54–55; Marxist and radical dissent within, 110, 185, 194, 227, 309; under the MNR regime, 63–64, 296–99, 306–10; Warisata's radical teachers and, 147–54

Indigenous laborers: corvée labor obligations of, 123, 382n35; and labor-sharing traditions, 27, 119, 370n32; racializing the Aymara workforce, 64–65; rural schooling as workforce training of, 63–69; as servile tenants on haciendas, 28, 45, 74–75, 81, 102–3, 120, 193, 203; Warisata's communitarian labor regime, 123–24, 126–28

indio lanzado (expelled or dispossessed Indian), 103

indio letrado. See lettered Indian

indio pongo (servile tenant), 27, 193–94, 208, 274

informal empire: Aymara critique of, 324–25; culture and politics of, 6, 17–18; leftist opposition to North America's, 252–60; pedagogies of, 7–10, 24–25, 49–53, 65–69, 235–52; Cold War geopolitics of, 161, 229–32. *See also* SCIDE; United States

Inter-American relations: 1940 Congress of Indigenistas and, 163–67, 397n10, 415n5; 1954 Congress of Indigenistas and, 315–21; US aid and diplomacy promoting, 232–35, 240, 247, 251

interculturalism: as contemporary pedagogical ideal, 334, 347–48n15, 419n49; Warisata's pathbreaking experiment in, 110–59

Inti Karka, 297, 306

Irurozqui, Marta, 54

Jáuregui Rosquellos, Alfredo, 192–93, 195, 204, 205, 386n1

Jesús de Machaca: 1921 uprising of, 91–92, 98, 118; núcleo escolar in, 118–19, 157

Juntas de Auxilio Escolar, 252

kallawaya (medicinal specialists), 205, 206, 209, 317, 389n34

Kant, Immanuel, 1–3, 5, 335, 345–46nn2–3

Katari, Tomás, 82

katarismo (resurgent Aymara movement, inspired by the memory of Tupac Katari), 321–25, 415–16n14, 416n15, 416nn18–20

La Calle, 382n32, 386n3

Lake Titicaca, 26, 73, 118, 120–22, 196, 271, 277, 302

land and landholding: Aymara legal campaigns for, 12, 74–80, 106–8, 360–61n9, 361n12; debate over Indian education vs. land question, 110, 185, 194, 227, 309; 1874 Law of Disentailment, 74, 78, 122; the escuela-ayllu vs. neighboring haciendas, 120, 122–24; intertwined struggles for literacy, schooling, and, 10–11, 78–80; latifundismo and conflict on the Altiplano, 73–75, 102–3, 122–23; MNR's agrarian reform, 279–80, 394n93; peasant land invasions and petitions for, 277–78, 282–86, 405–6nn16–17, 406–7n29

language: assimilationist policies, 38, 53, 63–64, 91, 307–9; Aymara political oratory, 138–40; bilingual communication in Warisata, 136, 137, 145, 147; census data on, 309–10; ethno-linguistic groups, 316, 319; hispanized linguistic nationalism, 224–25, 307–8, 380; intercultural, bilingual activism, 334–37; oral, aural, and written modes of communication, 291–93, 311–13; postrevolutionary spike in literacy and bilingualism, 303, 309–10, 412n92; trilingual peasant activists, 89, 130, 206, 390n37. *See also castellanización*

La Noche, 380n17

La Paz (capital city of): Aymara and cholo population in, 29, 31; ecology and commerce of, 29, 31; as lettered city, 28–29; as locus of Liberal oligarchy, 24–26; peasants' migration into, 269–70; postrevolutionary democratization of public space in, 273–75; urban metropole vs. rural hinterland, 9, 24–25, 26–28, 32, 35–38; white fear and siege mentality in city of, 32, 35–36, 43

La Paz (department of), topographic map, 30

La Paz (provinces of): Aymara political networks in, 75–80; epicenter of Bolivia's sprawling cacique-apoderado movement, 79–80; escalating land conflicts in, 74–75, 77–78, 360–61n9, 361n12; racial violence and fear throughout, 77–79; topography of, 73–74

latifundismo. See land and landholding

Le Bon, Gustave, 34, 346n10

Lefebvre, Georges, 210

Legión Cívica, 109

Lema, Vicente, 297–300, 307–8, 407–8n37, 410n72

Leonard, Olen, 291, 292, 313

lettered city (*ciudad letrada*): vs. Aymara hinterland, 27–28, 33; locus of La Paz's ruling oligarchy, 25, 28–29. *See also* La Paz (capital city of); Liberal oligarchy; Sucre

lettered Indian (*indio letrado; indio leído*): elite hostility toward, 8, 11, 92, 102, 139, 290; racial stereotypes of, 10–11, 101–2; in urban La Paz, 29, 31–32. *See also* cacique-apoderado movement; literacy

Liberal oligarchy: civilizing schemes of, 9, 7–10, 24–25, 26–28, 32, 36–38, 49–53; cosmopolitan educators and, 47–53, 355n62; critics of, 53–56; educational reforms designed by, 38–45, 68–69, 353n41, 354n50, 354n52; Indian problem debated by, 5, 26–38, 54–65, 113, 187–91; influence of North America on, 65–69; racial ideology and sentiments of, 9–10, 25–26, 44, 47–57

literacy: agrarian reform, village schools, and, 286–91, 291–94; Aymara demands for, 71–73, 80, 88–93, 97–98; Aymara insurgent practices of, 82–87, 291; Aymara literacy instructors, 91–92, 129–31, 201–2; barriers, denial, and suppression of, 83–85, 91–93, 96–97, 101–2, 129, 138–40, 310, 372–73n59, 374n76, 374n78; census data on, 303–4; emancipatory mystique of, 45–47, 81, 89, 269–70, 280, 282–86, 290, 293–94; ethnographic approaches to, 11–12, 71–72, 87, 95–96, 348nn20–21, 363n42, 366n75; gender inequality and, 309–10; Indigenous land claims, archives, and vernacular forms of, 73–80, 81–88, 348–49n22; MNR campaign for diffusion of, 292, 294, 306–14, 333, 410n72; peasant activism, orality, and, 72–73, 86–88, 210–14, 308–10; postrevolutionary upsurge of, 272–81, 291–94, 303–4, 309–10; suffrage and, 309–11, 354n52. *See also* Aymara school activism; caciques-apoderado movement; print culture

Llanos, David, 96

Llanqi, Faustino, 79, 91, 365n51

Llanqui, Marcelino, 91–92, 365n51

Llica, núcleo escolar in, 148, 157, 168, 402–3n64

MAC (Ministerio de Asuntos Campesinos), 242, 247, 273, 275, 297–98, 300–301, 303–4, 311, 409n59, 413n93

Maes, Ernest: on assignment in Bolivia, 235–42; career background of, 235, 266; mass media deployed by, 239–40; núcleo escolar adapted by, 240–42, 398n27; political opposition to, 258–62, 266; teacher-training workshops established by, 237–39

Magruder report, 396n7

mallku (Aymara; traditional Indigenous leader with authority over an ayllu or marka), 132, 135, 200

Mamani, Carlos, 76, 84

Mamani, Mauricio, 97

Mamani, Patricio, 77

Mamani, Serapio, 261

Manifiesto de Tiahuanacu, 324, 416n20

Mann, Horace, 48, 376n97

Mariátegui, José Carlos, 155, 185, 194, 327, 349n24

marka (Aymara; nested cluster of ayllus, usually oriented around a rural town): ancient, 111; Warisata's reinvention of, 141, 143

Marka T'ula, Andrés, 197

Marka T'ula, Santos, 76, 79; and the cacique-apoderado movement, 85–88, 197; collaboration with his scribe, 85–87; political persecution of, 85–86; and the subaltern archive, 85–86, 88; work with Centro Católico de Aborígenes Bartolomé de las Casas, 388n21

Marof, Tristan, 149, 185, 384n65

Martínez, Françoise, 39

Marxist ideology: Indian education vs. land question, 110, 185, 194, 227, 309; on the Indian problem, 149, 155, 185, 194, 326–27, 349n24, 384n65; and the mining proletariat, 395n100; radical indigenistas and, 147–54

mass communication: Aymara petition for channels of, 277; MNR deployment of, 20, 304–7, 311, 414n106; E. Pérez's use of, 157; via print culture, 291–93, 308–11, 313; via radio, 292–93, 305, 306; US technology of, 239–40

Mauck, Wilfred, 253–55, 401n52

Mayta, Mariano, 284

McBride, George, 360n9

Medinaceli, Carlos, 140, 386n87

Mendoza, Jaime, 64–65, 108, 358n106

Mercado, Bailón, 119

mestizaje (racial ideology of nationalism, promoting Indian assimilation into hispanized national culture): imported Mexican ideal of, 188–90; nationalist project of, 224, 297, 303, 306–7, 386n87, 393n88; neo-civilizing elites in quest of, 166, 186–91; and tutelary race-thinking, 4, 56, 356n79

mestizo and mestiza people (mixed-race label or identity): as bilingual, intercultural brokers, 75, 81, 85; mestizo towns and provincial violence, 32, 103, 119, 120, 123, 129, 143; stereotypes of, 32–33, 52, 55, 143, 175, 219–20, 393n82; theories about race-mixing, 186, 187, 189, 190–91. See also *cholo* and *chola* people

Mexico: agrarianist influences from, 203; Bolivian revolution and, 21, 321; delegates to 1954 Inter-American Congress of Indigenistas from, 316; 1938 Bolivian teachers delegation to, 152–55, 164; 1940 Congress of Indigenistas in, 163–67, 379n6, 380n11; Warisata and, 13–14, 127, 136–37, 166, 265

military: as arm of the neocolonial state, 5, 17, 118, 137, 139, 179, 191, 227–28, 402n61; Aymara conscripts in, 42, 89, 90–92, 98, 225, 364n49, 393n88; Chaco War recruits and veterans of, 202–4, 205–6, 224, 375–76n94; dictatorship and repression under, 325, 328, 333; racialized fear of Indigenous conscripts, 92, 247–48; universal conscription into, 42, 84

military socialist regimes, 111–12, 156, 158, 161, 169

mines and miners, 17, 64, 90, 130, 214; labor strife in, 175, 193, 215–16, 227–28, 258, 267; nationalization of, 349–50n29; Washington's strategic focus on, 230, 249

Ministry of Education, 98, 105, 116, 118, 124, 176, 196, 261, 282, 300–301, 306, 336, 356n69, 397n11, 399n32, 400n40, 409n59

MINK'A, 323, 324–25, 331, 416n18, 416n20

Miranda, Dionisio, 220

Miranda, Toribio, 201, 261, 388n25

MNR education reforms: CRE, organ of, 295–99; CRE's rural education plan, 306–10, 411n78; critics of, 301–3, 411n84, 412n87, 412n90; increase in rural elementary schools, 286–91, 303–4; V. Lema as architect of rural schooling, 297–99, 407–8n37, 410n72; mass media and didactic themes of, 304–6, 311–13; peasant petitions for, 270–71, 280–81, 282–86; SCIDE's influence on, 297–99; urban/rural caste divide reproduced in, 21, 299–303, 411n78; G. Villarroel's legacy and, 273, 281

MNR government, 15, 19, 216, 219, 226; Indian problem defined by, 21, 272; integrative nationalism of, 20–22; 1953 agrarian and 1955 education reforms of, 277–80, 286, 295–99; official indigenismo of, 297–98; party propaganda of, 304–10, 312, 408n40, 413n97, 414nn106–7; peasant and worker alliances with, 52, 227, 270, 286; and the peasantry, 276–78. See also COB; MNR education reforms

Montes, Juan Misael, 8; amended 1874 Constitution, 39–40; Conservative reaction to, 46–47; contract with Catholic missions, 39; as latifundista, 45, 102; Liberal Party search for literate Aymara voters under, 44, 354n52, 371n38; and policy of military conscription, 61, 91; public education reform under, 40–41; and G. Rouma, 57–58. *See also* Liberal oligarchy; Saracho, Juan Misael

Morales, Evo, 335–36, 337

moral memory: Aymara intellectuals and the decolonization of, 322–25, 327, 331, 389n29, 418n38; community archive as repository of, 87; erasure of indigeneity and, 320–21; and Indigenous acts of revindication, 261–62, 269–70, 282–83; oppression, oral testimony, and, 93–94, 96–97, 290–91; Warisata as contested icon of, 326–30, 331

Movimiento Nacional Revolucionario (MNR). *See* MNR education reforms; MNR government

MUSEF (Museo de Etnografía y Folklore), 419n42

NAFTA (North American Free Trade Agreement), 335

National Constitution: of 1874, 12, 25, 39–40, 42, 300; of 1938, 198–99, 386n2, 387n12; of 2009, 420n53

National Indian Congress (1945), 16–17; ceremonial staging of, 220–23; indigenous and state negotiations over, 215–19; platform on Indian education reform, 224–25; and regional congresses, 392n64; social repercussions of, 226–28, 273, 281; Villarroel's four decrees as finale of, 225–26

national pedagogy (*la pedagogía nacional*), 8, 24–25, 35, 55–56, 68–69, 107, 114, 350n1. *See also* tutelary race-thinking

National Revolution (1952–64): Aymara proposals for revolutionary reform, 282–86; the civic revolution from below, 272–73, 276–81; framing the era of, 19–22, 271–72; indo-mestizaje nationalism, 304–11; MNR's agrarian and education reforms, 278–80, 295–99; modern campesino as icon of, 297–98, 305–6, 311, 319; popular literacy and print culture during, 276–78, 291–94, 304. *See also* MNR education reforms; MNR government

nationhood and nation making: Aymara ethnic nationalism and multicultural ideals of, 106, 284–85, 318–19, 334–35, 406n29; imported French ideal of, 50; and linguistic nationalism, 50, 224–25, 307–8, 380; MNR's integrative, indo-mestizo ideal of, 19, 21, 56, 306–14; oligarchy's civilizing and assimilationist projects of, 9, 7–10, 24–25, 38, 42, 46, 49–53, 173, 186–91

Navarro, Cocha, 149

neocolonialism: endemic violence of, 330; ideological battles within, 174, 195, 284, 310, 314, 327, 330; ideological pillars of, 41, 68–69, 189, 191; resistance to, 269–81, 282–86, 309–11, 313–14. *See also* caste system; racial ideology; violence

networks: among cacique-apoderados, 76–79; of Chaco War veterans, 203–8; ethnography of subaltern networking, 391n46; among Indigenous teachers and labor organizers, 195–96, 210–15; and MNR propaganda, 20, 304–6, 413n97, 414n106; traditional webs of kinship, trading, and communication, 17, 36, 140, 210, 214; transnational circuits of cosmopolitan educators, 7–10, 24–25, 49–53, 65–69; of transnational solidarity movements, 154–55, 319, 325. *See also* communication

NGOs (nongovernmental organizations), 293, 316, 318–19, 323, 327, 333–34, 336, 347–48n15, 417n25, 420n54

Nina Quispe, Eduardo: Aymara victim of landlord violence, 102–3; career as teacher and activist, 103–6; collaboration with caciques, 105–6, 108–9; flight to city and early education of, 103; newspaper interview with, 103–4; a radical nativist project proposed by,

105–7; as target of political violence, 105, 107–9
1955 Education Code (*Código de la educación boliviana*), 22, 296, 299, 300–301, 308, 324, 411n78. *See also* MNR education reforms
Niño-Murcia, Mercedes, 11
núcleo escolar (ayllu-based school): agro-industrial potential of, 143–44; oligarchic assault on, 175–80; origins of, 140–44, 375n84; as reconstituted ethnic space, 141, 143, 384n57; SCIDE's takeover and diffusion of, 237–40, 398n27. *See also* Warisata

Omasuyos (province of): Achacachi, capital of, 122; cacique networks throughout, 86, 130, 371n42; latifundismo and land conflicts in, 13, 14, 73, 139, 200; locale of Warisata, 129, 142; Protestant missions in, 388n19
originario (claiming original, landholding membership in an ayllu), 278, 346–47n14, 361n18, 365n68
Oropeza, Samuel, 38
Oropeza de Pérez, Jaél, 114
Oruro: cacique-apoderado networks in, 76, 79, 196; mines in, 31; peasant organizing in, 205, 209, 211, 216, 219, 392n74; rural school activity in, 201
Otero, Gustavo Adolfo, 186, 187

Pando, José Manuel: education reforms of, 38–40; plans for *instrucción popular* and European immigration, 40
Paredes, Manuel, 38
parliament of *amautas* (council of wise elders), 131–36, 371–72n45. *See also* Warisata
Patiño, Simón, 230
patriarchy, 246–47, 330, 400n40
Pátzcuaro (Mexico): Inter-American Indigenista Congress in, 163–67, 171, 235, 382n32, 397n10
Paxipati, Dionicio, 97–98, 197
Paz Estenssoro, Victor, 269, 273, 279, 282, 285, 304

Pearce, Roy Harvey, 66
peasants: agrarian class politics of, 196, 203–5, 346–47n14; associations of Chaco war veterans, 203–8; MNR's ideal image of, 297–8, 305–6, 311, 319; racist stereotypes of, 183; rural poverty of, 33, 38, 39; rural strikes, unrest, and repression of, 17, 191, 219, 226–28, 392n74; syndicalism, citizenship practices, and popular education among, 7, 15–17, 205–10, 214–20, 277–78, 282–86; urban migration of, 178, 249, 289, 322, 412n90. *See also* indigenous laborers; land and landholding
pedagogies of praxis, 194–96. See also *concientización*; popular education
Peñaranda, Enrique, 160, 174, 200, 235
Pérez, Anita, 169, 178, 183, 375n84
Pérez, Elizardo: cofounder of the escuela-ayllu, 125–28; early field experiences and pedagogical ideas, 116–19, 144–46; first encounters with A. Siñani, 116–17, 120–23; on governance of Warisata, 131–32, 134, 137–39; government investigation of, 173–75; in charge of DGEI's Indigenal education, 156–59; intellectual formation of, 113–14; on the labor question, 126–28, 134, 370n32; memoir of, 112, 369n2; and the núcleo escolar, 140–44; from SCIDE's critic to collaborator, 259–60, 265–67; touring the ruins of Warisata, 258–59, 262
Pérez, Raúl, 128, 150, 169–70, 173–74, 181, 375n84, 375–76n94, 384n56
Peru: Bolivia-Peru border zone, 236, 240, 288, 301; on Indian problem in, 358n103; indigenous archive expeditions to, 81–82; introduction of núcleos escolares in, 240–41; Viceroyalty of Peru, 82
Platt, Tristan, 363n42
pongueaje (indentured servitude), 120, 193; demands for abolition of, 386n3, 405n6
popular education: katarista organizations and, 322–23; in Latin America, 3, 335; peasant political activism as informal sphere of, 7, 15–17, 194–95, 205–10, 227, 162; theories of, 386–87n85, 397n14

positivism: educational reforms influenced by, 4–5, 7, 23–24, 39–40, 47–49, 350n3; and theories of racial evolution, 4, 33–34, 50–51, 352n28

Posnansky, Arturo, 108

Potosí, 31, 46, 63, 76, 79, 82, 181, 196, 205, 209, 213; ethnography of Northern, 87, 360–61n9, 363–64n42

Pratt, Mary Louise, 12, 35

print culture: as breach of literacy/illiteracy divide, 291–93, 310–11; as medium of peasant insurgency, 210–12, 214, 218, 291–93; postrevolutionary profusion of popular literacy and, 308–11, 313

PROEIBANDES (Educación Intercultural Bilingue de Paises Andinos), 420n54

Protestant missions: and cultural hygiene, 245–46, 252; Indian schools organized by, 39, 88, 100, 200–201, 240, 284, 353n38, 355n65, 388n19; and US rural extension programs, 252, 266

Puiggrós, Adriana, 346n6

q'ara (Aymara; "peeled skin," referring to people of Spanish descent), 123, 370n27

qilqiri (scribe; secretary), 75, 86

Quechua people: Inca code of ethics, 201–2, 389n29; involved in agrarian syndicalism, 194–95, 202–8, 211, 215–16, 220, 316, 406n18; involvement in cacique-apoderado movement, 76–80, 361n19; local community archive of, 363–64n42; local school as ritual site of, 95–96; núcleo escolares among, 148, 150, 181–83, 375n84; racial categories, stereotypes, and typologies of, 55, 59–62, 346–37n14; social ecology of, 5, 7, 35, 55. See also Aymara people; peasants

Quintanilla, Enrique, 160, 174

Quispe, Cristina, 79

racial ideology: alleged Aymara savagery and theories of degeneration, 32–38, 356n79; the Aymara Indian as diagnostic object of, 27–28, 58–62, 64–65, 106, 189–90, 358; bio-cultural categories and labels of, 346–47n14; civilizing elites and the circulation of, 7–10, 24–25, 49–53; indigenista currents of, 55–56, 64–66; and Lamarckism, 51–52; national pedagogy informed by, 24–25, 55–57, 68–69, 350n1; and neocolonialism, 9, 41, 290; North American currents of, 65–69; and putative solutions to the Indian problem, 186–89, 306–7, 356n79; and typologies of national character and ethnic groups, 50–51, 59–63

railroads, 11, 26, 27, 28, 65; and labor unrest, 193

Rama, Angel, 2

Ramos, Mariano, 125, 126, 131, 135

Ramos Quevedo, Luís, 211–15

Ranaboldo, Claudia, 389–90n34

Rappaport, Joanne, 11, 22, 348n21

Reinaga, Fausto, 415–16n14

Rens, Jeffrey, 288

Revisita de títulos de composición (official review of colonial land titles), 77–78, 82, 85, 107, 197, 216, 278, 282, 363n34, 371n42, 387n12, 406n29

revolution. See National Revolution

Reyeros, Rafael, 150, 159, 166–67, 171, 186, 190, 380n12, 382n35

Rivera, Diego, 413n96

Rivera Cusicanqui, Silvia, 36, 109, 322, 324, 332, 418n38, 419n44

roads and transport: Andean traditions of inter-montane travel, 27–28, 390n44; backroad routes of Indian activists, 214; conscript and prison road gangs during Chao War, 137, 204, 205–6, 382n35; leftist critique of obligatory Indian labor in public works, 193; rural roads as MNR symbol of modernization, 305; subsidized by corvée Indian laborers, 27, 123, 193. See also Indigenous laborers; railroads

Rodriguez, Simón, 3

Rojas, José, 316

Rojas, Pedro, 131, 135, 139

rosca (derogatory term referring to Bolivia's parasitic ruling elite), 162, 227, 312

Rouma, Georges: background and trip to Bolivia, 57–58; Conservative critics of, 58; educational mission of, 57–58,

63–64; farm-school model advocated by, 63–64, 178, 263; influence on E. Pérez, 113–14, 119, 178; research on racial types by, 59–63, 357n94; rural normal schools established by, 63, 89, 113, 157; tutelary race-thinking as shaped by, 64, 67–69, 100, 113–14, 178, 263

Rousseau, Jean-Jacques, 1, 345n1

Rubio Orbe, Gonzalo, 271, 278, 287

rural extension education, 18, 225, 232, 252, 262, 399n32. *See also* SCIDE

rural poverty: and condition of schools, 38–39, 93–94, 99–100; and economic crisis in 1980s, 333–34; as endemic condition of neocolonial order, 33, 38, 39, 163, 180, 188, 190, 284; perpetuation of racial caste and, 38–39, 158, 217, 303–4, 330; rural schools as proposed solution to, 23, 145, 267, 272, 322; theories of racial backwardness as root cause of, 180, 188, 190; US aid for amelioration of, 233, 240, 267

rural schools and schooling: agricultural workforce training in, 63–69, 297–99; Aymara activism and community demands for, 71–73, 80, 88–94, 97–98, 196–202; classroom lessons in, 95–96; and community rituals, 95–97; conditions of, 38–39, 93–94, 99–100, 232–35, 300–304; contraband schools and oral memory of, 92–94, 96, 290–91, 292–93; elite perceptions of indigenous, 99–101; government reports on, 97–102; peasant political mobilization and, 205, 208–10; postrevolutionary proliferation of, 270–72, 280–81, 282–91, 303–4, 413n93; racial anxiety and violence toward, 91–93, 96–97, 102, 192–93; SCIDE's promotion of, 237–39, 242–52; state's logic of "separate and unequal" in, 9–10, 41, 300–303, 411n78; as symbol of Indigenous emancipation, 270–71, 282–86, 289, 290–91, 293–94, 309–11, 313. *See also* Aymara school activism; educational policy; Warisata

rural schoolteachers: as agents of the MNR's integrative revolution, 20, 286, 301, 304–8, 311, 378n123, 410n72; basic literacy instruction by, 8, 42–46, 90–91, 95–96, 101, 147, 201–5, 311, 334; as clandestine teachers, 88–93; IEB reforms and, 334–35; institutional discrimination against, 89, 99, 239, 301; instructional guides for, 234, 237–38, 240, 242, 254–57, 264; normal (teacher-training) schools, 157, 239, 300–301, 358n101; teachers unions, 297, 333, 384n65, 420n55; as victims of harassment, 54, 69, 91–93, 140, 170–73, 180, 184; Warisata and its corps of indigenista, 147–55, 326–28

rural syndicalism: agrarian class politics and, 215, 270, 395–96n103; as arena of peasant citizenship practices, 7, 15–17, 194–96, 218; under CSUTCB, 334; and escalation of peasant strike activity, 15, 195, 211, 215, 256, 395n101, 395–96n103; and fight for peasant unions and schools, 19–20, 195, 207–10, 293, 310–11; post–Chaco War spread of, 150, 162, 202, 207, 211, 308–10, 405n6, 406n18; postrevolutionary upsurge of, 280–81, 284, 288–89, 293; and teachers unions, 297, 333, 384n65, 420n55

Saavedra, Bautista, 47, 64, 102, 113, 116, 119, 140, 352n28, 366n69

Saénz, Moisés, 165, 166

SAI (Servicio Agrícola Interamericano), 232, 236, 262, 396n4

Salamana, Daniel, 109, 151

Salazar Mostajo, Carlos: arrival in Warisata, 136, 149–50; in the classroom, 151, 376n96; coming of age in Chaco War, 149–51; as director of Caiza D, 181–82; involvement in Marxist debates over the Indian question, 183–86, 384nn65–66; on the parliament of amautas, 132–33, 135, 136–37, 369n2, 373n64; photographic work of, 125–26, 149; solidarity work with leftist teachers of, 183–84; as teacher delegate to Mexico, 152–54, 184, 377n109; as Warisata's advocate, champion, and defender, 153, 157, 159, 175–76, 178, 181–83, 327–30, 377n111, 417–18n33

Salomon, Frank, 11
Sánchez Bustamante, Daniel, 49, 57, 91, 118, 168
Sánchez de Losada, Gonzalo, 334, 335
Sangines Uriarte, Marcelo, 286, 335
Sanjinés, Javier, 29, 55
Santiago de Huata, 98, 99, 120, 238–39, 251, 254–55, 257, 402n58
Saracho, Juan Misael: civilizing goal of, 43, 66; classroom pedagogy of, 42; as education minister under Montes, 40, 353n41; escuelas ambulantes established by, 42, 44–45, 118; modernization of public schools by, 40–46, 354n50; national curriculum of, 40–42; separatist school policy designed by, 41, 69
Sarmiento, Domingo Faustino, 3–5, 48, 355n66
SCIDE (Servicio Cooperativo Interamericano de Desarrollo Educativo): Aymara Indian as target of, 237–38; gendered curriculum of behavioral reform introduced by, 242–52; E. Maes, mastermind behind, 235–42; MNR's relationship to, 271, 298, 300, 410n72; núcleo escolar under authority of, 238–40; pedagogical goals of, 229, 234, 237–38, 241; E. Pérez's association with, 265–68; political opposition to, 256–60; school inspection tours by, 232–35; teacher workshops under, 239–49, 398nn21–22; US economic aid and bilateral program of, 17–18, 232–35, 396n4; G. Villarroel's relationship to, 235–36
scientific pedagogy, 9, 51, 57–58, 64, 65, 89, 114, 186, 263
SCISP (Servicio Cooperativo Interamericano de Salud Pública), 232, 239, 240, 262, 396n4
Scott, James, 58, 162
scribes, 3, 11, 75, 83–85. See also caciques-apoderado movement; qilqiris
Siles Suazo, Hernán, 295, 316, 320–21, 394n93
Siñani, Avelino: and the art of oratory, 138, 177; Aymara activist and literacy teacher, 128–30, 144–45; death of, 177–78; galvanizing community support for Warisata, 123–26; and J. Montes's political campaign, 371n38; E. Pérez's first encounters with, 117, 120–21; public commemoration of, 329, 336
Siñani, Julián, 129–31, 371n42
Siñani de Willka, Tomasa, 124, 176–78, 329–30, 369n2, 418nn35–36
Sindicato de Trabajadores Bolivianos, 193
Smithsonian Institute, 397n10
social Darwinism. See racial ideology
Sorata, 122, 131, 141, 142, 143, 374n80
Sosa, Rufino, 372–73n59
Spencer, Herbert, 33
SPIC (Subsecretaría de Prensa, Informaciones y Culturas), 311, 414n106
SRB (Sociedad Rural Boliviana), 226, 372n59, 378n123, 392n74
state-building: and the contemporary Plurinational State, 335–36; educational reform as tool of, 4, 143, 163; MNR's centralized project of, 269, 272, 295, 311. See also educational policy; Liberal oligarchy; MNR government; nationhood and nation making
Stepan, Nancy, 168
Stephenson, Marcia, 245
Suárez, Cristóbal, 301
Subirats, Ramón, 153
Sucre: colonial seat of Audiencia of Charcas and Archbishopric of La Plata, 82, 367n95; lettered city of national archive, high court, and legions of scribes, 81, 85; locale of Bolivia's first normal school, 57, 63, 113
Szuchman, Mark, 3

Tamayo, Franz: critic of the Liberal Party and its civilizing mission, 53–55, 56, 67; ideal national pedagogy of, 55–56, 114; intellectual influence on E. Pérez of, 114, 168, 259; Inti Karka editorial on, 306; as literary scion and telluric indigenista, 55–56, 114, 140
Tannenbaum, Frank, 153–54, 378n115
Tanqara, Francisco, 76, 79
Tapia, Luciano, 322

Taraqu, 103, 108, 196, 270, 272, 277, 282–83, 285, 295
Tarrifa Ascarrunz, Erasmo, 99
Tejada Sorzano, José Luís, 123
Tesis de Caranguillas, 406n17
THOA (Taller de Historia Oral Andina), 93, 332, 340, 360n3, 362n27
Thurston, Walter, 212–14, 226
Ticona, Esteban, 89, 90, 103, 364n48
Titirico, Gregorio, 197, 201–2
Toledo, Francisco de, 361–62n22, 387n15
Tornero, Ana Rosa, 104
Toro, David, 17, 156, 201, 217, 224, 225
Torres, Juan José, 326
Trotsky, Leon, 184
Trotskyism, 184, 227, 257, 376–77n99, 384n65, 395n102
Truman, Harry, 231
Tupac Katari rebellion (1781), 32, 331; and contemporary ethnic movements, 416n15, 416n18
Tuskegee Normal and Industrial Institute, 66–67
tutelary race-thinking: concept of, 8, 9, 51; driving the oligarchy's civilizing mission, 47–53, 68, 188–91; and neocolonial modernity, 65–66, 68, 331; and the quest for national pedagogy, 24–25, 55–56, 68–69, 229, 234; behind SCIDE's model of functional education, 247–48; among telluric indigenistas, 52–54, 58, 67, 140, 168. *See also* racial ideology
2010 Nueva Ley de Educación "Avelino Siñani y Elizardo Pérez," 336

UMSA (Universidad Mayor de San Andrés), 322, 342
UN, 231, 271, 275, 288
UNESCO, 21, 270, 296, 413n93
UNIBOL (Universidad Indígena de Bolivia), 336
United States: Bolivia's Indian problem as strategic concern of, 232–33, 396n7, 397n10; functional education introduced by, 237–38, 397n14; Indian and Black boarding schools in, 65–69, 353n30, 358n109; military aid and Cold War concerns of, 313, 323, 349–50n29, 395–96n103, 396n1, 398n19; postwar rural development projects of, 232–33, 396n4, 396n7; reports of political unrest and embassy surveillance by, 211–12, 226–28, 230, 235; rural extension programs of, 235–42, 242–52, 399n32; rural poverty and failing schools assessed by, 232–35, 302–3, 412n87; State Department envoys of, 402n60, 413n94; World War II and the tin factor, 230, 395–96n103. *See also* SCIDE

Vacas: núcleo escolar in, 148–49, 150, 157, 169, 236, 238–39, 251, 254, 393, 398n23; rural syndicalism in, 15, 257
Valcarcel, Luís, 240
Valencia, Alipio, 149, 183
Vázquez Martín: accused of fomenting rebellion, 83, 84–85; the archive expedition of, 81–82; exemplar of the "dangerous" lettered Indian, 81–84; involvement in the underground scribal economy, 82–88, 89, 362n25; status as cacique-apoderado of, 361n118; Velasco, Adolfo, 155
vecinos de pueblo (mestizo townspeople; rural elite), 92, 93, 96, 116, 118, 179, 181, 374n78
Villarroel, Gualberto: death of, 257; on the Indian problem, 394n93; military populism under, 216–17, 223–24, 228; 1945 Indian Congress under aegis of, 195, 206, 211, 212, 214, 219–20, 223, 236; official decrees and promises of, 225–26, 273, 281; and project of Indian assimilation, 224–25; relations with US envoys, 235–36
violence: cultural racism and symbolic forms of, 9, 32–38, 85, 175–78, 180, 188, 308, 346n14, 356n79; as endemic to neocolonialism, 13, 14, 97, 102, 103, 131, 135, 310; everyday forms of, 139, 180, 183, 200, 223; the lettered Indian as victim of, 8, 11, 81, 85, 92, 139, 290; peasant protest and state repression, 225, 273, 276, 280, 284, 293, 303, 309; peasant unrest

violence (*continued*)
  and incidents of state, 118–19, 226–27, 236, 256, 266; rural schools as target of, 13–15, 20, 73, 91–93, 96–97, 102, 170–72, 175–77, 192–93; Warisata and forms of state-organized, 14–15, 162, 163, 175, 176–77, 179–80. See also *gamonalismo*; racial ideology; Warisata

Vocalía de Educación Rural e Indígena, 180, 385n80. *See also* CNE

w'akas (Quechua; deities, often taking natural forms, guarding an ayllu or region), 95

Wañuco, Máximo, 376n98

Warisata (escuela-ayllu): agriculture, commerce, and crafts in, 125–26, 143–44, 147, 149, 376n95; Aymara cofounders of, 129–31; Aymara labor and construction of, 123–28, 133–34, 370n32, 382n35; boarding and normal school in, 375n93, 375–76n94; cacique-apoderado links to, 129–30, 371n42; classroom pedagogy, 376n96; geography, ecology, and land tenure in region of, 120–23; ideological battles over the legacy and memory of, 261–62, 326–30, 384n61, 368–9n2; integral curriculum of, 127, 146–47, 375n85, 376n97; interethnic origins of, 113–29; international solidarity networks with, 154–55, 377nn108–9, 377–78n112, 378n115; núcleo schools and territorial networks of, 140–44, 374n80, 375n84; the oligarchy's assault on, 162–75, 175–80, 381nn19–20; parliament of amautas in, 127, 131–36, 371–72n45, 372n50, 373n61, 373n64; pedagogical priorities in, 144–47; postwar generation of teachers and artists in, 147–52; as symbol and platform of Indian emancipation, 136–40, 146–50, 378n113; as target of gamonal violence, 138–40, 372–73n59, 374n76, 374n78; US administrative control over, 237–38, 262–68, 404n89. *See also* Pérez, Elizardo; Salazar Mostajo, Carlos; Siñani, Avelino

War of the Pacific (1879–83), 25, 104, 107
Washington, Booker T., 67, 105, 359n115
Weber, Eugen, 50
Whitehead, Laurence, 295
Willka, Rufino, 86, 98, 196, 197–202
Willkie, James, 301
World Bank, 418n36
World War II, 17, 161, 189, 229, 230, 231–32, 256

Yapita, Juan de Dios, 95–96
yatiri (Aymara; shaman), 363–64n42

Zampa, José, 388n19
Zárate Willka rebellion (1899), 36, 43, 331
Zavaleta Mercado, René, 395n100

www.ingramcontent.com/pod-product-compliance
Lightning Source LLC
Chambersburg PA
CBHW021847230426
43671CB00006B/291